CULTIVATING RACE

NEW DIRECTIONS IN SOUTHERN HISTORY

SERIES EDITORS
Michele Gillespie, Wake Forest University
William A. Link, University of Florida

Cultivating Race

The Expansion of Slavery in Georgia, 1750–1860

Watson W. Jennison

The University Press of Kentucky

Editorial and Sales Offices: The University Press of Kentucky
663 South Limestone Street, Lexington, Kentucky 40508-4008
www.kentuckypress.com

16 15 14 13 12   5 4 3 2 1

Maps by Dick Gilbreath, University of Kentucky Cartography Lab

Cataloging-in-Publication data is available from the Library of Congress.

ISBN 978-0-8131-3426-0 (hardcover : alk. paper)
ISBN 978-0-8131-3446-8 (ebook)

This book is printed on acid-free paper meeting
the requirements of the American National Standard
for Permanence in Paper for Printed Library Materials.

Manufactured in the United States of America.

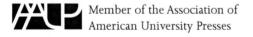 Member of the Association of
American University Presses

To Puck and Sue,

For all that you've done and continue to do

CONTENTS

ACKNOWLEDGMENTS

For more than a decade, Georgia, as Ray Charles memorably sang, has been "on my mind." Hardly a day has passed during that time when I did not consider some aspect of the state's rich history. Indeed, Georgia has been on my mind, in my head, and, occasionally, even in my dreams. In writing the monograph that resulted from this mild obsession, I incurred countless debts along the way. Consequently, I am grateful to a range of people whose support and contributions helped make this book possible.

I'd like to thank the folks at the University Press of Kentucky, especially Anne Dean Watkins, for bringing *Cultivating Race* to print. Dick Gilbreath also deserves special thanks for his many maps, which add an important dimension to the book. In addition, I'd like to express my appreciation to the series editors, Michele Gillespie, Bill Link, and Peter Carmichael, whose advice proved invaluable. Michele helped me in innumerable ways. Beyond my heavy reliance on her scholarship on Georgia, I benefited from Michele's sage advice. Michele read multiple drafts of the manuscript and offered several key suggestions, each of which I strove to implement; I have no doubt that her words of wisdom greatly improved the end product. Like Michele, Bill played an outsized role in the effort to bring this manuscript to publication. His counsel helped me navigate the sometimes rocky shoals of the academy and the publishing world. His guidance has been valuable, but I have benefited even more from his friendship.

While conducting research for this project, I visited numerous libraries and archives and benefited in myriad ways, both from the documents I viewed and from my interactions with the people who keep these institutions running. I'd like to thank the staff at the Georgia Archives (formerly the Georgia Department of Archives and History), the Georgia Historical Society, Alderman Library at the University of Virginia, Wilson Library at the University of North Carolina at Chapel Hill, Perkins Library at Duke University, P. K. Yonge Library at the University of Florida, and Hargrett Library at the University of Georgia. I would especially like to thank the Woodruff Library at Emory University for a generous research grant. I am also indebted to the staff in the interlibrary loan offices at Jackson Library at the University of North Carolina, Greensboro, and Alderman Library, whose prodigious efforts facilitated my search for sources on Georgia and whose resourcefulness always astounded me.

My years in Charlottesville were some of the best of my life. During that time, my intellectual universe expanded exponentially thanks to the faculty in the history department at the University of Virginia. A particularly loud shout-out goes to Edward Ayers, my advisor and good friend, for his part in this transformation. As a role model, he has few equals. His dedication to his students and his craft left a lasting impression on me, one that I can only aspire to emulate. His guidance deepened my understanding of southern history and all its contradictions and complexity. Courses with Grace Hale, Joseph Miller, Richard Drayton, Peter Onuf, Dylan Penningroth, Nelson Lichtenstein, and George Mentore broadened my historical perspectives and played an instrumental role in my development as a scholar. I benefited from the friendship and advice of Carl Bon Tempo, Aaron Sheehan-Dean, Andy Lewis, Phil Troutman, Li Fang, Charles Irons, Amy Murrell Taylor, and Syed Ali. I will always remember and value my late night gab sessions with John Riedl and Josh Rothman. While in graduate school I had the good fortune to find employment at the Virginia Center for Digital Humanities, where I worked on the Valley of the Shadow Project. I would like to thank Ed Ayers and Will Thomas for that valuable opportunity. I would also like to thank Reginald Butler and Scot French for hiring me for a summertime stint at the Carter G. Woodson Center at a time when I was deeply in need of a job.

Since arriving at the University of North Carolina, Greensboro, in 2003, I have had the pleasure to work with a superb group of colleagues. From the outset, members of the history department welcomed me into their ranks with open arms and made me feel at home. Their friendship and collegiality facilitated my transition from graduate student to assistant professor. I'd like to offer a special thanks to Chuck Bolton, Jodi Bilinkoff, Phyllis Hunter, and Tom Jackson, who read earlier drafts of chapters and offered helpful comments. In the years since my return to North Carolina, I've enjoyed the opportunity to reconnect with Jeff Jones, whose unfailingly sunny disposition and knowledge of UNC basketball history never cease to amaze me. Thanks also to Lisa Levenstein and Jason Brent, whose friendship and appreciation of all things "Can-con" have made my time here all the richer. Old colleagues, Peter Carmichael and Bill Link, as well as new colleagues, Benjamin Filene and Mark Elliott, provided and continue to provide a deeply satisfying intellectual community and social circle.

Without the support of my family, I can honestly state that none of this would have been possible. I want to thank my parents, Watson and Suzanne Jennison, for their love and support. Equally inspiring has been my daughter, Sheridan Lea, whose sweet smile and infectious laugh always kept me aware of what's really important in life. Encouragement from my grandmother Grace Sterling and my brother Alex Jennison has also sustained me through this process. I'd also like to acknowledge Cheddar, whose companionship kept me sane during the many long nights I spent working on this project. Although he did not live to see it through to its end, he lives on in my heart and memories. Finally, I'd like to express my deepest appreciation to Susanna Lee, whose love and unyielding encouragement helped me survive the dizzying emotional peaks and valleys (and everything in between) that I experienced while researching and writing this book.

INTRODUCTION

Austin Dabney was unique among Georgia's Revolutionary War heroes. He was black. One of the original settlers of the upcountry, Dabney came to Georgia from North Carolina in the early 1770s. He accompanied a white man named Captain Richard Aycock, reputedly his father, and moved onto the land ceded by the Creeks in 1773 in what would become Wilkes County. When the War of Independence broke out, Aycock offered Dabney as his substitute. Dabney performed bravely, fighting alongside General Elijah Clark and his band of upcountry Patriots. As one contemporary commentator noted, "No soldier under Clark was braver or did better service during the revolutionary struggle." Dabney fought in several major engagements, including the Battle of Kettle Creek in 1779. In 1782, during a skirmish near Augusta, he suffered a wound—a ball through the thigh—that would hobble him for the rest of his life. For his service during the war, Dabney received an annuity and a 250-acre parcel of land from the state authorities as well as a pension from the federal government.[1]

Throughout his life, Dabney enjoyed cordial relations with whites. When he was wounded at the Battle of Augusta, a fellow soldier named Giles Harris came to his aid and brought him to his home in Wilkes County to recover. After he recuperated, Dabney stayed with the Harris clan and later moved with them when they relocated to Madison County. After Harris died, Dabney supported the family financially and paid for the eldest son, William, to attend Franklin College and afterward arranged for him to study law with Stephen Upson, a prominent upcountry attorney and politician. In the years after the war, Dabney was a successful jockey and traveled throughout the region racing. He made quite a bit of money and became acquainted with many wealthy whites. Some of these men held prominent positions, men such as Judge John H. Dooly, whose father Dabney served with during the Revolution. Judge Dooly presided over Walton County's first superior court, and whenever he came to Madison County to hold court, Dabney visited him and socialized with the local lawyers, recounting stories about the war.[2]

One of the most revealing stories about Dabney's place in Georgian society occurred during a trip to Savannah in the late 1790s to pick up his pension. Dabney made the journey from the upcountry with Colonel Wiley Pope. The two men "were very intimate and social on the road," riding side by side until they reached the city limits, whereupon Pope advised Dabney to fall in behind him so as not to offend the racial sensibilities of local residents. Dabney obliged. Pope's fears proved unfounded, however. As Pope and Dabney rode through the streets, they passed by the governor's residence. Upon spotting the pair, Governor James Jackson bolted from his house and onto the street to welcome Dabney to town. The governor opened his home to Dabney and insisted that he accept his hospitality for the duration of his visit.[3]

By the 1820s, however, Dabney faced growing white hostility. The legislature granted the revolutionary hero an additional 112-acre plot of land in Walton County from the Creek land cession in 1821 despite state policy that restricted the distribution of land to whites only.[4] Dabney had been the recipient of goodwill from the General Assembly before, but this time some white Georgians did not endorse the legislature's decision to reward the revolutionary hero for his service. The vote of one legislator from Madison County in favor of the land grant set off a storm of controversy. The residents of the county divided into pro- and anti-Dabney factions. Those opposed to the law contended "it was an indignity to white men, for a mulatto to be put upon an equality with them in the distribution of the public land."[5] Times had changed since Dabney's trip with Pope to Savannah in the 1790s.

Dabney was clearly an anomaly, but his life illuminates the transformation in Georgia's racial order. Dabney's experiences embodied the trajectory of blacks in Georgia. In the late eighteenth century, Dabney had gained the respect of white Georgians through his Revolutionary War service. But by the early decades of the nineteenth century, many segments of Georgia's white population, particularly those in the upcountry, opposed granting privileges to free people of color, even war heroes like Dabney. A hardening of racial lines circumscribed the fluidity that had typified relations in early Georgia and that had allowed someone like Austin Dabney to flourish.

The emergence of white supremacy as the ideological foundation of Georgia's antebellum slave society played an integral role in the evolution of the state's racial order. The significance of this shift cannot be overlooked when exploring the creation of the bifurcated racial system that became synonymous with the slave South. In the late eighteenth century, the reliance on white supremacy to justify the use of slave labor was merely one of several rationales. By the mid-nineteenth century, however, most whites in Georgia embraced this ideology as the dominant rationale for the institution of slavery. This shift was not inevitable. Rather, it was the result of ideological struggle over the meaning of citizenship and race that played out between the founding of the nation and the rise of the Confederacy.

Historians have long recognized certain turning points in the South's history, such as Nat Turner's rebellion, which affected the region's racial order.[6] While it is clear that these insurrectionary scares had an impact on the passage of slave laws and the development of white racial attitudes, I argue that long-term structural and demographic changes played a more significant role in shaping the evolution of the racial order in Georgia. A confluence of factors contributed to the hardening of the racial order. The change in attitude toward race was influenced by the expansion of slavery along with the state's territorial boundaries as whites displaced Indians. Between 1750 and 1860, the lowcountry planter elite lost the ability to exclusively direct the machinery of government and, along with it, the ability to dictate social relations and determine the status of people of African and Indian descent. The growth of the white settler population in the upcountry in the decades after the Revolution repositioned the demographic, economic, and political center of the state and reformulated both the relationship between masters and slaves and that between poor whites and wealthy whites. The settlement of the interior and the emergence of the cotton kingdom fundamentally reordered relations among blacks, whites, and Indians. The forced relocation of the Indians and subsequent settling of Georgia's blackbelt shifted the demographic balance of the state, as whites and blacks, both slave and free, pushed onto the lands formerly held by the Creeks and the Cherokees. This shift gave whites in the upcountry increased political power, which they used to protect their economic interests and fashion society to fit their racial ideal. As whites settled the lands recently seized from the Creeks and Cherokees, a new society took root. While similar in many regards to the lowcountry society, the cotton kingdom drew more rigid lines between the races. Pockets of racial fluidity remained, but a rigid black/white divide wound up enshrined into law.

Cultivating Race argues that nonelite whites in Georgia not only benefited from the rise of white supremacy but pushed hardest to enact legislative changes to make Georgia conform to the tenets of the ideology.[7] White supremacy provided slave owners with an argument to counter the growing assault on slavery by northern abolitionists, but it also provided nonelite whites with a rationale to shape slavery in line with their interests. Contrary to depictions of white laborers and yeomen as subordinates manipulated or oppressed by their social and economic superiors, nonelite white men actively sought to protect their economic interests. By emphasizing both elite and nonelite white men as agents of change, this study highlights class divisions over issues of race and citizenship. The vast majority of nonelite white men in Georgia supported the institution of slavery, even in the late antebellum era, when rampant speculation inflated prices and placed slave ownership well beyond their means. But they also believed in republicanism and the revolutionary ideal of equality for all white men. Cognizant that their numerical advantage provided them leverage to shape policy and influence political debate, nonelite white men pushed for reforms that democratized slavery.[8]

This study also recognizes that whites were not the only actors contesting power in Georgia. Throughout the late eighteenth and early nineteenth centuries, blacks and Indians repeatedly obstructed white Georgians' efforts to expand the state's borders and impose race-based slavery. Whether as plantation slaves sabotaging production or warriors resisting American encroachment, blacks and Indians actively opposed white Georgians' attempts to subdue nonwhites living in the Southeast. Capitalizing on the political instability that characterized the region beyond Georgia's southern and western borders, blacks and Indians joined forces with one another as well as with the Spanish and British to form societies that offered an alternative to the racialized model embraced by white Georgians. Although white Georgians held the preponderance of power, the story of the interracial resistance should not and cannot be overlooked when addressing the history of Georgia. The decades-long struggle demonstrated that neither the spread of plantation slavery nor the narrow understanding of race espoused by white Georgians was inevitable. Moreover, the tenacity of black and Indian resistance shaped the white response, encouraging a bloodthirsty and extremist attitude toward nonwhites in Georgia.[9]

Edmund Morgan's *American Slavery, American Freedom* (1975) is the classic historical work on the making of race in the American South. Morgan chronicled the transition from the ambiguous racial boundaries in the early years of the Chesapeake to the bifurcated racial system in the late seventeenth century. *American Slavery, American Freedom* forced scholars to reconsider the way race had previously been portrayed in southern history. Morgan's study revealed that race did not just exist; it developed. He explained that, though it seemed counterintuitive, race was a product of material conditions instead of biology. Market forces and naked self-interest, he maintained, were responsible for the black/white divide. According to his celebrated interpretation, it was not until the second half of the seventeenth century that race replaced class as the most salient divide among the region's settlers. In the years since the publication of this seminal work, Morgan's argument has remained the fundamental blueprint for discussions on the creation of race in America.[10]

The development of the bifurcated racial order in the Lower South did not follow the chronology described by Morgan.[11] I argue that until the turn of the nineteenth century the region's racial system bore more resemblance to the slave societies of the Caribbean than it did to the Chesapeake. The continued presence of the Creek, Cherokee, and Seminole Indians in and around Georgia further complicated the development of the black/white divide. Ultimately, a bifurcated racial order did emerge in the Lower South, but the process did not occur until the second quarter of the nineteenth century—not coincidentally the same period when white Georgians removed the Indians and made cotton king.

Georgia serves as a microcosm for the development of the cotton South. In contrast to the other states along the eastern seaboard, where the coastal elite managed to maintain power over the objections of the residents of the interior, Georgia followed a different trajectory. Following the rise of cotton cultivation in the early nineteenth century and the attendant increase in the population and wealth of the upcountry, the balance of power shifted in the state. As upcountry whites exerted control over the levers of state government, they passed laws that reflected their values and beliefs. In doing so, they swept away the conventions that had stood at the heart of the slave system in early Georgia. Although Georgia deviated from the norm among the other colonies that formed the original thirteen states, it illuminates the pattern in the other states of the Deep South where cotton became king. As in Georgia, power in Alabama and Mississippi came to reside in the interior by the antebellum era. For this reason, Georgia offers a model to understand the social, political, and economic transformation of the cotton South.

Cultivating Race places early Georgia history within the Atlantic World context. White Georgians attempted to preserve slavery from attack by blacks and Indians and their British, French, and Spanish allies during a series of wars, including the American Revolution (1776–1783), French Revolution (1789), Haitian Revolution (1791–1804), Indian War (1787–1788), Muskogee War (1799–1803), Patriot War (1812–1813), Creek Civil War (1813–1814), War of 1812, and Seminole War (1817–1818). This book examines these conflicts as part of a larger trans-Atlantic struggle against slavery. White Georgians also looked to the larger Atlantic World as a model in developing their slave society.

Employing personal papers, newspapers, and official records, *Cultivating Race* offers a social, cultural, and political history of the rigidification of the racial system in Georgia. Personal papers, such as diaries, correspondence, and plantation records, reveal the struggles of daily life as different groups in Georgia and on its borders battled for power. Laws play an especially important role in this study. White Georgians did not always follow laws or the prohibitions contained in them. Laws, however, illuminate the "official" position, which in the colonial era reflected the ideals of the planter elite but by the antebellum era reflected the ideals of the white majority. When juxtaposed with political changes taking place over the same period, laws help to explain the social ramifications of the state's policies.

In recent decades, scholars have written a number of excellent studies of slavery in Georgia. Several recent works focus exclusively on the low-country. Building on Peter Wood's pioneering work, *Black Majority* (1974), these historians analyze the development of eighteenth- and nineteenth-century lowcountry society.[12] These studies explore the origins of slavery in Georgia and the conflicts that surrounded it. They investigate the development of rice cultivation and analyze relations between masters and slaves as well as between slaves and poor whites. Similarly, in the past three decades, a number of works on the upcountry have appeared. These studies trace the formation of the cotton kingdom. They examine the changing social, economic, political, and physical landscape in Georgia's vast interior, especially conflicts between slave owners and slaves and among different classes of whites living in the region.[13]

Although these studies have enhanced our understanding of the slave societies that took root in the respective regions, their geographical focus or periodization obscures important transformations that occurred in Georgia over the course of the eighteenth and nineteenth centuries. As a result, the historiography of slavery and race in Georgia during this period has fragmented.[14] This book seeks to rectify the chronological and geographical disjunctions in the historiography on Georgia. To find the origins of Georgia's antebellum slave society and understand the bifurcated racial system it spawned, scholars must examine the vast demographic and economic changes that occurred during this era. For this reason, *Cultivating Race* begins with the introduction of slavery in 1750, gives prominent coverage to the early national period, and extends to 1860. Moreover, this study examines slavery in both the lowcountry and the upcountry. Because of their localized nature, most monographs on slavery in Georgia do not consider the consequences of the transformation of the interior upon the older, coastal region where economic and political power traditionally had been concentrated. Recently, scholars have sought to join the histories of the two regions, thus creating a more complex vision of the Lower South. These studies portray a more dynamic relationship between the interior and the coast but generally focus on conflicts over economic and religious matters.[15] My study builds on this work by revealing both a symbiosis and an underlying tension between the regions but privileges race as the central factor in the ordering of the new American society.

The first chapter examines the abandonment of the founders' vision of a common man's utopia in favor a hierarchical slave society. The founders imagined a society based on small-scale agriculture and limited landholdings. The transformation to a slave society occurred quickly. Within two decades of the end of the slavery ban, a full-blown slave society had emerged based on the cultivation of rice. A planter elite rose to political power and created a slave society modeled on South Carolina and the West Indies. The planters' reliance on slave labor to fulfill their labor needs meant that there was little demand for most white skilled workers. And planters showed little inclination to place restrictions on their slaves.

The second, third, and fourth chapters explore the age of revolution in Georgia. The second chapter examines the impact of the American and Haitian revolutions on Georgia. The alliance between the British and slaves almost completely destroyed slavery during the American Revolution. Just as planters began the process of reestablishing the plantation regime, the events in St. Domingue disrupted the institution and influenced its development. The events in Haiti altered authorities' perceptions of people of African descent, both enslaved and free, and thus shaped decisions related to the slave order. In response to the Haitian Revolution, Georgia's authorities cracked down on arrivals of foreign people of color and enhanced the privileges of native people of color.

The third and fourth chapters analyze the impact of the American Revolution on Georgia's interior. Race in Georgia was more complicated than a black/white divide. The struggle for land in Georgia's backcountry created opposing racial orders as alternatives to the expansion of plantation slavery. Chapter 3 examines the Trans-Oconee Republic, an embryonic nation established on Creek land just beyond Georgia's established western border by frontiersmen who had battled Tories and their Indian allies during the War of Independence. Disillusioned by the turn of events following the ratification of the U.S. Constitution and the subsequent intervention of the federal authorities in their relations with the neighboring Indians, backcountry settlers, white and also possibly black, created a republic that fulfilled their visions of the American Revolution. The fourth chapter explores the establishment of the State of Muskogee, an entity that brought Indians, blacks, and whites together in the liminal space beyond the power of the authorities in Georgia and Spanish Florida. Bound together by a desire to resist the encroachments of white Georgians, the State of Muskogee created a multiracial society that stood in stark contrast to the emerging black/white world in Georgia and the South in general.

The fifth chapter examines white Georgians' drive to extend the state's frontiers and expand plantation slavery in the 1810s. Beginning in the early nineteenth century, the growing demand for cotton brought increasing numbers of white settlers and slaves to Georgia's southern and southwestern frontiers. The resulting pressure to expand brought white Georgians into conflict with the Creek and Seminole Indians, their British and Spanish allies, and the escaped slaves who found refuge in their midst. With the aid of federal troops, the Tennessee militia, and "friendly" Indians, white Georgians defeated their interracial foes in a series of brutal engagements that ultimately extended Georgia's boundaries and defeated the last remaining impediment to the spread of plantations across the Southeast.

The sixth chapter focuses on the political debates over the removal of the Cherokee Indians. White Georgians had few misgivings about expelling the Creek Indians in the wake of the wars of the 1810s, but the same was not true with the Cherokees. Within the state, a sizable population opposed forced relocation schemes. As migrants flooded into the Georgia upcountry, the number of residents in favor of Indian removal dramatically increased. These men shifted the demographic and political balance in the state. The new settlers possessed little wealth and arrived in search of land. They pressed for new priorities, especially a speedy resolution to the obstacles to white settlement on the remaining Cherokee lands and the creation of a white republic. That meant the expulsion of all Indians. It also meant that they expected all other whites to respect race as the paramount distinction in society. The Cherokee question became the defining political issue in the early 1830s. Where one stood reflected a deeper belief about the proper structure of society, specifically the nature of Georgia's commitment to white supremacy. The political power of upcountry settlers—as evidenced in their successful efforts to remove the Cherokees—signified an important shift in Georgia politics. In the subsequent decades, the number of migrants continued to swell and their voices grew louder. The politicians heard the cries and responded.

Chapter 7 examines the expansion of slavery to the Georgia interior. The rise of the cotton kingdom transformed life for blacks and whites in the antebellum era, collapsing distinctions among the former and opening up opportunities for the latter. Georgia's cotton kingdom introduced a new system of slavery to the state. Unlike the lowcountry or the Upper South, where slaves, particularly men, performed a variety of skilled and unskilled labor in addition to cultivating a cash crop, slaves in Georgia's cotton belt found themselves relegated to the harshest and most menial types of labor under the gang system. At the same time, cotton cultivation provided white men opportunities for social and economic mobility that were not possible in the lowcountry. In urban areas of the upcountry, nonslaveholders and white workers attempted to shape the system of slavery to benefit themselves. While most slaveholders believed they had the right to use their property any way they saw fit, nonslaveholders wanted a more restrictive form of slavery, one that removed blacks from most skilled occupations and limited them to the most menial and exhausting tasks in Georgian society.

By the 1850s, Georgia had emerged as one of the largest cotton-producing states in the South. In the course of a hundred years, it had transformed from a multiracial society in which people of European, African, and Native American ancestry contested for power into a slavery-based society where white and black had become synonymous with free and enslaved. Chapter 8 examines how white Georgians explained this transformation, how they told the history of their state's rise, and how they defended the emergence of the slave system that came to character-ize antebellum Georgia. Virtually all white Georgians agreed that slavery was superior to the free labor ideology found in the North, particularly in the face of growing abolitionist attacks on the institution, yet this con-sensus masked differences among white Georgians over the state's recent history, specifically the methods by which the Cherokee Indians were removed as well as the place of free blacks in society. In sections of Geor-gia that had been settled earliest, some whites continued to hold more nuanced views of race. By the antebellum era, however, their voices had been drowned out by those who espoused a more rigid interpretation of racial difference, a sentiment favored by whites who lived in Georgia's corner of the cotton kingdom. As representatives of this new Georgia rose to power, they rewrote laws to reflect their vision of idealized society. Similarly, they rewrote the state's history to provide a rationale to explain and to legitimate the reformulation of their society.

1

FROM A COMMON MAN'S UTOPIA TO A PLANTER'S PARADISE, 1732–1776

Georgia's founders established the colony as a haven for the common man, but within a generation their vision had evaporated. The countryside, once filled with inhospitable swamplands, gradually transformed into income-producing rice plantations. The transition to slavery came quickly in Georgia, with far-reaching social, economic, and political consequences for the colony's development. A mere twenty years elapsed between the repeal of the ban on slavery and the colony's emergence as a mature plantation society. In that span of time, a new planter elite arose, abandoning the utopian goals of the founders in the pursuit of wealth and political power. Georgia became a hierarchical society stratified by race and class. Planters relied on their slaves to perform all labor, both skilled and unskilled, marginalizing nonelite whites. At the same time, the influence of the Enlightenment as well as respect for slaves' intelligence prompted some planters to reform the institution. The racial hierarchy that emerged in Georgia, then, did not rigidly conform to a black/white divide.

After more than a year of preparations for the voyage, the *Anne* set sail on November 17, 1732, from Gravesend bound for North America. Over one hundred migrants, selected by the Georgia Trustees, received free passage and boarded the ship. The group included small tradesmen and artisans from the city but no soldiers or laborers from the countryside. After a quick crossing, the vessel arrived at Charlestown on January 13, where James Edward Oglethorpe, the group's leader, went ashore to seek counsel from the colonial authorities there and to secure supplies. Upon Oglethorpe's return, the *Anne* sailed south to Port Royal. After docking, the migrants disembarked in preparation for the last leg of their journey. Following a two-week respite, they boarded six vessels that carried them to a site selected by Oglethorpe on the banks of the Savannah River. On February 1, having reached their final destination, they climbed the Yamacraw Bluff, where they broke ground on a settlement that would eventually become Savannah. In the months that followed, new migrants arrived, composed of Jews, Scots, and Salzburgers, adding to the colony's fledgling population. Together this diverse group of settlers formed the nucleus of the Georgia colony, a social experiment unique in the annals of British North America.[1]

From the outset, Oglethorpe recognized that he had to establish good relations with the neighboring Indians if his utopian society was to have any chance of surviving. Soon after arriving, Oglethorpe initiated negotiations with Tomochichi, the leader of the Yamacraw Indians, the tribe that lived closest to the area where he hoped to build the first settlement. Though dismayed initially at the prospect of an English settlement, Tomochichi quickly came around to the idea. Like other Indian chiefs living nearby, Tomochichi understood that he could benefit from his new connection with the English. He recognized their value as potential allies and as a source of trade goods, particularly weapons and ammunition. In short order, then, Tomochichi and Oglethorpe came up with an agreement that allowed the colonists to establish a settlement. The relationship between the Yamacraws and Oglethorpe succeeded in large part due to the actions of Mary Musgrove, a mestizo woman, who mediated these first interactions and later served as Oglethorpe's interpreter. Musgrove and her husband, John Musgrove, also a mestizo, operated a trading house close to the Yamacraws. In addition to her keen business acumen, Mary possessed strong ties with nearby Creek towns. Oglethorpe put Mary Musgrove's diplomatic skills and connections among the Creeks to use when he successfully negotiated with the headmen of the eight most powerful Lower Creek towns that May for their recognition. Later, her efforts also aided Oglethorpe's push to establish a trading town in the backcountry in 1736. Indeed, Musgrove continued to play an active role in Oglethorpe's interactions with neighboring Indians in the years to come.[2]

Georgia's creation was the product of a convergence of interests. Since the founding of South Carolina in 1670, the English and Spanish had contested the area between the Savannah and Altamaha rivers. The English colonists in South Carolina and the Spanish colonists in Florida and their respective Indian allies fought a series of wars and battles in the decades that followed as each side sought to protect its interests. Gradually, by the turn of the eighteenth century, the English pushed the Spanish back to the St. Johns River, but their claim to the land remained tenuous and their settlements vulnerable to attack. Additionally problematic, the French began to exhibit greater interest in the Southeast. Facing a threat from both the Spanish and the French, the English hoped to secure the region to retain their hold on trade with the Indians in the interior. This impetus grew after the Yamasee War of 1715–1716, which decimated the Carolina frontier. The authorities in South Carolina pushed for the creation of a settlement south of the Savannah River to serve as a military deterrent. The settlers could defend against Spanish attacks. Several proposals were advanced in the years that followed, but it was not until 1730 that a plan with sufficient government and financial support emerged.[3]

In addition to imperial designs, philanthropy motivated the founding of Georgia. England at the turn of the eighteenth century was a deeply divided society. The economic changes brought about by the nation's expansion into the Atlantic World created enormous wealth for some but left many subjects behind. Unemployment and debt were rampant among the common folk. Workers found themselves struggling to survive in the new economic reality. Economic duress contributed to the social problems. An epidemic of alcoholism and crime seemed to take hold of the nation. Confronted with these economic and social ills, some members of the English elite looked for ways to ameliorate the conditions of their "inferiors." Among those who led this crusade was Oglethorpe, who became interested in the topic while serving in Parliament. Oglethorpe's work on a parliamentary committee that examined the conditions in the country's jails exposed him to the deprivations faced by England's poor and brought him into contact with like-minded individuals who shared his concern for the plight of the dispossessed. After securing the support of several wealthy philanthropists, Oglethorpe proposed creating a colony in America that would serve as a refuge for poor English workers, a place for them to begin their lives anew. With the proper supervision and regulation, he believed, the poor could find salvation and virtuous living. Motivated by nationalism as well as paternalism, he hoped to create a model society that would not only siphon off some of England's superfluous population but would serve as a model for England itself. With the help of the Earl of Egmont, Oglethorpe convinced the Crown to issue a royal charter in 1732 that authorized the Georgia Trustees to govern the area between the Savannah and Altamaha rivers for a period of twenty-one years. Settling Georgia with the worthy poor represented an opportunity to fulfill humanitarian goals while satisfying the Crown's military and economic interests.[4]

The trustees envisioned Georgia as a refuge for the common man. They consciously rejected the path toward cash crops and plantation slavery in place in much of British North America and the West Indies. Instead, they planned to base Georgia's economy around the production and export of silk and wine, two high-value commodities that would promote England's mercantilist interests but would not require slave labor to be profitable. Unlike sugar, rice, or tobacco, silk and wine production required specific skills that the trustees believed slaves did not possess. Since the trustees felt that free white labor could not compete on an equal footing with slave labor, silk and wine were perfect for the colony. Silk production alone, the trustees estimated, would create 40,000 to 50,000 new jobs for the poor and unemployed and would save England £500,000 per year, the amount spent annually on importing the luxury item, often from their European rivals. The trustees purposefully avoided the introduction of a cash crop in Georgia because they feared it would lead to the emergence of plantation slavery and, inevitably, to the concentration of land and wealth in the hands of a few colonists, thus undermining the entire project. To avoid such an outcome, they enacted a land policy that limited most migrants to fifty acres. Migrants who funded their own journey and brought four indentured servants, however, could receive up to five hundred acres. In addition, the trustees banned slavery in Georgia altogether, making it the only colony in British North America to impose such a prohibition.[5]

The trustees' decision to ban slavery was not based on abolitionist sentiment or concern for the fate of enslaved Africans. While governing Georgia, none of them expressed any hostility to the institution or questioned its value to Britain's colonial endeavors. Indeed, Oglethorpe had held high office in the Royal African Company prior to his involvement in the Georgia Plan. Instead, the trustees' opposition to the introduction of slavery in Georgia stemmed from their apprehension over the institution's impact on the colony's white population. In addition to their economic concerns, the trustees feared that if slavery were permitted Georgia would follow the same path as South Carolina or Barbados, societies where slaves performed all the labor while white settlers led lives of "luxury" and "idleness." This was exactly what the trustees hoped to prevent in Georgia. Only through hard work and discipline, the trustees believed, would the worthy poor achieve spiritual salvation and lead a virtuous life. In addition to slavery's potential impact on Georgia's moral fabric, the trustees believed the introduction of enslaved Africans would endanger the colony's security. The trustees hoped to avoid the violence that plagued virtually all slave societies in the Americas. To see the potential for problems, they had to look no farther than South Carolina, which experienced several significant slave revolts in the 1720s and early 1730s.[6] Moreover, the trustees recognized that the colony's proximity to Spanish Florida exacerbated the risk since authorities there promised freedom to runaway slaves from the English colonies. In fact, many of the male slaves who found refuge in Florida were incorporated into the colony's militia and given the opportunity to fight their former owners.[7] For the trustees, then, slavery posed a threat to the creation of their utopian society, a place where, under the tutelage and guidance of paternalistic elites, white commoners could find a semblance of equality.

Opposition to the trustees' vision of a nonslaveholding sanctuary quickly arose. Within months of the colony's founding, in fact, planters from South Carolina tried to bribe Oglethorpe to repeal the ban on slavery and the restrictions on land ownership. Despite Oglethorpe's outright rejection of their offer, South Carolinians continued to press for a change in Georgia's policies, though in a subtler manner. Although the South Carolinians were acting with their own self-interest in mind, they truly believed that slave labor was necessary to achieve any kind of financial success in the lowcountry's harsh environment. Articulating a sentiment shared by many of his peers, Samuel Eveleigh, a Charlestown merchant, declared that without slaves "Georgia can never be a Colony of any great Consequence."[8] In fact, some doubted whether the experimental colony could survive at all without slavery.

Within two years of the colony's founding, a proslavery faction formed in Georgia proper. Consisting mostly of Englishmen and Lowland Scots, these malcontents pushed relentlessly for the trustees to end the prohibition on bondage. They were mostly adventurers who paid their own passage to Georgia, where they hoped to make their fortunes. In contrast to Oglethorpe and the trustees, who viewed South Carolina and the British West Indian colonies as corrupt societies that corroded the moral character of their inhabitants, the malcontents aspired to emulate their economic success. Slavery, the malcontents argued, was not an obstacle to virtuous living but a vehicle for achieving prosperity. Patrick Tailfer, a Lowland Scot who arrived in Georgia in 1734, was one of the movement's earliest leaders. In a letter to the trustees in 1735, Tailfer communicated the malcontents' position. Their argument rested on a number of claims: whites could not labor in Georgia's oppressively hot climate without getting sick; white servants were more expensive than slaves and were more likely to flee; and, finally, Africans were accustomed to working in the heat and were more easily identifiable and therefore easier to recapture in the event of escape. The malcontents recognized that unlimited numbers of slaves could not be admitted to the colony without jeopardizing its security, but they felt that with the implementation of certain regulations these problems could be overcome. The malcontents also advocated restricting slaves to unskilled agricultural labor in order to protect white workers in Georgia and to attract more white migrants to the colony. They favored the introduction of a restricted system of slavery that would benefit the common man. Ultimately, the malcontents' initial efforts failed to persuade the trustees to alter the colony's laws, but they did lay the groundwork for future, more successful assaults on the trustees' land and labor policies.[9]

In the late 1730s and early 1740s, the trustees' utopian plans began to crumble. Thomas Stephens was the man most responsible for this change. Stephens moved to Georgia in 1737 with his father, William Stephens, who served as the trustees' secretary in the colony. Dissatisfied with the rule of law in Georgia and the colony's policies, Stephens attempted to remove Oglethorpe from power. When this failed, he submitted several reports to Parliament that detailed the colony's many troubles, specifically the land and slavery policies, which he thought doomed Georgia's success. By doing so, Stephens pulled Parliament into the debate over slavery in Georgia, which upended the dynamic between the trustees and the malcontents. His allegations found a receptive audience among critics of the Georgia Plan in the House of Commons, who used his tracts to assail the enterprise. Patrick Tailfer's publication of *A True and Historical Narrative of the Colony of Georgia*, written in 1741 after he abandoned Georgia for South Carolina, bolstered the proslavery cause. Like Stephens, Tailfer denounced

Oglethorpe's leadership and claimed the trustees' land and labor policies had condemned the colony to failure. Stephens gained some headway before halting his campaign in 1743 for unknown reasons and settling in South Carolina. Although Stephens ended his campaign before realizing his goal, his impact on shaping the debate over slavery is difficult to overstate.[10]

Not all colonists embraced ending the prohibition against slavery. Two groups in particular voiced support for the ban. The Salzburgers agreed with the trustees' guiding logic. They viewed slavery's effect on society as poisonous. Led by Johann Martin Bolzius, they settled north of Savannah at a location named Ebenezer, where they kept largely to themselves. Equally vehement in their opposition to slavery were the Highland Scots who settled near Darien. Slavery, they noted in a 1739 petition to the trustees, "is shocking to human Nature, that any Race of Mankind and their Posterity should be sentenc'd to perpetual Slavery; nor in Justice can we think otherwise of it, than they are thrown amongst us to be our Scourge one Day or other for Sins: And as Freedom must be as dear to them as to us, what a Scene of Horror must bring about! And the longer it is unexecuted, the bloody Scene must be the greater."[11] The Stono Rebellion in September 1739 confirmed slavery's opponents' worst suspicions and highlighted the danger posed by holding an enslaved population.[12]

Despite the trustees' lofty plans, Georgia struggled to survive. When the silk and wine industries failed to live up to the trustees' expectations, the economy stagnated, prompting an exodus from the colony. The population plummeted, falling in 1740 to one-sixth of its peak, according to one estimate. And those who remained "were in a starving and despicable condition."[13] Compounding matters, the charitable donations that had helped finance the experiment in Georgia dried up after 1740 as the philanthropic spirit dissipated in England. From that point on, the trustees relied on parliamentary grants to keep the colony afloat, yet even this source of funding became precarious as the complaints about Georgia's social, economic, and political problems by Thomas Stephens and his fellow malcontents filtered back to London. Members of Parliament expressed growing reservations about financing the colony unless the trustees changed the land and labor laws. The English victory over the Spanish at the Battle of Bloody Marsh, which essentially eliminated the Spanish threat to the English presence in the Southeast, undermined another argument against allowing slavery in Georgia.[14]

By 1743, the trustees' resolve had diminished. Under pressure, they gave in to their detractors' demand for the legalization of slavery. After extensive deliberations with officials and colonists in Georgia, the trustees removed the prohibition against bondage beginning on January 1, 1751. The following year the trustees' twenty-one-year tenure ended and control over the colony shifted to the Crown. It was the end of an era.[15]

The rise of royal rule marked a profound change in Georgia, not only in the colony's governance but in the colony's fortunes as well. It reversed the colony's decline, but the shift came with consequences that fundamentally undermined the original vision for the colony. The new policies reversed the sagging economy and population decline. They facilitated the move away from the production of luxury goods, such as wine and silk, to a more basic cash crop: rice. This shift also produced a change in the demography of the colony as enslaved Africans replaced English men and women as the primary workforce. The colony's new economy produced enormous wealth and proved far more successful than the trustees' earlier attempts. It also brought untold suffering. The profits were not distributed evenly; instead, they wound up concentrated in the hands of a few, mostly new immigrants to the colony. Benefiting immensely from new policies enacted under royal rule, this new planter elite had access to capital and owned the most land and the most slaves. The result was the creation of a society that mirrored its neighbor across the Savannah River, a society of profound inequalities. In short, Georgia became exactly what its founders had hoped to avoid.

Following its assumption of control over Georgia, the Crown imposed new land laws that facilitated the creation of a plantation system. While in power, the trustees had limited the size of the land grants given to settlers mostly to fifty-acre plots. The trustees enacted the policy in an effort to increase the size of Georgia's population; they were extremely concerned with settling as many people as possible to shore up the colony's defenses in case of a Spanish attack. They believed that allowing the accumulation of larger plots promoted the concentration of ownership and speculation, neither of which attracted prospective migrants. The policy, however, prompted complaints. Many settlers found the plots too small to start a farm and survive. Additionally problematic, land titles were not given to the individuals, which made it difficult for land to be passed down to heirs after the death of a husband or father. Following the transfer of power, the Crown implemented a new land policy that lifted these restrictions. The headright system removed the prohibition against ownership, enabling Georgians to pass land on to their heirs, and facilitated the accumulation of much larger tracts of land to individuals. As in Virginia's and South Carolina's earliest days, the law allowed men to claim land based on the number of their dependents, enslaved and free. The key criterion for distributing land under the new policy was whether it would be used productively. The result was that men who had political connections and owned slaves made out best. Settlements spread outward from Savannah along the Atlantic seaboard and into the many inlets that sliced into the shoreline.[16]

Attracted by the repeal of the prohibition against slavery and the implementation of the new land policy, newcomers flocked to the colony, where they scooped up vast swaths of coastal land. Having dropped from five thousand residents in 1737 to five hundred in 1741, the population rebounded after 1750 to new heights.[17] That the legal changes played a prominent part in this reversal was evident to those living in Georgia at the time. "It is true, our Georgia has been in times past, a despised land . . . in comparison with Carolina and other English colonies," Johann Martin Bolzius claimed. "But since [the colony received] those privileges which all English colonies completely enjoy regarding possession and use of the plantations, and trade and life, the disdain has stopped." The result, he noted, was that many new settlers "transport themselves and their families to us."[18] Statistics bore out his contention. By 1753, 2,381 white colonists resided in Georgia. By 1761 the white population had increased over twofold to 6,100, and by 1773 almost threefold again to 18,000.[19]

The new migrants brought with them a worldview that embraced plantation slavery. Unlike their earlier counterparts, many of those who immigrated after 1750 arrived from slave societies with substantial wealth, including slaves. Migrants from South Carolina led the way.[20] One of the first groups came from the Beach Hill Congregation, whose members abandoned their homes en masse and settled in Georgia in 1752. Soon after their departure, William G. DeBrahm noted, the "Spirit of Emigration" became "so universal" that "many rich Carolina Planters followed the Example of that Congregation, and came with all their Families and Negroes to settle in Georgia."[21] Having run out of new land to cultivate in South Carolina, they looked south of the Savannah River and saw the potential to expand their operations into seemingly virgin territory. Some of the wealthiest men in South Carolina established plantations in Georgia, including Henry Laurens, James Bulloch, Joseph

Tatnall, and the Gibbons brothers. In addition to the Carolina émigrés, a significant number of planters from the West Indies settled in Georgia. Men like Clement Martin, Edmund Tannatt, and Lewis Johnson bought land and hoped to emulate the success of lowcountry grandees.[22]

The white population increase, significant in its own right, did not compare with the black population increase. Despite the ban on slavery, a small contingent of blacks was present in Georgia from the colony's founding, having been brought there by Oglethorpe to help erect the settlement's first buildings.[23] After 1750, the scope of the black presence changed dramatically. The population increased exponentially in the first twenty years of slavery, growing from six hundred in 1751 to fifteen thousand in 1775.[24] The importation of slaves from the West Indies and Africa accounted for most of this growth and followed a clear pattern. From 1755 until 1765, most imported slaves came from the West Indies in small groups; the cargoes on board these ships usually included ten to twenty captives and rarely exceeded sixty total. The schooner Franklin, which plied the waters of the coastal and Caribbean trade, exemplified this trend. It docked in Savannah in late January 1756 from St. Christopher's with twenty slaves on board. In the mid-1760s, the shipments of slaves arriving in Georgia grew in size and frequency. Increasingly, the vessels came directly from Africa, rather than from the West Indies, and their cargoes routinely reached two hundred or more slaves. For example, the Constantine brought a cargo of 250 slaves from Angola in 1768.[25] The trade in slaves directly from Africa marked the ascent of Georgia's colonial plantation society to maturity.

Members of the slaveholding elite controlled the slave supply and profited handsomely from this role. After imported slaves arrived in Savannah or Sunbury, slave traders sold them in lots and by auction. Prices for slaves ranged from £30 to £50 for common laborers and £75 to £100 or more for skilled workers.[26] In 1772 alone, the total value of slaves imported to the colony reached £20,000.[27] Far from the caricature of the nineteenth-century slave trader as the marginalized outsider, the most prominent peddlers of African flesh in early Georgia counted themselves among the colony's elite. For example, this group included Joseph Clay and James Habersham Jr., whose firm imported 610 Africans to Georgia between 1768 and 1771.[28] Clay, Habersham, and other slave traders in Georgia made fortunes from selling Africans, which they invested in more land and labor, expanding their grip on the colony's economy.

Slaveholders exploited the labor of their slaves to create a thriving agricultural system based on rice production. Most of the slaves imported from Africa in the 1760s and 1770s came from Senegambia and Sierra Leone.[29] Having come to Georgia with the express purpose of establishing rice plantations, planter émigrés preferred bondmen and -women from these two regions because of their familiarity with this crop. The slaves' extensive knowledge of cultivation techniques made them a valuable commodity for Georgia's planters.[30] Under the trustees, settlers had shied away from rice cultivation under the assumption that it required labor unsuitable for whites. Instead they focused their energy on the production of silk and wine. With the restrictions against bondage removed, rice plantations took root south of the Savannah River and quickly spread down the Georgia coast.

Rice planting was a particularly expensive endeavor, thus rendering it an occupation undertaken exclusively by the rich. The crop grew only in certain types of soil and had to be produced on a large scale to be profitable. Consequently, individuals hoping to cultivate the crop needed a huge outlay of capital to begin operations. William G. DeBrahm estimated that it required at least £2,476 to purchase the two hundred acres of land, to buy the forty slaves, and to cover the other expenses needed to start production.[31] By contrast, Henry Laurens, a successful rice planter with operations in South Carolina and Georgia, believed it could not be done for less than three times that amount.[32] James Habersham agreed that any attempt to operate a rice plantation would be expensive. The lands near the coast, he asserted, "cannot be advantageously improved, but by people, who can purchase a number of Negroes, and many plantations from their peculiar situation require a large extent of land for reservoirs to water their fields, and other purposes, they are neither favourable to population, nor suitable to people in middling circumstances to cultivate."[33] Initially, those interested in purchasing land in Georgia could do so at moderate prices, but by the mid-1760s choice land had become scarce, at least at reasonable rates.[34] For example, Hutchinson's Island, located in the river before Savannah, was purchased during the trusteeship for £20 sterling, but by the end of the royal period the land could not be purchased for £10,000.[35] By the end of the colonial period, sixty individuals, fewer than 5 percent of all landowners, owned 20 percent of the land granted by the government, which amounted to 350,000 acres; twenty of them owned from 5,000 to 27,000 acres. These grandees owned an average of 2,500 acres worked by forty to forty-five slaves.[36] They dominated the economy, possessed the best lands, and owned the most slaves. Georgia's lowcountry became the domain of wealthy, white, slaveholding planters.

Georgia underwent a profound economic transformation after the introduction of plantation slavery and rice cultivation. The connection between the two did not escape the notice of commentators from the period. In his analysis of Georgia's economy, William G. DeBrahm recognized that as "soon as this Province became free from those prohibitions" against bondage, the colony's economy soared. Most, though not all, of the economic growth was tied to the establishment of rice cultivation. Between 1754 and 1770, exports grew more than five times over and the value increased by more than sixfold. The number of ships docking in Savannah increased over threefold. The rice crop grew from three thousand barrels in 1754 to almost fifteen thousand in 1769.[37] In addition to rice, Georgia exported indigo, skins, and timber and timber-related products, including shingles, staves, tar, and turpentine. Economic growth occurred steadily in the 1750s but accelerated in the mid-1760s, coinciding with the end of the Seven Years' War and the rise in the number of African slaves imported to the colony. The rise of the export economy brought great rewards for those able to afford the stakes. The result was that the enormous wealth produced by Georgia slaves ended up concentrated in the hands of a few individuals. Barring misfortune, like hurricanes or other natural disasters, rice planters whose slaves raised 350 barrels of rice a year could hope to make a profit of 25 to 30 percent annually.[38] The profit rates increased for those whose slaves also produced indigo or timber-related goods. By the mid-1760s, for example, James Habersham owned several thousands acres of land, two plantations, and more than two hundred slaves, which together earned him £2,000 annually.[39]

By the 1760s, a new leadership had coalesced in Georgia, composed mostly of émigrés from South Carolina and the West Indies. After displacing the men who had ruled the colony in its first two decades, the planter elite took control over the machinery of government and enacted legislation to suit its interests. The planter elite jettisoned the colony's initial slave laws, which tended to mitigate the power of slave owners, and moved society away from the vision offered by Oglethorpe and the trustees. Instead, the planter elite adopted regulations similar to those found in South Carolina and the slave societies of the British West Indies. That meant creating a slave code that gave slave owners maximum flexibility in terms of how they chose to use their property and that placed harsh new restrictions on the colony's slaves. The transition did not come without dissent, however. As the planter elite moved to secure its hold on power, it faced external opposition from groups that sought to place limits on its authority.

The change in the structure of government in Georgia from trustee to Crown rule created the planter elite as the new ruling class. Before 1750, the trustees, in conjunction with a body named the Georgia Council, governed the colony; after the Crown took over the system changed. The king appointed a governor to lead the royal government. The monarch also appointed wealthy men to the Council. The Council, made up of seven to twelve men, served as the upper house. Only men over the age of twenty who owned fifty acres of land or more voted in the elections for the Commons House of Assembly. The House initially consisted of nineteen men, but the number grew to twenty-five in 1760 following the creation of new parishes that year.[40] Planters dominated all branches of colonial government. In all, between fifty and one hundred men controlled the vast majority of wealth and power. Governor Wright alone owned eleven plantations on the Savannah, Ogeechee, and Canoochee rivers and 523 slaves. Georgia's leaders used their control over the system to create laws that suited their own interests. In his study of colonial Georgia, historian W. W. Abbot revealed the link between economic and political power in the colony: "In this small and unformed country the rising merchant or planter soon learned that his private interests were touched by every conceivable aspect of public policy. Every measure of the government . . . was likely to have an immediate and sometimes vital effect on his planting and trading interests." As a result, "The prudent man put himself in a position to exercise some control over the decisions made about these things." Abbot concluded that "As members of the Assembly, or less often of the Council, the merchants and planters asserted political as well as economic leadership, though political power had to be shared with the royal governor."[41]

Upon coming to power, the planter elite rewrote the colony's laws pertaining to slavery to provide slaveholders the greatest latitude and flexibility. There were substantive differences between the 1750 slave code and its successors. The laws enacted by the trustees placed constraints on the institution's growth and regulated whites' behavior. For example, the 1750 slave code imposed a four-to-one ratio on the number of slaves allowed in Georgia. In doing so, the trustees hoped to prevent a tremendous increase in the size of the colony's black population because they feared the danger it posed. They did not want to re-create the conditions in South Carolina that had contributed to the Stono Rebellion in 1739. The trustees also required whites to treat their slaves humanely. They allowed slave owners to punish their bondmen and -women, but their chastisements could not endanger the life or limb of the slaves. Similarly, whites who murdered blacks faced punishment as if the victims of the crime were white, which meant they could be hanged. The trustees also required slave owners to provide religious instruction for their slaves.[42]

By contrast, the slave codes of 1755, 1765, and 1770 represented a very different vision of slavery. Modeled on the laws in South Carolina and the West Indies, these slave codes regulated slaves' behavior rather than that of slave owners, placing a host of new restrictions on the colony's slaves and removing many of the slave owners' legal obligations. After 1755, slaves needed written permission to leave their plantations, consume alcohol, or buy or sell goods. They could not meet in groups without white supervision, nor could they beat drums or play loud musical instruments. Slaves faced capital punishment for a range of transgressions, from injuring whites to crimes against property. For certain offenses, the law called for extreme violence. For example, slaves convicted of poisoning could be burned alive at the stake. Planters further reduced slaves' legal protections when they gave themselves greater latitude to punish their slaves without fear of prosecution and dropped the provision that permitted whites who killed blacks to be hanged. Lastly, the new slave codes increased the permissible ratio to twenty slaves to one man "capable of bearing arms," which removed an important obstacle to the creation of large plantations.[43]

The rise of the planter elite did not come without opposition. Georgia planters and the Crown disagreed over the legal definition of slaves: Should the law treat slaves as chattel property or real estate? The controversy erupted in 1765 when the authorities in Georgia sent a copy of their latest slave code to the Crown for final authorization. Much to the planters' shock, the Council to the Board of Trade rejected the slave code. The Crown opposed the slave code because it wanted to limit planters' abilities to break up plantations and sell their slaves. Rather than a commodity to be exchanged like any other type of good, slaves, according to the Crown's reasoning, should be connected to the property, like feudal serfs or *encomiendera* Indians. The Crown had good reason for this. It hoped to establish a permanent presence in Georgia and feared that the provision in the 1765 slave code allowing planters to sell their slaves would undercut these efforts. The Crown desired stability and believed that restricting the rights of slave owners could accomplish this goal. The Crown feared that following a planter's death, his estate would be broken up and abandoned.[44]

The planter elite in Georgia defended chattel slavery as necessary to the maintenance and prosperity of rice-based plantation slavery. When the authorities in Georgia found out about the decision, they were flabbergasted. Passage of the 1765 slave code, as originally drafted, they contended, was "of the utmost Importance and without it we cannot well subsist." While the Crown saw its efforts as a means of establishing stability in Georgia, the colony's planters viewed the proposed provision in a completely different light. The restriction would have fundamentally undercut their rights as property holders. The fluid nature of cash crop production and slavery in the Americas necessitated absolute flexibility for planters, particularly in a newly developed colony such as Georgia. Rice cultivation required a significant outlay of capital and was fraught with risk. The planters needed the ability to move their slave property however they saw fit to maximize their profits or to liquidate their plantations in times of economic duress. "In a young and extensive Country like this," Georgia's authorities complained, "where Property must necessarily be frequently Aliened and new Settlements daily made, many cogent Reasons might be urged against" the Crown's efforts.[45] Planters launched a campaign to force the Board of Trade to reverse its ruling on the issue. The struggle persisted for several years before finally coming to a close in 1770, when Georgia successfully submitted a revised slave code. Ultimately, the authorities in Georgia prevailed in their struggle with the Crown. They retained the right to treat their slaves as chattel property and displayed their intention to exert their rights as slaveholders like their counterparts in other slave societies in the British Empire.[46]

The colony's nonslaveholders posed a more significant challenge to the colony's planter elite. The conflict between the slaveholders and nonslaveholders focused on a core argument: should owners be permitted to use their slaves, their property, however they saw fit? The trustees had conceived of Georgia as a sanctuary for white labor. Even after they agreed to allow slavery, they had hoped to preserve the colony in a way to mitigate the effects of slavery on society. The trustees crafted the slave code of 1750 to protect slaves and draw more settlers to the colony. To do so, they limited colonists to employing their slaves in agricultural work, with the exception of coopers and sawyers, who could use them as apprentices. Slaves could not hire themselves out. In developing the colony's slave laws on slave occupations, the trustees attempted to avoid the problems they discerned in South Carolina. There, Johann Martin Bolzius noted, "all kinds of craftsmen" were "necessary for the country, such as carpenters, masons, blacksmiths, locksmiths, shoemakers, tailors, saddle makers, cooper, carriage builders, tanners, gunsmiths, turners, weavers. But since the Negroes learn all kinds of common and useful crafts, the poor [white] craftsmen cannot succeed. In Georgia, Negroes are not allowed to learn a craft except the cooper craft." Consequently, he proudly noted, there "is still a shortage of carpenters, turners, brickmakers, carriage builders, and potters in Georgia."[47] The limitations on slave occupations under the trustees' vision created opportunities for white men as skilled laborers.

Georgia's mechanics embraced the trustees' logic related to slavery. Even before the ban on slavery was lifted, they had begun organizing themselves to protect their interests. Like Bolzius, they understood what unfettered competition with slave labor would do to their economic livelihoods. And they also hoped to avoid the fate of their counterparts in Charlestown, where slave mechanics dominated the trades. In 1746, mechanics in Savannah proclaimed their intent to set their own prices for their labor. They did so without consulting the trustees, who ultimately ignored the mechanics' actions. Although this effort failed in the immediate sense, eventually it did bear fruit. The mechanics made clear that they intended to protect their interests and were prepared to organize to achieve their goals. And unless the colonial authorities wanted to provoke the wrath of yet another group of potential malcontents, they would have to keep this in mind as they moved forward. In 1750 the mechanics formed the Union Society, a group devoted to promoting their interests. The trustees consulted the mechanics as they drafted the colony's first slave code of 1750. The provision restricting slaves to agricultural work no doubt reflected the mechanics' influence.[48]

Immediately after the transfer of power to royal rule, the planter elite began to exert its authority by chipping away at the restrictions on the rules pertaining to the employment of slaves. In 1755, they modified the slave code to allow slaves the right to self-hire; although the code kept many of the same restrictions on black skilled labor on the books, this shift undermined the intent of the law. Three years later, under pressure from the mechanics, the colonial authorities approved a new law that prohibited the introduction of slave mechanics into the colony, but the legislation came with a host of provisions that further weakened the stated intent of the law. The law did not apply to slaves who lived on farms. Slaves could be used as shipwrights, caulkers, sawyers, coopers, porters, or laborers. White handicraft tradesmen who owned one slave were allowed to use him. Further, if white carpenters, joiners, bricklayers, plasterers, or other tradesmen could not be found for a job, blacks might be employed with limitation after compliance with a few procedures. For the white mechanics, most likely the worst provision contained in the 1758 law called for the creation of a board to oversee their work and rates. Influenced by the planter elite, the body made sure that mechanics were not overcharging and that the colony's needs were being properly met. In instances where members of the board believed it appropriate, the restrictions against using slave labor could be removed entirely.[49]

The 1758 law highlighted the growing class conflict in Georgia. While anger with tradesmen's prices certainly factored into planters' designs to oversee the mechanics' operations, it was only one part of their rationale. Far more important, from the planters' perspective, was that they did not want to be told how they could use their slaves, especially by nonslaveholders. They chafed at restrictions against using slaves as skilled laborers. Many planters believed the mechanics exploited their position. The board was the product of contentious discussions that pitted the mechanics against the emerging planter class. Five wealthy opponents of the bill argued that artisans only wished to "indulge the Greediness and insatiable Thirst after Gain."[50] John Graham led the effort and later served as the lieutenant governor of the colony and as a member of the board. In the latter position, he worked assiduously to deny mechanics any type of labor protection.[51]

When the 1758 law targeting slave mechanics expired, the legislature failed to renew it. Without restrictions, slaves took over a significant portion of skilled work in Georgia's cities and towns. By the Revolution, slaves performed much of the unskilled and skilled work in Georgia, more so even than in South Carolina. They formed the nucleus of the building construction trades as carpenters, painters, and bricklayers. They could be found working as blacksmiths, coopers, mechanics, and tanners as well as in less skilled capacities as porters and draymen. Whether working for hire or directly under their owners, the result was the same. They undercut their white competition and reduced the need for white nonslaveholders in Georgia, particularly those bent upon protecting their economic rights at the expense of the planter elite.[52] The conflict between the planter elite and white mechanics revealed, first, that white nonslaveholders posed a challenge to the planter elite's power in Georgia and that their presence could be detrimental to the planter elite's economic interests, and second, that the planter elite believed that slaves could meet virtually all of its labor needs. The new slave code represented a fundamental reversal in policy toward slaves and had dramatic consequences for relations among whites. The rise of the planter elite came at the expense of the colony's white nonslaveholders, particularly the mechanics.

The introduction of slavery and the plantation complex in Georgia fundamentally altered the colony's labor system and social relations. Whites in Georgia commonly accepted the wisdom that only Africans could labor in the colony's harsh climate. This was particularly true when it came to rice cultivation. Despite the fact that rice brought vast wealth to planters in South Carolina, Georgia's early settlers had shunned the crop because of its association with slave labor. Soon after the ban on slavery was lifted, rice plantations became an ubiquitous sight along the Georgia coast. The vast majority of slaves who arrived in the colony after surviving the middle passage wound up on these plantations, where they struggled to adjust to their new lives in America.

Rice cultivation in the lowcountry underwent a significant transformation that roughly coincided with the repeal of the prohibition against slavery in Georgia. In the five decades after the crop first emerged as a viable export commodity in South Carolina in the late seventeenth century, rice had been cultivated in inland swamps. In the middle of the eighteenth century, however, new techniques emerged that altered how and where rice could be grown. The new system relied on tidal flows to irrigate the fields. As a result, planters began to establish plantations in areas that had previously been viewed as unsuitable for the cultivation of rice or any other crop. Tidal flow rice production bore striking similarities to the methods used to grow rice in West Africa, which has led some historians to the conclusion that the African slaves imported from this region in the mid-eighteenth century introduced these new techniques. Slaves' knowledge and engineering skills, historians argue, made possible the revolution in lowcountry rice cultivation, which, ironically, substantially increased the annual yields and the planters' profits, thus allowing them to invest in more slaves. While the degree to which African slaves can be credited with the innovations in rice production remains open to debate, it is clear that tens of thousands of West African slaves arrived in Georgia and South Carolina in the mid-eighteenth century and their labor proved essential to the efforts to transform coastal Georgia's landscape from tidal swamps into productive rice fields. Using only their bare hands, simple tools, and buckets, slaves moved literally millions of cubic feet of soil to construct the earthen banks, which reached six feet high and fifteen feet wide, that surrounded the rice fields and made tidal cultivation possible. Slaves abhorred this type of labor, known as "mudwork." The one benefit of tidal production to field slaves was that it shortened the time they spent weeding. Regardless of the changes in the system of production, however, one thing remained constant: the dismal conditions in which the slaves labored. For much of the day, slaves worked in knee-deep water. This insalubrious environment fostered illnesses, such as dysentery and malaria, that ravaged slaves' health and shortened their lives.[53]

The work regime for slaves on rice plantations in Georgia was strenuous, periodically exhausting, and year-round. The initial stage in the process occurred between late December and March, during which time slaves burned the stubble from the previous season and cleared and leveled the fields in preparation for planting. In two separate stretches, from mid-March to early April and late May to early June, slaves then sowed seeds in the fields. In July and August, the fields underwent a series of controlled floods, and after each the slaves hoed and weeded to remove all unwanted growth. The process yielded two crops per year. The harvest began in late August and continued until October. Slaves collected the rice by hand using a sickle. After the slaves finished gathering the final crop, they started the last and most physically demanding stage of the cycle: milling. Using a mortar and pestle, slaves, usually females, threshed millions of pounds of rice each year, a process that took upward of two months and often lasted until it was time to recommence the routine all over again. Exacerbating the slaves' travails at this point in the cycle was the fact that they had to perform the onerous task of fixing the earthen banks that enclosed the rice fields in advance of the preparation for planting the following year's crop. In addition to their work cultivating rice, and the ancillary activities associated with it, slaves were required to erect and mend fences and, on most plantations, grow their own food. Most planters supplied some food for their slaves, but not enough to survive.[54]

The dominant system of labor on rice plantations in Georgia, as well as South Carolina, was the task system. The task system differed in fundamental ways from the gang labor system prevalent throughout most of the Chesapeake. Under the gang system, slaves had to labor for a set number of hours each day, usually from sunup to sundown, under the direct supervision of a white overseer who set the pace of work. Under the task system, by contrast, slaves had to perform a set amount of labor each day. The quantity of work that constituted a completed task changed depending on the type of labor. After they finished their task, slaves could use their remaining time to pursue other activities. For most slaves, that meant supplementing their families' diets through gardening, hunting, or fishing. What their families did not consume from these activities, they sold for a profit, enabling some slaves to accumulate modest amounts of cash and property, including cattle, pigs, horses, and even wagons, that rivaled and sometimes exceeded the holdings of some poor whites. The slaves' entrepreneurial spirit did not escape the notice of Georgia whites, who recognized the "skilful and industrious" efforts of the bondmen and -women. At times, however, the slaves' business acumen prompted vitriolic responses from whites. When female slaves came to dominate the market in Savannah, for example, the city's white residents chafed at what they deemed to be exorbitant prices charged by the black market women. Yet, because these women supplied virtually all of the produce in the region, there was little that whites could do. Although completing the daily work requirement was by no means a simple feat, the task system did offer slaves greater control over their daily lives and working conditions.[55]

The origins of the task system are unclear. Planters likely would have preferred to retain as much control over the pace of labor as possible. They would not have benevolently and magnanimously bestowed the task system on their slaves. Instead, the task system probably emerged as a product of negotiation between planters and slaves. Indeed, the terms of the task system demonstrate that Africans, who possessed essential knowledge about rice cultivation, compelled their owners to compromise on a work regime that granted them a degree of flexibility in return for their labor. The task system, then, was a testament to the agency of the lowcountry's enslaved population, whose expertise was an essential element in the cultivation of rice.[56]

While slaves primarily enriched their masters through the cultivation of rice, they labored in secondary industries as well. Following in the footsteps of their counterparts in South Carolina and the West Indies, many planters experimented with indigo. The crop was difficult to produce, yet it proved a lucrative addition for those willing to invest the time and effort to cultivate it properly. For many planters, timber-related products offered a simpler solution. For these "industrious people," the swamplands of the lowcountry provided a bountiful natural resource. Their slaves felled fir, oak, and cypress trees in the marshlands and turned them into a range of goods, such as building lumber, ships' masts, shingles, and barrels, which planters exported to Europe and the West Indies for significant profit. Of course, logging came with an added incentive: as the slaves cut down the forests, they cleared more land for rice cultivation. For the planters, then, logging was doubly beneficial. Another profitable secondary enterprise for Georgia's planters was brickmaking and bricklaying. As the colony prospered after 1750, demand for bricks grew. Men such as Thomas Lee, who owned a brickyard in Savannah, sought to capitalize on this trend.[57]

Georgia rice planters strove to make their plantations self-sufficient, which meant they needed slaves who could perform a range tasks beyond those directly associated with agriculture. In addition to their field laborers, many planters kept a retinue of slave craftsmen, including sawyers, mechanics, carpenters, and coopers. John Graham, for example, owned almost twenty-seven thousand acres of land divided between two plantations, Monteith and Mulberry Grove. More than 150 slaves labored on his estates. While most of this group consisted of field hands, thirty of them served as house servants, including a coachman, a steward, a tailor, waiting boys, cooks, and a midwife. In addition, another group of eight to ten male slaves performed skilled labor, including a driver, two carpenters, two boatmen, four sawyers, two carters, and one cooper. This legion of slaves met virtually all of Graham's needs.[58] Even on smaller plantations, planters kept slaves with specialized skills, even if they did not use these laborers exclusively in that capacity. By using their slaves to do skilled work on their plantations, planters lessened the need for white workers, which discouraged nonelite white migrants from settling in Georgia.[59]

Slaves' abilities to perform highly skilled tasks as well as or better than white workingmen undercut the validity of white supremacy and undermined the notion that blacks, or more precisely, black men, were inferior to all white men. Owners came to recognize the value and intelligence of these slaves. James Habersham, for example, bragged about the talent of his cooper; the man filled a critical role in Habersham's operations and represented an important asset. Consequently, the planter "had no Intention to part with him" regardless of the circumstances. According to Habersham, this cooper was not an exception, but the rule. In recognition of the talent of Georgia's skilled slaves, Habersham asserted that "daily Experience evinces, that there are many ingenious Mechanicks among them, and as far as they have had Opportunity of being instructed, have discovered as good abilities, as are usually found among people of our Colony."[60] This knowledge forced some whites to reevaluate or ignore blanket assumptions about intelligence and race. Many planters formed relationships with their slaves that, while clearly paternalistic, did not preclude them from judging the value of a black man's opinion to be superior to that of a white man's. Planters consulted leading slave men about the state of the plantation and even asked them for planting advice. These planters recognized and respected leaders among the slaves. Nowhere was this more evident than in the relationship between planters and black drivers.

By law, planters were required to maintain a ratio of one white man for every twenty slaves they held on their plantations. Since many planters preferred to reside in Savannah, St. Mary's, or Darien rather than in the countryside, they resorted to using overseers to watch over day-to-day operations. Yet many planters expressed nothing but contempt for this class of worker, though there were some exceptions. Planters complained that overseers often tried to deceive their employers or, conversely, were deceived by their slaves.[61] Consequently, some planters chose to forego using white overseers altogether. Instead, they installed "the most loyal Negroes as Negro drivers" to run their plantations.[62] For example, Savannah merchant and planter Samuel Douglass opted to place a black driver in charge of his plantation on Skidway Island rather than hire a white overseer.[63] The practice had developed in South Carolina, where planters often flouted a similar law; as a result, one contemporary claimed, it was commonplace in some parts of that colony to see plantations with one hundred or more slaves without any white supervision.[64] When the plantation complex spread to Georgia, so too did the custom. Slave drivers who oversaw plantation operations had to be extremely knowledgeable about cultivation, labor supervision, and engineering. They had to know when to plant, irrigate, and weed. Habersham understood the value of a good driver. When Jacob, the driver on his Dean Forest plantation, became ill, the planter was beside himself. Jacob was such a "valuable Negro and excellent Planter" that Habersham admitted that "cou'd I preserve his Life I wou'd not take any Money for him, not even £150 sterling." Slaveholders recognized their slaves as valuable property, but they also recognized them as "excellent Planter[s]" in their own right.[65] Slaves were not just beasts of burden; they possessed skills and intelligence that made them capable of supervising other slaves and plantation operations.

Georgia became a slave society at roughly the same time that the first protests against the institution were emerging. Many of those opposed to slavery based their position on humanitarian ideals that advocated a universal understanding of mankind. Planters in Georgia neither relented on their commitment to slavery nor ridiculed the assumptions that lay at the core of antislavery arguments. Instead the planters embraced them, at least in part. Hoping to soften the image of slavery as a brutal and coercive system of labor, some members of the planter elite made a self-conscious effort to create an ameliorated version of slavery. Tapping into crosscurrents of philosophy, such as the Enlightenment, these planters aspired to create a new, more humane institution. The spread of this new ideology influenced the way that planters in Georgia shaped slavery and their relations with their slaves. Increasingly, elite planters came to think of themselves as patriarchs who ruled over both their white and black families. These planters expressed newfound concern in their slaves' personal lives and for their material and spiritual well-being. This change was the product of an emerging sense of humanity that included those previously considered beyond the pale of civilized society. That these planters began to "care" for the well-being of their slaves does not mean that they were on course to abandon the institution. On the contrary, planters believed that amelioration strengthened the institution. Their recognition of slaves' humanity did not pose a significant challenge to the morality of owning another person.[66]

Historians have documented the influence of South Carolina on slavery in Georgia. The cash crop, the system of labor, and even the individuals who formed a significant portion of the planter elite all had their origins in Georgia's northern neighbor. For that reason, it was only natural that, when drafting their earliest slave codes, Georgia's authorities initially turned to South Carolina as a model slave society. Of the historians who study early Georgia, Betty Wood has done the most to highlight the links between the two colonies as reflected in their respective slave laws. In her important work *Slavery in Colonial Georgia*, Wood notes similarities in the language used in the slave codes of Georgia and South Carolina. Pointing to changes in the form of punishments and restrictions on slaves, she demonstrates the degree to which Georgia's authorities relied on their more experienced counterparts in South Carolina.[67]

White Georgians initially turned to South Carolina as a model slave society. But, by the mid-1760s, as Georgia's slave society matured, the colony's planter elite sought a new model, one that better reflected their vision of a well-ordered society. Although there had been and continued to be close connections between South Carolina and Georgia, planters in the latter colony increasingly pursued their own path. Before drafting a revised slave code for the colony in 1765, Governor James Wright noted that Georgia's authorities had consulted "with great care & attention" the "Negro Laws of Jamaica, So. Carolina & Virginia."[68] By blending successful aspects of other slave societies, the officials believed they had improved the institution. In contrast to the colony's first slave code under royal rule, which "was framed on the plan of that of So Carolina," they felt that the 1765 slave code was superior because "it was framed on more extensive and humane principles than our former Law or that now in Force in So Carolina."[69] The comments of the Duc de la Rochefoucauld-Liancourt, a French visitor to the lowcountry region, suggest that the authorities in Georgia achieved at least a modicum of success in their endeavors. After visiting both, he asserted that "the laws affecting slaves are more moderate in Georgia than in Carolina. They are also of English origin, but since they are thirty years more recent than the other, they have been influenced by the spirit of philosophy and humanity that has characterized the writing of the latter part of this century, and with some exceptions they seem to me to be about as moderate and fair as possible for a system."[70]

One outgrowth of Georgia planters' humanitarian zeal was a new concern for their slaves' welfare. As owners came to recognize the humanity of their slaves, they developed emotional attachments to them. By the time the plantation regime had matured in Georgia, some owners and slaves had known each other for more than a decade. James Habersham, for example, expressed genuine sadness when one of his female slaves died in 1764. The woman had been a family "favorite" who had nursed his daughters. He noted that the woman's husband was "inconsolable." The woman's death left Habersham shaken: "I must own the sight of her has affected me more than all the negroes I have ever lost." His grief was so intense it left him emotionally devastated for weeks. Eight years later Habersham experienced similar heartache when a slave boy died from rabies. The child "was in every respect worthy of regard" and "had made such an Impression on me, that I believe, will never be blotted out of my memory." In all his years as a slaveholder, dozens of his slaves had died, but none had affected him in this way. "I have buried near 80 Negroes, little and big, but their Deaths, I have received as common accidents, and have acquiesced in the Dispensation of divine Providence, as I hope I do in this." This boy's death was different. "I cannot divest myself of Humanity—The Cries and Intreaties of the Mother begging her Child to be put to Death, the dreadfull shrieks of the Boy, and his more than pretty Behaviour in his taking leave of all around him has run such a Peal in my Ears, that I never can forget, and which it is impossible for me to describe, and hope never to meet with the like again." Habersham considered himself so affected by the scene as a natural result of his own humanity and his recognition of the humanity of his slaves. The leave-taking between the boy and his mother particularly struck him. When referring to the episode, he noted that a "very shocking Circumstance has happened in my Family."[71] Whether or not the slave considered himself part of his master's family, Habersham considered him a member.

Planters' newfound concern for their slaves extended to the work regime. Profits were the chief concern of planters and the primary reason for investing in plantation slavery in Georgia, but by the 1760s some members of the planter elite placed less emphasis on the bottom line. They expressed the need to strike a balance between their economic needs and their slaves' suffering. Consequently, they tried to ease the labor demands placed on their bondmen and -women. By 1765, James Habersham, having made a fortune, could afford to play the benevolent patriarch. His plantations produced seven hundred barrels of rice a year "without Hurry and too much driving," which he declared was quite satisfactory. He did not want to tax his slaves too much.[72] When John Channing left his Georgia estates in the hands of Edward Telfair while he was in England, he impressed on Telfair that his first concern was with the way his slaves would be managed. "I wish them to be treated as reasonable creatures," Channing stated, "that is, with humanity and kindness." Similarly, Henry Laurens declared in 1773 that he preferred an overseer who "makes less rice with more hands but treats my Negroes with Humanity" over "one who should make twice as much Rice & exercise any degree of Cruelty towards those poor creatures who look up to their Master as their Father, their Guardian, & Protector, & to whom there is a reciprocal obligation upon the Master." Many of the same planters resorted to bribery to cajole their slaves to do more than the customary amount of labor. In July 1773, Josiah Smith provided the slaves on the plantation he managed with clothes, beef, and liquor "to Encourage their Perseverance" while they performed the onerous task of weeding the summer rice fields. He claimed it would give him "pleasure" to give the slaves "some little articles, to make them more comfortable, as long as they continue to deserve it." Concern for slaves' welfare extended to those hired out as well. Some owners refused to hire out their slaves to whites who had reputations for treating slaves poorly, for fear it would undermine their slaves' trust in them. Mary Dedingfield refused to hire out her female slave Matt to a man "who is Reputed by the Negroes . . . to be one of the severest masters." Matt would end up resenting her situation and run away, Dedingfield feared. These slaveholders believed that they had imposed a labor regime based upon the dictates of humanity and kindness.[73]

As some members of the planter elite embraced the new humanitarianism, they came to rely less explicitly on physical coercion and punishment to force their workers to act according to their wishes. They found other ways to accomplish their objectives. When James Habersham wanted one of his slaves to do something against his will, he insisted, "I do not chuse to make use of force and violence" to get them to heed his word. Yet his aversion to physical coercion did not mean his slaves did not suffer serious consequences for their "misbehavior."[74] Their pain was felt in different ways. Increasingly, planters used separation to threaten or punish recalcitrant slaves. Consequently, sale became the choice of punishment for some "enlightened" planters. John Houstoun tried to sell two of his recalcitrant slaves: "I find my Negroes have begun their old pranks. I wish you would be good enough to make some Inquiry and find whether the blame lies altogether on the Black side. If so I am of opinion Jacob and Pompey must at all counts be shipt off—this I'll do even if I get but £5 a piece for them."[75] Planters praised themselves for resisting the urge to sell individual slaves because they did not want to divide families. Yet they showed little concern about selling a slave as punishment. Henry Laurens, for example, refused to sell individual slaves to Elias Ball unless he bought the rest of the family as well. He opposed "this unnecessary division of Fathers, Mothers, Husbands, Wives, & Children who tho' Slaves are still human creatures & I cannot be deaf to their cries least a time should come when I should cry & there shall be none to pity me." Yet Laurens decided in 1764 that his slave Abram had to be sold, as an example to his fellow slaves, for repeated bad behavior. Laurens meticulously listed Abram's five faults, including his over "Fond[ness] of Women," against his eight good qualities, including sobriety. Ironically, once planters came to recognize the humanity of their slaves, they used it against them.[76]

Just as some planters expressed concern for their slaves' physical well-being, they hoped to do the same for their spiritual well-being. When the trustees enacted the colony's first slave code in 1750, they included a provision that forbade slaves from laboring on the Sabbath and required owners to provide religious instruction for their slaves. This mandate proved extremely controversial among some planters, particularly after the trustees, in conjunction with the Society for the Propagation of the Gospel, arranged for Joseph Ottolenghe to go to Georgia and minister to the colony's slaves. Despite the law, most planters initially refused to allow their slaves access to religious instruction. Some feared the consequences of teaching their slaves the Scripture, while others believed Africans to be too ignorant to comprehend the Gospel. For many planters, the underlying motive was that religious instruction took precious time away from developing their plantations and cultivating their crops. Opposition to instructing slaves came from West Indian planters, in particular, who felt that Christianized bondmen were "ten times worse" than those in a "State of Paganism."[77] As a result of their protests, the authorities dropped the provision on religious instruction when they drafted the slave code of 1755.

Reform-minded planters embraced religious instruction for their slaves even without legislative mandate and even in the face of opposition. By the 1760s, a growing number of influential and wealthy planters had come to the conclusion that, in their roles as patriarchs, they were required to provide religious instruction to their bondmen. To that end, they employed men with religious training to preach to their slaves and teach them to read and write, despite the prohibition against doing so. One of the most sustained and well-funded attempts to bring Christianity to Georgia's slaves followed the death of the Anglican rector of Savannah, Reverend Bartholomew Zouberbuhler, in 1766. Zouberbuhler, who prospered in the brick business, left a significant portion of his estate to pay for a catechist for his slaves. The executors of his will hired Cornelius Winter, a Methodist under the influence of George Whitefield, to come from England to serve in that capacity. Winter arrived in 1769, and from the outset he faced spirited resistance from a contingent of planters who resented his efforts to proselytize among slaves from neighboring plantations. They viewed this expansion of his mandate to be a clear (and potentially dangerous) breach of etiquette. The controversy sparked by

Winter's actions highlighted the continued divisions over religious instruction for slaves. For James Habersham, one of Winter's most ardent supporters and a chief proponent of reform, the opposition to exposing slaves to the teachings of Christianity was unforgivable: "It is to me unaccountable, that any people calling themselves Christians, should have any objections against having their Servants instructed." Ultimately, Winter returned to England when objections to his efforts mounted, yet his departure did not end the attempts by Habersham and other elite planters to proselytize among their slaves because they believed that such instruction was essential for their slaves' salvation.[78]

The decision to instruct slaves in religion was significant because it illustrated that planters believed their slaves could improve themselves. They had the intellectual capacity not only to do skilled work as well as any white artisan but to comprehend the divine truths of Christianity as well. All they needed was the opportunity. James Habersham understood the slaves' potential, and he looked forward to the day when slaves would create a "Church of Africans" who could rejoice "at their being made partakers of our own common salvation, to which bond and free are equally intitled."[79]

In spite of the lofty rhetoric about improving slavery, slaves themselves continued to express contempt for the institution by running away. Slaves fled to Savannah or Charlestown, seeking refuge and anonymity. Others fled south toward Florida, where the Spanish authorities granted runaway slaves from South Carolina and Georgia their freedom. They also fled to swamplands and other areas that had yet to be developed. These bands of maroons found sanctuary on the islands that dotted the Savannah River and managed to evade authorities from both South Carolina and Georgia. This area remained a popular destination for runaways throughout the eighteenth century. Slaves also rebelled, particularly in the 1760s, as their numbers grew through importations.[80]

Many planters, however, did not embrace the humanitarian reform of slavery. The slave codes of 1755 and 1765 granted planters the legal sanction to discipline their slaves and allowed brutal punishments for serious transgressions. Runaway slave advertisements with their descriptions of scars and mutilations testify to the brutal character of slavery in Georgia despite the reformers' efforts. Some owners branded their slaves, sometimes with the owners' initials. Others forced their slaves to wear leg or neck irons. Outsourcing the unpleasantness of slave discipline allowed some masters to retain their sense of themselves as benevolent patriarchs.

Georgia's Parishes–1773

Authorities erected a slave workhouse in Savannah in 1763 where owners could send their slaves for punishment. The state sanctioned the most
brutal penalties, executing at least eighteen slaves before the Revolution,
either by hanging or burning at the stake. In 1774, the state burned alive
a slave women who allegedly poisoned her owners.[81]

Despite the best intentions of the founders, the white man's utopia that
they envisioned descended into a hierarchical society stratified by race
and class. Georgia's founders created a society that banned slavery and
limited landholdings. But white Georgians clamored for the prosperity
that slavery enabled. Georgia's planters created a society that maximized
wealth in slaves and land. Planters dominated Georgia society through
their wealth and political power, silencing the voices of the nonelite.
Slaves faced permanent disfranchisement, harsh punishments, and ex-
ploitive labor. Yet blacks' standing did not unilaterally define the racial
order of colonial Georgia. All whites were free and only Africans were
enslaved, but this truism obscures the murkiness of race and class rela-

tions in colonial Georgia. Whiteness was a requirement for those who had power, but whiteness alone did not bestow power. Planters tended to regard nonelite whites with veiled contempt. At the same time, planters valued and respected the skills of their slaves. Planters created a slave society that benefited the elite class at the expense of the nonelite class. Georgia's colonial slave society, however, would unravel as quickly as it emerged.

2

The Contagion of Liberty, 1776–1804

Americans inaugurated the age of revolutions with their War of Independence in 1776. Patriots were not the only people who sought liberty from tyranny. Slaves took the opportunities provided by the American Revolution to escape from their plantations and seek their freedom. In the aftermath of the war, white Georgians sought to rebuild the institution. In the midst of these efforts, however, the revolutionary cycle initiated by the revolutionaries in North America came full circle, returning to its birthplace. Having spread from the United States to France to St. Domingue, becoming increasingly radical at each step of the way, the revolutionary spirit threatened to return to the nation of its birth with deadly consequences. The Haitian Revolution unsettled slave societies throughout the Americas and shattered long-standing beliefs about race. White Georgians responded to the threat initiated by the Haitian Revolution by altering the state laws related to people of African descent, both enslaved and free. The revolution exerted complex effects: on one hand, the rebellion convinced whites of the need to crack down on the foreign slave trade to the state; on the other, it led to the bestowal of greater protections on slaves and the enhancement of privileges and rights for free people of African descent. By the end of the age of revolutions, liberty had become a dangerous contagion.

Planters in Georgia, latecomers to the Patriot cause, supported a conservative revolution that preserved the institution of slavery and the elite status it afforded them. White Georgians, then, viewed slaves as property to be protected rather than as fellow Patriots in the revolutionary cause. Slaves, however, took advantage of the presence of the British and their offers of freedom to strike against slavery. Blacks fought their own revolutionary war even after the official end of the hostilities. The combined efforts of the blacks and the British severely weakened slavery during the war.

The revolutionary spirit arrived late in Georgia. In contrast to South Carolina, Georgians expressed far less enthusiasm about the prospects of forming their own union in the 1770s. Georgia did not send delegates to the first Continental Congress in 1774; it was the only colony not to do so. In South Carolina, the Liberty Boys had led the call for rebellion, but the movement failed to gain traction in Georgia. The elite in Georgia had greater control of the colony than their counterparts in South Carolina. Members of the elite were unwilling to jeopardize the system that they had spent the past two decades creating and so resisted following the lead of the other colonies. And even among Georgia's nonelite, the desire to join the revolutionary cause elicited a more tepid response. Recent arrivals who had settled on the 1773 cession were particularly apathetic to the Patriot cause.[1]

Two principal reasons accounted for white Georgians' reluctance to embrace the Revolution early on: security and economics. Located at the southern extreme of the thirteen colonies, white Georgians felt exposed to numerous threats. With a large slave population inside the colony and an even larger Indian population surrounding it, they felt vulnerable to attack on two fronts. As one group of Georgians lamented, "Not one of the thirteen United Colonies is so weak within, or so much exposed from without." Relations with the surrounding Indian nations, which had never been cordial, worsened in the second half of the eighteenth century, particularly after the 1773 land cession, which left many Creek warriors disaffected. Adding to the insecurity, the population of slaves had grown tremendously between 1765 and 1775. In some parts of Georgia, the ratio of blacks to whites rivaled that in the West Indies; there were more than enough, the Georgians wrote, "to subdue us."[2] The colony had only a limited number of white men who could potentially take up arms. Joseph Clay, a Georgia planter and merchant, estimated the number to be between fifteen hundred and two thousand white men, hardly enough to take on Indians or slaves, let alone both.[3] For this reason, slaveholders and nonslaveholders viewed a break with Britain with trepidation. After all, they relied on British soldiers to provide military protection against Indians and slaves. Could Georgians rely on other colonists to come to their assistance if they left the empire? As part of the British Empire, Georgians could count on British troops to aid them in their time of need. If the colony broke from the empire there was no guarantee that the other colonies would send troops to help them. A second motive for rebuffing calls for revolution, at least among the elite, was economic. Rice was white Georgians' primary cash crop, which they sold to the slave societies of the Caribbean. They risked losing their market should they opt to leave the empire. Most of their imports and exports originated or went to the British West Indies. If Georgians were blocked from this market, their economic survival would be sorely tested.

With the revolutionary fervor sweeping through the rest of the colonies, Georgians finally embraced the independence movement in 1775. That summer Georgian rebels convened a congress in Savannah and created the Council of Safety. The rebels gradually usurped power from the royal government in late 1775. Several months later, the first violent event of the Revolutionary War in Georgia broke out when British ships arrived in Savannah seeking supplies. A small melee ensued, and when the ships pulled out in February 1776 Royal Governor James Wright was on board. In the summer of 1776, Georgians began forming a permanent state government. In the wake of the royal governor's departure and the apparent end of royal rule, many of the merchants and members of the planter elite who had avoided siding with the Patriots pledged their allegiance to the new rulers. Other loyalists, including hundreds of planters, fled Georgia instead. With their slaves in tow, they relocated to other British colonies that offered similar conditions to their former homes and permitted them to resume their plantation operations.[4]

Ideology appears to have played a limited role early in the war. With the situation remaining volatile, planters repeatedly changed sides. When it appeared that the experiment was destined to flounder, many early Patriots joined the exodus of loyalist planters from the state to Florida and the Bahamas. As Joseph Clay explained, economic more than political concerns shaped the planters' decisions. He noted that "much has been said & propagated about the Disaffected in this State—that they are many Disaffected in it is past any Doubt—but I believe no greater proportion than in any other State, & I believe fewer from Principle than in most— Fear from the very exposed situation of this State has operated very powerfully on many well Affected Citizens, who if a proper force had been Early Sent into this State wou'd have declared themselves & Acted very differently—this undoubtedly was wrong in them, but it must be considered rather as a human frailty than a Crime."[5] Georgians had tried to stay out of it, but when they were pulled into the tempest, they did not know which way to go because, for them, the war was not ideological. What those on both sides wanted was to protect their property, particularly the slaves that planters had spent so much to acquire in the previous decade.

Georgia planters countenanced a conservative revolution with limited political, social, and economic change. Having only recently established the plantation system, they opposed any course that might imperil their fortunes. The elite in Georgia tried to thwart an all-out assault on their power. To do so, they conceded political rights to the nonelite. They lowered the requirements to vote and altered the political system. The constitution in 1777 enfranchised all white males twenty-one and over who owned property of at least £10 or who labored in the mechanical trades. The constitution divided Georgia into eight counties—Wilkes, Richmond, Burke, Effingham, Chatham, Liberty, Glynn, and Camden. Before the Revolution, the parish that contained Savannah exercised the most power within the colony. The elite agreed to a new constitution that conceded some of the power of this area to the interior and other parts of the state. Under the new state government, Georgia created a powerful legislature that selected the governor, his council, and other state officials. The lowcountry planter elite offered concessions to less wealthy newcomers to the state, many of whom had only recently relocated to Georgia's interior to settle on land obtained from the Creek Indians by the royal governor. Georgia planters envisioned a limited political revolution, not a radical economic experiment in the redistribution of wealth or a restructuring of the social order.[6]

Georgia elites especially hoped to protect the institution of slavery from revolutionary incursions. They prohibited blacks from joining the state militia or from filling the state's quota in the Continental Army. In the North, black soldiers fought in the earliest battles of the War of Independence but were briefly prohibited from joining the Continental Army and the state militias. As the Patriot demand for soldiers increased, the policy was rescinded. By 1777, only Georgia and South Carolina banned black soldiers. Although the Continental Congress left the decision to the states, members of the body pushed for the states to reverse their stand. Legislators in Georgia refused all entreaties to reverse their decision. They feared the consequences of allowing slaves to be armed for security reasons, but they also feared the larger consequences on the slave system.

Totally reliant on slave labor to cultivate the state's main cash crop, rice, they refused to pursue a pragmatic approach. Indeed, rather than offer to include slaves as part of the revolutionary coalition, Georgia authorities instead offered slaves as bounties to entice white recruits.[7]

Although the vast majority of Georgia planters opposed allowing blacks to join the army or militia, several critics condemned the policy. John Laurens, one of the most vocal critics, supported raising an army of three thousand slaves in Georgia and South Carolina. In return for their service, the slaves would receive their freedom at the end of the war. The owners of the slaves in question would receive $1,000 for each slave. Congress approved of the idea. Still, state officials rejected the proposal.[8] The refusal to arm slaves obstructed the military effort after the British invasion of Georgia in late 1778. Without sufficient resources to send to counter the British, American military commanders predicted dire consequences should the ban on black soldiers remain. General Nathanael Greene, the commander of the Continental Army in the South, observed that the "natural strength of this country, in point of numbers, appears to me to consist much more in the blacks than whites." He speculated that the incorporation and employment of blacks in the army would offer "double security." They would "make good soldiers" to protect the country from enemy attack and would "rather tend to secure the fidelity of the others, than excite discontent, mutiny and desertion among them." He charged that "if the national strength of this country could have been employed in its defence, the Enemy would have found it little less than impracticable to have got a footing here."[9] Despite the dire warnings, Georgia's authorities remained intransigent.

The notion of using black soldiers was not farfetched, even in the Lower South.[10] In the early eighteenth century, colonists in South Carolina and Georgia had employed slave-soldiers in the various wars against the Spanish and Indians.[11] Indeed, in Spanish Florida, the militia contained a significant portion of black men.[12] The 1755 militia act in Georgia had required planters to keep a list of trusted slaves who could be called on to defend the colony in the event of attack.[13] In the region as a whole, in fact, black soldiers were not uncommon. The decision by the authorities in Georgia and South Carolina truly represented a unique response to the changes unleashed by the war.

Georgia authorities feared upheaval and hoped to bring the revolutionary forces under control. To that end, they employed a conservative approach, which left little room for flexibility when it came to slavery and race. Georgia whites generally viewed slaves as objects and not ac-tors. They treated their slaves as property to be protected rather than as possible Patriots to strike for freedom. Georgia whites refused to include slaves in the revolutionary coalition in order to preserve the institution of slavery. Yet, ironically, this approach provided inroads for the British to exploit, almost leading to a complete collapse of the institution of slavery in Georgia.

The British were pragmatic and flexible, if nothing else, in their ap-proach toward colonial rebellion and slavery. They recognized the value of slave labor to Georgia's economic success, yet victory in the war took precedence. They hoped to punish the rebels, using any means to accom-plish their objective. The best way to accomplish this feat, the authorities surmised, was to threaten the colonists' biggest investment. They were willing to liberate slaves who pledged their loyalty in order to suppress rebellion. In the early stages of the conflict, the British undermined the institution by accepting runaway slaves of Patriot owners on their ships. The British also offered freedom to slaves who joined the British Army. Yet they were not abolitionists by any means. They did not want to de-stroy slavery. The institution had brought great riches to many of the loy-alists. While they hoped to prevail in the conflict, they did not intend to forego the benefits derived from slave ownership. After the British seized Georgia in late 1778, the royal authorities did not end slavery. In fact, they pursued policies similar to those put in place by the Patriots—they distributed the property of their rivals who fled, including the slaves. Slaves constituted the prize for remaining loyal.[14]

Blacks in Georgia saw the Revolution in a different light than did the Patriots or the British and their loyalist allies. It offered them an oppor-tunity to escape from bondage or at the very least reform the plantation system. They were actively involved in the battle for liberty in Georgia. They refused to sit by while the opportunity for freedom lay within reach. They consciously supported the side that provided them with the best possible situation. And that meant the British, even though they did not promise abolition.[15]

War created chaotic conditions in the countryside and brought disorder to the plantation system in Georgia. With armies marauding throughout the lowcountry and slave raids a constant threat, plantations fell into disrepair and security all but vanished. Discipline disappeared. According to Ann Rabenhorst, the mere presence of British troops nearby emboldened her slaves to defy her authority. She stated in 1777 that she was "a little afraid on account" of her slaves after Tories passed through her neighborhood. In an effort to protect their investments, some planters took their slaves and fled to more secure locales. Others chose to divide slave families to ensure the loyalty of their bondmen and discourage insubordination.[16]

Blacks used the uncertainty of the war to press for improved conditions on their plantations. Many refused to follow the prewar labor regime. Instead, they grew cotton and food crops. Cotton appears to have served as a compromise crop, which could be used to supply planters and slaves with otherwise scarce textiles to make their clothing. Planters may have even given slaves an added inducement to remain and cultivate cotton by allowing them to sell on their own account.[17]

For thousands of slaves in Georgia, renegotiation of work conditions, regardless of its extent, was not enough. They seized the opportunity presented by the chaos and fled their bondage. Between two hundred and three hundred runaways escaped to British ships off the Georgia coast in the first few months of 1776 alone. They claimed to support the king and sought refuge. In the months and years to come, several thousand more sought their liberty. Many flocked to Savannah, where they claimed status as freedmen or women. Others followed a path similar to Chance, an enslaved man who fled to Cockspur Island in the summer of 1778. Cockspur attracted runaways from across the lowcountry who hoped to spot a passing British ship. In Chance's case, he boarded a man of war and sailed to St. Augustine along with several other runaways, including two others from his owner, Joseph Clay. As a cooper, Chance no doubt hoped to market his skills and begin his new life in Florida as a free man. Yet, as some runaways found out, freedom was far from guaranteed. In 1777, a slave belonging to Abraham Markoe fled his plantation and managed to get on board a ship to Charleston. En route, the captain of the vessel discovered the runaway's status and forced him to commit a robbery. While performing the crime, the runaway was caught and committed to jail upon arrival in Charleston. Untold numbers faced an even bleaker fate when, after making it on board British ships, they found themselves taken against their will to the West Indies by unscrupulous captains who sold them back into slavery.[18]

Perhaps the clearest evidence that blacks refused to play the role assigned them by the Patriots was their efforts on behalf of the British Army. Their participation proved crucial and began at the outset of the campaign in Georgia. Black pilots helped British ships navigate the treacherous waterways on the state's coast. When British forces landed in 1778, blacks led them along hidden paths unknown to local whites, which allowed the invading troops to mount a surprise attack on the Patriots and capture Savannah with minimal resistance. One particularly useful guide named Sampson led British troops in their initial assault and continued with them in later forays as they moved through the Georgia lowcountry and into South Carolina. He participated in several raids carried out by coastal cruisers that helped to liberate slaves owned by Patriots. By far the largest contribution to the British war effort came from the five hundred blacks, some of whom volunteered while others were forced to labor, who built the defensive fortifications that protected Savannah.[19]

Blacks' most prominent role in the British war effort, however, came through enlistment in the British Army. Several hundred blacks, most of whom were runaways, joined in the wake of the British invasion of Georgia in 1778, including 250 to 300 who fought in the Siege of Savannah, where they provided an essential component of the British defense. Black soldiers absorbed the brunt of the Patriot attack led by General Benjamin Lincoln and four thousand to five thousand men and a contingent of French troops led by the Count d'Estaing. Ironically, the French force contained a contingent of black and colored troops from St. Domingue, including several who would later lead the insurrection in that colony. The black pioneers earned praise for their efforts in rebuffing the rebel forces. Governor Wright singled out the black soldiers for special commendation by noting that "they contributed greatly to our defense and safety."[20]

British policies toward incorporating slaves in Georgia into the effort to defeat the Patriots proved successful, but the British could not control the former slaves as pawns. Blacks understood their role in routing the Patriots, and they had their own ideas about what victory meant for them. Service in Georgia's defense emboldened black soldiers and laborers. Blacks refused to return to their plantations or to surrender their weapons when the tumult calmed. Instead, they took over shops and abandoned houses in Savannah, engaging in trade—much to the "terror and distress" of the white residents.[21] Armed and unsupervised slaves roamed in bands around Savannah after the siege, refusing to return to the fields. Other blacks joined their ranks after British troops returned from an expedition into South Carolina in the spring of 1780 accompanied by three thousand runaways. The new arrivals erected houses around Savannah and established a settlement called Durnford Village outside of the city. The Assembly appointed several commissioners in March and April 1781 to manage idle and runaway slaves as well as deserted property. Apparently their efforts were not enough. In late October the Christ Church Parish commissioners complained in the newspaper about the "many idle, disorderly, and runaway negroes, wandering about town and country, committing acts of theft and plunder."[22] Slaves in Georgia and the British shared a common goal—the defeat of the rebels—but they diverged sharply in other respects. To the British, the goal of the war was to bring the rebels back into the fold; for blacks, the war represented an opportunity for freedom.

When the British evacuated Savannah at the end of the war, a significant portion of the colony's slaves left with them. According to one historian's estimate, it "is well possible that between 7,000 and 8,000 slaves left Georgia during 1782" alone. Most of those slaves who left Georgia with their owners wound up in Jamaica and East Florida.[23] The state government did its best to keep as many slaves in Georgia as possible by trying to buy slaves from departing loyalists, but most refused the American entreaties.[24] Georgia's blacks joined an exodus of tens of thousands of ex-slaves departing from other American port cities, men and women who shed their slave status for an unknown future. Some found new homes in Nova Scotia or London, while others made their way to Africa. They left behind a world they knew for the unknown. Some of them ended up in better circumstances. They found freedom in cities where they created new identities.[25]

The Revolution destabilized the institution of slavery throughout the lowcountry. Blacks continued to wage their own revolution even after the official cessation of hostilities. Enslaved men used the opportunity presented by the Revolutionary War to run away. But they did not flee from the area. The region around the Savannah River, on the Georgia–South Carolina border, had attracted maroons since slavery's first introduction. A group of over one hundred armed black men encamped there in the mid-1780s. Some of these maroons had served with the British and had defended Savannah during the siege. Still wearing their British uniforms and calling themselves "King of England's soldiers," they mounted a guerrilla campaign by raiding nearby plantations on both sides of the border.[26] Their continued presence in the region threatened the reconstruction efforts that began after the war. Many planters feared their numbers would only grow the longer they remained on the loose. The presence of maroon societies enticed slaves to flee their plantations for the swamps and freedom. "The freebooty they make & the independent state they live in," General James Jackson reported, "have strong charms of allurement, of course their numbers are increasing." The consequences, he recognized, could be serious if not dire unless immediate steps were "taken to put a stop to their marauding." If the rebels were not dealt with harshly and quickly, he cautioned, "there is no knowing how far the revolt may lead." The maroons did not shy away from confrontation. General Jackson complained that this "daring banditti of slaves," "as dareing as any" rebels, even attacked two detachments of soldiers from Georgia and were dislodged from their camp only after great exertion.[27] Their violence was not random, but strategic and retributive. For example, twenty maroons crossed into Georgia in search of William Molmar, whom they accused of killing one of their leaders; the man had belonged to Molmar before running away. The maroon leader's body was desecrated after his death; he was decapitated and his head stuck on the end of a pole and placed on a roadside. The rebels were outraged and hunted Molmar for revenge. Molmar managed to escape with his life but little else when the maroons arrived at this house to seek retribution.[28] In another example, the rebels targeted one planter for repeated attacks, seizing "whole Stacks of rice" in retaliation for an assault by state troops on their camp and the resultant destruction of the "incredible magazine of provisions" stored there.[29] As late as 1787, black men dressed in British uniforms continued to raid the nearby plantations in the South Carolina–Georgia border region.[30]

The black men refused to recognize an end to the Revolutionary War. Treaties had been signed and amends made between Britain and her belligerent ex-colonies, but these agreements made little difference to them. The maroon threat illustrates that the slaves' revolutionary zeal and desire for freedom continued long after the last British troops had left the state. Their raids against the surrounding plantations were a continuation of their struggle for freedom, one that had begun with the outbreak of the Revolution.

Prompted by planters' complaints, Georgia authorities sent the militia from nearby districts to put down the rebels, but their efforts fell short, at least initially. The situation was so dire that the governors of South Carolina and Georgia agreed to work together to bring the armed black men down. The governors' recognition that they needed to battle the maroons together illustrates the extent of the threat they posed. The South Carolina governor's recognition of the "expediency of a joint exertion" constituted an admission that the embers of revolution had not been quelled and that they threatened to reignite under the correct conditions.[31] When the state troops located the rebels' camp, they found it extremely difficult to penetrate. The maroons had built two houses surrounded by a four-foot-high breastwork made of logs to defend themselves. In addition, they placed large logs across the creek leading to their position to prevent boats from sailing within attacking distance. The rebels may have learned to construct these forts while defending Savannah during the siege in 1779. The maroons planted rice and potatoes, suggesting that they intended to remain there on a semipermanent basis at the very least. In May 1787, General James Gunn led an assault on the camp with several dozen militia men and claimed to have routed his foes.[32] The maroons were still operating that fall, however. Indeed, Jackson claimed that since regrouping after the attack, "they are in fact much more troublesome."[33]

The American Revolution did not destroy slavery, but it did leave the institution weakened. The Revolution sharply reduced the number of slaves in Georgia; those who remained were radicalized. Slaves in Georgia demonstrated that their desire for freedom was stronger than their attachment to their owners, regardless of their benevolence. Slave owners could modify their rules and make slavery less severe as an institution, but slavery paled in comparison to even the remote possibility of obtaining liberty. The seeds sown by the Americans' war for independence would bear revolutionary fruit several more times among the slaves in years to come. The Revolution did not, however, dampen white Georgians' desire to retain slavery.

The Revolutionary War had come close to destroying Georgia's slave society. In the aftermath of the war, Georgians attempted to rebuild their slave society, but the revolutionary spirit unleashed by American independence had long-lasting consequences, both direct and indirect. Not only did the American Revolution create a new nation, but it also crossed the Atlantic, setting off the French Revolution. Like the so-called triangular trade, the revolutionary spirit recrossed the Atlantic to ignite the Haitian Revolution, then reverberated once again in Georgia. The effects of the Haitian Revolution spilled out beyond the colony's borders, affecting life in Georgia repeatedly over the 1790s, just as white Georgians were in the process of reconstituting the slave system. This far-off insurrection profoundly shaped white Georgians' perceptions of slavery and induced them to question their assumptions about the state's racial order. In the process, white Georgians themselves divided over these same issues. The policies adopted by the authorities in Georgia prompted heated debate at times, revealing sharp divisions over white Georgians' visions for the future. In the time it took for the insurrection in St. Domingue to become the Haitian Revolution, Georgia's racial order transformed. Spurred by the tumult in the West Indies, white Georgians reevaluated the institution of slavery. The rebellion hastened the end of Georgia's participation in the Atlantic slave trade and pushed planters to see their bondmen as less expendable. Aware that slave labor held the key to the state's future prosperity, yet equally aware of the risks, white Georgians initiated reform to save the institution before it destroyed Georgian society. Increasingly, whites came to espouse a more insular view of their society, with masters and slaves all being part of a large family. In addition to identifying those excluded from Georgian society, the Haitian Revolution prompted state authorities to codify the status of those included in Georgian society. The authorities moved to clarify the position of those who occupied the nebulous space between free and enslaved and black and white in an effort to protect Georgia from the ravages of racial insurrection.

Victory in the Revolution gave Georgia's Patriots their independence, but at a terrific price, particularly for lowcountry planters. Throughout the region the scars of war remained long after the British troops left the state. The war brought dislocation and destruction of the plantation districts and produced massive social upheaval. Abandoned estates littered the landscape. Josiah Smith described a chaotic scene at his plantation. He reported that his rice dams were broken and would most likely remain so for the foreseeable future. Some of his slaves had run away, while the Tory overseer had absconded with several others. Those still remaining could do little since several of them had smallpox. Rice fields sculpted from the muddy marshlands of the lowcountry fell into disrepair with little prospect of returning to their former glory. Many would have to start from scratch.[34] George Ballie noted that the "resettling of plantations that are so intirely gone to ruin must be attended with nearly as much expense and difficulty, as the first settling of them."[35] Similarly, another Georgia planter asserted that the dismal state of Georgia "will oblige many of us, as it were to begin the World again."[36]

As planters began to rebuild, demand for slaves soared. By the end of the war, nearly two-thirds of the slave population had fled to freedom, been removed from the state by loyalists, or died. Without their labor, planters lamented, any effort to reconstruct Georgia's economy was destined to fail. Slavery had been the lifeblood of Georgia before the war and would continue to be after the conflict's conclusion. Joseph Clay, a planter-merchant and one of Georgia's largest pre-Revolution slave traders, recognized the potential for profit. Seeking to capitalize on the business opportunity, Clay sought out his overseas contacts, including British financiers, even before the war had come to an end. The "Negro business," he noted, "is a great object with us, both with a View to our Interest individually, & the general prosperity of this State & its commerce, it is to the Trade of this Country, as the Soul to the Body, & without it no House can gain a proper Stability, the Planter will as far as in his power sacrifice every thing to attain Negroes." In addition to supplying lowcountry planters who had lost the bulk of their chattel property, he expected to sell slaves to newcomers to the state, hundreds of whom had moved to the interior at the end of the hostilities with England, hoping to take advantage of the cheap and fertile land. To meet the state's needs, Clay planned to reestablish slave importation directly from Africa, yet he recognized that economic and logistical challenges meant that Georgia planters would also have to rely on slave imports from the "W. Indies particularly the French Islands" to supplement their workforce in the immediate future.[37] By 1790, it appeared as though Georgia planters had resurrected the slave regime. Through a combination of imports from Africa, the West Indies, and other states, Georgia's slave population increased to almost thirty thousand.[38] Lowcountry plantations returned to profitability, and slavery penetrated deeper into the backcountry.

Yet, despite all the planters' success, dark clouds were gathering on the horizon. The first sign of trouble was word of an uprising in the French colony of St. Domingue led by Vincent Ogé, a free man of color, in 1790.[39] Though the French authorities managed to put down the rebellion, the revolutionary spark had been lit. In August 1791, slaves in the northern region of the colony rose up, initiating what would become the Haitian Revolution.[40] In the two years after Georgians first learned about the outbreak of the slave insurrection in St. Domingue, it had little impact on their lives. The conflict there had not produced a steady stream of violence; rather, the events exploded periodically before calming down. There was no reason to believe that this slave revolt would somehow be different than any of the others that preceded it. At some point, the insurrectionists would be subdued and things would return to the status quo.[41]

Two episodes in the fall of 1793 brought the Haitian Revolution to

U.S. shores.[42] White Georgians learned of the first threat from Philadelphia in fall of 1793. The city received several hundred refugees from St.
Domingue who had fled the French colony. Initially, white residents of
Philadelphia welcomed them, but their hospitality diminished following
the outbreak of yellow fever in the city. The city authorities first attributed
the sickness to an annual outbreak of "fall fever," but as the number of
victims grew, by one account reaching close to one hundred deaths per
day at its worst, they determined that the epidemic was in fact yellow
fever, carried to Philadelphia on a ship that had recently arrived from
war-torn St. Domingue, where the disease ran rampant. The authorities
quarantined parts of the wharf but failed to halt the pathogen's spread.
The disease carried panic and dislocation through the sweltering streets
of Philadelphia. Residents with the means fled. Commerce in the city
ground to a halt. According to one estimate, within a month of the outbreak one thousand people had died from yellow fever while another
fifteen to twenty thousand had fled the city.[43]

Disease was not the only threat emanating from St. Domingue in
the 1790s. Nearly simultaneously, white Georgians learned of a second
threat involving individuals from the French colony in South Carolina.
On October 1, a stable belonging to a French émigré in Charleston was
set ablaze. Suspicion immediately fell on slaves and free people of color
who had arrived in the city with the French refugees from St. Domingue.
The group was part of a sizable population of free people of color and
slaves who had come to the United States after the rebellion began. Their
arrival caused considerable consternation among whites wherever they
landed. The fire in Charleston confirmed these fears.[44]

Roused from their complacency by the events in Philadelphia and
Charleston, the authorities in Georgia moved quickly to halt the spread
of disorder into the state. The city council in Savannah responded first. As
the state's chief port of entry for people and products, Savannah stood on
the front line. Its authorities imposed a quarantine on vessels originating
from Philadelphia and all other locations known to be afflicted by yellow
fever and sent a cutter to patrol the coast for potential violators. The city
council also enacted new restrictions on all arriving foreign people of
African descent and ordered a census of the city's slave population. Upon
receiving word of the situation in Savannah, Governor Edward Telfair embraced the city council's actions. The crisis necessitated vigilance. Conflat-
ing the two threats, Telfair asserted that the introduction of foreign blacks
into Georgia would spread "contagious disorders of a fatal tendency and

many abuses and inconveniences not to be tolerated." To avoid this outcome, he called for stepped-up enforcement of state laws related to "the introduction of contagious disease, as well as those for maintaining the peace and good order of the community, by punishing and suppressing the infractions" of foreign people of African descent.[45] A few weeks later, the Georgia General Assembly enacted a new law to "prevent" slave importation to the state by imposing a tax of £50 for each seasoned slave imported from the West Indies or Florida for sale in Georgia. Significantly, however, the legislature left the African trade unaffected.[46]

Foreign people of African descent, both free and enslaved, were increasingly becoming synonymous with disease, as pathogens of destruction, carrying death and violence everywhere they landed. Outbreaks of yellow fever were a frequent aspect of life in American coastal regions and often coincided with episodes of bloodshed and strife in the Caribbean. The continued bloodshed in the West Indies prompted white Georgians to view foreign people of African descent with greater suspicion. Sporadically over the next decade, Georgia's authorities quarantined suspected instances of yellow fever (and smallpox) at the same time as strife and sickness in the Caribbean produced thousands of refugees, many of them people of color in search of new homes. The disease was both physical and ideological. In addition to protecting Georgia from disease, then, the quarantine served as a means of vetting all arriving people of African descent. And as the authorities understood, conveyors of the most dangerous contagion—insurrectionary ideals—did not exhibit physical symptoms. As one future governor noted, French people of color did not have to participate actively in the rebellion to make them dangerous; indeed, merely having observed the "horrid scenes of massacre which of late years have been so barbarously practised in the West Indies" was sufficient to render them a threat to public safety.[47] The spread of disease was as much metaphor as reality.

White Georgians recognized that their state was not immune to the Haitian epidemic. But rather than impose absolute restrictions, like in South Carolina, where the state government imposed an outright ban on the importation of all African and West Indian slaves, the authorities in Georgia chose a less drastic course of action.[48] White Georgians adopted a pragmatic approach in the face of the threat posed by St. Domingue. With Georgia's economy still recovering from the devastation caused by the War of Independence and the loss of thousands of slaves who escaped or were removed from the state, legislators agreed to modify the rules governing the slave trade but not to ban it altogether. The slave trade was too essential to the state's economy. With the trade with Africa left untouched, planters could count on a continued flow of slaves to the state. As an additional benefit, the closure of Charleston to slave traffic left Savannah as the South's premier port of entry for slaves, thus further enriching lowcountry planter-merchants, a politically powerful constituency. Of course, attitudes among white Georgians were not monolithic, and some had favored copying South Carolina's route. In fact, legislators debated whether to include a provision that placed African slaves among those banned by the bill, but this proposal failed to attract sufficient support.[49]

In choosing to enact a tax on slaves imported from the West Indies rather than a total ban on their introduction into Georgia, the state authorities included a loophole in the law that appears to have been designed to attract wealthy West Indian planters fleeing their island homes. The tariff was costly enough to deter speculators from importing cheap slaves from the region to sell in Georgia but did not affect West Indian planters who wished to relocate to the state with a segment of their most trusted and valued slaves. The authorities proved willing to tolerate a limited number of spoken-for slaves from St. Domingue, but their owners would be held liable for their actions. The law represented a balanced approach toward safeguarding security and continued prosperity in the midst of tumult. Georgia's authorities, intent upon the repopulation of their state, wanted to lure wealthy planter émigrés and so rejected any prohibition that might deter them.

Georgia's authorities had long relied on the arrival of settlers from the West Indies to help boost the population. Among the thousands of émigrés who had come in search of cheap land and opportunities were men like Charles Thiot. Born in 1753 in the French port city of Nantes, Thiot came to the New World as a young man to make his fortune. Thiot settled in St. Domingue and established himself as a planter and merchant in Grand Gossier, a small port southeast of Port au Prince. There he cultivated coffee and cotton on his plantation and traded his crops and those of his neighbors in markets throughout the Americas until the slave insurrection broke out in 1791. Around that time, Thiot and his family moved to Pedernales, a small town on the border between the Spanish and French colonies on Hispaniola. From there Thiot continued his business as best he could. By June of the following year, he had left Pedernales and settled in Jamaica, bringing twelve slaves as well as his family. At some time over the next year and a half, Thiot returned to St. Domingue, most likely following the British invasion of the island in 1793. In December 1794, he permanently quit the colony, sailing to Jamaica once again. Ships sailing between Savannah and Jamaica enjoyed a brisk business in the first three months of 1795. During this period, no less than seventeen vessels made the trip, one of which carried Thiot to his new home. In September 1795, he arranged for the passage of his family and slaves to join him. When he tried to bring his slaves into the state, Thiot found himself embroiled in a swirl of controversy over whether to allow blacks from St. Domingue into Georgia.[50]

In the four decades following the repeal of its ban on slavery in 1750, Georgia had absorbed thousands of immigrants from the West Indies with little or no cause for concern. But the influx of French refugees in 1795 raised new concerns about the possibility of importing insurrection. White Georgians sympathized with the plight of the French refugees, but the arrival of the émigrés that summer of 1795, accompanied by hundreds of slaves and free people of color, struck fear in their hearts. Until that point, the events in St. Domingue, despite the fears of Savannah's residents, had had limited impact on life in the state. A few distressed ships from the colony had limped into Savannah's harbor in 1793 and 1794, but none had contained large numbers of slaves.[51] The arrivals of 1795 and the possibilities of further swarms of foreign people of African descent convinced Georgia's authorities that their solution in 1793 had been inadequate. The French émigrés who arrived in 1795 differed from their predecessors. Unlike the previous waves of refugees who arrived in Savannah, they had not fled in haste, and therefore managed to bring more of their property—significantly, slave property—with them. Yet, as they came to discover, their relatively well-orchestrated departure had its own drawbacks. Some of the French refugees in 1795, like Thiot, arrived via Jamaica, where they had previously relocated. The first French planters to settle in the English colony landed soon after the initial outbreak of the insurrection in St. Domingue.[52] Jamaican authorities greeted the French planters with a mixture of sympathy and suspicion, but in subsequent years, as their numbers (and their slaves) multiplied, the planter émigrés came under increasing scrutiny. In late 1794, the situation reached a crescendo when a ship carrying 271 black "disaffected persons and brigands" from St. Domingue arrived, leaving the island's whites "exceedingly alarmed." In response, Jamaica's authorities imposed new restrictions on the admission of "negroes and other slaves" from foreign colonies, spurring an exodus of French planters.[53] Some French refugees had relocated to Jamaica, hoping to start their lives anew; for others, however, the English colony served as a way station, a temporary residence until they could return to their former home or travel to the United States.

Once the authorities in Savannah realized that several hundred French slaves had been brought into the state in the previous five months, they moved to halt the flow. The extent of the potential problems became clear when a ship carrying more than one hundred French slaves docked in Savannah on July 1. The white residents of the city complained that the "safety of this city and of the country will be much endangered by suffering the said slaves to land."[54] To ensure the city's safety, the aldermen barred the ship from landing its cargo or passengers and ordered its captain to proceed downriver for quarantine. In what was becoming a routine event, white residents assembled at a town meeting the next day to discuss the situation and plot a strategy. With unanimous support, the city council enacted extreme measures to halt the flow of West Indian people of African descent to the city as a necessary means to prevent the spread of insurrection. The mayor called for the city council to implement restrictions based on those employed in South Carolina and the British West Indies. In turn, the city council prohibited vessels carrying "seasoned" slaves and people of color from docking in the city's harbor. Violators of the statute faced the prospect of immediate expulsion from the harbor at the expense of the boat's owner. To enforce the provisions, residents agreed to the creation of a Committee of Inspectors staffed by local citizens and "unanimously" pledged to assist the city council in its effort to monitor the coast.[55]

While it is unclear whether Thiot ever secured the release of his slaves, at least one émigré named Borel succeeded in spite of the city council's efforts. Borel's slaves arrived in July 1795 aboard the ship from Jamaica with one hundred slaves. The authorities refused to allow the slaves to be landed in Savannah. Borel appealed to the city council to regain his slaves. After taking "the opinion of their Fellow Citizens, who . . . unanimously" opposed such an action, the city council refused his request. Outraged, Borel contacted the governor to appeal. Unlike the scare in 1793, when Governor Edward Telfair rubber stamped the city authorities' decisions, Governor George Mathews in 1795 rejected the city's ruling. He forced the city to release Borel's slaves and to return them. As a compromise, Borel removed his slaves from the city to a plantation on the St. Mary's

River, near the Georgia-Florida border, where a cluster of French émigrés had settled. At least some of Borel's neighbors were none too thrilled about the presence of the French slaves, and they continued to complain about them to the authorities for the next several years.[56]

The struggle between the city authorities and Borel reflected a larger conflict over the institution of slavery and the future of Georgia. First, it highlighted the tension between white Georgians' desire for economic profit and their security. Second, it illustrated that the lowcountry elite no longer had the kind of political power that they had previously held. Before the Revolution, the planter elite in Savannah and its environs had controlled the colony politically. In most debates, their word ultimately carried the day, regardless of the opposition. By the 1790s, this was no longer the case. The lowcountry elite found its interests trumped by the desires of other segments of the population in the state. The goal of protecting Savannah's security was clearly desirable and necessary, but the means called for by the city authorities to achieve this objective came into conflict with a greater good for the state—encouraging émigrés, particularly wealthy planters, to settle in Georgia and boost the state's population and economy.

Although the fear generated by the arrival of the French slaves subsided by the end of the summer, the specter of French-inspired insurrection continued to plague the residents of Savannah in the months to come. That fall reports of planned revolt emerged, prompting the city authorities to purchase all of the gunpowder in town to ensure that it did not fall into the hands of "some Negroes, or improper persons."[57] Weeks later the authorities discovered that one of the alleged leaders of the St. Domingue insurrection was imprisoned in Savannah. The city council ordered the slave's owner to immediately remove him from the city.[58] The rebel's presence reflected Savannah residents' worst nightmare: the possibility that insurrectionary slaves would be imported into Georgia, where they would spread the "contagion" of revolt. The following year, a series of suspicious fires broke out, including a massive conflagration that consumed more than half of the town's buildings, which many whites assumed represented the work of black arsonists. Despite the persistence of the seemingly French slave–related violence, the General Assembly refused to prohibit completely the introduction of West Indian slaves. The legislature did, however, concede some measure of control to the authorities on the coast when it amended a law allowing the Chatham militia to apprehend all people of African descent arriving in Georgia from the West Indies, free or enslaved, and hold them until they could be examined by the city officials in Savannah to determine whether they should be allowed to stay in the state.[59]

With their focus on West Indian slaves, white Georgians paid little attention to African slaves. The authorities quarantined African slaves but did not regard them as especially rebellion-prone. Consequently, merchants imported thousands of West Africans into the state after the War of Independence. Many planters preferred Africans, specifying, as Joseph Clay did, that "tis from the Coast only we wish to receive them."[60] Many of these Africans wound up in the upcountry, where planters integrated the newly arrived slaves into their labor force. The region developed at a quick pace in the 1790s as the tide of immigration to the state continued. As the Duc de la Rochefoucauld stated, "It is a fact that the population of blacks is as abundant on the other side of Augusta as it is on this side; of course there are no large planters who assemble a great number of them on their plantations, but all the small farmers try to get some slaves as soon as they have saved enough money to buy them." Cotton drove up the demand. "At present everyone is vying with one another in planting cotton, and it is considered to be the principal staple of trade as mentioned above."[61]

White Georgians became concerned with the African slave trade after a slave insurrection in early 1797. The incident occurred in February on Hergen Herson's plantation in Scriven County when a group of "new negroes" revolted. Four months earlier Herson had traveled to Savannah, where he had purchased eight Africans—seven men and a woman—from a shipment of slaves that had recently arrived from Africa. The slaves reportedly caused few if any disturbances after arriving, but on the morning of the fifteenth their true sentiments became clear. The slaves initiated their plot by luring Herson from his home, ostensibly to examine their work. Once Herson made his way to the fields, the slaves struck him in the head with their axes, then attacked his overseer. The second man died instantly, while Herson held on for twenty-four hours before finally expiring. After killing the overseer and fatally wounding Herson, the rebels rushed the planter's house in search of his wife. Before they could find her, however, one of the family's other slaves, who "had long lived with them," hid the woman in the cellar and escaped to a nearby plantation to raise the alarm. On hearing of the revolt, a collection of white men from the neighborhood assembled and took off in pursuit of the rebels, who, after ransacking the house, had fled. Eventually the white men overtook the insurrectionists, but they resisted. In the ensuing fight, the whites killed three of the Africans and seriously wounded another. Two other rebels subsequently surrendered and one escaped. After interrogating the rebels, the captors burned the ringleader alive when he admitted his role in the scheme.[62]

In the wake of the Scriven rebellion, opposition to the slave trade grew. All slaves, not just slaves from the West Indies, appeared affected by the contagion of rebellion. The notion that Georgia could avoid the kind of violence that had occurred in the Caribbean simply by cutting off the supply of West Indian slaves seemed foolhardy. The incident raised the possibility that the slave trade itself, not just the origins of the slaves, posed the threat of violence. For example, the grand jury of Wilkes County repudiated the trade as a vile institution. "We conceive it to be greatly injurious to the welfare of the inhabitants thereof, and highly repugnant to the principles of a free government, and do earnestly recommend it to the next legislature to prohibit the same."[63] The importation of slaves to the state had become a serious security issue for many white Georgians. They came to question whether the state's economic growth trumped basic safety concerns.

Legislators responded to the concerns raised by the recent spate of slave-related violence by imposing a total ban on further slave importations, a truly drastic course of action in a society based on slave labor. When the General Assembly met at the beginning of 1798, legislators enacted new laws derived from the lessons learned over the past year in Savannah, Scriven County, and, most recently, Charleston, South Carolina, where whites uncovered a conspiracy by French slaves to set fire to the town.[64] The legislators amended the act regulating the importation of slaves, imposing more severe restrictions than were in the initial bill in 1793. In contrast to the earlier measure, which only sought to "prevent" the importation of slaves from the West Indies by imposing a tax on slaves intended for sale, the new law prohibited the introduction of slaves "from Africa and elsewhere," including the West Indies, into Georgia and set steep fines for those who did; for each slave illegally imported, an individual faced a $1,000 penalty. The prohibition against importation extended to slaves from other states as well. Individuals faced a $500 fine for their first offense and the fine doubled for each additional infraction. So broad was the language contained in the act that it even barred new immigrants who moved to the state from bringing their slaves. The legislature did, however, later amend the importation act to allow planters who relocated to Georgia from other parts of the Union to bring their slaves. The law represented a reappraisal of the policies that had allowed the importation of several thousand foreign slaves to Georgia in the five years since the initial restriction in 1793. Legislators wanted no other whites to suffer Herson's fate at the hands of African slaves. The economic imperatives that had prompted the earlier decision no longer outweighed the risk in light of the recent violence.[65]

Some white Georgians called for reforms in the institution of slavery in order to stave off insurrection. To them, the Herson murder demonstrated that slavery itself, not just the origins of the enslaved, spurred violence. It meant that the solution to the problem, then, extended beyond closing the state to further slave imports. The institution of slavery itself needed reform, they contended. Some whites believed that a key cause of the violence in St. Domingue was the maltreatment of slaves by the colony's planters. White Georgians condemned the insurrectionary violence perpetrated by the slaves, but they recognized the role played by whites in sparking the rebellion. This opinion was self-serving. It allowed whites in Georgia to find fault for the insurrection in the French colony—not in the institution of slavery itself, but merely in the way that the French planters had conducted themselves. In an effort to stave off rebellion, whites had to approach their chattels in a more nuanced manner; native slaves, especially those who displayed their loyalty, had to be drawn closer, while the others, particularly foreign slaves, had to be blocked from entering the state. The episode at Hergen Herson's plantation had made this message clear. In addition to providing important lessons for white Georgians on the danger of foreign slaves, the revolt on the Herson plantation demonstrated the wisdom of cultivating the loyalty of native slaves. The quashed rebellion in Scriven reveals important inter- and intraracial divisions that had emerged in Georgia in the last decade of the eighteenth century. Mrs. Herson became a widow rather than a victim herself only through the protection of a loyal native slave. Moreover, this same slave roused the alarm among neighborhood whites and enabled the swift capture of the rebellious African slaves. He had lived with the Hersons for some time, which apparently led the slave not only to eschew participating in the revolt with the African slaves, but to put his own security at risk.[66] Even if he had not endorsed the actions taken by the Africans, he could have chosen to hide rather than imperil his own safety. His actions illuminated the divide within the slave community between Africans and "native" slaves. The slave who saved Mrs.

Herson may have acted pragmatically in recognition of the impossibility of a successful slave rebellion, but whites interpreted his act as a sign of his devotion to his mistress. To avoid the violence that had played out in Scriven but on a grander scale, white Georgians recognized the necessity of ensuring the loyalty of native slaves.

The editors of the *Columbia Museum and Savannah Advertiser* understood the value in cultivating loyalty among native slaves. After providing a grisly account of the insurrection in Scriven in which they emphasized the role played by the loyal family servants, they concluded the article with a query: In view of what had transpired, they asked, what "species of reward ought to be bestowed on the faithful negro, who at the risque of his own, saved his mistress's life, and gave the alarm to the neighbouring families?"[67] The tumultuous times necessitated a flexible approach toward slaves; the fires in Savannah in late 1796 and the revolt in Scriven were part of a larger trend that threatened slave societies throughout the Atlantic, and unless some changes were made Georgia could follow the same path toward destruction as St. Domingue.

One of the most outspoken proponents of reform was John E. Smith, the editor of the *Augusta Chronicle and Gazette of the State,* who condemned the inhumanity of the slave trade and castigated masters who did not practice a benevolence worthy of their position as patriarchs. In September 1797, Smith penned an editorial calling on planters to assess the situation in Georgia. In the wake of the "deeds of horror" that had "desolated" St. Domingue, Smith warned planters to avoid the barbarities practiced in the French colony if they hoped to avoid the wrath of their slaves. It was in Georgia planters' best interest to treat their bondmen well, he intoned; after all, a "poor wretch enfeebled with hunger, and the lash, cannot earn as much in the day, as one well fed, and free from pain." Yet, instead of recognizing this fact, some Georgia planters continued to treat their slaves with "satanic depravity." Inverting the common characterization of whites and blacks, Smith accused these masters of acting like "savages" whose pursuit of economic profit jeopardized not only their own place in heaven but the safety of Georgian society as well. As a result, Smith concluded, laws were necessary "to restrain the rage of taskmasters, and to protect, from their tortures, the hapless race of Ethiopians, whose lot in life should command our pity." Doing so, he confessed, "is a dangerous experiment," yet few other options remained. If the members of the General Assembly failed to "give to those *bearers of heavy burdens,* already among us, the protection of such laws, as the common principles of humanity dictate," Smith asked, "how can they expect their country to flourish?" Such "laws are not merely acts of mercy. They are acts of justice not only to the unhappy bond-men, but to" the planters "themselves."[68]

Smith stressed that he was not advocating abolition or any "other illiberal motive"; rather, he sought to call attention to the "crimes against humanity" that endangered Georgia's security if left unchecked. He affirmed his belief in hierarchy and the notion that "subordination is altogether indispensible" for society to function properly. He acknowledged the necessity of punishment to maintain order. But his chief concern, he reiterated, was slave owners' excessive cruelty and ill treatment of their chattel, which would lead to ruin if not checked.[69]

In the midst of the chaos caused by the Haitian Revolution, Smith looked to Jamaica as a model slave society. The decade before the slave uprising began in Haiti, the authorities in Jamaica had begun to implement new policies to improve the plight of their bondmen and bondwomen as part of a project to ameliorate slavery.[70] This attempt to reform the institution of slavery appeared to have rendered Jamaica immune to the contagion that spread slave insurrection. Despite its proximity to St. Domingue, Jamaica had remained largely unaffected by slave unrest.[71] For this reason, then, Jamaica served as the perfect model for white Georgians in search of precautionary preventatives to rebellion. As an alternative to Georgia's slave code, which offered little in the way of protections for bondmen and -women, Smith urged Georgia planters to consider emulating the course taken by Jamaica's colonial assembly, which had recently adopted new measures that shielded slaves from inhumane treatment and imposed serious punishments on whites for transgressing those laws. Smith cited five of the laws, three of which dealt directly with violence perpetrated against slaves, as examples to illustrate his point. By taking these steps to ameliorate slavery, Smith contended, the authorities in Jamaica had shown a humanitarian spirit that would help them avoid the kind of slave discontent that had roiled St. Domingue.[72]

To avoid a similar outbreak of violence among slaves in Georgia, delegates to the constitutional convention in 1798 took steps to ameliorate the system of slavery in Georgia by including a provision that mandated that whites who "maliciously" wounded or killed slaves would be penalized as if their victims were free whites. In effect, the law gave blacks the privileges of whiteness, but only after they had suffered an attack. The reforms were modest, but they did provide (at least in theory, if not in practice) a modicum of protection for slaves against the worst abuses.[73]

There is no clear indication in the minutes of the *Journal of the 1798 Constitutional Convention* that the delegates considered Smith's calls for reform before drafting the new protections for slaves.[74] But as Smith was the editor of one of the state's few newspapers, it seems likely that his advice proved influential in the discussions. The authorities could have pursued a range of options in the wake of the slave unrest in the states; the most obvious would have been to clamp down on the slave population. Yet the authorities chose to do the opposite: they enacted a measure to regulate the behavior of whites. While it is true that their decision reflected more of a concern for the security of the state than any sense of altruism or sympathy for the enslaved population, it would be wrong to dismiss the significance of the reform out of hand. In combination with the ban on slave importations, the law testifies to the potential powers of the slaves— a recognition that they could shape the destiny of the slave society.

Of the changes to the institution of slavery in 1798, the ban on slave importation generated the most opposition and revealed a growing regional division in Georgia. The passage of the 1798 ban reflected a general fear among most white Georgians that the continuation of the slave trade was not in the state's best interests. Some white Georgians, however, judged the measures adopted by the legislature too extreme. The prospect of halting the flow of slaves to the state carried serious repercussions for the state's economic growth. The most urgent appeals came from the state's backcountry, a region where most settlers had only recently arrived in the state.

Many émigrés hailed from Virginia. The migration had kicked off immediately following the peace with Britain. George Mathews had led a group of five hundred families from Virginia to Georgia in 1783. He had first noted Georgia's advantages when he traversed the state as an officer in the Revolutionary War. Thousands more followed in their wake. Most settled in Wilkes County, near the Broad River. In contrast to earlier settlers to the region, the Virginia émigrés tended to be well off. They came not because they lacked access to land in their former homes but because they were impressed with Georgia's potential. These men came with families and slaves, not individually, and settled in enclaves. Samuel Butler, for example, came to the state in 1784 with two other white men from Hanover County, Virginia. After several weeks of searching, Butler finally located a promising plot and bought it. He paid for his land with three slaves, at least one of them female. He then returned to Virginia, collected his family and slaves, and set off for their new home in the

Georgia backcountry. Butler used his slaves as currency; like many slave-holders, he apparently thought nothing of trading his slaves for goods and lands. It was business, the business of buying and selling teenage boys and girls. Men like Butler established plantations in the upcountry where they initially hoped to grow grains and tobacco but eventually embraced cotton as a more lucrative crop. These migrants came with the intent of making money, and the ban on slave imports threatened their continued prosperity.[75]

It was not only the wealthy residents of the backcountry who chafed at the ban. The prohibition on the importation of slaves increased their price and put them further out of reach for yeomen and settlers, thus widening the economic divide between slaveholders and nonslavehold-ers. Traders found ways around the ban and continued to smuggle slaves into the state, thus exacerbating the situation. The contraband slaves brought into Georgia further upset the balance among whites because it enabled only the wealthiest to benefit from slave labor.

Judge George Walton raised the issue of slave importations. Though a Virginian, Walton's history followed a different trajectory than most of his émigré counterparts. Orphaned, he arrived in Georgia penniless before the war and rose rapidly through the ranks of society in the revolution-ary years. Appointed governor in 1779 and again in 1789, he maintained his presence in Georgia politics in the years after as a judge on the west-ern circuit of the superior court. Judge Walton recognized the potential for development in Georgia's hinterland. Walton believed Augusta would serve as the perfect commercial hub for the flow of goods from planters in upcountry Georgia as well as Tennessee and the Cumberland to the coastal merchants. Cotton, tobacco, and other staples would flow from the interior. The trade would bring great prosperity to Augusta.[76] As the country expanded westward, the region's relevance would only grow. Slavery played a pivotal role in his vision.

From his position on the bench, Judge Walton advocated for reform of the law banning the interstate slave trade in a case in 1801. The case involved a man named William Aftline, called before Walton's court to face charges for illegally introducing slaves into Georgia with the intent to sell. The trial revealed that Aftline had only overseen the transportation of the slaves found in his possession. Aftline intended to deliver the slaves to the purchaser, Robert Hughes. Three years earlier, the legislature had altered the state constitution to allow for the importation of slaves to the state by masters who intended to use the slaves themselves but outlawed the practice of bringing slaves into the state to sell. Judge Walton argued that the ban was difficult to enforce and therefore "defective." He called for the legislature to "repeal or amend" it.[77] Three months later, Judge Walton returned to the controversy when he addressed the grand jury of Scriven County. In his charge, Walton complained about "a novel and grievous evil," the rising number of slaves smuggled into Georgia from the North and Chesapeake.[78]

Not all residents of the backcountry favored relaxing the prohibition. Some settlers living in the counties bordering the Creek and Cherokee Indians were philosophically opposed to slavery. They viewed the institution as a corrupting force in society and resented the added economic and political clout planters gained through their ownership of slaves. These backcountry settlers found refuge living on the state's periphery and hoped that eliminating slave imports would prevent plantation society from reaching them in the near future. They hoped to slow the process, but they faced an uphill battle. Slavery's spread seemed inexorable.

Support for the ban on slave imports among white Georgians in the backcountry also came from the counties bordering South Carolina. In fact, some residents complained that the law in its current form did not go far enough. Too many slaves continued to be imported illegally into the state. These critics complained that the slaves smuggled into Georgia from the Upper South behaved in an "obstinate" manner, and they feared "their introduction" tended "to excite discontent and insurrection among the unhappy people of their color heretofore in our possession."[79]

Events in Virginia and North Carolina at the turn of the nineteenth century appeared to confirm white Georgians' worst suspicions about slaves from the Chesapeake region. White Georgians were no doubt distressed by news in the summer of 1800 that the authorities in Richmond, Virginia, uncovered an insurrectionary plot led by Gabriel Prosser, an enslaved blacksmith.[80] Reportedly aided by two French agents, Prosser's plan probably involved hundreds of slaves from Richmond and the surrounding countryside. The rebels intended to carry out a "general massacre of the whites," except for the Frenchmen. They hoped to seize the magazine of arms, then they planned "to issue a proclamation to the negroes to come rally around their standard."[81] Vast in its scope and well-planned, the scheme fell apart when a torrential downpour disrupted its start. Evidence found on the rebels indicated contact with individuals in Philadelphia, Norfolk, and Petersburg, suggesting a much broader conspiracy. That the insurrection was uncovered before it came to fruition offered little consolation to whites in Richmond and the surrounding area. They remained unnerved by its discovery, and for good reason. An account of the planned rebellion that appeared in the *Augusta Chronicle* made clear their rationale: Gabriel's Revolt made it "evident that the French principles of Liberty and Equality has been infused into the minds of the negroes, and that the incautious and intemperate use of these words by some whites among us, have inspired them with the hopes of success."[82] A little over a year later, the authorities in eastern Virginia and North Carolina found large quantities of arms and ammunition in the possession of several groups of slaves, creating yet another furor. In the wake of the discovery of the various plots, the *Augusta Chronicle* insisted there was "no room to doubt but a horrid massacre of the whites was intended by the Negroes of this and the adjoining states."[83] White Georgians believed the effects of revolt in St. Domingue had incontrovertibly arrived on American shores.

For those in favor of repealing the ban, the timing could not have been worse. When the General Assembly met in 1801 and 1802, legislators who supported reopening the slave trade repeatedly attempted to amend the law to permit at least limited importation. The violence in the Chesapeake had done little to dissuade them. The potential for profits simply outweighed any concerns they had about the safety of the bonded laborers they wanted to bring to the state. But those who supported the resumption of the trade found their efforts thwarted by a faction of lowcountry legislators led by George Troup who vehemently opposed attempts to loosen the restrictions. The result was legislative gridlock.[84] Economic considerations undoubtedly influenced some legislators to oppose the proposed changes. After all, those who already owned slaves (as many of the lowcountry representatives did) stood to gain the most if the supply of slaves remained closed. For most, however, fear played the most significant role in the decision-making process. Many agreed with Governor Josiah Tatnall, who believed that slaves tainted by the toxic ideology of racial equality had spread everywhere, even to the United States. The conspiracy in Richmond had demonstrated as much. "The importation of negroes" into Georgia, "particularly those of North Carolina, Virginia and Maryland, has increased to an alarming extent." Yet, Tattnall warned, the "industrious and faithful slave is seldom to be purchased, more especially at a low price." Consequently, it was highly unlikely that imported slaves could be trusted. The "speculator finds it in his interest to seek them in jails and other places of confinement, from whence on account of their infamy of character" problem slaves could be purchased at "very low" prices. These are the ones, Tattnall assured the lawmakers, traders generally brought into Georgia. "Already we have so ma[n]y of them, that I fear the evil has taken root."[85]

The actions of the slave rebels in St. Domingue initiated a conversation about the safety of the slave trade that ultimately led to the total ban on the practice. The decision had wide-ranging consequences. It had an impact on the development of the black community by halting the flow of foreign slaves, African or West Indian, to Georgia and accelerating the process of creolization. The fight over imports created a wedge that pitted slaveholders against one another, a new paradigm from the earlier conflicts that generally pitted slaveholders against nonslaveholders. It complicated the sectional divisions within the state. It resulted in the widespread fear among the whites in Georgia of "foreign" slaves. It even raised the possibility that the Haitian contagion could infect "native" slaves and incite them to bloodshed. The slavery-inspired violence led to renewed calls for the reform of the institution and the treatment of bondmen. The debate remained a constant source of friction over the course of the following six decades. The Atlantic upheavals raised white Georgians' suspicions of all slaves and prompted reform of the slave system.

As white Georgians attempted to reform the institution of slavery, they also reconsidered the status of free people of color. As in other parts of the Atlantic World, free people of color in Georgia were viewed as potential supporters of the regime. White Georgians and the authorities were relatively tolerant in their treatment of free people of color in their midst in the decades after slavery was introduced. While we tend to focus on whites' suspicions of free people of color, some whites viewed them as allies. After 1794, with the abolition of slavery in the French colonies, white Georgians' assessment of free people of color became more complicated. As French black citizens spread throughout the Atlantic, white Georgians encountered difficulties determining the status of people of color. As whites struggled with the changes, they contemplated ways to avoid the spread of insurrectionary violence to Georgia. The troubles in the West Indies had an ambivalent impact on free people of color in Georgia. On the one hand, white Georgians distrusted foreign free people of color. On the other hand, they viewed native free people of color as potential allies, even recognizing some as "citizens of the state." The 1790s paradoxically represented a time of promise for Georgia's free people of color.

While planters and slaves in the colonial era have received considerable attention, the same is not true for free people of African descent. Historians of colonial Georgia have largely directed their energies to other topics, while historians of free people of color in Georgia have skipped over the period, focusing instead on the nineteenth century, when the state began to systematically crack down on them. And to a certain degree, these omissions make sense since free people of color constituted a rather small portion of the colonial population. Estimates place the number at fewer than one hundred in the mid-1760s.[86] Their importance, however, is greater than their numerical size. Their treatment reveals the flexibility of slavery and the racial system. It demonstrates that racial differences were not as entrenched as they would later be. The position of free people of color in society indicates that, at least in the eighteenth century, the rigidly bifurcated racial system that came to dominate the South in the antebellum era had not yet taken hold.

Barbara Galphin provides an indication of the social mobility that characterized the lives of some slaves and free blacks in colonial Georgia. Galphin was born sometime around 1760 at Silver Bluff, an area near Augusta. She was the daughter of an enslaved woman named Rose and an Irish émigré named George Galphin. Though born a slave, Barbara went on to become a fairly wealthy woman in early Georgia, gaining her freedom and considerable land along the way. She owned several thousand acres of property in the backcountry of South Carolina and Georgia as well as considerable livestock. She also had the use of several dozen slaves to work her fields. She was reportedly well educated and must have operated in polite white society with some ease. As a young woman, she married a white man named William Holmes, and together they had four children who went on to have successful and prosperous lives. Some of her descendants became prominent members of southern society, including legislators.[87]

Barbara Galphin's biography highlights the fluidity of race in early Georgia and the difficulty of relying on legal status when determining the place of people of African descent. Masters and mistresses could grant freedom on their own authority, so manumission left few records. The prevalence of free people of color among the population of people of African descent is difficult to determine. Legally, Barbara did not receive her official freedom until her father manumitted her in his will when he died in 1780, yet her history strongly suggests that she was not treated like a slave by her father or by other whites that she dealt with.

Rather, her birth to a powerful white man who considered her his own child made her life very different from that of the numerous other slaves that he owned.

The story of Barbara Galphin's father similarly reveals the fluidity of race relations, but from a different perspective. George Galphin emigrated from Ireland to British North America in the 1730s. He became an Indian trader and moved to the backcountry to carry out his work. He traded and dealt extensively with the Lower Creeks, becoming an extremely wealthy man through his business dealings, amassing more than forty thousand acres of land and more than one hundred slaves by his death. All told, he apparently had nine children from six different women. His wives included native women and white women as well as women of African descent. These relationships indicate that it was fairly acceptable for white men of means not only to have sexual relations with women of color but also to acknowledge the paternity of and care for the children of those relations. Galphin was not an outlaw or rogue on the fringes of acceptable society. Instead, he was a patriarch whose large family reflected his wealth. In fact, he was of sufficiently good standing that one of his daughters, Martha, married John Milledge, a governor and one of Georgia's most prominent politicians from the revolutionary and early national eras.[88]

George Galphin did not see race as the sole or even primary factor in his relations with his wives or his children. His will provides a lens to view the complex web of race and class that shaped the Galphin family hierarchy and influenced its internal dynamics. With his will, the first thing Galphin did was establish the freedom of all of his children. But he did not treat all of his children equally. Judging by the contents of the will, he regarded certain of his progeny in a higher standing than the others. Three of Galphin's children, whom he identified as two "mulatto" girls and a "half-breed Indian girl," received their freedom and little else. Apparently Barbara Galphin was part of the more select group. She, noted as "his mulatto girl," along with five of her half-siblings—a white son and daughter whose race he left unspecified and three Indian children, marked as born to Metawney, "an Indian woman"—inherited most of their father's land, property, and slaves.[89] Galphin exhibited a type of favoritism that bestowed on them a higher rank in society. This enabled Barbara to live among the elite of society. Neither her race nor her slave birth blocked this social and economic ascent.

Barbara Galphin and her father, George, are both important historically, but for different reasons. Barbara Galphin is important as an exception. Her life story shows us the potential heights to which people of African descent could climb in early Georgia. By contrast, George is important because of his typicality, at least in certain ways. He may have represented an extreme in terms of the number of wives he took and children he fathered, but his rather fluid conceptions of race and status were not unique. Indeed, his views appear to have been widespread not only among other Indian traders but among the rest of Georgia's political and economic elite as well.[90]

One key piece of evidence that suggests the general acceptance of mobility for some free people of color comes from the colony's 1765 slave code.[91] This code was the colony's third iteration since repealing the ban on slavery. It included a few changes to the previous code from ten years earlier, including new draconian punishments for certain crimes when committed by those in bondage. The authorities were particularly fearful of poisoning, having mandated burning at the stake for those convicted of the crime. More importantly, the slave code of 1765 included a passage that, amazingly enough, actively encouraged free people of African descent to immigrate to Georgia. Until that point, the authorities in Georgia had failed to offer any kind of protection or special privileges to attract free-born "mulattoes" and "mestizoes" to the colony; thus the provision represented a kind of amends. The legislation decreed that "All Persons male and Female of what Nation or colour soever being born of free parents . . . may be intituled to an Act of Assembly for Naturalizing them . . . whereby they, their Wives and Children may have, Use and enjoy, all the Rights, Privileges, Powers and Immunities" enjoyed by "any Person born of British parents . . . except to vote for or be Elected a Member to serve in the general Assembly."[92]

In effect, the authorities promised to grant free-born people of color the same status that whites enjoyed except voting and officeholding. They were not to be tried in the same manner as regular free blacks who obtained their freedom but were not born free. Similarly, they did not face the same kinds of punishments as spelled out in the new slave code, which called for harsh new penalties against blacks, enslaved and free. The law introduced distinctions among the population of free people of African descent, setting up a hierarchy based on official rights and privileges. The law, then, treated free-born people of color as it did Jews. They enjoyed partial rights as subjects. The law appears to have been unique among the colonies of the British North American mainland.

Ultimately, no free person of color took advantage of the measure because the Crown rejected the entire slave code for an altogether different reason before it was implemented. When the Crown and Georgia's authorities finally agreed on a revised slave code five years later, the provision was not included, though it is unclear why. Though the Crown ultimately rejected the 1765 slave code, the provision demonstrated that Georgian authorities were not averse to extending privileges to people of African descent. Prior to the Revolution, then, blackness did not preclude free people of color from becoming an accepted part of society.

Although historians disagree over the motives and significance of the law, they all agree that its passage seems strange given the structural changes that Georgia was experiencing at the time. In the midst of a huge increase in the number of slaves imported to Georgia, it seems counter-intuitive that the authorities would pass legislation enticing people of color to settle in the colony just as the plantation complex was hitting its full stride. It does not fit with the prevailing narrative on the rise of plantation slavery in Georgia, one that focuses on the decline in the treatment of slaves and a concomitant hardening of racial attitudes. That the authorities could simultaneously elevate the status of some people of African descent seems to defy logic.

The apparent anomalies of the law can be explained by examining the links between Georgia and the wider Atlantic World. In particular, the law suggests that white Georgians tightened the bonds on slaves even as they loosened the bonds on free-born people of color. And they did this, at least in part, by drawing on the Jamaican example. The law was not an anomaly but rather reflected the kind of society that authorities hoped to create, one that allowed and acknowledged the benefits of a loyal population. As noted previously, Georgia's authorities had consulted "with great care & attention" the "Negro Laws of Jamaica, So. Carolina & Virginia" before drafting a revised slave code for the colonies in 1765.[93]

That Wright listed Jamaica first among the slave societies whose laws Georgia's authorities consulted was significant (and should come as no surprise). In fact, there was good reason for Jamaica to stand out since it was the most important of the British West Indian colonies. By the middle of the eighteenth century, Jamaica had the largest slave population and produced enormous wealth for both the island's planters and the metropole. Jamaica's rise had not come without problems, of course; as elsewhere in the Americas, Jamaica's past was marked by bloodshed connected to slavery. Yet in spite of these periodic bouts of insurrectionary violence, Jamaica's authorities had managed to create a slave society that on the surface at least appeared to be in control. Consequently, it made perfect sense for white Georgians to look to the island in hopes of emulating its success. After all, conditions in the lowcountry mirrored those found in Jamaica's plantation districts.

Jamaica provided an example of a seemingly successful slave society that recognized gradations among free people of color. The authorities there divided free people of color into three categories, each with distinct legal privileges. The first comprised those born as slaves and subsequently manumitted. They were allowed no other mode of trial beyond that of a common slave and were prohibited from testifying against whites or other free-born persons. The second class, consisting of free-born people of color, was allowed trials by jury and could give evidence against one another in civil and criminal cases, but only against white persons or against free persons of color endowed with superior privileges in civil cases. Individuals in these two classes were not allowed to vote.

The third group consisted of what would be considered the colored elite, individuals who by private acts of assembly were granted "the same rights and privileges with other English subjects born of white parents." Now, their rights were not absolute. Legislation defined the range of rights and privileges that they could enjoy. For men, the private acts almost always came with the caveat that the extension of rights did not include the right to vote for assembly members, though in a few rare instances they did. The number of people who could qualify for the status was not large. Often they were educated, baptized Anglican, and possessed considerable property. Many of these individuals were quite wealthy, owning plantations and large numbers of slaves.[94]

Georgia's naturalization portion of the 1765 slave code called for official recognition of a class of free people of color very similar to this third group in Jamaican society. The same methods employed by Betty Wood—that is, comparison of language in the respective slave laws—suggest that authorities in Georgia modeled the 1765 law on similar legislation passed in Jamaica.[95] The inclusion of the naturalization law highlights the broader connections between Georgia and the Atlantic World and indicates that whites in Georgia considered themselves part of a larger community that extended beyond the mainland colonies. As in Jamaica, Georgia's authorities envisioned a legal structure that recognized distinctions among free people of color, which reflected the authorities' beliefs about race as well as class. Elite whites in both colonies understood that free people of African descent were not all equal, as was the case with the respective white populations. Factors such as birth and wealth stratified people into different social categories. Moreover, free people of African descent were not necessarily considered enemies of the state and a potential fifth column. Even though the 1765 naturalization law did not end up on the books permanently, its real significance lies, as Carl Degler suggested, in the fact that the authorities considered it at all. It demonstrates that Georgia whites could and did hold views on slavery and race that may seem completely contradictory but were fairly commonplace throughout the Americas. Their slave system became crueler in its punishments and more restrictive in its regulation of black life. But their slave system did not preclude a degree of social mobility in the racial order for free-born people of African descent. Colonial slavery, then, was not predicated on the assumption that race alone qualified people of African descent for enslavement and disqualified them from certain rights, privileges, and protections.

The American Revolution brought about tremendous political changes in Georgia, but it was unclear what effect it would have on free people of color. Elite Georgians had protected the rights of some free people of color in the colonial era, but they were not certain they could continue to do so in the new postrevolutionary order. Joseph Clay embodied this ambivalence. In 1784, one of his friends died and he found himself in charge of the man's two mulatto children. Clay's friend clearly felt a responsibility for his mixed-race children, illustrating the connections between some elite whites and free blacks. This affinity extended to Clay, who took his duty to look after his friend's children seriously. Clay, however, did not know what to do with them. He noted that "these young Folks are very unfortunately situated in this Country" because "their descent places them in the most disadvantageous situation." The law protected them "as Free persons," but "they gain no rank in Life." On the one hand, "White Persons do not commonly associate with them on a footing of equality." On the other hand, "so many of their own Colour (say the mixt breed) being Slaves, they too naturally fall in with them, and even the Negro Slaves claim a right to their acquaintance & Society." As a result, "their future Prospects" in Georgia included neglect by "the most respectable Class of Society" and forced intermixture "with the lowest." He concluded that "the most eligible plan that I can recommend is that they be sent to Europe—this alone can save them." In Europe, where "no such distinctions [would] interfere with their happiness," "they might both be made usefull Members of Society."[96] While Clay was unclear what would be the best course of action, he clearly wanted to do the right thing. He opted to send the children abroad rather than risk a diminution of their status in postrevolutionary Georgia.

Despite Clay's fears, free people of color did find a place for themselves in Georgia. While most of them failed to achieve any type of substantial prosperity, some did. They continued to establish and strengthen business and social relationships with members of the state's white elite. Some found employment as skilled artisans. Others obtained land and became yeomen farmers. A handful owned slaves. A few even found relative acceptance among members of white society. One key measure of success was the growth in the state's population of free people of African descent, which rose from 398 in 1790 to 1,919 in 1800.[97] The increase came from natural reproduction, manumissions, and, surprisingly, immigration. Free people of color from South Carolina, the Chesapeake, and even the West Indies flocked to Georgia in the decade and a half after the end of the War of Independence. Like their white counterparts, black émigrés came in search of new opportunities. In some ways, then, the 1790s were a decade of possibility for free people of color in Georgia.

Events in St. Domingue raised free people of color as an issue in Georgia. Although the slave rebellion in St. Domingue began in 1791, the first stirrings of trouble had occurred the year before, when Vincent Ogé, a free person of color, returned to the colony after successfully lobbying in Paris for rights for this class. Free people of color had enjoyed some rights in the mid-eighteenth century, but by the late eighteenth century they had begun to lose their status. While authorities in Paris agreed to bestow rights on free people of color, authorities in St. Domingue refused. Ogé initiated an uprising but was defeated and brutally executed. Because the authorities continued to withhold their rights, free people of color eventually joined the slave rebellion.[98]

White Georgians remained tolerant toward free people of color in Georgia even after the outbreak of violence in St. Domingue. Some white Georgians sympathized with the plight of free people of color in St. Domingue even as they criticized their methods. They opposed the use of force but realized that the situation was not necessarily their fault. Although they could not condone the use of violence by free people of color to achieve their goals in St. Domingue, some white Georgians blamed white colonists, at least in part, for the eruption of violence there. If they had granted free people of color the basic rights they deserved, the *Augusta Chronicle* maintained, much of the bloodshed might have been avoided: "The miserable fate of the whites may, in a great measure, be attributed to their obstinate hatred and opposition of every law and attempt made by the commissioners to restore the free mulattoes to the natural rights of citizenship, to which they were not only born, but have doubly qualified themselves to enjoy the blessings of freedom—many of those mulattoes have received very liberal educations, and would make a very respectable figure in any station of life."[99] White Georgians could imagine a place for "mulattoes" in "respectable" society. They believed that the failure to recognize and reward the potential of free people of color created resentment that could explode into violence.

When the effects of the revolt in St. Domingue spread to U.S. shores in the fall of 1793, many white Georgians continued to resist the notion that all free people of color were dangerous. When Governor Telfair received word that French blacks were linked to a string of arsons in Charleston in September 1793, he urged legislators to impose a total ban on the arrival not only of slaves but of free people of color as well.[100] He viewed these free people of color as extremely dangerous to the state's security. Some white Georgians called for extreme measures when dealing with them, but this view seems to have been in the minority. Legislators chose to ignore Telfair's warning. Instead of banning arrivals, they enacted a new guardianship law requiring all free people of color who entered the state to find a white man within three months of their arrival to vouch for their trustworthiness.[101]

On the surface, the law represents a clear diminution of liberty for free people of color. In actuality, the law did not represent the repudiation of the tolerance that had marked earlier relations between whites and free people of color. Requiring free people of color to find guardians was considerably less draconian than some of the alternatives pursued by other slave societies. After all, Georgia legislators could have followed their South Carolina counterparts' lead by banning the entry of all free people of color, as Governor Telfair had requested.[102] Instead, we should interpret the guardianship law as an attempt to find a practical solution to what must have been a quandary. The law allowed them the "privileges of residence" provided they registered with the clerk in their county within thirty days and secured a certificate from two magistrates within six months attesting to their "honesty and industry."[103] This provision, like the provisions concerning slaves, adopted a moderate stance. Georgia's legislators permitted free people of color to continue immigrating to the state so long as they convinced free-holding whites in their communities to vouch for their characters. By requiring guardianship, legislators demonstrated that free people of color continued to be a trusted group, even if that allegiance had to be verified. They envisioned a place for free people of color in Georgian society, as long as that place was under the patronage and approval of respectable whites. The provisions of Georgia's 1793 law illustrate yet again that whites did not amalgamate all blacks together as a homogeneous racial group. State legislators distinguished between people of African descent who had secured the confidence of their masters or other white patrons and those who were unknown and possibly dangerous. They welcomed the former and banned the latter.

Guardianship, in fact, could be mutually beneficial both for whites who agreed to serve and for their charges. It promoted alliances between the two groups. Guardianship was an essential part of the process through which free people of color could gain the trust and support of white Georgians. Some members of the lowcountry elite had extensive relations with free people of color.[104] These bonds facilitated the development of a patriarchal order from which both groups benefited. Richard Stites, a planter and merchant from Chatham County, served as guardian for Simon Jackson, Jane Habersham, and London Dolly. Stites had extensive financial dealings with Jackson, a well-known free man of color in Savannah, which even included purchasing a slave cook from Jackson for $200. Stites also employed Charles Senseny, a free man of color from Martinique, to care for his horses and serve as his carriage driver. In fact, Stites relied upon people of African descent to satisfy all his labor demands. When his slaves could not meet his needs, he employed free blacks or rented slaves. He did not look to poor whites, though. The bonds of clientage and patronage that joined whites in other parts of the country did not form in the lowcountry. Instead, those bonds joined white planters to their black employees and slaves.[105]

Free people of color understood the value of having a member of the planter elite represent their interests.[106] Because of their birth, free people of color faced certain limitations on what they could achieve. They could not hope to attain equal status with Georgia's wealthiest white planters, economically or politically. But their identity did not restrict them absolutely. As such, they hoped to climb as high as they possibly could. The only way to achieve that was to have a patron, a white man who could vouch for their character and give them his business.[107] Without white support, an endeavor, whether for an individual or a group, had little chance of gaining the city government's approval. When a group of people of color petitioned the Savannah City Council to allow them to hold church services, the alderman granted the request, but they did so primarily because the petitioners' motion was "supported by [a] respectable number of citizens."[108]

Indeed, connections to prominent whites were especially handy when a free person of color was charged with committing an infraction. Forced to appear before the city council for "suffering his five Negro slaves" to work without the appropriate badges, John McIntosh, a free person of color, relied on his guardian, Dr. James Houstoun, to explain the circumstances behind his actions to the authorities. Evidently Houstoun managed to convince the aldermen that there were "several matters in mitigation of the offence," which benefited Houstoun as well, since he was held responsible for his charge's wrongdoing.[109]

Many whites did not believe that free people of color uniformly threatened the institution of slavery. For example, whites believed that Andrew Bryan, a black preacher in Savannah, instilled in his flock an appropriate subservience to their masters. In his petition to establish his own church, white patrons stressed that unruly slaves had become docile under his ministrations.[110] Moreover, as the example with McIntosh indicates, some free people of color owned slaves. Though elite whites formalized the boundaries of the racial order, some free people of African descent participated in it wittingly and wholeheartedly. Unlike the practice in the Upper South, these slave owners were not related to their bondmen.[111] Exploitative slave owners of color accepted with little reservation the tenets of the slave society because it granted them a relatively privileged position in the hierarchy. The fact that their slaves were of African descent would not have weighed too heavily on their shoulders because they likely felt little racial affinity. They were "people of color" and their slaves were "Negroes." Divisions within Georgian society, as whites understood, did not clearly fall along racial lines.[112]

Of course, not all relationships were between wealthy whites and people of color.[113] Bonds, though less official than guardianships, could unite poor whites with slaves and free blacks as well. Planters, however, feared these associations, believing that only harm could result. Consequently, they used their power to regulate relations between poor whites, slaves, and free people of color by enacting legislation to discourage specific types of racial interaction. Authorities cracked down on white men who operated "houses of entertainment" frequented by slaves and free blacks, believing them to be impediments to maintaining order.[114] In these establishments, far from the sight of the planters or city authorities, the people at the bottom of the hierarchy came together to engage in all sorts of nefarious activities. Officials were most concerned with illicit trade, which they believed transpired between the two groups. Laws restricted the kinds of commercial activities that poor whites could engage in with slaves and imposed hefty penalties for any transgressions. The punishment imposed on those who engaged in trade with slaves was disproportionate compared to the penalty for having slaves work without the proper authorization or on a Sunday. In Savannah, slave owners were usually fined 25 cents for the infraction committed by their slaves in their name, while poor whites who traded with slaves were fined $10 or $20 for each infraction.[115] The discrepancy demonstrated the dominance of the planter elite and its ability to legislate measures that reflected its members' interests.

The abolition of slavery in the French colonies fundamentally altered what it meant to be a free person of African descent in the Atlantic World. Desperate to protect the achievements of the French Revolution in St. Domingue in the face of an invasion of British and Spanish troops, the National Assembly in France abolished slavery in the French colonies in 1794. By liberating French slaves, the French government vastly increased the number of free people of African descent in the Atlantic World. These free people of color were darker and less distinguishable from slaves. They shared few of the attributes of other free people of color. Ex-slaves were firmly committed to the French nation and were among its most ardent supporters. They offered their services in the army and navy, where they hoped to fight to protect the revolution and spread its message. By allowing ex-slaves to become soldiers and sailors and then sending them throughout the Atlantic World as the vanguard for the French Revolution and its radical ideology, the French government created a new group of free people of color that had no desire to protect the slave system. Tainted with the contagion of revolt, these free blacks threatened to destroy slavery throughout the Atlantic World just as they had done in St. Domingue before gaining their freedom.[116]

As French free blacks began spreading across the Atlantic World, white Georgians faced new challenges determining the allegiances of people of African descent. They could no longer assume that free people of color would support the slave regime. White Georgians repeatedly faced these questions as black sailors arrived in their ports in the second half of the 1790s. Despite the threat of the revolutionary contagion, some white Georgians refused to view people of color monolithically and continued to draw distinctions among the population.

Newly free people of color arrived in Georgia in the summer of 1795 and immediately threatened the racial hierarchy. At the end of June, the French ship *La Vengeur* docked at Savannah's port, creating a panic among the town's white residents. The ship was a privateer commissioned by the French authorities; it apparently arrived with several prizes it had taken before reaching Savannah. What caused a stir was the multiracial composition of the ship's crew. The men appeared to have a swagger about them. After they docked, the sailors strutted through the city's streets, armed with pistols and knives. Clearly, they did not display the humility that white Georgians expected of all people of African descent, whether bond or free. Unnerved by the sailors' display, the white residents of the town held an emergency meeting where they decided to quarantine the ship and its sailors while they determined how to proceed.[117]

Within days of the ship's arrival, an article appeared in the *Georgia Gazette* offering evidence of the danger posed by the French ships plying the seas in the wake of the 1794 decree. Purportedly written by a French émigré who had recently settled in Savannah, the piece offered a firsthand account of the intentions of those on board. The émigré related a harrowing story. While en route to Georgia from Jamaica, his ship had been attacked and taken by the *Vengeur*. The privateers stole the white passengers' belongings, placed them in chains below deck, and threatened them with violence. The sailors treated the slaves belonging to the Frenchmen in a completely different manner. They attempted to lure the slaves away, promising them freedom and encouraging them to return to St. Domingue. They offered them an inversion of the power structure, with blacks in control and whites in submission. To illustrate their point, the sailors performed mock executions of the white prisoners and sang revolutionary ballads. Their message was clear: their actions signaled the ascent of a new world of radical egalitarian ideology put into practice.[118] The émigré's message was equally clear. His article represented a warning to the white residents of Savannah and Georgia as a whole. The decision by the French to free their slaves and send them out on the seas to spread the revolutionary message represented a direct challenge to the institution of slavery. And if they were not careful, he argued, Georgia would end up like St. Domingue.

For many white residents of Savannah, the sight of the armed black

Frenchmen and the account of the émigré clearly had an impact. Faced with what seemed like an existential threat to their world, they opted to abandon the relatively tolerant stand that had marked their dealings with free people of color in the past. Part of the problem, of course, was that it had become impossible to determine which free people of color were really free in the wake of the 1794 decree. Consequently, they urged the city authorities to expel the ship and the sailors on board.[119]

Yet the decision was not unanimous. Apparently some whites in Savannah disagreed with the decision to treat the sailors as a threat simply because of their color. The initial decision to quarantine the ship had been based upon a finding by the city's health officer in accordance with the law stipulating such a course for ships with ten or more "negroes." Shortly before the city council issued its ruling, the health officer revised his finding and called for the ship's and sailors' release. He had initially counted several of the "Spaniards & Portuges" as "negroes," an error that had subsequently been pointed out to him by a sympathetic white. As a result, the ship had fewer than the ten "negroes" required to mandate a quarantine. Although the city council moved forward with its plans to expel the ship, the new evidence had an impact. Members of the council divided five to four over the issue.[120]

The *Vengeur* incident highlighted the difficulty of determining the status of people of African descent in a world undergoing profound change. Clearly, the physical appearances of the men in question had not changed in the time between their initial arrival and when the health officer revised his opinion. Only his perception of racial difference shifted. The events in St. Domingue had altered the way whites looked at people of African descent. Until then, relatively clear markers identified those who were free and most likely sympathetic to slavery (or at least not likely to challenge the institution). After the mass manumission of French slaves, these assumptions could no longer be counted on. As the health officer demonstrated, teasing apart the differences between race and nationality and status as free or enslaved was hardly straightforward. Yet, in spite of this uncertainty, sympathetic perspectives persisted. Whites did not abandon the notion that some people of African descent could be trusted and deserved at least a modicum of rights.

The arrival of people of African descent with unknown provenances and histories continued to be an issue for Georgian authorities in the years after the *Vengeur* episode. In late 1797, the *Exuma* arrived in Savannah with two dozen men who had been picked up at sea after their ship sank.

Georgian authorities learned that the sunken ship had carried black prisoners of war and free people of African descent as passengers. Conflicting stories emerged over whether the free people of color had been dropped off before the ship sank.[121] Without clear indications of the men's status, the Savannah authorities placed the men in custody. Although some of the men wound up hired out, the city's authorities permitted two of the men to sign on with departing ships and contracted with a ship captain to have fourteen of the men removed from the state, rather than placing them in bondage. The survivors were not "Negroes (*slaves*)" brought into Georgia to be sold. They were brigands who had been captured in battle; their arrival in the state was completely accidental. To enslave the men, the city council contended, would "illegally, and unconstitutionally, without accusation or trial, deprive *freemen* of liberty."[122] The authorities in Savannah regarded the *Exuma* refugees as prisoners of war, not slaves, who could not be allowed to stay but also could not be deprived of their rights. Black skin did not automatically translate to slave status.

Clearly, then, some white Georgians believed that free people of color, even those who were foreign, deserved some rights. They were freemen and like all freemen, regardless of color, they could not be deprived of basic legal protections. But an important question remained: exactly how far should the state extend these rights? The question was even more complicated for free people of color from Georgia. They were not slaves and yet they were not free white citizens. They occupied a nebulous middle ground. Under British rule, the issue had not created the same kind of problems. As subjects of the Crown, individuals, whether white, colored, or black, were placed on a sliding scale in which race was one of several factors that determined their place and rights in society. After independence, the graded hierarchy gave way to a binary system in which individuals were ostensibly citizens or not. This theoretical formulation left a huge chasm, however. Part of the problem was that early legislation remained unclear on who qualified for citizenship. What were the criteria? What rights did citizenship convey? Georgia did not codify the status of free people of color as citizens.

There is considerable evidence that Georgia's authorities experimented with giving some people of African descent citizenship rights in the late eighteenth century. Without a codified policy in the state, a handful of people of color in Georgia took the initiative in the late eighteenth century and pressed the state to recognize their elevated social and economic status. Through private acts, the authorities in Georgia extended some privileges and rights of citizenship to certain people of African descent. As in Jamaica, the people of color who received the special economic and legal rights had connections to prominent white men. A clear pattern emerged in which white men appealed to the state government to officially recognize the rights of their "mulatto" children and wives. In 1796, for example, the Georgia General Assembly granted an enslaved woman named Chany and her nine children their freedom and considerable land and property through the will of Anthony Haynes, who was most likely the father of the children. In addition to bestowing official recognition of the manumission, the legislature inserted language into the act authorizing members of the family "to take, hold, and enjoy property of every kind, in like manner as if they were free citizens of this state."[123]

In another example three years later, the legislature manumitted Sylvia Posner and her son David and granted them legal rights that exceeded those bestowed upon regular free people of color. At the behest of Sylvia's white husband, the authorities conferred upon the mother and son some privileges of whiteness. In the manumission act, the legislature "declared [them] to be . . . utterly, clearly and fully discharged from slavery, as if the said Sylvia and David, had been born free." Furthermore, the law declared that if they were ever charged with a crime, they would be "tried for such offence in the same manner, and be entitled to the same defence in the courts of this state, as allowed to free white persons in likes cases."[124]

These examples draw attention both to the vast social and economic differences among people of African descent and the fact that the state authorities appeared to recognize these distinctions and to grant various gradations of citizenship accordingly. In specific situations, Chany and her children were guaranteed recognition as "free citizens" while Posner and her son were guaranteed treatment as "free white persons." The language contained in the legislation made clear that their status was different from the rest of the state's free blacks and free people of color, who were only to receive the "privileges" that "free people of color are entitled to by the laws of this state." As with Barbara Galphin, these examples illustrate the difficulty of using African descent to determine an individual's place in society. Like Galphin, Sylvia Posner and Chany had technically been slaves, yet their lived experiences were most likely far removed from the drudgery and physical exhaustion that marked most slaves' lives in Georgia. An analysis of the private acts approved by the legislature suggests that gender played a prominent role in the process.[125]

The terms used in these statutes appear to echo those provided by the

Jamaican authorities.[126] They reflect an understanding that all people of African descent were not the same. While most were deemed deserving of few rights beyond the right to be free from slavery, others came from families with solid reputations, were owners of land and property, were educated, and had connections to white families, often familial ones. Clearly, then, a graded notion of status was necessary to ascertain their proper place in society. Although the 1765 law that called for some free people of color to receive naturalization rights was never actually placed into law, it appears that the state did implement its provisions on an individual basis through private acts after the Revolution.

If Georgia's legislature toyed with establishing a graded notion of citizenship with its extension of rights to well-placed manumitted slaves, it took a much bolder step in that direction at the end of the decade when it granted citizenship to a handful of people of color who were already free. Without a codified policy in the state, three free people of color petitioned the state authorities in 1799 to recognize their standing in society. The General Assembly acquiesced, passing legislation that explicitly stated the petitioners were "entitled to all the rights, privileges and immunities belonging to a free citizen of this State."[127] Rather than singling out certain privileges and rights at their disposal, as in the Posner case, the legislature provided a broad grant of citizenship and stipulated specific limitations. They could not testify against whites, nor could they vote or hold office. Beyond these exceptions, however, these "citizens of the state" were entitled to all the benefits of freedom that whites enjoyed.

The free people of color granted status as "citizens of the state" were very different than the free people of color who obtained partial citizenship earlier in the 1790s. Thomas Going, for example, was neither a woman nor the mixed-race son of a wealthy white planter. Instead, he was a male adult who came from a long line of free people of African descent, some of whom appeared lighter than others, but a family that was generally known as black and not "mulatto." He did not possess any particularly intimate relations with white Georgians that set him apart from other free people of color. He and his family were yeomen. The Goings were free blacks of a different, more middling, sort. Recognition as a "free citizen of the state" to Thomas Going suggests a broadening of rights to a larger segment of the free population of African descent, not limited just to the wives and children of the white elite.

The experience of the Going family suggests that some blacks secured at least some measure of success and stature in the backcountry.

The Going clan traced its origins to a Virginia enslaved man, John Gowen, who gained his freedom in 1641.[128] His descendants Moses and Sherwood fought in the Virginia militia during the Revolutionary War.[129] Moses traveled to Georgia to claim land offered to veterans in 1786. After inspecting the land, he returned home to prepare for the relocation of his family. Around 1789, Moses Going and his wife, Agnes, moved their family to Georgia; other members of the family followed, creating a community of transplanted black Virginians. The Goings were materially well situated. Moses owned substantial land holdings: 575 acres in Wilkes County and 684 acres in Franklin County. He was also a millwright and operated his own mill on his property. The women in the family were also employed as weavers. The sons were similarly well off. The Going clan appears to have enjoyed a modicum of status in their community. Their children sought enhanced rights through the legislature. In 1796 Reuben and John were granted a special privilege by the General Assembly allowing them to own property.[130] Three years later, their brother, Thomas, who was a doctor, benefited from legislation that made him a "citizen of the state."[131] Going men appear to have even received land from the state authorities in subsequent land lotteries in 1803 and 1806.[132]

In a society in which the rights of individuals were still being determined, these select people of color codified the privileges that they enjoyed, even if they did not amount to full political rights. In colonial Georgia, not all men possessed the right to vote. The 1777 constitution did extend suffrage rights to virtually all white men in the colony. In the immediate aftermath of the Revolutionary War, however, many white men did not bother to vote, and voting itself was not as important as it would become in the antebellum era. Status as "citizens of the state" was meaningful to these men and women despite the accompanying restrictions. Exemption from whipping meant more in their everyday lives than voting on election days.

The decision to grant these people of color rights was not so unique when compared to what was taking place elsewhere in the Americas. In 1794, France moved immediately to grant citizenship to former slaves in its colonial possessions. Although the abolition of slavery in the French colonies marked a significant turning point in the history of the Americas, the decision to make the ex-slaves citizens of the republic had equally profound consequences. The decision granted the ex-slaves a stake in society and radicalized the concept of equality. Georgia's authorities rejected the French model and instead apparently followed the Jamaican model, where the practice of bestowing rights and privileges to free people of color was growing. This was particularly true after the 1795 maroon uprising.[133]

In spite of the restrictions, the possibility of obtaining official citizenship rights prompted another eight free people of color to petition the General Assembly two years later.[134] After initially opening the door to partial citizenship for some free people of color, however, the General Assembly appears to have retreated from this position. Legislators approved a petition for citizenship from the second group of free people of color in the House but tabled it in the Senate for unknown reasons.[135] The legislature left no written record of their deliberations. There are several possibilities: Perhaps they were unnerved by news of a conspiracy in late 1799 in Jamaica allegedly led by free people of color and a white Frenchman with connections to the French émigré community in Charleston.[136] The plans came to naught, however, when the authorities arrested one of the conspirators, who, in turn, revealed the details of the scheme. Officials quickly detained the suspects and executed them soon after. For white Georgians, the alleged slave plot in Jamaica demonstrated that revolt could spread anywhere. Even Jamaica, with its amelioration of slavery, could not remain immune to the disease of insurrection. Georgia's borrowings from Jamaican law and society no longer seemed adequate protection. Perhaps the census numbers from 1800 left the legislators apprehensive.

Having increased by close to fivefold in the previous ten years, the population of free people of color may have appeared far more menacing than it had earlier. With such a substantial and rapid growth rate, legislators may have feared that free people of color would soon overrun the state. Regardless of the legislators' rationale, however, for free people of color it made no difference. The decision to halt this brief experiment marked the end of an era in which racial fluidity flourished in Georgia. In the decades that followed, free people of color would see their position in Georgian society continue to diminish as a new, more rigid racial system emerged.

In the quarter century following the outbreak of the American Revolution, Georgia's racial order underwent a transformation. Having survived the chaos and destruction of their own war of independence, Georgia's planters revived their slave society only to be confronted by the effects of revolution abroad. Spurred by the tumult in the West Indies, white Georgians reevaluated the institution of slavery. The rebellion in the Caribbean hastened the end of Georgia's participation in the Atlantic slave trade and pushed planters to see their bondmen as less expendable. Aware that slave labor held the key to the state's future prosperity, yet equally aware of its risks, white Georgians initiated reform to save the institution before it destroyed Georgian society. Increasingly, whites came to espouse a more insular view of their society, with masters and slaves as all part of a large family. In addition to identifying those excluded from Georgian society, namely foreign slaves and free people of color, the Haitian Revolution prompted state authorities to codify the status of those included in Georgian society. The authorities moved to clarify the position of those who occupied the nebulous space between free and enslaved and between black and white in an effort to protect Georgia from the ravages of racial insurrection. The impact of the Haitian Revolution extended well beyond the coast, where plantation slavery had taken root in Georgia. The same forces that created chaos on the Georgia coast affected the interior, but the consequences for the racial order would be very different. Instead of narrowing the opportunities for black people, it opened them. Geopolitical rivalries produced divergent racial systems in the interior as the Americans, British, Indians, and Spanish competed for control. The Trans-Oconee Republic and the State of Muskogee emerged as two challenges to the expansion of American plantation slavery.

3

THE TRANS-OCONEE REPUBLIC, 1794

We are happy to find that you honors have met,
The soldiers, we hope, you will never forget.
We flatter ourselves, so honest a band,
Will immediately pay the soldiers their land.
You ne'er in your lives, saw such a d——d pother,
As the soldiers have made among one another.
Some have given their goods, clothes, money, and ponies,
For the lands that you promis'd beyond the Oconies,
Such fighting and squabbling you never did see,
For the rights of state soldiers on the Oconee.
When his honor the Governor issued his Proclamation,
We were ready to fight the whole Creek nation,
"Bravo!" says one—"huzza!" says another,
And each son of Mars would encourage his brother.
When the war was gone through and they came to disband,
A few certificates you gave them, but where is their land?
                            —*Augusta Chronicle and Gazette of the State,*
                                    November 20, 1790

The author who penned this poem in late 1790 expressed the resentment felt by many Revolutionary veterans in Georgia who believed that their contributions on behalf of the nation had not been rewarded. The men had received promises of land in return for their service during the Revolutionary War, but seven years after the conflict's official end they had yet to obtain their recompense. As part of its efforts to raise troops during the Revolutionary War, Georgia had offered bounties of land to men who fought in the state militia or Continental Army. This land, however, lay beyond the colonial borders, beyond the Ogeechee River, on territory still claimed by the neighboring Creek Indians. After the war ended, the state set about obtaining a cession to compensate the veterans. In the meantime, it issued certificates to be redeemed at a future date. These certificates served as currency in the backcountry's economy as veterans anticipated receiving their land. By the publication of the poem, many of the veterans who had "given their goods, clothes, money, and ponies" in exchange for additional promissory notes on the lands "promis'd beyond the Oconies" felt they had waited long enough. Anger at the failure of the state and federal government to obtain the disputed lands eventually pushed some veterans and other frontier residents in Georgia to create a new nation, the Trans-Oconee Republic, just across the southwestern border in these disputed lands.[1]

Established in 1794, the Trans-Oconee Republic lasted less than six months before crumbling. Despite its brief existence, the republic represented a significant episode in early Georgia. Its history offers insight into important differences over republicanism, land, and Indian policies that emerged among white Georgians during the revolutionary era. Race played a central part in this story. The dominant history of race in Georgia focuses on the lowcountry and the development of the plantation economy. The Revolution, however, affected the racial order in the backcountry as well, though in different ways. It unleashed an era of hostile relations with the Indians. Backcountry frontiersmen coveted Indian lands as their revolutionary inheritance. They viewed Indians as savages to be removed or exterminated and rejected the premises underlying the "civilization" program. In their hostilities with the Indians and their attempts to obtain land, backcountry settlers developed their own version of republicanism, one shaped by the realities of frontier life. In the backcountry, settlers determined worth and belonging through fighting skills against the Indians. Backcountry republicanism excluded Indians but possibly included blacks. In any case, backcountry republicanism stood as a challenge to the extension of plantation-based agriculture.

The decision to abandon Georgia and the United States could not have come easy to the men who joined the Trans-Oconee Republic. It was not the product of rash thinking or exuberance; instead, it was the product of the complex (and at times contradictory) political struggles that occurred in the last quarter of the eighteenth century. The 1790s were a turbulent decade in the backcountry of the United States. Riots and rebellions, including the Whiskey Rebellions in Kentucky and Pennsylvania, broke out repeatedly over the course of the decade.[2] Regionalism in Georgia was not the typical story about festering western hostility toward the eastern elite. The backcountry did not explode as a result of long-standing grievances ignored by the authorities. Backcountry settlers had not suffered at the hands of the lowcountry planter and merchant elite. Of all the groups involved in the Revolution in Georgia, the frontiersmen benefited the most, which they deemed fitting since it was they who had sacrificed the most within the state to bring the nation into existence. The War of Independence, in addition to securing the thirteen colonies' freedom from British rule, served as a catalyst for more far-reaching changes. Since 1754, the planter-merchant elite in the lowcountry of Savannah and its hinterland had dominated Georgia's political institutions. The Revolution upended the status quo. Through a combination of demographic change and the exigencies of war, residents of Georgia's backcountry assumed a more prominent role in the governance of Georgia. Backcountry settlers, then, actually held power in the state and set the agenda for Indian and land policies in the 1780s. After 1790, however, they found their power diminished. As their grip on the machinery of government slipped, backcountry settlers found their interests sacrificed in the name of promoting peace with their avowed enemies. By the middle of the decade, some had begun to question not only the wisdom of ratifying the Constitution but their commitment to the nation.

Before the American Revolution, British-negotiated land cessions expanded Georgia's boundaries, resulting in explosive growth in the backcountry. Governor Wright secured a cession of land from the Creeks in 1763. Thousands of migrants, mostly poor farmers from the Carolinas and Virginia, flocked to the colony to take advantage of generous offers of land. Before long, migrants had settled all the ceded land and had begun to push illegally onto the Indian land. In an effort to defuse the tension with the Indians and to alleviate the clamor for more land, Wright negotiated another treaty with Creek chiefs in 1773. The cession effectively doubled the size of Georgia and drew thousands of additional settlers to the colony. The backcountry accounted for much of the colony's population growth between 1760 and 1773, when it went from 9,000 residents to 33,000.[3]

During the Revolution, backcountry settlers chose their loyalties according to Indian policies, initially supporting the British but eventually embracing the Patriot cause. Backcountry residents originally supported the British because the British had opened the land for settlement. In addition, backcountry residents believed that British troops would aid them in their future struggles with the Indians. By contrast, the coastal elite, from which the Patriot cause in Georgia drew its strength, had proven themselves unsympathetic to backcountry settlers on issues related to land and Indians. In the early stages of the war, state authorities focused their meager resources on protecting the slave plantations of the southern border with Florida rather than the family farms of the western backcountry. When presented with the possibility of attack on both frontiers but the ability to defend only one with a reasonable chance to emerge victorious, state authorities selected the plantation belt. Dissatisfaction with the British governor's Indian policies, however, eventually drove the backcountry settlers into the arms of the Patriots. The shift in the settlers' allegiance stemmed from an episode in which Governor Wright failed to pursue and punish Creek warriors after they launched a series of raids in the backcountry in 1774. By aligning themselves with the Patriots, backcountry settlers gained the promise of support against the Indians. Their decision to abandon the British amplified their political power.[4]

The success of the Patriot cause in Georgia owed much to the backcountry. At the outset of the conflict, the Patriots forced Governor Wright into exile in February 1776, but the British retook control in December 1778 when Lieutenant Colonel Archibald Campbell landed in Savannah and restored the governor to power. British forces established control of the lowcountry and extended their authority to the midpoint between Savannah and Augusta, effectively dividing the colony in half. As the prewar status quo returned to the lowcountry, the center of Patriot activity shifted to the backcountry. The Patriots established a government at Augusta, where they ruled for two years before British forces captured the town and its hinterlands in 1780. Unlike lowcountry settlers, who generally acceded to the restoration of British rule, backcountry settlers, numbering approximately eight hundred to nine hundred men, primarily from Wilkes County, waged guerrilla warfare to challenge British control over the interior of the state. The conflict continued until 1781, when the backcountry Patriots, with the aid of Continental troops, drove the British from the region and gradually extended their control over the entire state. Although initially latecomers to the Patriot cause, backcountry residents showed themselves to be its most faithful adherents. Without them the movement would have expired in Georgia.[5]

Georgia's new state government reflected the importance of the back-country to the Patriot cause. The 1777 constitution mandated a new system of representation, lowered suffrage requirements, and provided for compulsory voting. Each of these measures gave backcountry residents a greater say in forming the state government and influencing its policies. After the Revolutionary War, the reconstituted Assembly recognized the backcountry's contributions to the Patriot cause by making Augusta the co-capital along with Savannah, the traditional bastion of power.[6] In continuing the fight long after lowcountry Patriots had abandoned the cause, the backcountry Patriots understood themselves as the true heirs of the revolutionary cause and thus the true leaders of the new republic.

Greater representation from the new constitution combined with the reputation of the veterans from Wilkes and the other frontier counties empowered backcountry settlers. With their newfound power, backcountry politicians used the machinery of state government to enact their agenda: to remove the neighboring Indians, seize control of the disputed territory, and distribute it to veterans and new settlers. The state authorities enacted a series of land laws and treaties to legitimate their claims to the land and also provided material and military support. Contrary to the myth of westward expansion as a venture accomplished through the rugged individualism of early Americans, the settlement of the contested lands of the Oconee River was a state-sponsored enterprise. State policy during the initial stages of the Revolution had favored the plantation districts; with the rise of the backcountry in the Patriot cause, settlers were able to enact their frontier agenda.[7]

Attempts to shape government policy regarding land laws and Indians began soon after the organization of the Patriot government and continued throughout the war. In 1781, the reconstituted state government enacted legislation to entice settlers to the state in an effort to shore up the region's defenses by populating the land between the Ogeechee and Oconee rivers, the area beyond the colonial borders, with diehard Patriots. The state authorities also issued bounties for land to men who volunteered to serve as part of the state's contribution to the Continental Army. For many backcountry Patriots, the revolutionary cause was one of land.[8]

When the British conceded their defeat, the backcountry Patriots argued that the Indians had similarly been vanquished and forfeited their claim to their lands. State authorities negotiated three treaties with the Creeks, in 1783, 1785, and 1786, each under dubious circumstances. Georgia's officials negotiated with the Fat King, the Tallassee King, and a small ensemble of chiefs who conducted the treaties without consulting other headmen of the nation. In the first treaty, signed in Augusta, the commissioners from Georgia acquired a huge swath of the Creek hunting ground between the Ogeechee and Oconee rivers. Two years later at Galphinton, they negotiated for a tract of land lying southeast of the fork of the Oconee and Ocmulgee rivers. At Shoulderbone the next year, the two sides agreed to an accord confirming the earlier territorial cessions.[9]

Most Indians, however, refused to give up the land. Fat King failed to foresee the potential opposition to the agreements from the people he claimed to represent. He completely underestimated the depth of resentment and anger that the land cessions would produce among the rest of the Creeks. The chiefs who signed the agreements did not enjoy broad support among the Creek towns. They, therefore, spoke for very few. And the land they offered to cede to the state was not really theirs to give. Several towns considered the land to be communal hunting lands. Most Creeks, then, regarded the treaties as illegitimate. They were shocked when informed that the Americans expected them to cede their lands. For the Creeks, the victory of the Americans over the British presented a host of problems, the most important of which was the settlers' belief that the Indians had lost the war and therefore had lost their lands as well.

Because the Indians refused to relinquish their lands, settlers relied on state-sponsored armed might to seize the disputed territories. Backcountry leaders secured weapons and ammunition from the state as well as militia support. Along the border, the state constructed blockhouses, which provided refuge for settlers from Creek attacks. Gangs of settlers also used the blockhouses to organize their "counter" raids on the Indians. Territorial expansion followed a general pattern of encroachment, attack, and counterattack. Settlers encroached on land, sometimes within agreed-upon borders and other times well beyond. Angered by the settlers' actions, warriors responded to white encroachment by attacking the settlements. Conflict then erupted between settlers and Indians. The settlers then appealed to the state for aid, which, once received, allowed them to mount an attack that far exceeded the level of violence perpetrated in the initial raid. Elevating the level of violence created a vicious cycle of revenge and ensured that the state authorities would remain vigilant in protecting Georgia from what had become its greatest enemy: Indians.

Bands of men organized raids on Indian villages on the slightest pretexts. But in the cycle of attack and counterattack, the settlers' initial act of aggression often became obscured. The state provided support to the settlers even when they clearly acted as the aggressors. Reflecting the power of the backcountry, the state authorities devoted their attention to the western border. Planters on the southern border complained constantly that they did not receive adequate protection.[10] The expenditures told the story. The state provided Franklin, Greene, and Washington counties from six to sixteen times as much as one imperiled southern county.[11] When Fat King signed the treaty granting the Georgians the Oconee territory, he did so believing that he was resolving the major stumbling block to peace between the Creeks and their neighbors. Fat King believed that by "giving up this land we observed, that the white and red people might meet on the land and that they must take each other by the hand."[12] He erred in thinking that the Georgians would be sated by the cession. Once they settled the region, it was clear that they would continue pushing west. He misunderstood the settlers' motivations; he did not comprehend that peace was the last thing they wanted. Instead, they coveted confrontations precisely because conflict advanced their agenda.

Georgia's aggressive expansion policies may have satisfied the wishes of the backcountry settlers, but they provoked a hostile response from the Creek Indians. The Creeks rejected the American contention that the Indians had lost the war and were therefore required to cede land as restitution. As opposition to the land cessions coalesced, Alexander McGillivray emerged as a leader of an alliance between the Upper Creek and the Lower Creek towns. Claiming that he represented the Creek Nation, he immediately denounced the land cessions as illegitimate.[13] While he probably exaggerated his own importance, he did command considerable respect among the Creeks. McGillivray possessed valuable skills in negotiations with Americans. As the son of a Scottish trader and a Creek woman of a prominent Coweta family, McGillivray was adept in negotiating both white and Indian worlds.[14] Resistance to Georgian encroachments came in two forms: armed warfare and diplomacy. McGillivray insisted that the Creeks would not sign any agreement until the Oconee was cleared of settlers. Consequently, between 1785 and 1788 he sent waves of Creek warriors to terrorize the settlers in an attempt to forcibly expel them from the disputed territory.[15]

On the diplomatic front, McGillivray pursued a nuanced agenda. He initiated talks with the chiefs from the Choctaw, Chickasaw, and other

Indian nations to form an alliance to block further American encroach-ment on their lands. McGillivray had little faith in the Georgia state gov-ernment as long as it remained in the hands of the backcountry settlers. Georgia's authorities had belied their inability to treat the Indians with justice or respect on numerous occasions. They sided with the settlers whenever an incident occurred that resulted in the death of an Indian. On the rare occasion in which whites stood trial for the death of an Indian, inevitably the white jury refused to convict. McGillivray complained that "the upper Georgians never will suffer satisfaction to be given, for killing an Indian; and, indeed, every month affords instances of felons among them being rescued from justice, when condemned for the most atro-cious offences."[16] McGillivray carried on an extensive correspondence with the authorities in Georgia, but the two sides could rarely come to an agreement about the nature of the problem or the solutions. By the end of 1789, McGillivray had thoroughly lost faith with state authorities and looked to the federal government.[17]

The formation of a new federal government under the Constitution and the implementation of a new state constitution brought a new phase in Indian relations to the Georgia backcountry. Georgia took less than three months from the arrival of the first copy of the Constitution in early October 1787 to ratify the document. Fittingly, word of the document reached the authorities as they assembled in a special session of the leg-islature to address resurgent violence with the Indians. White Georgians were quite pleased with the move to grant the federal government more authority, though largely for self-interested reasons. Under the Articles of Confederation, the state had received little if any financial or mili-tary aid in its struggle against the Creek and Cherokee Indians. Conse-quently, many hoped that a new federal government would translate to greater support. Indeed, in late 1789, shortly after the implementation of the Constitution, the authorities in Georgia appealed to Washington for federal assistance to force the Creeks to cede the disputed Oconee lands. Frustrated by the pace of negotiations with McGillivray, the As-sembly complained that the "blood of our citizens has been spilled, our public resources greatly exhausted, and our frontiers still open to fresh ravages."[18] The federal government responded to Georgia's call for inter-vention, but not with the kind of intervention Georgia intended. Most settlers would later have cause to wish that the federal authorities had not interfered.

Under President George Washington, the federal government inaugurated a new era of Indian relations on the Georgia border. Washington wanted to preserve the integrity, security, and prosperity of the nascent nation. His long-term goals mandated peaceful relations with the Indians in the Southeast because their numbers were substantial enough to undermine any effort to place the region under American control. With the Spanish in Florida and with British and French forces not far off in the Caribbean, Washington understood that the Americans' hold on the Southeast was precarious. He also wanted access to the Mississippi River, which would be difficult to secure without peaceful relations with Spain and the Creek Indians. To maintain the security of America's southwestern border and achieve his diplomatic ends, Washington needed to lure the Indians from the Spanish orbit, but the persistent strife between Georgia and the Creeks hampered his efforts. The Creeks held the balance of power in the region, and neither the Americans nor any of the competing European powers could place the area under their "sovereignty" without the Indians' consent. Consequently, as hostilities on the frontier worsened, Washington initiated a meeting with McGillivray and sent U.S. troops to monitor the border between the Georgians and the Creeks.[19]

Washington's treatment of the Indian negotiators contrasted starkly with their treatment by Georgia's authorities. He invited McGillivray to New York in the spring of 1790. The arrival of McGillivray and his entourage in July inspired a frenzied period of celebration. As the dignitaries sailed up the Hudson River, soldiers honored them with a federal salute. Upon landing, a welcoming party, composed of the Society of St. Tammany, dressed in full regalia, along with General Malcolm and a detachment of the City Artillery and Infantry, escorted the Creek chiefs to the home of the secretary of war, General Henry Knox. After meeting with members of the delegation, Knox introduced them to the president. That evening the Creek chiefs met the governor of New York and dined at the City Tavern with several luminaries.[20]

With the power invested in him by the Constitution, Washington negotiated the Treaty of New York with McGillivray without the input of the Georgians. The provisions of the treaty were complicated. It placed the Creek Nation "under the protection" of the United States but guaranteed to the Creek Nation all their lands within the limits of the United States beyond the agreed-upon boundary with Georgia. It required the Creeks to cede the land called for in the two other agreements with Georgia, but it annulled the terms of the Treaty of Galphinton, which pertained to Tallassee lands, a fertile swath of territory coveted by both parties.

Georgia's Counties–1790

Complicating matters, whites had settled the Tallassee land soon after the Treaty of Galphinton in 1785, which meant that complying with the Treaty of New York would entail their dispossession. The treaty granted certain powers to the Indians. The treaty stipulated that American citizens who settled beyond the line—that is, on Indian land—"forfeit[ed] the protection" of the United States and would be punished by the Indian authorities. Settlers who wanted to enter the Creek land had to obtain a passport from the U.S. Indian agent.[21] Not only did Washington fail to consult with the Georgians, but the treaty also stipulated that the Creek Nation could make treaties only with the federal government and not with any individual state.[22]

Federal authorities possessed very different evaluations of Indians than Georgia's frontiersmen, who viewed the Indians with nothing but contempt. Georgia's authorities had repeatedly demonstrated this contempt in their relations with Indians. Perhaps nothing summed up this sentiment better than General Elijah Clark's refusal to shake hands with Fat King at the Treaty of Augusta.[23] In contrast, federal authorities regarded Indians with greater respect. Influenced by enlightened thought, federal authorities held that the Indians, with the proper direction and support, could progress from their primitive state. The Treaty of New York called for the United States to aid the Creeks' efforts to "civilize."[24] In a 1791 speech, Washington elaborated on this treaty, pledging federal aid for the Creeks for the development of industry, agriculture, and trade and calling for the creation of a regulated method of obtaining Indian land and trade. He suggested stern penalties for whites who violated Indians' rights, because they endangered the peace of the Union and infringed on the treaties.[25] When Washington visited Georgia in 1791, he emphasized this policy of goodwill with the Indians, telling the people in Midway, "Continue, my fellow citizens, to cultivate the peace and harmony which now subsists between you and your Indian neighbors—the happy consequence is immediate, the reflection, which arises on justice and benevolence, will be lastingly grateful."[26]

The response to the Treaty of New York and Washington's intervention was decidedly mixed and broke along sectional lines. The divisions mirrored an emerging rift over federal power within the state. The backcountry had been empowered under the 1777 state constitution during the Confederation period. A new state constitution in 1789 diluted backcountry power by creating a state senate, which was dominated by the older sections of the state, particularly the lowcountry. The Senate welcomed the federal government's assumption of relations with the Indians, pleased that the "subject of peace and war, is wisely placed under the direction of the Executive of the United States." The body also praised the fact that "the measures adopted by the general government clearly demonstrate [that] peace is preferred to war."[27] The lowcountry elite praised federal intervention. In Savannah and Midway, citizens thanked Washington for bringing peace to the frontier, which they apparently attributed to the Treaty of New York. They extolled Washington's leadership and pledged support for his policies, including his efforts to bring calm to the southwestern border. They looked upon federal intervention in favorable terms and credited Washington for the "present tranquility."[28] Many of these men were planters who desired peaceful coexistence with the Indians; they feared an Indian war would have a disruptive impact on their plantations and slave labor force.

Some elites in the long-settled regions of the state were willing to view the Indians as partners in peace and important allies, not as fiendish savages beneath white contempt. They believed that, in time and with the help of whites, Indians could possibly become worthy of citizenship.

These elites maintained long-standing relations with Creek and Cherokee Indians. In some cases, whites, especially traders, even intermarried with Indians.[29] These whites celebrated peace with the Indians for social as well as economic and safety concerns.

On the frontier, however, settlers condemned Washington's intervention. These settlers in the backcountry, especially in Wilkes, Franklin, Greene, and Washington counties, were less inclined than their wealthier counterparts on the coast and along the Savannah River to listen to Washington's words of peace.[30] Backcountry settlers believed that federal officials had sacrificed white Georgians' interests by denying the legitimacy of treaties signed prior to the ratification of the Constitution and by recognizing the Creeks' claim to the disputed lands. Washington may have furthered the nation's long-term objectives, but he had done so at white Georgians' expense.[31] For months, backcountry settlers called for the state to repudiate the treaty.[32]

Settlers charged that the federal government subverted the achievements of the Revolution and betrayed true Patriots. Instead of securing the state's "rightful territory," one Georgian declared, the federal authorities "have ceded it to the enemy." He noted that white Georgians had "bravely fought and freely bled" for "the glorious cause of freedom." Now, when it came time to distribute the spoils of war, "instead of supporting the honor of those intrepid heroes," the federal authorities "promoted over their heads, an avowed enemy to the cause." White Georgians, consequently, fought "without reward" and now subsisted on a "course and scanty fare."[33] Many of them had fought in the War of Independence, but, in the wake of federal authorities' intervention in the state's affairs with the Creeks, they questioned what had happened to their revolution.

Race infused much of the commentary. The lowcountry elite possessed long-standing personal relationships with Creek and Cherokee Indians, which made their views on Indians similar to those of the Washington administration. Settlers on the frontier, in contrast, were particularly shocked that federal officials debased themselves by negotiating with "savages." The actions of the federal government caused some white Georgians to doubt their commitment to a Union that did not protect the interests of white men. They accused the federal government of compromising their rights and overstepping its constitutional bounds, all in an attempt to appease Indians at the expense of white men.

The Treaty of New York managed to establish relatively peaceful relations on the frontier. Occasional murders and horse thefts continued to plague both sides of the border, but, for the most part, peace reigned. Even Governor Telfair, no friend of the Indians, had to admit more than a year after the agreement that "the Creeks at large are well disposed towards the people of the State."[34] But the settlers did not want peace. They thrived on conflict, which justified their attacks on surrounding Indian villages. In late 1792, the level of violence on the frontier spiked. At least part of the blame for the rising tensions rested with the Indians, but the lion's share of the responsibility fell on the settlers since they broke the peace. They repeatedly engaged in reprisals that were far more severe in scope than the initial incident and were largely meted out in arbitrary yet collective ways. They used the smallest pretense to wipe out entire villages and kill any and all Indians they encountered. In early 1793, for example, a group of Indians stole sixteen horses from a white settlement on the frontier, prompting local militiamen to pursue the raiders. The militiamen managed to regain five of the stolen horses. In the process they also killed an Indian and burned three towns. Raids such as this prompted the federal officers monitoring the border between Georgia and the neighboring Indians to intervene in an effort to halt the escalating violence. The federal officers recognized the aggressions of the militia and settlers and attempted to arrest the perpetrators and to block raids on the Indians, and this federal intervention resulted in settler acrimony. The federal officers' intrusions, Elijah Clark complained, thwarted the will of the settlers and "disincorages the frontiers very much."[35]

While the federal officers saw the state militiamen who patrolled the frontier as the chief aggressors, settlers viewed them as avengers and the federal officers as the Indians' collaborators. "The frontier situation of Georgia," Judge William Stith explained at the Franklin County Superior Court's January 1793 term, "induced her as early as possible to accede to the Federal Constitution, the readiness with which we made that adoption, and our infantile state, gave us (as we thought) a well-grounded hope that the potent arm" of the federal government "would in all times of danger be cheerfully incited in defending us against the savage enemy." But "since the adoption of the Federal Government," we "have experienced a continued series of the most inhuman butcheries and robberies committed on our frontiers," yet "scarce a singe ray of Federal protections." Stith asserted that federal betrayals accounted for the behavior of those settlers who committed violence against the Indians. They were "justified . . . by that great and first principle of nature, *self defence*."[36]

Although the federal government failed to provide the kind of support the settlers expected, the state government proved more sympathetic to the settlers' cause. Throughout the winter and spring of 1792 and 1793, Clark and other militia officers on the frontier issued a series of appeals to Governor Telfair, imploring him to provide guns and ammunition to the settlers so that they could continue their struggle against the Indians. If he failed to oblige their demands, they warned, it would surely result in the demise of most frontier settlements.[37] The grisly murder of the Thrasher family in Greene County by a group of Creek warriors in April 1793 bolstered the militia officers' claims.[38] Despite the strong opposition of the federal government, Governor Telfair did not disappoint them. In the wake of the attack, he ordered the erection of fourteen blockhouses on the state's three-hundred-mile border with the Indians. Telfair also ordered Generals John Twiggs and Elijah Clark to mobilize their respective militia divisions to defend against an Indian attack. The generals sympathized with the settlers' plight and promised to "give them every assistance" in their power to aid them in their struggle against the Indians. By May, General Clark reportedly commanded a twenty-five-hundred-man force, ready to launch an expedition into the Creek territory. In the midst of the preparation for war, the federal government's Indian agent, James Seagrove, desperately worked to avoid an escalation of the conflict. He informed the governor that the "alarming accounts from the frontier are much exaggerated, if not totally without foundation."[39] Moreover, he noted, most of the Creek Nation did not want war; instead, he asserted that blame for the current spate of violence on the frontier rested with the "restless, vicious disposition of some white people" in Georgia.[40] Despite the fact that Telfair had no authority to initiate an offensive war against the Creeks and that Seagrove and other federal officials contradicted the reports that the Creek Nation was preparing for all-out war against the Americans, he ordered the state militia to commence their assaults. General Twiggs and the nine hundred men under his command crossed the Oconee River into the contested area in early June and moved forty miles toward the Ocmulgee River, where they prepared to build a fort.[41] In the end, however, no fighting actually occurred. Before the militia could engage its foe, General Twiggs abandoned the campaign.

The official story blamed the failure of the expedition on a number of incidental factors—it was the wrong season, the horses were tired, the troops lacked supplies, the generals feared that they might mistakenly attack friendly Indians.[42] But in the weeks that followed contradictory, and more accusatory, reports emerged. "A Volunteer" wrote in to the paper to criticize the sanitized account and to cast blame. He charged that the expedition failed due to "mutiny," especially among the troops from the older regions of the state. General Twiggs first discovered discontentment in the ranks shortly after crossing the Oconee. Twiggs called the commanding officers together to determine which units would continue. Only General Clark and three officers under him voted to continue. Twiggs decided to abandon the operation. But before all of the troops left, General Clark and his officers circulated the camp trying to muster support for a nonsanctioned assault on the Creeks. The only enthusiasm for the expedition came from two frontier counties. The cavalry from Greene County and about two hundred militiamen from Wilkes County agreed to join Clark. Among troops from other regions, Clark's appeals fell on deaf ears. "A Volunteer" ridiculed:

> It is by no means to be wondered at, that the failure of the late intended expedition should be imputed to a want of provisions; especially by those who deserted before they left the settlements, or could form any tolerable conjecture of what might happen, except the probability of being obliged to face Indians in battle [*horrid idea*]; and *more* especially by those (of which the number was not small) who made the want of provisions a pretence for mutinying, and . . . threw away *very considerable quantities* of excellent beef, and other articles of provision . . . in consequence of their fears.

"A Volunteer" charged that the troops from the older regions of the state lacked the courage to face Indians in battle. A resident of Augusta defended his county's militiamen by suggesting that frontiersmen were "backward" and bloodthirsty. Speaking of Augusta, he commended "the people in this quarter of the country [who] never have made general professions, even of willingness to enter upon Indian warfare, much less to boast their ability and inclination to extirpate the Creeks from the state of Georgia."[43]

The failed assault on the Indians revealed deep racial and political fissures that had festered just beneath the surface since the arrival of the settlers in the 1770s. For people on the frontier, depredations were a feature of routine life. But for those residents who lived in the older, settled regions of the state, Indians did not produce the same degree of hatred that they did for settlers. Not only did residents from the older sections of the state refuse to sanction violence against the Creeks, but they criticized settlers' boasts as distasteful and even savage. The elites also doubted whether the settlers were worthy of the protection that the state afforded them. They believed that white settlement of the interior posed a potential financial disaster for the state. They doubted that frontiersmen who moved to the disputed borderlands would pay either their taxes or their share of the state's debt, thus leaving the residents of the older sections of the state to bear an unfair economic burden. Residents of the older sections expressed reservations about the state's capacity to exercise any semblance of authority over the region. But equally important, they feared that rampant population growth in the interior of the state would dilute the power of the planter elite.[44]

Despite the outcome, residents of the frontier applauded Telfair's decision to attack the Creeks. Petitions from militiamen in Greene, Elbert, and Wilkes counties praised the governor for initiating the assault. To secure the land for white Georgians, settlers urged offensive action against the savage Indians. "Oconee-Ensis," a correspondent to the *Augusta Chronicle*, asserted that the best way to protect the state was through expansion. "To keep the war out of our own country," he argued, "we carry it into the heart of the enemy's." He suggested that "it is no longer a time to talk of treaties, or to halt between the duty of preserving ourselves and an overweening, if not a criminal, attachment to peace."[45] "Oconee Planter," another correspondent to the *Augusta Chronicle*, agreed, arguing that "Georgia never was better fit for war than what she is at this time."[46] Because they could not imagine a place for "savages" within the state, the settlers envisioned no solution for the problem of Indians on the border other than extermination.

The settlers, however, also harbored economic motives for their attacks on Indian settlements. Many settlers believed the Creek land to be "among the richest in America, and at every convenient distance most happily pierced with rivers." Blessed with a water system to transport crops to market, the region promised to enrich its settlers, even those with the most meager means. Settlers thought they could easily recruit volunteers to fight in a war against the Creeks by promising bounties in return for their service. "Oconee Planter" informed his readers that "my biggest boy plagues me for a plantation . . . and says he will go out [and] volunteer if I will give him a fat horse and a gun—he is thirteen—do you think he will do?"[47] The land between the Oconee and Ocmulgee rivers served as the ultimate inducement to young men who desired an opportunity to gain their independence.

After General Twiggs's failed campaign, Telfair, despite the opposition of the federal government, surreptitiously authorized a series of raids by Clark and others across the Oconee in September and October 1793 in which armed Georgians committed a variety of atrocities. In one of the more gruesome examples of frontier violence, a group of more than eighty men commanded by Colonel William Melton crossed the Oconee in mid-September ostensibly in pursuit of seven Indians who had allegedly stolen horses from settlements on the border. They pursued the Indians for several days until they encountered a small Creek town called the Little Oakfulkees, under the direction of White Lieutenant, a "friendly" chief who cultivated peaceful relations with James Seagrove and other federal officials. The Georgians attacked the town, killing and scalping six men and taking eight female prisoners, then plundering and burning the town before returning to Georgia on September 26 and bragging about their achievements.[48] Upon learning about the raid, Seagrove criticized Telfair for sanctioning the assault, which he construed as a direct attempt to subvert relations with the Creeks, particularly his frantic efforts to work out a peace agreement with them. "I have every reason to believe," he wrote the governor, "it was done chiefly with a view to destroy all hope of my being able to effect a peace." Seagrove was correct. As one of the militiamen involved in the raid acknowledged, his primary goal was "destroy all Indians he came across, whether friend or foe; and that he was opposed to peace."[49] The settlers undertook the raids in hopes of undermining peace efforts. Indeed, the settlers took steps to neutralize all those involved in the talks, including Seagrove. In addition to Melton's men, two other groups of militiamen from the frontier counties crossed the Oconee. The first sought the party of Creek chiefs believed to be en route to meet with Seagrove, whom they intended to kill. The second targeted Seagrove himself, whom many settlers detested for his efforts on behalf of the Indians. In mid-October, militiamen on the frontier initiated a second series of raids, though this time they went even further. Several men from the settlements stole their neighbors' horses, brought them over the Oconee, and claimed that the Indians had stolen them so that they could justify another attack. With that rationale, two hundred militiamen from Washington and Greene counties organized at Carr's Bluff to launch a raid against the Chehaw towns. When General Jared

Irwin heard about the militias' intentions, he ordered them to desist, but they refused. After authorizing the surreptitious raids, Telfair had lost control of the men.[50]

Governor Telfair's inauguration of war on the border and his inability to control the situation wounded him politically. From the perspective of Georgians in the more settled areas, the war against the Indians had gone too far. Killing Indians was one thing, but targeting an agent of the U.S. government was altogether different. In the midst of the growing violence on the border, the General Assembly met and elected a new governor. The vote highlighted a divide among the legislators. In the state house, Telfair received the most votes (21), while General Irwin came in second (17) and George Mathews came in third (15). The ultimate arbiter, the state senate, disproportionately composed of members from the older areas of the state, selected Mathews.[51] In choosing Mathews, the Senate chose a more prudent and cautious approach to Indian affairs and repudiated the violence sanctioned by Telfair. Many of the state's elite, especially those in the older areas, increasingly felt misgivings over Telfair's war against the Indians.[52] Mathews, a Revolutionary War hero, had a proven track record of fighting Indians, but he advocated a less aggressive stand toward the neighboring tribes. Rather than foment violence, he sought a more conciliatory relationship. In light of the fall campaign against the Creeks, Mathews's selection represented a reassessment of the state's Indian policy by the political elite and a rebuff to the settlers, whose aspirations for more land would be put on hold.

Governor Mathews immediately pursued a more moderate policy toward the Indians than his predecessor. He met with Tuskatchie Micco, a Cusseta chief, weeks after taking over the executive office in an effort to hammer out a peace with the Creeks. As a clear indication of his intentions, Mathews traveled to the frontier in early 1794 to meet with the headmen. He also cultivated better relations with James Seagrove, assuring the Indian agent that he would put forth his "best endeavors to give the Federal Government a fair Opportunity of trying their favorite Object of peace with the Creek nation."[53] Mathews's program, then, signaled a break from the past emphasis on confrontation with the Indians and an embrace of the president's peace initiative. It was a rebuke not only of Telfair's handling of the war with the Creeks but of the state's clumsy and unforgiving approach toward relations with the surrounding Indians since the Revolutionary War. In that time, the state had come to adopt policies toward the western lands and Indians that benefited the settlers.

At first, with the threat of Indian attacks ever present, white Georgians from the settled sections of the state had condoned the violent methods employed by the frontier militia. They had overlooked the appalling treatment of Indians or pretended that the victims deserved their fate. By the mid-1790s, this approach proved too costly to maintain. And the frontiersmen, those intrepid men who had helped to bring to life the nascent nation, had become liabilities. Their incessant warring threatened to forestall the state's development and seemed anachronistic in peacetime.

Empowered and then seemingly disempowered, backcountry settlers became disgruntled as state and federal authorities failed to support their efforts to obtain their inheritance from the Revolution. The Trans-Oconee Republic emerged within contests over the true nature of the American Revolution and the French Revolution that it helped spawn. The Trans-Oconee Republic represented a particular vision of radical republicanism, one with patriarchal, militaristic, and possibly multiracial overtones. The fledgling republic generated significant sympathy in the backcountry. State and federal efforts, however, ultimately succeeded in disbanding the Trans-Oconee Republic.

Disputes over the fruits of the American Revolution became caught up in contrasting views on the French Revolution. White Georgians initially welcomed the French Revolution as a validation of their own revolution. In time, however, as the French Revolution grew more radical, white Georgians splintered. Some Georgians, generally elite merchants and planters in the lowcountry, were alarmed by the Jacobins' rise and embrace of egalitarianism and revolutionary violence. Support for the French centered in the Georgia backcountry, where settlers embraced the radical turn of the French Revolution. They also viewed the French as critical allies in the larger struggle against the imperial powers of Britain and Spain, which they blamed for supporting and encouraging the Indians to mount attacks along the frontier. Backcountry settlers resented the continued power of the coastal elite, whom they viewed as antirepublican.

For backcountry settlers, the antirepublicanism of the lowcountry was made clear in the summer of 1793 when a privateer licensed by the French ran aground off of the coast near Savannah. The survivors were picked up by the local authorities and brought before a federal judge, who placed three men in custody and freed a fourth individual. The liberated man was immediately taken by a mob, which proceeded to tar and feather him and then drag him through the streets of Savannah before finally setting him loose.[54] When news of the episode spread, it produced considerable outrage among backcountry settlers, who chafed at the actions of the "anti-patriots of Savannah."[55] According to one backcountry observer, the assault was evidence that Savannah was "governed buy a monocratic junto" whose antirepublican attitudes he compared to "black drivers in their fields" whose sole desire was to impress their owner, in this case President Washington. If, as many northerners believed, Savannah was the "most civilized part of Georgia," he continued, then "civilization means neither more nor less than forming peoples [sic] minds for slavery."[56] This backcountry critic identified lowcountry elites as slaves and Washington as their master. Backcountry republicanism, then, was simultaneously an assertion of independence from political enslavement to the coastal and federal elite and possibly a disavowal of the institution of slavery. The episode was emblematic of the divide between the lowcountry elite and the residents of the backcountry over control of political power within the state, the direction of the country, and the meaning of the Revolution. In the years since the ratification of the federal constitution and the new state constitution, backcountry settlers had seen their power within the state diminish as the power of the federal government's proxies, the coastal elite, grew. Some backcountry settlers believed that this incident confirmed white lowcountry residents' abandonment of the revolutionary principles that had guided the nation in its earliest years and marked an ominous turn toward aristocratic rule.[57]

The arrival of French diplomat Edmond Genêt exacerbated the rift among white Georgians over the French Revolution and provided backcountry residents an opportunity to act on their grievances and fulfill their version of the Revolution. With their rise to power in 1792, the Jacobins began spreading the French Revolution and challenging their enemies wherever they could. As part of this agenda, Genêt arrived in the United States in early 1793 to set in motion a plan to attack Spanish Florida. French agents fanned out across the southern United States to enlist participants in the winter of 1793–1794. When the agents arrived in Georgia's backcountry, they found a receptive audience. Many settlers welcomed the opportunity presented by the French. Elijah Clark heeded the call. Clark resigned his commission in the state militia in February 1794, citing his health and age as an excuse. He apparently made an amazing recovery, because two days later he agreed to join the French army with the rank of brigadier general and a salary of $10,000.[58] The terms that the French required were quite simple: in return for their services,

Clark and his followers would be allowed to form their own government after the war to take East Florida, provided it be a "strictly democratically Republican Governm't" with a "constitution" based on the "Rights of Man."[59] Over the next few months, Clark traveled throughout the back-country of Georgia and the Carolinas recruiting men for an expedition to seize Spanish Florida.[60] For Clark and his would-be co-conspirators, the attack on the Spanish offered an opportunity not only to defeat a hated foe but also to build their ideal society. Corrupted by the machinations of the state's merchant and planter elite and the federal authorities, the republican experiment in Georgia had failed to live up to their expectations. Disillusioned with the direction of the American Revolution and increasingly alienated from the political process in Georgia, backcountry settlers believed Florida promised a new beginning.

The attack on Florida never came to fruition. Alarmed by reports of men mobilizing on the frontier, Governor Mathews issued a proclamation prohibiting Georgians from joining the French-inspired adventure.[61] Despite the warning, several hundred settlers flocked to Clark's camp in Greene County, and from there they began their trek to the Georgia-Florida border in early April. By the time the men arrived at the St. Mary's River, across from their intended destination, French support had already unraveled. Deserted by their erstwhile allies, Clark and his followers had few options available to them. Dejected, they left their camp on the Florida border and returned to the backcountry, traveling along the western bank of the Oconee River.[62]

Despite the failed expedition to Florida, the men refused to return to Georgia. Rather, they chose to remain on the Creek side of the boundary once they arrived parallel to Greene County. There they began construction on the first of what would be a string of forts, housing settlers and their families. These structures and their occupants formed the nucleus of what would become the Trans-Oconee Republic. With two large blockhouses, Fort Defiance and Fort Advance, anchoring its defenses, the nascent republic quickly assumed the character of a permanent settlement.[63]

The Trans-Oconee Republic drew many migrants across the border. No precise counts of citizens of the republic survive. But the alarm of state and local authorities in Georgia suggests that the Trans-Oconee Republic achieved some success in attracting settlers. Many of these men relished the opportunity to pursue a more aggressive strategy against the Indians, unhindered by the restrictions imposed by the political elite at the state and federal level. Rather than placate the Indians, they hoped to remove them completely. They hoped to accomplish against the Creeks what Clark and his men had managed to do to the Cherokees during and after the war—kill them or expel them from the area. In the Trans-Oconee Republic, they could achieve their vision of the American Revolution.

The Trans-Oconee Republic offered the promise of land to young men with little prospects on the Georgia frontier. The republic offered 640 acres of land to those who joined.[64] Settlers who remained more than a year received the promise of even more land. Many migrants were young men whose fathers had been Revolutionary veterans. For example, Micah Williamson staked his claim as a citizen of the Trans-Oconee. His father had fought alongside Clark in the Revolution. Williamson, like other settlers, was a junior officer in the Georgia militia. Williamson settled in the Trans-Oconee Republic as a part of a larger group of settlers connected through marriage or various other "kin-like" connections. Other Trans-Oconee rebels were linked through these sorts of arrangements.[65]

The Trans-Oconee Republic also drew soldiers from the federal forts on the Georgia side of the border. Clark ordered the erection of forts directly across the river from the federal forts, locations clearly designed to serve as beacons for soldiers frustrated by the authorities' apparent lack of concern about Indian violence on the frontier. Officially, Clark denied encouraging federal troops to desert their posts. In practice, the Trans-Oconee Republic welcomed federal soldiers.[66]

Blacks may also have numbered among the new residents of the Trans-Oconee Republic. Free blacks had a long history on Georgia's frontier. They were some of the first settlers in the region. Even before the land was officially ceded in 1773, at least two free blacks were among the men who acquired warrants for land in what would become Wilkes County.[67] After the war, the frontier continued to attract free blacks. In 1790, Wilkes County housed the largest population of free people of African descent in Georgia, with 180 listed there (out of a total of 398 in the state), a considerably higher tally than Chatham County's 112.[68] Chatham, with Savannah as its capital, served as the center of the free black population for most of the antebellum era. In the late eighteenth and early nineteenth century, however, free blacks flocked to the frontier. But it does not appear that they stayed in one place. Instead, they seem to have moved with the center of the action. In the 1780s, Wilkes County was a hotbed of settlement and a flashpoint between the Indians and frontiersmen. By the 1790s the flashpoint had moved southward to Washington County, which had been created in 1784. Populated with large numbers of new settlers and revolutionary veterans, Washington County, along with Greene County, became the new frontier. The free black population followed the frontier. The 1800 census recorded a substantial decrease in the size of Wilkes County's free black population, which contracted to sixty-three. By contrast, Washington County's population grew from two in 1790 to 451 (of a total 1,919 for the state) in 1800.[69] Doubtless some of the decrease in Wilkes County was due its division and incorporation into new counties, but the shift to Washington was undeniable. The frontier offered free blacks the opportunity to establish themselves away from the plantation regions. Life on the frontier focused less on color than on the contributions of the individual to the protection of the community, at least when it came to blacks. The experience of the Going family, discussed in the previous chapter, suggests that some blacks secured at least some measure of success and stature in the backcountry.

While we are uncertain of the Trans-Oconee rebels' relations with blacks, we do know that Elijah Clark had good relations with a least one black frontiersman, Austin Dabney, a Revolutionary War hero. Dabney reportedly saved Clark's life at the Battle of Kettle Creek when his horse was shot out from beneath him.[70] Like Clark, Dabney was part of the first wave of settlers to arrive on the frontier after the cession of 1773, served in the state militia during the Revolution, and fought in several of the backcountry battles. After the war, when questions of Dabney's status arose, Clark helped establish Dabney's freedom and secured him an annual pension from the state.[71] It is unclear if Dabney ever crossed the river to join the citizens of the Trans-Oconee Republic, but the evidence suggests that he did not. During the Revolutionary War, Dabney suffered an injury that left him partially disabled. In any case, Dabney's relationships with whites point to the ease with which some backcountry residents cast aside racial differences to fight a common foe trying to kill them both.[72]

The republic's constitution did not restrict citizenship by race and made no distinctions by race whatsoever. Because the Trans-Oconee Republic left no census of its citizens, it is impossible to determine with certainty whether or not blacks numbered among the rebels. It is possible, however, that blacks composed at least a small segment of the fighting population. Census numbers suggest that blacks followed Indian violence. The exigencies of frontier living, especially the necessity for armed defense, allowed blacks like Dabney and the Goings to achieve a measure of status and respect. White Trans-Oconee rebels may have carried this tolerance across the river. The Trans-Oconee Republic needed fighters, and blacks had proven themselves in the backcountry to be just as good Indian killers as whites. Clark, who clearly played an influential role in shaping the Trans-Oconee Republic, owed his life to Dabney.

Few of the documents produced by the Trans-Oconee Republic lasted much longer than the experimental nation itself, but from the shards of evidence that did survive it is clear that the enterprise meant more than just an illicit land grab. Its creation was deeply ideological as well. The founding fathers of the Trans-Oconee Republic brought forth in the backcountry an alternative vision of republicanism. The founders passed a constitution that guaranteed citizens basic rights, including a republican form of government under the authority of a Committee of Safety, just like in the earliest days of the Revolution. Trans-Oconee republicanism emerged from the exigencies of frontier living. The constitution of the Trans-Oconee Republic granted an "equil right" to all men who brought in four men who could fight. Clearly, then, the ability to fight, an important necessity for life on the frontier, was pivotal to Trans-Oconee citizenship.[73] This requirement for citizenship represented a conscious rebuke of Georgia's leadership, a group comprising newcomers to the state and men who had avoided combat during the Revolution and the subsequent Indian wars. Backcountry settlers forged their sense of citizenship in the Revolution. Settlers' desire to secure their revolutionary inheritance—the land—through Indian war if necessary further reinforced their link between citizenship and militarism. The founders of the Trans-Oconee Republic brought a patriarchal orientation with them across the Georgia border. The social structure of the backcountry was clan-based and patriarchal. Contrary to the myth of individual settlers battling alone on the frontier, these backcountry settlers relied on social networks for support. Trans-Oconee republicanism, then, melded radical republicanism, patriarchy, and militarism.

The debate over the Trans-Oconee Republic among white Georgians split largely along predictable lines. Those in the older, more settled areas of the state expressed outrage over the scheme. Residents of the frontier sympathized with the grievances of the Trans-Oconee settlers, but some disapproved of their course. Debate over the Trans-Oconee Republic centered on the meaning of republicanism.

Residents of the older regions of the state viewed Trans-Oconee rebels as illegitimate insurrectionaries who upset the fragile peace in Georgia. In August 1794, the grand jury of Burke County labeled the creation of the Trans-Oconee Republic "the greatest grievance that the state of Georgia ever experienced" and "an open violation of law and government."[74] That same month, the grand jury of Chatham County expressed similar sentiments, castigating Clark and his followers for putting the state in jeopardy. While the Trans-Oconee rebels viewed the American government as subversive of their interests, the Chatham grand jury viewed the American government as "most conducive to the general happiness." Patriots in the American Revolution had thrown off tyrannical government. The grand jury of Chatham, however, did not see the Trans-Oconee rebels as analogous. According to these citizens of Chatham, the Trans-Oconee rebels were "licentious and ill disposed citizens" who acted "in contempt of law and good government, and in direct violation of the rights of property."[75] Residents of the older regions of the state suggested that the Trans-Oconee settlers subverted the American Revolution. Judge George Walton, an acclaimed jurist and a former of governor of the state, expressed this perspective in a well-received address to the residents of Richmond County. Walton highlighted his friendship with Clark, a man whose "virtues" he "esteemed." Clark, he noted, "stands high in the lists of revolutionary patriots and soldiers" whose efforts during the "long and arduous war . . . produced our liberty and independence." And yet Walton could not help but express his disappointment that Clark had turned his back on the Revolution and its principles. The traditional elite in Georgia's older areas insisted that the Trans-Oconee rebels could not simply throw off their American citizenship without repercussion. Like the grand jury of Chatham that referred to the Trans-Oconee settlers as "citizens," Judge Walton dismissed as ludicrous the notion advanced by Clark and his supporters that the men who formed the Trans-Oconee Republic "simply expatriated" themselves by crossing the river and disavowing their status as Americans. They were "either citizens or insurgents." If the state and federal government allowed Clark's adventure to stand, Walton cautioned, "civil war" would threaten to tear Georgia apart.[76]

Beyond ideological concerns lay the issue of land. Supporters of the Trans-Oconee Republic claimed that wealthy planters opposed the Trans-Oconee Republic because they hoped to reserve the land beyond the Oconee for themselves. Judge Walton argued that the lands beyond the Oconee River belonged to the state, regardless of the Treaty of New York or any other agreement. The people of Georgia, he argued, owned the disputed land collectively. He viewed the establishment of the Trans-Oconee Republic as an attempt by backcountry settlers to unilaterally lay claim to land that should be the heritage of all Georgians. In this criticism, Walton exposed his desire for the more settled regions to receive a stake in the Trans-Oconee lands.[77]

Frontiersmen, however, offered their support to the Trans-Oconee Republic. Backcountry supporters filled the pages of the *Augusta Chronicle* with denunciations of the state and federal authorities as well as attacks on the wealthy "patricians." "Oconee" railed against the "federal government and its patrician coadjusters" in Georgia who worked together to deprive the settlers access to the Oconee lands.[78] The criticisms extended to President Washington: "Had he exhibited the same coercive spirit in protecting the state of Georgia against the Indians, as . . . his present attempt to protect them against these new settlers, the contest would never have existed."[79] They contended that Washington's actions displayed "traits of monarchy." Proof of Washington's antirepublican stance, they argued, was evident in his decision to support the claims of the Indians over the rights of whites. In December 1794, the president made clear these sentiments when he spoke before Congress, suggesting that the federal troops patrolling Georgia's border were there to protect the Indians against the encroachment of the settlers.[80] These criticisms clearly linked republican ideology, which on its face was race neutral, with whiteness. One commenter accused President Washington of abandoning the veterans "who raised him to his present pinnacle of glory" and of failing to respect the desires of "the patriotic bands of South Carolina and Georgia, who wished to be French Republicans." Consequently, that individual had come to question the notion that the nascent United States was truly a land of liberty and freedom.[81]

Trans-Oconee republicanism contained class and race dimensions. One supporter of the Trans-Oconee Republic declared, "I am sure there is not a sound republican in the state, but must feel it his indispensible duty to be on general Clarke's side; for if he is on the other, he fights to wrest the vacant territory from the state, for the benefit of the federal Nabobs, and to enslave himself."[82] He favored the settlement of "vacant" (meaning Indian) territory for the benefit of the common man. Backcountry settlers leveled a race- and class-based critique of federal policies. Their understanding of republicanism was rooted in a racialized understanding of rights that also corresponded to their notion that the nonelite should benefit from the formation of the new nation. Trans-Oconee republicanism was malleable enough to include black men but not malleable enough to include Indians.

Local officials in the backcountry seemed unwilling or unable to take a stand against the Trans-Oconee Republic. When Governor Mathews is-sued a warrant for Clark's arrest, Clark was so sure of his support in the backcountry that he turned himself in to Wilkes County officials. The justices of the peace apparently accepted Clark's argument that he was be-yond the jurisdiction of the United States and had not committed a crime in Wilkes County, because they quickly discharged him. Vindicated by the justices' decision to dismiss the charge against him, Clark returned to the Trans-Oconee Republic, convinced that there was not enough support in the state to bring an end to his experiment in backcountry democracy. Should the authorities in Augusta make the mistake of sending troops to disperse the garrisons of the Trans-Oconee Republic, he advised his com-manders to "refuse with a firmness ever becoming the Brave," but should the authorities persist, to "cheerfully submit to be tried by a jurry of your Fellow Citizens." They had little to fear from sympathetic neighbors who openly supported their cause. If they encountered federal authorities, he prescribed a very different response, however. He told them to deny the legitimacy of their authority outside of the United States.[83]

Clark's appearance before the justices of the peace in Wilkes was an important test, but its outcome was never in doubt. He was related to several of the county officials and had known the others for years. More-over, whites who committed offenses of any sort against Indians rarely suffered repercussions. His appearance represented an overt symbol of defiance to the state and federal authorities and convinced other residents of the frontier who sympathized with his cause but were sitting on the fence, waiting to see how the authorities would respond, that it was safe to join the republic. And it appears to have worked. Reports indicate that the number of recruits grew in the wake of Clark's "deposition."[84]

Clark also returned comforted because he felt that neither the militia nor the U.S. troops stationed in the state would intervene or in any way im-pede his efforts to set up the Trans-Oconee Republic. In one instance some troops not only refused to undertake a mission against the Trans-Oconee Republic but also promised to punish those who did. Members of the mi-litia stationed at Fort Republic informed participating troops that "if they were to fight General Clark's men, they should never reenter the fort alive." In fact, there was at least one episode in which men stationed on the Amer-ican side apparently caused a commotion that may have resulted in the death of the commander of the federal fort. Soldiers were not unanimous in their support for Clark's cause, but most seem to have been receptive.[85]

Residents of the backcountry, however, did not unanimously embrace the Trans-Oconee Republic. The divisions on the frontier were apparent as early as March 1794, when Thomas Houghton, Robert Alpin, G. W. Foster, and John Armor wrote to the governor to inform him of the mobilization of men taking place in Greene County on the eve of the aborted raid on Florida. Houghton and the others were concerned that Clark's efforts would produce a backlash among the Indians, and they feared that they would suffer the consequences. Another motivating factor was the way in which Clark's men went about recruiting volunteers. Led by Adam Carson and others, a band of forty to fifty men had ridden into Greensborough, where they intimidated local men, brandishing weapons and threatening them with violence. They broke into one house and took some men prisoner for a short time. At the end, they asked the men to join their ranks.[86]

Houghton and the others were not alone. Consider the example of the Adams clan from Hancock County. The Adams men clearly shared a visceral hatred for the Indians and were angered by the intervention of the federal authorities on their behalf. The patriarch of the family was a Revolutionary War soldier and continued to play an influential role on the frontier. He thought that Seagrove was a traitor and blamed him for tension between the frontiersmen and the federal government. He called for the Indian agent to be punished. Adams's sons also played a crucial role on the frontier. They targeted friendly Indians in an effort to disrupt negotiations between Creek chiefs and federal and state officials. The first episode occurred in December 1793, when Seagrove brought White Bird Tail King to Augusta to begin discussions with Governor Mathews. John Adams and three other men attacked a party from the Creek delegation, killing two of them. The Indians were camped out across from Fort Fidius, on the western side of the Oconee, waiting for the rest of the delegation to return.[87] A second instance took place in May 1794 under similar circumstances. One of the Adams men led a group of 150 militiamen on a raid against a group of Creeks who were camped out at the same location while their chiefs were in Augusta brokering a peace. The militiamen stole horses and other property from the Creeks, who sought refuge in Fort Fidius. The group included Tim Barnard, an American trader who lived among the Creeks and was well known to Seagrove.[88] Clearly, then, the Adamses were known as individuals opposed to any peace plan with the Indians—so much so in fact that Clark hoped to solicit their support for his enterprise. Clark wrote to Adams in an effort to recruit him, but apparently Adams opted not to join the republic.[89]

That Adams agreed with Clark's anti-Indian sentiments was clear. But the Adams clan and others like them in Hancock refused to abandon the American experiment. Rather than blame President Washington, they blamed intermediaries. They feared that federal officials misrepresented them to Washington, causing him to "withhold that care the federal Government otherwise would hastily afford us."[90] They thought that federal officials had misled Washington about the true situation on the frontier and if he knew the truth he would surely side with them. Consequently, they organized themselves into a board to represent the county's interests. Rather than go through the state or federal authorities, they petitioned Washington directly:

Convinced . . . by a long and faithful trial, that our language of liberty is that of yours and equally conscious our United Sufferage has confirmed you the gratest ruler, Among the great, we are happy as men of Arms and citizens in unity to State our greviances to you in language becoming to freemen—Thus we hope pleas with that Spirit we have acted and thus we Shall indeavour to pay the Strictest obedience to the laws, maintain the Independent greatness of america & the Glory of our Generalisimo Perhaps our prudence may appear to have failed in our defensive opperation at the Very moment we strove to void the Censure of our Superiors. Yet as we have on all occasions been actuated from principals to repel the danger of the Savage Scalping Knife, by which our friends of every age & Sex have reiterably fell sacrifices to an unrelenting Savage cruelty. The magnitude of our Stated Sufferings should . . . entitle us to your care & patronage of the General Government. . . . it will not be denied that had the Atlantic Citizens sufferd by the pirates in a manner similar to what we have long undergone their resentment would have been equally roused and would have exclaimed no less. Should a baseness have been found to report in favour of the aggressors. . . . and it is the United voices of the frontiers that dictates many of whome once assiduously fought under your Banner thus Situate and confident that a simple stated truth will be acceptable to you we present our address by the adjutant Gen. of the State who is personally acquainted with Our Grievances. Let him return to us with a permission to be lodged with the Commander in Chief of the State Occasionally to vanish the savage Invaders from Our frontiers; Consider their depredations as National, with an assurance that no misrepresentation shall disturb the Confidence we have in your wisdom and directions for the militia to Guard Our Citizens, and we shall be happy.[91]

In calling upon Washington to allow them to "vanish the savage Invaders," they positioned themselves as peaceful citizens of a republic dedicated to liberty, emphasized their revolutionary service, and represented their cause as one of national concern. These backcountry settlers shared the concerns of settlers of the Trans-Oconee rebels but could not bring themselves to believe that the revolution that they helped bring about had failed them.

The complaints from those who opposed Clark revealed that the fissures within Georgia were more nuanced than simple geographical or socioeconomic divisions. Some residents on the frontier opposed the Trans-Oconee Republic. Most backcountry settlers shared the Trans-Oconee rebels' disdain for the Indians surrounding them and for federal policies toward the Creeks, but they could not bring themselves to break with the United States—or Georgia, for that matter.

Authorities across the border, both state and federal, took determined action to suppress the Trans-Oconee Republic. The creation of the Trans-Oconee threatened to undermine the terms of the New York treaty and to unsettle relations with the Creeks. The actions of Clark and his followers angered Washington and frustrated his efforts to establish peace on the southern border. Federal authorities wanted to eradicate the Trans-Oconee Republic before its existence further upset relations with the Creeks. State authorities worried that failing to uproot the Trans-Oconee forts would provoke a violent response from the Creeks and the wanton destruction of property. The governor of Georgia faced the difficult task of following the president's bidding and quashing a popular movement with a sizable following while at the same time averting a backlash. From the beginning, the state and federal efforts to suppress the Trans-Oconee Republic were hindered by local support in the backcountry.[92]

When Governor Mathews first learned of the existence of the Trans-Oconee Republic in May, he dispatched General Irwin on a mission of destruction. Irwin declared success, but reports surfaced in July that men continued to linger in the area around Fort Fidius on the border. Mathews then ordered Irwin to negotiate with Clark in an effort to convince him to abandon the Trans-Oconee settlement. Mathews knew that sympathy and support for the Trans-Oconee Republic was deep in certain areas and that the state's ability to enforce its will there was limited. Finally, in September 1794, Mathews mobilized a large force and sent it to the frontier. Before any violence occurred, Twiggs finally convinced Clark to give up. Surprised that the state authorities had managed to recruit enough men to overwhelm the republic's defense, Clark and most of his followers agreed to leave the settlements and return to the American side of the Oconee. The threat of violence dissipated, but hard feelings on both sides remained.[93]

After the disbanding of the Trans-Oconee Republic, at least some of the men refused to return to the Georgian side of the river. A group of twenty to twenty-five men led by Adam Carson held their ground.[94] Carson had played an important role in Clark's plans from the outset. He and a group of forty men had recruited in Greene County in March 1794 for the attack on Florida.[95] He also had been a key figure in the fighting that had plagued the frontier in the months before the Trans-Oconee Republic.[96] Carson and his fellow diehards highlighted the fact that the motivation to join the Trans-Oconee Republic went far deeper than a simple desire to follow Clark. They had been shaped by their experiences on the frontier, which for most had been a series of brutal raids and counter-raids. They were young men committed to the notion that they had a right to the Oconee land and that they would not be thwarted by anyone. Carson made clear his sentiments when, after members of the state militia confronted him and the other remaining men holed up at Fort Defiance, he proclaimed that he would occupy the post "at the risk of his life & bid defiance to the Laws of this state & the United States."[97] Despite Carson's fiery rhetoric, the men capitulated to the much larger force surrounding them.[98]

The Trans-Oconee Republic made clear to the federal and state authorities that the land question in the western country needed to be resolved. Unlike the other states in the Union, Georgia had refused to cede control over its western territory to the federal government. As officials negotiated a resolution to Georgia's western land claims, frontiersmen instigated attacks on the Indians. State officials eventually reached a compromise to transfer Georgia's claims to the western lands to the federal government with the promise that the latter would remove the Indians to allow white settlement.

State authorities sold Georgia's western land claims off through a piece of dubious legislation. When the General Assembly met the month after the demise of the Trans-Oconee Republic, legislators enacted the Yazoo Act.[99] Passed largely through bribery, the law sold most of the disputed land to a group of investors, many of them linked in one way or another to many of the legislators, for a pittance. The law provoked a maelstrom of controversy. Men from all sections of the state condemned the authorities for selling the state's patrimony. In one instance, Robert Thomas, a member of the legislature, was reportedly killed when it was discovered that he received $4,000 to vote in favor of the measure.[100] The outcry produced a "wholesale turnover of legislators."[101] Virtually all whites in Georgia, regardless of their socioeconomic status or their residency, agreed in their denunciation.[102] The antagonism toward the law ran so deep, in fact, that when legislators met at the next session of the General Assembly, they not only repealed the land sale but also burned the books containing all of the pertinent information.[103]

President Washington tried a different approach to resolve the land question. He focused his efforts on diplomacy with Georgia's neighbors. Hoping to tamp down the tensions on the Georgia-Florida border and, at the same time, gain access to the Mississippi River, Washington sent his envoy, Thomas Pinckney, to negotiate an agreement with the Spanish authorities. The result was the Treaty of Lorenzo in 1795.[104] Concurrently, Washington continued his attempts to establish a lasting peace with the Creeks. Extending an olive branch to the chiefs, he convinced them to meet at Colerain in 1796, where the U.S. commissioners acceded to most of the Creeks' demands despite the vocal and strident opposition of the delegates from Georgia.[105] The net result of actions taken by the federal government combined with the attempted sale of the western lands undertaken (then revoked) by the state authorities was continued confusion over the fate of the western lands.

The instability on the frontier was compounded by the state authorities' failure to deal with those who joined the Trans-Oconee Republic. The officer in charge of the militia, Jonas Fauche, himself a resident of Greene County, arrested Adam Carson and the other ringleaders, but much to his chagrin the men managed to escape from custody not long after being subdued. For Fauche, the escape of the rebels pointed to a much larger problem facing the state's authorities: the episode highlighted the government's inability to enforce the state's laws on the frontier. As a result, he argued, it was necessary for the state to make an example of the men who had led the effort to create the Trans-Oconee Republic;

they had to face prosecution for their actions. Fauche urged the governor to hold courts-martial to deal with the "delinquents" and demonstrate to the general public, particularly those on the frontier, the state's dedication to the rule of law. Should this fail to occur, he warned, it would prove exceedingly difficult to raise volunteers for the militia, since most frontiersmen "think of getting more land than to defend the ground they are in possession of."[106] The Trans-Oconee Republic had revealed a deep fissure in Georgian society that even after its collapse threatened to turn the state's residents against one another.

Dealing harshly with the rebels would have amplified the animosity of the settlers toward the state authorities. Despite Fauche's appeals, former Trans-Oconee rebels returned home to disappointment. Clark went back to his homestead in Wilkes County, but he did not go into retirement. He continued to harbor grievances. When a second opportunity to be part of a French-inspired attack on Spanish Florida arose the next year, Clark seized the opportunity.[107] Unfortunately for him, the proposed mission met a fate similar to the first. Clark returned home "disgusted" with Georgia and actively sought to leave the state in search of a new home, one whose residents possessed a republican worldview like his own.[108] Part of Clark's disgust with Georgia had to do with the changes that had taken place in the backcountry as the frontier pushed westward. Each time settlers succeeded in pushing the boundary with the Creeks, they just freed up more space for the spread of plantation agriculture and its corresponding hierarchies. But Clark resisted. While Clark served as foreman in 1797, the Wilkes County grand jury called for a ban on the importation of all slaves by "land or sea" to Georgia. The grand jury declared the slave trade to be "greatly injurious to the welfare of the inhabitants thereof, and highly repugnant to the principles of a free government."[109]

By the end of the decade, however, even in Wilkes, the county that Clark had helped to settle in the early 1770s, a new order had emerged, one dominated economically and politically by a plantation elite. The rise of the plantation order was evident in a Wilkes County grand jury presentment in 1798, which called for the repeal of the ban on importing slaves to Georgia to allow the importation of slaves from other parts of the Union. The grand jury argued that "the price of produce has not until lately been sufficient to stimulate to active industry. This said industry must be rendered abortive if we are prohibited purchasing slaves to work our land."[110] Planters wanted slaves to work their land, but the scarcity of slaves drove prices up, prompting many to smuggle slaves into the state. The grand jury argued that slave importation was necessary to develop the backcountry and keep slave prices at an affordable rate. While Clark had once led the grand jury of Wilkes County to denounce the slave trade, just under two years later the grand jury had reversed its opinion. Not long after, Elijah Clark died. He was eulogized as an American hero, though one who had fallen briefly during his Trans-Oconee adventures. Though celebrated, Clark was disappointed by what had happened to the nation he had helped to create.

Clark's removal from the scene represented the end of an era, but not the end of hostilities on the frontier. In the post–Trans-Oconee Republic period, settlers at certain key junctions along the border continued to instigate attacks on the frontier, hoping to start a war with the Indians. Their methods grew increasingly daring. An example of the depths to which some of the settlers were willing to descend occurred in October 1795 at Carr's Bluff in Montgomery County, which had been carved out of Washington County two years before. Located at the fork of the Oconee and Ogeechee rivers, the county was home to a sparsely settled mixture of farmers and frontiersmen, several of whom had been actively involved in the War of Independence and the subsequent Indian wars. Among this group was Benjamin Harrison, a captain in the state militia. A "large man with a black beard, a cloth tied over one of his eyes, and a piece out of his nose," Harrison embodied the stereotype of the Indian killer and lived up to those expectations.[111] He had amassed considerable experience in the art of raiding Indian settlements in his time on the frontier. On the eve of the negotiations at Colerain, Harrison led a group of settlers in a massacre of twenty-two Creek men, many of whom were well known to be "friendly" to the United States.[112] Their intent was clear: following a pattern established in the first half of the 1790s, they hoped to scuttle the impending negotiations between the Creeks and the U.S. commissioners by inviting a retaliation by the Indians, which, they hoped, would renew the war. In fact, Harrison reportedly stated as much when bragging about his role in the massacre. Not long after the incident he told William Scarborough "that there Should Never be a peace with the Indians whilst his Nam was Ben Harrison for he was abel to raise men enough to kill half the Indans that might cum to aney Treaty."[113]

The massacre was appalling even to those inured to the barbarity commonplace on the frontier. One witness to the scene declared the slaughter to be "shocking to humanity."[114] Members of the General Assembly concurred, expressing similar disgust upon hearing the details of the murders.[115] They called for Harrison's arrest not only because of the gravity of the crime but because they recognized that the repercussions would be severe if he and his co-conspirators did not face justice. The following spring Harrison and the other men responsible for the massacre were arrested, but apparently they were not convicted of the crime because Harrison was back out on patrol by the summer.[116]

State officials attempted to restrain the backcountry settlers from forays against the Indians. Not long after Harrison's raid, Judge Talifero addressed the grand jury in neighboring Hancock County, itself the home of considerable strife with the Creeks. He most likely had the massacre in mind when he spoke:

> Experience has taught us, that there are some among us, who, regardless of treaty, laws, or the more sacred ties of humanity, would involve their country in scenes of bloodshed for the ill timed gratification of killing a single Indian—if no possible ill could result from the perpetration of acts like these, there is something so shocking to every humane and benevolent mind, in wanton and unprovoked effusion of human blood that I cannot suspect a good man, or a well disposed citizen, of a wish to commit a crime so horrid; but when we reflect that retaliation is to be the inevitable consequence, without knowing when, or where the fatal blow will fall, whether on the person whose commission of the act, or on whose families of innocent and defenseless women and children; how can we forbear to censure the man who has been the author of such mischief.[117]

Occasionally the authorities intervened to stop or disrupt raids, but in doing so they put themselves at risk and highlighted their impotence in the backcountry. An episode in which local residents in Hancock accosted a group of federal officers is a perfect example. The officers had gone there to arrest William Yarborough, Obadiah Morris, Ephraim Moore, and Miel Monk for crossing to the Creek side of the Oconee River. The men claimed that they were just hunting. As the officers tried to depart with the men, the locals prevented them from leaving. Surrounded, outgunned, and overpowered, they were at the crowd's mercy. Violence was prevented only by a timely intervention by the arrested men, who managed to quiet the crowd and convince them to disperse.[118]

The election of James Jackson to the governor's chair in 1798 promised to resolve some of the divisions between the regions. He had returned to the state after hearing about the Yazoo scam and won the election by promising to find a solution to the western problem.[119] Jackson pushed hard to restrain the backcountry settlers. He stopped the erection of a mill on the Oconee because he felt it might imperil relations with the Indians; this stood in marked contrast with the state authorities' earlier consent and subsidization of expansion.[120] Jackson also issued a hefty $100 reward for the capture of men responsible for shooting an Indian.[121] He also enforced his Indian policies. Jackson made sure that Henry Gaster would be prosecuted for his role in nefarious activities in Montgomery as part of his effort to start a war with the Indians. Gaster was a major in the Montgomery militia and was the highest ranking officer in the county. He had conspired with James Ford, another officer in the militia, to kill an Indian in an attempt to start a war with the Creeks. The men planned to lure an Indian across the river to trade, then murder him, a strategy that had been used several times before. Before the plan to murder the Indian came to fruition, John Jones, a man from the county, informed the governor of the illicit trade and the scheme. The governor ordered Gaster's arrest to face trial before a military tribunal. Gaster refused to attend the hearing and resigned his commission instead. In his absence the military jury convicted him of several charges and expelled him from the militia. In the governor's mind, he acted correctly in ordering Gaster's arrest because "less damage has been sustained from Indian depredations, and . . . not a man has been called into service, of course not a shilling expended, for Indian defense . . . a circumstance unparalleled since the first settlement of the state."[122]

Jackson also placated backcountry settlers. He recognized that without backcountry support, however grudging, he would not achieve his goal of a peaceful resolution to the issue of western lands. The biggest prize that the backcountry won was a new system of apportioning representatives to the General Assembly; the new system, part of the 1798 constitution, gave the frontier counties greater power within the legislature.[123] After mollifying the critics on the frontier, Jackson moved to settle the matter. He pushed through a bill that allowed the state authorities to negotiate with the federal authorities a plan to grant the federal government control of the western lands. The land east of the Chattahoochee would be part of Georgia. After he completed this part of his goal, he left the executive chair and ran for Congress, where he hoped to shepherd the process along. With his help, the state ultimately reached an agreement with the federal government whereby it received $1.25 million to cede the western lands as well as a promise "to extinguish the Indian lands claimed by Georgia as soon as possible."[124] The system of distributing the land changed. Beginning in 1803 the state gave the land away through lotteries in which all citizens were eligible; this was different, more egalitarian, than the prior system in which land was simply given away by the state to individuals, or lately by county officials—both of which were prone to corruption.

Backcountry settlers briefly rose to power in the revolutionary era. For a short time, they used their power to implement their revolutionary goals: possession of land through the dispossession, even extermination, of Indians. Alarmed by violence on the frontier, residents of the more settled areas of the state as well as federal authorities asserted their influence. In response, backcountry settlers crossed the river and declared themselves citizens of the Trans-Oconee Republic. These rebels understood themselves as the true guardians of the American Revolution. Their republic, founded on the principles of "equil rights," offered an alternative to the slavery-based and, in their view, aristocratic republicanism developing in the rest of the state.

Elijah Clark and the Trans-Oconee have largely been ignored or treated as an historical footnote in the history of early Georgia.[125] In part, this results from a scarcity of historical documentation. But, perhaps more significant, this story is little told because it complicates our understanding of Georgia's revolutionary past and therefore sits uneasily within the revolutionary narrative. Clark was remembered as a revolutionary hero. The attempts by Clark and other Trans-Oconee rebels to achieve their own revolution have been forgotten. The story of the Trans-Oconee Republic reveals clashing racial ideologies through the pervasiveness of rabid anti-Indian sentiment among residents of the border counties and the more tolerant attitudes of the lowcountry elite. It illuminates the complexities of racial "othering" as hostilities with Indians created space, both physically and socially, for blacks on the frontier. It demonstrates that some Georgians had different ideas about the meaning of the Revolution, what kind of society it created, and whose interests it should serve. The story of the Trans-Oconee Republic shows that the expansion of plantation slavery into what would become the "Cotton Kingdom" was not inevitable but that racially exclusionary republicanism in the American context certainly appeared so.

4

THE STATE OF MUSKOGEE, 1799–1803

The short-lived State of Muskogee, in existence from 1799 to 1803, constituted a threat to the expansion of American plantation slavery. Members of the nation came primarily from the Seminoles in the Mikasuki towns situated along the Apalachee River, but also included a significant contingent of Indians from other towns as well as a sizable group of blacks and whites. They allied to resist expansion efforts by Spain and the United States and the growing centralization of power among the Creeks through the Creek national council. The State of Muskogee was a multiracial society where race played little role in defining internal hierarchies. Its racial system, then, deviated from the rest of Indian and Georgian society. Although the Muskogees did not express or adhere to an overtly ideological opposition to slavery, their opposition to American and Spanish expansion nevertheless constituted a substantive challenge to the institution. It was a hybrid society in terms of both its racial policies and the basis of its economy. Because of these positions, the State of Muskogee became a rival for power with the Americans and Spanish. Although the exact size of the State of Muskogee's population remains unknown, its importance to the history of the Southeast at the turn of the nineteenth century is considerable. In its four years of existence, the nation profoundly shaped geopolitics in the region and left a legacy that extended well beyond its demise in 1803.

When traveling through the Southeast in the mid-1770s, the naturalist William Bartram could scarcely believe the raw beauty and abundant resources of the area near the present-day Georgia-Florida boundary. The "swampy, hommocky country," he wrote, "furnishes such a plenty and variety of supplies for the nourishment of varieties of animals, that I can venture to assert, that no part of the globe so abounds with wild game or creatures fit for the food of man." The land provided the perfect sanctuary as well. The land, he noted in his *Travels*, was "naturally cut and divided into thousands of islets, knolls, and eminences, by the innumerable rivers, lakes, swamps, vast savannas and ponds," which "form so many secure retreats and temporary dwelling places, that effectually guard them from any sudden invasions or attacks from their enemies." The inhabitants enjoyed "a superabundance of the necessaries and conveniences of life, with the security of person and property, the two great concerns of mankind." The residents of the paradise "appear as blithe and free as the birds of the air, and like them as volatile and active, tuneful and vociferous. The visage, action, and deportment of the Siminoles, form the most striking picture of happiness in this life; joy, contentment, love and friendship, without guile or affectation, seem inherent in them, or predominant in their vital principle, for it leaves them but with the last breath of life." The only threat to its existence, he noted, was the white man. "They seem to be free from want or desires. No cruel enemy to dread; nothing to give them disquietude, but the gradual encroachment of the white people."[1]

The white man did disturb the serenity of the Seminoles in the twenty-five years following Bartram's trip. The outbreak of the American Revolution and the rise of the new nation upset geopolitics in the region. The new conditions exacerbated political and economic differences among the Indians of the Southeast. Confronted by the new situation, some Seminoles chose to band together to form the State of Muskogee. In their opposition to the expansion of plantation slavery, Seminoles allied with whites like William Augustus Bowles and slaves who had escaped from Georgian plantations. The Muskogees created a hybrid nation not only in population and culture but also in economy, all of which posed a threat to white Georgian society.

The Seminole Indians whom Bartram described were recent arrivals to Florida. They moved from Creek towns located in central and southern Georgia beginning in the 1720s following the Yamasee War. They replaced the former inhabitants, the Apalachee and Timucua Indians, who were killed or taken prisoner by raiding parties of Creek and Yamasee warriors and, later, by settlers from Carolina. The Seminoles' numbers grew in the second half of the century and their villages spread in clusters across the panhandle of Florida and into the eastern prairies.[2]

The Creek towns were part of a confederacy that had formed in the late seventeenth and early eighteenth centuries, bringing together a host of different native groups that coalesced in the wake of the destruction of the southeastern chiefdoms during the Mississippian Period the century before. The confederacy represented a form of political organization that was decentralized, unlike the hierarchical institutions prevalent in the Mississippian chiefdoms. The towns were independent and acted according to their own dictates. The flexibility of the system allowed towns to join one another when their headmen desired, and only then. There was no mechanism for compelling towns to act in unison with the others that formed the confederacy. The towns acted independently and considered themselves distinct politically and even culturally. Each town had a council; each township had a central town where the town council met. The Indians who had formed the confederacy had come from a number of different societies, possessing different cultures and speaking a variety of different languages, though Muskogee was dominant. One key marker was geographic; an individual's town was an integral part of his or her identity. The Creek towns were divided into two main groups. The Upper Creeks lived in settlements in and around the fork of the Tallapoosa and Coosa rivers in present-day Alabama, while the Lower Creeks resided along the Flint and Chatahoochie rivers in present-day central and southern Georgia. The Creeks who moved to Florida and would later become the Seminoles were mostly from the Lower Creek towns.[3]

By the 1780s, the two largest Seminole settlements in Florida were the Mikasuki and the Alachua. The Alachua towns were located in north central Florida, while the Mikasuki towns were located on Lake Mikasuki, thirty miles north of the Spanish fort San Marcos, close to the Georgia-Florida border. The Mikasuki towns became the largest settlement. The leader of the settlement was Kenighe, who along with his followers moved to the region following the Revolution. The Alachua towns were led by Payne. The leaders of the towns were very different in their dealings with their neighbors. Payne developed a much closer relationship with Spanish officials; Kenighe harbored deep resentment toward both the Spanish and the Americans. The towns were loosely connected to one another, but authority over each as well as decisions concerning war, diplomacy, and trade rested among the chiefs of each village rather than with a common council.[4]

Pinpointing an exact date for the creation of the Seminoles would be impossible. The origins of the term *Seminole* are also unclear. There are two competing theories. Some say the name comes from *cimarrones*, the Spanish term used for runaways, usually slaves, while others attribute the term to Muskogee for "wild men."[5] Regardless of the sources of the term, the notion that they were renegades was well established by the late eighteenth century. The transition of the Lower Creeks to Seminoles evolved over several decades. By the end of the 1790s, though, the rupture had clearly emerged. In the time since the Lower Creeks resettled on the Florida-Georgia border, the cultural and political differences between the Seminoles and the Creeks, particularly those in the Upper towns, had grown. Disagreements over slavery, the place of blacks within society, and how to deal with the Americans and Spanish led to a permanent break. The divide took hold in the wake of the American Revolution and grew over the course of the 1790s.

Over the course of the eighteenth century, social, economic, and political divisions between the Seminoles and the Creeks emerged over very different conceptions of how society should be ordered. As the British and Spanish penetration of the interior increased during the mid-eighteenth century, certain segments of the Creeks began to adapt their way of life. They embraced key tenets of what would emerge after 1790 as the civilizing program, initiated by the federal authorities under President Washington and his successors. Among the Creeks, particularly the leading men among the Upper towns, western notions of property and power gained increasing acceptance in the decades after the Revolution. Among the Upper Creeks, a small but significant group of leading men adopted farming and ranching, deviating from the traditional organization of labor. Indeed, in some pockets of the Upper and Lower Creek towns, Indians embraced plantation slavery, using African slaves to cultivate cash crops. The institution gained sway in towns in the region around the confluence of the Coosa and Tallapoosa rivers. In these areas, new notions of private property emerged, ones that conflicted with more traditional modes. Many of those who embraced this new lifestyle had connections, often familial ones, with whites. Several of the most prominent were the sons of European traders and Indian women. Many of these mestizo Creeks spent time in white society and proved adept at operating in white as well as Indian society. They prospered financially from their relationships and managed to translate their economic success into political power among the Creeks. The shift to plantation slavery and its attendant social and political relations proved extremely controversial within the Creek population. Indeed, many Creek Indians reacted warily to the changes.[6]

The Seminoles, in contrast, rejected "civilization" on European-American terms and decided to establish their own communities. Far from the Upper and Lower Creeks towns and well beyond the pernicious influence of the Spanish and British settlements, the Seminole villages developed their own unique culture over time. This culture did not represent an outright rejection of European culture in favor of the traditional past. Instead, the Seminoles blended aspects of Indian and European-American culture to create an alternative to the American-style plantation slavery that had emerged in the Southeast and had been adopted by some Creek leaders.[7]

American officials viewed the emergence of a slave-based agricultural economy in the Southeast and its integration into the larger Atlantic system as a sign of modernity.[8] The antithesis of this portrait of modernity was the stereotypical lifestyle of the Indian hunter, a world removed from consumer society and at one with nature. From the perspective of these officials, Indians were backward savages who lived off the hunt and did not make use of the land. The idea that Indians either embraced modernity or remained trapped in tradition presents cultural change as an all-or-nothing concept. This false dichotomy hardly reflected the lives of the Seminoles who would form the State of Muskogee. The Seminoles did not embrace the plantation complex, but neither did they strictly rely on hunting. And yet the Seminoles were undeniably caught up in the larger Atlantic World. While traveling near the Georgia-Florida border in the fall of 1799, for example, Stephen Minor reported that he ran across vast fields of "fine corn, rice, peas, beans, sweet-potatoes, musk-mellons, water-melons, cucumbers." Minor also noted that "most of the Indians have fowls, hogs, and cattle in plenty" and that he saw "several Negroes" there as well. The inhabitants of the region seemed to "live very comfortably," he concluded.[9] This depiction of life among the Indians along the Georgia-Florida border illustrates the subtle ways in which life among the Indians was not all that "traditional." From the crops they grew, like rice, to the people growing the crops, blacks, to the practice of husbandry, the Seminoles were a hybrid society. The Seminoles still engaged in the hunt, but agriculture had grown to play an increasingly important role in their culture. But unlike in the Spanish or American settlements, they did not rely on coerced slave labor, nor did they strive to produce a surplus for the market.[10]

Slave escapes from South Carolina and later Georgia to Florida had a long history.[11] At first, most runaways fled to Spanish Florida, where the authorities, beginning in 1693, offered asylum to those who agreed to convert to Catholicism. By the time the Spanish authorities reversed this position in 1790, hundreds of American slaves had escaped their bondage and fled southward in search of freedom.[12] The change in policy did not halt the flow of runaways, however. In the wake of this decision, runaways turned increasingly to the Indians for refuge instead. This trend was not entirely new. Slaves from Georgia had looked to the Indian tribes in Florida for sanctuary since the introduction of slavery in 1750.[13] By the turn of the nineteenth century, the volume of the runaways increased and the black population among the Seminole towns reached several hundred strong.

The relationship between the Florida Indians and the blacks who joined them was complicated. Though characterized by some contemporary whites as a master-slave relationship, the social contract between them more resembled feudalism than chattel slavery. Blacks lived in their own villages, independent of the Seminoles, but provided tribute to the Indians in the form of corn and other crops. According to William Bartram, for example, "slaves, both male and female, are permitted to marry amongst them; their children are free, and considered in every respect equal to themselves; but the parents continue in a state of slavery as long as they live."[14] While those terms fell short of full freedom and independence, they exceeded those offered by masters in Georgia. Word spread that a better life could be found among the Seminoles. As a result, blacks ran to the Seminoles seeking refuge. Some men of African descent commanded considerable respect among the Lower Creeks and Seminoles. Ninnywageechee, for example, played an instrumental role in the raids on the plantations along the Georgia-Florida border in the spring of 1793.[15] He was an "Indian and negro mestizo" trader among the Lower Creeks who lived within a clan "low down" on the Flint River.[16] Philatouche, or Black Factor as he was also known, lived among the Chehaws and was another prominent black Indian. His town became a center of the black population among the Lower Creeks in the 1790s.[17] With their incorporation of slaves, along with their rejection of plantation slavery, the Seminoles had become figuratively and literally a separate people from the Creeks by the end of the eighteenth century.

The two decades following the American Revolution were a tumultuous period for Indians in the Southeast. Georgians pushed hard after the war to secure the land. As the Americans sought to legitimize their claims to the region through land cessions, the question of who represented the Creeks emerged as a central issue. This was particularly true in the late 1780s and 1790s as a cadre of Creek chiefs and headmen, mostly from the Upper towns, tried to assert control over the nation's diplomacy while claiming the right to speak for the nation. The drive to centralize power created an immense divide among the Creeks and Seminoles. A group of dissidents later formed the State of Muskogee.

Fearful of the Americans' insatiable appetite for land, the Seminoles understood the need to block their plans for expansion. Facing this existential threat, the Seminoles along with other Indian nations in the Southeast allied together to oppose the Americans. They particularly took issue with the American assertion that, by virtue of the terms of the Treaty of Paris, Americans now owned the lands held by those who had allied with the British. Georgians pursued their own peace with some Creeks, making several treaties of dubious legitimacy in the mid-1780s. Other Indians, however, organized a resistance to confront the Americans. Alexander McGillivray, the son of a Scottish trader and an Indian woman, served as the movement's spokesman. McGillivray orchestrated attacks on the settlers who moved to the disputed land between the Ogeechee and Oconee rivers. The resistance struck out against the Americans in 1787–1788 in what some Georgians called the "Indian War." Through his actions, he rose to prominence and gradually tried to assume greater power within the nation.[18]

In the negotiations with state and federal officials to end the violence on the southern frontier, McGillivray claimed that his status as leader of the Creeks entitled him to speak for the Seminoles. His claim was part of his effort to centralize control over the Creeks' diplomatic affairs. In the wake of raids conducted by Seminole warriors in which they took twenty-five to thirty slaves from plantations chiefly in Liberty County on the southern Georgia border, state officials called upon McGillivray to explain his relationship with the Seminoles, implicitly challenging his claims to represent the Indians. Of the "Simanolies," they noted, "we know not whether they belong to any part of the Creeks." McGillivray assured them that he indeed possessed authority over the Seminoles. He offered a brief history lesson, explaining the supposed relation between the Creeks and Seminoles that justified both his claim to lead and the need to subjugate the Seminoles to his authority. "The Semanolies are Creeks who after the extinction of the Floridas and Apalachians removed to & inhabit that Country." They "got that appellation Semanolie which signifies a murderer, because a few only first settled in that part and those that fled from punishment, others afterward following they are now numerous." McGillivray informed the commissioners that he had traveled to the Lower towns and "harangued them on Account of the complaints from Georgia." Consequently, he assured Georgia officials that "I believe no mischief will be committed by them thru the Winter."[19]

In spite of claims by McGillivray and would-be successors, the Seminoles had very different ideas about their relationship to the Creek Confederacy and their obligations to the entity. As early as the mid-eighteenth century, Seminoles had begun to think of themselves as distinct from the Creeks. In 1757, for example, Cowkeeper proclaimed the independence of his people. He denied the right of the Creek Confederacy to speak for him and the Indians who settled in his town. In the decades that followed, other Seminoles expressed similar sentiments. Kenighe, the leader of the Mikasuki, stopped attending the national council, claiming that he and his people were not represented by the Creek Confederacy but would speak for themselves. Over the course of the 1790s the chasm between the confederacy (and later the national council) and the Seminoles, particularly the Mikasuki, continued to grow. The divisions centered on claims to political power.[20]

Hoping to quell the violence on the nation's southern frontier, President Washington invited McGillivray to New York to reach an agreement to halt the bloodshed and establish peace. When McGilivray negotiated the terms of the Treaty of New York in 1790, he claimed to speak on behalf of the "Upper, Middle, and Lower Creeks and Seminoles, composing the Creek Nation of Indians." Of course, his entourage did not include representatives from the Seminoles. Making matters worse, McGillivray agreed to give up land claimed by the Seminoles and Lower Creeks, land he had no right to cede. The inclusion of several secret provisions in the treaty also brought dividends for McGillivray. For example, he was made a brigadier general by the Americans, with an annual salary of $1,200.[21] McGillivray left a hero, but he returned with a sullied reputation. Many Creeks and Seminoles were outraged that McGillivray had ceded land. The goodwill that McGillivray had accumulated for his earlier role in the struggle against the Americans dissipated as the reality of his duplicity in the negotiation process became known. By 1792, McGillivray's standing in the nation had sunk so low that, according to one resident trader, he had "given up all pretentions of commanding the nation" and fled to Spanish Florida fearing for his safety.[22] He died soon after.

Resistance to the Treaty of New York and McGillivray's actions among the Creeks and Seminoles split along geographical and generational lines. The opposition was centered among the Lower Creeks and Seminoles. By establishing a peace agreement with the Americans, McGillivray angered young warriors who believed the land cession in the treaty meant the loss of important hunting grounds, which would result in fewer economic opportunities at the same time that property ownership was becoming increasingly important in Creek society. The young men also charged that the agreement would put an end to the raiding of the settlements, which had become a means for establishing masculinity in times of peace.[23]

The tensions turned violent in late 1792 and early 1793. In the spring of 1793, warriors from the Lower Creek and Seminole towns launched a series of attacks on plantations along the Florida-Georgia border, which resulted in the capture of considerable property and several dozen slaves and the exacerbation of tensions with frontier whites.[24] Timothy Barnard, an Indian trader, related that only a small portion of the nation, primarily within the Lower Creek towns, caused mischief. Not only were they committing acts of violence, he complained, they "are very saucy and say that the white people were afraid." More problematic, they were ridiculing the Indians who did not join them in their resistance and "telling them that they are slaves to the Americans."[25]

A significant portion of headmen from the Upper towns and a smaller number from the Lower towns chose to follow McGillivray's path and pursued a more conciliatory approach to the Americans. They had a mixture of motives for their position. Some embraced the civilizing plan and accepted western ways, while others recognized that the balance of power in the region had shifted following the Revolution and understood the infeasibility of overt resistance. Working extensively with James Seagrove, the U.S. Indian agent, and his successor, Benjamin Hawkins, these Creek headmen strove to maintain peaceful relations with the Americans and promised to do everything in their power to control the dissidents and the young men who opposed the treaty.[26]

Relations between and among the Creeks and Seminoles deteriorated in the second half of the 1790s as the chiefs allied with the Americans attempted to consolidate their power. The first step in this process occurred in 1796 at Colerain. At the urging of Georgia's authorities, federal officials convinced chiefs from mostly the Upper but also some Lower towns to meet in an effort to sort out the contested lands.[27] The Georgians hoped to obtain the area between the Oconee and Ocmulgee rivers, but the assembled chiefs thwarted their designs. Claiming to represent "the whole of the chiefs of our nation," the headmen who agreed to negotiate with the U.S. commissioners refused to cede any further land; however, they did agree to carry out the terms of the Treaty of New York, which had largely been ignored in the years since the agreement's signing in 1790.[28] The Treaty of Colerain recognized the land cessions promised by the earlier treaty, which affected the Lower Creeks disproportionately and had rather limited impact on the Upper Creek chiefs who made the agreement. The negotiations also produced a promise to allow the survey of the boundary between Georgia and Florida at some point in the near future.[29]

Those headmen who cast their lot with the Americans faced opposition from their fellow Creeks as well as from white Georgians who strove to foment conflict between the two nations. For some the results proved fatal. At the height of the violence in 1793, for example, soldiers and white settlers killed David Cornels, a trusted Creek translator, and three other Indian men as they traveled to meet James Seagrove to negotiate an end to the conflict. Cornels's killers targeted him specifically because of his efforts. The soldier assigned to accompany the Creek men to the meeting with Seagrove reportedly played a central role in the murders, informing troops stationed at Colerain of their route so that they could waylay the party. The incident proved sufficiently embarrassing to the authorities in Georgia to spur the prosecution of the soldiers. In the end, however, the local militia officers who oversaw the proceedings declared the men not guilty.[30]

Soon after the Treaty of Colerain, the rift among the Creeks and Seminoles deepened in the wake of the reorganization of the national council. Composed predominantly of Upper Creek chiefs, the council emerged as a powerful force within the nation between 1797 and 1799. Centered in the Creek towns of Tuckabatchee and Coweta, the council passed a series of regulations designed to protect property rights, an issue of increasing importance as a portion of the Creeks came to embrace western ways, and to deter young warriors from committing acts of violence on the American settlements along the frontier. To enforce these laws, the council created a proto-police force entrusted with far-reaching powers to punish offenders.[31]

This centralized model of governance deviated from the ways in which the Creeks had traditionally governed themselves. There had been no uniform set of laws. With no uniform set of laws, the Creeks had traditionally meted out justice through a localized clan-based system. Property crimes and corporal punishment had been alien concepts. Despite their claims to the contrary, the men on the council did not represent the wishes of the majority of the Creeks. They ruled in a manner that benefited themselves, usually at the expense of the rest of the nation. Moreover, they reaped material and political benefits from siding with Hawkins and the United States, but at great cost.[32] The national council thoroughly divided the nation and angered most Creeks, even those not predisposed to attack white settlers. But most worrying to some was the national council's claim to speak for all Indians.

American involvement among the Creeks increased after 1796 when Benjamin Hawkins took over from James Seagrove as Indian agent in the Southeast. Hawkins became a fierce proponent of the civilizing plan. He celebrated Indians' acceptance of the civilization plan, though they clearly represented a minority of the Creeks. Hawkins played an integral role in the reorganization of the national council in the late 1790s. At his prompting, chiefs allied with the United States formed the body "to make general regulations for the welfare of the nation."[33] He had several motives for his actions. While he most likely believed that the council's newest iteration was superior to its predecessor, he probably also hoped that centralizing the tribe's authority in the hands of few men would accelerate adoption of civilized ways and facilitate negotiations with the federal government for land cessions.[34]

In the spring of 1798, Hawkins met with the national council, which he identified as the "chiefs of the towns of all the upper, and a deputation from the lower Creeks and Simanolees." Hawkins made two demands. He ordered the group to stop "encouraging negros to leave the service of their masters to come into the Creek land and there find protection from Indians who claim them." This "evil," he told the group, "was of a serious and alarming nature."[35] Hawkins also told the group that they would have to follow the terms of the treaty they signed in 1796, which included allowing the boundary between Georgia and Florida to be drawn. The decision to draw the line produced "much uneasiness" among many of those attending the sessions, however.[36] The chiefs representing the Lower towns showed some apprehension about the prospect of convincing the warriors whom they led to respect this part of the treaty obligations. Even though these Lower Creek chiefs recognized the authority of the national council, they knew the terms Hawkins demanded would not be accepted. The speaker of the national council, Efau Hadjo, chose to ignore the warnings. He issued a decree, informing the Seminoles that they would have to fall in line behind the decisions made by the Four Nations—Chickasaws, Choctaws, Cherokees, and Creeks—and would have to consult with them before undertaking any raids or similar actions. "The Simanolees must mind and not take any step without the consent of the four nations. . . . You must all look on Colonel Benjamin Hawkins as the agent of the four nations, and you must do nothing without the consent of the four nations."[37] The national council may have demanded Seminole acquiescence, but it was unclear whether the Seminoles would follow their dictates.

When word of the imminent survey of the land reached the Seminole Indians living along or near the proposed boundary, they vowed resistance. Rumors circulated in the area that once the line was drawn, "the men would be made slaves of to work the ground for the Spaniards, and their women and children would be kept and taken care of; and that all their land would be taken from them . . . [and] that Indians who fell into the American side would be served in the same way." Noting that the Seminoles living in the area would defend their homes from any such incursion, Methlogey, a Mikasuki chief, explained that they "are determined sooner than submit to such treatment, to engage in a war against any nation or people, and sooner sacrifice their lives to a man, than be robbed of their lands, which is their only support."[38] In early August, as the surveyors prepared for their expedition, a group of sixty Seminole warriors led by Kenighe confronted Andrew Ellicott and Stephen Minor and ordered them to desist in their efforts, promising violence if they ignored the warning. Rather than heed the threat, the surveyors pushed ahead. On September 17, as they camped at the head of the Flint and Chatahoochee rivers, Seminole warriors returned as they had promised they would and plundered the surveyors of their valuables and sent them fleeing for safety.[39]

The attack on the surveyors produced a crisis in the region. Observing the events among the Indians, one trader declared that the "Whole Nation" was shaken by the actions of the young warriors and that many expected "nothing else but a rupture."[40] The national council had authorized the drawing of the line and the Seminole warriors undermined their authority. Prompted by Hawkins, the national council sent a delegation of seventy-two warriors from the Upper and Lower Creek towns to punish the offenders and impose its will. In late October, the warriors caught up with the chief who led the raid, Mankiller (Mannioc), and some of his men. The council's representatives brutally chastised the man, beating and mutilating him before executing him, burning his house, and destroying all his property. They beat two others, but the rest managed to escape. The lesson was made painfully clear: those who challenged the authority of the national council did so at considerable peril. The national council had whipped offenders for stealing property. This was the first time it (at Hawkins's prompting) executed offenders—and not for property crimes, but for disobeying its authority. In doing so, the national council insisted on its authority to monopolize violence, similar to the rule of law in the western sense.[41]

The execution of Mannioc served as a catalyst for the creation of the State of Muskogee. Seminoles under the leadership of Kenighe formed the State of Muskogee as part of a calculated response to oppose the American expansion, which was being aided and abetted by the national council. Faced with the apparent prospect of dispossession on the basis of an agreement that none of them had even seen, let alone signed, these Seminoles took action to protect themselves. To do so, they used the same tactics as the Creeks who had formed the national council. They created a legislative infrastructure that emulated the structure of a western-style government and claimed a monopoly on the use of force to preserve the paradise Bartram had described.

The man most identified with the State of Muskogee was William Augustus Bowles, its director-general. Bowles was an unlikely man to lead the State of Muskogee. Born in Maryland in the mid-eighteenth century to white, middling parents, Bowles left home as a young teenager to join the British Army when the Revolutionary War began. Bowles's time in the military brought him to the West Indies and finally to Florida, where, after being discharged, he joined some Creek warriors who allowed him to return with them to their town. Bowles immersed himself in Indian culture and married the daughter of a prominent chief. In the latter stages of the Revolutionary War, Bowles returned to duty briefly but was captured and spent several years away before coming back to the Southeast. For Bowles, the homecoming was bittersweet, however. The Treaty of Paris in 1783 had brought about an end to the hostilities between the British and the rebellious colonies, but it had failed to bring about a lasting peace in the Southeast. No sooner had Bowles returned to his wife and her family than he found himself in conflict with the Americans and Spanish once again. Bowles helped to organize the Lower

Creek and Seminole resistance to the expansion of settlers from Georgia and Florida. In the process, he was taken prisoner by the Spanish. As their captive, Bowles was first transported to Havana and then to Spain, where he spent time in Madrid and Cadiz before finally being transferred to the Philippines. Bowles remained in Asia for several years, until the Spanish governor sent him back to Spain. While en route, Bowles managed to escape and found his way to an American ship that carried him to England. Bowles used the opportunity to solicit the Crown on behalf of the Creeks and Seminoles before returning to the Southeast in the fall of 1799 to resume the struggle anew.[42]

On his way from England to the American Southeast, Bowles visited the West Indies, where he became a minor celebrity. In Jamaica, he had "the reputation of Very learned Man," which, in conjunction with his decision to sport Indian dress, made him "much researched by every class of people" there. Bowles introduced himself to the "best company in the island, where every Mark of Respect & Attention was paid him by the Governor, Sir Hyde Parker, Gen. Churchill, & other leading personages of the place."[43] He served as an ambassador for the Indians, promoting their cause wherever he went. His exploits were fairly well known, so much so that he appeared in the 1802 edition of *Public Characters*, a veritable who's who of the Anglo world, in a twenty-four-page biography.[44] The piece suggested that Bowles had gone "native." It was true. He had become an Indian.

Most whites rejected Bowles's self-identification as an Indian. On the eve of his return to the Southeast, Thomas Forbes wrote to William Panton to advise him on the man's impending arrival. It "will be no surprize to inform you that Mr. Bowles is now here on his way to *his own Country as* I am told he gives out." Later in the same letter, Forbes noted that while in Jamaica Bowles had spoken of "driving out all the *English* from *his* Country the Creeks."[45] Forbes doubted Bowles's sincerity as he identified Indian country as "his own Country." Like most whites, Forbes considered Bowles to be an imposter and his Indian followers to be dupes. "Under the title of *General* and with much cunning he imposes this nonsense upon the Weak & the ignorant." Yet Forbes also claimed that Bowles was "*without followers*."[46] Many other American and Spanish officials shared Forbes's sentiments. They dismissed the significance of the State of Muskogee, cast aspersions on Bowles's sincerity in his assertions of Indian identity, and portrayed the Seminoles who joined Bowles as fools unwittingly dragged into his dangerous gambits for self-aggrandizement.

William Augustus Bowles, by Thomas Hardy, 1791. Courtesy of the Upton House, Warwickshire, England, National Trust, London.

In the first half of the twentieth century, early American historians also rejected Bowles's self-identification as an Indian. They vilified Bowles for his actions in creating the State of Muskogee, viewing him as an "adventurer" seeking fame and fortune, someone who used the Indians as tools in his unjustified and unlawful fight against the United States and

Spain.[47] In more recent decades, historians have continued the trend of portraying Bowles as an adventurer, but they have minimized his influence among the Indians.[48] Doing so de-emphasizes the importance of the State of Muskogee. Focusing on Bowles, the individual, rather than the collective effort of the State of Muskogee, loses sight of the nation's significance, not only to American and Native American history but to Atlantic World history as well.

This view seems to overlook an important aspect of the relationship between Bowles and the Indians. Ignoring the State of Muskogee trivializes its resistance to the spread of plantation-based slavery across what would become the Deep South. We should see the Indians who did join Bowles to form the State of Muskogee not as dupes to the whims of an Anglo "adventurer" but as agents fully cognizant of the benefits of their alliance with him. Indeed, rather than being used by Bowles, the Indians, in fact, used him. Surrounded by their enemies and facing increased pressure—even violent coercion—to cede their land, the Indians who formed the State of Muskogee recognized Bowles's value as an intermediary to the larger world. Most likely, they found him to be a valuable (if not completely reliable) ally. For the Seminoles, then, Bowles represented an alternative to working with the Spanish or Americans, and his help came with fewer strings attached. Unlike those who sought to "civilize" the Indians, Bowles assimilated to an Indian lifestyle and asked virtually nothing of them.

To say the State of Muskogee was composed of Seminoles would be an oversimplification. The State of Muskogee drew its supporters from Mikasuki and the surrounding towns. The chief of the Mikasukis, Kenighe, provided a refuge to those alienated by the changes taking place in the Southeast, including young men from the Upper and Lower towns and warriors from Coweta, Tallahasee, Apalachicola, Hitcheta, Uchee, Oseooche, Oconee, Eufaulau, and Oketeyocenne.[49] Kenighe refused to heed the demands of the national council, which denied the sovereignty of the State of Muskogee and Bowles's claim to represent the Muskogee people. He had no time for other "Seminoles" either, however. He repeatedly ignored pleas from Payne and other Seminole chiefs to stop the raids on the Spanish and American settlements. When Spanish officials pressed Payne to explain this refusal, he noted a simple but telling truth: he could make peace with the Spanish, but he could not speak for the Mikasuki because, he explained, "we are a people to ourself."[50]

In addition to Native Americans, the State of Muskogee included a sizeable population of blacks. Building off what had been the norm for Seminoles, Bowles and the State of Muskogee welcomed all dissidents from plantation slavery. The state was a beacon to slaves from Georgia.[51] In 1799, for example, an enslaved man escaped from a Liberty County plantation owned by Andrew Walthour. He was presumed to have reached the growing black population within the State of Muskogee. The man fit the pattern of runaways to the Indians; he was described as a "villain" with "marks about his body" from the multiple whippings he had endured.[52] In 1803, Walthour lost three more slaves who joined their compatriots among the Indians.[53] Sightings of Bowles and his fellow warriors frequently pointed to the mixed racial composition of the men. Newspaper articles and reports in letters almost always took note. Black, white, and red all traveling and fighting together subverted the entire structure of the world white Georgians hoped to expand. Bowles's previous experiences in the Southeast indicated that he regularly had black confidantes upon whom he relied to conduct important affairs. The State of Muskogee adopted this practice. Blacks occupied positions of trust, authority, and prominence. They served as warriors, translators and negotiators, and guards for white prisoners.[54]

The State of Muskogee also included whites beyond Bowles.[55] The white men who joined the State of Muskogee, like the black men, formed a critical component of the nation's armed forces. A few of the recruits came from the West Indies, where Bowles traveled to garner support for the fledgling nation.[56] He also won the support of some white men from the area around the Georgia-Florida border, including traders Peter Shuggert, John Hague, William Harris, William Gray, and William McGirth.[57] The authorities in Georgia took his recruiting efforts seriously enough to issue a proclamation prohibiting Georgians from accepting Bowles's overtures to join the State of Muskogee. Governor James Jackson denounced him as "a common plunderer and vagabond, and a common disturber of the peace of nations," yet Jackson also understood that Bowles and the nation attracted followers, even among white Georgians.[58] Bowles also recruited whites from among the Anglo-Spaniards who settled in the region after the War of Independence.[59] They had initially welcomed Spanish rule but soon became disaffected. Several of the men were implicated in plots to overthrow the Spanish authorities in Florida, including the aborted 1794 Genêt scheme.[60] Bowles contacted Richard Lang, one of the leaders of the uprising, inviting him "into our land and service." Bowles made the offer contingent upon the men Lang could provide to "voluntarily bear arms against the Spanish King." Bowles offered to provide those men with land and protection "in the full enjoyment of all the rights of citizens of Muskogee."[61]

The State of Muskogee stood in stark contrast to the increasingly racialized society that was emerging in the southern United States. Like the United States and Spanish Florida, the State of Muskogee was a polyglot and multiracial society. But the State of Muskogee also appears to have been relatively racially inclusive. This flexibility proved an essential part of its survival strategy. Race had little to do with citizenship in the State of Muskogee. Instead, the key criterion for citizenship appears to have been an individual's ability to contribute to the security or prosperity of the nation. The State of Muskogee was an attempt to create an alternate nation, which included blacks and whites, an Indian-African-European hybrid.[62] The members of the State of Muskogee were rogues on the periphery of the Atlantic system. They were a liminal people occupying a liminal space wedged between the Spanish, the Americans, and the Creeks. They failed to fill the roles assigned to them by the emerging Atlantic system. They were all marginal peoples who banded together in common cause against the expansion of plantation slavery.

The multiracial component of the State of Muskogee threatened whites in the area, particularly Georgians. "A Planter" complained about the "banditti" that plagued the region, raiding plantations and "stealing" slaves. He emphasized the instability they created and castigated the authorities for their failure to subdue them. The groups conducting the raids, he noted, were composed of "Indians, Negroes and vagabond white men" from the nation. Their goals were to "plunder Negroes, Horses, and Cattle" while sowing chaos and fear to "break up all the settlements in East Florida." Among those who joined Bowles and the State of Muskogee were the "notorious horse thief" Robert Allen, with "three vagabond negro men, (stiling themselves free) from their Town in the Lotchaway country."[63] The four men arrived in Colerain, proclaiming their freedom and virtually defying white authority. Through their alliance, Muskogees defied the emerging racial orthodoxies associated with plantation slavery.

Trade was a persistent point of contention between the southeastern Indians and the Spanish and the Americans. The Indians' only outlets to trade were through individuals authorized by the Spanish and the Americans, which left them at the whim of their white neighbors. Both the Spanish and the Americans made agreements with delegations claiming to represent the Creeks and Seminoles that guaranteed a monopoly on trade with them.[64] For years leading up to the altercations in the fall of 1799, the Indians had complained about the high prices, low quality, and limited range of goods available at the stores set up by the Spanish and Americans to service their needs.[65] They also charged that both the Spanish and the Americans used trade as a privilege rather than a right.[66] As such, they restricted or halted trade to the Indians at times to force them to accede to their demands or to compel them to change their behavior in one way or another.[67] In return for access to American-supplied goods, Hawkins expected the Creeks and Seminoles to become "civilized," which meant abandoning the hunt and taking up agriculture.[68] Though supportive of efforts to improve the conditions of the Indians, the Spanish called for more modest concessions; they allowed for hybridity. They were no less rigorous in blocking the Indians' access to outside trade, however.[69] This policy set the Spanish authorities on a collision course with the State of Muskogee.

Even as they came to rely more on agriculture to fulfill their needs, hunting remained a fundamental part of the Seminoles' lives. The hunt was integral to the maintenance of Muskogee traditions. It was a gendered activity that provided young warriors the opportunity to prove their worth and practice their battle techniques during times of peace.[70] But perhaps most importantly, the hunt was the Muskogees' ticket into the Atlantic economy. Unlike the planters and farmers in Georgia and Spanish Florida, the State of Muskogee did not cultivate surplus crops for export. Instead, the deer the Muskogees killed provided the currency that they used to exchange for the goods that they desired and, in the case of ammunition and guns, needed. "The hides of deer, bear, tigers and wolves, together with honey, wax and other production of the country," William Bartram noted, "purchase their clothing, equipage, and domestic utensils from the whites."[71] For the Muskogees, then, the struggle to keep their land in the face of increased encroachment was a matter of the utmost importance. The deeper the Americans and Spanish pushed the borders of their settlements, the fewer forests the Indians had to hunt for deer and the less land to raise their cattle.

The Muskogees welcomed Bowles into the State of Muskogee largely because of the importance of trading. Surrounded by their enemies and facing increased pressure, even violent coercion, to cede their land, the Muskogees recognized Bowles's value as an intermediary to the larger world. Through Bowles, they gained essential commercial and diplomatic contacts beyond the Spanish and the Americans. When Bowles returned to the Southeast in 1799, he promised to help establish contacts with the English government and commercial agents in the British West Indies. Offering such services, some Seminoles welcomed him back. Bowles fulfilled his promises, traveling to Jamaica and Barbados, where he received enthusiastic welcomes.

Trade brought the State of Muskogee into contact with other marginal characters in the Atlantic economy, among whom race played a similarly subdued role. Trade brought them into contact with men like those on board the twelve-gun schooner that sailed up the Apalachee River to drop off goods for the State of Muskogee. The ship was "chiefly man'd with negroes, mulattoes" from Jamaica.[72] The ship carried arms. The State of Muskogee paid for the goods with skins and cattle. In July 1801, Bowles received a vessel, the schooner *Vulture*, captained by William Brice. The vessel carried twenty men, eight carriage guns, and dry goods.[73] The State of Muskogee operated as part of a larger underground network of trade. The Muskogees embodied the "motley crew," a multiracial rabble resisting the encroachment of plantation slavery.[74]

The State of Muskogee was clearly a fledgling entity, yet both the Spanish and the Americans recognized the danger that it posed through its mere existence. If allowed to take root and grow, the State of Muskogee would have had dire consequences for both the U.S. South and Spanish Florida. Inevitably it would have continued to draw runaways from both regions, further undermining the development of racially based plantation slavery, a labor regime that was not yet dominant in the area. The State of Muskogee challenged claims by the United States and Spain to extend sovereignty over the area, offering an alternative system to the civilizing program. It actively sought trading partners outside of the United States and Spain. In doing so, it undermined one of the key levers used by the Americans and Spanish to influence and in some cases compel the Indians to conform to their demands.

The State of Muskogee posed the most significant threat to Spain. The Spanish tried to destroy the nation and capture Bowles because they feared that he could help unite the Seminoles and Lower Creeks in opposition to Spanish rule in the area if he successfully established a consistent line of trade. The Spanish began their campaign to pressure the Indians to surrender Bowles shortly after they received word of his arrival. They threatened the Muskogees for giving Bowles sanctuary.[75] After initially dismissing the significance of Bowles's return, Vincente Folch reported that the Spanish authorities dispatched a small expedition from New Orleans to seize him with the help of Indians sent by Hawkins. Folch noted that the raid would have symbolic importance in addition to ridding the authorities of a tiresome troublemaker: "This expedition will be very Usefull in order to Show to the turbulent & daring Siminolies that if they behave ill, we will know how to go to the heart of their nation to Chastice them."[76] The expedition would also prevent Bowles from launching raids and block the Indians' access to the outside world. In February 1800, Spanish galleys attacked a fleet of three ships coming to trade with the State of Muskogee as they sailed up the Apalachicola. The Spanish then proceeded to patrol the mouth of the river. They also destroyed a village and took its residents as prisoners.[77]

The State of Muskogee responded to the provocations by declaring war against Spain.[78] Its first target was Fort San Marcos, located near the border with Georgia. A group of sixty warriors—comprising thirty Indians, twenty-one whites, and nine blacks—assaulted the Spanish fort in May 1800 and, after a brief siege, defeated the garrison and took possession of the fort.[79] With the help of several Spanish soldiers who deserted their posts and joined their attackers, the warriors held the fort for a couple of weeks, during which time they took everything of value, then abandoned it.[80] The decision to attack San Marcos was both tactical and symbolic. On a practical level, the fort represented an affront to the State of Muskogee's sovereignty, but it also had a more direct, tangible effect on their lives: it served as an obstacle to the establishment of trade with the outside world.[81] The seizure of the fort established the State of Muskogee's legitimacy in the area and attracted followers.[82] Benjamin Hawkins, the U.S. Indian agent, recognized the significance of the attack in a region rife with competing claims to governance. He predicted that the State of Muskogee, galvanized by its victory, would try to expand its zone of power to include Pensacola and St. Augustine. If the Spanish were not careful, he warned, the "whole property within their power will change owners."[83]

Shortly after the seizure of the fort at San Marcos, the State of Muskogee embarked on a campaign against Spanish plantations in East Florida. The raid carried out by a "large party of Indians, Negroes, and vagabond white men" in June 1800 was emblematic of these expeditions. The twenty-five warriors who formed the group attacked plantations near the

St. Johns River, destroying buildings and seizing "negroes, Horses, and cattle" along the way.[84] The warriors' strategy served dual purposes. Their actions terrorized Spanish colonists living in the countryside, forcing many of them to abandon their settlements and seek refuge in protected towns. In doing so, they undermined Spanish claims to the land and offered proof of the State of Muskogee's sovereignty and strength. Equally important, the raids garnered recruits from the slaves they liberated. Incorporated into the State of Muskogee, these former slaves provided essential labor for the nation and bolstered the ranks of its fighting force. The planters in the region, particularly those who lost slaves, cast the bondmen and -women taken in the attacks as "stolen" or "plundered," ignoring the agency of those involved. While there were a few examples of slaves who joined their owners in resisting the Muskogee warriors, most slaves appear to have put up little or no resistance, suggesting that they welcomed the opportunity to be "seized." The raids continued intermittently for eighteen months and proved to be an effective strategy for the State of Muskogee. By early 1802, in fact, the instability they unleashed left some white inhabitants of the region convinced that "all the settlements in Florida will be totally broke up."[85]

In addition to its efforts on land, the State of Muskogee battled the Spanish on the high seas. In one of the more intriguing episodes in the history of warfare in the Southeast, the State of Muskogee established a navy to confront its adversaries. Although its naval force never exceeded more than a handful of ships, the State of Muskogee Navy did disrupt Spanish trade in the northern portions of the Gulf of Mexico and limited the Spanish authorities' ability to resupply their forces stationed in the region. Privateers commissioned by the nation seized at least twelve Spanish ships in 1801 and 1802 and transformed them into State of Muskogee vessels.[86] One of the most successful of these expeditions involved the cutter *Tostonoke*, which left port in November 1801. Captained by Richard Powers, a white man who had become a citizen of the State of Muskogee two years earlier, the ship captured six vessels during its cruise, three of which were detained and condemned as prizes.[87] Like the nation itself, Powers's crew (and the navy as a whole) was multiracial, comprising Indians, blacks, and whites.[88] Indeed, as a measure of the social mobility offered to those willing to join the State of Muskogee, one of the captains commissioned by the State of Muskogee appears to have been of African descent.[89]

The Spanish authorities' inability to subdue the State of Muskogee militarily weakened their stature among the Indians in Florida. Spanish agents among the Creeks and Seminoles understood that the nation's appeal would only grow if left unchecked. The situation was tenuous even among those Indians who "are Staunch friends," warned John Forrester, a Spanish agent working among the Seminoles. Earlier appeals by the State of Muskogee to abandon the Spanish had failed in the past, "but god knows how long they remain So. I am a little uneasy, that they will be able to hold out . . . as they [the State of Muskogee] have people constantly among them, trying to corrupt and destroy their friendship toward this province."[90] In an effort to shore up their support among their Indian allies and undermine Bowles's standing, Spanish officials enlisted several Lower Creek and Seminole chiefs to appeal to Kenighe, the leader of the Mikasukis. Among this group was King Payne, the chief of the Latchua towns, a powerful Seminole settlement located in East Florida with whom the Spanish authorities had a relatively good relationship. On multiple occasions, Payne, accompanied by the other chiefs and hundreds of warriors, visited the Mikasukis and spoke to Kenighe, but to no avail. Kenighe refused to bow to their pressure.[91] The Spanish went so far as to place a bounty on Bowles, offering $4,500, but none of his supporters took the bait.[92] The nation had proven its ability to withstand military and political pressure.

The rise of the State of Muskogee posed a danger not only to Spain's interests but to America's as well. The authorities in Georgia viewed the nation as a threat because it drew slaves away from the plantations within the state and offered runaways a refuge. The authorities also feared the State of Muskogee would entice white men living in the southern section of Georgia who hoped to break free of the state government's control. In fact, Governor James Jackson was so worried about the prospects of white Georgians joining the State of Muskogee that he issued a proclamation prohibiting men from doing so.[93] Finally, the authorities in Georgia feared the State of Muskogee's actions could jeopardize the negotiations between Georgia and the federal government over the fate of the western lands.

The State of Muskogee represented a challenge to the federal government's geopolitical designs for the region. American officials had worked assiduously in the 1790s to gain access to the Mississippi River to protect the nation's economic interests, only to see their efforts potentially undermined by events at the end of the decade. The first was the return of Louisiana to French control in 1799. The second was the rise of the

State of Muskogee, which, in effect, nullified the authority of the Spanish government in large portions of Florida and upset the balance of power in the Southeast. Confronted by this menace, Benjamin Hawkins, the U.S. Indian agent, predicted dire results for both Spain and the United States should the Spanish fail to act. The "officers of Spain must give up the Floridas or fight for them. If the officers of Spain will not act with vigour and a show of force on their part . . . they will be embarrassed and embarrass us. Our Indians near them will join" the State of Muskogee.[94] Should that happen, Hawkins understood, American plans for the region would unravel.

With the prospect of growing unrest in the Southeast, the U.S. government stepped up its efforts to strengthen its relations with the Indians living there. Beginning in the summer of 1801, U.S. commissioners fanned out across the region to meet with representatives of the Cherokee, Chickasaw, and Choctaw Indians. Although the Americans did not secure all the concessions they had hoped for from the chiefs, they did reach several agreements granting the United States new land cessions, authorizing the construction of new roads within the Indians' territory, and finalizing plans for the survey of borders.[95] The following spring, the commissioners, James Wilkinson, Benjamin Hawkins, and Andrew Pickens, traveled to Tuckabatchee, where they met with Efau Hadjo and thirty-two other chiefs from the Creek national council. Most of the chiefs came from the Upper towns, though there was a small contingent of chiefs from the Lower towns as well. The commissioners' "primary object" was to obtain the Tallassee lands, the region south of the Altamaha River. Coveted by white Georgians for its "magnetic charm," the region had drawn thousands of illegal settlers since the 1780s and had served as a constant source of friction between the United States and the Indians in the intervening years.[96] When informed of the commissioners' demands, however, the Creek chiefs expressed deep reservations about ceding the land. The problem, they noted, was that the land was not theirs to give away. It belonged to the Seminoles, and they had chosen not to send delegates to the meeting.[97]

The commissioners did not take the rejection lightly. Instead, they pressed the Creek chiefs even harder. Wilkinson led the attack. He denounced them for insulting his and the other commissioners' integrity, and he questioned their honor. That the chiefs refused to surrender the contested land to the Americans because the "people who claim it, are not here" left Wilkinson near apoplectic. If the chiefs were truly the "masters" of their "land," he declared, they would not allow the "fools and mischief-makers, who run after the lying vagabond Bowles" to deter them from making these important decisions. Appealing to their masculinity, he demanded that they "stand up like men." After assailing the chiefs for their reluctance to act, Wilkinson pursued a more conciliatory approach, offering to provide them with military aid "to all those who may oppose your will."[98]

The pressure eventually succeeded. After weeks of wrangling, the chiefs finally succumbed to the commissioners' demands, at least in part. The two sides reached an agreement, called the Treaty of Fort Wilkinson, on June 16 that required the Creeks to cede the Tallassee land and an area in the fork of the Oconee and Ocmulgee rivers that had largely been overrun by settlers already, but they refused to relinquish any other territory.[99] In essence, the treaty did not involve any serious sacrifice on their chiefs' part since they resided predominantly in the Upper towns. But it did come with potential ramifications. Word of the treaty would no doubt anger the Seminoles, who refused to recognize the legitimacy of the national council to speak on their behalf. Cognizant of this fact, the headman of the national council, Efau Hadjo, issued a declaration to the Seminoles informing them of the terms of the treaty and demanding their compliance. "You must no longer persist in the conduct you have hitherto pursued, you must listen to the voice of the chiefs of the nation," he admonished. "I am speaking from the whole Creek nation."[100] Despite Efau Hadjo's air of confidence, some "old chiefs" believed the accord would prove extremely unpopular among their young warriors and might spur them to join the "partizans of Bowles" and further "divide the nation."[101]

Although Wilkinson's harsh words served an essential function in the negotiations with the Creek chiefs, it was Benjamin Hawkins's efforts behind the scenes that played the most important role in bringing about the treaty. The Creek chiefs' assent to the terms in the agreement and, in particular, their pledge to disrupt relations between the Seminoles and Bowles represented an important victory for Hawkins. Since Bowles's return to the Southeast in 1799, Hawkins had pushed relentlessly to destroy his rival's influence among the Seminoles and Creeks while at the same time promoting his own. Hawkins's efforts to portray Bowles as a charlatan and liar failed to persuade many Lower Creeks but found fertile ground in the Upper towns, in part because most of the chiefs living there had little or no knowledge of Bowles. Indeed, Efau Hadjo, the headman of the national council, had never met the man, but that did not prevent him from ridiculing the notion that Bowles had any standing among the Creeks while simultaneously declaring his people's support for Hawkins. "We never had a White Chief," he told Hawkins, "This man says he is a chief of our land, he is our director General, he lies." "The only white man is yourself, you are our beloved man, and the Representative of the President."[102] In 1801, Hawkins sent a delegation of chiefs from the Upper Creeks to appeal to Kenighe and the Mikasukis to break off their relationship with Bowles, but Kenighe refused the request out of hand.[103] For Hawkins, then, the Treaty of Fort Wilkinson both secured much-sought-after land cessions for the United States and offered a new chance to pressure the Mikasukis and other Seminoles and Lower Creeks to renounce their association with the State of Muskogee.

Bowles, too, expressed a deep antipathy toward his rival. As director-general of the State of Muskogee, he repudiated Hawkins's authority in the nation and actively promoted his downfall. In fact, one of the Bowles's first acts upon assuming the post was to issue a proclamation requiring all foreign agents, specifically those working for Spain and the United States, to leave the nation. Those who ignored the edict faced arrest and punishment.[104] In theory, at least, the proclamation was designed to stop the pernicious influence of the agents from both of the State of Muskogee's neighbors. In reality, the declaration targeted one man, Benjamin Hawkins, as the primary proponent of the civilizing program, which had exacerbated divisions among the Seminoles and Creeks.[105] When word of the proceedings at Fort Wilkinson reached Bowles and the other headmen of the State of Muskogee, they denounced the negotiations and criticized the Creek delegates in attendance for engaging in a "drunken frolick" rather than looking out for the nation's best interests. But they laid the greatest blame on Hawkins. Bowles and the other headmen recognized that as long as Hawkins retained his sway over members of the national council and other Indians who collaborated with the United States, he would continue to thwart the State of Muskogee's plans to break free of foreign interference.[106]

In addition to the Treaty of Fort Wilkinson, the State of Muskogee suffered a string of setbacks in 1802 that impaired its ability to operate. In early spring that year, warriors from the nation launched another assault on Fort San Marcos, which failed after a brief siege.[107] A far more serious blow came when England signed an accord with Spain to end the hostilities between the two nations. Following the Treaty of Amiens,

England severed its ties with Bowles and the State of Muskogee, unwilling to jeopardize its relations with Spain over the struggle taking place in the Southeast. Complicating matters further for Bowles, most of his associates in the Bahamas either left the colony or lost their offices.[108] These contacts had provided an essential trade link for the State of Muskogee and had publicized the Indians' plight in newspapers published in New Providence.[109] Nor could the State of Muskogee count any longer on the Court of Admiralty in the Bahamas to recognize the legitimacy of the prizes its privateers captured, even though the court had previously done so. The captains and crews of several State of Muskogee ships found themselves subject to prosecution for piracy.[110] This change in policy followed the appointment of a new judge with ties to Bowles's enemies. In justifying his rulings against the State of Muskogee's privateers, the judge questioned whether Bowles could actually speak for the State of Muskogee. The judge also disputed the notion that Indians had the right to field a navy because, as Indians, he argued, they inhabited the interior of the mainland while the European colonizing powers held the coast. The policy was to "treat & consider them as living under the protection, & as dependent on the Sovereign or Nation who possesses the Sea Coast," which positioned the Muskogees as residents of the "interior part of the Spanish Colonies of East & West Florida."[111] According to his logic, Indians did not have the right to conduct war like a civilized European state. They had to "act" like Indians, and any deviation from the traditional norm was unacceptable in his mind. In the face of mounting difficulties in the Bahamas, many of Bowles's remaining allies there counseled him to make peace with the Spanish, yet he rejected the suggestion out of hand. Neither he nor the headmen of the State of Muskogee were willing to concede quite yet. They were down, but they were not out.

By the start of 1803, the conflict between Bowles and the State of Muskogee and Hawkins and the United States reached a climax. News that Hawkins planned to convene a general congress at Hickory Ground in May 1803 to discuss the treaty reached the previous summer provided a perfect opportunity for Bowles and Kenighe to confront Hawkins and appeal directly to the other Indian nations of the Southeast. To salvage the State of Muskogee, Bowles and Kenighe decided to travel to Hickory Ground in 1803 to curry the support of other southeastern Indians. They hoped to dissuade them from allying with the Americans and becoming a dependent nation. Their project proved unsuccessful. Hawkins and several Creek leaders conspired to capture Bowles. They delivered him to the

Spanish authorities, who transported him to Havana. En route, Bowles escaped, but the Spanish soon recovered the fugitive. Bowles died in prison two years later, in 1805.

To root the State of Muskogee's embrace of blacks on pragmatism would miss an important part of the story. Clearly pragmatism played a role, but the decision to create a racially inclusive society represented a political statement. Members demonstrated that their opposition to the spread of the plantation economy and slavery outweighed concerns about racial differences. If taken on its own, it is easy to dismiss the State of Muskogee as a quixotic effort to resist the inexorable expansion of slavery, a mere historical footnote. When considered in the light of Atlantic history, however, the creation of the State of Muskogee illustrates that the emergence of a plantation-based economy in what would later become the Old South was not predestined or uncontested. The State of Muskogee was one of many experiments in nation-making that occurred in the tumultuous 1790s, a time when long-standing shibboleths about race and citizenship were coming under increasing scrutiny. Though not explicitly ideologically antislavery in the western liberal tradition, those who joined the State of Muskogee were functionally antislavery, at least in their opposition to the expansion of American plantation-based slavery. The State of Muskogee, had it survived, may have developed into a more explicit threat to slavery or it may have developed into a slave society of its own. We will never know. But, in its brief existence, American and Spanish officials recognized the State of Muskogee as a danger to the institution of slavery.

Historians have likened the Seminole resistance in the Georgia-Florida area to a form of maroonage. And while this comparison is apt in some ways, ultimately it fails to convey the complexity and nuance of the State of Muskogee's existence. Maroon societies resisted slave-based plantation agriculture and generally entailed isolation from the modern Atlantic economy. The State of Muskogee, like a maroon society, resisted slave-based plantation agriculture. But unlike a maroon society, it did not isolate itself from the Atlantic World. Through its trade connections and its navy, the State of Muskogee embraced modernity, but the particular form of modernity that developed there differed from the model that emerged within the American South. Bowles did not simply graft European-style modernity onto an Indian nation. The Muskogees adopted aspects of modernity, like a navy, in keeping with their goals and interests.

Yet there was a certain paradox to their situation: the State of Muskogee relied on the Atlantic economy, an economy based on slave labor, to resist the encroachment of plantation slavery. To paraphrase historian Eugene Genovese, in a different context, the State of Muskogee was in, but not of, the Atlantic World.

The Trans-Oconee Republic and the State of Muskogee both originated in disputes over land in the 1780s. The immediate impetus for both societies was a backlash against an attempt to centralize power—by the U.S. government in the former case, and by the Creek national council in the latter. Both offered alternatives to the expansion of American plantation slavery. Of course, significant and irreconcilable differences separated the two groups and the men who joined them. In the long term, their views gained increasing prominence. White Georgians gradually embraced the tenets of the Trans-Oconee rebels, specifically adopting an extreme position on Indian removal. Indians on Georgia's southern border increasingly accepted the necessity of warfare through a multiethnic army to block American expansion. The descendants of these movements would come into conflict in the early 1810s over control of the interior.

5

Borders of Freedom, 1812–1818

John Spaniard escaped from his master in Georgia sometime in early 1812. Carrying "several kinds of clothes" and possessing the ability to speak English, Spanish, and French, Spaniard most likely hoped to remake himself into a freeman.[1] To achieve this objective, he did not have to travel far. Unlike subsequent generations of Georgia slaves who would have to cross vast distances to the northern United States or Canada in their quest for freedom, Spaniard faced a far less arduous and lengthy journey to freedom in Florida. If the escape of Spaniard had been an isolated incident, the expression of a lone slave dissatisfied with his master's treatment, and if hunger and exposure had eventually forced his return to his master and had reduced him to submissiveness and repentance, then his escape would not have represented a threat to the system of slavery and the structure of race relations in Georgia. Unfortunately for white slave owners in Georgia, Spaniard was not unique. Indeed, John Spaniard represented just one of thousands of Georgia slaves who bolted their lives of bondage and battled for their freedom.

For slaves in Georgia in the early nineteenth century, the geography of freedom was reversed. Slaves looked south to Florida when contemplating their escape from bondage. Like generations before them, slaves in Georgia knew that just beyond an invisible border with Florida lay societies that offered runaways the promise of more autonomous lives, if only they could reach them. Faced with the prospect of lifelong servitude in this portion of Georgia's burgeoning cotton belt, slaves found the decision simple. Between one thousand and two thousand slaves fled southern Georgia between the tumultuous years of 1812 and 1818. As they had during the War of Independence, Georgia's slaves seized the opportunity and escaped to freedom. More important, runaway slaves from Georgia, in one of their first acts of freedom, took up arms to defend their freedom against their former masters.

The 1810s marked a violent decade on Georgia's southern border. The United States fought in four military conflicts on the Georgia-Florida border in the span of seven years: the Patriot War from 1812 to 1813, the Creek Civil War from 1813 to 1814, the War of 1812, and the Seminole War from 1817 to 1818. Most scholarship on these wars treat them separately, as isolated phenomena outside the American experience.[2] These four conflicts, however, were the products of tensions created by continued American expansion, which repeatedly exploded into violence. Though the British and the Americans initiated the War of 1812 far from Georgia's borders, the hostilities in Georgia quickly adopted the pattern of previous conflicts. In all of these conflicts, the incessant incursions of settlers from Georgia onto lands south and west of the state upset the already fragile relations with their Spanish and Indian neighbors. Though commonly portrayed as isolated Indian-white disputes in the historiography, these wars included blacks as pivotal players.

The names for these conflicts adopted by contemporary observers and subsequent commentators obscure the central role of people of African descent. Officially, the Americans' opponents in the various wars were the Spanish, the Creeks, the British, and the Seminoles. But in each of these conflicts, black runaways joined forces with Georgia's enemies to resist American encroachment. Indeed, escaped slaves frequently defended their adopted homes with the fiercest resistance. Having fled bondage in Georgia, former slaves understood what awaited them should they fall back into American hands. Although histories separate these conflicts into four different wars, on the Georgia frontier these conflicts constituted one sustained struggle against American expansion. Rather than a series of wars, the hostilities represented a long string of battles between Americans, led by white settlers from Georgia bent upon seizing the land from its occupants, and their opponents, a multiracial army, which included runaways from Georgia whose continued freedom depended on checking their foes' advances into Florida.

The participation of armed blacks lent these conflicts a darker meaning. Americans legitimized their involvement in affairs beyond their na-

Georgia's Counties–1810

Indian

Lands

tion's borders with the argument that their southern neighbors gave sanctuary and, even worse, weapons to black runaways from Georgia. Though white Georgians focused on the foul deeds of their southern neighbors in provoking slaves to escape, black Georgians needed no encouragement to resist their bondage through escape and armed combat. The participation of blacks transformed these conflicts into race wars, which threatened the security of the state and destabilized the very foundation of southern society. Since the advent of social history, scholars of American slavery have largely focused their attention on the day-to-day resistance of slaves rather than on overt and violent forms of resistance. For example, Eugene Genovese argues that, with the exception of famous conspiracies, like Denmark Vesey's and Gabriel Prosser's, and ill-fated revolts, like Nat Turner's, American slaves refrained from engaging in open insurrection because it was sure suicide. As a result, Genovese contends, armed slave rebellions were few and far between, particularly by the nineteenth century; therefore they had little relevance in slaves' lives.[3] The conflict on the Georgia-Florida border in the 1810s contradicts this assertion. The focus on everyday acts of resistance by scholars has added an important dimension to the study of slave life, but it has come with a price: it has obscured actual resistance just beyond the American border.

During the 1810s, white Georgians faced the task of incorporating a large population of slaves. Despite the 1798 ban on importations, white Georgians witnessed an explosion in the size of their enslaved population. In 1817, one estimate placed the number of slaves introduced to Georgia in the three prior years at twenty thousand, most of them coming from the Upper South.[4] The entrance of such a large number of new slaves alone had the potential to destabilize plantation life in the state. The fact that little or nothing was known about the newly arrived slaves only compounded matters. Whites in Georgia had good reason to fear that the continued violence on the southern border, combined with the demographic changes, posed a serious challenge to the stability of society.

The years had not been kind to former governor George Mathews. His reputation had declined in the years after his tenure as governor. White Georgians condemned his signature on the bill authorizing the Yazoo sale and his persistent efforts against Elijah Clark and other upcountry settlers.[5] In the late 1790s, Mathews sought to rehabilitate his good name by moving to the Mississippi Territory in 1797 to start anew, but his efforts came to naught. In 1810, however, Mathews's fortunes seemed to brighten. That year, President James Madison enlisted the former governor to lead a covert attempt to secure Florida from the Spanish. The resulting "Patriot War," as it was known, represented an unsuccessful attempt to root out black resistance on the Georgia border.

Finding little support among Anglo-Floridians for his plans, Mathews began recruiting among white Americans for an invasion of Florida.[6] Mathews found considerable support among Georgians for his enterprise, especially among the residents of Camden County on the state's southern border. These Georgians deeply resented the Spanish, whom they accused of harboring runaway slaves. As an added incentive, Mathews offered bounties of fifty acres to each recruit and promised future appointments to the territorial government once under American control. A range of Georgians joined his enterprise, including some of the county's wealthiest planters, such as William Ashley, Lodowick Ashley, and John Houstoun McIntosh, who yearned for access to the fertile lands of the Alachua plains in Florida. Mathews also secured the support of General John Floyd, commander of the Camden militia, whose influence extended to the governor. With this volunteer army, Mathews intended to seize Florida, which would then be absorbed by the U.S. government.[7]

After more than a year of preparation, Mathews's army finally embarked on its mission in the spring of 1812. Composed chiefly of Georgians and a smaller number of actual residents of Florida, Mathews's group—the self-styled "Patriots"—left Georgia and headed for Florida. In mid-March they secured the surrender of Amelia Island, just south of the Georgia-Florida border, in a rather bloodless affair. They then declared themselves independent from Spanish authority, drafted a constitution for an independent republic, and requested annexation by the United States. Shortly thereafter, the Patriots marched on St. Augustine, the center of Spanish control in Florida. The Patriots reached San Marcos on the outskirts of St. Augustine by the end of the month.[8]

From their initial assault until their arrival at San Marcos, the Patriots proceeded largely unimpeded and encountered little organized resistance. On arriving at San Marcos, however, their fortunes began to change. Unlike their counterparts on Amelia Island, the Spanish authorities at St. Augustine refused to surrender to the invaders. In response, the Patriots established a camp at the ruins of Fort Mose, a black garrison previously devastated by white Georgians in the 1740s and rebuilt in the 1750s, and laid siege to the city.[9] The Patriots waited for additional help from the U.S. government. Unfortunately for the Patriots, Federalists in Congress questioned the decision to attack a country at peace with the United States. Under pressure from the Federalists, President Madison removed Mathews from his post and disavowed the purported revolution when details of the annexation plot surfaced in Washington.[10]

Madison's rejection of the Patriot cause represented a serious blow, but of all the obstacles facing the Patriots, the most serious was the determination of the black troops in Florida and of residents of St. Augustine to resist any effort to annex Florida. The militia and the Florida free black community were ethnically and linguistically diverse, including blacks from the West Indies (such as Afro-Cubans from Havana), Africans, and, most important, slave runaways from Georgia. Together, the polyglot black community resisted American encroachment with all its might. The black militia held firm in its defense of St. Augustine. For blacks, the conquest of Florida by the Americans represented more than a blow at the Spanish Empire's geopolitical interests; American rule meant the end of their freedom. Under Spanish governance, they enjoyed privileges unknown by slaves in nearby Georgia, privileges that they would lose should the Patriots succeed in overthrowing the Spanish authorities and should the United States subsequently absorb the Florida colony.[11]

Indeed, blacks in the Patriot-occupied areas quickly felt the fist of American rule. As one of his first directives, Georgia's Governor David Mitchell, who had assumed charge after Mathews's recall, cracked down on blacks in the Patriot-occupied areas.[12] The Patriots feared that blacks under their authority might rise up in rebellion, that they spied for the Spanish, or that they intended to ally with the Indians. American-appointed officials routinely harassed blacks. They passed legislation to monitor their movements, including a nightly curfew on all blacks, free or enslaved. They also threatened imprisonment for blacks caught without written passes by owners, guardians, or employers.[13] The Patriots also promised execution for any free black associated with a plot against them.[14]

The Patriots envisioned no place for free blacks in their Floridian society. In the constitution for their self-proclaimed republic, they restricted citizenship rights to white men.[15] Later, as the conflict descended into a guerrilla war, one Patriot leader, Buckner Harris, made clear his sentiments toward free blacks when he executed two after a battle. According to one witness, Harris killed the men for "no other crime than being free blacks." The witness related that the Patriots "say they will not leave free any black or colored person who falls into their hands."[16] Ostensibly, white Georgians depicted the invasion of Florida as an attempt to spread republicanism and overthrow monarchal rule. In reality, rather than extending the rights and privileges of most residents of the Spanish colony, the invasion and occupation of Florida resulted in a serious reduction in the rights of black residents. In contrast with their status under the Spanish, free blacks found themselves reduced to little more than slaves. Consequently, free blacks tied their interests to the Spanish presence on the mainland and fought to preserve it.

The Patriots predicted total collapse of the system of slavery in the South if the black Spanish troops were not defeated. John Houstoun McIntosh, the leader of the Patriots, informed Secretary of War James Monroe that the "army of negroes" "excited" the slaves to rebellion. In pleading his case, McIntosh reminded Monroe that the stakes were potentially enormous should the United States fail to come to the Patriots' aid. The Patriots in Florida stood at the front line in the defense of slavery and "if we are abandoned," he argued, "what will be the situation of the Southern states, with this body of black men in the neighborhood." McIntosh relayed his own dire predictions: "St. Augustine, the whole province, will be the refuge of fugitive slaves." From there, he warned, emissaries "no doubt will be detached, to bring about a revolt of the black population of the United States." He concluded that "a nation that can stir up the savages round your western frontiers to murder will hesitate but little to introduce the horrors of St. Domingo into your Southern country."[17]

Supporters of the Patriot cause in Georgia viewed the black population in Florida as a threat to the security of the state in both a literal and a figurative sense. Indeed, supporters of the Patriot cause routinely represented the invasion as a preemptive strike against the growth of the black population in Florida—and most of all, against the presence of the black militia. Both Mathews and his successor, Governor David B. Mitchell, focused on the role played by blacks in defending the Spanish territory as a rationale for supporting the Patriots and keeping American troops in Florida. Mitchell accused the Spanish of arming "every able-bodied negro within their power," which included two companies of black troops recently arrived from Havana. But Mitchell understood that the true threat lay less with the actual firepower of the black troops and more with what they represented: freedom. Black troops embodied living proof that feasible escape from slavery existed nearby should the slaves in Georgia find the opportunity to leave their plantations. Mitchell believed that if the black troops remained in East Florida their presence would surely lead to "a state of insurrection" on Georgia's southern frontier as slaves abandoned their plantations for freedom in the Spanish colony.[18]

In the summer of 1812, the Seminoles, both "red" and "black," fearing that they would be the Patriots' next victims, joined the Spanish side and broke the stalemate in the Patriot War.[19] In the months before the Patriot invasion, George Mathews and the Patriot leadership had made several sloppy attempts at diplomacy with the Seminoles. Aware that the Patriots' chances of success would be greatly diminished should the Seminoles ally with the Spanish, Mathews hoped to secure their neutrality but managed to infuriate them instead. During one fateful visit to Chief Payne's town, Mathews announced in the village square that he intended to drive the chief from his land. In another stunning display, John Houstoun McIntosh sent a message to another Seminole chief that he intended to make him "his waiting man."[20]

Mathews's interpreter during the negotiation, a Florida slave named Tony whom Mathews had stolen from his master, was instrumental in convincing the Seminoles to side with the Spanish. After Mathews's party departed, Tony escaped and returned to the Alachua towns and related the Patriots' true designs. He informed them that "they're going to take your country beyond St. John's. The old people will be put to sweep the yards of the white people, the young men to work for them, and the young females to spin and weave for them." Tony encouraged the Seminoles to forge an alliance with the Spanish. Though initially in favor of remaining on the sidelines of the struggle between the Patriots and the Spanish authorities, the Seminole chiefs acquiesced to their warriors' demands to join the war against the Patriots. Black warriors led the cry for action.[21]

The involvement of the Seminoles provided white Georgians, particularly those close to the border with Florida, with yet another reason to support the Patriot cause. White Georgians detested the Seminoles because they provided an asylum for escaped slaves. The commander of the Camden County militia, General John Floyd, saw the Patriots' expedition as the perfect opportunity for expelling the Spanish from the peninsula and the perfect opportunity to destroy Seminole towns on the Spanish side of the border. In Floyd's estimation, the black towns represented "an important evil growing under" the "patronage" of the Indians. Thus the Patriots' assault provided a "desirable pretext for the Georgians to penetrate their country" and destroy the offending settlements.[22]

In July and August 1812, the Seminoles went on the warpath. Warriors, black and red, joined troops from the black Spanish militia and scoured the no-man's land outside of St. Augustine. Together the Seminoles and the black militia raided the Patriots' settlements in Florida, sending many home to protect their farms and plantations. They killed a white plantation owner and five slaves, then liberated another twenty-five slaves. Shortly after, the Seminoles recruited seventy to eighty more slaves to fight the Patriot invaders.[23] Black Spanish soldiers from Fort San Marcos and their Indian allies ambushed Americans who ventured too far astray from their encampment. In one incident, blacks and Indians killed ten Patriots. In another incident, they captured a Patriot who had been delivering a note from the main encampment to a nearby blockhouse. They then sent a gruesome warning that the American invaders would be dealt with in a severe manner: they cut off his nose and genitals in addition to scalping him. These mutilations made clear their determination to resist American encroachment and inflict retributive justice on their enemies.[24]

September proved a decisive month in the struggle between the Patriots and Florida's defenders. The first clash occurred at the beginning of the month, when a group of Seminoles in concert with the Spanish black militia succeeded at breaking the stalemate at St. Augustine. Led by Prince, a free black man, an interracial band composed of black militiamen and black and red Seminoles ambushed twenty Marines and sixty to seventy Patriots as they escorted a supply wagon train traveling through the Twelve Mile Swamp. In the battle, the Seminoles killed the commanding officer of the American troops. Although the battle lasted little more than two hours, its consequences were dramatic. The Seminole assault broke the Patriot supply line, forcing the American troops outside of St. Augustine to abandon their siege.[25]

A second clash occurred at the end of the month. Colonel Daniel Newnan (an officer in the Georgia militia) and a body of approximately one hundred troops, composed of U.S. soldiers, Patriots, and Georgia volunteers, set out to destroy the Alachua villages and settle on the lands. Seven miles from the towns, the approaching Americans encountered a mounted party made up of Chief Payne and his warriors. The fighting lasted for two hours before the outnumbered Indians retreated to seek reinforcements. Newnan and his men used the lull to scalp the slain warriors and to construct fortifications to hold off the imminent Indian attack. Once word of the initial battle reached the black settlements connected to Payne's towns, armed men poured forth to fight the American invaders. Numbering more than two hundred, the Seminole warriors, red and black, attacked at dusk. In the face of the onslaught, Newnan and his men suffered severe casualties and ultimately found themselves pinned down. After enduring a week-long siege, wracked by hunger, wounds, and disease, Newnan and his men escaped at night, skulking off across the St. Johns River to recover from their humiliating defeat.[26]

In the various military engagements that summer, blacks played a prominent role, both in leadership and actual combat. Their participation turned the tide in favor of the Spanish and the Seminoles both at St. Augustine and at the Alachua villages. Even Newnan, hardly a champion of blacks, had to acknowledge the bravery of his black adversaries, whom he characterized as "their best soldiers." Slaves in Georgia surely heard the rumors of armed blacks successfully fighting against whites in nearby Florida. Rebellion against white masters may have previously seemed futile, but the Florida example raised the promise of freedom for Georgia's slaves. Many slaves risked the possibility of capture and punishment by whites to escape to Florida. Governor Mitchell noted that "most of our male negroes on the sea board are restless and make many attempts to get off to Augustine, and many have succeeded."[27]

In the wake of these two military defeats, Governor Mitchell became increasingly troubled by the potential for instability in the South should the free black population on Georgia's border continue to grow unchecked. He appealed to Secretary of State James Monroe for help in dealing with the tumult in Florida. Mitchell argued that direct federal involvement was necessary to halt the epidemic of runaways and stave off insurrection among Georgia's slaves. He predicted that "nothing short of the whole military strength of the state" was necessary to vanquish the "Indians and negroes" and save Georgia from the "worst evils imaginable."[28]

Governor Mitchell also called upon the General Assembly to aid the Patriot cause. In particular, he condemned the Spanish use of black troops as "so savage and barbarous, that it is impossible for an American to hear of it without feeling the utmost indignation and resentment against the power that commands or even permits it." Black troops, Governor Mitchell asserted, "we cannot tolerate." To safeguard their "immediate interest" as well as their "future peace and happiness," Governor Mitchell urged members of the legislature to act quickly. When the legislature met in Georgia that November, the Florida invasion as well as the racial composition of the province's militia figured prominently in its discussions. The General Assembly passed a resolution that called on the federal government to take "possession and occupancy" of Florida. The legislature justified the seizure as a necessary precaution to halt the flow of runaways to the fort at San Marcos, which they complained offered an asylum for "outcasts of society and disaffected of our own country."[29]

In response to Georgia's appeals, President Madison authorized an additional detachment of U.S. troops to cross the Florida border in December 1812. In early February 1813, in a combined force of more than five hundred men, with Georgian militiamen leading the way, they commenced their mission: to destroy the Alachua towns and punish the warriors they blamed for the attacks on Newnan, to drive the Indians from their land, and to capture for resale or repatriation any blacks they encountered.[30] The American forces converged first on two Alachua towns, first Payne's town and then Bowlegs's, but found both virtually deserted. Aware that their depleted ranks could not overcome the American forces, the Seminole warriors had hidden their families in the swamps for protection. The Americans immediately plundered the villages. Their greed so overpowered them that they failed to notice their enemy regrouping. The Seminole warriors launched several unsuccessful assaults and harried the invaders, but they were vastly outnumbered. Ultimately the Seminoles' attack forced the Americans to leave, but not without their plunder. After killing thirty-eight Indians and burning nearly four hundred houses, the Americans withdrew from the Alachua lands in possession of four hundred head of horses and cattle, hundreds of bushels of corn, and seven prisoners.[31] With the offending Alachua towns destroyed and their inhabitants dispersed, the federal authorities wiped their hands clean of the situation, leaving the Patriots to their own devices.[32] Abandoned by the federal authorities, the Patriots began to disintegrate. Growing numbers returned to Georgia to resume their former lives.

After the departure of the American troops, blacks in Florida continued to harass Anglo-Floridians who had sided with the Patriots. One veteran of the Patriot cause reported that the blacks were "getting very bad, and oppressive on the Inhabitants of East Florida." Several Anglo-Floridians had attempted to seek pardon from the Spanish government for siding with the Patriots but failed to follow through after threats and harassment. Blacks promised that any Anglo-Floridians who accepted a pardon would be "governed by the Negroes if they remain in the province and that they would slap any white man's jaws who would dare say something not pleasing to them."[33] Blacks, once slaves in Georgia but now free men in Florida, asserted their own superiority.

But even with the depletion of their ranks, some veterans of the Patriot War continued their efforts to gain Florida. In June 1813, William Ashley, a justice of the Inferior Court in Camden County, wrote to Governor Mitchell decrying the conditions in Florida and southern Georgia. Ashley had participated in the initial assault on Florida but had resigned his commission in the Patriot army and returned to Georgia shortly after the attack stalled outside St. Augustine. Ashley continued to support the cause, however, by lobbying the governor to intervene on the Patriots' behalf. Ashley alerted the governor that white residents in Florida, particularly Anglo-Floridians who had supported the Patriots, faced great danger if they remained in that province.[34]

The Patriots' renewed efforts to woo Georgia's authorities to intervene on their behalf failed to persuade either Governor Mitchell or his successor, Governor Peter Early, who took office in November 1813. There were several reasons for their reluctance to involve the state in another conflict with Florida. First, state authorities objected to the new Patriot leadership. Most of the original Patriot leaders had returned home, leaving Buckner Harris in charge. Harris roamed the region and plundered property and slaves, prompting retaliatory strikes by his Indian victims on border counties in Georgia. His methods proved odious to the state authorities, who increasingly viewed the Patriots as a source of insecurity. Second, Governor Early began to doubt the Patriots' accounts of Spanish venality after he received communications from other Georgia residents who traveled to Florida and found their treatment at the hands of black troops more respectful than did the Patriots. Third, Governors Mitchell and Early were consumed by other security-related matters, most notably the outbreak of war with England in 1812 and a civil war among the Creeks.[35]

When it became clear that neither federal nor state aid would be forthcoming, Buckner Harris and a new band of Patriots crossed the St. Johns River and proceeded toward the Alachua lands, from which the Seminoles had been forced off only months earlier. Along the way, they stopped occasionally, picking up new recruits by promising them plots of land. In a process repeated thousands of times in the centuries since encounter, the Patriots plowed under the remnants of the Seminoles' existence and built their settlements on top. The process of settling the area was made easier by the work of the previous inhabitants, whose efforts at clearing and planting allowed the invaders to slide more comfortably into their lives than other pioneers. Harris unsuccessfully petitioned the U.S. authorities to annex the Patriots again in April. Harris did not have long to dwell on his failure, however, because he died the next month when a group of Indians and black scouts caught him and exacted retribution. After Harris's death, the remaining Patriots dispersed, leaving the Alachua lands and bringing to a close the Patriot War. But the main story—black opposition to American expansion—would remain a key consideration even as the scene of battle shifted.[36]

Within months of the American troops' departure from Florida in the spring of 1813, U.S. soldiers returned to the region in order to help a different set of allies and to promote the cause of American expansion. This time the "Friendly Creeks," as white Americans termed them, needed military aid. The outbreak of the so-called Creek Civil War in 1813 represented the culmination of a growing divide among the Creeks that dated back three decades, to the emergence of a propertied class within the nation. The Friendly Creeks were primarily planters and members of the propertied elite who favored the centralization of power within the Creek

Nation under the auspices of the national council. Rather than offering futile resistance against American expansion, they allied with the Americans. Their opponents within the nation, the "Redsticks," so named after the red clubs they brandished, challenged the authority of the Friendly faction.[37] White Americans sided with the Friendly Creeks in the Creek Civil War because their enemies constituted both an Indian and a black threat to white expansion.

The immediate source of the trouble began in the fall of 1812, when the Creek national council executed a number of Creek warriors as punishment for their participation in a series of raids conducted on the Georgia and Tennessee borders. The council performed the executions on the advice of Benjamin Hawkins, the U.S. Indian agent living in the Creek Nation. The national council's actions generated considerable acrimony in the nation because they violated traditional methods of Creek governance. The controversy over the executions aggravated an already tense situation. The year before, a Shawnee warrior named Tecumseh had met with leaders of the Choctaws, Cherokees, Creeks, and Seminoles in an effort to form a pan-Indian army to fight the Americans. Indian leaders in the Southeast divided over Tecumseh's message. While the Friendly faction opposed joining forces with the movement, Tecumseh's anti-Americanism resonated among some of the younger Creek warriors, who increasingly came to view the national council as illegitimate. In the spring of 1813, the situation reached a breaking point when Hawkins again pressured the national council to act after a party of Creeks led by Little Warrior murdered several white settlers in Ohio. The warriors were returning home after conspiring with northern Indians and hatching a plot against the Americans. The executioners trapped many of the warriors in a house, then set it on fire and killed the men when they fled. The executions set off a civil war within the Creek Nation. The Redsticks organized to defeat the national council and its faction.[38]

The Creeks divided over the place of blacks within their society. Creek planters, who largely supported the Friendly faction, had adopted American agricultural and racial practices. They had embraced farming by holding black slaves in bondage to labor for them on their plantations instead of laboring themselves, traditionally women's work in Creek culture. They held racist views similar to those of their white counterparts in Georgia, which they used to justify their enslavement of blacks. They were often "mestizo," having a white male ancestor. Traces of African heritage served as the primary marker of lower social status. Creek planters offered blacks no more incentive to ally with them than did white masters.[39]

Blacks, in contrast, did join the Redstick cause. The Redsticks demonstrated less inclination to consider black skin as a signifier of inferiority and welcomed black men as allies in their fight against American expansion. On their way back from Pensacola in the summer of 1813, after picking up ammunition and guns to continue their fight with the Friendly Creeks, Redstick warriors attacked settlements and then overran Fort Mims, where they killed as many as 250 of its occupants, mostly mestizoes and whites, including women and children. The Redsticks spared blacks, though they did kill some in the battle, liberating 243 from an adjacent stockade and the surrounding plantations. These men joined the Redsticks in their battle against the Americans.[40]

The Redsticks and their black allies maintained an advantage through the first engagements of the war and gained even greater support within the nation as a consequence of their success, but the tide turned with the entry of American troops, led by the Georgia militia, in late 1813 and early 1814. White Georgians feared that the Redsticks, if victorious in their war against the Friendly Creeks, would attack the Georgia frontier and undermine slavery. Americans sent a force of twenty-five hundred Georgia militiamen under the command of General John Floyd. These Georgians joined Tennessee militiamen and U.S. troops. Between November 1813 and March 1814, American forces in combination with Friendly Creek warriors destroyed Upper Creek towns, the centers of Redstick strength, killing more than fifteen hundred warriors, including more than eight hundred at Horseshoe Bend alone.[41]

The Creek Civil War came to an end. In June and July of 1814, the surviving Redsticks fled south from the nation into Florida, seeking refuge in the area around Pensacola. There, they joined other refugees of American expansion—Seminoles, red and black, and escaped slaves from Georgia—and regrouped in preparation for another stand against the advancing American armies. In a strange twist of irony, the Friendly Creeks signed a treaty with Andrew Jackson the next month to end the hostilities. Cooperation with the Americans came at a steep price. In exchange for helping them defeat the Redsticks, Jackson required the Friendly Creeks—their covictors—to cede a huge swath of their land to the United States.[42]

The War of 1812 reached Georgia's shores in the summer of 1814. When war broke out between England and the United States in 1812, white

Georgians were already preoccupied with the events in Florida. The British threat became imminent only in the summer of 1814 when reports reached Georgia that a large British fleet had set sail from Bermuda to launch an attack on the American coast. Prior to this time, the conflict had been centered in the northern United States. Georgians initially assumed that New York would be the British target. In early September, however, they discovered that the British fleet intended to attack the southern coast. Soon after, Georgians sighted British privateers offshore. The British troops threatened to undermine slavery by offering slaves a chance to escape to their freedom, just as they had during the American Revolution.

Georgians worried that without protective measures, their state, especially the institution of slavery, would be devastated by British attack. Members of the Savannah Committee for Defense warned the public that "your crops will be destroyed and your Negroes stolen." In response to the threat, authorities in Georgia began preparations to defend the coast. The governor reconvened the legislature a month early to address the impending invasion. Officials in Savannah, assuming that their city would be the point of embarkation, called for volunteers to form an armed defense. In addition, they appealed to planters to supply slaves to build fortifications to repel any attack. In mid-October, anxieties increased when officials in Savannah warned residents that they expected British vessels to shell the city. Tensions mounted as the weeks wore on without the threatened assault.[43]

White Georgians feared that the British authorities would lure their slaves away. Having just recovered from the slave depopulation caused by the Revolution, white Georgians hoped that the War of 1812 would not have a similar result. Earlier that year, on April 2, British vice admiral Alexander Cochrane, like Lord Dunmore during the Revolution, had issued an order from Bermuda offering freedom to any American slaves who left their masters. During the British raid on the Chesapeake that summer the consequences of the declaration became clear when hundreds of slaves left their masters for the uncertain promises of the British invaders. The British offered the slaves two choices: they could either join the British Army and fight their former masters or they could secure passage to a British colony, where they would receive land. Most of the slaves who fled to the British opted for relocation to a colony, but a substantial portion chose to join the struggle against the Americans. Cochrane's blatant attempt to undermine the very structure of society outraged white

Georgians. Terrified at the prospect that their slaves would take up Co-chrane's offer, white Georgians attempted to keep the information from reaching them. Though knowledge of the offer surely circulated among white Georgians, they made no mention of the declaration in their state's newspapers. The attempts at secrecy mattered little, however, as broad-sides announcing the proclamation were posted in Fernandina, on near-by Amelia Island in Spanish Florida, within one month of Cochrane's announcement.[44]

The city council in Savannah understood that any successful defense required the support of the entire population, including the black popu-lation, and offered rewards to win their allegiances. They included blacks in the city's defense, beyond their forced labor on the city's fortifications. The authorities offered a $200 reward for the person, regardless of race, who first spotted the enemy's ships. They especially targeted one category of slaves: the boatmen who transported goods down the rivers to mar-ket. But their value extended beyond mere labor. Their knowledge of the treacherous inlets of the Georgia coast would make them invaluable to an attacking navy. Their possible use by the enemy was made clear in one incident in which a British ship captured a local vessel while conducting a preliminary raid off the Georgia coast. Among their prisoners, the Brit-ish sailors captured a black pilot. They attempted to convince him to join their cause, but the pilot refused before he somehow managed to escape. The pilot then returned to Savannah, where he divulged all he knew to the authorities. After presenting the pilot's actions as heroic, the editors of the Columbia Museum endorsed granting him a "liberal" reward for his actions.[45]

In spite of white Georgians' best efforts, the British did launch an in-vasion early in 1815 and Georgia's slaves did flee to their lines. Bypassing heavily defended Savannah, the British began their assault at the south-ernmost point of the state. In mid-January, over two thousand troops, half of them white and half of them black, including slave recruits from the Chesapeake, landed on Cumberland Island. In the ensuing days, British soldiers fanned out across the region and recruited slaves to join them. Several hundred blacks responded to the call and escaped to the British headquarters. On January 28, three of the fleet's ships departed for the nearby islands of St. Simons and Jekyll, home to some of the state's largest plantations. Once there, the British found similar success in convincing black slaves to join their forces. When they returned to Cumberland Island two weeks later, several hundred additional blacks accompanied them.[46]

Planters in Georgia experienced the departure of their slaves as both economic and psychological blows. Many planters believed that their slaves had been content with their status. They were therefore shocked when not only their field slaves but also their most trusted house servants rushed to the British invaders despite uncertainties that the British would fulfill their promises of freedom. Almost all planters in the region suffered losses, but virtually every slave absconded on some of the largest plantations. On St. Simons Island, the three wealthiest planters, James Hamilton, Pierce Butler, and John Couper, lost close to 450 slaves combined.[47] To discourage runaways, white Georgians spread rumors that the British sold escaped slaves to the West Indies. Despite these rumors, the number of slaves in the British ranks only increased.

Altogether, around fifteen hundred slaves left to join the British during their two-month occupation.[48] Slaves cleared out from the plantations, though sometimes one or two older slaves remained. Those who left represented a cross-section of the slave community: families and individuals, skilled and unskilled. The exodus illustrates the slaves' overwhelming desire for freedom, of course, but the pattern of the exodus reveals something more. The differences between slaves who escaped and slaves who remained tells much about the nature of slavery in coastal Georgia and the dynamics of interracial relations. The experiences of Pierce Butler, John Couper, and Thomas Spalding demonstrate the range of experiences of slaveholders.

Of the plantations on St. Simons Island, Pierce Butler's had the reputation for the harshest discipline. Butler was an absentee planter who lived in Philadelphia. Through his overseer, Roswell King, Butler managed his plantation like a military camp. He sought to regulate all aspects of his slaves' lives. A prohibition from traveling off the plantation and a ban on marriages off the plantation were just two of Butler's many rules. Violators were severely punished with whippings. Butler's slaves surely chafed under these restrictions. In addition, Butler had recently changed his slaves' labor regime. Just that year, Butler had planted a sugar crop on his plantation. Perhaps many slaves resented the new demands imposed on them by the recent introduction of sugar cultivation. Whatever the reason, most of Butler's slaves abandoned his plantation as soon as they could. Slaves could perceive little benefit from remaining there.[49]

John Couper, also a planter on St. Simons Island, fared better in retaining his slave population. Unlike Butler, he lived on his plantation. When the British arrived, half of Couper's slaves fled. Half of the slave population represented a significant proportion but did not approach the virtual depopulation experienced by Butler. Apparently, the slaves who stayed followed the advice of Salih Bilali, one of the plantation's Muslim drivers. By all accounts, Bilali, a literate and religious man, had gained status as a leader among the slaves. Prior to coming to Georgia, he had been a slave in the Bahamas for a decade or so. Bilali convinced half of the slaves to remain by telling them that he had lived under British rule and that they had been worse masters than the Americans. Bilali's ability to convince the slaves to stay, combined with importation patterns, suggests that Couper's plantation may have included a sizable Muslim population. But Couper's slaves did not blindly follow the advice of their religious leader. They probably recognized that Couper was a relatively lenient master in comparison to masters like Butler. Possibly, Bilali, as driver, alleviated some of the harshest aspects of slavery, such as whippings. This segment of Couper's slaves may have been reluctant to risk their relatively lenient treatment for an uncertain fate at the hands of the British.[50]

Bilali probably chose his path because he had reached an acceptable accommodation with his master. Bilali and Couper shared a hierarchical view of the world. Bilali had been born into a wealthy family in West Africa, where he became familiar with African forms slavery, forms not based on the chattel principle. In Africa, slaves could achieve relatively high rank and high status. Most likely, Bilali had his own slaves before being captured by traders as a teenager. Bilali might have believed himself to be superior to the rest of the slave population because he understood himself as a Muslim first and foremost. Couper divided the world racially and considered himself as a white man to be superior to his black slaves. Despite his belief in his own superiority, Couper could recognize distinctions among his slaves and could recognize Bilali as an exception to the rule of black inferiority and therefore grant him greater authority and greater privileges. For his own part, Bilali recognized the conditions of his enslavement as being the result of unfortunate circumstances in being captured by slave traders rather than being the result of any inherent inferiority of "Africans," a racial category he would not even have recognized. For these reasons, Bilali probably faced few moral qualms in allying with Butler and convincing the slaves to stay. Butler later rewarded Bilali for his loyalty. The next year Butler placed Bilali in charge of five hundred slaves as the head driver of the Hopeton Plantation.

Thomas Spalding, on nearby Sapelo Island, fared the best of the wealthy plantation owners. Spalding did not lose a single slave during the invasion. Spalding, like Couper, had a Muslim driver, but the best explanation for Spalding's retention rate lies in his ideas about slavery and race and his style of plantation management. Before becoming a planter, Spalding had opposed slavery. On inheriting his father's slaves and property, however, he had a change of heart. In reconciling his conflicting sentiments, he attempted to ameliorate the conditions of enslavement as much as possible. He never sold a slave and he stopped purchasing slaves in 1819, suggesting distaste for the exchange of human flesh for money. In contrast to the other planters in the area, Spalding allowed his slaves far greater latitude in their everyday lives. Spalding expected his slaves to work according to specific guidelines, but he chose not to interfere with their social affairs. His slaves organized their housing along an African model. They probably practiced their religion without interference. In addition, Spalding relied on his slaves as leaders and routinely placed them in positions of authority. There were no white overseers on his plantations; instead, Spalding trusted his driver Bu Allah as his second-in-command. Spalding seems to have taken great care in ensuring Bu Allah's happiness. For example, he purchased Bu Allah's numerous sons and at least seven daughters in the Bahamas. Spalding also granted other slaves positions of authority and sought out slaves with experience directing plantations. On one hand, it could be argued that Spalding's behavior embodied the paternalistic and benevolent characteristics that apologists sentimentalized.[51] On the other, the relationship highlights blacks' abilities to carve out freedoms under slavery. In any case, when the British threatened invasion, Spalding trusted his slaves enough to arm them, relying on them to defend the plantation as well as Sapelo Island. The British forces heard about the defenders and did not even attempt to recruit among them.

In addition to revealing the depth of white Georgians' fear of insurrection and the true sentiments of slaves toward their conditions, the British attack highlighted the diversity of slavery on the Georgia coast. The planters of the region thought deeply about all matters related to agriculture; these concerns extended to their management of their slaves. Just as the planters experimented with new crops and methods of cultivation, they experimented with their labor systems in their quest for greater efficiency. At one extreme, Butler operated his plantation under military-like conditions. While it was profitable, life there was so intolerable that slaves took the first opportunity to leave, despite the uncertainty of their fate. At the other, Thomas Spalding managed his plantation and slaves on a model closer to feudal lines. Apparently, Spalding's slaves found their treatment tolerable enough to resist the British promise of safe passage and freedom. Into the second decade of the nineteenth century, therefore, a uniform standard for slave management had yet to emerge.

The Treaty of Ghent brought the end of the War of 1812, but it did not end the British presence in the Southeast. At the same time that British ships departed Cumberland Island in May 1815, British commanders Colonel Edward Nicholls and Captain George Woodbine oversaw the completion of a fort at Prospect Bluff, just miles away from the Georgia border. With six sides and thick walls, the fort was an imposing structure. What made the fort most menacing to the Americans was the composition of its defenders. The sixteen-hundred-man army stationed at the fort included Redsticks, Seminoles, whites, and at least 250 blacks, many of them runaways from Georgia. The fort's presence just over the Florida border improved the odds for a slave to make a successful escape to freedom. Slaves knew that all they had to do was reach the fort. Once there, they would be given an opportunity to take up arms against their former masters.

The story of the creation of the "Negro Fort," as white Americans dubbed it, began the summer before, when Nicholls and Woodbine landed in Florida. Armed with the same decree granting freedom to runaway slaves used with great effect by Cockburn in the War of 1812, they organized an interracial army south of the Georgia border to attack the Americans. They mobilized the Redstick survivors and Seminole Indians to travel the region and recruit slaves. The British contributed three hundred Royal Marines from the West Indian Brigade.[52]

The Negro Fort became an even greater threat in the wake of Andrew Jackson's November 1814 attack on the Redsticks and escaped slaves serving under British command at Pensacola. Once confronted with a sizable American force, they fled to the Negro Fort. These reinforcements transformed the fort into a serious challenge to the economic and social stability of southwest Georgia. Planters feared the fort because as it grew in stature it attracted more slave runaways. The Spanish authorities in Florida, a spent force only able to control St. Augustine and its immediate surroundings, could offer no aid to the Americans. In the rest of the region, the interracial army serving at the Negro Fort constituted the most significant obstacle to American expansion settlement.

The actions of Nicholls and Woodbine in building and manning the Negro Fort outraged commentators and officials in Georgia. Benjamin Hawkins, the American agent among the Creeks, railed against the British for establishing the fort and "garrisoning it with negros and Indians and making it an asylum for runaway negros belonging to people of the United States."[53] In fact, he knew firsthand the potential disruption in plantation discipline that the fort could cause. Working in concert with Seminole warriors, five of his slaves had fled from his plantation.

In addition, Hawkins feared that Nicholls would unite Indians and blacks against white Georgians. Hawkins believed "he is set to free the negros, compel the Americans to restore back the lands to the Indians, and make everything submit to him as he marches along." Hawkins compared Nicholls to William Bowles, his principal antagonist of the previous decade. Hawkins believed Nicholls intended to incite insurrection among the region's slaves, just as Bowles had done in the late 1790s. He also accused Nicholls of meddling in his fiefdom and regarded him as a potential rival for power within the Creek Nation. Nicholls, like Bowles, took it upon himself to serve as an interlocutor, or interloper as Hawkins would term it, on behalf of the Seminoles. Hawkins and Nicholls squabbled over who really represented the Indians of the Southeast. The American feared that Nicholls could sway the Indians to his side, a worrisome eventuality for the United States. Several Friendly chiefs who had signed the 1814 treaty with Jackson had begun expressing second thoughts about their decision. Deceived by the Americans and disenchanted with their relationship, they turned increasingly to the British, who promised much more, including a return to the 1811 borders.[54]

Georgia's slaves took the opportunity for freedom offered by the Negro Fort. Within just a few months of the erection of the fort, in the spring of 1815, slaves fled from their masters and were welcomed by Woodbine and Nicholls. One American spy reported that "the British are determined to keep the negros."[55] Escapes from Georgia plantations surged the following spring of 1816 as blacks capitalized on the opportunity for freedom brought by the change in season. Twenty-four slaves, for example, escaped from the vicinity of Hartford, a Georgia border town, to claim their freedom at the Negro Fort.[56] Georgia planters offered little that could compete with British promises of liberation. Once at the fort, these former slaves, now freemen, armed themselves for defense against their former masters.

Whites monitored the happenings at the Negro Fort and grew increasingly alarmed. Timothy Barnard, a white trader in the Creek Nation, warned in February 1816 that "if that fort is not broke up soon, the citizens of Georgia will lose a number of their negros before the coming summer is over."[57] Georgia planters complained that their slaves escaped to the Negro Fort, and not just any slaves. General Floyd noted that "many of the most active, and intelligent male slaves, have fled from their Owners."[58] Slaveholders feared that if the fort continued undisturbed, only the most feeble and elderly slaves would remain. More alarmingly, an American spy related that the slaves "have joined them as soldiers and they have given them their freedom."[59]

Governor Early kept informed about the situation at the Negro Fort through his correspondence with Hawkins. They shared a mutual interest in preserving peace on the Georgia-Florida border. They knew that the presence of the Negro Fort impeded settlement near the border and destabilized the institution of slavery in Georgia. The increased frequency of their correspondence mirrored the increased severity of the situation. In each message, Hawkins elevated his level of urgency as he raised his estimation of the total number of black soldiers manning the fort.[60]

Hawkins recognized that Georgia troops offered the best defense against an attack from the Negro Fort, since assistance from Washington inevitably would be slow in coming. In April 1815, he warned Early that should the Georgia militia not mobilize additional men to counter the threat, the residents of the state's southern frontier might find "themselves in a perilous situation."[61] By mid-February of the following year, Hawkins estimated that the number of blacks at the Negro Fort had reached 350. He argued that unless "some decisive steps are taken to correct this abuse" Georgia would have much to fear.[62] Governor Early almost always acquiesced, but he could contribute only so much and still retain sufficient troops to defend the state's frontier.

In southern Georgia, the situation appeared bleak. In April 1816, General Floyd joined the chorus, urging the governor to intervene. He complained that the fort had grown to "such magnitude, as to demand the adoption, of decisive, and energetic measures" to uproot it. He lamented that the "seeds of Emancipation are already sown, and are taking strong hold in a Situation so well Calculated to encourage its growth." Moreover, he added, "the facility with which escapes are capable of being made, gives such encouragement to the practice as to render its frequency alarming." Floyd advised Governor David Mitchell to destroy the fort and recapture its inhabitants. The threat of an interracial army proved too intolerable to fully articulate. Floyd could not bring himself to identify explicitly the interracial soldiers mobilizing at the Negro Fort. His description of these men rendered them almost inhuman. He referred to the army as "composed of Materials capable of becoming a formidable Engine in the hands of an Open or disguised foreign Enemy from their intimate acquaintance with the local Situation of our Country, without interruption they will accumulate Strength."[63]

Hawkins knew that Georgia's authorities could not spare enough soldiers to destroy the Negro Fort while still garrisoning the region's numerous forts and protecting its border, so he recruited Friendly Creeks as slave catchers. He recognized that "something must be done, and very soon, or Georgia will be despoiled of all their negros on their frontiers." He suggested to the Friendly Creeks that recovering Georgia's slaves from the Negro Fort would ingratiate them with the American authorities. In April 1816, Friendly Creeks began preparations to assault the Negro Fort and to recover escaped American slaves. In his instructions to the Friendly Creeks, Hawkins warned: "Act justly towards your white neigbours and remain peaceable and friendly, and you have nothing to fear. If you do not, you will see settlements making and heming you in towards Alachua. Get rid of the negros without delay or their masters will be after them and involve you in difficulties. If they come, you will lose more land. If you deliver them up, their masters will stay at home and be peaceable and friendly and your paths of peace and trade will be free and open."[64] If the Friendly Creeks followed orders, they would be rewarded. If they did not, they would be punished. The Friendly Creeks asked only for provisions from the Americans, but Hawkins also offered a $50 bounty for each American slave on delivery.[65] By the beginning of May, the Friendly Creeks had completed their preparations for battle. Hawkins vowed to "take by force the negros."[66]

Meanwhile, federal authorities grew alarmed at the situation on the border. In the summer of 1816, after mobilizing a sufficiently large number of troops, the Americans adopted the offensive. General Andrew Jackson ordered the destruction of the Negro Fort, which he accused of "stealing and enticing away our negroes."[67] Colonel Duncan Clinch, with a company of 116 men and a force of Friendly Creeks led by William McIntosh and reinforced by two armed American vessels, arrived at the Negro Fort. Surveying the fortification, they confronted an impressive edifice—a large structure with a "parapet fifteen feet high and eighteen thick." Defended by ten cannon, the fort was situated on a beautiful and commanding bluff, with a river in front, a large creek just below, a swamp in the rear, and a small creek just above, all of which made it largely immune to artillery. The Americans dispatched a patrol to probe for weaknesses, but the effort turned fatal when soldiers from the fort ambushed them, killing all but one.[68]

The Americans suffered another indignity when they sent a delegation of Friendly Creeks to request the fort's surrender. The defenders, led by their commander, Garçon, a runaway slave from the Spanish, scoffed at the offer and abused the delegation before sending them on their way with a message: Garçon, belying his name, promised manly action to destroy any ship that approached the fort and swore he would blow the fort up rather than surrender. Finding little success with assaults by artillery and by infantry, Clinch directed the boats to fire on the fortification on the morning of July 27. Like earlier American attempts, the initial volleys had little effect as they bounced harmlessly away. The fifth shot, however, proved lucky. The Americans fired a hotshot, a cannonball heated red, that struck the fort's magazine, causing an enormous explosion and massive carnage.[69] Clinch claimed that he killed far more of the fort's inhabitants than he most likely did. Many blacks had left the fort in the months preceding the assault. Faced with the American invasion and with the prospect of defeat and reenslavement, they fled to the Suwanee towns, to live in black settlements surrounding Bowlegs, and to Tampa Bay, another black Seminole stronghold.[70] Those who stayed, like Garçon, had determined to make a stand for their freedom or die trying.

Clinch valued the booty he acquired from the Negro Fort at $200,000. Among the contents Clinch reportedly found inside were five to six hundred pounds of powder and three thousand weapons.[71] But the true value of the fort's destruction lay in its symbolism rather than the sum of the property seized. With the destruction of the Negro Fort, the Americans rendered the territory safe for the expansion of settlement and for the expansion of slavery. Denied an avenue to freedom on their doorstep, slaves would have to find new methods and new destinations to escape bondage.

The destruction of the Negro Fort marked the disappearance of a beacon for black freedom, but it did not bring an end to the violence on the Georgia-Florida border. Georgian and American troops had fought against blacks and Indians in the Patriot War, the War of 1812, the Creek Civil War, and finally at the Negro Fort. Each time, the military power of the Americans had defeated their black and red enemies. But each time, blacks and Indians regrouped to continue their resistance against American slavery and American expansion. The last chapter of interracial armed resistance, the Seminole War of 1817 and 1818, pitted black and red Seminoles, who had been involved in the Patriot War and the Negro Fort, against the Americans.[72]

The renewed conflict in the border region began when a group of whites, remnants from the Patriots, conducted raids on Seminole villages in the months after the demolition of the Negro Fort, plundering goods and stealing cattle.[73] In the process, they killed several Seminoles. Though aggrieved, the Seminoles did not immediately seek revenge. Instead, they asked the Georgia authorities to enact justice against the murderers. The Seminoles waited in vain. By February 1817, their patience had grown thin. Whites had killed their people and they expected justice. When justice through the American legal system did not materialize, they resorted to more traditional methods of exacting retribution. A group of Seminole warriors attacked several Georgia farms and plantations in Camden County. During the raid, they killed the wife and two children of a man they believed had been involved in the murders. In response to the raids, white settlers abandoned their farms and plantations and relocated to more settled areas. This flight represented a victory for the Seminoles, who had been disgruntled over continued white encroachments upon their lands.[74]

When the Americans demanded justice, the Seminoles refused to appease them. In the wake of the Seminole raids on the Georgia frontier, General Edmund Pendleton Gaines, the U.S. Army commander at Fort Gaines, instructed several Indian towns to surrender the murderers. The responses he received were not what he expected or desired. The chief of the Mikasuki did not deign to reply. The chief of the Ten Towns reversed the equation. Instead of promising to deliver the murderers, he demanded three additional deaths of whites to even the tally between the Indians and the whites. The chief of Fowl Town warned the Americans "not to cut another stick on the east side of the Flint River."[75] Even though the Negro Fort had been destroyed and even though their Creek allies had been defeated, the Seminoles refused to cower before the white man.

The Seminole settlements attracted large numbers of slave runaways from Georgia. Gaines, for example, charged that the towns harbored "many of my black people."[76] Unfortunately for slaveholders, the Seminole towns on the southwestern border were accessible to the region of

Georgia witnessing the largest growth in the slave population. In addition, some of the black residents of the Negro Fort had fled before its destruction. Americans estimated that approximately six hundred black warriors and an equal number of Indians drilled at Suwanee. According to reports, these blacks yearned for vengeance against Americans in retaliation for their defeat at the Negro Fort the year before. They welcomed another opportunity to meet the Americans in battle.[77]

General Gaines used the Seminoles' harboring of runaway slaves as a justification for an American offensive. One white Georgian explained that "the refuge which fugitive Slaves from this State, and more particularly from its Southern borders have from time, to time, found" among the Seminoles has "long since been Viewed" by slave owners as "a Serious, and growing Evil."[78] Georgians had targeted the maroon societies on the Georgia-Florida border during and after the Patriot movement of 1812, but they had repeatedly failed to destroy them. They succeeded in forcing blacks to flee, but they proved unable to eliminate them. The escaped slaves had simply moved to another location. To convince Georgia's Governor William Rabun of the necessity for intervention, Gaines emphasized the reports of hundreds of blacks living in the Seminole towns. He reminded the governor that these black insurrectionists plotted within 120 miles of Fort Gaines and Georgia's border. Indeed, Gaines emphasized that their numbers increased with "the addition of every runaway from Georgia able to get to them." According to Gaines's sources among the Friendly Creeks, the British were once again active in the Southeast; they had promised to send British forces to assist the "hostile party" and blacks in their struggle against the Americans.[79]

General Gaines naively boasted that he would easily triumph over the Seminoles. He arrogantly explained that "I feel little faith in their threats, and believe their numbers to be overrated." Nevertheless, he acknowledged that he might need more help against the reported twenty-seven hundred warriors. With these additional troops, he bragged that he could "put an end to the little war in this quarter, in the course of this or the next month."[80] Gaines greatly underestimated the strength and resolve of the black and red Seminoles arrayed against him.

In the beginning, it appeared as though Gaines's boast would come true; the Americans won two initial skirmishes. But the Seminoles emerged victorious from the third, a far more deadly strike. At the end of November, a party of warriors estimated at five hundred ambushed a ship carrying about fifty troops and military supplies from Alabama as it sailed up the Apalachicola River. The Seminoles killed almost everyone on board, including soldiers' wives, allowing only six men, four of them wounded, to escape. The incident shocked Gaines and forced him to request additional help from Georgia. The governor sent two additional brigades commanded by Generals Thomas Glascock and Francis Hopkins to the frontier, where they met Gaines and 250 friendly warriors from the Chehaw village who had agreed to fight against the Seminoles.[81]

Even with an enlarged force, however, the Americans proved unable to defeat the Seminoles and only succeeded in emboldening them further. Gaines complained that "some of their Chiefs have triumphantly asserted that we cannot beat them! that we never have beaten them, except when we had 'Red People to help us.'" He noted that they "*must be beaten before we can reasonably calculate upon peace.*"[82] The Seminoles and the Redsticks continued their attacks on Georgia settlements and expanded their targets to include travelers heading for Alabama.

By making the road unsafe for travel, the Indians succeeded in slowing the invasion of Alabama and sending settlers into a panic. Residents in the counties of Wayne, Camden, and Glynn felt "much alarmed" by the state of affairs on Georgia's southern border. Conditions all along the southern frontier between Trader's Hill and Hartford had deteriorated to the point that most families had already relocated to the "more thickly peopled settlements for safety." Those remaining on the contested land would "soon follow their example" unless they received assistance. "Such is the state of alarm in this county," one resident complained, that "more than one half of Camden county will be deserted" if the authorities did not put a halt to the Seminole raids. In fact, the situation was so serious that it prevented county officials from holding court in the spring term.[83]

With the tide of the war sliding toward the Indians, the federal government decided to intervene. In January 1818, General Andrew Jackson received an order to muster the Tennessee state militia and proceed to the Georgia-Florida border. Instead of following the order, Jackson chose to mobilize not the state militia, but a group of men from the plantation districts of western Tennessee who had fought with him on prior interventions into the area. Jackson also secured the aid of the Friendly Creeks.[84] Like the Americans, the Friendly Creeks had lost their slave property to the marauding Seminole warriors. After meeting with white Georgians and Friendly Creeks in March, the army, numbering over three thousand soldiers, advanced across the border into Florida. Jackson and the Americans easily routed the defenders at St. Mark's in Florida, most having fled upon learning the size of the approaching American force. Meanwhile McIntosh and his Friendly Creek warriors attacked the Mikasuki towns, though most residents had likewise fled rather than confront the approaching Indian army. Before rendezvousing with the others, the Friendly Creeks, along with some Georgians and Tennesseans, killed thirty-eight Indians and took a large number of prisoners. In addition, they razed the Mikasuki towns and the surrounding black satellite towns and stole everything they could carry.[85]

The American soldiers and Friendly warriors joined forces again in mid-April and proceeded to the Suwanee towns, which had been the goal from the outset. One British observer put it best: "The main drift of the Americans is to destroy the black population of Suwany."[86] Bowlegs, the chief of the town, and his followers had fled to the area following the Georgian and Tennessean raid on their homes in Alachua in February 1813. The Americans led by Jackson and the Friendly Creeks led by McIntosh attacked the Suwanee towns in April 1818, but as was the case in the earlier raids, residents of the towns had been warned in advance, allowing them to move their families and property to safer locations. When the battle actually did take place it was anticlimactic. Vastly outnumbered and outgunned by their foes, the black and red Seminoles opted to flee after a brief skirmish. The American and Indian invaders destroyed the villages and seized all objects of value, but they failed to kill more than a handful of their opponents. With the Suwanee towns destroyed, the Georgians turned toward home on April 20 to be mustered out.[87]

White Georgians had not been strong enough by themselves to defeat the Indians on their southern border. White Tennesseans from the western plantation districts demonstrated solidarity with white Georgians by coming to their aid when they seemed poised for defeat. Friendly Indians sided with the Americans to affirm their allegiances to the new slavery-based order. With these defeats, the last armed force blocking American expansion was removed. Finally, the hostile Indians on the border had been pacified, opening the way for the spread of slavery. This war marked the end of the refuge for slaves on the southern border and consequently the end of the interracial alliance blocking the expansion of slavery. But the involvement of the Friendly Indians, though strained, demonstrated that the interracial alliance to extend slavery had not yet shattered.

The thrill of victory proved short-lived, as the Chehaw massacre, which occurred at the tail end of the war, shifted attention away from the success of the American expedition against the Seminoles. In late April

1818, about the time of Jackson's raid on the Suwanee settlements, Governor Rabun used the confusion occasioned by the war to order Captain Obediah Wright to destroy two villages, Hoponnee and Phelemmee, which he blamed for sending warriors in multiple attacks on the Georgia frontier. Commanding 270 Georgia militiamen, Wright left immediately to carry out his orders, but became hopelessly lost. When they finally reoriented themselves, they had only a couple of days before their enlistments expired. Wright and his men attacked the Chehaw town on April 23. Claiming to have destroyed all the buildings and killed forty or fifty of the village residents, including twenty-three warriors, Wright and his men bragged about their military exploits and proudly displayed their war booty on their return. In his report to Governor Rabun, Wright judged the mission a success, describing the assault and the efforts of his men in glowing terms. "The conduct of the officers and soldiers on this occasion," he praised, "was highly characteristic of the patriotism and bravery of the Georgians in general."[88]

There were several problems with Wright's story. First and foremost, the Chehaw village had been friendly. Wright's men lived to brag of their "patriotism and bravery" because the Chehaw men had been off fighting with Jackson and the American troops against the Seminoles and runaways on the Florida-Georgia border. In need of rations and extra power, Jackson and his troops had passed through the towns on their way south, gathered food and men, and chosen not to harm them. Second, reports of individuals who saw the aftermath of the raid contradicted Wright's account. They depicted the incident at the Chehaw town in a more grisly light. Rather than slaying twenty-odd warriors, Wright and his men had butchered six old men and an old woman. Another Georgia officer who happened upon the scene of carnage shortly after Wright's departure described it as "one of the most infamous outrages that ever disgraced the human form." He accused the perpetrators of behaving as a "band more barbarous than the most savage Indians." Survivors reported that "a party of mounted men had entered their town with a white flag and fired on them, while the hand of friendship was extended to them." After suffering a wound when the troops fired their first round, the town's old chief fell to his knees and begged for mercy. He told them he "wished no war," but his pleas did not deter their "inhumanity." The troops fired another round at him, and "after they had murdered him, the ornaments were torn from his ears." Wright and his men then burned "all their houses" and "plundered everything they could lay their hands on" before making "a precipitate retreat."[89]

When Jackson learned of the raid on the Chehaw village, he was livid. Jackson consoled the victims and their families: "I cannot adequately express my feelings on the outrageous and inhuman attack of captain Wright." Jackson expressed regret, but he cautioned the survivors against retaliation and further bloodshed. Warning them to leave the matter in his hands, Jackson assured the victims and their families that he would find and punish the men responsible for the raid. For Jackson, the connection was closer than usual. McIntosh, the Coweta leader and his trusted military ally, lost an uncle at the hands of the attackers. Jackson ordered Wright to stand trial, but Wright secured a writ of habeas corpus and gained his release from prison. The writ characterized Jackson's orders against Wright as "informal" and containing "no specific charges." Outraged, Jackson wrote to Governor Rabun calling for Wright's rearrest and extradition to Fort Hawkins. Rabun acquiesced to part of Jackson's demands. He arranged Wright's arrest on May 29, but rather than deliver him to Jackson, Rabun confined Wright in Georgia until he received instructions from the president. In a message that Rabun deemed "as inflammatory and indecorous, as it is unbecoming a gentlemen and a soldier," Jackson demanded that Rabun reverse his decision. Rabun, however, remained steadfast. Any fears Jackson may have entertained about the reliability of the Georgia officials proved well founded when Wright apparently escaped from prison on July 27 while waiting for the president to make his decision. Rabun's reward of $500 did not accomplish Wright's recapture.[90]

Like Jackson, many prominent whites in Georgia expressed shock at the brutality committed by Wright and his men. The editors of the *Augusta Chronicle* denounced "The burning and massacre of the Chehaw town" as "one among the most infamous transactions that ever blackened the page of humanity." They argued that those responsible for the attack should face a military tribunal and deserved the most "severe reprehension," an opinion shared by their counterparts at the *Georgia Journal*. The governor quickly moved to distance himself from the massacre, citing his order, which called for an attack on two other villages, as proof of his innocence. The General Assembly passed a resolution condemning the attack.[91]

But after the initial outrage died down, any appearance of unanimity on the matter dissipated as Georgians divided over the legitimacy of placing white men, Americans, on trial for killing Indians, regardless of their status as "friendly" or not. After all, many believed, today's friendly

Georgia's Counties–1820

Indian was merely tomorrow's enemy. Originating in counties on the southwest border and interior of Georgia, these sentiments reflected a less sanguine assessment of the presence of Indians on the frontier. This group included planters from the southern section of the state as well as yeomen from the west. In contrast to the vitriolic denunciations made against Wright by their counterparts in the Savannah and Augusta newspapers, the editors of the *Milledgeville Reflector* articulated a more nuanced analysis. They recognized that Wright's actions may have been wrong, but ultimately they placed the blame on Jackson. They could not condone the arrest and imprisonment, in irons no less, of a white man for actions taken against an Indian. In short, they concluded, the decision to proceed with the prosecution of Wright was "unjustifiable" and "irrational."[92]

The debate over Wright illustrates a rift among whites in Georgia over the nature of race and the structure of race relations. White Georgians all agreed that Indians were not the equals of white men, but they held different ideas about hierarchy. Was it absolute or graded? Those indignant at Wright's behavior tended to be found in the older sections of the state. Like Jackson, who vigorously denounced the Chehaw massacre, they recognized distinctions among Indians as well as among people of African descent. Those Georgians knew that the Chehaws did not represent an obstacle to the expansion of America or the expansion of slavery. Those Georgians saw no contradiction in allowing nonwhites to participate in the defense of Georgia's slave-based society. The tens of thousands of white newcomers to the state, like Wright, came from the mid-Atlantic and the North and did not share the racial views of Georgia's traditional elite. Wright and his supporters did not possess that kind of respect for Indians or blacks, regardless of their status. With their enlistment almost expired and their chance for a fight almost gone, Wright and his men did not think twice when the opportunity arose to sack a town and obtain war trophies. They killed the Chehaws for sport.

Through the Patriot War, the War of 1812, the Creek Civil War, and the Seminole War, white Georgians waged a crusade against escaped slaves and their Indian allies on their southern border. Though the names of these conflicts grant little recognition to the roles of blacks, white Georgians at the time centered their fears and anxieties on the vision of armed blacks combating slavery. In striking out for freedom and arming themselves against their former masters, escaped slaves threatened the stability of slavery in Georgia and undermined the notion of blacks' inherent suitability for enslavement. In raiding and destroying black settlements and attacking blacks' allies, white Georgians eradicated the threat of black rebellion from their borders. Armed might by state and federal officials secured the safety and longevity of the institution of slavery.

The significance of these military engagements cannot be calculated simply in terms of casualties, numbers of forts destroyed, or value of war plunder. While battling free blacks and their Indian allies, white Georgians settled important questions over the place of nonwhites within Georgian society. As they extended their state's sovereignty over the recently ceded Creek lands and as cotton began to contest rice's dominance as the state's chief crop, white Georgians would export their vision of slavery and their ideas about race into the state's upcountry.

6

MAKING GEORGIA BLACK
AND WHITE, 1818–1838

The defeat of the Seminoles in 1818 brought peace to the southwestern frontier. White Georgians had long claimed the territory as their own, and now they could finally begin settling the area. Indians, however, remained on the lands white Georgians had long coveted. Although historians typically have presented white Georgians in monolithic terms, they were divided along class and regional lines and over their thoughts concerning the proper treatment of the Indians, their abilities to assimilate into American culture, the modes of their removal, and their place in society.[1] Between 1820 and 1840, the white population in Georgia exploded, doubling from 189,570 to 407,695. Although some of the new arrivals came as families, the new immigrants were mostly single, landless men, who flocked to the periphery of the state, to the counties bordering the Creek and Cherokee Indians. These settlers called for the immediate expulsion of the Indians, through violent means if necessary. Georgia's dramatic demographic changes affected the state's politics, which in turn shaped how the state government dealt with Indians. The population explosion in the 1820s enabled upcountry residents to control a much greater share of power in Georgia. As a result, the machinery of government increasingly represented their views and marginalized Indians' allies among the traditional elite. The situation resulted in a realignment of state politics, as governors and state legislators retooled their message for an evolving constituency. To appeal to upcountry residents, politicians in Georgia adopted a more aggressive approach to western lands and Indians. During this period of enormous population growth, Georgia became a white man's republic.

Land cessions and population growth had a symbiotic relationship. Each land cession triggered a wave of immigrants to the frontier. As the area came under cultivation, planters moved in, raising land prices and pushing yeoman to seek cheaper land beyond the stipulated border. Settlers, citing overcrowding, continually appealed for more land. The promise of prosperity from cotton cultivation exacerbated the trend. In the wake of the Treaty of Fort Jackson in 1814, Georgians pushed for further land cessions from the Creeks, resulting in a series of treaties—in 1818, 1821, 1826, and 1827—that removed the Creeks from their territory within Georgia's claimed boundary. Upcountry settlers achieved these successes as a result of their increasing political power within the state.

White Georgians in the 1810s and 1820s targeted the Creeks for several reasons. The Creek lands were rich and fertile and desirable for cotton cultivation. Moreover, white Georgians considered the Creeks savage, particularly in comparison to the Cherokees, who had made such headway in the civilizing program. With a few exceptions, the Creeks had largely failed to embrace the western way of life. They had fought against Americans in the French and Indian War, the American Revolution, and the War of 1812 but had lost each time. They had blocked American expansion in the years after the Revolution. And white Georgians were not a forgiving people. Having feared the Creeks for so long, whites were not in the mood to treat the Creeks kindly. The Creeks' removal from the state prompted little debate in Georgia. Whether planters or frontiersmen, virtually all white Georgians endorsed annexing the Creeks' lands as the price of defeat. They had posed a formidable enough foe to limit western migration in the first decades after the Revolution, but now white Georgians took their revenge. The Creeks fit white settlers' ideas of savage Indians whose fates embraced only one of two options: removal or extinction.[2]

For the thousands of men who came to Georgia in the first three decades of the nineteenth century, there were no "friendly Indians" or distinctions between tribes and villages. The migrants arrived with little prior contact with Indians and no exposure to the complexities of Indian-white relations. For them, the past had no relevance. It did not matter that the Friendly Creeks had helped the Americans subdue the Redsticks and the Seminoles. It did not matter that some areas of the Creek Nation had come to accept the tenets of the civilizing plan. It did not matter that some of the prominent members of the tribe had familial connections to members of Georgia's white elite. All that mattered was that the Indians occupied some of the most fertile land in the South, and for this reason they had to be removed. The arrival of these immigrants transformed a minority opinion into the majority opinion.

By the 1810s, in the wake of the treaty with the Creeks in 1814 and the resultant immigration to the state, the older sections of the state, particularly the lowcountry, began to realize the dissipation of their power. The waning power of the lowcountry became fully clear in 1816. For the first time, in 1816, the congressional delegation from Georgia included no coastal representatives. In each session of the U.S. Congress since the nation's founding, Georgia's delegation included at least one resident from the state's coastal region, usually from Chatham. Indeed, in many early sessions coastal residents comprised most of those elected. Georgia's most established and well-known lawyers called the region home, and the coast also benefited from the at-large electoral system, especially after the population of other regions of the state grew in the late eighteenth and early nineteenth centuries. The 1816 congressional election demonstrated that the coast had lost its ability to select the state's representatives because it could not compete with the numerical superiority of Georgia's western counties. The coastal elite responded to evidence of the changing demographic and political conditions of the state with bitterness and anger. The *Savannah Republican* editors criticized "our Western Brethren" for viewing lowcountry residents as a "distinct people, not as brethren of the same family." By electing only congressmen from the interior, westerners allowed their "jealousy of the riches and commercial importance of this District" to triumph over the interests of the state as a whole. Lowcountry residents condemned the west's "sectional partialities," which rendered residents of the older parts of the state "insignificant and unimportant."[3] For the first time, coastal elites feared they would become passive spectators in state politics. The gubernatorial election in Georgia in 1819 further underscored the growing power of the interior of the state. Following Governor Rabun's sudden death, John Clark, an upcountry militia general, won the election for governor (after two failed attempts, in 1813 and 1817), beating his rival by thirteen votes, 73 to 60, in the General Assembly tally. The *Savannah Republican* noted that the "election was very warm and bitter on both sides and the result not dreamed of twelve months ago."[4] Clark's victory represented a stunning upset and came as a shock to most observers, who assumed that his opponent and longtime nemesis, Colonel George Troup, would win easily. Troup, a planter from Savannah, along with William Crawford, headed a powerful party, which had often allied upcountry and lowcountry planters.[5]

Governor John Clark benefited from the rise of the upcountry and personified and represented its interests. Clark was the son of Elijah Clark, the founder of the failed Trans-Oconee Republic. He was his father's son. He had fought alongside his father in the Revolutionary War. Like Elijah, he was a frontiersman with little education, rude manners, and a disdain for aristocrats. Also like his father, Clark represented the interests of frontiersmen and western farmers. After his father's death in 1799, John Clark continued the struggle. Clark's victory in the gubernatorial race represented the culmination of the struggle that his father had begun when he arrived in Georgia on the eve of the War of Independence.[6] Upon assuming power, Governor Clark promoted an agenda that benefited the poor and western farmers, those who had long felt aggrieved by the state government's failure to meet their needs. He called on the General Assembly to establish free schools, lamenting that the state's "literary institutions" had failed in their professed objective—to enlighten the populace. He argued that the limited educational opportunities for the state's common folk perpetuated the dominance of the planters. He also urged the General Assembly to adopt internal improvement projects. The lack of adequate transportation to bring crops to market from the upcountry hindered its economic development. Clark repeatedly called for the construction of better water and road routes to upcountry markets. He understood that the successful settlement of the interior was contingent on the ability of farmers to transport their goods to markets on the coast. A steady flow of settlers to the interior increased the potential number of voters for Clark and his party.[7]

As the first governor from the frontier, Clark's most important goal was obtaining Indian lands and the property taken by Indians. Of the various issues that divided the settlers on the frontier and the residents of the older, settled areas, land hunger still stood as the greatest rift. Clark's primary concern was pushing the federal authorities to adhere to the promises made in the Compact of 1802, which he and other settlers believed obligated the government to remove the Indians from the boundaries claimed by the state as quickly as possible. Other governors had advocated the implementation of the treaty's terms, but none as relentlessly as Clark. At the governor's urging, the General Assembly issued a memorial to the president complaining about the federal government's refusal to fulfill the terms of the compact. The federal government had secured two land cessions from the Creeks, the first after the Treaty of Fort Jackson in 1814 and the second in 1818, both of which they found unacceptable. The memorialists dismissed the Indian cessions as a "tract of country scarcely sufficient to invite our attention."[8] Heeding the continuing complaints from Georgia, President James Monroe authorized federal commissioners to negotiate the Treaty of Indian Springs in 1821. Under the treaty, the Creeks, represented by William McIntosh and other chiefs from the Lower towns, ceded a parcel of land located between the Ocmulgee and Flint rivers.[9] The Indian Springs cession brought a renewed sense of hope to upcountry Georgians. They believed that their troubles with the federal authorities were coming to a close.

To distribute the lands gained through the Indian Springs cession, Governor Clark implemented a system that would benefit poor farmers. In conjunction with his agenda of promoting the interests of those who had long been denied justice, Clark called for the land to be distributed by lottery. With "no hesitation," he touted the system "as being calculated to do equal justice to the poor and to the rich, and to insure a speedy population of the country." Some of the land would remain for public purposes; its sale would be used to fund internal improvements and the free schools, which "are beneficial to all."[10] Every male white citizen eighteen or older was entitled to enter the draw; those with dependents were eligible to draw twice. Widows and orphans were also eligible. To make sure that the lottery could not be manipulated to benefit speculators, the General Assembly divided the land into 202-acre plots and passed a law mandating a $100 fine for selling lottery tickets without the government's authorization.[11]

Clark's program to benefit the interior proved a politically wise strategy. He won his reelection bid in 1821, once again against the low-country candidate, Savannah's George Troup. In his second term, Clark continued to push for additional land cessions. Under his authority, the General Assembly passed resolutions in 1821 and 1822 urging the federal authorities to pursue the rest of the state's land claims under the Compact of 1802.[12]

In his second term, Clark concentrated his efforts on a democratic reformation of the electoral process. From the Revolution onward, a protracted controversy over representation had divided the residents of the state. As the state's population expanded, the issue grew in importance.

Upcountry residents struggled for greater control over the machinery of government while those in the older sections of the state, particularly the coastal region, struggled to maintain a semblance of the power they once held.[13] The attempt to further democratize the electoral system focused on altering the method of electing the governor. Since the Revolution, the state's legislative body had selected the governor. The reform movement sought to grant that right to the people instead. Toward the end of his second term, Clark supported the direct election of the governor. "The privilege of choosing those who rule over us," Clark argued, "is one of the most inestimable rights of a free people, and the surest guarantee of their liberties." That this privilege had been "unrighteously withheld" from the citizens of Georgia represented a travesty of justice.[14] Though Clark's declaration may have reflected the true feelings of the citizenry, his support for electoral reform did not preclude other, less selfless reasons for advocating the changes. He surely knew that by altering the voting system residents of the upcountry, those settlers and western farmers from whom he garnered his support, would gain greater control of the state's political machinery. Though it took several years, the attempt to secure direct elections of the governor succeeded. Because the bill warranted a constitutional change, it required the approval of two successive legislative assemblies. Direct elections became a central issue in the gubernatorial election campaign in 1823. Clark and his supporters prevailed, and the bill to alter the constitution to allow direct elections for the governor passed the General Assembly in 1823, though complete victory would have to wait until the following session of the legislature in 1824. Before the gubernatorial reform went into effect, George Troup, in his third attempt, defeated the Clark faction candidate, Matthew Talbot, in a close race (84 to 81) to become Georgia's next governor.

The rising power of the upcountry combined with the likelihood that electoral reforms would soon be passed in Georgia spurred Clark's successor, Troup, to take a firm stand on the Indian question.[15] Normally elites from the older sections of the state exhibited more moderate stances on the Indian question. William H. Crawford, who along with Troup headed the Troup-Crawford Party, exemplified this approach toward the Indians. He favored preserving Indians' rights to their lands. Arguing that the "utter extinction of the Indian race must be abhorrent to the feelings of an enlightened and benevolent nation," he suggested that it should be "the true policy and earnest desire of the Government to draw its savage neighbors within the pale of civilization." To preserve "civil liberty and social happiness," he advised, "let intermarriages between them and the whites be encouraged by the Government." He concluded that it "will redound more to the national honor to incorporate, by a humane and benevolent policy, the natives of our forests in the great American family of freemen, than to receive with open arms the fugitives of the old world, whether their flight has been the effect of their crimes or their virtues." Crawford envisioned a future for the Indians within Georgia's borders, more so than for white foreigners.[16] The growing population in the up-country, however, had no patience for such views. Troup's actions during his term would demonstrate his break from his party's views. After the fall of 1824, when the General Assembly passed the bill mandating direct elections for governor, Troup would need to secure the support of the general population in order to win a second term. Consequently, he embraced Creek removal to broaden his appeal beyond his traditional power base in the older section of the state.

White Georgians in the upcountry feared that the federal government had little interest in removing the Indians. History suggested as much. President Monroe's address to Congress in 1823 on the question of Indian removal explained that he wished that the Indians could be relocated west of the Mississippi but that unless the Indians agreed, his hands were tied. He asserted that he needed the "special sanction" of Congress and did not have the power to forcibly remove the Indians. Monroe strongly disagreed with Georgians' contentions that Indians possessed no title to their lands: "I have no hesitation, however, to declare it as my opinion that the Indian title was not affected in the slightest circumstance by the compact with Georgia." He further insisted that "there is no obligation on the United States to remove the Indians by force." The compact only called for the federal government to obtain the land when it could be done "*peaceably* and on *reasonable* conditions." Moreover, he declared that "an effort to remove them by force would, in my opinion, be unjust."[17]

White Georgians justified the removal of the Indians on the basis of their uncivilized natures. Legislators in the General Assembly sent Monroe a memorial complaining about his position on the Indian question and portraying the Indians as unworthy and incapable of advancement. They asserted that "the exhausted state of the game affords a scanty and precarious subsistence to the hunter, and a dispersed and wandering population are not in a condition to become the objects of the benefits of civilization." According to this logic, the Indians could neither live as they had in their "savage" state nor adapt to "civilization."[18]

Closer to the truth, white Georgians feared that the Indians' adoption of white ways would only make them more difficult to remove. The document exposed fundamental flaws of logic and revealed the true source of the memorialists' alarm. After denigrating the ability of the Indians to alter their "savage" ways, the petitioners grudgingly acknowledged a sign of the Indians' acceptance of capitalist principles, especially changing attitudes toward private property. The memorialists stressed the need to act quickly because "every day diminishes the disposition of the savage to abandon his accustomed haunts, and consequently increases the price which he will demand for their surrender." On one hand, the memorialists insisted the Indians were beyond the pale of civilization; on the other, the memorialists revealed their dismay that the Indians had learned the monetary value of their land and refused to accept anything less.[19]

Governor Troup avoided racial arguments, which might have alienated his lowcountry supporters, in favor of apparently race-neutral legal arguments. Troup insisted that, as a result of the agreements signed in the 1780s and the Treaty of Ghent, the Indians were "mere tenants at will" on the lands claimed by Georgia. The guaranties contained in the accords only granted them the "right of hunting on the grounds," which was dependent on Georgia's magnanimity.[20] "The Indians are simply occupants—tenants at the will—incapable of transferring their naked possession, except through the instrumentality of the United States, to the state of Georgia." By arguing that Georgians were entitled to the land and that Indians had no title to the land, Troup changed the contours of the debate.

Currying upcountry favor, Troup engineered a new treaty with the Creeks. The treaty, signed in February 1825 under fraudulent conditions, required the Creeks to cede between 4 and 5 million acres, one-third of which was believed to be "good land," in return for $400,000 and an equal tract of land west of the Mississippi River. The treaty also required the Creeks to leave the land by September 1826. The commissioners' heralded their agreement, but the celebration of their success omitted the more nefarious events that led to the treaty. The commissioners asserted that the Creek signatories constituted the most important chiefs in the nation. In fact, the chiefs who signed the document spoke for only a fraction of the Creek people, only eight of the fifty-six Creek towns. For their actions, William McIntosh and the other chiefs received roughly half of the amount to be paid to the tribe and the promise of protection by the U.S. authorities.[21]

Responding to demands by frontiersmen, Troup, upon receiving word of the treaty's ratification, moved forward with his plan to take control of the contested territory. Despite a provision in the agreement stipulating that the ceded land would remain under the authority of the Creeks until September 1826, Troup decided to have the land surveyed in advance of the official turnover date in an effort to facilitate the transfer of sovereignty to the state authorities and the division of plots for settlers. To do so, he capitalized on some of the lowcountry's ties to the Indians and appealed to his cousin, McIntosh. After initially balking at Troup's demands, McIntosh finally acquiesced.[22]

The Creek majority exacted revenge against McIntosh for his collaboration in its dispossession. At the end of April, one hundred warriors surrounded McIntosh's house and, after allowing the women and children inside to leave, set it on fire. When McIntosh and one of his associates fled the burning structure, the warriors shot him. The next day, warriors shot and seriously wounded Ben Hawkins (the former Indian agent's son and McIntosh's son-in-law). In the wake of these attacks, McIntosh's allies, including his son, Chilly, fled to the "settled parts of the frontiers" of Georgia to avoid "the vengeance" of the Creeks. The national council made clear that its actions were not directed at the Americans, yet whites in Georgia sympathetic to the plight of McIntosh and the others chose to ignore the distinction. Instead they provided refuge for members of the "emigrating party" and issued dire warnings that the violence would eventually spill over the border into the state.[23] In his zeal to win upcountry votes, Troup sacrificed his cousin to save his own political life by pushing him to survey the land before the election instead of waiting for the agreed-upon post-election date. He did so because he needed to demonstrate progress on the issue of the Indian lands before the impending election. To undermine criticisms of his aristocratic bearings and to appeal to the emerging majority in the upcountry, Troup had to be able to show that he could get the same successful results as Clark when it came to the Indian lands.

Although Troup's aggressive pursuit of the contested Indian land earned him many admirers in Georgia, not everyone in the state appreciated his methods or motives. An opposition composed of disparate elements emerged in the months after the ratification of the Indian Springs treaty in 1825. Some were Clark supporters in the upcountry who feared that Troup would succeed in his attempt to co-opt the issue that Clark had long championed—the pursuit of the Indian lands—and thereby cut into the Clark Party's support among its traditional upcountry constituency. The prospect of this occurring had serious ramifications, particularly in 1825, the year of the first direct election for governor. Traditionally, the residents of Savannah and Chatham County, particularly the wealthy planters, represented Troup's core constituency, but many had become alienated by his pursuit of upcountry votes. Troup's opponents in the lowcountry condemned his support for a lottery to distribute the Indian lands as a cynical ploy to garner votes among the poor. For example, on the eve of the extra session of the General Assembly scheduled for the spring of 1825, residents of Savannah and Chatham County met "for the purpose of expressing opinion with regard to the disposition of the lately acquired territory from the Creek Indians." Those in attendance called on the state authorities to hold on to the lands. As "public property," it should be used to benefit the "*People*," a feat that could be accomplished through a number of means. The land could be sold and the proceeds used for internal improvements or free schools or a host of options other than giving it away to attract political support.[24]

Relations between Troup and federal authorities deteriorated over the course of the summer as revelations about the treaty emerged. Federal authorities in Georgia concluded that the Creek signatories had lacked the authority to negotiate. Troup promised to defy President John Quincy Adams should the federal government decide to repudiate the treaty. As the war of words escalated, fears of an armed conflict between Georgia and the United States surfaced. Added to the mix, northerners became more vocal in denouncing the extreme nature of the terms contained in the treaty and questioning why Indians could not be absorbed into Georgia. Forced relocation seemed draconian, particularly in light of the Creeks' expressed desire to remain on their ancestral lands.[25]

Upcountry whites became increasingly convinced that the federal government intended to treat Indians as their equals. The suggestion of Indian citizenship, placing them on par with whites, struck at the very foundation of the white Georgians' racial hierarchy. "Atticus," one up-country observer, complained that "the Indians have been thrown in upon us, under circumstances presenting the odious alternative, to be acknowledged an independent nation, in our very bosom, or to be incorporated in color, and identified in privilege, with the Georgians." Atticus charged that "the general government has commenced and fostered by every means, a regular and concerted system of civilization." The Indians received money for schools, farm implements, and any additional help they requested. "And this glaring outrage is attempted to be forced upon us under the hypocritical cant of christian benevolence." Atticus asked incredulously: "Do they believe that our people will consent to mix with that unfortunate race? And can they for a moment suppose that they ought to remain in the very heart of the state a sovereign and independent nation, a sanctuary for villainy and a harbor for refugee slaves." He complained that the federal officials "receive them in the character of *ambassadors*, hold diplomatic correspondences with them (a thing unheard of with other Indians)," and "countenance their reproaches of us, by listening to their complaints against us." Atticus condemned the actions of federal authorities, which "put them upon a footing with the citizens of Georgia." By treating the Indians with respect, Atticus concluded, the federal government treated Georgians with "mortifying disrespect."[26]

The Indian treaty was an integral part of the election campaign for governor as Georgians prepared to go to the polls in October 1825. Troup made the election a referendum on his performance in pursuit of the state's patrimony.[27] The election pitted Troup against Clark, who came out of retirement to compete against his longtime rival in a third head-to-head battle for governor. Only this time the people would directly elect the new governor. Both camps portrayed their opponents in characteristic fashion: Clark was uneducated and rough-hewn, "possessing physical and not intellectual industry," while Troup was the leader of "the aristocratic few who have so long withheld the important elections from the people."[28] But now Troup supporters could counter this claim by pointing to his two-year struggle with the federal authorities to get land for the state, land that was to be distributed by lottery so that all Georgians had a chance to prosper. Reversing the dynamics of the traditional upcountry-lowcountry divide, Troup's supporters cast Clark as an opponent of expansion. Clark, they asserted, "displayed in various ways his opposition to the Treaty for extending the limits of the State and acquiring a large quantity of valuable land for its citizens."[29]

Troup's hijacking of the Indian issue won him enough upcountry votes to win the election, if only by 688 votes (20,545 to 19,857), an extremely narrow margin. His relentless clamoring for the Indian lands and incessant demands on the federal authorities paved the road to victory. Troup managed to split the upcountry vote.[30] Ironically, he did so by co-opting the rhetoric of secession and resistance to federal encroachment championed by John Clark's father, Elijah, and his supporters in the 1790s. Troup lost in the counties on the immediate border with the

Creeks, but not by much. His drive to obtain the Creeks' lands earned him support there and chipped away at Clark's advantage. Troup fared even better in the counties just removed from the frontier, counties that had undergone the transformation from wilderness to plantation districts. On those lands where Creeks hunters had roamed only decades before, cotton now thrived. The planters in these areas, like the settlers on the frontier, longed for expansion. Troup benefited from a common interest between the two groups. These voters made the difference in the election.

In 1826 and 1827, the conflict between Georgia and the federal government continued. Much to the consternation of white Georgians, President Adams nullified the Treaty of Indian Springs and negotiated another agreement with the Creeks in its place. The new treaty contained several important features distinguishing it from its predecessor: it reserved some land within Georgia's boundaries for the Creeks and it did not require them to leave. Georgia's congressional delegation protested against the new treaty. An enraged Governor Troup and President Adams exchanged threats. A major confrontation appeared to loom on the horizon.[31]

But in the end, Georgia achieved its goals. The Creeks possessed neither the white allies nor the resources to combat their removal. Through the various treaties in the 1810s and 1820s, Georgians acquired virtually all the Creek lands the settlers had coveted. The Creeks were pushed out and the state extended its sovereignty to its present-day limit with Alabama. The expansion of the border opened the door to further immigration. The demographic changes exacerbated the shifting balance of power within Georgia, a trend that would continue in the decades to come as king cotton came to dominate the state's economy.

The Creek lands were not enough. The attention of land-hungry settlers then turned toward the Cherokee lands in the northwestern corner of Georgia. With the Creeks forced from the state, white Georgians pushed for the expulsion of the remaining Indians within the disputed territory. More so than the Creeks, the removal of the Cherokees would entail complicated questions about race and racial boundaries. The Cherokees, unlike the Creeks, had embraced the federal government's program of civilization.[32] A significant proportion of the Cherokee population adopted the trappings of southern culture, including slaveholding, Christianity, and patriarchy.[33] Some of these "civilized" Cherokees even socialized with members of the white elite and gained their support as allies in their attempts to retain their privileges and lands.[34] These Cherokees appeared very different from white settlers' stereotypes of the savage Indian. In the end, the successful removal of the Cherokees marked an increasing ideological simplification of race in Georgia.

Troup's appropriation of the Indian question contributed to the eventual breakdown in the party system in Georgia. Troup's hard-line approach to the Indian lands deprived the Clark Party of the issue that had stood as its hallmark. In the wake of the election, a defeated Clark left the state and relocated to Florida, leaving his party to founder without its leader. In the gubernatorial election of 1827, John Forsyth, the Troup-Crawford Party's candidate, defeated the Clark Party's candidate, Matthew Talbot, in a landslide, thus extending the party's hold on the executive for a third consecutive term. The *Savannah Mercury* noted that the party had become "so completely *disjointed*, that every *member* has been in the habit of following its own *lead*. The Clark *party* no longer exists. There is no longer a *head*, a rallying point, and each individual is left to look out for himself." Ironically, Troup's efforts also led to the demise of his own party. Without an organized opposition, the party turned against itself. In the gubernatorial election of 1829, the party elite selected Joel Crawford as the nominee. The decision provoked a backlash from within the party's ranks. This faction viewed Crawford as the embodiment of the aristocratic privilege that had long characterized the party. Rather than fall into line, the members of the faction backed a dark-horse candidate from within the party's ranks, George Gilmer, on a platform of democratic reform.[35]

Gilmer appealed to a broad cross-section of white Georgian society. His family came from the Virginia Piedmont along with others in the immediate aftermath of the Revolution and settled with them along the Broad River. Though well-off, he considered himself a kind of people's man, eschewing the trappings of privilege that many Virginia migrants embraced and rejecting the aristocratic bearing that had formerly characterized his party. A former congressman and state legislator, Gilmer ran for the governorship on a pro-reform platform. He pledged his support to continued democratization of the political process and the creation of free schools. Gilmer ultimately won by a landslide, receiving substantial support from former Clark men in the northwestern section of the state who agreed with his stand in favor of the continued democratization of the political system. Voters in the counties bordering on Cherokee land, including Habersham, Hall, and Gwinnett, overwhelmingly supported Gilmer.[36]

George Gilmer, by George Mandus. Courtesy of the Georgia Capitol Museum, Office of Secretary of State, Atlanta, Georgia.

Despite Troup's best efforts to neutralize the Indian question as a political issue, during Gilmer's time in office it reemerged as a point of contention. The year before Gilmer's election, the General Assembly had decided to annex the portion of the Cherokee territory that the state claimed as its own. Following the same route pursued against the Creeks,

the state authorities simply announced their intention rather than waiting for the federal government to act, as required according to the Compact of 1802. The General Assembly unilaterally declared its intention
to place the disputed lands under the state's sovereignty beginning in
June 1830.[37] The state's position put it at odds with its Cherokee neighbors, the federal government, most states in the Union, and even a portion of its own residents. There had always been a range of opinions
among white Georgians regarding the Cherokees, but in the 1820s these
positions crystallized into two competing camps. The positions held by
politicians and voters relative to these questions revealed divergent perspectives on the ideal structure of society.

A substantial (and growing) proportion of white Georgians discerned no space for Indians within Georgia's borders. They held a simpler
view of the state's racial order, a binary world of black and white, one
without Indians. They supported total Indian relocation. They preferred
for the Cherokees to leave of their own volition, but they were not averse
to the use of force to accomplish their objective if necessary. Many of the
men who held these sentiments resided in the northwestern counties
of the state, which bordered the Cherokees. This area had experienced a
massive influx of white men in the late 1820s. Within the span of less
than five years, between five thousand and ten thousand men had arrived
in the area. Many of them poor, these men loathed all pretense of aristocratic privilege.[38]

In contrast, another group argued that the Indians should be given
an option to stay or leave after the state extended its authority over their
land. Those who shared these sentiments tended to be concentrated in
the eastern blackbelt and older counties of the state, in the lowcountry
and along the Savannah River. They were acquainted with the Cherokees
and in some cases linked by blood and marriage to them. These Georgians believed in the tenets of the civilizing program. To suggest that
Cherokees should be summarily removed from their ancestral lands so
that poor whites could claim the territory was unthinkable. They believed
that proximity to whites had led to considerable suffering for most Cherokees, but they recognized that some Cherokees had successfully adopted
"civilized" ways and deserved to be treated accordingly. As a result, they
supported an emigration policy that encouraged the Cherokees to relocate to Arkansas, but they drew the line at forced removal. Indeed, they
insisted that the more enlightened Cherokees should be allowed to stay
and receive the rights and privileges of citizenship. "It has been the object

of humanity and wisdom," Governor Gilmer proclaimed, "to separate the two classes among them, giving rights of citizenship to those who are capable of performing its duties and properly estimating its privileges, and increasing the enjoyment, and probability of future improvement to the ignorant and idle, by removing them to a situation where the inducements to actions will be more in accordance with the character" of Indians.[39] This attitude was not new or unique. A few, like Robert Campbell, a Savannah resident, believed that Cherokees should be left alone entirely. He adamantly opposed the removal of the Cherokees. He called upon the General Assembly in 1829 to reconsider the "impolicy, injustice, and disgrace" of their Indian policy. In contrast to representations of the Indians as "savages," Campbell described the Cherokees, indeed all Indians, as "kind, confiding and generous," recounting their services to the white man from the arrival of Columbus forward. Campbell recognized the Indians' rights to their lands and asserted that the "white man had no authority for settling upon the lands inhabited by these Indians." From his perspective, the legislature's embrace of Cherokee removal in violation of their rights "will justly entail upon Georgia the odious charges of being Faithless—Covetous—Ungrateful—and Inhuman."[40] Campbell's legal arguments notwithstanding, most white Georgians accepted that the state government possessed the authority to place Indian lands under its control, but they differed over the timing and, more importantly, over the ultimate fate of the Indians living on the disputed lands.

As the state prepared to extend its authority over the disputed territory, the Cherokee question became the main political issue in Georgia. With the prospect of placing thousands of Indians under its laws, the General Assembly faced several pressing questions: How would the state treat the Cherokees? Would the Indians enjoy the privileges of citizens? Or would they be relegated to the margins of southern society and treated the same as free blacks and free people of color? Factions within both bodies of the legislature bickered over the issue. Those with more moderate views believed the Cherokees were entitled to protection of their person and property. Their opponents saw nothing wrong with denying Indians all rights. If anything, they hoped, such treatment would spur them to relocate west of the Mississippi. Granting them even basic rights gave them the wrong impression that there was a place for them in Georgia's future.

The first controversy arose in 1829 and centered on Indian testimony. That year gold was discovered on the Cherokee land, which accelerated the migration of white men to the region, many of whom settled illegally on the Indian side of the border. Cherokees as well as many wealthy white Georgians disdained the new arrivals. "These intruders were the most lawless and turbulent of men; they set all the laws of the state and the laws and treaties of the United States at defiance," Junius Hillyer noted. In addition to the miners, "thousands of thieves, gamblers and murderers were among them—men of the most corrupt and turbulent character—quarrelsome, drunken, malicious, revengeful, unjust and cruel, forming altogether a lawless [un]governable community."[41] Many of these men preyed upon the Indians, committing crimes against their person and property. In an effort to stem this criminal behavior and provide a modicum of protection for the victims, legislators in Georgia who held a moderate position on the Cherokee question attempted to reverse a ban on Indians testifying against whites in courts. The ban had only been passed in 1828 after multiple attempts in the 1820s. In the wake of the surge of violence near the gold mines, those who sympathized with the Cherokees understood that "great inconvenience and injustice have resulted" from the law because white men had plundered "the unfortunate Indian with impunity," knowing they "could not be convicted on Indian testimony."[42] Consequently, these legislators advocated returning to the earlier status quo, when Indians had been permitted to testify in the state's courts and judges and juries had determined how much credence to give their testimony. Having extended its authority over the Cherokee territory, the state had to protect its residents, even the Indian ones. One legislator even suggested that the state should treat Indians like aliens. "Perhaps we should neither extend to them the rights of citizens nor impose on them the disabilities of free persons of color, but extend to them the rights and protections similar to those enjoyed by aliens."[43]

Not everyone agreed, however. An indignant minority of legislators expressed outrage at the prospect of reversing the ban. They condemned attempts to allow "savage" Indians to testify as an assault on their privileges of whiteness. Led by men from the areas recently ceded to Georgia by the Creeks or on the border with the Cherokees, twenty-three representatives protested any proposals that granted Indians any measure of equality with whites. They criticized the provision allowing Indian testimony as "a measure fraught with dangerous consequences, and calculated to corrupt the stream of justice at its fountain head, to prostrate sacred rights of personal liberty, personal security and private property, at the feet of savage ignorance and barbarity."[44] This vocal minority did not

derail the effort to reverse the 1828 ban but did succeed in placing restrictions on the provision that curtailed its efficacy. In the end, the General Assembly in 1829 allowed Indians to testify in cases involving whites
only in limited instances.[45] Even after its defeat, however, the minority
continued its struggle by publicizing its protest. Trying to curry favor in
the court of public opinion, the minority submitted its resolution to the
Georgia Journal for publication in an attempt to shame its opponents for
their stand in favor of Indian testimony regardless of the circumstances.[46]

In the year following the acrimonious debate over Indian testimony,
the controversy over the Cherokee question mounted, at both the national and state levels. A divided Congress enacted the Indian Removal
Act of 1830, which authorized the federal government to negotiate the
removal of Indians east of the Mississippi. Meanwhile, violence in the
Cherokee country continued unabated. Gilmer pursued a moderate solution to the Cherokee question by dispatching armed guards to the Cherokee land to prevent both whites and Indians from mining for gold. He
then called the General Assembly into session early and urged its members to pass legislation to protect the gold mines as well as the rights of
the Cherokees. He called specifically for the removal of all white men
from the Cherokee territory. This action targeted the "lawless intruders"
who had moved illegally into the mining districts and victimized the
Indians as well as white men who lived peaceably among the Cherokees. Gilmer as well as large numbers of white Georgians accused these
white men of improperly influencing the Cherokees' decisions to resist
removal for their own economic self-interest. Gilmer recommended that
the legislature grant the Cherokees the same protections that the federal
government had previously provided, arguing that the Indians would be
"exposed to continual vexations and disturbance, unless their rights are
so secured as to enable them to obtain redress of their violation." Gilmer
supported removing the limitations of the 1829 law to expand the cases
in which Indians could testify against whites. He insisted that "the present law exposes them to great oppression, whilst its repeal would most
probably injure no one."[47] Gilmer's endorsement of these policies, however, did not signify a retreat from his view that relocation west of the
Mississippi offered the best long-term solution to the Indian question. To
accomplish this, he advised the legislature to grant the Cherokees land in
fee simple reserves, which, he argued, was the "policy best calculated . . .
to obtain their peaceable removal." This course of action, he contended,
would speed up the process of removing the Cherokees who wanted to

leave the state while allowing those who had achieved a sufficient state of "civilization" to remain.[48] While some, like the editors of the *Augusta Chronicle and Advertiser*, questioned the need to remove the Indians at all, Gilmer believed that it was in the best interests of white Georgians and the Cherokees for the Indians to find a refuge away from the negative influences of the white man.[49] Although Gilmer came to office rejecting the elitist principles that characterized the Crawford faction of the Troup-Crawford Party, he embraced its Indian policies, including support for the civilizing program. Gilmer averred that two distinct classes among the Cherokees had emerged over the course of the preceding decades, one consisting mainly of "half-breeds" with "both wealth and intelligence" and another "composed of unmixed aboriginal people" who were "deprived of their former pride of character" and "corrupted by . . . degraded vices."[50] He believed that the "unmixed" Cherokee population had to abandon the region for its own survival, but, like other moderates, he felt strongly that the "rights of citizenship" should be granted to Cherokees who had adopted civilized ways and were "capable of performing its duties and properly estimating its privileges."[51] These Indians would in effect become Americans.

Since members of Gilmer's party held the majority of the seats in the legislature, he had good reason to believe the body would heed his requests. Much to his consternation, however, a significant number of them refused his entreaties. Instead, they pursued a more radical program designed to forcibly remove all Cherokees and survey the contested land in preparation for immediate settlement by white Georgians. The committee charged with initiating the legislative agenda produced a report completely contradicting the governor's goals. Dismissing opposition from both outside and inside the state to the immediate settlement of the Cherokee lands by whites, the committee pronounced the efforts to civilize the Cherokees a failure. Indeed, rather than uplift the Indians, the civilization program had stalled the removal process. When the Cherokees enjoyed "all the happiness incident of savage life," the report explained, white Georgians had felt sympathy "for their weakness and their ignorance." Since the introduction of the "arts of civilization," however, Cherokee leaders had assumed a more confrontational "political attitude" regarding removal. This type of progress, the committee members lamented, only served to excite white Georgians' "national pride and their resentment" toward the Indians. Similarly, the committee report blamed "intermarriages" between Indians and whites as another cause of the

deteriorating relations between the Cherokees and Georgians. In contrast
to Gilmer and other moderates, who shared a generally positive view of
"mixed" Cherokees, or at least of their accomplishments and potential
for achievement, members of the committee offered a much bleaker assessment. The committee members contended that rather than serving as
role models to the rest of the Cherokee Nation, as Thomas Jefferson had
suggested in 1806, or constituting a group that could one day be incorporated into the American body politic, as Gilmer opined, the "mixed"
products of intermarriages represented a scourge to both the Cherokees
and Georgia. The "day must and will come and it is not far distant when,"
the committee report proclaimed, "by constant intermarriages between
the Indians and whites, the original Indian character will in a great degree be lost and yet the half or mixed breed will retain so much of that
character as to be incapable of enjoying the civilized life, and so much
of the character of the white man as to be illsuited for the savage state."
The report concluded, "Here then will be a sort of mongrel population
in the bosom of Georgia, unfit for the character of citizens, and unfit
for the wilds beyond the Mississippi."[52] Legislators who supported immediate removal depicted the Cherokees as weak and ignorant "savages"
and therefore unworthy of American citizenship. The Cherokees provided
clear examples that some Indians could indeed adapt to American ways.
Yet the committee members refused to acknowledge this fact. To admit
that the Cherokees could actually become "civilized" contradicted arguments in favor of their forced relocation. Predicting only a "mongrel
population," the committee members argued that there was no real hope
for the Indians east of the Mississippi.

The debate over how to proceed with the Cherokees dominated the
1830 legislative session. "The Indian question is the all-absorbing subject
of the time," the *Augusta Chronicle's* correspondent to the legislature noted.
From the moment "it was taken up," he continued, "scarcely anything
else has been talked of or thought of."[53] As the depth of the chasm over
the controversy became clear, two competing sides coalesced in the General Assembly. Yet, reflecting the fluid state of the party system in Georgia
in the late 1820s and early 1830s, the divisions did not fall along orderly
political lines. "Indeed," one observer noted, "it is by no means a party
matter."[54] Instead, the Cherokee question had become a sectional and
class issue. Both the House and the Senate witnessed fierce debate over
the survey bill between proponents and opponents of Cherokee removal.
A clear alliance of legislators sympathetic to the plight of white settlers

emerged, especially in the House. A core group of moderates, primarily senators from the older regions of the state, resisted attempts to take over control of the disputed land by stalling the proceedings and inserting poison pills into the language of the bills. The two sides battled over the details of the bill, subjecting each section to close scrutiny. The debate over the survey bill encompassed twenty-three speeches and consumed eighteen hours of "solid speaking," more time than any other issue before the General Assembly.[55]

The marked shift in the tone and substance of the debate over the Cherokees shocked moderates observing the legislative proceedings. Referring to the proposal to survey the Indian land and expel the Cherokees, the *Augusta Chronicle* correspondent expressed genuine disbelief. "How such a bill can be the subject of a moments consideration in a christian land, is to me a subject of the deepest astonishment," he remarked. Many "intelligent men," he continued, "who look upon it as one of the most important and dangerous questions that has ever agitated the State, are deeply fearful of the result."[56] The *Milledgeville Recorder* hoped that calmer heads would prevail in the discussion over the Cherokee territory and that the General Assembly would not "proceed hastily" in making policy concerning it.[57]

Much to Gilmer's vexation, the extremists succeeded in passing a law in 1830 to survey and distribute the land annexed just six months earlier. Moderates failed in their attempt to halt the state's course toward removal, but they did manage to secure some protections for the Cherokees. Moderates insisted on banning anyone who had mined for gold after June 1, when the state officially took over the land, from participating in the land lottery. The law granted the Cherokees their right to legal protection of their property, at least until the General Assembly decided to do otherwise. Prospective settlers who drew lots where Indians resided could not, according to the law, force them to relinquish their land. In addition to the survey law, the General Assembly approved a law to prohibit whites from moving to the disputed territory and to provide a guard for the mines. The General Assembly required all whites living in the Cherokee Nation to register with the state authorities after March 1 of the next year. The moderates, however, were not able to remove the restrictions against Indian testimony. In addition, extremists scored a victory in declaring all contracts involving Indians null and void. One key concession left the determination of when to begin the survey in the hands of the governor. The balance had shifted in favor of the radicals.

The struggle over the Cherokees altered the political landscape in Georgia and endangered Gilmer's political career. The controversies concerning the extension of the state's jurisdiction over the Cherokee territory, the survey of the land, and the removal of the Indians left him despondent. It was the "time in my public life," Gilmer complained, "when I had to struggle with the greatest difficulties, and was the object of the vilest abuse."[58] Gilmer had come to power by forming an alliance with disaffected members of Troup-Crawford faction and former Clark men, based on their mutual opposition to the Crawfordites' aristocratic ways, but his coalition disintegrated as the difficulties connected to the Cherokee question increasingly took center stage. A crucial segment of his support had come from the newly settled areas of the state, but as Gilmer's moderate position on the issue became clear he lost the support of these areas. Unfortunately for Gilmer, it was these areas that experienced the most significant gain in population in the two years that followed his election in 1829. The population grew enormously as white men came to the state and settled on the border with the Cherokees, where cheap land was accessible. In effect, the demographic landscape of the state had changed virtually overnight, speeding a process that had been unfolding for decades. This demographic transformation would have serious implications for the state's political system.

The 1831 gubernatorial election served as a referendum on Gilmer's stand regarding the Cherokees, exposing rifts in Georgia over notions of white supremacy. The unusually long, ten-month campaign began just weeks after the contentious 1830 legislative session came to an end, indicating the depth of the divisions. Dissatisfaction with Gilmer had mounted in the upcountry, where some residents feared the next legislative session might even bring a repeal of the survey law. Hoping to avert any policy reversal, these residents sought a candidate to champion their interests. They recruited Wilson Lumpkin to lead the challenge to Gilmer.[59] Lumpkin's public life began early; he was elected to the state legislature in 1804 at the age of twenty-one. He served in Congress from 1815 to 1817, was reelected in 1826, and remained until 1831. Lumpkin empathized with the plight of upcountry settlers. Having lived on the frontier during his formative years, he had encountered Indians on a regular basis in his youth. His early interactions with the Cherokees, at a time when the residents of Georgia's border counties were in frequent conflict with their Indian neighbors, left him more skeptical about the prospects of peaceful relations than his rival, Gilmer. Moreover, Lumpkin doubted the

Wilson Lumpkin, by J. T. Moore. Courtesy of the Georgia Capitol Museum, Office of Secretary of State, Atlanta, Georgia.

potential for Indians, even Cherokees, to adopt civilized ways, believing them incapable of changing their innate savageness. Consequently, Lumpkin noted, "I knew my policy on the Indian subject would differ from his [Gilmer's] on some very important points."[60]

The *Milledgeville Federal Union* suggested that "if there is any subject upon which Mr. Lumpkin deserves, as he has won, the confidence of the people of Georgia, it is upon this very subject of our Indian claims." Lumpkin had a long history of working on issues related to Indians. He served in multiple instances as a U.S. commissioner responsible for overseeing the surveying of boundary lines between the United States and its Indian neighbors. In his second term as a congressman, he served on the Committee on Indian Affairs, where he worked tirelessly to remove the Cherokees from within Georgia's claimed boundaries. At the vanguard of the movement, Lumpkin encountered opposition from critics in Georgia who "considered me in haste and premature in introducing my emigration policy." His colleagues from Georgia in Congress "pronounced my effort nothing more than a popularity-seeking affair." They claimed he was trying to do more than Troup.[61] By 1831, his views resonated with a larger portion of the Georgia public, particularly new arrivals.

Lumpkin's supporters used race and class to appeal to the changing demography of the state. In a reversal of the previous election, they cast Gilmer as beholden to the interests of the "monied aristocracy" because he advocated state control over the gold mines rather than their distribution to the people through the land lottery. More damning, however, was the charge that Gilmer favored "hostile, ignorant, depraved barbarians" over "his fellow-citizens, whose safety he is bound by the most solemn obligations to protect." The Milledgeville Federal Union emphasized that "Mr. GILMER believes that INDIANS OUGHT TO BE ADMITTED AS WITNESSES IN OUR COURTS, IN CASES AFFECTING THE RIGHTS OF WHITE PERSONS" and that he had exerted "extraordinary influence" to "impose this disastrous policy" on the state's white population. The paper called on white Georgians to "Let every man who would dread to subject his property, his reputation, his liberty, his life, to the awful hazards of HOSTILE INDIAN TESTIMONY, unite with us in removing from executive office, a man who has exercised its high authority in attempting to introduce a policy so subversive of justice, so fatal to the safety of the people of the State." The Federal Union specifically targeted upcountry residents, asking, "If Indians are allowed to testify against white men, under the present state of our Indian relations, what is to become of the white people in Carroll, Campbell, DeKalb, Gwinnet, Hall and Habersham?"[62] The Indian issue appealed to those counties on the border with the Cherokee territory, the area of the state with high concentrations of recently arrived white men. Lumpkin's supporters also linked Gilmer with the dangerous doctrine of miscegenation. Highlighting Gilmer's sympathy for the "mixed-blood"

Indians, Lumpkin's supporters reminded voters of Gilmer's association with William Crawford, who in 1816 had suggested the best way to deal with the Indian question was to promote intermarriage. In an article entitled "Crawford's Axiom," the editor of the *Federal Union* asked: "does he still wish our sons to marry *squaws*, and our daughters, *Indian men*, to civilize them?"[63] By linking Gilmer with Crawford, Lumpkin's supporters yet again emphasized that Gilmer did not share the same racial views as white residents of the upcountry.

The tactic worked. Lumpkin won the election, though by less than fifteen hundred votes, defeating Gilmer 27,305 to 25,863.[64] In two years, from 1829 to 1831, the number of voters grew by close to 25 percent (from roughly 40,000 to just over 53,000). Much of the increase came from voters in the border counties, who had voted for Gilmer in the previous election but had turned against him for his support of Indian rights. Lumpkin trounced Gilmer there, much as Gilmer had beaten Crawford in 1829. The margins were almost identical. Gilmer understood the ramifications. "I was defeated," he lamented, "by those who had been previously my most clamorous advocates."[65]

Lumpkin's victory represented more than a symbolic changing of the guard. His election produced a fundamental reorientation in the state's policies toward the Cherokees. The differences between the outgoing and incoming administrations were evident when the legislature met in the fall of 1831. In his last communication to the General Assembly, Gilmer issued a final plea to the body to pursue a cautious approach to the Indian question. His words betrayed a concern that extended beyond the state's welfare. Gilmer feared that the survey and distribution of the Cherokee lands, according to the law passed the previous year, would "deprive our Indian population entirely of their possessions without their consent and without any equivalent." He insisted that "the character of the State, the interest of the Union, respect for public opinion, and the rights of the Indians, forbid that so gross an act of injustice should be committed."[66] When Lumpkin addressed the legislature days later, members received a very different message, one that demonstrated more sympathy for the white settlers. He argued that the Indian crisis jeopardized "the interest and prosperity, if not the peace and safety of the State." He blamed the impasse, at least in part, on elite Georgians, asserting that "some of our most distinguished citizens have thrown almost insuperable obstacles in the way of a speedy termination of our Indian difficulties." The only solution to the problems facing the state, he declared, was to establish a "settled, freehold, white population" in the contested region. To accomplish this, he advocated the "immediate survey of the Cherokee Territory."[67]

The state government moved to open Cherokee land to white settlement. Despite the fact that a majority of the seats in the legislature remained in the hands of Lumpkin's opponents, the General Assembly acted to honor the governor's request. As the previous legislative session had demonstrated, party loyalties proved to be of secondary importance on issues related to the Cherokees. The legislature authorized Lumpkin to begin the surveying of the Cherokee country into individual 160-acre plots by the following April and granted him the right to decide when the distribution of the land should begin. As soon as the surveyors completed their assignment that fall, Lumpkin ordered the land lottery to commence. Shortly thereafter, thousands of white Georgians poured into the ten new counties carved from the contested area, establishing new settlements surrounding the Cherokees. The 1831 survey law provided a boon to frontier residents in several ways beyond simply settling the question of occupancy of the Cherokee territory. In a concession to white settlers, the General Assembly reduced the residency requirement from four to three years, thereby making men who had flooded to the state in the first days of the gold rush eligible for the lottery. In this way, the law reversed a portion of the 1830 law that had banned squatters who arrived after the discovery of gold from participating in the lottery. The law also repealed a provision prohibiting men convicted of mining on the Cherokee land after June 1830 from participating in the land lottery. Moderates had insisted on the inclusion of these provisions the year before as a way to punish the "lawless intruders" who had victimized the Indians and defied the state's authority. But the balance of power in the legislature had shifted in the year since. The moderates, who championed Cherokee rights and supported Gilmer's plea to proceed cautiously, continued to resist the radicals' demands for immediate action, but their ability to influence policy had diminished. Just one year previous, the state's politicians had vilified the men on the frontier as violent criminals. In that year, the state had undergone a metamorphosis; those previously disparaged found themselves the core of the political establishment.[68]

Advocates of the survey law assumed that the arrival of thousands of whites would convince the Cherokees to relocate. Lumpkin hoped they would accept President Jackson's invitation to negotiate an agreement to sell their land and move west of the Mississippi. Despite the deteriorating conditions in their nation, the Cherokees remained resolute in their posi-

Georgia's Counties–1840

tion. They maintained their conviction that the federal authorities would eventually intervene on their behalf. The U.S. Supreme Court's ruling in March 1832 affirming the Cherokees' claims to the land reinforced their beliefs in federal assistance. To Lumpkin's dismay, the result of the high court's opinion made "the prospect of a treaty . . . less flattering now, than it was some time since."[69]

By the end of his first term in office, Governor Lumpkin succeeded in fulfilling his goal of placing white settlers in the Cherokee country and establishing the state's clear authority over the area. He failed, however, to achieve his second objective: the removal of the Cherokees. Using the machinery of government, he created what he had hoped would be the necessary conditions to convince the Indians that there was no place for them in Georgia's future. Hoping to steer clear of a showdown with the federal government, he had avoided deploying outright coercion in the pursuit of his goal. In his second term he would show less restraint.

As in his first race for the governor's seat, race and class factored prominently in Lumpkin's reelection campaign. Lumpkin's supporters highlighted his achievements in the state's quest to place the contested territory firmly under its control. They cast his efforts as part of a larger struggle on behalf on Georgia's growing poor white population, one in which he strove to bring a semblance of equality to those who had fewer resources at their disposal than did the state's wealthier residents. He had accomplished this by opening the up the Indian country to immediate occupancy through the land lottery, which offered all white Georgians a fair chance at obtaining self-sufficiency and maybe even social mobility. Thanks to Governor Lumpkin, the editor of the *Federal Union* reminded his readers, the Cherokee country "has been organized and the people are industriously delving out its golden treasures, and realizing its agricultural products. Many a poor man has been rendered comfortable—thereby a destitute family, cheerful and happy."[70] Economic inequality was a growing concern in Georgia in the 1820s and 1830s, as the plantation economy heightened the gap between the wealthy and the rest of the population. Obtaining the Indian lands for settlement, then, was a clear testament to Lumpkin's concern for those left behind in the state's new economy. This strategy offered Lumpkin a means to draw a stark contrast with his opponent, Joel Crawford. As in the previous election, when Lumpkin's supporters portrayed Gilmer as an elitist who cared little for the common man, they castigated Crawford as an aristocrat. Indeed, Lumpkin's platform centered on his opposition to all aristocrats, white or red. His efforts paid off once again. Lumpkin won the election by twenty-five hundred votes, gaining a clear majority in the newly established counties. By contrast, Crawford took the lowcountry. In the state's broad middle, residents split their votes, though Crawford won in the counties with large plantation districts. In broad terms, the state's voting patterns remained largely the same as they had since the Revolution; the difference was in the distribution of the state's population.[71]

Having secured his victory, Lumpkin embarked on an aggressive campaign to remove the Cherokees from within Georgia's borders. His efforts focused on eliminating the predominantly "mixed-blood" leadership, whom he blamed for blocking previous attempts to reach an agreement. Asserting that "mixed-bloods" "have already done their own people, the State of Georgia, and our common country, great and serious injury," Lumpkin contended that they had taken control of the Cherokee government and worked against the wishes and interests of the Cherokee people. Lumpkin's abhorrence of the "mixed-blood" Cherokees offered yet another striking example of the differences between the radicals and the moderates on the Indian question. Whereas moderates, such as

Gilmer, resented the "mixed-blood" leadership for its intransigence, they envisioned a place for at least some of its members in Georgia once they halted their opposition to Georgia's annexation of the contested territory. Lumpkin, like other radicals, had nothing but contempt for this racially impure group. Like the Committee on the State of the Republic, which had undermined Gilmer's agenda in 1830, Lumpkin loathed the prospect of a "mongrel" race settling in Georgia's "bosom." In particular, the governor despised a certain "class" of Cherokees who had agreed to take fee simple lots in 1817 and 1819 and become U.S. citizens, but had subsequently sold their improvements, then moved back to the Cherokee land and begun to make new improvements again rather than go out west. Not only had these "mixed-blood" Cherokees hindered Lumpkin's project, but they had benefited from the provisions contained in the 1831 survey law that protected their property from confiscation, which, he believed, prevented white settlers from their deserved patrimony. "In our anxiety to provide for the welfare and protect the rights" of the Cherokees, he reasoned, "we have in some instances, given advantages to the native population over our white citizens." These policies, he continued, have become "oppressive to our white population." Whites, he declared, were certainly "not less entitled to the protection of our laws, than the native race."[72]

When the General Assembly convened in 1833, it took up the governor's call to action. By this time, the political realignment begun in the late 1820s was largely complete. Two new parties had emerged: the Union Party, which included former Clark men and a contingent of former Troup-Crawford supporters who sided with President Jackson, and the State Rights Party, which included the remnants of the Troup-Crawford Party. The State Rights Party attracted wealthier men and found its greatest support in the lowcountry and in the eastern counties of the state, while the Union Party drew more common folk and found its greatest support in the northern and western sections. The Indian question served as one of the core issues dividing the parties. With a clear majority in the legislature, the Union Party enacted a new law designed to rectify the shortcomings of the earlier legislation identified by Lumpkin. Members of the State Rights Party tried to block these efforts, though their numbers precluded them from succeeding at anything beyond weakening some of the more draconian provisions.

The new law targeted civilized Cherokees for special persecution and offered new incentives to poor whites to move to the new counties. "The

provisions of this act have met the sanction not only of the General Assembly, but the views and wishes of a large majority of the people of
Georgia, especially those residing in and near the Cherokee region of
the State."[73] Frontiersmen secured several important victories. The law
circumscribed the Cherokees' rights, particularly their rights to own
and occupy the land. The law outlawed all contracts, written or verbal,
between Indians and whites unless two "respectable witnesses" could
vouch for it. The law dispossessed Cherokees who had sold their lots
taken in 1817 and 1819 and moved back to the Cherokee land rather
than out west. The law mandated that Cherokees were eligible for lots
no larger than 160 acres and limited the number of improvements they
could make on their lots. This provision explicitly targeted some of the
wealthiest Cherokees, who owned plots with significant improvements.
The law subjected all other land to the lottery and occupation by whites.
Finally, to restrict economic advancement, the law prohibited Cherokees
from hiring slaves, free blacks, or whites to work on their plantations.
Lumpkin declared that "We must meet the crisis when it comes; and I am
resolved to be in readiness to act with promptitude and decision. Before
the close of the year it may become necessary to remove every Cherokee
from the limits of Georgia, peaceably if we can, forcibly if we must."[74]

Beyond depriving wealthy Cherokees of their means of subsistence,
the law sought to define the meaning of "Indian" and "white" and force
individuals to fit one category or the other. By prohibiting the Cherokees from hiring slaves or white men, the General Assembly restricted
their abilities to act as planters, as many "civilized" Cherokees had done.
American authorities had offered training and tools to transform Indians
into "civilized" agriculturalists, but once the Cherokees achieved this goal
Georgian authorities deprived them of their ability to earn a living. White
settlers argued that the Indians' savage state required their removal, and
the General Assembly took steps to ensure that the Cherokees remained
as uncivilized as possible. The state was also willing to make a white
man into an Indian if he refused to live like a white man among his own
kind. The law forced white men to choose between their privileges of
whiteness and legally becoming an Indian by residing with their Indian
families. This law represented the state's attempt to simplify the racial
order. Extremists accused white allies of the Indians of being traitors to
their race, and the law reflected this perspective. The act granted a white
man's Indian family, meaning his wife and children, possession of their
property, leaving the white man with "no rights but that of the Indian use

and occupation." This stood in marked contrast to laws in Georgia that made men the absolute power in the family. Should a white man opt to become an Indian, he would face the same restrictions that true Indians faced. Failure to follow the law would result in a forfeiture of the land.[75]

Passage of the new law heightened tensions in the Cherokee country, resulting in a series of violent encounters across the region. White settlers interpreted the legislation as a license to use any means necessary to rid themselves of their Indian neighbors. In June 1834, for example, white men terrorized the residents of Hickory Log and Sixe's Towns in two particularly brutal episodes. They raided the towns under the pretext that the Indians were plotting an armed foray against white settlers living in the area. The episode began on May 13 when a notorious Indian outlaw, known to victimize both Indians and whites, shot and injured a white man. The Cherokees arrested the shooter and handed him over to the authorities for prosecution. Their actions failed to mollify the white residents of nearby Etowah, who decided to send an armed posse against the two principal Cherokee towns in the county. The posse seized several men, reputedly the leaders of the plot, and disarmed the rest of the towns' residents. Before leaving, they threatened the inhabitants, declaring their intent to kill three Indians at random for each white settler found dead in the future.[76] One white resident of the region, Thomas G. Barron, captured the sheer brutality of the attacks in his description of the events. Noting that the "whites have butchered some, taken the arms from others, and frightened the balance of the Indians out of their wits," he accused the settlers of using the injury suffered by the white man "in order to justify some of the most cruel measures and wicked acts that have ever disgraced any people, calling themselves civilized."[77]

Beyond illuminating the brutality of the process of Cherokee removal, the events were notable because they highlighted whites' hypocrisy over the issue of Indian character. White settlers had led the effort to ban Indian testimony in courts, arguing that their word could not be trusted. Yet the white residents of Etowah who assaulted the Cherokee towns relied on the testimony of a young Cherokee woman to justify their actions. After allegedly overhearing the leaders of the plot as they laid the groundwork for their scheme, she informed local whites about the plans. When the Cherokees discovered that the woman was the source of the information, they assumed whites would ignore her story since she was known, among the Indians, to have "the most notoriously bad character." Unfortunately for the Cherokees, the white settlers did not do so. Indeed, they expressed a very different view of the woman, whom they described as "an intelligent Indian girl." The basis of their appraisal of the woman's character was simple: she lived in a white town and "had been raised and educated in a white family" and "spoke English." As the example illustrates, whites could overcome any reservations they held regarding Indian character when it served their interests.[78]

In addition to the violent attacks led by the settlers, Lumpkin initiated his own campaign of intimidation against the Cherokee elite. Shortly after passage of the law, state officials fanned out across the Cherokee country to remove wealthy Cherokees from their homesteads and place white settlers on the disputed properties. The evictions followed a similar pattern: the officials, accompanied by a group of armed thugs, appeared at the doors of the victims and informed them that they had to vacate their property within a specified time frame, usually two or three days, or face forcible removal. Resisters risked life and limb. In theory, the individuals targeted by the agents fell into one or more of the categories laid out by the legislature in the 1833 law. In practice, however, the agents selected those Cherokees known to harbor anti-Georgia sentiments and who owned properties with substantial improvements that whites coveted. Moreover, the agents often distributed the contested plots to individuals with political connections to the Union Party rather than to the legitimate drawers of the land. One of the most egregious violators of the law's terms was the man personally selected by Lumpkin to oversee the process, William Springer. On multiple occasions, Springer removed Cherokees from their homes based on dubious—and perhaps fraudulent—claims. The agent defended his actions, maintaining that while they did not conform to the letter of the law, they did achieve the legislature's "intended" results. Springer had little use for formalities, particularly when they stood in the way of the objective he relentlessly pursued: the removal of the Cherokees.[79]

As the harassment and intimidation began, members of the Cherokee leadership sought solutions to halt the process of evictions through "civilized" legal channels. With their defenders in the General Assembly incapable of halting the legislative onslaught directed against them and the U.S. Supreme Court's decisions ignored by the state authorities, the Cherokees had few options available. After consulting their lawyers, they turned to the state judiciary to intervene on their behalf. The decision made sense. Unlike the General Assembly, the state courts remained less susceptible to the settlers' zeal for Indian removal and proved unwilling to rubber stamp the legislature's assault on the Cherokees. They had previously received justice from the state courts. Augustus S. Clayton, the judge of the superior court of the western district, had demonstrated his independent streak by proclaiming his resolve to treat Indians fairly once the state extended its authority over the disputed territory. Clayton had recognized that his course would encounter opposition among the white population in the upcountry, but he had insisted that the state must mete out justice equally and that the rights of the Indians "must be respected." He had promised the Indians that "they have nothing to dread, as far as they are concerned, either from the character of our laws, or their mode of administration, for if *we can* live under them, *they* surely can, and no distinction shall be made in their execution."[80] He ruled in favor of a number of Cherokee litigants, which suggested he meant to abide by his word.[81] Clayton's successor, John W. Hooper, pursued a similar course. Judge Hooper, a resident of Cass County, sympathized with the plight of the Cherokees. Over the course of 1834, Hooper issued a series of opinions favorable to Cherokee defendants and claimants, which included injunctions to block the confiscation of property in several high-profile cases involving members of the Cherokee elite. Hooper based his decisions in these cases on an 1832 law that granted Indians limited rights to testify in cases involving the protection of their persons, property, and land. Contrary to the legislators' original intention, Hooper argued that this law placed Indians on the "same footing as free white citizens of the State." Ironically, Lumpkin had requested the enactment of the law after white settlers began moving to the Cherokee country. Even he had recognized the disastrous consequences that would ensue if the Cherokees were completely deprived of this right.

Hooper's principled stand polarized white Georgians. Mirroring the divide in the legislature over the Indian question, a substantial minority in the state, even in the Cherokee counties, defended the judge. Generally, his supporters tended, like him, to support the State Rights Party. For example, party members in Lumpkin County praised his "independent, fearless, and conscientious discharge . . . of the duties of his office."[82] Similarly, residents of Murray County signaled their "high respect for the judicial character" of Hooper and offered their "unabated confidence in his integrity."[83] Hooper also enjoyed the backing of a substantial number of lawyers and the majority of the state superior court justices, who affirmed his decisions in the cases involving the Cherokees.[84]

Most white Georgians rejected the legitimacy of Hooper's rulings, however. Many of them shared the *Federal Union*'s belief that "the course pursued by Judge Hooper is fraught with injustice to many citizens of the state."[85] They expressed outrage at his perceived bias in favor of the Cherokees, which, they asserted, came at the expense of white settlers. This was particularly true of those residents of the western circuit over which Hooper presided. William Bishop articulated the sentiments of many such individuals when he protested that the Indians claimed "Judge Hooper was their friend, and opposed to the Georgians." Hooper's detractors also blamed him for giving the Cherokees the misguided impression that he "would get back for them their country."[86] William Springer, Lumpkin's agent, offered an especially harsh rebuke of the judge for his "interference" in this regard. Hooper's actions on behalf of the Indians, he grumbled, have "altogether put the Cherokees more out of the notion of removal than ever. They are made to believe . . . that they have only to hold out, and they will eventually succeed in having the whites driven from among them, and that they will be permanently settled on the soil of Georgia."[87] Of course, the individual most disturbed by Hooper's deeds was Governor Lumpkin. After word of the judge's first injunction reached Lumpkin in January 1834, he immediately began plotting Hooper's removal. Incensed by the judge's audacity, Lumpkin initially intended to have Hooper impeached, though he ultimately opted to pursue a different course. Instead he hired a team of lawyers to contest Hooper's rulings and bided his time. He worked assiduously over the next ten months to develop a plan to punish the judge and his backers in the State Rights Party.[88]

When the General Assembly met in the fall of 1834, it moved to censure Judge Hooper. Spurred to act by Lumpkin and protests from the residents of the Cherokee country, the legislature considered a range of sanctions for Hooper's willful undermining of the 1833 Indian law, which the body noted had the backing of the majority of the state's people, particularly those from the frontier. After extensive debate, the legislators settled on an investigation of Hooper's judicial administration as the best way to proceed.[89]

Convened haphazardly in the middle of the legislative session, the investigation was more political theater than anything else. Dozens of witnesses drawn from the Cherokee country as well as the surrounding counties appeared before the panel.[90] The group included lawyers, civil officials, and private individuals. Their testimony offered competing, and often contradictory, perspectives on Hooper and social relations in the disputed region. Those who supported Hooper portrayed the judge as a man of conviction who remained steadfast in his application of the law even when that forced him to make unpopular decisions. He strove to treat all who appeared before him equally, regardless of whether they were Indian or white, and when rendering his judgments he consistently displayed this impartiality.[91] Yet it was precisely this trait that vexed his critics most. To them, this posture demonstrated a wholly inadequate support of white supremacy. But their protests went well beyond his courtroom behavior. These witnesses complained that Hooper and his associates, most of them members of the State Rights Party, socialized with his Indian neighbors in Cass County, which was home to a sizable number of wealthy "mixed-blood" Cherokees. They attended barbecues and other functions together, where they discussed politics and plotted strategy. Worst of all, according to his critics, Hooper chose to lodge at the homes of wealthy Cherokees when traveling rather than with whites of more modest means.[92] This behavior represented the ultimate racial insult, associating him with the classism of the State Rights Party and before that the Troup-Crawford Party. Earlier in the state's history, this type of criticism had posed some problems for those accused of such charges, but in the wake of the dramatic growth of the state's population in the 1820s and early 1830s and concomitant democratization of the state's political system, it now posed a far more serious liability.

In the end, the investigation produced little of substance. It embarrassed Hooper and damaged his credibility, but the panel overseeing the process took no action against the judge. The General Assembly did, however, enact a couple of significant pieces of legislation affecting the judicial system. The Union Party, having increased its majority in the legislature yet again, chose to follow Lumpkin's admonition not to impeach Hooper. Instead, its members passed a law that eliminated his and all other superior court judges' ability to issue injunctions against white land claimants.[93] The legislature continued its assault on the state judiciary by replacing seven State Rights Party judges on the superior court with Union men.[94] And lastly, the legislature initiated proceedings to create the state's first court of error.[95] At the time, Georgia did not have a state supreme court, a system that many citizens of the state cherished, particularly those in the upcountry, because it allowed justice to be dispensed according to local sensibilities. The controversy with Hooper apparently convinced some legislators of the need to alter this tradition. In the wake of the electoral reform that brought about direct elections for the governor and the ascendancy of the Union Party in the legislature, the courts had remained a bastion of racial moderation. But now that was coming to an end as well. In addition to the judicial reforms, the legislature amended the 1833 Indian law to remove the passages that the Cherokees' lawyers and Hooper had exploited. The legislature's actions neutralized the Cherokees' final allies within the state.[96]

After witnessing Georgians' hostility toward one of their own, many Cherokees recognized removal to be inevitable. A faction led by John Ridge negotiated a treaty with the federal authorities in 1835. The treaty divided the tribe, but even opponents realized the futility of their fight against white Georgians. In 1838, federal troops forcibly removed the Cherokees from their ancestral lands. Four thousand Cherokees died on the "trail of tears" to their new homes west of the Mississippi.[97]

Many of the white men who came to Georgia during the late 1820s and early 1830s had ideas about race and Indian relations that differed in fundamental ways from those who had traditionally held power in the state. Radicals viewed Indians as inherently savage and inferior. Moderates recognized class distinctions among Indians and accepted the possibility of their inclusion into Georgia society. There had always been a cadre of men with an extreme position relative to the Indians, but, with the exception of a few scattered years in the 1780s and 1810s, those who held this view had largely remained out of power. The influx of new settlers transformed a minority view into the majority. The demographic shift, along with the democraticization of the state's political system, made possible the removal of the Creeks in 1828 and the Cherokees ten years later. Their views increasingly became the official policy of the state government. Radicals' success in removing the Creek and Cherokee Indians created Georgia as a white man's republic in which white supremacy and white privilege became sacrosanct. With the "savage" red man gone, white Georgians could work toward further simplifying the racial order. Now they set out to make blackness synonymous with slavery and whiteness with freedom. On the lands obtained from the Creeks and the Cherokees, white Georgians created their corner of the cotton kingdom.

7

THE DEMOCRATIZATION
OF SLAVERY, 1820–1860

In the wake of the removal of the Creek and Cherokee Indians from Georgia, plantation slavery quickly spread throughout the interior of the state. In short order, cotton plantations emerged from the forests where Indian warriors had hunted for game not long before. The slave society that took root in Georgia's blackbelt differed in fundamental ways from its predecessor in the lowcountry. These transformations democratized the institution of slavery. This chapter illustrates the democratization of slavery in two different but interrelated ways: first, by examining the rise of cotton as the state's primary crop and exploring the social and economic consequences of this shift, and second, by exploring the diversification of the state's economy in the middle third of the century and the struggle among whites over the appropriate use of slaves.

Through cotton, white southerners democratized slavery in the upcountry. The financial requirements for cotton cultivation placed economic and social mobility within the reach of a much larger portion of white families than had been the case with rice cultivation in the lowcountry. At the same time, white slaveholders used cotton to create an institution of slavery that relegated slaves to menial and unskilled labor. In addition, the development of Georgia's cotton belt spurred internal improvements as well as industrial endeavors that relied on slave labor and benefited all white Georgians. Cotton enabled the elevation of whites to equality and the reduction of blacks to subordination.

The rise of the cotton kingdom produced enormous wealth for

planters in Georgia, but it also brought increased divisions among whites within the state. Although virtually all white men in the state supported slavery, they disagreed over the specific roles of blacks within society. While most slaveholders preferred to retain maximum flexibility in their use of their slave property, nonslaveholders favored prohibiting slave workers from most skilled occupations. White slaveholders may have embraced the changes in the economy and the new opportunities to employ their slaves, but nonelite whites expressed considerably more apprehension. The rise of industry and manufacturing brought new possibilities to find steady employment, but without proper rules in place, the result for nonelite whites was greater competition with slave labor and a race to the bottom. Nonelite whites pushed not for the abolition of slavery but for restrictions on the institution that would solidify its benefits, not just for slaveholders but for nonslaveholders as well. Nonelite white workers in the urban upcountry defined whiteness from below to successfully impose their vision of slavery at the local level and possibly, as their numbers grew, at the state level as well.

When Frederick Law Olmsted toured the South in 1852 and 1853, he spent considerable time in the Georgia lowcountry. Olmsted, a northern journalist, took two different journeys, spending a total of fourteen months in the region. His observations on the South formed the basis of his study, a trilogy known as *The Cotton Kingdom* (1861).[1] He provided a finely nuanced analysis of the region, one that offered rich details about the nature of life in a society governed by a profoundly unequal system. Olmsted was not a proslavery ideologue or even remotely sympathetic to the southern cause, but his opposition to the institution did not prevent him from revealing the complexity of life there. While his title indicated the way people from outside the region had come to think of it, his study highlighted the variety of Souths that actually existed. Perhaps the title was a nod to the fact that cotton interests had taken over the South economically and politically by that point. In any case, his work undermined the monolithic stereotypes associated with the South. He described a land in transition, a people on the move, pushing westward in search of fresh land and new opportunities. And yet his account of lowcountry slave society would have been recognizable fifty or even seventy-five years earlier. Clearly lowcountry society had evolved over this period of time, but it built upon the structure set by the rise of the plantation complex in Georgia following the introduction of slavery.

During one visit to Georgia, Olmsted stayed at Dr. Richard Arnold's plantation, a sprawling estate in the rice district. Arnold owned two plantations, located close together. Both produced rice and sea island cotton. Between the two, about two hundred slaves of various ages (one hundred of them "prime hands") cultivated seven hundred acres. The region was the province of large planters, rice grandees, who owned slave forces that often numbered in the hundreds. According to the census, there were fifty-six planters in the lowcountry who owned one hundred slaves or more.[2] The demography of the region remained like the Caribbean. Slaves represented the vast majority of the population in the lowcountry, accounting for upward of 75 percent in some parts.

The conditions of labor in the lowcountry were harsh. Field laborers continued to work in malarial swamplands, spending most of their days bent over cultivating the crop at one stage or another. The work was brutal, and disease was rampant. "The negroes do not enjoy as good health on rice plantations as elsewhere," Olmsted observed. The climate produced high mortality rates among the slaves, particularly infants, and confirmed "that the subtle poison of the miasma is not innocuous to them."[3]

The system of labor remained relatively similar, as slaves completed work according to the task system. Planters divided male and female slaves into four categories, from full hand down to quarter hand. Slaves usually worked in groups of twenty or so. Each slave had their work marked out before them, depending on their labor. They worked from sunrise until they finished their tasks, primarily growing rice and long-staple cotton. The addition of cotton in the early national period had a limited impact on labor, however, since slaves still employed the task system.[4]

Despite the harshness of the work conditions, the task system did offer slaves some advantages. Once slaves finished their allotted tasks, they worked on their own behalf. Masters did not provide rations sufficient for subsistence and instead required slaves to grow food to meet their dietary needs. According to Lafayette Delegal, a slave driver on H. H. Delegal's plantation in Liberty County, "hands" had "all the time they could make by completing their task." He did not know a single slave who worked by the day, from "sun to sun."[5] Some finished early enough to allow them time to work on their gardens or to hunt or fish. As Olmsted described one plantation, each family had a half acre to use as a garden. Out front of the cabins there were "coops of fowls with chickens, hovels for nests, and for sows with pig." The slaves' hogs were allowed to run around and each owner had a personal mark to distinguish them from one another. They were free to sell what they produced in their gardens and through tending their swine; the owner's family purchased their eggs and poultry from the slaves. The only provision was that they could not purchase liquor, but they often flouted this rule. Some slaves managed to accumulate property. Evidence of the achievement was that slave cabins had doors with locks and keys and the slaves locked up before they left in the morning for the fields.[6]

When visitors to the lowcountry wrote about rice cultivation, they almost always made a point to note the task system and the relative autonomy it provided slaves. Olmsted was no different. "The system of working slaves by tasks, common on the large cotton plantations of the Atlantic States, as well as the rice plantations, has certainly great advantages," he declared. "The slave works more rapidly, energetically, and, within narrow limits, with much greater use of discretion, or skill, than he is often found to do elsewhere."[7] Basil Hall, a British traveler who stayed at a plantation on St. Simons, one of the sea islands, more than two decades earlier, offered a similar analysis. He claimed that slaves "prefer[red]" the task system "to any other." He observed that "Active hands get through their proportions generally by the middle of the day, others in two-thirds of the day, after which, they are left to employ the balance, as it is rather well called, or what remains of daylight, in their own fields, in fishing, or in dancing;—in short, as they please."[8] While Hall failed to fully capture the slave perspective, his description does convey the benefits of the task system to the slave population. Olmsted and Hall noted the task system because it represented an alternative mode of organizing labor compared to the gang system that prevailed elsewhere and seemed to contradict many of the stereotypical characterizations of slavery. It highlighted the degree to which slaves had carved out customs and traditions over time, which maximized their autonomy under a coercive system. As Olmsted noted, "In nearly all ordinary work, custom has settled the extent of the task, and it is difficult to increase it. . . . if it should be systematically increased very much, there is a danger of a general stampede to the 'swamp'—a danger the slave can always hold before his master's cupidity. In fact, it is looked upon in this region as a proscriptive right of the negroes to have this incitement to diligence offered them; and the man who denied it, or who attempted to lessen it, would, it is said, suffer in his reputation, as well as experience much annoyance from the obstinate 'rascality' of his negroes."[9]

Custom applied to the pervasive use of black drivers, some of whom wielded considerable control over daily life on their plantations. As in earlier times, black drivers continued to play a prominent role in low-country slave society. Selected for their intelligence and leadership skills, black drivers enjoyed the respect of the other slaves as well as their owners. It was not uncommon for black drivers to actually manage the plantations, ostensibly performing the overseer's job. In certain instances, the "advice of the drivers is commonly taken in nearly all the administration," Olmsted noted, "and frequently they are, *de facto*, the managers." Valued for their extensive agricultural knowledge, some black drivers made important decisions related to the plantation economy. Their opinion was so respected, Olmsted asserted, that it "is often left with them to decide when and how long to flow the rice-grounds—the proprietor and overseer deferring to their more experienced judgment." Some planters' estimations of their black drivers were so high, in fact, that they would have preferred to forego using an overseer if the law had permitted. Conversely, they held white overseers in low regard and believed that they were "almost universally drunken and dissolute, and constantly liable to neglect their duties." As a consequence, Olmsted related, "Where the drivers are discreet, experienced, and trusty, the overseer is frequently employed merely as a matter of form."[10]

The main driver on Arnold's plantations was a slave named Amos Morel. Arnold referred to him as the "watchman" and trusted him more than "he would any overseer he had ever known." Morel was in charge of the daily operations, supervising virtually everything. In fact, Olmsted explained, "his authority was superior to that of the overseer." Morel had the keys to the storage area for provisions, tools, and materials as well as the produce. He weighed and measured out all rations for the slaves and the cattle and even the overseer, who received his private allowance of family provisions from him. Morel superintended the mechanics and made and repaired, as was necessary, all the machinery on the plantation, including the steam engine. A "favourite house-servant" since his childhood, he was educated with the white children while very young. Although initially employed as a waiter, he expressed a desire to learn skilled work and was subsequently trained to be a blacksmith. When he displayed a proclivity for fixing gins on the plantation, his owner arranged for him to learn to be a machinist working with steam engines. Once trained, he became an engineer and was rented out and was allowed to keep some of his wages. The owner brought him back to the plantation after Morel enjoyed his freedom a little too much. Despite his status as a slave, the watchman was a fairly wealthy man, whose possessions included at least three horses. Part of the money for the horses came from the owner, who "frequently encouraged his good behavior with handsome gratuities. He receives, probably, considerably higher wages, in fact (in the form of presents), than the white overseer. . . . The watchman has a private house, and, no doubt, lives in considerable luxury." Olmsted was clearly impressed by the man. The "watchman was a fine-looking fellow" who "had passed us, well dressed and well mounted, and as he raised his hat, to salute us, there was nothing in his manner or appearance, except his colour, to distinguish him from a gentleman of good breeding and fortune."[11]

Like their predecessors, many antebellum lowcountry planters strove for self-sufficiency. As such, they continued to rely on the work of skilled slaves, particularly mechanics, to take care of their plantations' needs. Black drivers may have represented the apex of the slave hierarchy, but black mechanics, who were far more numerous, occupied a rank not too far below. Whether designing and constructing buildings or repairing agricultural implements, skilled slaves provided valuable services to their owners. Richard Arnold clearly understood the worth of their contributions. When giving Olmsted a tour of his estates, Arnold displayed considerable pride in the accomplishments of his blacksmiths, carpenters, and other mechanics. During their inspection of the plantation shop, Olmsted noted, Arnold "called my attention to the excellence of their workmanship, and said that they exercised as much ingenuity and skill as the ordinary mechanics that he was used to employ in New England. He pointed out to me some carpenter's work, a part of which had been executed by a New England mechanic, and a part by one of his own hands, which indicated that the latter was a much better workman."[12] Arnold's compliment of his slaves' abilities undercut the foundation of white supremacy.

In the lowcountry, planters relied to a considerable extent on the labor of their slaves in sawmills, rice mills, and cotton presses. Slaves' labor in these industries carried on the lowcountry custom of relying on slaves for a variety of skilled and unskilled labor, sometimes at the expense of white workers. These industries were the logical outgrowth of the region's agricultural production. There was a symbiotic relationship between them. The region's forests were cut down to make way for rice and cotton fields. By the 1850s, in fact, Georgia led the Lower South in lumber production.[13] Most workers in the sawmills were black. The Savannah Steam Saw Mill had a predominantly slave labor force, as did the Royal Vale Mill, which worked forty blacks. Both of Savannah's rice mills owned a substantial number of slaves. The Upper Steam Rice Mills owned sixty-six slaves and employed another fifty black women seasonally.[14] In addition to the large mills, some lowcountry planters constructed mills on their own property. Indeed, some planters relied on slaves not only to work in the mills but to supervise their operations. Frank, the head driver, and Ned, the engineer, oversaw the steam mill on the Butler Island plantation.[15] In addition to the saw and rice mills, slaves worked in the cotton presses in Savannah.

Some planters in the lowcountry embraced the amelioration of slavery in the mid-nineteenth century, in part as a response to northern criticisms of slavery. These planters followed their mid-eighteenth-century predecessors who had hoped to soften the harder edges of slavery through reform. Planters like Charles C. Jones promoted efforts to Christianize slaves. A major religious figure in the state, he penned *The Religious Instruction of the Negroes* in 1842, which laid out his vision of the proper relationship between slave owners and slaves and their mutual obligations.[16] He viewed slavery as a vehicle for improving the state of uncivilized Africans and exposing them to Christianity. Understanding himself as a benevolent paternalist, he and like-minded slave owners cast slavery as a more equitable system of labor than free labor because masters cared for the welfare of their slaves.[16]

Despite their protestations to the contrary, many slave owners failed to meet their ideal. In *A Journey in the Seaboard Slave States,* Olmsted noted that one of Arnold's neighbors put a slave on the market simply to make money. He "sold an excellent man to a trader, without any previous intimation to him that he intended to do so, without having any fault to find with him, and without the slightest regard, apparently, to the strong ties of kindred which were ruptured in the transaction." He was "considered a 'pious' man" yet he "was evidently under no social taboo" against selling slaves within most circles.[17] So Arnold and some other proponents of amelioration may have claimed to sell slaves only very rarely (three in twenty years for Arnold), but others certainly did with great frequency and little hesitation. Olmsted noted another instance in which one of Arnold's neighbors, "while in a drunken frolic, not only flogged a number of his negroes, without cause, but attempted to shoot and stab them." Olmsted related that the slave owner stopped short of killing the slave only because the infraction might not have been considered "an act of insubordination to be justifiably punished with death."[18]

As in plantation slavery in the lowcountry, urban slavery in the lowcountry developed along the lines set in the late eighteenth century. Savannah and other towns of the region continued to be centers of life for the lowcountry elite who chose to reside in the towns rather than in the countryside. As in rural areas, slaves continued to perform a wide range of occupations, from the most menial to the most skilled, and most white residents continued to rely on them to fulfill virtually all of their labor needs. While many white residents owned the slaves who worked for them, many others rented their bonded labor instead. Indeed, slave hiring and slave self-hire remained integral elements of the urban slave system in the lowcountry. The towns, like the country, remained bastions of planter power and privilege.

Throughout the antebellum era, Savannah remained the state's largest and most diverse city. As Georgia's key port, Savannah's fortunes were directly tied to the economy of the export trade. In 1820, the total population was 7,253; over the course of the subsequent decade, a period of slow economic growth, the population stagnated, increasing by less than 250 individuals. The population rebounded over the course of the following twenty years, reaching 11,214 in 1840 and 15,312 in 1850. The racial composition of Savannah's population's remained roughly the same over the three decades between 1820 and 1850. The city's slave and white populations grew in tandem. Paralleling the increase of the city's white population, the slave population more than doubled between 1820 and 1850, growing from 3,075 to 6,231. Throughout most of this time, slaves accounted for four of every ten residents of the city. Over the course of the 1840s, the pattern began to shift, however, as the proportion of the slave population grew, peaking at 46 percent in 1848 before dipping to slightly less than 40 percent two years later.[19] The city, then, retained a significant black presence throughout the antebellum era.

Urban slaves in the lowcountry were not relegated to menial labor. Rather, they worked in a range of occupations and dominated certain fields. Their labor proved essential to the everyday workings of Savannah. Slave women worked in a number of fields, usually connected to domestic labor: They labored as washerwomen, seamstresses, cooks, housekeepers, and shopkeepers. Some slave women found employment as vendors of small wares, while others sold produce and eggs in the market. Black women continued to dominate the city market. Dolly Reed, for example, traveled to the countryside every three months with a rented wagon and returned carrying bacon, tobacco, flour, molasses, and sugar, which she traded for eggs, chickens, or cash. She also traded in the city market.[20] Many slave men provided personal services as barbers, butlers, coachmen, and waiters. Some transported goods, both on land and water, to and from the docks and wharf. Others served as stevedores, loading and unloading goods that passed through the city's port. In addition to manual and semiskilled labor, several dozen slave men worked as mechanics. By 1848, seventy-four slaves were identified as mechanics in Savannah. Many found employment in the building trades—as carpenters, coopers, sawyers, masons, whitewashers, and plasterers—working for master craftsmen.[21] Whites employed slaves in these trades because they believed it economical and because they thought slaves were more than capable of performing the requisite labor.

While many slave mechanics lived with their owners and worked alongside them in their shops, others negotiated with their owners for the right to sell their services as they pleased. Self-hire was a prevalent institution in Savannah, not only for mechanics but for slaves in all occupations, and had been since the colonial era.[22] Slaves were responsible for finding their own work; they paid their owners weekly, monthly, or sometimes annually. As many as 60 percent of the slaves in the city lived apart from their owners. The practice had become so ubiquitous that when Joseph Bancroft conducted his census of Savannah in 1848, he opted to record where slaves lived as opposed to where their owners lived when assigning residences.[23]

Controlling their own time provided slaves great latitude in conducting their affairs. Many used the freedom to amass small and sometimes fairly substantial savings. Charles Ball recognized the flexibility of Savannah's slave system. "In Savannah, I saw many black men who were slaves, and who yet acted as freemen so far that they went out to work, where and with whom they pleased, received their own wages, and provided their own subsistence; but were obliged to pay a certain sum at the end of each week to their masters." Ball related that "One of these men told me that he paid six dollars on every Saturday evening to his masters; and yet he was comfortably dressed, and appeared to live well." Ball also worked for a slave in Savannah who hired his time and paid his owner $250 a year for this privilege. The slave performed "job work, which consisted of undertaking jobs, and hiring men to work under him, if the job was too great to be performed by himself." In addition to Ball, the slave hired

seven or eight additional men in order to load a thousand bales of cotton on a ship.[24] As long as these slaves stayed out of trouble, or at least
avoided getting caught, and made their payments to their owners, they
were free to pursue their own lives.

While self-hire brought benefits to slaves who obtained the privilege, there can be little doubt that the practice would not have lasted
had it not produced tangible rewards for slave owners. Indeed, self-hire
proliferated precisely because it generated profits for slave owners while
requiring the bare minimum of oversight. One of William Grimes's owners purchased him specifically to allow him to hire out his own time
in Savannah. He left Savannah on business for an extended period and
had Grimes send him the $3 a week while he was away.[25] Slave owners
received a steady income without the bother of supervising the slave,
which made it an ideal system for urban women, particularly widows.
For example, most of Mary Ann Cowper's income in the 1840s came
from her ten slaves, who hired their own time. The men paid $10 to
$12 a month.[26] Richard Arnold undoubtedly spoke for many among this
class of slave owners when he asserted that hiring out slaves produced "a
better interest than the amount of their value would bring in any other
investment."[27]

To regulate the hiring of slaves, Savannah's authorities required
virtually all slaves who worked for someone other than their owner to
purchase a badge. The badge system originated in the colonial era and
evolved over the subsequent decades. By the mid-nineteenth century,
the system served an essential role in the city's efforts to govern its already chaotic labor market. Equally important, the fees garnered from
the licenses helped to pad the city's coffers. Costs varied depending on
occupation and sex: cabinetmakers, carpenters, caulkers, bricklayers,
blacksmith, tailors, barbers, or butchers paid $10.56 per year; coopers,
painters, sawyers, pilots, fishermen, boatmen, and grass cutters paid
$8.56; porters and laborers paid from $3.06 to $4.56. The last category
included women's work, which Savannah's officials taxed at a lower rate.
According to one historian's estimate, by the Civil War approximately
half of the adult male slaves living in Savannah purchased badges. The annual receipts from the sale of slave badges accounted for a sizable portion
of the city's budget, reaching close to $10,000.[28]

Although the slave system that emerged in the lowcountry may have
satisfied the interests of slave owners, it infuriated many nonelite urban
whites, particularly those living in Savannah. Urban white workers be-

lieved the slave system, particularly self-hire and hiring out, placed them at a clear disadvantage when competing for work, and they resented the fact that some slave men worked in skilled occupations. From the time the planter elite first emerged in Georgia in the 1750s as a potent political force, white workers in Savannah, particularly mechanics, had struggled to protect their economic interests, though they had largely failed in their efforts. There were moments such as in the 1790s when the city's mechanics organized themselves, but these efforts did not accomplish any substantial change.[29] In the first decades of the nineteenth century white workers' efforts flagged, only to be revived in the 1830s with the reemergence of the Savannah Mechanics' Association. The white mechanics determined that they would support candidates "who would make it a penal offense to hire a negro in preference to a white man."[30] They met often to discuss ways to protect themselves from competition with black artisans. A grand jury in 1845 in Chatham declared that "practice of slaves being permitted to hire their own time or labor for themselves" was "an evil of magnitude" that "is striking directly at the existence of our institutions." The grand jury believed that "It is but the beginning of the end . . . and unless broken up in time, will result in the total prostration of existing relations."[31]

Although the conflict between white and black mechanics drew the most scrutiny, the rivalry between nonelite whites and slaves extended to less venerated occupations as well. Indeed, it was precisely the fact that slaves worked in almost all capacities in Savannah that left nonelite whites fuming, because they could not avoid competition with them. And the badge system, they complained, made it all possible. The dominance of black women in the city market left many whites, even some supporters of the hiring-out system, particularly aggrieved. "Anti-Mulatto" in the *Savannah Republican* in 1818 illustrates the antipathy toward blacks in Savannah. He ranted about the practice of allowing elderly slaves to sell their wares in Savannah, which he contended deprived whites of the opportunity to prosper. He complained that the council refused to rectify the situation. From his perspective, the council had sided with blacks and betrayed whites. He also railed against planters who sent their superannuated slaves to the city, thereby passing along the responsibility of monitoring and caring for slaves. But the problem was equally objectionable if done by free blacks because poor whites suffered the consequences. He argued that "Many a widow and orphan, now struggling in the stream of adversity" were "too proud to take up the calling to which the most abandoned of the sable race invariably cling." If Savannah banned the practice of allowing black street peddlers, the worthy white poor "will then open small shops and live happily." In the long term, he suggested, "By such means many children, who for lack of instruction might live in vice and die in misery, would be enabled to initiate themselves into all that is requisite to mould them into useful and respectable members of society."[32] When the Chatham County grand jury convened in January 1818, it condemned the practice of granting badges to colored and black women to hawk goods on the city streets, which it labeled "an evil of great magnitude." The women monopolized the market for certain items, enabling them to make a handsome profit at the expense of whites, who had no alternative. The process affected "poor inhabitants," leaving them disproportionately "distressed." "They encourage theft; deprave our domestics, and by their evil influence and dissolute lives endanger the safety of our city." For this reason, the grand jury called on the authorities "to repeal this ordinance."[33]

In spite of the nonelite whites' complaints about the slave system, the authorities in Savannah left the offending ordinances in place. Throughout most of the antebellum era, planters and slaveholders dominated the city government, and they had no interest in implementing new restrictions that could limit the way they deployed their property. The slave system benefited slave owners and their slaves at the expense of working white men. Nonslaveholding white working men clearly felt the sting. The apparent alliance between planters and their slaves undermined nonelite whites' position in society, particularly their claims to superiority through whiteness. This fact angered nonelite whites, especially skilled working men, because it adversely affected their economic livelihoods.

Lowcountry slavery may have changed little in the first half of the nineteenth century, but the institution underwent a far more dramatic transformation as it spread to the interior of the state and took root on the lands ceded by the Creek and Cherokee Indians. There, material conditions—a different crop, a different climate, a different labor regime, and a different demography—all combined to create a new slave society, one that bore similarities to its coastal counterpart but whose distinctive characteristics pointed to the rise of a new and unique system of slavery. In the upcountry, slavery collapsed distinctions among blacks, contributed to greater social mobility for whites, offered fewer opportunities for slaves to excel or display their talents, and introduced the gang labor system. Greater equality for whites and more restrictions for blacks characterized society in the upcountry. In this way, the rise of the cotton kingdom democratized the institution of slavery for white men.[34]

In the wake of the land cessions by the Creeks in 1821, 1826, and 1827, Georgia's state officials quickly took steps to settle the contested territory and extend their authority over its residents. Affordable land combined with the cotton boom following the Napoleonic Wars created favorable conditions for personal enrichment, which attracted a broad range of migrants to the upcountry. Planters from the Georgia lowcountry and other southern states carried their slave property to the blackbelt. Legions of unattached, young white men looking for opportunity joined them. Most white settlers who arrived in the upcountry in the 1810s and 1820s shared the same antipathy toward Indians as the frontiersmen of the 1790s, but they were more supportive of the institution of plantation slavery. By 1830, twenty-three new counties with a total population of 116,323, which accounted for more than one-fifth of the state's population, had been carved out of the former Creek lands.[35]

The addition of the western lands effectively doubled the size of middle Georgia and facilitated the spread of cotton cultivation. In short order, this region became the heart of Georgia's cotton kingdom, the western section of the blackbelt, which stretched from the border with South Carolina across the middle of the state to the border with Alabama. By the middle of the decade, Georgia's blackbelt emerged as the center of the South's burgeoning cotton kingdom and rose to become the world's largest cotton producer, though other southwestern states would in later decades overtake the state. Planters in the upcountry had first grown short-staple cotton in the 1790s as part of a diverse range of crops. With the increase in prices and the emergence of the cotton gin, planters boosted output exponentially. Production grew from one thousand bales in 1790 to twenty thousand in 1801 and doubled again by 1811. After 1821, cotton production accelerated even quicker, increasing from 90,000 to 399,276 bales in less than twenty years.[36] By the eve of the Civil War, Georgia produced 521,472 bales annually. It did not take long for cotton to become king in Georgia.

Unlike rice cultivation, cotton did not require a significant outlay of capital to commence operations. Whites in the upcountry, at least early on, benefited from a plethora of available land suitable for cotton cultivation, while whites in the lowcountry confronted a scarcity of available land suitable for rice cultivation. Cotton planters could grow their crop on smaller holdings, but rice planters needed to grow their crop on a large scale to keep it cost-effective. Cotton cultivation in the upcountry could be begun without any slave labor; whites in the lowcountry required a small army of slaves to cultivate rice. In contrast to rice cultivation, then, cotton cultivation was a bargain. Cotton production placed planter status within the reach of any white settler.

Cotton cultivation laid the promise of acquiring wealth open to all white men and provided an attainable threshold for social mobility.[37] Through cotton, yeomen farmers could imagine a more prosperous life. The purchase of a slave constituted merely the first step in the process of becoming a planter. With some luck and a good harvest or two, a farmer could hope to expand both his land and his slaveholdings. And the more hands a farmer had at his disposal, the more cotton he could grow and the more money he could amass. For many white men of modest backgrounds, then, economic mobility was a distinct possibility in the Georgia upcountry.[38] Thomas Stevens, a planter in Baldwin County, exemplified the pattern. Stevens began his working life as a poor jobbing carpenter. Later, he abandoned his employment as a struggling artisan to set up a still. With the profits he made from distilling whiskey, he purchased a farm and began to buy slaves, whom he put to work in his cotton fields. Yet, even as he moved into the planter ranks, Stevens continued his liquor business on the side.[39]

These conditions resulted in a high degree of economic and social diversity among planters. While visiting Georgia's cotton belt, A. T. Havens commented on the "small class of Planters" who "are the roughest looking beings I ever saw. I refer to those who have but few negroes, work themselves, and are in many instances extremely ignorant." But, he continued, there "is another Class of Planters, as well as Business and Professional Men, who have all the comforts and even luxuries of life."[40] C. D. Arfwedson, another traveler, similarly observed that "The manners of the people were uncouth to a degree, which made It equally disagreeable and hazardous for a civilized person to remain" among them. "Many individuals, there called gentlemen, would in other places receive a very different appellation."[41] Although the two visitors' comments belied a clear class bias, they did reveal the extent to which cotton cultivation had altered the class composition of the "elite" in Georgia. To speak of a planter class in the state's cotton kingdom, then, was to refer to a broad range of men, not a monolithic group.

This mobility in the upcountry contrasts with its absence in the lowcountry. A stark divide separated the rice grandees from the rest of white society in the lowcountry, while a continuum characterized the social hierarchy in the cotton kingdom. Yeomen in the lowcountry could not as successfully and frequently achieve grandee status. The amount of capital required to buy and operate a lowcountry rice plantation successfully precluded the possibility. Yet in the cotton kingdom such rags to riches stories for white men were not uncommon, at least in the first decades of the nineteenth century.

The democratizing effects of slavery in the cotton kingdom extended even to white men who did not own slaves. Slavery in Georgia's cotton belt benefited nonelite whites because it provided them with employment opportunities. Even white men who could not afford slaves could accept a position as an overseer or learn a skilled trade. With the profusion of plantations in the region, the need for overseers increased. For white men, particularly young ones without access to capital or property, such employment offered a step toward independence and, eventually, land and slave ownership.[42] For white men with artisanal skills, the upcountry proved even more promising. When purchasing slaves, planters, particularly those with smaller holdings, generally preferred cheaper bondmen without special skills because, more often than not, they would be used in the fields. Since the majority of plantations in the region had fewer than twenty-five slaves, most planters fell into this category. Upcountry planters, then, relied on white mechanics for skilled labor, in contrast to their lowcountry counterparts, who employed skilled black slaves. Most planters were unwilling to spend the extra money required to purchase a slave artisan whose skills would only be put to use on occasion.[43] Cotton expanded opportunities for whites by limiting opportunities for blacks.

Georgia's upcountry was home to the state's largest concentration of blacks. Upcountry slaves were part of a massive redistribution of the nation's black population from the Upper South to the Deep South. Between 1790 and 1860, slave owners forcibly relocated nearly 1 million slaves. Without this massive internal slave trade, the transformation of the Deep South into the cotton kingdom would not have been possible. Despite multiple periods when slave importation was illegal in Georgia, the overall black population of Georgia grew steadily between 1810 and 1840, from 60,000 to 280,944, each decade increasing by a little more than 50,000. In the decade between 1840 and 1850, the population exploded by more than 100,000, reaching 381,682. The number reached 436,631 ten years later. The vast majority of this growth occurred in the blackbelt, on the grounds recently departed by the Creek and, to a limited degree, Cherokee Indians.[44]

Most slaves imported to Georgia in the antebellum era came from the Chesapeake, Virginia in particular, and the lowcountry. Some came with their owners in search of new land. Others were sold to speculators who prowled through plantation districts in the Upper South, trawling for slaves to bring to Georgia to be auctioned off to the highest bidder. Regardless of how slaves arrived in Georgia, their departure from their homes almost always included heartache. Many forced south were teenagers and young men and women. Ripped from their families, they were sent south and forced to reconstitute their worlds under very different conditions than they had previously lived. The process caused emotional trauma for those taken and for those who remained. John Brown was separated from his mother at the age of ten, sold to a speculator, driven in a coffle down to Georgia, and sold again. Even as a child, Brown understood that a black life had a clear price. "Owing to the considerable rise in the price of cotton, there came a great demand for sales in Georgia." His owner was "in want of money" because he was building a new house, so he made a deal with a speculator to sell him by the pound. The speculator weighed him and agreed on a final price. "Within five minutes after," he recalled, the slave trader "paid the money, and I was marched off. I looked around and saw my poor mother stretching out her hands after me. She ran up, and overtook us," but the speculator refused to allow her to say goodbye to her son. "That was the last time I ever saw her."[45] The internal slave trade uprooted families, decimated communities, and left a devastating emotional impact on those who endured it.

While not as lethal as its Atlantic counterpart, the internal slave trade was a physically brutal ordeal. After a grueling six- to eight-week journey across hundreds of miles, slaves arrived in Georgia. Some were sold as the coffles made their way through the countryside. Others wound up on the auction block in the towns and cities that dotted the interior. Cities such as Augusta, Macon, Louisville, and Columbus had large slave markets. Columbus served as a gateway to the Southwest. Planters from surrounding areas, including eastern Alabama, patronized Georgia's slave markets.[46]

As cotton pushed ever westward, slave prices increased and traders prospered. In 1800, the price for a prime field hand was $500; in 1860, the price reached $1,800. But prices fluctuated over that time, paralleling the dips and swoons in the southern economy and the cotton market. The price swelled dramatically in the 1850s as a wave of speculation swept the

Number of Slaves, 1790

One dot • represents 200 slaves

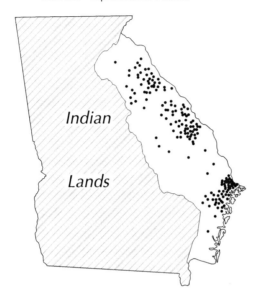

Number of Slaves, 1860

One dot • represents 200 slaves

state and the South. The price soared almost 80 percent over the course of the decade.[47] Prices varied depending on the age and condition of the slave. Slaves with knowledge of a trade or a special skill were also valued. In the cotton South, prospective buyers particularly coveted slave women with proven fertility, known as "good breeding women."[48] The rise of the cotton kingdom placed preeminence on slave women's reproductive labors. Since slavery's introduction to Georgia, Africans had been valued primarily for their labor. By the antebellum era, however, slave women's ability to create wealth through reproduction assumed greater importance. Slave women represented valuable future investments. Whites who purchased pregnant and "likely" women clearly hoped to profit from the fruit of their wombs.[49]

For slaves in the Upper South, the threat of being sold "down South" loomed ever present. Frequently, owners used the prospect of sale to control unruly slaves, a method often more effective than physical discipline. Threats of sale left no scars, at least no visible ones, marring the value of an owner's property.[50] William Grimes, a slave in Virginia, noted that his owners constantly threatened to send him south should he misbehave. For "any trifling offence," his owners made abundantly clear that they would sell him to a "negro buyer from Georgia." His life there would be terrible, they told him. He would "have to eat cotton seed and make indigo" and he would "not have corn bread to eat" as he did in Virginia.[51] Grimes's words illustrate that while separation from one's family was clearly the most traumatic aspect of being sold to the Deep South, slaves faced other concerns as well, principally their working and living conditions once there. Slavery throughout the South existed as a violent and coercive system, which denied enslaved humans basic legal protections. But by the early nineteenth century, slaves in the Chesapeake and low-country had slowly chiseled out a degree of autonomy for themselves in society. Slaves in those areas had managed through custom to negotiate improved conditions.[52] They feared that removal from the Upper South would entail a loss of these privileges. Their fear was not misplaced.

In many ways, Georgia's blackbelt deserved its reputation for harshness. These differences were reflected in the treatment of slaves. As with rice grandees in the lowcountry, some of the largest cotton planters in the blackbelt adopted a benevolent paternalism in their relations with the slaves; their wealth insulated them from the need to drive their bondspeople to squeeze out profits. With farmers and smaller planters (and even some wealthy planters), the situation was often quite different.

They drove the slaves to their physical limits in the pursuit of profits. And because these slave owners vastly outnumbered their wealthier counterparts, their treatment of slaves, in effect, became the norm in Georgia's cotton kingdom. Slaves transported to the Georgia upcountry endured a severe work regimen. The first generation of slaves in the upcountry labored under brutal conditions, clearing the vast forests that covered the land. Axmen lived tough lives, a frontier existence in which, in addition to their everyday exertions, they feared attack by Indians opposed to black and white settlement. But even as the frontier transformed into settled plantations, slaves' working conditions did not improve markedly. Though less physically demanding than clearing forests, cotton cultivation required long days, from sunup to sundown, to maintain the plants and protect them from pests.[53] For Charles Ball, a slave transported from Maryland to Georgia in the early nineteenth century, the fact that he had entered a different world became clear shortly after he saw his first cotton fields. He witnessed "a gang" of slaves at work "hoeing cotton by the roadside, nearby them, attended by any overseer in a white linen shirt and pantaloons, with one of the long negro whips in his hands." The scene made clear the systematic domination of slaves' behavior at all times by whites in the cotton South. "It was manifest that I was now in a country where the life of a black man was no more regarded than an ox, except as far as the man was worth more money in the market."[54] Skills were not valued as much as sheer brawn.

On larger plantations, the day usually began with the overseer blowing a horn at 4:00 A.M. Slaves fed the livestock and prepared the draft animals for the day's work before making their way to the fields. They took their breakfast in the fields, paused for a brief break for lunch, and then worked until dark. At certain times of the year even darkness did not bring an end to fieldwork; usually during harvests slaves worked well into the night, by torchlight if necessary. After finishing their fieldwork, slaves retired to their quarters, but their day was not over. Women were required to spin and weave, while men repaired utensils and buildings, hunted, and fished. Exhausted by their daily routine, many slaves collapsed once they completed their work. Most slaves received Saturday afternoon and all day Sunday off to recuperate. The only respite from this routine came at Christmas, when slaves enjoyed a brief holiday.[55] Slaves in the cotton kingdom labored under better physical conditions than their lowcountry counterparts; though unbearably hot during certain times of the year, the conditions in the cotton fields of the blackbelt were not as harsh as the malarial swamplands on the coast. Yet improved working conditions did not bring slaves increased autonomy.

Slaves in the blackbelt found themselves subjected to far greater white supervision and control than lowcountry slaves. Slaves who moved from the lowcountry to the interior attempted to make the task system the norm, but they possessed little leverage. Cotton planters possessed their own ideas about the proper methods of slave management. Many preferred a system that reduced their slaves' autonomy and limited their access to provision fields. They doled out subsistence-level rations rather than allowing slaves to grow their own food. This practice was intended to enhance masters' image as providers and their slaves' as dependents. Many blackbelt planters had arrived from the Upper South, where the gang system predominated, and they resisted implementation of the task system, preferring instead to use a more managed form of labor.[56] Some planters from the lowcountry experimented with the task system on their blackbelt plantations. For example, Alexander Telfair used the task system on his cotton plantation near Augusta, but he employed a white overseer and no black drivers.[57] By the 1830s the gang system became pervasive in the blackbelt. The gang system did not possess the same incentives for efficient labor. In an effort to maximize the amount of labor from their slaves, white slave owners and overseers therefore resorted to the whip to maintain a steady working pace.[58] Slaves recalled the punishments that occurred when individuals failed to meet their daily quota, which on most plantations ranged from 150 to 200 pounds.[59] Whipping became an everyday part of life in the cotton South, leaving the victims emotionally and physically scarred but able to resume work after a few days off.

While violence characterized slavery everywhere, slave owners in the blackbelt relied on the whip for everyday discipline. The whip had always been used, but in the cotton lands masters and overseers used it in a different way. Rather than employing incentives, like the lowcountry's task system that rewarded efficient work with free time, planters in the cotton kingdom used disincentives, like physical punishment, for failing to meet daily quotas set at extremely high standards. Planters and overseers used the whip to enforce work pace and as a means of punishing transgressions, but also just to terrorize and to maintain a sense of superiority. They employed arbitrary violence to instill among slaves the power and scope of white supremacy. Strong black men became the targets of white violence. Slaves felt the sting of the lash for a range of other transgressions, real and imagined. Some of the most contentious interactions between slaves and owners took place on plantations and farms with small holdings, between fifteen and thirty slaves. The owners were middling folks who employed no overseer and enjoyed few amenities.[60]

Many skilled slaves imported to Georgia's cotton kingdom faced a future with limited work options compared to their former homes. The result for some was a reduction in their status, since there were few occupational opportunities beyond growing cotton. In the blackbelt, slaves endured a more circumscribed role in the economy. The crop's high price helped fuel this transformation. Planters devoted virtually all their lands to cotton cultivation at the expense of other crops. Planters wanted bodies in the fields to profit from the increase. Moreover, white artisans performed most skilled work in the blackbelt, in both rural and urban areas.[61] The situation was particularly tough on enslaved men taken from the Upper South. They had departed a society that had transformed in the decades following the Revolution. Partly as a result of soil degradation and partly as a result of the drop in the market price for tobacco, planters in the Chesapeake had shifted to a more diversified agricultural base. This period also witnessed a growth in manufacturing in the region. The changes in the economy brought a greater diversity to the Upper South and proved the malleability of slavery as an institution. Even those who labored in the countryside performed a variety of tasks. Relying less on tobacco, farmers and planters grew wheat and corn and branched out into manufacturing. Spurred by changes in the international tobacco market, this transition to a mixed economy meant that slaves worked in a variety of capacities. Some slaves performed specialized labor on the plantations, like husbandry and other occupations related to the shift to mixed agriculture. Others were apprenticed to skilled craftsmen, then hired out on a short- or long-term basis. Some men were involved in transportation or service industries, which brought them off the plantation, an additional bonus. Most, though not all, of the opportunities for skilled work were usually open only to men. The fields of the Upper South became the province of women as men found employment in other areas.[62] For slaves from the Chesapeake, getting sold down south meant separation from loved ones as well as increased physical hardship and less variety in the work regime.

Charles Ball's story exemplifies the hardships faced by slaves sold to the Georgia upcountry. He was brought to South Carolina and eventually Georgia, where he was put to work on a cotton plantation. His work was less rewarding than in Maryland. He went from being a fisherman to being a cotton picker.[63] Ball was not pleased by the changed labor regime. Indeed, he described plantation life in the cotton belt as a "dull and monotonous existence" and cotton picking as a "fatiguing labor . . . one to which I never became reconciled." The labor regime in the cotton kingdom delegitimized and deskilled black labor and contributed to the collapsing of distinctions among people of African descent.

Ball, like other slaves arriving in the cotton belt, quickly discovered that cotton cultivation required skills that could not easily be acquired if attempted too late in life. "Picking of cotton may almost be reckoned among the arts," claimed Ball. Common wisdom predicted that a man who learned to pick cotton after the age of twenty-five could never become a "*crack picker.*" Indeed, the first time Ball picked cotton proved a humbling experience. "I had ascertained that at the hoe, the spade, the sickle, or the flail," he declared, "I was a full match for the best hands on the plantation." When it came to cotton picking, he admitted, "I was not equal to a boy of fifteen." His first haul amounted to only thirty-eight pounds, well below what was expected from a prime hand. Two other men his age picked fifty-eight and fifty-nine pounds, respectively. "I hung down my head, and felt very much ashamed of myself when I found that my cotton was so far behind that of many, even of the women, who had heretofore regarded me as the strongest and most powerful man of the whole gang." After a couple of days Ball improved his performance so that only three other hands—two men and a woman—could pick more than him. He expressed a genuine sense of pride in this accomplishment, yet he never reconciled with the fact that "in every other kind of work I was called a first rate hand, whilst in cotton picking I was hardly regarded as a *prime hand.*"[64]

Though his labor under slavery was coerced, Ball nevertheless took pride in his work, not necessarily to garner the praise of the overseer or the master but to savor the admiration of the slave women on the plantation. He lamented the fact that the women had regarded him as the "strongest and most powerful man of the whole gang" of slaves until they saw him pick cotton. Like most men of the period, his status as superior to women, at least in terms of labor, formed an integral part of his identity as a man. Yet the very nature of the work regimen in the cotton belt deprived many male slaves of that claim. Having arrived in the cotton kingdom as men, they lacked the skills necessary to make them superior laborers compared to young men or even women. This, combined with their inabilities to claim rights in their women, emasculated new transplants to the cotton South.

While cotton cultivation tended to deskill and emasculate enslaved men, it could elevate slave women. Men and women worked side by side, doing many of the same tasks. Women plowed, cut wood, hoed, and picked cotton just like men.[65] Nancy Boudry, a slave in Columbia County, "had to work hard." She plowed and "split wood jus' like a man."[66] Sally Brown was put in the fields when she was five years old, picking cotton and hoeing. After her first owner died she found herself transferred from plantation to plantation. The one thing that remained constant in her life was that she "worked hard always." She, too, split wood like a man.[67] Many female field hands were proud of the fact that they were the equal of their male counterparts. Ferebe Rogers was a slave in Baldwin County, the oldest of thirteen children. She was not the fastest one with a hoe, but no one, man or woman, was superior to her with the plow. She was so proficient that she considered herself raised "twix' the plow handles."[68] Julia Rush felt the same way. Working in the fields with her mother and three sisters, Rush contended that she could "out plow" any man.[69] Paradoxically, cotton was the great equalizer in terms of gender and work among the slave population.[70]

The subjugation of slaves to the worst kind of labor in upcountry Georgia was a critical component of the effort to solidify the ascent of white supremacy in the state. Cotton cultivation was brutal and most other occupations were off limits to slaves. Unlike in the Upper South, where the diversification of the economy had allowed blacks to branch out into fields beyond those connected exclusively to tobacco, or the lowcountry, where skilled slaves made up a significant portion of the total slave population, the cotton belt offered few options. That field work in the cotton belt became gender neutral moved in the opposite direction from other areas in the South, where a gendered division of labor was the norm. Cotton cultivation was tedious and arduous but not so physically difficult as to make it the exclusive province of men. It was hard work, but *anyone* could do it, male or female, young or old.

The conditions of slavery in the Georgia upcountry in the 1830s rendered unlikely the kind of insurrectionary violence that had characterized the state's early history or had roiled the Caribbean and South America. Slaves understood that rebelling meant certain death. As such, those without death wishes tended to avoid outright insurrection. Though they outnumbered whites in certain pockets of the state, overall, slaves represented a minority of the population and had virtually no access to the weapons necessary to mount a successful rebellion. Slaves faced even greater scrutiny after the publication and dissemination of David Walker's *Appeal to the Coloured Citizens of the World* in 1829 and Nat Turner's rebellion in Virginia two years later. Shocked and horrified by the number of whites killed during the failed uprising, white Georgians, like their counterparts throughout the South, clamped down on their slaves. Occasionally rumors of impending slave conspiracies spread in the state, yet many of these scares proved little more than false alarms.[71] Periodically slaves, individually or in small groups, did commit murders or other violent acts against whites, but these examples were the clearly the exception to the rule and usually represented the actions of slaves who had been pushed too far.

Yet, as in the lowcountry, slaves in the blackbelt did not simply accept their condition. Most slaves channeled their anger into various kinds of everyday resistance. Perhaps the most popular way slaves resisted was through shirking their work obligations. They feigned illness. They slowed down the pace of work when the overseer turned away. They broke tools. They turned to arson. Property crime constituted one of the most common forms of petty resistance in the blackbelt. Slaves stole goods, usually cotton or another agricultural commodity, and bartered them with white men. Frequently slaves took—or stole, according to the planters—food when presented with an opportunity. Many blamed their actions on their limited diets. Others understood their actions as a reappropriation of the fruits of their labors, which their masters had unjustly stolen from them.

A minority of slaves pursued a more radical approach. In a handful of cases, slaves from Georgia's blackbelt succeeded in escaping to the North.[72] The most famous runaways were William Craft, a cabinetmaker, and Ellen Craft, a domestic servant, of Macon. After obtaining passes from their owners to give themselves a head start, Ellen posed as an elderly white gentleman and her husband posed as her waiting man. In this manner, they traveled by train and steamer to Savannah, then Charleston, then Wilmington, then Richmond, and then finally to freedom in the North in 1848.[73] Most runaways could not aspire to freedom beyond the boundaries of the state. The border to the closest free state was a thousand miles away. The defeat of the Seminoles in 1818 and the subsequent annexation of Florida by the United States had left slave runaways few avenues of escape. When aggrieved by their treatment at the hands of the overseer or owner, some slaves showed their displeasure by running away for brief periods of time. Usually, they found shelter in wooded areas, living off the land or relying on the assistance of sympathetic slaves on nearby plantations.[74]

The rise of the cotton culture, then, provided mobility for white Georgians but immobility for black Georgians. Slavery in the cotton-producing regions of the upcountry provided opportunities for white advancement by opening plantation slaveholding to a greater proportion of the population and creating opportunities for white skilled and unskilled labor. For newly arrived slaves, enslavement in the upcountry meant less autonomy in their daily lives, both in the fields and in the quarters. The work was tedious and back-breaking. It reduced virtually all slaves to the same level, male or female, and offered fewer opportunities for stratification or improvement. Worst still, slaves faced greater white oversight and increased violence.

While the vast majority of slaves in Georgia's blackbelt cultivated cash crops, thousands of slaves worked in nonagricultural occupations. Over the course of the nineteenth century, slavery emerged as a dynamic institution that proved useful in a range of settings. As Georgia's economy diversified, so too did slavery. Slave labor played an essential role in the development of the state's infrastructure and the nascent industries that took root beginning in the 1820s. The use of slaves in constructing internal improvements represented one way in which slavery benefited all white Georgians, even nonslaveholders. Entrepreneurs relied on slaves to spur nascent industries, which contributed to the economic diversification and self-sufficiency of the state. Though slaves remained key laborers in saw and rice mills in the lowcountry, white laborers had largely pushed black workers out of mining and textile mills in the upcountry by the late 1840s. Railroads remained the one main exception, continuing to employ black labor. Nonagricultural slave labor, especially in the upcountry by the late antebellum era, then, had developed into a system that profited a significant proportion of the white population, both elite and nonelite.

As Georgia's borders expanded and plantation slavery spread to the lands ceded by the Creeks and Cherokees, the development of the state's infrastructure became a paramount concern for planters, yeomen, merchants, and politicians. The rise of new transportation technologies and the rapid growth of cotton cultivation spurred experimentation in a number of different directions. Though white Georgians sometimes disagreed over the best method of connecting the fields of the interior to the markets of the coast, they agreed that, regardless of the type of transportation, slave labor would play an integral role in its construction and maintenance. From the rather rudimentary efforts to clear the state's rivers to the construction of a vast network of railroads, Georgia's internal improvement projects relied on slaves to carry out most of the work that allowed Georgia's economy to grow and prosper in the antebellum era.[75]

The first concerted effort to develop Georgia's transportation needs using slave labor focused on the state's rivers. The state first appropriated funds to purchase slaves for its internal improvement campaign in 1815. The program began with the Oconee River and expanded to the state's other major rivers in the 1820s. The legislature appointed commissioners to supervise the projects and manage the slaves. As the number of projects increased, the authorities hired a state engineer, Hamilton Fulton, to oversee the various endeavors. When questions arose over the direction of the program, Fulton advised the state authorities to continue on its path. "I feel satisfied from the experience I have had in the Southern States that it will be impossible to go with such operations in an expeditious and satisfactory manner, unless there are a number of negroes purchased by the State," he noted. "It appears to me it would be the most economical plan for the State to purchase as many slaves as the nature and extent of the proposed improvements will require."[76] In 1829, the legislature heeded his words, centralizing control over the state's internal improvement projects and doubling its investment in slave labor. The state authorities removed the public hands from the river stations and redeployed them to the largest nearby towns, placed them under the authority of two superintendents, and enlarged the scope of the program to include roadwork as well. The law mandated the number of slaves for each station: Columbus, twenty-five; Macon, twenty-five; Milledgeville, fifteen; Savannah, twenty-five; Flint River, twenty-five; Augusta, seventy-five. An overseer selected by local authorities managed each site and possessed the power to designate where the slaves were to be deployed.[77] By the early 1830s, the state had spent more than $100,000 on its public hands program and owned more than two hundred slaves. These state-owned public hands benefited the white public in general through their labors.

Despite this massive investment, the program came to an end in 1833 when the legislature adopted a new approach toward internal improvements and sold all of its bondmen at public auction. The demise of the public hands program did not signify a break with the practice of using slaves to construct the state's infrastructure, however. Even as the state abandoned its policy of slave ownership, white Georgians continued to rely on black men to provide the essential labor for the construction of the state's infrastructure.[78]

Even as the General Assembly was spending tens of thousands of dollars to clear the state's roads and waterways in the late 1820s, urgent new appeals emerged, calling for a radical redirection of the state's internal improvement efforts. Faced with competition from Asia, Africa, and South America, the South's monopoly on cotton production for Europe had eroded. As profits plummeted, Georgia's planters, farmers, and merchants sought new ways to protect their interests. The best way to keep the producers competitive was to reduce the cost of transporting goods to the coast for shipment. To accomplish this objective, the legislature created the Board of Public Improvement to oversee the development of the state's infrastructure. Legislators debated the merits of various modes of transport but concluded that canals and railroads offered the best value. Railroads, in particular, were "the most practicable and useful, at least for the middle and upcountry." Although railroads required substantial initial outlays, the investment would prove most cost-effective in the long run. According to one estimate, the state's farmers and planters could reduce their transportation costs by 80 percent if the changes were adopted.[79]

While legislators may have debated which mode of transportation offered the greatest benefits, they agreed that slaves should provide the bulk of the labor used to construct the various projects. Slave labor, they estimated, cost less than a third of comparable free white labor. By contrast, "Hired labor is objectionable from its uncertainty and expensiveness; uncertain from the constant liability to desertion and . . . expensive from the enormous price demanded by that class of our population whose labor can be thus obtained under the necessary restrictions to ensure a fulfillment of their promise."[80]

As in much of the nation, the canal building craze came to Georgia in the 1820s and 1830s following the completion of the Erie Canal in 1825. Construction on at least two transportation canals in the state involved slave labor. White residents of Savannah led the campaign to build the first project, the Savannah, Ogeechee, & Altamaha Canal. The city's mayor at the time, William C. Daniell, proposed the idea and the city council agreed after extensive discussions, chartering prominent local merchants and planters to carry out the work. Laborers dug sixteen miles of the proposed route, successfully linking the Savannah and Ogeechee rivers, before abandoning the remaining portion of the planned extension.[81]

The second project, the Brunswick Canal, began construction in 1837. Conceived as a means to connect the Brunswick and Altamaha rivers, the canal enjoyed the support of several prominent lowcountry planters, including Thomas Butler King of Glynn County, who served as the company's treasurer. Like its predecessor, the Brunswick scheme faltered when its backers failed to secure sufficient financial backing. The effort came to a final end in 1839 when funding dried up completely.[82]

Both projects employed a mixture of enslaved and free labor. Canal contractors did not purchase slaves to labor on the projects; instead they paid $15 to $20 a month to rent slaves from their owners. In general, contractors preferred enslaved over free workers because they perceived them to be more docile and less likely to cause any serious problems. Because most native-born white men in Georgia, and the South in general, viewed ditch digging as beneath them, most of the white workers who found employment with the canals were foreigners who had only recently arrived in Georgia.[83] These laborers were notorious for their propensity to engage in strikes and other kinds of labor actions that slowed the progress of the work. In 1837, for example, 150 Irish workers marched on Savannah over a wage dispute and were only thwarted in their attempt by the intervention of a priest and the arrival of militiamen.[84] Equally troublesome, contractors complained, the Irish displayed antagonistic, even hostile, behavior toward slaves, which made some slave owners reluctant to hire out their bondmen to work on the canals. Violent encounters between the two groups were not infrequent. As a result, one observer noted, the "Irishmen and these slaves are not allowed to work together, but are kept apart at separate stations on the canal." This was necessary because of the immigrants' "insolence toward them, and hatred of them."[85]

In the wake of the abortive canal-building phase in Georgia, boosters and legislators enthusiastically embraced railroads. The Central Georgia Railroad, which connected Macon and Savannah, began construction in 1835. In the decades that followed, railroads proliferated. New routes connected towns and cities across the piedmont with one another and with the coastal markets. By 1861, Georgia boasted eighteen railroad companies in the state and fourteen thousand miles of track, making it the leader in train transportation in the Lower South and second only to Virginia in the South as a whole.[86]

Slaves remained the core of the workforce used in the construction of railroads. Railroad companies experimented with various kinds of labor systems, but most ultimately relied on slave labor. Although exact numbers are difficult to determine, it is clear that companies and contractors employed thousands of slaves to build and maintain the railroad system in Georgia.[87] As with canals, authorities rented slaves to perform the labor. Often the companies hired slaves from planters whose property was close to the line. Advertisements in antebellum newspapers were a common sight and testify to the extent of the practice. For example, the classified section of the *Savannah Daily Georgian* included an announcement from the Central Railroad that it sought "One hundred able Bodied Negro Men" to work on the line between Macon and Savannah for one year. The company promised slave owners "liberal wages" for the use of their bondmen.[88] Slave owners would profit both from access to the trains and from the $15 to $20 paid per month for each slave they provided. Companies usually paid with a mixture of cash and stocks when they hired slave laborers. Wealthy planters stood to benefit from the arrangements that brought the railroad to their backyard and paid them for doing so. Hiring slaves to the railroads helped to absorb surplus labor and could be quite lucrative. For example, the planter Farish Carter netted $6,048 when he supplied "30 good able bodied Negro men" and "2 good men" as hewers and two women as cooks to work on the Milledgeville & Gordon Railroad for a year.[89] Because the potential for conflict between slaves and white laborers remained a concern for planters, the railroad companies strove to assure owners that their property would be protected. For example, the Muscogee Railroad Company assured owners in 1852 that "The Negroes will be worked in Co's separately and at a distance from any white laborers who will be employed in the same line of work."[90]

While most railroad companies relied on hired slave labor, the Central Georgia Railroad Company opted to purchase them instead. The Central employed a workforce of five hundred men, most of whom were black. The company had used free white labor for three years in the 1840s before switching to slave labor almost entirely. The president of the company judged slave labor far more efficient and less prone to delay from labor actions. The switch followed a disturbance between different groups of white workers. The president complained that in "the course of two or three months, it was manifest that the plan adopted would soon bring the company to ruin. The waste of fuel, the turbulence and general confusion were fearful." As an alternative, the company employed slave-owning contractors for the grading work and purchased $40,000 worth of slaves for the shop and road work. A combination of the slaves' "great-er expertness and efficiency" and the "ability at all times to control their services" made slave labor the best labor system for railroads, according to the president of the Central.[91] After 1845, railroad companies increas-ingly followed this business model, shifting away from free white labor and toward a greater reliance on slave labor, both hired and purchased.[92]

White Georgians profited from more than improved transportation and economic opportunities through slaves' labor on railroads. Governor Joseph E. Brown called for the state authorities to invest a portion of the revenues from the Western & Atlantic Railroad in the state's public schools to promote democratization and white equality. The profits from the railroad, built with slave labor to maximize savings, would benefit white Georgians collectively while simultaneously lifting poor whites' fortunes. "Let the children of the richest and the poorest parents in the State, meet in the school-room on terms of perfect equality of right. Let there be no aristocracy there but an aristocracy of color and conduct."[93] Legislators approved his initiative and increased the funding for educa-tion from $29,569 in 1859 to $149,565 in 1860.[94] In this way, state authorities used black labor as a leveling mechanism for whites.

Slave labor, then, was essential in developing Georgia's infrastructure. Through slave labor on the construction of roads, canals, and railroads, the institution benefited slave owners who sold or hired their slaves as workers, nonslave owners who worked as overseers, and white Georgians in general who reaped the opportunities generated by improved trans-portation networks. New transportation routes, especially railroad lines, opened the interior of the state to overseas markets. Slave labor in state infrastructure further served the white collective good by funding the public school system.

In addition to their labor on state infrastructure, slaves provided another source of nonagricultural labor in the Georgia upcountry. Slave labor enabled entrepreneurs to experiment with manufacturing and industrial opportunities. Georgia's economy experienced significant growth in the antebellum era. Although the rise of cotton cultivation ac-counted for most of the increase, manufacturing and industry played an integral role in the state's development. In addition to the production of timber-related commodities, which had played a small but crucial part of the economy since Georgia's founding, white Georgians developed new industries in the antebellum period. While not as advanced as those in New England, Georgia's nascent industries led the way in the Deep South.

These industries, which differed by region, relied on slave labor to varying degrees. By the 1840s, however, this labor shifted toward nonelite
white Georgians.[95]

Georgia whites increasingly saw their fates tied to diversifying the
region's economy. There were several reasons for this position: they were
at the mercy of the cotton prices that fluctuated wildly in the late 1820s
and 1830s; they were economically vulnerable because of their reliance
on the North to purchase their cotton and supply them with finished
goods; and they believed such problems highlighted the shortcomings
of the southern "way of life" and provided fodder for northern critics who decried the economic backwardness of the region. As a result,
white Georgians, even planters who stressed the importance of agriculture, embraced efforts to modernize the economy through industrial development. The vicissitudes of the world cotton market spurred many
white Georgians to consider the need to break free of their reliance on
the crop. Economic diversification also ensured southern self-sufficiency
amid the growing sectional crisis. The *Southern Whig* argued that "The encouragement of the mechanic arts alone can affect our emancipation
from Northern thralldom, and render our country what it was intended
to become, the garden-spot of the World."[96]

In middle Georgia, whites attempted to diversify in the second
quarter of the nineteenth century. Textile manufacturing led the way.[97]
Harnessing the power of the Oconee and Savannah rivers, entrepreneurs
erected the first cotton mills near Augusta and Athens. Boosters championed the new source of revenue as a much-needed addition to the
region's increasingly stagnant economy. With abundant natural resources,
proximity to the source of raw material, and a cheap labor source, white
residents of the region envisioned a lucrative future in manufacturing.
"The capacity of the Southern States for manufacturing their great staple,
is no longer a matter of speculation," proclaimed the *Georgia Courier* in
April 1828. "Practical experiment has demonstrated, not only their capacity to manufacture, but to manufacture their own staple at a cheaper
rate than any part of the Union!"[98] In a short time, Augusta and Athens
were home to a number of profitable mills. Success bred imitation. In
the 1840s, textile manufacturing spread west to Macon and Columbus,
to the heart of the state's cotton kingdom. Within the decade, Columbus
became a center of textile production. With two "extensive" cotton factories operating in 1848, the *Milledgeville Federal Union* noted, Columbus had
become the "Lowell of Georgia."[99]

From the outset of the textile industry in Georgia, owners employed slave labor. Indeed, many of the first Georgians to invest in textile mills were mechanics who used their own bondmen and -women. In other instances, factory owners hired slaves from nearby planters to work the looms. For many white Georgians, slave labor represented a logical choice for factory work. They agreed with the *Macon Telegraph*'s assertion that "slaves are most profitable of all operatives (in the manufacture of cotton goods)....They are more docile, more constant, and cheaper than free men."[100] Few whites doubted the intellectual and physical capacity of slaves to perform the work. After visiting several textile mills in Georgia, the English traveler James Silk Buckingham noted that "negroes here are found to be quite as easily taught to perform all the required duties of spinners and weavers as the whites, and are just as tractable when taught."[101]

Despite the fact that slaves proved adept at factory work, no consensus emerged on the use of bonded labor in textile mills. Factory owners experimented with their workforces in the first decades of the industry. Although some mills continued to rely on slave labor exclusively, others used free white labor or a mixture of the two. By the time of Buckingham's tour in the 1840s, however, factory owners were increasingly turning from slave to free labor.[102] The main reason for this shift was financial. With the arrival of thousands of new immigrants desperate for work, the price for white labor had declined to the point that it made more economic sense to rely on white workers than slaves.

In Cherokee country, slaves also performed a key role in the region's early industrial development.[103] The discovery of gold there in 1829 precipitated a rush that played a critical role in the state's annexation of the Cherokees' territory. Soon after word spread, thousands of men and boys descended on the contested land. The men and boys were mostly poor and landless whites, but some blacks joined the rush. In the weeks and months that followed, anarchic conditions prevailed. The scene, as one observer described it, "presented a most motley appearance of whites, Indians, halfbreeds and negroes, boys of fourteen and old men of seventy—and indeed their occupations appeared to be as various as their complexions comprising diggers, sawyers, shopkeepers, peddlers, thieves and gamblers, etc."[104] By the mid-1830s, after the state extended its authority over the Cherokee country, the lawless character of the mining industry largely disappeared. With the establishment of order, production became more organized and the number of slaves used in mining grew.[105]

As in other industries, mining companies relied on a mixture of rented and owned slaves to perform labor. Some mining companies purchased slaves as a means to guarantee a steady labor supply. Others sought slaves to hire at $10 month in the 1830s. The use of rented slaves provided an outlet for planters who had a surplus of slave labor. This must have been especially true in the late 1830s and early 1840s, when the price of cotton sagged. However, the industry had its own unique dangers that made many slave owners reluctant to hire out their bondmen. A group of slaves, for example, was killed when support beams collapsed at the Franklin Mine in Cherokee County. The nature of the work prompted some planters to refuse offers to lease their slaves.[106]

In other instances, cotton planters brought large groups of their slaves to work the mines. For example, John C. Calhoun transported twenty of his slaves from his plantation in South Carolina to Georgia to mine for gold during the lull in the cotton planting season.[107] Working the mines provided what some planters believed to be an excellent source of off-season labor for their male slaves. As nineteenth-century mining engineers Henry Nitze and Henry Wilkens noted, "Farming and gold-digging went, in many cases, hand in hand. When crops were laid by, the slaves and farm-hands were turned into the creek-bottoms, thus utilizing their time during the dull season."[108] The use of slaves meant less time for the bondmen to recover from the rigors of the planting and harvesting season but produced steady—and sometimes remarkable—profits for their owners. For example, Thomas Lumsden, the owner of a mine in the Nacoochee Valley, claimed that his slaves produced $30,000 worth of gold in a single season.[109] Mining offered more proof that agriculture and industry did not have to be at odds and could in fact be complementary.

The use of slaves in the mines declined precipitously in the 1840s. The decline was directly linked to structural changes in Georgia's mining industry, which reached its apex of production in the middle of the decade and then suffered flagging fortunes. A number of factors contributed to the decline. Most prominently, it became more difficult to extract the gold. When panning and other simplistic methods no longer produced the kind of astonishing results they once had, mining companies shifted to new methods that relied less on slave labor and more on machinery. The discovery of gold in California in 1849 played a role as well, draining many of the miners away.[110]

Despite the vast changes in Georgia over the course of the first half of the nineteenth century, slavery emerged as a remarkably plastic institution, capable of accommodating itself to virtually any setting. Slavery flourished in rural and urban as well as skilled and unskilled settings. And it could be redirected instantly. Unlike a machine that could be used for one purpose, slaves, white Georgians recognized, could be deployed in an infinite number of ways. Free-labor advocates in the North may have disagreed, but slavery in the upcountry proved to be a dynamic institution.

Slavery's ability to morph proved a boon to planters and slave owners who weathered the changes in the state's economy in the antebellum era. But this malleability spurred renewed debate over the proper use of slave labor. How absolute were property rights in a society ostensibly devoted to republicanism and white supremacy? Did they supersede the rights of nonslave owners to earn enough to support their families? Georgia's towns and cities became the battleground in the struggle over these questions. In this conflict, nonelite urban whites, led by mechanics, used the power of their numbers to shape the laws related to race and slavery. Mechanics organized movements at the state and local level and pushed for restrictions on blacks to bar them from most forms of skilled and semiskilled labor. The movements waxed and waned during the antebellum era. Yet, by the eve of the Civil War, mechanics and other nonelite urban whites had helped to reform slavery to reflect their views and interests.[111] Their success was not complete, nor was it felt uniformly through the state. But the political dominance enjoyed by the planter elite in early Georgia and its ability to construct the laws of slavery so that they benefited slave owners, even at the expense of other citizens of the state, were no longer tolerated.[112] Nonelite whites in upcountry urban areas pushed to ensure that Georgia lived up to the promises guaranteed to all citizens of the slaveholding republic, to in essence democratize slavery. Though they did not succeed in shaping slavery on the state level, they did achieve some successes on the local level.

The banning of self-hire in the most populous towns in the interior of the state between 1827 and 1834 was a clear indication that slavery in the upcountry differed dramatically from the pattern set by slavery in the lowcountry. Passed by the General Assembly, the laws prohibited slaves from hiring their own time and living apart from their owners in Sparta, Augusta, Clinton, Macon, and Milledgeville as well as four upcountry counties.[113]

The laws had dual intentions: they were designed to avoid the anarchy of Savannah and to offer a form of protection for white laborers working in those cities, a level of protection that their counterparts in Savannah did not enjoy. The laws opened employment opportunities for whites and ensured that blacks had fewer opportunities for economic advancement. The practice of self-hire in the lowcountry contributed to the fluidity of the racial order. Whites in the upcountry imposed restrictions to prevent the near freedom experienced by the slaves who enjoyed the right to self-hire in Savannah. The laws prevented unregulated competition between white mechanics on one hand and planters and their skilled slaves on the other. As relatively new slave societies, upcountry towns possessed no established traditions or beliefs on issues of slavery and race. Thus, white nonelites enjoyed some flexibility in creating a system of slavery that suited their interests.

By the mid-1840s, agricultural and "mechanic interests" exhibited significant contention. The Panic of 1837 had a profound impact in Georgia's agricultural industry, particularly cotton production. The price of cotton plummeted, reaching a low of two and a half cents per pound in January 1845.[114] Both land and slaves declined in value in the aftermath. In Athens and its hinterlands, for example, the price of slaves dropped from $1,200 to $200–$300 and the price of land dropped to $2–$3 an acre.[115] As a result, many planters cut back on cotton cultivation, but this decision meant they needed far less labor. Rather than sell their slaves at a steep loss, some planters responded to the decline by training their slaves to perform mechanical labor and hiring them out; many planters sent their skilled bondmen to towns and cities in search of employment. In doing so, the planters protected their own interests, but their actions undermined the economic livelihood of white working men, particularly skilled ones, who resided in the upcountry. Charles Lyell, a touring Englishmen, noted that black workers were as capable as their white counterparts and all indications suggested that they would continue to advance.[116] In several cities, towns, and counties, the authorities enacted laws to protect white workers and halt black advancement, but in the wake of the economic decline in the late 1830s and early 1840s planters increasingly ignored these proscriptions against allowing their slaves to hire themselves out. The arrival of black skilled laborers in the cities of the cotton belt, therefore, represented a direct assault on the ability of white mechanics to find work.

The economic decline had devastating consequences for the state's white workers. Increased competition with black laborers for employment heightened white nonelite anxieties. As unemployment and economic insecurity grew, rising inequality among white men became a topic of concern in the 1830s. Addressing contractors who chose to use skilled black laborers, John J. Flournoy expressed the frustrations of many white workers: "I am aware that most of you have too strong antipathy to encourage the masonry and carpentry trades of your poor white brothers, that your predilections for giving employment in your line of business to ebony workers have either so cheapened the white man's labor, or expatriated hence with but a few solitary exceptions, all the white masons and carpenters of this town." "The right, then, gentlemen, you will no doubt candidly admit, of the white man to employment in preference to negroes, who must defer to us since they live well enough on plantations, cannot be considered impeachable by contractors. . . . As masters of the polls in a majority, carrying all before them, I am surprised the poor do not elect faithful members to the Legislature, who will make it penal to prefer negro mechanic labor to white men's."[117] His words proved prescient.

In the 1840s, white mechanics in the upcountry mobilized to meet the growing threat posed by skilled slaves. They appealed to local and county officials to crack down on the practice of allowing slaves to self-hire as mechanics.[118] These efforts spawned a statewide drive. Agitation continued to mount, culminating in the passage of a state law in 1845 that banned blacks, both free and enslaved, from contracting their labor in the construction industry.[119] Legislators representing the interests of white mechanics had initially tried to enact legislation that would have prohibited black laborers from all trades, but the effort failed to garner sufficient support in the General Assembly. Nevertheless, the 1845 law did represent a significant achievement for white workers since black skilled laborers were disproportionately represented in the building trades.

The law illustrated the growing influence of white workers in the state. Harnessing the power of the democratic system, one that limited the right to vote to white men, white laborers succeeded at chipping away at the power of slave owners. The only way to minimize competition was to use their democratic rights and legislate against them. There "are numbers of colored mechanics in all these southern states very expert at trades requiring much more skill and knowledge than the functions of ordinary work-people in factories," Charles Lyell noted. The passage of the 1845 law against black mechanics, he asserted, "proves that not a few of the negro race have got on so well in the world in reputation and fortune, and in skill in certain arts, that it was worth while to legislate against them in order to keep them down, and prevent them from entering into successful rivalry with the whites. . . . Hence, they are using in Georgia the power given to them by an exclusive franchise, to pass disabling statutes against blacks, to prevent them from engaging in certain kinds of work."[120]

The 1845 law represented the high-water mark of the mechanics' efforts to bring about legislative change regarding slavery at the state level.[121] The 1845 law, however, did not mark the end of their struggle nor their last success, especially if we shift our attention to municipalities in the upcountry.[122] The years immediately following the law's enactment brought white mechanics some relief, but by the late 1840s the conflict over slavery resumed. As tensions rose, the mechanics' movement revived. Centered initially in Macon, the movement spread throughout the blackbelt before expiring in the early 1850s. Though it bore many similarities to its mid-decade predecessor, the latter movement was more radical in that it called for a broader ban on slave mechanics. No longer satisfied with a proscription on self-hire, many white urban mechanics pushed for a complete prohibition on all black mechanics.

Situated on the Ocmulgee River and established in 1823, Macon prospered as a depot for most of the goods produced in the upper part of the state. Cotton production in the region increased dramatically in the first few years after the city's founding.[123] Macon became a key trade and transportation hub by the 1830s; by the end of the decade, one-third of the state's cotton crop passed through the town on the way to the coast for shipment to the North and overseas.[124] By the late 1830s, however, the rise of railroads and the opening up of the Cherokee territory threatened Macon's prosperity and continued success. As one observer noted, "Rival towns and rival interests are springing up on every hand." Fearful of being eclipsed by rival towns, civic leaders and businessmen in Macon embraced manufacturing to avert an apparent inevitable decline in their town's fortunes. "Our only hope then is a change in pursuits. We must become manufacturers and sustain our own mechanic interests."[125] As a result, in the 1840s Macon became home to a number of burgeoning enterprises.[126]

Mechanics emerged as a significant political force in Macon. Many of the city's leading mechanics played a central role in the reestablishment of the Mechanic Society of Macon (MSM) in 1849; an earlier version of the group had flourished in the 1830s before disbanding in 1840. The new MSM differed in important ways from its predecessor. Although the new group carried its predecessor's name, members of the latest iteration of the MSM embraced a wider spectrum of views concerning slavery and slaveholders' rights, some more radical than others. Unlike the earlier version, the new society took a more overtly political stand and expressed a willingness to challenge slave owners' perceived rights. Mechanics in Macon enjoyed influence over political affairs in their city. For example, the mayor in the mid-1840s sympathized with their cause. In one of his first acts upon taking office in 1844, James Nisbet cracked down on slaves who hired their own time. The practice, he proclaimed, was one of "two evils" that white Georgians had to eliminate because it "engenders habits of idleness, dissipation, theft, and all manner of unrestrained indulgence in the slaves who are thus allowed to release themselves from the salutary control of their owners." The other evil—the practice of black mechanics making contracts—had the potential for even graver consequences if not addressed. The practice, he asserted, led inevitably to a situation where the "distinction of color is broken down," which was "incompatible" with slavery. He also complained that black mechanics created "competition" that "is highly prejudicial and unjust to our white mechanics and artisans." "If such competition be tolerated," he warned, it would have the "effect of discouraging and driving away, from amongst us, substantial and skillful white mechanics," whose presence ensured the community's "wealth and prosperity."[127] After Nisbet's term expired, his successors continued the policy and further expanded the restrictions on the city's slaves.[128] Macon's white mechanics, it seems, had friends in high places.

The immediate catalyst for the reemergence of the mechanic movement in the late 1840s was a speech delivered by S. T. Chapman, the owner and editor of the *Georgia Journal and Messenger*, in May 1849. Speaking before the MSM, Chapman offered a scathing critique of slavery's effects on nonslaveholding whites in Georgia, particularly the state's mechanics, and proposed banning blacks from all mechanical trades as the solution. If not properly regulated, he declared, slavery undermined the nation's "great principles," mainly that "all men must stand on the common plain of republican equality." By allowing slaves to compete with white mechanics and undercharge them, slave owners undermined this basic right and punished the "respectable mechanic who cannot afford to live, much less support his family." In addition to the economic defense for his position, he offered philosophical justifications. The "great evil" of permitting blacks to labor as mechanics threatened to undermine the entire slave system, he proclaimed. "This competition blends the pursuits of the classes—it breaks down the dividing barrier which slavery has wisely instituted between the races—it slackens the chords which bind the negro in his proper place—it makes him to some extent equal to the white man—it leaves him a slave only in name."[129] An indirect product of allowing slaves to work as mechanics, he argued, was a direct assault on white supremacy. Chapman envisioned creating a slave system that benefited slaveholders, but not at the expense of nonslaveholders—a system that preserved the rights and status of *all* white men and relegated *all* blacks to subordination and unskilled labor.

White mechanics in Macon agreed that the institution needed reform to operate successfully in a society designed to simultaneously protect white equality and property rights. Yet even as they agreed on this basic principle, they differed in fundamental ways on other related issues. For example, members of the MSM empathized with the plight of poor white mechanics, but they also believed that a different cause was responsible for their suffering. In their official response to Chapman's lecture, they broke with him on one of the key tenets of his argument. The problem was not black mechanics per se, but self-hire. Slave owners who permitted their "negroes to make contracts and dispose of their own time," the MSM declared, were "virtually emancipating and placing negroes upon an equality with white laborers, and by such a course are practically effecting in part, what the abolitionists and other[s] unfriendly to the institution of the South desire." As slaveholders themselves, some members of the MSM found the demand for the removal of slaves from all mechanical occupations far too broad to accept. Consequently, they advocated extending the terms of the 1845 law prohibiting black mechanics and masons from contracting for the erection and repair of buildings. The MSM urged the legislature to broaden the law's "prohibitions to all other classes of colored mechanics."[130] Chapman's analysis of the problems facing mechanics in Georgia clearly resonated with the members of the MSM, even as they stopped short of fully embracing his demands.

As word of Chapman's speech spread in the days and weeks that followed, it touched off a storm of controversy throughout Georgia's blackbelt. Many upcountry planters viewed his lecture as an assault on their rights as slave owners and accused him of fomenting class warfare. Moreover, they categorically rejected his claims about the pitfalls of allowing competition between black and white skilled laborers. Their message was clear: planters needed absolute flexibility in how they deployed their property if slavery and the South were to survive. The greatest danger to the South came from the reluctance to diversify slave labor; if not undertaken the South would perish. Cotton-belt newspapers sympathetic to the planters' position provided a forum for diatribes against Chapman and his supporters. The editor of the *Rome Southerner* declared that the white mechanics' demands represented the first salvo, for "if driven from one field, they will drive them [the slaves] from all."[131] The editor of the *Georgia Telegraph* concurred, insisting that white mechanics who supported restrictions on slave labor undermined the entire slave system and even white supremacy itself. The "institution must be preserved in its totality, or go down," he avowed. While white artisans highlighted the conflicting economic interests among whites, the editor emphasized their common racial identity. "Here the interests of the whole white race, are homogeneous, and are all embarked in the same vessel, whether holders or nonholders of that sort of property." He charged that the "white laborer who weakens this institution with a view to his personal interest," instead of the common good, "would destroy the source of employment and wages, with no compensation but ruin for himself and his country." The *Telegraph* editor therefore opposed "any policy that looks to compromising, or tampering with the tenure and value of slave property."[132]

Some blackbelt slave owners discerned a dangerous movement among Macon's white artisans, which threatened to extend to the entire state. "Observer" predicted that the "move begun in Macon would not stop there; from the black mechanics it would extend to other pursuits." While he could not imagine that "respectable intelligent men will allow themselves to be led to so stupid and wicked a movement," he nevertheless called on the slave owner to "arise in his might" and condemn the "white mechanic who should follow Mr. Chapman's lead."[133] "Cotton Planter" repudiated the notion that white mechanics needed protection from unfair black competition as an example of "good Northern doctrine."[134] The editor of the *Rome Southerner* viewed it as an "assault upon slave *labor*, as an insidious attack upon slavery itself." He predicted: "Fill the minds of all our mechanical classes with such ideas, set them to forming associations for operating upon *public opinion*, let artful political demagogues attach themselves to these associations and give them a *political* direction" and the consequences would be "a war upon the 'abstract right,' of slaveholders." Soon, "We shall see them banding together as a political party, and entering the field to ballot against what they have thus been taught to regard as oppressive and thus degrading."[135] If left unchecked, they asserted, the movement would inevitably result in the rise of abolitionism in the state. In the midst of political uncertainty, calls for the creation of a new movement sounded like a direct strike at slavery to some planters, evidence abolition had spread to the region. While some of the rhetoric in the escalating war of words was clearly just that, rhetoric, it did resonate with some planters whose suspicions of white workers, particularly mechanics, were confirmed when they read or heard calls to use their vote to effect change.

In actuality, the vast majority of white mechanics in the upcountry (as in the rest of Georgia) were not abolitionists.[136] The spread of conspiracy theories and heated rhetoric led upcountry critics of the mechanics to overestimate the mechanics' unity and underestimate their commitment to slavery. There were a handful of white men who embraced abolition.[137] But, like John J. Flournoy, most did so solely with an eye toward improving the condition of white workers, not as a result of any sense of humanitarianism. In one well-publicized case, for example, a carpenter employed at the iron works of Cooper, Wiley & Co. in Cass County proclaimed his support for emancipation because he believed it would increase his wages to $2 a day once he no longer had to compete with slave laborers.[138] They simply believed that controls within the slave society were necessary to guarantee a modicum of success for white workers; that was the compromise for their support of the slave system. Mechanics had called for change for generations, but at that moment in the midst of the growing sectional crisis, their appeals for change took on increased significance.

Chapman's speech and the subsequent controversy galvanized Georgia's white mechanics and sparked interest in a renewed mechanic movement throughout urban areas in the upcountry. In the *Albany Patriot, Georgia Journal and Messenger, American Mechanic, Georgia Citizen, Muscogee Democrat,* and other blackbelt newspapers sympathetic to the mechanics' perspective, white workers voiced their grievances. They complained that competition with slave labor degraded white labor and drove down wages. "Justice" offered a class-based analysis of the situation. The "long continued conflict of Capital against Labor is reviving its energies and arraying its force with more than ordinary rapidity," he noted. "Capital is not satisfied in owning and monopolizing all the best lands and their productions, but it now aims at depriving the white mechanic of all means to protect or advance their interests." The solution, he argued, was for mechanics to protect themselves: "Let not one white mechanic, employ, work with or instruct a negro in any branch of trade. 'Self preservation is the first law of nature.' It is your right, you are entitled to the protection and respect of all good men. Protect that right for yourself and others. Assert it, and stand up to it, fearlessly. You will be sustained and supported in doing so, by your fellow laborers, by an enlightened and healthy public opinion, and by men who desire 'to live and let live.'"[139] "Romeo" agreed that nonelite mechanics had to take a stand; however, he believed the agent of change lay elsewhere: the ballot box. "But as long as they—not content with the produce of their slave labor, upon the richest lands in the country, which they hold—seek, through their negroes, to monopolize the mechanic's trade, so long should the poor white man of the South, refuse to support for any office of profit or honor, any man that would not pledge himself to discountenance by all legal means—negro mechanics, whether bond or free."[140]

Tapping into broad currents of unrest among nonelite white workers, mechanics organized local societies in towns and counties across the blackbelt to advance their interests.[141] They were joined by thousands of white men who poured into the state in the two years following the lecture. Most of the new arrivals came with their skills and little else, hoping to take advantage of the state's reviving economy. As the ranks of nonslaveholding white laborers increased, so too did calls for reform of the state's slave laws. As a movement coalesced, the MSM and its leading officers tried to harness the energy. Hoping to build on the growing enthusiasm, they called for mechanics to meet at a statewide convention in Atlanta on Independence Day.

On July 4, 1851, five hundred delegates, representing eighteen upcountry counties and Chatham County, gathered at Walton's Springs in Atlanta alongside two thousand of their supporters. Those in attendance ate barbecue and listened to a host of orators and singers over the course of the day. There was business, too, of course. Before departing, the delegates passed a preamble and six resolutions that laid out an agenda for the state's mechanics.[142]

Slavery figured prominently, though not exclusively, in the delegates' deliberations at the convention. Three main issues absorbed the lion's share of their attention. First, delegates called for the establishment of a mechanical institute to train the next generation of young men in skilled crafts. Second, they demanded an end to the practice of training and employing convicts to perform mechanical labor. Last, they repudiated the use of slaves as mechanics as "inexpedient, unwise, and injurious to all classes of the community." Delegates offered several reasons for this position. In addition to blaming "the pernicious influence" of slave mechanics for "nearly all the escapes of slaves from Georgia and several Southern States," they claimed that "a few Negro Mechanics in towns and and [sic] cities, have done and can do more practical injury to the institution of slavery and its permanent security, than all the ultra abolitionists of the country." Moreover, they complained, slave mechanics degraded the labor of white men who performed the same tasks and caused white youths to reject the mechanical pursuits as a potential occupation. "As Mechanics and Southern men, by birth or by adoption, and as slaveholders," they appealed to their fellow citizens to empathize with their position. "We ask only for such encouragement as will raise our calling in the scale of respectability and usefulness, as well as secure, on a permanent basis, the peculiar institution of the South, and promote the general welfare of the people."[143]

The Atlanta convention represented a mixed bag for Georgia's white mechanics. On the one hand, the large number of delegates and supporters who attended the function illustrated the potential strength of the movement, as did the resulting anxiety of its critics. On the other hand, the proceedings demonstrated that there were deep, intractable divisions over slavery not only between planters and mechanics but among mechanics themselves. Despite the inclusion of a distinctly moderate position relative to the use of slaves as mechanics, the body could not reach a unanimous position. In fact, one faction of the convention, led by William Anderson of Coweta County, called for the complete removal of the provisions contained in the convention's preamble and resolutions related to slavery. Although his effort was rejected by a "large majority" of the delegates, the divide highlighted the structural changes that had shaped Georgia's economy in the previous twenty years as economic mobility became increasingly difficult and rare for journeymen mechanics.[144] In the first two decades of the nineteenth century, differences between master craftsmen and journeymen had seemed temporary. Journeymen experienced significant economic and social mobility. By the 1830s and 1840s, however, artisans divided between the master craftsmen, who owned slaves and had entered the middle class, and the journeymen, who were largely relegated to the status of wage earners with limited chance for economic mobility. White mechanics complained that "every opening in their trades was closed to them, because black artisans were employed by their owners in preference."[145] Nonslaveholding artisans viewed competition with blacks, free and enslaved, as an evil that needed to be sharply restricted or removed altogether. They based their position on their claim to whiteness; they were white men deserving of some protections, especially because they lived in a slave society whose foundation rested on the inferiority of blacks, a society in which slave labor supposedly benefited all whites, even nonslaveholders. After all, they were expected to help in the defense of the society and therefore felt they should reap some of its benefits. White nonslaveholding mechanics, those who were journeymen, called for the restriction of blacks, both slave and free, from their occupations. Slaveholding mechanics favored the flexibility to employ their slaves as they saw fit. Differences over restrictions on slaves, then, divided nonslaveholding and slaveholding mechanics.

In the wake of the meeting in Atlanta, delegates returned home to implement the convention's agenda. In the months that followed, the initial excitement over the movement gradually dissipated. While the split over slavery definitely played an integral role in this development, there were other causes for the movement's diminishment. The most prominent was the growing sectional crisis over slavery's expansion in the West and the Compromise of 1850, which distracted white Georgians from their conversation over the appropriate use of slave labor. One key consequence of the controversy was the destruction of the Second Party System in Georgia. The implosion of the Whigs and the subsequent rise of the Know-Nothings further stratified Georgia's white men. By the mid-1850s, wealthier mechanics gravitated toward the American Party while journeymen and wage earners leaned toward the Democratic Party. Ultimately, the splintering of the mechanic movement in 1851 highlighted the limitations of a movement dedicated to the uplift of an occupation rather than a class.[146]

Though white workers in the upcountry did not achieve their goals in the 1851 movement, demands to eliminate black mechanics grew in the late 1850s, coinciding with Governor Joseph Brown's ascent to power and the Panic of 1857.[147] As they had when the economy stagnated after the Panic of 1837, white mechanics attempted to protect themselves from slave competition. The Columbus Enquirer stated its support for prohibiting "the learning of the mechanic trades to negroes" and insisted that "laws ought to be enacted to prevent it in the future." Slaves currently trained in such trades should be allowed to continue; to stop them would be "unjust." "Slaveholders ought to reflect upon the policy of continuing a system which may prejudice any class of white laborers at the South against its peculiar institution, and ought to readily concur in the prohibition of the practice in the future."[148] The *Milledgeville Federal Union* agreed with the *Enquirer*, contending that "many good citizens" entertained similar views. "The policy of teaching negroes the various trades, instead of putting them on the plantations, where they belong, tends to make the rich richer, and the poor poorer, or by bringing slave labor into competition with white labor, and thus arraying capital against labor, (for the negro is capital) and this will produce a sprit of antagonisms between the rich and the poor.—Such a policy . . . tends to elevate the negro at the expense of the poor white man; and makes the poor mechanic at the South the enemy of the negro and the institution of slavery."[149] Increasingly, those who claimed to stand for the interests of white nonelites invoked the specter of class warfare to bolster their case for reforming slavery, a threatening development as the tensions between the North and South deepened.

Though white workers did not mount another statewide movement in the last few years of the antebellum era, they continued their efforts in their localities. Atlanta represented the pinnacle of white working-class power and solidarity that characterized the upcountry. Atlanta was in many ways the opposite of Savannah: in geographical position, history, and demography. Atlanta was a newer city, incorporated in 1847 on Cherokee lands, while Savannah was the oldest city in the state. Atlanta's economy was tied to railroads and the emerging industrial order in North Georgia, while Savannah's economy was organized around plantation agriculture and the marketing of cash crops. Atlanta, more than Savannah, represented the future of the state.

The region in which Atlanta was located, northern Georgia, experienced accelerated economic diversification in the two decades before the Civil War. Although agriculture continued to be the state's mainstay, manufacturing and industrial production assumed an increasingly important role. There was little growth in the percentage of men employed in manufacturing between 1820 and 1840. Between 1840 and 1860, however, the number grew much quicker. By 1860 there were nearly 1,890 establishments employing 9,511 men and 2,064 women.[150] The development of industry was particularly pronounced in the northern section of the state on the lands ceded by the Cherokees in the 1830s. In that region, cotton played a much smaller role in the economy since the lands were less suited to the cultivation of the crop. Instead, smaller farms and subsistence agriculture were the norm.[151] As a result, the demography of the area diverged sharply from the rest of the state. In contrast to the black majorities in the lowcountry and blackbelt in middle and southwestern Georgia, there were far fewer slaves and free people of color.[152] Equally relevant, the ranks of the planter elite were much smaller, which meant that white nonslaveholders gained a greater say in the region's political affairs.[153] While many white settlers flocked to the area to take advantage of cheap land, others arrived with the intention of joining the growing ranks of wage laborers employed in the various industries that had taken root there. Skilled and semiskilled white workers found employment in the foundries, mines, and factories that dotted the region's burgeoning urban areas and their hinterlands. Georgia became known as the "Empire State of the South," and North Georgia was the center of industrial development within the state.

In the 1850s, Atlanta became the economic focal point of North Georgia, a hub connecting the industrial, commercial, and agricultural sectors of Georgia's interior. The city was home to fifteen major manufacturers, including four machinery and steam engine shops and two metalworking shops, employing 319 white workers receiving a total of $110,484 in wages.[154] The growth of the railroad industry in the 1840s and 1850s created even more industrial jobs. With four major lines converging on the city, white workers flocked to Atlanta to take advantage of its employment opportunities. Atlanta experienced explosive population growth in the years after its founding. From five hundred residents in 1847, the population increased by approximately one thousand people per year throughout the following decade. By the eve of the Civil War, over eleven thousand people resided there, an expansion "unexampled in the history of the South."[155] And like the region as a whole, the population of Atlanta was disproportionately white compared to that of most other cities in the state. In contrast to Savannah, whose white population amounted to 65 percent, or Macon, Columbus, and Augusta, whose populations were 69 percent, 62 percent, and 67 percent, respectively, Atlanta's white population amounted to 80 percent.

White mechanics made up a significant portion of Atlanta's population. The city was buzzing with activity in its first years as builders struggled to keep up with demand for homes and stores. As one early historian of the town remarked, "The place was full of mechanics attracted from an hundred miles around to get work. Wages were good for that day, and employment to be had for the asking."[156] By 1860, in the state as a whole, one in ten adult white males in Georgia was a skilled worker.[157] The numbers were even more pronounced in urban areas. Leading the state was Atlanta, where white skilled workers represented 51 percent and 44 percent of Atlanta's working population in 1850 and 1860, respectively.[158] It was with good reason, then, that one early resident claimed, "The mechanical element prevails in our city."[159] Skilled white workers were concentrated in urban areas, and Atlanta had the highest concentration.

Atlanta was an entrepreneurial city for those on the make. Commentators noted that the white population was generally younger, more business-oriented, and more attuned to "democratic impulses" than elsewhere in the state.[160] Mechanics were a major force in the city. As the *Atlanta Daily Intelligencer* noted, "Atlanta probably more than any other city of our State, is dependent upon her mechanical population for everything that constitutes wealth and power." The paper rooted the town's prosperity in "this class of worthy and useful citizens," speculating, "Take away those in our midst who compose this useful class of our population, and our city would soon dwindle into insignificance and decay."[161] This made Atlanta a white man's town with a power structure that favored mechanics.

The mechanics' demographic strength in Atlanta translated into political influence. White mechanics helped elect a Democratic mayor and slate of city councilors into office in 1855, breaking the stranglehold over power by their rivals.[162] After just one term, the Democrats lost power for two years before sweeping back into office in 1858. In the years that followed, the Democrats consolidated their hold on local power.[163] And the city's mechanics constituted a critical part of the vote that made their victories possible. In contrast to other cities in the state, white workers were relatively well represented in Atlanta. The year the Democrats swept to power, in fact, they placed "two or three practical mechanics" on the city council.[164] Atlanta's political world was not dominated by planters. In fact, they appear to have played a rather minimal role in the city's political scene.[165]

Race and class factored prominently in the Democrats' attempts to attract the support of nonelite workers. The *Atlanta Intelligencer,* one of the city's Democratic Party organs, highlighted these themes repeatedly in articles in the weeks prior to elections, particularly the 1858 contest. The editors complained about the conditions that white workers were forced to endure. The paper reported on a series of local episodes in which white mechanics reportedly suffered at the hands of the white elite, usually those with a direct association with the American Party. In one case a man named Hunicutt—"a poor man, with a wife and a large family of children to support"—was almost fired from his job after a politician from the American Party complained to the man's employer about his behavior at a political meeting. "In this country, every white man is supposed to be free, to support or *oppose* whom he pleases, for public office," the editor noted relative to Hunicutt's predicament. "At least, that has heretofore been our impression, as to the *rights* of free white men, in such matters."[166] In another story designed to tap into the readers' class antipathy, the *Intelligencer* reported that a "Know-Nothing boss carpenter in town, has commenced the work of dismissing from his service, every man suspicioned of entertaining a determination to vote" for the Democrats in the upcoming election.[167]

Perhaps the most sensational episode in the run-up to the election centered on the city's night watchman, H. H. Bankston. Hired by the American Party when they were in power, Bankston gained notoriety when it was alleged that he was actually a "*free man of color.*"[168] Although Bankston denied the allegation, he stepped down to avoid further scrutiny.[169] The Democrats refused to let the story die, however. The *Atlanta Intelligencer* invoked Bankston repeatedly in the weeks leading up to the 1858 municipal election.[170] Apparently, their coverage had the desired effect. Stoking the flames of racial and class hostility, the Democrats stormed into office in a clean sweep, winning the mayor's seat and all ten spots on the city council.[171] The role of the city's mechanics and laboring classes in bringing about this political shift was clear. Their votes carried tremendous sway in the city, the fastest growing one in the state.

The election results in the late 1850s had clear consequences for white mechanics. In the wake of the Democratic victories, the new city government enacted strict laws monitoring blacks in the town and limiting their economic actions. For example, the practice of allowing slaves to hire themselves out had already been banned, but the law became even more severe after 1855 when the city council also prohibited slaves from living apart from their owners.[172] White workers, particularly mechanics, pushed for even greater restrictions on black labor when the Democrats returned to power in 1858. Galvanized by the party's success at the polls and confident of their role in the victory, they called for new restrictions on black mechanics. Shortly after the election, two hundred white mechanics in Atlanta signed a petition calling for the creation of new laws to prohibit slave mechanics from operating in the city. The white mechanics complained that "there exists in the city of Atlanta a class of persons who in the opinion of your memorialists are of no benefit to the city. We refer to negro mechanics whose masters reside in other places, and who pay nothing toward the support of the City government & whose negro mechanics can afford to underbid the regular resident citizen mechanics of your city, to the great injury and without benefiting the city in any way." The white men called upon Atlanta authorities to "afford protection to the resident citizen mechanics of your city."[173] Despite the appeal, the authorities failed to enact the reforms, at least initially. It appears the council could not reach an agreement and put off making a decision as a result. When, in the midst of the secession crisis, the city's mechanics petitioned the city authorities a second time in early 1861, the mechanics had better luck. Not willing to jeopardize the support of such a critical group of citizens as the state embarked on the unknown, the city council moved to enact a $100 tax upon each slave mechanic whose owner resided outside of the city limits.[174]

In a town like Atlanta, predicated on the notion that white working men, particularly mechanics, formed the core of the populace, the authorities enacted the restrictions so that white men would not have to compete for skilled labor jobs with blacks. White workers in Atlanta worked to exclude blacks from virtually all occupations except menial and agricultural work. This contrasted with Savannah, where planters rebuffed attempts to rein in their slaves and the practice of hiring them out to compete with white artisans. In targeting planters' prerogatives to use their slave property as they saw fit, white workers felt emboldened to challenge elite autonomy. In Atlanta, more so than in Macon or Columbus, white workers enjoyed political influence that allowed them to block the rights of slave owners, restricting what they could and could not do with their slaves. This was the democratization of slavery.

The events in Atlanta were not unique. Indeed, they were part of a broader political shift taking place throughout Georgia in the 1850s as the state's nonelite exerted growing political influence through the Democratic Party. Even in Savannah, that bastion of planter power, nonelite whites made some moderate headway in their efforts to limit black competition. This shift was directly linked to the demographic changes in Savannah in the late antebellum period. During that time, the city became increasingly paler. Between 1850 and 1860, Savannah's population rose from 15,312 to 22,292. Almost 80 percent of this increase came from the growth of the white population, which reached 13,875. Whites constituted 65 percent of the city in 1860, up from 52 percent twenty years before.[175] Much of the expansion in the white population came through foreign immigration. Indeed, the biggest burst came between 1848 and 1852, when the city's population rose by more than 50 percent as whites from the northern states and Europe, particularly Ireland, arrived en masse. By 1860, two-thirds of all adult white men in Savannah were from the North or were foreign born.[176] The arrival of the migrants transformed the city in myriad ways.

Savannah's black residents were the first to feel the impact of the city's changing demography. The arrival of the immigrants placed new pressures on the city's slaves. The immigrants competed with them not only for skilled occupations but also for more menial positions. Most of the Irish immigrants, in particular, had few skills or experience beyond fieldwork. As a consequence, many Irish men competed with slaves for employment as common laborers, often on the city's wharfs unloading and loading ships, while Irish women vied with slave women for work as domestics, seamstresses, and laundresses.[177] In addition to the economic realm, blacks and the newcomers battled over housing. With few financial resources at their disposal, many of the migrants moved into the city's poorer neighborhoods, areas that were home to most of Savannah's black populace.[178] The struggle over jobs and housing produced deep antagonisms between blacks and the newcomers. Yet, despite the immigrants' poverty and lack of skills, they did have one thing that gave them a distinct advantage in this conflict: their white skin. And in time, as they gained citizenship, they used this privilege to push for greater restrictions on Savannah's black population. In doing so, they struck at the city's slave laws as well as the prerogatives of the slave owners who benefited from the status quo.[179]

The influx of immigrants had a dramatic impact on Savannah's political system. Once they obtained the right to vote, they flocked to the Democratic Party, bolstering the political power of the city's nonelite whites. The Irish played a pivotal role in this development. They formed the party's base and wielded considerable influence within the organization. When their votes helped the Democrats secure control of the city government in the mid-1850s, they were rewarded with patronage positions.[180] The Democratic ascent had broader implications for the nonelite. Under their watch, the city authorities implemented some modest reforms to the slave system. While white workers' biggest issues—slave self-hire and the hiring out system—were too well entrenched to eliminate, the authorities did successfully chip away at some of the privileges enjoyed by slaves in the city.

The butchers' story provides a clear example of the changes. As one historian of the lowcountry has noted, the biggest struggle between white and black artisans occurred over meat.[181] White butchers tried repeatedly to eliminate their slave competition, beginning in 1822, when they petitioned the authorities to ban black butchers. Members of the city council listened to their petition and initially indicated their sympathy with the white butchers' plight, but ultimately they refused to act. The white butchers tried several more times to bar blacks from the meat trade, petitioning the city council in 1825, 1829, and 1842, with similar results each time. In fact, in the last instance the white butchers' appeal was met with a petition from unnamed white residents who complained that any such law would restrict blacks' right to sell meats.[182] In 1854, however, the white butchers finally scored a modest victory when the council enacted an ordinance stipulating that "no slave shall act as a butcher unless in the presence of a . . . white person."[183] The law was designed to halt independent economic activity by slaves who were competing with whites. But it still allowed slaves to work as butchers; therefore, it did not totally impinge on slave owners' rights. The struggle over the butchers exemplified the conflict between nonelite, white skilled laborers on one side and planters and slaves on the other. And by the late antebellum era, white workers, even in Savannah, were gaining power.

By the 1850s, nonelite white men in the upcountry and northern section of the state, including white workers and yeomen, represented a formidable political force. Their numbers and relative voting strength gave them the power to influence laws related to slavery and the racial order. Their views on these issues could not be ignored; planters may have filled the seats of the assembly, but the votes that put them there came from nonslaveholding white men who entertained different ideas about the role of slavery in society. As their numbers and political muscle increased, the state's slave laws came to reflect their views.

Together, nonelite whites throughout the state gained greater political power in Georgia in the 1850s. This alliance helped to elect Governor Brown to office in 1857. Brown hailed from North Georgia and was recognized as the governor of the poor. And though he tirelessly advocated on behalf of the nonelite, he embraced slavery as a vehicle for improving their lives. It was, he stressed, the best system for poor whites because it created a mudsill class that placed blacks at the bottom of society while simultaneously elevating all whites. Even white workers who could not afford slaves benefited both economically and socially from the institution. The white southern laborer "received higher wages for his labor, than does the laborers of any other portion of the world, and he raises up his children, with the knowledge, that they belong to no inferior cast." "Among us the poor white laborer is respected as an equal," he argued. "He feels and knows this. He belongs to the only true aristocracy, the race of white men." Consequently, these "men know, that in the event of the abolition of slavery, they would be greater sufferers than the rich, who would be able to protect themselves," and hence they would "never permit the slaves of the South to be set free among them and their children as equals."[184] Brown represented the nonelite white view that slavery, when properly regulated, produced dividends for all whites in southern society.

8

Rewriting Georgia's Racial Past, 1850s

By the 1850s, Georgia had become a black and white society. The state's population had changed dramatically from its colonial beginnings. New arrivals to Georgia between 1820 and 1840 had become an important constituency and had shifted the balance of political power in the state. Driven by greed, they successfully restricted the state's black population, both free and enslaved, and removed the state's Indian population, both "civilized" and "uncivilized." They tightened the racial divide by collapsing the differences among people of African descent, and they opened vast swaths of land to the expansion of slavery and plantation agriculture. White Georgians replaced the racially fluid society of the colonial and revolutionary years with a racially bifurcated society in which race and status became absolute corollaries. In the process, they faced criticism by northern religious organizations for their treatment of the Creeks and the Cherokees and by northern antislavery and abolitionist organizations for the institution of slavery. White Georgians during the sectional crisis of the 1850s grappled with their history to account for what the state had become. White Georgians rewrote their past in the 1850s in both history books and judicial opinions to legitimate the bifurcated racial order that would become synonymous with the antebellum Lower South.

In 1854, George White published *Historical Collections of Georgia*, five years after his first book, *Statistics on the State of Georgia*.[1] His second book expanded on the first, which offered detailed geographical and historical

277

information about each of the counties in the state. "This work does not assume to be a consecutive History. It is but a collection of materials for the use of the future historian." He visited archives for ten years, compiling the information contained in the book. In addition to the documents he collected, he also consulted "the oldest inhabitants of many of our towns and villages." He asserted that "This oral tradition, indeed, furnishes, the warm flesh and blood of the body of History, while documentary evidence can be relied on for the putting together of the dry skeleton."[2] Other Georgians, however, nurtured an alternative oral tradition. White's book prompted a bitter debate between George Gilmer and Wilson Lumpkin as they both claimed responsibility for Cherokee removal. These conflicts reveal white Georgians' efforts to rewrite their past and also highlight the class divisions over the Indian question.

White's account of Georgia's past included Indians. He was not the first to do so. Earlier treatments of the state's history had mentioned Indians, but only as bit players, usually one-dimensional characters, in the larger drama. Beyond their role as signatories to treaties or in attacking settlers, they played little role in the histories of Georgia. Accounts focused on the "good Indians" who had worked with the colony's early leaders but ignored the more recent past. White, by contrast, offered compelling portraits of Indians. He recognized them as pivotal actors who shaped Georgia's past, even when they worked against white Georgians' interests. For example, White's book portrayed the Creek chief General Alexander McGillivray in a manner that stood in marked contrast to contemporaneous representations of the chief. He referred to the Creek chief as a "remarkable man" and waxed on about his physical stature, accomplishments, intelligence, and diplomacy. "His face was handsome, and indicative of quick thought and much sagacity."[3] White detailed McGillivray's many achievements, including his organization of a resistance to Georgians' encroachment in the 1780s, which resulted in the loss of considerable property and the deaths of Georgians. He noted his wily dealings with U.S. and Georgia commissioners in the years after the War of Independence. In contrast to most white Georgian contemporaries, who regularly cast him in diabolical terms, the book offered a positive assessment of his diplomatic skills, even though he used them to pit the British and later the Americans against the Spanish while protecting his own personal interests as well as the Creek Nation's. McGillivray was not the only Indian portrayed in a positive manner. Indeed, White included an entire section on "Distinguished Indians," to complement his section on "Distinguished Men."[4] The "Distinguished Indians" section offered detailed biographical sketches of important Creek and Cherokee men. The list included men who fought alongside the Americans in the various wars and military engagements that took place on the border between Georgia and the neighboring Indians in the late eighteenth and early nineteenth centuries. The group comprised "full-blood" and "mixed-blood" Indians: Hopoethleyoholo, Timpoochee Barnard, Major Ridge, John Ridge, Paddy Carr, Tustennuggee Emathla, Tomochichi, and General William McIntosh. Like McGillivray, McIntosh received a lengthy and admiring tribute extolling his physique, manners, and military achievements.[5] "He was intelligent and brave. In person he was tall, finely formed, and of graceful and commanding manners." The sketch extolled his military achievements in the Creek Civil War and in the Florida campaign that followed. "Having been thrown into the society of the more polished of our people, and having been the associate of our officers in the war of our Southern borders, he had acquired all the manners, and much of the polish, of a gentleman."[6] White portrayed both McGillivray and McIntosh as civilized Indian gentlemen.

Beyond including stories of the individual "distinguished Indian," White made clear the pivotal role of Indians in the development of Georgia history. He emphasized the intertwined relations between Georgia and the surrounding Indian nations in his discussion of the conflicts that preceded the state's expansion in the 1820s and 1830s. The book included sections on the "Difficulties with the Creeks and the General Government" and the "Difficulties with the Cherokees." He also devoted considerable attention to Indian removal.[7]

White's account of Indian removal was paradoxical. On the one hand, he painted the Indians as noble savages who could have easily been absorbed into American society. He seemed to embrace the ideological basis of the civilizing program that cast the Indians as having the potential to become part of the body politic, and the individuals he labeled as "distinguished" clearly fit that category. His book included segments that praised the achievements of the Cherokees, such as Sequoyah's development of the Cherokee alphabet. Consequently, he seemed to lament their disappearance from Georgia. On the other hand, he suggested that removal was the only option; anything less would have hampered Georgia's development and caused the Indians irreparable harm. He had "no doubt that by their removal their condition has been greatly improved."[8]

While White's depiction of Indians may have raised a few eyebrows,

William McIntosh, by Nathan and Joseph Negus, 1821. Courtesy of the Alabama Department of Archives and History, Montgomery, Alabama.

his account of the history of removal proved far more contentious. His treatment of the state's conflicts with the Indians, specifically the Cherokees, reopened wounds that had not completely healed. White credited Governor George Gilmer with finding a solution to the "complicated and delicate" problem while maintaining the state's integrity. He presented Gilmer as a learned man. "The situation of the Cherokee Indians—the injustice said to have been practised upon them by the State of Georgia—the conflicting opinions of the United States Government and the constituted authorities of Georgia, all conspired to render Governor Gilmer's administration anything else than pleasant." As such, "Wisdom, prudence, and firmness were requisite to conduct the helm of State at this critical period; and we believe we utter the sentiments of every thinking man in Georgia, when we say that Governor Gilmer's administration was marked by all these attributes."[9] White's portrait of Governor Wilson Lumpkin stood in marked contrast as a basic biography with few laudatory comments. In writing his book, White reignited the debate over the Cherokee question, prompting the men who held the executive chair during the most acrimonious moments of the controversy, George Gilmer and Wilson Lumpkin, to contest the struggle over the memory of removal. Both men offered their respective versions of the past shortly after the publication of *Historical Collections*.

Gilmer was the first to join the fray, when he published *Sketches of Some of the First Settlers of Upper Georgia, of the Cherokees, and the Author* in 1855.[10] Gilmer's study ostensibly focused on the history of the first settlers, but he actually devoted the vast majority of the book to an examination of his public life, specifically his first term as governor, between 1829 and 1831. Following White's model, Gilmer interspersed relevant documents from the era with his recollections of the most salient events in an effort to redeem his handling of the Cherokee question. Attempting to do what was best for the state while at the same time considering the needs of the federal government and the Cherokees, he found himself caught in the middle of these conflicting goals. With few, if any, good options available, Gilmer asserted that he had faced an unenviable situation. Even his successor, Lumpkin, Gilmer claimed, had been daunted by the task and had possessed no clear ideas on how to proceed. Under the circumstances, Gilmer asserted, he had done the best he could.

Throughout the portion of *Sketches* that dealt with Indian removal, Gilmer repeatedly stated that the policy had benefited both Georgia and the Cherokees. "It is a source of pride and pleasure to those who were responsible for the conduct of Georgia towards the Cherokees, to know that what they did has tended to the good both of the Indians and Georgians." Removal had taken the Cherokees away from the harmful influence of dastardly white men who preyed upon them while simultaneously granting them the space they needed to develop into a civilized people. He wrote that "the Cherokees, instead of being controlled in their public affairs, and corrupted in their morals, by profligate white men, as they were when within the limits of Georgia, are now in a country the best suited to their peculiar instincts and habits of living."[11] More important to Gilmer, removal had allowed Georgia to grow and prosper. Where the Indians had once hunted, thus failing to make proper use of the land, white settlers had turned the interior of the state into an agricultural paradise. "The Cherokee country, instead of being wandered over by listless, objectless, ignorant savages, whose only satisfying employments were destroying the beasts of the forest and their fellow-men, and being the receptacle of the lawless from every where, is now cultivated by a population rapidly advancing in all the arts of civilized life. Fine houses, valuable farms, beautiful meadows, schools, colleges, churches, and railroads have taken the places of wigwams and scalp-poles."[12]

Gilmer's declarations came with a caveat, however. He agreed that although forced relocation had been "absolutely necessary" for "preservation of all the unmixed" Cherokees, the same had not been true for the Indian countrymen, their Indian wives, and their "mixed-blood" offspring. He maintained, as he had at the time of the controversy, that in fact there were "two classes among the Cherokees, very widely separated from each other."[13] For those Indians who had been "civilized," Gilmer continued to believe that citizenship should have been an option. Consequently, he lamented the fact that many white Georgians had failed to discern important differences among the Indians. In an effort to highlight his misgivings on the subject, Gilmer included a letter he wrote in 1831 to John Rogers, a white man who lived in the Cherokee territory with his Cherokee wife and their sons in the midst of the turmoil. Gilmer, who had known Rogers since 1814 and was well acquainted with his family, expressed concern for the man's family when Rogers explained his family's desire to remain in Georgia and become citizens of the state. Although Gilmer believed that Rogers's sons were well qualified for citizenship despite their Indian heritage and would have contributed to Georgia's development, he acknowledged that most white Georgians would disagree. "However respectable, industrious, and intelligent your children may be, they never can associate upon an equality with our people," he noted. "Many individuals among us may be free from prejudices against the Indian people, but it will be long before our society will become so."[14] As a result, Gilmer opined, the Rogerses' best prospects lay west of the Mississippi.

The inclusion of the letter not only made clear Gilmer's personal beliefs about the wisdom of complete removal but offered an implicit message: poor whites were to blame for what had happened. Although he did not explicitly identify prejudiced whites as poor whites, the main division that Gilmer repeatedly emphasized among whites was between the nonelite migrants from North Carolina in the interior and the elite migrants from Virginia. If Gilmer and others of his ilk had had their way, some Cherokees, the elite, would have been given an opportunity to stay. White Georgians of substance, such as Gilmer, could recognize similar qualities in others, even if they had different color skin. Or put another way, not all whites were equal. Class and heritage were almost as important as race.

While Gilmer's primary objective in writing *Sketches* was to vindicate his name, the book also served as a means to gild the reputation and legacy of his people, the families who formed the Broad River settlement in what became Wilkes County. In the opening section of his book, Gilmer recounted the histories of the most prominent individuals and families of this group. Drawn principally from Virginia, the immigrants settled in the Georgia backcountry immediately after the War of Independence came to an end. Most had enjoyed relatively privileged lives before the Revolution, but the conflict with Britain and its aftermath had limited their economic opportunities. The decision to relocate to Georgia, therefore, reflected their desire to start anew. In the decades that followed their arrival, Gilmer noted, they succeeded. The settlers from Virginia and their children prospered in their new home. Many became wealthy planters. "The descendents of George Mathews were worth several million dollars as were those of Frank Meriwether, Nat Barnett, Micajah McGehee and Mrs. Harvie. Nicholas Johnson's family was worth two million as was the kin of John Gilmer while Thomas Gilmer was worth one million." Some achieved political success. "One of them has been a prominent candidate for the Presidency. Three have been Governors of States. Three have been Judges of the highest courts. Two have been Presidents of the Legislature of Georgia and other Southern States; and many have been members of the Congress of the United States, and two of them have been electors of

President and Vice President of the United States." For Gilmer, the group's many achievements offered proof of their industry and their upstanding moral character. "Not a descendant of any one of the Broad River people is now know to be so poor, as to be dependent on others for support. Not one has been lost to society by continued gambling, drinking, or other violations of morals and law."[15]

In addition to the Broad River people, Gilmer chronicled the history of a second stream of early settlers to the Georgia upcountry: immigrants from North Carolina. Linked by blood and marriage, they created their own community near Long Creek. Although the settlers from North Carolina and Virginia resided in relative proximity to each other, Gilmer's depiction of the two groups made clear that vast social and economic differences separated them. In stark contrast to his descendants, Gilmer noted, the people who came from North Carolina were dirt poor. "Many years passed before they owned hogs and sheep enough for bacon and clothing." He described them as poverty-stricken and living barely better than the Indians. Of their eating habits, he noted, "Food was eaten then with the greatest relish, which the lady descendants of the settlers would be horrified to see on their tables now. An opossum, with its full dish of gravy, occupied the place of the sucking pig at present." Of their manufacturing, he wrote, "There were no tanneries then to prepare leather for shoes, nor well-instructed shoemakers to manufacture them. Skins, taken from the cattle killed for beef, and those that died with the hollowhorn, were hung in running streams until the hair could be slipped off, and then put into troughs with bark until they became what was called fit for manufacture. . . . Most went without shoes the greater part of the year." Of their living conditions, he remarked, "The first houses were log cabins, with dirt floors and clapboard coverings. Vile toads and venomous serpents were often found crawling over them, and occasionally on the beds." The signs of civilization—the church and schools—were slow to arrive. He identified migrants as scoundrels, either "drunken Irishman or dissolute Virginians, who found the restraints of society in the old countries too binding for their comfort."[16] Few residents received newspapers and most were illiterate. They died with nothing to show for their work. Gilmer's portrait of the North Carolinians was not all negative. He did acknowledge, grudgingly, that they had played a pivotal role during the Revolution in Georgia, helping to defeat the Tories in the backcountry. For their effort, he noted, they had received several positions in the post-revolutionary state government. Yet he tempered his praise by pointing out that some of them had abused this power during the land distribution scandals that took place in the decades following the end of the conflict with the British. Moreover, he also included an account of the exploits of the most famous of member of this group, Elijah Clark, the founder of the Trans-Oconee Republic in the 1790s, whom he implicitly represented as a traitor.[17]

In Gilmer's analysis, both Virginian and North Carolinian migrants consisted of whites. But as he did with the Cherokees, he identified class distinctions within the race. Unlike the North Carolinians, who had no past to speak of, the Virginians who came to Georgia came from blue blood. They were strong, hardy, and industrious folks who were among the first English settlers to arrive in Jamestown. Not only could they claim status as original settlers, some could even claim connections with the original southern nobility, Princess Pocahontas.[18] The Virginians may have arrived in Georgia after the North Carolinians, but they were first in all other ways. Gilmer's book, then, was a commentary on class, race, and politics.

Like Gilmer, Wilson Lumpkin worried how history would judge his role in the Cherokee removal saga. Indeed, in the years after his time in office he began to collect documents related to the controversy so that he would be able to offer a defense of his actions. Lumpkin feared that his critics would have the final say and that his memory would be maligned. His actions while in office touched off backlash. "I was often assailed and misrepresented in religious newspapers, in magazines, pamphlets, and books. . . . this immense mass of published matter, disseminated throughout the country, has, to some extent, left a false impression."[19] The result was a two-volume manuscript that chronicled his time in public office from 1827 to 1841.

If a general apprehension spurred Lumpkin to begin the process of writing his memoir, the catalyst to finish his effort came from the publication of White's *Historical Collections*. While writing his book, White had asked Lumpkin to contribute an article on the controversy between Georgia and the Cherokees, but Lumpkin declined the request because "justice could not be done to such a subject in so limited an article as he proposed" and because he felt he would have to censor himself "to make his book agreeable to everybody and offensive to none."[20] Lumpkin did agree to provide documents, however. When White sent him the finished product, a thirty-three-page article, and asked him to comment, Lumpkin was floored. After reading it, he judged the article "an *entire failure*." Not only was it "inappropriate and calculated to mislead and pervert, rather than to enlighten," Lumpkin complained, but it increased "the cloud and fog which already hangs over the history of Georgia, in connection with her Indian affairs." Lumpkin informed White of his misgivings and White arranged a time to visit with him to correct the mistakes. White failed to turn up, however; instead he went ahead with publication without consulting Lumpkin again. Offended by this assault on his honor, Lumpkin requested that his name be removed from the list of those consulted for the article.[21]

Although Lumpkin was clearly troubled by White's interpretation of the Cherokee controversy, he did not fault the reverend alone. In fact, he believed that, in coming to his conclusions, White had been "misled by selfish and designing men." By this, he meant one man in particular: George Gilmer. Lumpkin had long detested his gubernatorial predecessor Gilmer. From the time he replaced Gilmer as governor, Lumpkin had held him in low regard. "I have long considered him very deficient in the necessary qualifications to make an efficient, useful, public man. His undying prejudices and prepossessions have never allowed him to examine and judge calmly and impartially of men or measures." Lumpkin's estimation of the man plunged further still in the wake of his disagreement with White, which Lumpkin blamed primarily on Gilmer. Lumpkin believed that Gilmer had been trying for years to take the credit for settling the controversy with the Cherokees, and White's article on the dispute simply reinforced his convictions, as did Gilmer's book. "I have for several years past been apprised that Gov. Gilmer was making a great effort to pervert the truths of history in regards to his Cherokee subject. The publication of Rev. Geo. White's Statistics gave me the first reliable evidence of Mr. Gilmer's movements." By compiling relevant documents and recording his version of the events, Lumpkin hoped "to place the labors of my own life in their proper and true position before posterity."[22]

In his assessment of the Cherokee removal, Lumpkin reaffirmed his commitment to the policies he promulgated while in Congress and as governor. Unlike Gilmer, who hinted at remorse for the absolute nature of the laws enacted by the authorities in Georgia, Lumpkin declared his complete satisfaction with the state's policies. "I believed at the time, and I believe yet, that her policy for which she has been most censured was wise humane and philanthropic towards the Indians. To the vigorous policy of Georgia in hastening the removal of the Cherokees, and which was violently opposed at every step, do that people owe their present tranquil enjoyments and future prospects of advancement and success."[23] He conceded that the policies were harsh, but he claimed that he had no alternative. By the time he came to office in 1831, he contended, the Cherokees had become intransigent; they were averse to removal and refused to negotiate a treaty because they "felt assured that their cause was every day gaining strength throughout the country." Lumpkin blamed Gilmer for the state of affairs. "The Indians had become accustomed to Mr. Gilmer's heightened, spicy 'paper bullets.' They disregarded his splutter. They viewed him as a man of words, but not of deeds." Consequently, Lumpkin pushed hard "to legislate the Cherokees into a peaceful willingness to leave the States." Although Lumpkin had faced considerable condemnation from both within and outside of the state for these policies, he repudiated his critics out of hand. His insistence on forcing the Cherokees to leave Georgia, he averred, demonstrated that he had "been their best and most constant friend for forty years past." "If the policy of their leader, Ross, and his Northern fanatical friends . . . prevailed," Lumpkin proclaimed, the Cherokees "would chiefly have perished from the face of the earth."[24]

In addition to providing an outlet to proffer his version of events surrounding the Cherokee controversy, Lumpkin's memoir served as a vehicle to settle old political scores. Lumpkin took his critics and opponents to task for their transgressions against him and his policies. Among those he reproached was William H. Crawford, whose death did not stop Lumpkin from airing grievances that he had nurtured for decades. Lumpkin reserved his most caustic condemnation for George Gilmer, however. Indeed, Lumpkin devoted the final seventeen pages of his manuscript to an all-out assault on his former rival's character and his book, *Sketches*, which Lumpkin labeled a "book of *old wives' fables*."[25]

While differences of opinion over the Cherokees clearly factored into Lumpkin's disdain for Gilmer, Lumpkin's enmity also stemmed from Gilmer's elitism and arrogance, which were revealed in his depiction of the settling of "Upper Georgia" in *Sketches*. Lumpkin resented Gilmer's implication that the Broad River settlers were superior to other white migrants to the region. Even though Lumpkin's family also migrated from Virginia, he scoffed that Gilmer depicted his "*kinfolks* (Broad River)" as the "whole world *of good*" while all others paled in comparison.[26] Yet, Lumpkin noted, Gilmer's claims were completely unfounded. Indeed, Lumpkin equated Gilmer's "Broad River *kinfolks*" with John Ross, the Cherokee chief who had led the resistance to removal, and his "*kinfolks* who had become the wealthy aristocracy of the Cherokee people"; both groups, Lumpkin suggested, had achieved their material and social success through dubious means.[27] For Lumpkin, then, Gilmer and his people served as a stand-in for a larger problem facing Georgia. They represented the continued existence of an elite whose unjustified claims to authority and leadership hampered the state's development and progress.

Despite their differences, both Gilmer and Lumpkin wrote of Indians in Georgia in the past tense as a relic of history rather than a reality of the late antebellum era. As far as they were concerned, white Georgians had successfully removed Indians from the state. While this was certainly the case for the most part, a small population of Indians resided in Georgia. In fact, a number of them succeeded in securing rights and privileges similar, and in some cases identical, to those of whites. Beginning in 1838, dozens of Cherokees gained citizenship in Georgia. A couple of these individuals obtained white status, granting them all the privileges of citizenship. The others gained status as "free citizens"; this also meant that they no longer faced laws applicable to Cherokees, those passed in the 1820s and 1830s to spur them to leave Georgia. The laws, however, carefully stipulated that the petitioners could not advance claims to lands they had formerly held as Indians. Status as "whites" or as "free citizens" necessitated giving up claims as Indians. The first act granted twenty-two Cherokee families citizenship in Georgia; nine of the families were Indian men and their children; the remaining thirteen were wives and children of white men. The law was specific in declaring them "free citizens of this State."[28] The next year, the General Assembly granted four more Cherokee families "citizenship" and removed their "legal disabilities" as Cherokees. They were "liable to do and perform all and singular the duties of citizens of Georgia."[29] The 1839 law included a provision prohibiting them from initiating a suit to recover any land that had been or would be granted by the state "to which they may claim title as Indians or the descendants of Indians." In 1840 the General Assembly granted seven adults from four more Indian families citizenship. The families were also prohibited from suing for land. Most significantly, there was also a provision that transformed Daniel Sills, of Marion County, into a white man. He and his family were "authorized to exercise and enjoy all the privileges of white citizens of this State."[30] In 1842, one family of a white man gained citizenship as well as three adults.[31] In 1845, one woman and her family and Neely Justice received status as "free citizens."[32] That same year two Cherokee men, George Michael Lavender and Matthew Thompson, officially changed their names and received "all the rights and privileges that appertain and belong to the free white citizens of this State," including a repeal of "all disabilities."[33] Grants of citizenship then abruptly ceased. The bestowal of the rights and privileges of citizenship on these Indians represented the continuing influence of men like Gilmer, who recognized that some Indians could be incorporated into society, over men like Lumpkin, who insisted on complete removal. Elite and well-connected Indians, however, possessed this room to maneuver in isolated instances because of the triumph of Indian removal.

The dispute between Gilmer and Lumpkin reflected class tensions among whites over matters of race. The resurrection of the debate over the removal of the Cherokees in the 1850s revealed that divisions over race, at least relative to Indians, had not disappeared in the two decades since the controversy first erupted. The debate highlighted the continued role of class in the framing of these divisions. Like Gilmer, some elite whites continued to see race and socioeconomic status as intertwined phenomena rather than absolutes. They lamented the rigid application of racial lines. By contrast, Lumpkin, embodying the beliefs of the common man, represented a less flexible approach to the subject; for this group, the notion that Indians could progress beyond their semicivilized state was absurd. The Cherokees were not, nor would they ever be, ready to meet the requirements of citizenship. As such there was no place for them in Georgia. Yet the conflict between the two sides was academic. Both sides agreed that Indian removal had served the best interests of the state. The Cherokees had long since left the state and no one, not even their most righteous defenders, imagined that the situation could ever change. But it was precisely this fact that made it possible for debate to flourish. The public could tolerate the romanticization of "distinguished" Indian men when those Indian men no longer lived within the boundaries of the state. When it came to racial matters related to blacks, the same was not true.

Of all the men in antebellum Georgia, State Supreme Court Justice Joseph H. Lumpkin, the brother of Governor Wilson Lumpkin, had the greatest impact on the state's laws regulating race and slavery. He was the architect of the state's slave regime, having authored the opinions in more than half of the sixty most important cases related to those issues during his twenty-one years on the bench. Through these rulings, Lumpkin molded Georgia's antebellum legal code to conform to his vision of a properly ordered slave society. Across the region, whites were pushing for changes in the racial order that entrenched slavery and reduced the rights of free blacks. In his reshaping of Georgia's slave law, Lumpkin stood at the vanguard of a southern movement promoting proslavery ideology in the legal realm.[34]

In his opinions, Lumpkin ruled that free blacks were not, never had been, and never would be citizens in Georgia. Indeed, he defined the free black population as the antipodes to Georgia's white citizenry. Lumpkin's rigid interpretation of the correct form for a slave society left no room for free blacks. He read the history of the racial past in dichotomous terms, literally black and white. He erased free blacks from Georgia's early history and reduced their diversity in status to a simple stereotype. Lumpkin cast white Georgians' perceptions of free blacks in monolithic terms that defied historical reality. But his vision contradicted a more ambiguous stand toward free blacks in the past, a sentiment that still existed in pockets of the state. Indeed, a small group of free people of color even obtained some of the rights and privileges of citizenship in the 1790s. Yet, despite his errors, Lumpkin had a profound impact on southern law and national law. Moreover, it was his vision that served as the basis for future scholarship on race and the place of free blacks in society by legal scholars and historians. Thus, while Lumpkin may have lost in the immediate sense, the legacy of his opinions long outlasted his life.

That Lumpkin would emerge as the key defender of slavery in Georgia was far from clear during his early years. Lumpkin was born in 1799 in Oglethorpe County. His family had migrated to Georgia from Virginia and settled on the Broad River in the late 1700s. As a young man, Lumpkin attended the University of Georgia and later Princeton University. Soon after his return from the North, Lumpkin took up the study of law. During this time, he met and married his wife and, following her lead, became an evangelical Christian. Lumpkin's conversion shaped his worldview. Influenced by his newfound religious convictions and the perfectionist impulse, Lumpkin was drawn to national reform movements in the 1820s and 1830s. Like most evangelicals, Lumpkin embraced the temperance movement. In time, however, he gravitated toward abolitionism, going so far as to join the American Colonization Society (ACS). The depth of Lumpkin's commitment to the movement became clear in 1833 when he delivered a speech in Boston in which he tacitly endorsed emancipation. That Lumpkin chose to name his son after William Wilberforce, the famed English abolitionist, provided further proof of his convictions.[35]

And then all at once, Lumpkin completely changed course. After flirting with the abolitionist movement, Lumpkin backed away in the late 1830s as the sectional conflict over slavery escalated.[36] This reversal pushed him in the other direction; he embraced the proslavery ideology with the zeal of a reformer. His earlier ambivalence dissipated. In the mid-1850s, he broke formally with the ACS over the group's direction and objectives. "I was once, in common with the great body of my fellow citizens of the South, the friend and patron of this enterprise. I now regard it as a failure, if not something worse; as I do every effort that has been made, for the abolition of negro slavery, at home or abroad."[37] All blacks, he believed, should be enslaved. With this change in his convictions, he adhered to a rigid application of these principles in forming his legal opinions.

Lumpkin's embrace of slavery came at a particularly auspicious moment. Having jettisoned his reservations about bondage, Lumpkin rose to prominence in Georgia at a time when the state's legal system was undergoing a radical transformation. Unlike other states in the Union, Georgians had resisted the creation of a state supreme court in the years after independence, preferring instead to rely on a series of superior courts to mete out justice. By the second half of the 1830s, opposition to the state supreme court began to wane, culminating in the establishment of the tribunal in 1846. Recognized by most Georgians as one of the state's leading attorneys, Lumpkin was the natural choice to lead the court. He served from 1846 until his death in 1867, and although he was not made the official chief justice until 1863, he was widely regarded as the court's leading jurist from the outset. From his position on the bench, Lumpkin led the effort to standardize the state's slave and racial laws.[38]

Lumpkin's shifts on slavery paralleled a broader transformation in proslavery thought in Georgia and the South as whole. In the revolutionary and early national periods, apologists defended slavery as a necessary evil when countering critics' condemnations of the institution. They acknowledged that slavery posed some ethical and moral quandaries in a nation founded on freedom and equality, but, they reasoned, whites were ill-suited to the rigors of rice cultivation, which meant that African slavery provided the only solution to develop the area commercially. By the second decade of the nineteenth century, however, a transition was well under way. No longer willing to concede the principled high ground to their foes, slavery's defenders portrayed bondage as a positive good. Slave ownership was framed as a republican virtue that required no apology. Governor George Troup's words reflected the changed mind-set: "If this matter be an evil, it is our own—if it be a sin, we can implore the forgiveness of it; to remove it, we ask neither their sympathy or assistance—it may be our physical weakness—it is our moral strength. If, like the Greeks and Romans, the moment we cease to be masters, we are slaves."[39] In the 1830s and 1840s, as the abolition movement grew in force in the North, proslavery advocates increasingly looked to religion, history, and science to legitimate their position.[40]

By the second quarter of the nineteenth century, religious justifications came to play an integral role in the defense of slavery. Countering abolitionists' reliance on Christian doctrine with their own scriptural interpretations, white Georgians galvanized their support for slavery. Tracts such as *Bondage a Moral Institution, Sanctioned by the Scriptures of the Old and New Testament, and the Preaching and Practice of the Savior and the Apostle*, published in Macon in 1837, carried the divine message throughout the state. As the sectional divide deepened, the rhetoric escalated. The parishioners of the Hopewell Presbytery declared that the Bible did not promote emancipation as a duty of a master to his slaves but did emphasize obedience as a duty of a slave to his master. The Presbytery denounced any ecclesiastical attempts to interfere with the institution as "tyrannical and odious."[41] While serving in the second of his two terms as governor, Joseph Lumpkin's brother, Wilson Lumpkin, assailed northern abolitionists in even harsher language. Castigating opponents of slavery as "vile incendiaries who are laboring to stir up insurrection and rebellion in the southern States," he argued that the "principles of the Christian religion can never be brought to the aid of these monsters, whose proceedings are marked by the most reckless blood thirsty spirit that ever disgraced the American name."[42]

Drawing on the Bible, proslavery ideologues in Georgia as in other southern and even northern states embraced slavery as a divinely sanctioned institution, not a necessary evil. As a deeply committed evangelical, Judge Lumpkin relied on the Bible for moral and ethical guidance as well as historical evidence to support his opinions on slavery. Lumpkin idealized slavery as an essential component of the South's perfect society. Invoking Christianity to sustain his position, he asserted that slavery "—like government itself—is of God. That being recognized and regulated by the Decalogue, it will, we have every reason to believe, be of perpetual duration. That it subserves the best interests of both races, and that we will persevere and defend it at any and all hazards."[43] Central to the biblical justification of racial slavery was the identification of Africans as the descendants of the "tribe of Ham." According to the Book of Genesis, Lumpkin claimed, blacks were "cursed" and "judicially condemned to perpetual bondage."[44] Lumpkin viewed this decree as "unreversible. It will run on parallel with time itself. And heaven and earth shall sooner pass away, than once jot or title of it shall abate."[45] By the grace of God, they could not escape their fate, destined to remain enslaved forever.

Proslavery advocates also increasingly offered their own historical interpretations that vindicated benevolent southern slaveholders, often at the expense of greedy northern merchants. Thomas Cobb, one of Lumpkin's disciples, told the story of how slavery arrived in the New World and gradually reached perfection in the U.S. South. He traced the history of slavery from ancient times, through the middle ages, and ultimately to the Americas. In his discussion of the origins of plantation slavery in the New World, Cobb praised Bartolomé de Las Casas for his rejection of Indian slavery in favor of African slavery. He acknowledged that the Spanish were "brutal" and that the early revolts had much to do with their behavior, but he ultimately excused their actions because he believed their primary goal to be civilizing them. By contrast, Cobb condemned the Atlantic slave trade and vilified northerners, particularly the Puritans, for their role in the enterprise. As part of his analysis, Cobb compared slavery in the West Indies and the U.S. South, which he asserted were "totally different." In the islands, slaves were merchandise, worked to death because it made economic sense to do so. In contrast to the "vast plantations" worked by legions of slaves owned by absentees, "the English colonists on the continent were generally men of moderate means, who had sought a home in the New World." As a result, he claimed, "No tempting market enticed him to forget humanity in his search for gain." In fact, Cobb portrayed the emergence of cash crop production on the mainland as a sacrifice on the part of masters, something they had taken up as a form of Christian charity; the profit motive was not mentioned. Tobacco, cotton, rice, and silk were all introduced to Georgia, he claimed, "to furnish employment for the slaves." He portrayed the relationship between slaves and their owners as a form of benevolent paternalism. "To take care of the sick, to shelter and provide for the children, to feed bountifully and clothe warmly, became the interest of the planter, and soon his pride. The natural result of the all these causes was sympathy between the master and slave unknown upon the islands."[46]

To support his benign portrait of slavery, Cobb rewrote the history of slave resistance in the South. "Having been generally well-treated, the slaves have never exhibited that disposition to revolt so frequently seen in the West Indies," he claimed. "No Maroons have infested our mountains; no war of the Maroons stain our annals." Overlooking the multiple slave insurrections in the nation's past, including Turner's Rebellion only two decades earlier, he contended that Gabriel Prosser's revolt in 1800 was the sole slave uprising to occur in the South. In doing so, Cobb ignored the strong black and Indian resistance to the spread of plantation slavery in the early nineteenth century and retained his benevolent portrait of slavery.[47]

As the nineteenth century wore on, proslavery ideologues increasingly relied on science to prove blacks' racial inferiority and to therefore justify their enslavement. Cobb portrayed Africans and their descendants as naturally suited for slavery, a condition he suggested they had always suffered. Like many nineteenth-century intellectuals, Cobb believed biological differences separated the races and rendered Africans mentally inferior and perfectly suited to slave labor. The "physical, intellectual, and moral development of the African race are promoted by a state of slavery, and their happiness secured to a greater extent than if left at liberty," Cobb argued. "But remove the restraining and controlling power of the master, and the negro becomes, at once, the slave of his lust, and the victim of his indolence, relapsing, with wonderful rapidity, into his pristine barbarism." To further bolster his argument, Cobb relied on the latest trends in the natural sciences and zoology to demonstrate the supposed pervasiveness of slavery in the natural world. He anthropomorphized relations among various creatures to find analogous social systems to those among humans. Asserting that blackness in nature was synonymous with inferiority, he claimed that "servitude, in every respect the counterpart of negro slavery," existed even among "lower animals." "It is a fact, well known to entomologists, and too well established to admit of contradiction," he stated, "that the red ant will issue in regular battle array, to conquer and subjugate the black or negro ant, as he is called by entomologists. And, that these negro slaves perform all the labor of the communities into which they are thus brought, with patience and an aptitude almost incredible." Accordingly, he concluded, "negro slavery would seem to be perfectly consistent" with "the law of nature."[48]

Lumpkin also relied on the slaves' supposed racial inferiority to justify their condition. Without the direct aid and supervision of whites, he claimed, slaves were incapable of taking care of themselves. As proof,

Lumpkin pointed to Liberia, which freed American slaves had founded in the early 1820s with the aid of the American Colonization Society. "Liberia was formed of emancipated slaves, many of them partially trained and prepared for the change, and sent thousands of miles from all contact with the superior race; and given a home in a country where their ancestors were natives, and supposed to be suited to their physical condition. Arrived there, they have been for a number of years in a state of pupilage to the Colonization Society, in order that they might learn 'to walk alone and by themselves.' And at the end of a half century what do we see? A few thousand thriftless, lazy semi-savages, dying of famine, because they will not work!" He repudiated all emancipation and repatriation efforts as futile. Any "experiment, whether made in the British West India Islands, the coast of Africa, or elsewhere, will demonstrate that it is a vain thing for fanaticism, a false philanthropy, or anything else, to fight against the Almighty." "Under the superior race and nowhere else," Lumpkin concluded, "do they attain to the highest degree of civilization."[49]

Lumpkin and other proslavery thinkers recognized that Georgia and the South as a whole were entering a new era. As one of the last three remaining slave societies in the Americas, the South could no longer look to the West Indies or South America for inspiration or guidance. White Georgians no longer took their cues from others on how to run their slave society. Fifty years earlier they had looked to the Caribbean for a model; now they turned inward and to God for inspiration. By the 1850s, the suggestion that white Georgians should look elsewhere was beyond the pale. That virtually the rest of the Atlantic World opposed the continuance of slavery did not matter. It was supported by the white residents of the state and God, and that was good enough. Indeed, in Lumpkin's estimation it made Georgia divine. With slavery abolished almost everywhere else and abolitionism growing, it was time that Georgians charted their own path. These ideas served as the foundation for Lumpkin as he ruled in supreme court cases related to race and slavery.

Created in 1845, the state supreme court had its roots in racial matters.[50] From the state's founding, white Georgians had largely preferred a decentralized judicial system that allowed laws to be interpreted according to the will of local residents. Without a supreme court in the state, this had remained possible. The system highlighted the regional divisions at play when the state was first formed and tensions between whites in the backcountry and on the coast. Neither group fully trusted the other. They had different backgrounds and values and held divergent ideas about the proper way to structure society. When delegates drafted the state constitution in 1789, they chose not to establish a court of errors. Instead they opted to rely on a regionally based system of circuit courts to administer the law, a compromise that satisfied the concerns of the state's white residents. In the years that followed, the state authorities experimented on occasion with ways to standardize the courts' rulings, but in each instance they abandoned their efforts soon after implementation. As a result, the judicial system remained decentralized for the next four decades, accommodating the physical expansion of the state and the population growth by adding new circuits. By the mid-1830s, however, new calls to reform the judicial system had emerged.[51]

Advocates favoring the supreme court framed their efforts in class terms. One of the court's most outspoken supporters was Judge Hiram Warner, a superior court justice who argued in 1835 that the court would "protect the poor and weak against the encroachments of the strong, the rich and the powerful." The wealthy and strong, he recognized, could protect themselves. The poor and obscure, however, needed "the arm of the Judiciary, to shield and protect them." He presented a state supreme court as the common man's "sheet anchor of American liberty, the bulwark of freedom."[52] Governor Charles McDonald offered a similar argument in favor of judicial reform in 1841. He complained that the "decisions of the circuit judge are final and irreversible, except at his will. His power, in cases involving the life, property and liberty of the citizen, is absolute and appalling; and, but that we have been so long accustomed to its exercise by a single individual, it would not be tolerated for a day. . . . The principle is anti-republican." He promoted the state supreme court as a democratic measure. Because the reports of the decisions would be published, he argued, "an opportunity will be afforded every man to understand the authoritative interpretation of the laws."[53] The court, according to the governor, would become another tool of the people. After a lengthy legislative process, the General Assembly finally agreed to found the state supreme court in 1845.[54]

Proponents explicitly emphasized class, but the racial subtext remained an integral aspect of the movement to create a supreme court and should not be ignored even if it was not openly addressed. Widespread revulsion at Judge John W. Hooper's rulings in favor of Cherokee litigants in 1834 served as the catalyst for the establishment of a court of error. Many nonelite whites, particularly yeomen and mechanics in North Georgia, felt that the lower courts did not reflect their interests and specifically their interests in white supremacy. They charged that Hooper's rulings favored Indians at the expense of common white men. They demanded that the judicial system, the last bastion of moderation in the state government, demonstrate a clear commitment to white supremacy, regardless of legal principle. Nonelite whites remained suspicious of their wealthier counterparts' commitment to absolute white supremacy.[55]

The composition of the court and the timing of its creation reflected the altered balance of power in the state. The court's creation coincided with the rise of the interior of Georgia, the cotton kingdom. Interestingly, all of the men who served as justices before 1865 came from the upcountry.[56] Not a single one came from the lowcountry. The majority came from the newer sections of the state. Thus the attitudes of the upcountry whites were well represented on the court while lowcountry whites, particularly those who held differing views of slavery, were largely excluded.

Race remained a central issue for the court in the years after its establishment. Rather than a check on its law-making abilities, Georgia's legislators envisioned the court as a legitimizing body whose rulings would add constitutional heft to the state's laws, particularly those related to slavery, at a time when the South was coming under increasing fire from abolitionists. Justice Lumpkin agreed. He viewed the relationship between the legislature and the supreme court as complementary as well. And he, too, believed some of the most important work facing the two arms of the government lay in reforming the slave system. In 1847, for example, the General Assembly asked the judges of the supreme court to examine the state's legal code and issue a report identifying any defect in the laws and suggesting remedies. In his reply, Justice Lumpkin called on the legislators to continue their efforts to remake slavery. "In the present state of the union and of the world, the law of slavery should undergo the most thorough examination, and its various details and provisions, be made to conform to the exigencies of the times. If duty to ourselves, as well as our slaves require increased severity, by way of security, let it be imposed, regardless of the hypocritical cant and clamor of the fanatics of our own or other countries. If on the other hand, it shall be found that existing enactments may be relaxed or ameliorated without prejudice to our safety or rights of property, let us not be deterred from doing what is right and just, as Christian masters."[57]

Cobb and other proslavery intellectuals provided Lumpkin with historical and legal evidence to further solidify his position. For Lumpkin, this information was only part of his larger argument. Lumpkin considered himself a reformer with a mission. He recognized the unique nature of antebellum slavery in the South and the need for it to evolve to survive. He envisioned a society in which slave-based agriculture and free white mechanical labor coexisted. In these ways, Lumpkin represented the sentiments of a large segment of white Georgian society, especially in the interior of the state. The "Southern people must, to a certain extent, abandon their accustomed paths, and devise new plans for their future prosperity; that the interest of agriculture, laying aside every other consideration, imperatively demands a diversity of employment; in short, the manufactures must be combined, to a great extent, with agriculture; the one stimulating the other, and contributing to its emoluments."[58]

For its part, the supreme court contributed mightily to the reform effort. Between 1846 and 1866, the justices ruled on nearly 3,800 cases, 330 of which related to slavery. Of the justices, Lumpkin had the biggest impact on the court's rulings on race. Despite the existence of a system that was supposed to assign cases equally, he presided over a disproportionate number of the slavery-related cases that came before the state supreme court and authored the opinions in more than half of the sixty most important cases.[59] Under the leadership of Lumpkin, the supreme court issued a series of rulings that legitimated the institution in Georgia so that the laws reflected the racial views dominant in the cotton kingdom. In addition to establishing a uniform set of legal standards, then, the supreme court added another layer of legitimacy to slavery in Georgia.

By presenting slavery as a civilizing school for foreign pagans, Lumpkin envisioned a properly ordered slave society that had a place for everyone—everyone except free people of African descent. Like his larger worldview, Lumpkin's attitude toward race was bifurcated, with no gradations. Influenced by his religious convictions to see the world in Manichean terms, all issues became black or white, good or evil, right or wrong. And unfortunately for free people of color, they contradicted his perfectionist vision of the slave South, a world where African descent and slavery were increasingly synonymous. Consequently, Lumpkin decried the very existence of free blacks: "To him there is but little in prospect but a life of poverty, of depression, of ignorance, and of decay. He lives amongst us without motive and without hope. His fancied freedom is all a delusion. All practical men must admit, that the slave who receives the care and protection of a tolerable master, is superior in comfort to the free negro."[60] Indeed, he considered the mere suggestion that any person of African descent should enjoy his or her liberty as an abomination. Free blacks offered proof of the falsity of his portrait of slavery. Free blacks, then, had to disappear. To that end, Lumpkin issued a series of opinions designed to halt the growth of the state's free black population and to reduce their legal status to roughly equal that of a slave. In the process, Lumpkin ignored the ambiguity that had characterized the state's stand toward free people of color in the first decades after the Revolution, substituting a more contemporary and rigid view of race. In justifying his position, Lumpkin relied on two central arguments: that free blacks and slaves were roughly equivalent and that it had always been that way. These principles shaped his legal interpretation, which, by virtue of his position on the court, became in effect the state's official position.

Georgia's policy toward free people of color and free blacks changed over the course of the nineteenth century. In the first twenty-five years after independence, authorities displayed a flexible approach toward free people of color. Some free people of African descent gained citizenship status during the revolutionary era. Although the push to expand the rights of some elite free people of color dissipated in the first decade in the nineteenth century, most whites in Georgia did not view free people of African descent as being the same as slaves. In the antebellum era, whites' attitudes toward race hardened. As both potential economic competition and a security risk, free people of color found few friends when the authorities cracked down on them. To most white Georgians, they came to represent a fifth column.

As they battled blacks on their borders in the 1810s, white Georgians further subordinated blacks within their borders. In the midst of the various wars, the General Assembly passed a series of laws in the 1810s that steadily eroded the rights of free people of color in the state. In their efforts to root out potential enemies of the state, legislators targeted free people of color. In 1812, the General Assembly approved a law hiring out free people of color who neglected to pay their taxes.[61] In 1816, the assembly ordered free people of color to be tried in the same manner as slaves.[62] Just months after the fall of the Negro Fort, the General Assembly sentenced free people of color who aided runaway slaves to one year's hard labor followed by sale into slavery. The restrictions against free people of color increased as the decade wore on, culminating in the passage of a series of harsh new reforms in 1818, months after the defeat and destruction of the Seminole towns around Suwanee.[63] In the aftermath of the Seminole War, the General Assembly again cracked down on free people of color and nominal slaves. Complaining of the burgeoning population of free people of African descent in the state, the General Assembly blocked the immigration of free people of color to the state and mandated strict registration requirements for free blacks, imposing enslavement as the penalty for noncompliance. The General Assembly removed a loophole from the 1801 prohibition against manumission that had allowed owners to free their slaves in their wills.

Free people of African descent faced a host of new restrictions in the antebellum era, often in connection with rising fears of racial violence. In 1818, the same atmosphere of distrust and heightened racial fears that led to the manumission ban resulted in a general crackdown on the free people of color in the state. Similarly, in the wake of the discovery that copies of David Walker's *Appeal to the Colored People of the World* had been successfully smuggled into Georgia, the General Assembly prohibited black sailors from coming ashore while their vessels docked in the city port. The sailors were barred from contacting vessels and were forced to undergo quarantine. The law reflected the severity of white Georgians' concerns. Those convicted of spreading the pamphlet faced execution. Laws made it illegal to teach any person of African descent to read or write. They also banned slaves and free people of color from working as typesetters.[64] The possibility of blacks reading the incendiary material scared whites more than anything to that date. It was the spread of ideas, they knew, that represented the biggest threat.

Even as the legislature took an increasingly harsh stand toward free blacks in the antebellum era, the courts continued to recognize rights for free people of African descent, as late as 1831. That year Judge William Crawford ruled in *State v. Philpot* that there was a "very broad and obvious distinction between the rights and conditions of slaves and free persons of color." The case centered on the rights of free people of color, specifically the right to writs of habeas corpus. Crawford noted that "with but a single exception known to the court, the decisions and practice throughout the State are now and have been uniform, to extend to this class of persons the benefit of the writs of habeas corpus." The judge declared that, like a "Frenchman, Englishman, or other foreigner who might come among us," free blacks deserved such protections. Quoting from the 1798 state constitution, Crawford noted that the document stipulated that "all persons shall be entitled" to this right, regardless of the "particular complexion of the individual."[65] While acknowledging that slaves did not have the right to habeas corpus, he stressed the differ ence between the two: "Let it be remembered, while these positions are examined, with a view to ascertain their bearing on the present question, that it is not whether a slave may have the writ, but whether it may be legally awarded to a free person of color." Clearly they were not the same. For those who conflated the two together because of "the general presumption against the liberty of the slave race," he wrote, "this is carrying the presumption of law too far." It "would be a very hard and unreasonable construction of a mere rule of evidence, to make it reduce a whole class of free people to a level with slaves, deprive them of the most effectual means of protecting their personal liberty, and subvert a constitutional provision. This is a very broad and obvious distinction between the rights and condition of slaves and free persons of color."[66] In this instance, Crawford regarded free people of African descent as little different from other nationalities. Whether free blacks had rights, therefore, had more to do with their status than their skin color. Race clearly was an important marker in Georgia, but in the first decades of the nineteenth century, it was only one of several key identifiers.

Invoking the 1798 state constitution as a source of legitimacy was not simply a rhetorical device designed to support an opinion. Rather, it pointed to an era when free people of color were able to access a range of the rights and privileges associated with citizenship. In contrast to Lumpkin, who stated that it was unnecessary for the court to go beyond 1818 to ascertain the condition of free people of African descent, Crawford knew that in the early decades of the nation the situation had been different. He understood that, in that time of racial and legislative flux, the place of free people of African descent had not yet been fully determined.

In the years after the *Philpot* decision, racial attitudes among white Georgians shifted. There had always been white Georgians who viewed race in absolute terms, those who believed blacks had no rights, but by the middle third of the nineteenth century their numbers had grown substantially. Numerous interrelated factors contributed to this shift, including the spread of slavery to the interior of the state, the rise of cotton cultivation, the removal of the Cherokee Indians, the subsequent increase in the white population (particularly of nonslaveholding whites), and the growth of abolitionist sentiment in the North. Black resistance also played a role. The rising fear of slave insurrection and the discovery of multiple plots inspired a belief among whites that a large-scale insurrection was inevitable, and many assumed that free blacks would join it. The flexibility that had characterized the state's earlier treatment of

free people of African descent had dissipated. Reflective of the growing antipathy toward free blacks, Georgia legislators passed a host of
laws that imposed new scrutiny on free blacks' behavior and restrictions
on their economic activities. Laws passed in 1833 and 1835, when the
General Assembly enacted the new penal code, continued the assault on
free blacks' rights. Blacks were banned from being druggists. Free people
of color were prohibited from owning or using firearms. Free people
of color could not secure credit without written permission from their
guardian. They could be involuntarily bound out to pay their debts. They
could be whipped for aiding runaways, instead of fined, as mandated by
the 1770 code. They were required to provide proof of their free status
for the previous five years. They could not leave the state for longer than
six months and could travel only to surrounding states. They could be
denied the right to register if shown to be of "bad character." The state
government sought to debase free blacks and free people of color to the
status of slaves. These restrictions came at the same time as the laws making white men into Indians if they stayed with their Indian families and
denying Indian men the option of acting as planters. Just as white Georgians defined white men living with Indians as Indians, state legislators
defined free blacks as little more than slaves.[67]

Efforts to erode the distinctions between slaves and free blacks continued in the 1840s. Anticipating a later decision by Chief Justice Roger
B. Taney in the Dred Scott case, the legislators declared that free blacks were
not eligible for citizenship under the Constitution, because the fram-
ers did not intend to include as citizens those "who were not so at the
time of the adoption of the Federal Constitution." The General Assembly
passed a resolution asserting that "negroes, or persons of color, are not
citizens, under the Constitution of the United States; and Georgia will
never recognize such citizenship."[68] The following decade, the legislature tightened restrictions on the registration rules, granted the inferior
courts the right to bind out free black children, tightened the prohibitions against free blacks settling in the state, and granted whites the right
to arrest any free person of color they deemed to be "leading an idle,
immoral or profligate course of life" and charge them with vagrancy.[69]

Clearly some of the laws were drafted as protection to ensure the
state's security, but some of them were passed with the intention of de-
basing free blacks and free people of color. The democratization of slavery
shepherded a collapsing of distinctions between slaves and free blacks. It
attacked the privileges that free people of color had traditionally enjoyed.

It destroyed the fluidity that had characterized the racial order in the first decades after the introduction of slavery. A more rigid and simplified hierarchy emerged, one based exclusively on race.

Georgia's supreme court dealt with a number of important cases pertaining to free blacks, but it was Lumpkin's decisions in the *Bryan v. Walton* case that established their legal standing in the state. The suit made it to the supreme court three times before coming to a conclusion.[70] Ostensibly the case pitted two white men, Hugh Walton and Seaborn C. Bryan, against one another over the ownership of a group of slaves, but at its core it answered a fundamental legal question concerning the status of free people of African descent in Georgian society. The man who sold the slaves in question was Joseph Nunez, a free person of color from Burke County. The case turned on whether Nunez had the right to do so. In his ruling, Lumpkin declared the importance of the issue at hand. "This is a grave question," one that "involves a great principle" and "establishes an important precedent."[71] The opinion in the *Bryan* case defined the legal status of free people of African descent in Georgia both in the present and, as importantly, in the past.

According to Lumpkin, free people of African descent were virtually identical to slaves before the law. Indicative of his effort to draw a clear-cut divide between black and white Georgians while simultaneously lumping all free people of color and free blacks with slaves, Lumpkin referred to them all as "Africans," a curious decision since the Atlantic slave trade had ended more than four decades earlier. In doing so, Lumpkin erased differences of wealth, birth, and caste among free people of color and emphasized their foreignness. The "*status* of the African in Georgia," he remarked, "whether bond or free, is such that he has no civil, social or political rights or capacity." Blacks, regardless of their status as free or enslaved, could "never enjoy" civil freedom among whites.[72] "Like the *slave*," Lumpkin declared, "the *free* person of color" was associated "with the slave in this State in some of the most humiliating incidents in his degradation." As proof, he pointed to a list of laws that reduced free people of color to the status of the slave, including prohibitions against voting or holding office, testifying in court against whites, carrying firearms, preaching without a special license, selling or making drugs and medicines, learning to read or write, or working in any occupation that required those skills.[73]

Believing free blacks to be indistinguishable from slaves, Lumpkin declared that they could never be citizens of Georgia. The free black man, he proclaimed, "resides among us, and yet is a stranger. A *native* even, and yet not a citizen. Though not a *slave*, yet he is not free. Protected by law, yet enjoying none of the immunities of freedom. Though not in a condition of chattelhood, yet constantly exposed to it." To "be civilly and politically free, to be the peer and equal of the white man—to enjoy the offices, trusts and privileges our institutions confer on the white man, is not now, never has been, and never will be, the condition of this degraded race." Lumpkin concluded that "He is not and cannot become a *citizen* under our Constitution and Laws."[74]

Not only did Lumpkin contend free blacks and slaves were synonymous, he also insisted that it had always been that way. He depicted a static vision of Georgia's racial order, relying on biological and biblical justifications to support his position. He rooted free blacks' "social and civil degradation" in "the taint of blood, [which] adheres to the descendants of Ham in this country, like the poisoned tunic of Nessus." He asserted, "The blacks were introduced into [Georgia], as a race of Pagan slaves. The prejudice, if it can be called so, of caste, is unconquerable. It was so at the beginning. It has come down to our day."[75] His explanation was religiously inspired and eternal.

Lumpkin's efforts to deny the existence of a free black past as distinct from the slave past were essential to legitimate the ideology of slavery that emerged in the antebellum era. With slavery abolished almost everywhere else and abolitionism growing, it was time that Georgians charted their own path. In this context, Lumpkin and other white southerners faced the prospect of forging a new proslavery ideology alone. To do so, they rewrote history to justify their actions. The true history of free blacks in Georgia, indeed in the South, contradicted the rationale underlying white southerners' claims that slavery was necessary. By collapsing the broad range of distinctions among the state's free people of African descent, ruling repeatedly that their status in Georgia was the equivalent of slaves, and asserting that it had always been this way, Lumpkin created a new history of free blacks in order to counteract the assault on slavery.

The graded notion of citizenship secured by free people of color in the 1790s contrasted with Lumpkin's absolute notion of citizenship in the 1850s. According to Lumpkin, Georgians fell into one of two categories: citizen or slave. There were no gradations, just absolutes. Free blacks, in Lumpkin's reasoning, could be justifiably equated with slaves because of their racial inferiority but also because they had not been granted the

right to vote. In focusing on suffrage, Lumpkin offered a masculine definition that ignored the citizenship status of white women. When speaking of free blacks, Lumpkin envisioned them as men, specifying "he" and
never "she" in his decisions. This allowed him to use free white men as
a foil, positioning all white men as equal citizens while simultaneously
placing all free people of African descent into the same category—black
men completely devoid of the political rights and privileges of citizenship that all white men enjoyed. Lumpkin projected a black/white bi-
furcation back in time, imagining racial rigidity where there had been
racial flexibility and equating blackness with slavery and whiteness with
citizenship.

Despite the confidence of his declarations, Lumpkin's views of free
people of color in Georgia and their past were ahistorical. As proof of
their degraded place in society, he invoked a series of laws that restricted
the rights of free people of color, but he did not mention that most of the
laws had been enacted only in the past three decades. Rather, Lumpkin
portrayed the prohibitions against blacks as having been on the books
forever.[76] The court records and legislative acts demonstrate that state authorities had afforded free people of color greater rights than Lumpkin
maintained and that some free people of color even obtained citizenship.
While it was true that by the antebellum era most whites in Georgia
shared Lumpkin's views of free blacks, this attitude was not monolithic,
nor had whites always felt this way. In fact, as late as the 1850s, there
continued to be pockets in Georgia where whites tolerated mobility and
status for certain free people of color, places where an earlier racial sen-
sibility persevered despite the rise of the cotton kingdom.

Lumpkin used the *Bryan v. Walton* case to argue that free blacks in Georgian society had always been equivalent to slaves, but ironically the facts
in the case demonstrate that Lumpkin's portrait of the racial order in
the past was wrong. Evidence from the Nunez family proved his error.
Testimony revealed that Joseph Nunez's father, James Nunez, was a free
man of color who in spite of his racial background had become an accepted part of white elite society in Burke County in the late eighteenth
and early nineteenth centuries. James Nunez's wealth and the standing of
his father, Moses Nunez, who was part of a well-known Sephardic family that emigrated to Georgia in the 1730s, provided status in the community. James Nunez was particularly accomplished and well known. He
was educated and met regularly with white men in the neighborhood.
One white woman claimed he "was received by them as on a footing

with whites." He was admitted to society functions and held a respect-able position in the community. He attended social events with whites, including dances. He and a white woman named Lucy Anderson "lived together as husband and wife." As evidence of Nunez's status among his white neighbors, Lucy Nunez did not lose her standing in the commu-nity for having a nonwhite husband. She met regularly with other white women in the neighborhood. James Nunez's neighbors knew "he was of color" but were unsure as to what his mixture was. Some whites believed he was a "respectable Indian and white blooded man," while others were convinced he was a "free mulatto." His appearance offered few clues: he had "black and tolerably straight hair" and "a nose like a white man—not flat." His lips "were not very thick." As for his skin color, he "was a dark complected man," though there were "some white men darker than he was."[77] Regardless of his exact racial mixture, however, one fact was clear: he was a wealthy planter. And for most whites in his community that was enough.

When Lumpkin reached his opinion in the Bryan case, effectively defining the place of free people of African descent in Georgia, he dis-missed most of the testimony regarding James Nunez's place in society. In reaching his decision, Lumpkin ignored this evidence because it con-tradicted his rigid and simplistic worldview. Instead, he simply projected his understanding of race back in time. In assessing the rights of free blacks in Georgia, Lumpkin fixated on the political component of citizen-ship—specifically, voting—and thus he ignored evidence that pointed to a history that contradicted his static vision of racial divisions in Georgia's past. Despite Lumpkin's failure to acknowledge as much, Georgia's policy toward free people of color had changed over the course of the nine-teenth century. In the first twenty-five years after independence, authori-ties had displayed a flexible approach toward free people of color. Some free people of African descent gained citizenship status during the revo-lutionary era. Although the push to expand the rights of some elite free people of color dissipated in the first decade of the nineteenth century, most whites in Georgia had not viewed free people of African descent as the same as slaves. The history of the Nunez family, as presented in Bryan v. Walton, shows that white attitudes and state government policies toward free people of African descent underwent a significant transformation between the turn of the century and the midpoint.

By the time the Bryan case reached the supreme court, the world of James Nunez had long since passed. For Joseph, James's son, his choices in life were much narrower than his father's. Though phenotypically lighter than his father, he lived life as though he were much darker. Instead of a white woman, he married one of the slaves he inherited. His social circle was composed not of white planters but of other free blacks and slaves. Unlike his father, he faced a host of restrictions based on his racial status, including a requirement that he register with the state officially as a "negro." Gone was the racial ambiguity that had characterized earlier times.

Just as Lumpkin's portrait of his state's past was clearly faulty in failing to convey the complexity of the racial order, so too was his depiction of his state's present. His assessment of race and the status of free blacks may have reflected life in large pockets of the state, especially in the upcountry. But white attitudes in Georgia were not monolithic, nor were the experiences of free people of African descent. The result was a patchwork of areas, usually on the coast and along the Savannah River, where free people of color found sanctuary from the imposition of state and local restrictions against them. In these areas, some prospered under the protection of whites who held views on race that deviated sharply from Lumpkin's and those of others who agreed with his racial perspectives.

The status of free people changed over time along with the size of their population and their geographic distribution. After a rapid and substantial increase between 1790 and 1800, the number of free people of color in Georgia grew at a much slower and uneven rate in the decades that followed. By 1860, the population reached thirty-five hundred.[78] In the first decades of the nation, the free black population concentrated on the state's periphery, a trend that continued until 1830. In the wake of the state's annexation of the Cherokee territory, however, free blacks abandoned the "frontier" counties. By the late antebellum era, free blacks were few and far between in the Georgia interior, scattered across the blackbelt and Cherokee territory in singles or in dozens. By contrast, the largest concentrations of free people of color were in the oldest counties in the state, areas along the Atlantic coast and the Savannah River. Beginning in 1810, for example, Chatham County emerged as the center of the population of free people of color in Georgia, and it remained so until the Civil War. Urban areas reflected this geographical imbalance, and the difference was striking. In 1860, Savannah and Augusta alone accounted for more than a quarter of the state's total free black population, with 705 and 386 respectively. Pushing toward the interior, to the newer areas of the state, cities such as Macon and Atlanta, with twenty-two and twenty-

Number of Free People of Color, 1860

One dot • represents 10 free people of color

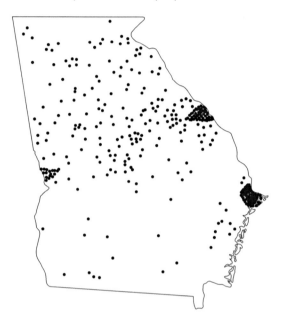

five, respectively, contained significantly smaller numbers of free blacks. Columbus, in the state's southwest, was somewhat of an exception to the rule in that it had 141 free blacks, yet this number was still far below the older cities.[79]

That the demographic patterns emerged the way they did was not by accident. White attitudes toward free blacks had an impact on the population distribution. How free blacks were treated and assessed by whites differed depending on region. In certain parts of the state, whites made it difficult, if not impossible, for free blacks to live among them. Through taxes and economic restrictions, local and county officials effectively made their towns off limits to free blacks. Two cities, Atlanta in the upcountry and Savannah in the lowcountry, provide excellent examples.

In governing a center of white worker militancy, Atlanta's local authorities went to great lengths to appease their constituents. White workers feared competition with free people of color for employment, believing it would degrade their labor and drive down their wages.[80] And as with the laws related to slavery in Atlanta, the scope and magnitude of the restrictions increased significantly following the rise of the Democrats to power in the city. Responding to local residents' wishes, city officials enacted ordinances to dissuade free people of color from relocating there, including a $200 tax on those who moved to the town. Those who failed to pay the tax were subject to being arrested and bound out to pay the amount owed.[81] This was not an idle threat. City authorities arrested Robert Harden, a free man of color, in 1855 for failing to pay the tax and sentenced him to be auctioned off to the highest bidder.[82] In 1859, the city authorities increased the penalties in a further effort to deter the undesirables from moving there. In addition to the possibility of being sold off, free people of color who violated the ordinance could face a daily whipping of thirty-nine lashes for every day they remained within the city limits.[83] Those free people of color who could pay the money also needed to have a local guardian to vouch for them before the city council, and even then permission was not always granted.[84] In addition, the authorities imposed an annual poll tax of $5 on free black residents.[85] The *Atlanta Daily Intelligencer* expressed the sentiment of most white residents of the city when it noted, "We are opposed to giving free negroes a residence in any and every Slaveholding state, believing as we do, that their presence in slave communities is hurtful to the good order of society, and fraught with great danger to our 'peculiar institution.'"[86]

Those free blacks permitted to settle in Atlanta faced a host of restrictions on their economic activities, including prohibitions from engaging in even the most basic forms of petty commerce. In June 1856, for example, the city council even refused a petition on behalf of a free person of color, Jo Miller, who sought a license to sell ice cream, not the most sought-after occupation. Council members opposed the endeavor on principle alone, defending their actions on the premise that it "would be unwise, unjust, and impolitic." They explained that "it is not our policy to train negroes, whether bond or free, to become tradesmen, merchants, or speculators and to make exceptions . . . would be, not only highly prejudicial to the well being and contentment of those classes, but a source of envy and dissatisfaction to others."[87] In 1860, the authorities broadened the restrictions on the economic activities of free people of color by banning them from virtually all commercial activity in the city.[88] In this way, they denied economic mobility to free people of color in order to limit class and race tensions. The authorities suggested that

Roderick Dhu Badger. Courtesy of the DeKalb Historical Society Collection, DeKalb History Center, Decatur, Georgia.

allowing blacks entry into white occupations would make whites angry and blacks dissatisfied.

And yet, there were a handful of people of color who could retain a measure of autonomy and status even in Atlanta. In 1859, a group of "aggrieved ... Southern citizens" petitioned the city council to prohibit the city's sole black dentist, Roderick Badger, from practicing his craft. The petitioners failed in their efforts. Despite the complaint, the city council did not act. In 1861, the petitioners again asked the city council to prohibit Badger from continuing to practice his vocation. As in the first instance, the city council denied the request.[89] Badger likely benefited from his connection to the white elite, which afforded him protection against the complaints. He was the son of a prominent local white man, who trained him in his craft. Moreover, Badger was the "favorite dentist of many prominent white citizens."[90]

Despite exceptions like Badger, it is little wonder that the free black population only grew from nineteen in 1850 to twenty-five in 1860. In Atlanta, then, free people of color faced significant restrictions on their economic opportunities and enjoyed little autonomy. The upcountry in general proved hostile to free people of color. Their status as "free" seemed merely nominal and, in the words of one historian, they existed as little more than "slaves without masters."[91]

In contrast to their counterparts in Atlanta, Savannah's free people of color benefited from significantly fewer restrictions and relatively greater acceptance by whites.[92] Some elite whites in Savannah recognized "mulatto" free people of color as racially superior to black slaves. For example, Richard Arnold questioned the prevailing ideas about race, namely that any African blood "tainted" a free person of color. In countering this perspective, he remarked that "a mulatto is not a negro any more than he is a white man."[93] Arnold believed that a "mulatto" was different from both a "negro" and a "white," amounting essentially to a third race. In some respects, Arnold considered "mulattoes" closer to "whites" than "negroes." Mulattoes, like whites, were incapable of laboring in the rice fields. Speaking for his class, he claimed, "With us no man would buy a mulatto for field work."[94] Arnold, in contrast to Lumpkin, recognized degrees of racial mixture, not absolutes. Arnold was not a fringe character in antebellum Savannah; he was one of the city's most influential men, a prominent planter and doctor and heavily involved in city politics, eventually serving as mayor in the 1850s and 1860s. Many elite whites in Savannah shared Arnold's beliefs about race in general and free people of color in particular. Elite whites regarded Andrew Marshall, a wealthy free "mulatto" drayman and preacher in Savannah, as possessing "elements which would of necessity have made him a leading character anywhere." According to one observer, "prominent native citizens were always among his tried friends; and some of the most respectable gentlemen in Savannah, of different denominations, acted as trustees for his church." They understood his superiority as racially based and rooted in his whiteness. "His Anglo-Saxon temperament made him superior to his African race."[95] These "mulattoes," who by virtue of their "Anglo-Saxon" blood stood as superior to "negroes" and "Africans," constituted approximately 70 percent of Savannah's free black population.

These elite whites maintained deep connections with elite free people of color. Arnold, for example, exerted great efforts to protect those free people of color under his guardianship, including Georgiana Kelly, Hannah Cohen, and Maria Cohen. Other prominent elite whites in Savannah served as guardians, including Richard Richardson for Andrew Marshall, Richard Stites for Simon Jackson, and Mordecai Myers for Jack Gibbons.[96] There is some evidence to suggest that elite whites regarded these dealings as something more than a superior-inferior relationship. Solomon Zeigler became guardian for David Waters when, as Zeigler described it, Waters "made me his confident."[97] These relationships often took the form of sexual relationships, as the numbers of "mulattoes" in the city indicates. Sarah Ann Black, who became nominally free when her mother purchased her freedom at the age of fifteen, considered herself "married" to John Robinson, a white man. Black also relied on a different white man to serve as a guardian and hold her property.[98]

Elite white toleration and acceptance of free people of color contributed to greater economic opportunities for them in Savannah compared to Atlanta. Free blacks in Savannah labored in both skilled and unskilled occupations, even dominating certain fields.[99] Some free people of color capitalized on Savannah's economic opportunities and accumulated significant wealth. For example, the city's wealthiest and most influential free person of color, Andrew Marshall, possessed assets worth an estimated $25,000 to $30,000 by the 1850s.[100] In aggregate, the city's women of color fared even better financially than the men, prospering throughout the antebellum era. Susan Jackson embodied this success. As the owner of a bakery, six slaves, and twenty-three buildings, she owned property valued at $15,000.[101] As in Charleston and New Orleans, slave ownership among the free people of color was not uncommon, though the practice peaked in the 1820s when twenty free people of color owned a total of fifty-eight slaves. Many of these slaveholders were artisans who used their bondmen in their workshops.[102] In other instances, owners appear to have lived off of the income generated by their slaves, whom they hired out or allowed to work for themselves. Unlike the pattern in the

Upper South, it seems these slaves were not related to their owners and were used to create wealth. The conditions in Savannah, and the Georgia lowcountry in general, facilitated the rise of an elite class of free people of color whose economic status, if not their political or legal status, exceeded that of most white Georgians.

Some free blacks outside of Savannah also enjoyed relatively privileged lives and considerable respect.[103] For example, Solomon Humphries was a well-known merchant who lived in Macon. He did business with, socialized with, and even worshiped with whites. He even managed to convince the legislature to manumit his wife and father at a time when the General Assembly had all but ended the practice.[104] Still, examples like Humphries were rather isolated occurrences in the upcountry. Elite free people of color clustered in Savannah and, to a lesser degree, Augusta. Of course, not all free people of color in Savannah or Augusta enjoyed special status, but a disproportionate share of the state's elite free people of color resided in lowcountry urban areas.

Perhaps the best illustration of blacks' relative advantages in Savannah as well as elite whites' respect of that status was black fire companies. Black men, both free and slave, volunteered for the city's fire companies. The role of black firemen went back to the great fire of 1796, when several black men died while trying to extinguish the blaze. They served in an organized capacity by 1821, when seventy-five free blacks were made part of the fire company. The number of black firemen grew in subsequent decades. By the late 1850s, more than seven hundred free blacks and slaves served with the Savannah Fire Company.[105]

Black men clearly relished the opportunity to participate, taking pride in their accomplishments and service. There also were clear financial motives for blacks to join the fire companies. Free black firefighters were exempt from the annual head tax of $6.25, and slave firefighters were paid 12.5 cents per hour for their time.[106] But the rewards extended beyond the economic realm. Serving on one of the fire companies brought a certain degree of respect and gratitude from local blacks and whites. This was evident during the firemen's parades, an annual event every May attended by much of the city's population and concluded with a review by the mayor. The parade was one of the most important events in Savannah's black *and white* social calendars. Mayor Richard Arnold praised that "No where besides Savannah are there to be found so large and orderly a body of colored firemen, and under such admirable control, or more gentlemenly or efficient set of officers than those composing the Savan-

nah Fire Department."[107] Accounts in the city's newspaper celebrated the
parades as amazing spectacles. After describing the "fine body of men"
marching in their "gay uniforms," accompanied by their "engines, lan-
terns, and brightly polished torches, tastefully decorated with flowers,"
one white writer enthused that "We have rarely seen a healthier, finer
looking body of men than were out on this parade. They numbered about
four hundred stout, strong, happy-faced fellows—the *elite* of the colored
population of Savannah."[108] Another article examined the "four hundred
stout fellows—the pick of the colored population, devoted to the protection of the city from the ravages of the devouring element,—gaily
dressed, steadily marching, and cheerfully and enthusiastically chanting
their peculiar refrains." Complimenting the black firemen, the author
noted, "It is seldom that so athletic and healthy looking a body of men
can be found, and in the class of the community to which they belong,
they are certainly without parallel in any other country." More significant, the writer experienced the parade as "a subject for extreme gratifi-
cation to our citizens to witness" and, though "an exhibition peculiar to
us," "a just cause for that feeling of pride which springs from evidences
of patriotic feeling in every class of the community."[109] Though whites
distinguished between the black firemen and the white citizens as different "classes of the community," they understood the spectacle as a
celebration of black manhood that both blacks and whites could feel as
a moment of pride. Firefighting offered black men an outlet to express
their masculinity publicly in a manner that could not be construed as
representing a security risk. White men in other cities in the state, particularly across Middle and North Georgia, pushed black men out of the
job or denied them access to this opportunity altogether.

Of course, not all whites in Savannah agreed with Arnold and the
others who lavished praise on black firemen. Although black men held
a virtual monopoly on firefighting in Savannah for most of the antebellum era, they were joined by several white companies that formed in the
late 1840s and 1850s. From virtually the moment the white fire companies were established, a pattern of conflict between white and black
firemen took hold in the city. Disputes routinely arose between the two
groups, usually in midst of actually fighting the fires! The question of
which company should take the lead proved a constant source of tension. When white firemen arrived on the scene of a fire, they expected
to take command of the extinguishment effort, even if they arrived after
black companies had begun putting the fire down. They expected white

supremacy to ensure their place and were outraged when their demands to join or replace black firemen were ignored by the white commanding officers. Often violence erupted when black and white men exchanged words or came into contact while in action.

Two of the worst instances in which black firemen suffered violent assaults came at the hands of the Oglethorpe and Young America fire companies in 1853 and 1856, respectively. The circumstances in each case were similar: arguments over who should lead the effort to quell the blaze resulted in heated words, fisticuffs, and, for some, arrest. In both episodes, the commanding officers sided squarely with the black firemen. They accused the white firemen of Oglethorpe Fire Company of having a "disposition to riot and beat negroes."[110] In both cases, the allegations against the white firemen were part of a broader set of charges leveled by the Savannah Fire Company that included insubordination and failure to follow protocol. Commanding officers complained that the firemen of the Young America Fire Company treated them with "contempt and disobedience."[111] The managers found the Young America Fire Company "guilty of insubordination and conduct subversive of good order and destructive of the authority and discipline of the Department."[112] The Savannah Fire Company deemed the episodes alarming enough to justify seizing both offending companies' engines as punishment.[113] The Savannah Fire Company's decisions to confiscate the engines proved enormously controversial.

White firemen, like those of the Oglethorpe and Young America companies, maintained that the managers denied them the privileges of free white citizenship. They complained that "we were not even allowed to vote for the officers under whose command we were to serve, and to whom we were to yield implicit obedience." They were white men without the vote, they asserted, denied the opportunity even to select their own leaders. "They seem to forget altogether that those two officers have a constituency of free, white citizens, more numerous by far than their own body, perhaps as intelligent and as competent to judge of the fitness and worthiness of their officers."[114]

White firemen chafed at their treatment relative to black firemen. They wanted to claim firefighting as a kind of white man's labor and complained that the officers were effectively trying to degrade their labor. They demonstrated their desire to distinguish themselves from black firemen with their insistence that only white firemen should wear uniforms.[115] They suspected that the officers preferred working with black firemen, who were content in their subordination, and disliked working with white firemen, who refused to be treated as subordinates. They charged that the commanding officers did not recognize that the white firemen were their equals and treated them as though they were black. According to James Oliver, the foreman of the Oglethorpe Fire Company, the department's "*Opposition to White Fire Companies,*" which had been "apparent from soon after the organization of" the first "white company" in 1846, was the true cause of the difficulties. One of the leaders of the Young America Fire Company expressed a similar sentiment, noting that his men would pay greater heed to the manager's words so long as he "recollect that my men are not negroes, and if you would speak to them in a more gentlemanly manner, there would be no difficulty."[116]

The members of the Oglethorpe and Young America fire companies, along with their supporters, questioned the legitimacy of the fire company's rulings and appealed to the city council to intervene on their behalf in both instances. They were not satisfied with the fire company's excuse that in "time of fire" white firemen "may occupy the same position and relative value with" the other companies, even if "they may be worked by negroes. They cannot in hours of emergency and danger expect precedence, and hardly etiquette."[117] White firemen regarded their treatment as a more weighty issue than mere etiquette. They hoped that the city council would be more receptive to their demands than had the board of the Savannah Fire Company, which was not elected but appointed. Much to the white firemen's consternation, however, the city council failed on both occasions to reverse the Savannah Fire Company's decision to seize the engines. Instead, the council praised the white firemen as "free" and "fearless" but warned that they had "forgot the necessity of implicit obedience."[118] In this decision, the city council approved the fire company's contention that the white firemen had not been properly subordinate and rejected the white firemen's complaints that their status as white citizens had not been protected. The struggles between white and black firemen and the response by the fire company as well as the city council demonstrate the divide between elite whites and nonelite whites over the status of blacks and especially free people of color. In particular, they reveal that some free men of color could gain a measure of status and respect, even at the expense of nonelite white men.

Treatment and attitudes toward free people of color, then, exhibited significant diversity, especially regionally, with the upcountry being less tolerant and the lowcountry being more tolerant. As the antebellum era wore on, upcountry whites attempted to impose their vision of white–free black relations on the state as a whole. From early on in the century, periodic attempts had been made to remove all free blacks from Georgia, but these efforts never brought tangible results. In 1858, P. E. Moore of Clarke County in the upcountry spearheaded a new effort that gained considerable traction. Moore charged free blacks with a litany of offenses. He regarded free blacks as a criminal class; living by themselves without supervision, their residences had become repositories for everything slaves could steal. The "trading and trafficking between free negroes and slaves, free negroes and vagabond white people, has become a tax upon the rich, and an intolerable burthen upon the middle class." He charged, "without hesitation, that the free negroes and slave mechanics have done us more harm than all the Abolitionists of the whole world combined." Moore viewed free blacks as a threat to both slaves and whites. Free blacks served as a demoralizing influence on slaves. "There is not a slave in five miles of a city in Georgia who does not want to quit the fields and go to town to learn a trade, that he too might dress fine, ride in buggies, and smoke cigars." Worse still, free blacks "are exerting an influence still more appalling; the degradation of the whites. Having much more property, and dressing much finer than many of our degraded poor white citizens, they are looked up to by them as their equals, and in numerous instances are their associates." These interactions further upset Moore's understanding of the proper racial hierarchy by providing free blacks with a false sense of their own equality. Moore complained that "every day" free blacks felt themselves "more independent, bold and daring," until "Casting their eyes upward to that high position which we now occupy, they have presumed to amalgamate with the white." As a solution, Moore proposed that "In the South there should be but two classes: bond and free. Any intermediate class only serving to pull up the one and drag down the other. . . . they are an incubus, a curse, a plague upon them. And it is for this reason I would have Georgia to get rid of the institution altogether."[119]

Many elite whites in Savannah in particular and the lowcountry in general opposed such attempts to eradicate the free black population. Opponents of the campaign to remove free blacks did so for a variety of reasons.[120] Some opposed the bills because they felt that free blacks should be sent to Liberia or Haiti rather than simply evicted or enslaved.[121] Others disagreed because they felt that free blacks had "some rights, by the law of this state, vested rights, as inalienable as the rights of white man," that the state could not trample.[122] One group that played a major role in resisting the removal of free blacks was the delegation from Chatham County, which sought the addition of an exception to the bill that would have allowed the city's free blacks to remain untouched.[123] As for their reasoning, the representatives made quite clear that they needed this population not only for its contributions to the city's coffers but also for the service they provided the city through firefighting. In their opposition, they demonstrated that they regarded free blacks as essential members of the community.

But these views were not represented on the state supreme court, which, before 1865, was solely composed of upcountry justices.[124] Lumpkin did not believe that free blacks should have rights, that they offered any valuable contributions to the state, or that they counted as members of Georgia society. Lumpkin did not embrace the perspectives of the lowcountry white elite, like Arnold and other grandees. Lumpkin's opinions on free people of color, which were largely shared by his fellow justices, may have reflected the views of most whites in Georgia, but, as the Savannah elite's support of black firefighters demonstrates, not all, in spite of Lumpkin's assertions to the contrary.

As the foregoing indicates, the attempt to relegate free blacks and free people of color in Georgia to the status of slaves reflected a growing reality, especially in the upcountry, but not a full reality, especially in the lowcountry. More significantly, the state's incorporation of pro-slavery interpretations ignored a complicated history under which free blacks and free people of color had enjoyed some rights and privileges of citizenship, if not full equality. Lumpkin's flat portrait of free black life failed utterly to convey the historical or actual experiences of free black life. Real life was more complex. Yet it was Lumpkin's perspective that emerged as the official voice of the past, present, and future. When Thomas Cobb compiled and codified Georgia's laws in *The Code of the State of Georgia* and wrote *An Inquiry into the Law of Negro Slavery in the United States of America*, he relied on Lumpkin, his chief mentor, to legitimate many of the laws related to race and slavery. Cobb's account provided little sense of the history of the recent legal past. Like Lumpkin, he pointed to laws that placed restrictions on free blacks' rights without acknowledging how recently they had been enacted. Cobb's books, and their foundation in Lumpkin's rulings, would go on to provide the legal foundation for a number of important cases across the South in the few years before the end of slavery.[125]

Early historical scholarship about the place of free blacks and their rights in Georgian society relied on the definitions offered by the law and the courts. Like the jurists before them, historians of Georgia's past offered similarly flat portraits of free black life in Georgia history. They were static portraits that framed race much as Lumpkin had, as unchanging absolutes. As Ralph Flanders wrote in 1932, "Far down the scale of Georgia society, slightly superior to their more lowly brethren, the slaves, stood the free persons of color." Flanders argued that "Throughout the South as a class they were held in low repute, being viewed as an injurious by-product of slavery." As a result, "constant attention was fixed upon them, great care taken to prevent their increase, and their activity sharply circumscribed." Flanders's historical account looked to the legal past to support his argument. "The low regard in which the Negro was held is likewise seen in his status as defined by law," he noted.[126] Flanders presented free people of color as virtual slaves. He relied heavily on Cobb's *Digest* and *Code of Georgia, 1861*, which, in turn, was drawn from Lumpkin's 1853 opinion in the *Bryan* case, to support his account of free blacks. But, in the process, Flanders perpetuated the same misrepresentation made by Lumpkin and Cobb; he let his contemporary understanding of race shape his understanding of the past and swept away inconsistencies that undermined his depiction of a world of racial absolutes. His Jim Crow world had more in common with life in the cotton belt in the late antebellum era than it did with the world of early nineteenth-century lowcountry Georgia, a world that had largely disappeared by the time he wrote his piece.

White Georgians in the 1850s reflected on their past. Political partisans resurrected the class divides over the potential of Cherokees for "civilization" but recognized that Cherokee removal overall had served the interests of the state. White Georgians agreed that the opening of Indian lands to white settlement and the spread of slavery and cotton cultivation served as the foundation of the state's prosperity. With the relocation of most Indians, including elite Indians, white Georgians did not feel the pressing necessity to explain away Indians' achievements in order to promote white supremacy. Joseph Lumpkin's efforts to deny the existence of a free black past as distinct from the slave past, in contrast, provided the necessary legitimation for antebellum proslavery ideology. The true history of free blacks in Georgia, indeed in the South, contradicted the rationale underlying white southerners' claims that slavery was necessary.

If the authorities in Georgia had once considered granting free blacks partial citizenship, it meant that the whole notion that slavery was a civilizing school was wrong. It meant that slavery was an exploitative system that stole the labor from blacks. Lumpkin erased the free black past in order to preserve the future of slavery.

NOTES

Introduction

1. "An Act to Emancipate and set free Austin a mulatto, also Harry, a Negro fellow," 14 August 1786, vol. D, Enrolled Acts and Resolutions, House and Senate, Legislature, RG 37-1-15, Georgia Department of Archives and History (hereafter cited as GDAH); Austin Dabney Petition for Land Grant (1786), in "Negroes Box 1," GDAH; "In council 4th Feb. 1788, From Executive Council Journal, Jan. 7–Feb, 15, 1788," 56–59, in Austin Dabney File, GDAH; "Pension Statement of Austin Dabney, Free Person of Color from the National Archives and Records Service, Washington, D. C.," in Austin Dabney File, GDAH. Although Dabney was reportedly born free, he petitioned the legislature for his freedom to protect himself against a claim made by Aycock, who had heard about Dabney's heroics. In addition to ensuring Dabney's freedom, the 1786 manumission act granted him an "annuity allowed by this State to wounded and disabled soldiers." The quote in the paragraph is drawn from George R. Gilmer, *Sketches of Some of the First Settlers of Upper Georgia, of the Cherokees, and the Author*, rev. ed. (Americus, Ga., 1926), 165. Gilmer included a rather flattering biographical account of Dabney's life in his study of the early inhabitants of the backcountry (see pages 164 to 167). Gilmer authored a similar biographical sketch of Dabney for George White's work, *Historical Collections of Georgia: Containing the Most Interesting Facts, Traditions, Biographical Sketches, Anecdotes, Etc. Relating to its History and Antiquities, From its First Settlement to the Present Time* (New York, 1854), 584–585. There are conflicting accounts about the time and place of Dabney's injury. Gilmer asserts that he was wounded at Kettle Creek in 1779. In *The Negro in Revolutionary Georgia* (Atlanta, 1977), Alton Hornsby Jr. contends that Dabney sustained his injury three years later at Augusta.

2. Gilmer, *Sketches of Some of the First Settlers of Upper Georgia*, 164–167.

3. Ibid.

4. *Acts of the General Assembly of the State of Georgia, Passed at Milledgeville, at an Extra Session, in April and May, 1821* (Milledgeville, 1821), 20.

5. Gilmer, *Sketches of Some of the First Settlers of Upper Georgia*, 164–167.

6. For a recent interpretation that focuses on slave rebellions as turning

points, see Lacy K. Ford, *Deliver Us from Evil: The Slavery Question in the Old South* (New York, 2009).

7. The degree to which whiteness unified white southerners has been a historiographical topic of debate for decades. As expressed by Ulrich B. Phillips in his seminal piece "The Central Theme of Southern History," *American Historical Review* 34, no. 1 (October 1928): 30–43, a common white identity drew whites, rich and poor alike, together, smoothing over all social, political, and economic conflicts in the process. In subsequent decades, historians increasingly questioned whether southern white society was as devoid of conflict as their predecessors had argued, yet Phillips's views on whiteness continued to hold sway, even if altered to varying degrees.

For examples of studies on whiteness in general, see Alexander Saxton, *The Rise and Fall of the White Republic: Class Politics and Mass Culture in Nineteenth-Century America* (New York, 1990); David R. Roediger, *The Wages of Whiteness: Race and the Making of the American Working Class* (London, 1991); Noel Ignatiev, *How the Irish Became White* (New York, 1995); Matthew Frey Jacobson, *Whiteness of a Different Color: European Immigrants and the Alchemy of Race* (Cambridge, Mass., 1998); Karen Brodkin, *How the Jews Became White Folks and What That Says about Race in America* (New Brunswick, N.J., 1998); and Thomas A. Guglielmo, *White on Arrival: Italians, Race, Color, and Power in Chicago, 1890–1945* (New York, 2003). The pioneering work of W. E. B. Du Bois's *Black Reconstruction: An Essay toward a History of the Part Which Black Folk Played in the Attempt to Reconstruct Democracy in America, 1860–1880* (New York, 1935) remains the classic interpretation on the topic.

For an opposing view of whiteness studies, see Peter Kolchin, "Whiteness Studies: The New History of Race in America," *Journal of American History* 89 (June 2002): 154–173; Eric Arnesen, "Whiteness and the Historians' Imagination," *International Labor and Working-Class History* 60 (fall 2001): 3–32; Kevin Kenny, "Diaspora and Comparison: The Global Irish as a Case Study," *Journal of American History* 90 (June 2003): 134–162; Frank Towers, "Projecting Whiteness: Race and the Unconscious in the History of Nineteenth-Century American Workers," *Journal of American Culture* 21 (summer 1998): 47–57; Bruce Laurie, "Workers, Abolitionists, and the Historians: A Historiographical Perspective," *Labor Studies in Working-Class History of the Americas* 5, no. 4 (2008): 17–55.

For an interpretation of relations between nonelite whites and slaves and free blacks in lowcountry Georgia that differs from the one presented in this study, see Timothy James Lockley, *Lines in the Sand: Race and Class in Lowcountry Georgia, 1750–1860* (Athens, 2001). Rather than fighting to maintain their rights as whites and exclude all others from those privileges, Lockley argues, nonelite whites supported class-based alliances with poor blacks that targeted wealthy planters and merchants. Accordingly, Lockley contends that support for slavery among nonelite whites remained tepid at best and racial attitudes toward blacks failed to develop into a visceral racism.

8. In 1971, George Fredrickson offered a new variant on the role of white supremacy in the antebellum era. In *The Black Image in the White Mind: The Debate on Afro-American Character and Destiny, 1817–1914* (New York, 1971), he argued that a "*Herrenvolk* democracy" emerged in the South as a means for the elite to appease the "democratic" demands of the "plain folks" while maintaining their "*de facto* hegemony" (64–70). In effect, the elite embraced the rhetoric of white supremacy to paper over broader disagreements within white society. While I agree with those historians who view whiteness as an integral part of the development of the antebellum southern identity, my work explores white supremacy as it was generated both from above and below. Rather than portray white supremacy as an organic part of southern society or as a means of controlling the masses, I argue the nonelite whites employed white supremacy to promote their own interests when in competition with elite whites or slaves. They utilized the democratic system to elect lawmakers who reflected their views and pushed for the enactment of legislation to benefit their self-interest. In some instances, in fact, these laws came at the expense of the rights of slaveholders. My work on nonelite whites focuses on urban workers, who, like their counterparts in the North, pushed for legislation to protect their interests from above and below. They feared domination by white elites and competition from black laborers.

For studies that challenge the notion that the white elite politically dominated southern society, see Fletcher M. Green, "Democracy in the Old South," in *Democracy in the Old South, and Other Essays*, ed. J. Isaac Copeland, 65–85 (Nashville, 1969); Clement Eaton, *The Growth of Southern Civilization, 1790–1860* (New York, 1961), 172–175, 308–309; and Charles S. Sydnor, *The Development of Southern Sectionalism, 1819–1848* (Baton Rouge, 1948), chapter 12.

9. Here, I build upon the work of Herbert Aptheker, *American Negro Slave Revolts* (New York, 1943); Kenneth W. Porter, "Negroes on the Southern Frontier, 1670–1763," *Journal of Negro History* 33, no. 1 (January 1948): 53–78; J. Leitch Wright, *Creeks and Seminoles: The Destruction and Regeneration of the Muscogulge People* (Lincoln, 1986); Jane Landers, *Black Society in Spanish Florida* (Urbana: Univ. of Illinois Press, 1999); Claudio Saunt, *A New Order of Things: Property, Power, and the Transformation of the Creek Indians, 1733–1816* (Cambridge, 1999); Adam Rothman, *Slave Country: American Expansion and the Origins of the Deep South* (Cambridge, Mass., 2005).

10. Edmund S. Morgan, *American Slavery American Freedom: The Ordeal of Colonial Virginia* (New York, 1975). For instance, Morgan's influence is quite apparent in Barbara Jeanne Fields's article "Slavery, Race, and Ideology in the United States of America," *New Left Review* 181 (1990): 95–118.

11. For a monograph on Georgia history that adheres more closely to the Morgan model, see Ben Marsh, *Georgia's Frontier Women: Female Fortunes in a Southern Colony* (Athens, 2007). According to Marsh, Georgia's racial system "fell smartly into line with its northern neighbors," in effect following the same pattern that occurred in Virginia once a sufficient number of white women were pres-

ent in the colony (145). Marsh argues that the authorities established fixed racial boundaries in the 1760s and 1770s as part of the colony's transition to a "'southern' slave society," which, in effect, made it like any other "British American (mainland) plantation society" (146). This interpretation stands in contrast to other recent work on the lowcountry, which stresses the differences between the slave societies and concomitant racial systems that took root in the colonial Chesapeake and the lowcountry, respectively. For more on the regional differences in slavery, see two excellent comparative studies of early slavery: Ira Berlin, *Many Thousands Gone: The First Two Centuries of Slavery in North America* (Cambridge, Mass., 1998), and Phillip D. Morgan, *Slave Counterpoint: Black Culture in the Eighteenth-Century Chesapeake and Lowcountry* (Chapel Hill, 1998). For a perceptive historiographical essay on the evolution of scholarship on race and slavery in the colonial era, see Rebecca Anne Goetz, "Rethinking the 'Unthinking Decision': Old Questions and New Problems in the History of Slavery and Race in the Colonial South," *Journal of Southern History* 75, no. 3 (August 2009): 599–612.

12. Betty Wood, *Slavery in Colonial Georgia, 1730–1775* (Athens, Ga., 1984); Betty Wood, *Women's Work, Men's Work: The Informal Slave Economies of Lowcountry Georgia* (Athens, Ga., 1995); Lockley, *Lines in the Sand*. See also Julia Floyd Smith, *Slavery and Rice Culture in Low Country Georgia, 1750–1860* (Knoxville, 1985); Alan Gallay, *The Formation of a Planter Elite: Jonathan Bryan and the Southern Colonial Frontier* (Athens, Ga., 1989); Philip D. Morgan, *Slave Counterpoint: Black Culture in the Eighteenth-Century Chesapeake and Lowcountry* (Chapel Hill, 1998); Robert Olwell, *Masters, Slaves, and Subjects: The Culture of Power in the South Carolina Low Country, 1740–1790* (Ithaca, 1998); Jeffrey Robert Young, *Domesticating Slavery: The Master Class in Georgia and South Carolina, 1670–1837* (Chapel Hill, 1999); William Dusinberre, *Them Dark Days: Slavery in the American Rice Swamps* (New York, 1996); Erskine Clarke, *Dwelling Place: A Plantation Epic* (New Haven, 2005).

13. Joseph P. Reidy, *From Slavery to Agrarian Capitalism in the Cotton Plantation South: Central Georgia, 1800–1880* (Chapel Hill, 1992); J. William Harris, *Plain Folk and Gentry in a Slave Society: White Liberty and Black Slavery in Augusta's Hinterlands* (Middletown, Conn., 1985). See also Steven Hahn, *The Roots of Southern Populism: Yeoman Farmers and the Transformation of the Georgia Upcountry, 1850–1860* (New York, 1983). For examples from other southern states, see Christopher Morris, *Becoming Southern: The Evolution of a Way of Life, Warren County and Vicksburg, Mississippi, 1770–1860* (New York, 1995); Daniel S. Dupre, *Transforming the Cotton Frontier, Madison County, Alabama, 1800–1840* (Baton Rouge, 1997); John Hebron Moore, *The Emergence of the Cotton Kingdom in the Old Southwest: Mississippi, 1770–1860* (Baton Rouge, 1988).

14. For an exception to this trend in the historiography, see Michele Gillespie, *Free Labor in an Unfree World: White Artisans in Slaveholding Georgia, 1789–1860* (Athens, Ga., 2000). For an older monograph on bondage in Georgia that covers this time frame, see Ralph Betts Flanders, *Plantation Slavery in Georgia* (Cos Cob, Conn., 1967 [c. 1933]). Flanders's exhaustive study details many important aspects of

slavery in Georgia; however, his analysis, like most scholarship on slavery written in this period by white historians, reflects clear racial biases. As such, Flanders presents slavery in largely benign, if not benevolent, terms.

15. Joyce E. Chaplin, *An Anxious Pursuit: Agricultural Innovation and Modernity in the Lower South, 1730–1815* (Chapel Hill, 1993); Christine Leigh Heyrman, *Southern Cross: The Beginnings of the Bible Belt* (Chapel Hill, 1997). For a study with an investigative scope similar to the one presented in this book, see Rachel N. Klein, *Unification of a Slave State: The Rise of the Planter Class in the South Carolina Backcountry, 1760–1808* (Chapel Hill, 1990); J. Mills Thornton III, *Politics and Power in a Slave Society: Alabama, 1800–1860* (Baton Rouge, 1978).

1. From a Common Man's Utopia to a Planter's Paradise

1. Kenneth Coleman, ed., *A History of Georgia* (Athens, Ga., 1977), 16–19.

2. David H. Corkran, *The Creek Frontier, 1540–1783* (Norman, Okla., 1967), 82–102. For more on early relations between the white Georgians and the Yamacraws, see Julie Anne Sweet, *Negotiating for Georgia: British-Creek Relations in the Trustee Era, 1733–1752* (Athens, Ga., 2005). For more on Mary Musgrove Matthews Bosomworth and her role in early negotiations, see Michele Gillespie, "Sexual Politics of Race and Gender: Mary Musgrove and the Georgia Trustees," in *The Devil's Lane: Sex and Race in the Early South*, ed. Catherine Clinton and Michele Gillespie, 187–201 (New York, 1997); Rodney M. Baine, "Myths of Mary Musgrove," *Georgia Historical Quarterly* 76 (summer 1992), 428–435; E. M. Coulter, "Mary Musgrove, 'Queen of the Creeks': A Chapter of Early Georgia Troubles," *Georgia Historical Quarterly* 11 (1927): 1–30.

3. Kenneth Coleman, "The Founding of Georgia," in *Forty Years of Diversity: Essays on Colonial Georgia*, ed. Harvey H. Jackson and Phinizy Spalding, 4–20 (Athens, Ga., 1984).

4. Ibid.

5. Milton L. Ready, "Philanthropy and the Origins of Georgia," in *Forty Years of Diversity: Essays on Colonial Georgia*, ed. Harvey H. Jackson and Phinizy Spalding, 46–59 (Athens, Ga., 1984).

6. Peter H. Wood, *Black Majority: Negroes in Colonial South Carolina from 1670 through the Stono Rebellion* (New York, 1974), 285–307. Of the various uprisings that occurred in South Carolina during this time, the 1739 Stono Rebellion had by far the biggest impact. For more on the Stono Rebellion, see Mark M. Smith, "Remembering Mary, Shaping Revolt: Reconsidering the Stono Rebellion," *Journal of Southern History* 67, no. 3 (August 2001): 513–534; John K. Thornton, "African Dimensions of the Stono Rebellion," *American Historical Review* 96, no. 4 (October 1991): 1101–1113; Edward A. Pearson, "'A Countryside Full of Flames': A Reconsideration of the Stono Rebellion and Slave Rebelliousness in the Early Eighteenth-Century South Carolina Lowcountry," *Slavery and Abolition* 17, no. 2 (1996): 22–50.

7. For more on slave runaways from South Carolina and Georgia to Florida, see Jane Landers, "Gracia Real de Santa Teresa de Mose: A Free Black Town in Spanish Colonial Florida," *American Historical Review* 95, no. 1 (1990): 9–30.

8. As quoted in Wood, *Slavery in Colonial Georgia*, 15–16.

9. Wood, *Slavery in Colonial Georgia*, 25–26; Patrick Tailfer, M.D., Hugh Anderson, and M.A. David Douglas, *A True and Historical Narrative of the Colony of Georgia, In America, From the First Settlement thereof until this present Period: Containing the most authentick Facts, Matters and Transactions therein. Together with His Majesty's Charter, Representation of the People, Letters, &c. And A Dedication to His Excellency General Oglethorpe* (Charles Town, S.C., 1741).

10. Wood, *Slavery in Colonial Georgia*, chapter 3.

11. "Petition of the Inhabitants of New Inverness to his Excellency General Oglethorpe," January 1739. For more on the Darien Petition, see Harvey H. Jackson, "The Darien Anti-Slavery Petition and the Georgia Plan," *William and Mary Quarterly*, 3rd ser., 34, no. 4 (October 1977): 618–631.

12. For more on the impact of the Stono Rebellion, see Wood, *Black Majority*, chapter 12.

13. David Douglass, William Sterling, and Thomas Baillie to the Georgia Trustees, 10 August 1740, as quoted in Ready, "Philanthropy and the Origins of Georgia," in *Forty Years of Diversity*, ed. Jackson and Spalding, 53–54.

14. Wood, *Slavery in Colonial Georgia*, 77–78.

15. For more on the period between 1743 and the repeal of the ban on slavery, see Wood, *Slavery in Colonial Georgia*, chapter 5.

16. W. W. Abbot, *The Royal Governors of Georgia, 1754–1775* (Chapel Hill, 1959), 14–18; Gallay, *The Formation of a Planter Elite*, chapter 4; Wood, *Slavery in Colonial Georgia*, 90–91; Kenneth Coleman, *Colonial Georgia: A History* (New York, 1976), 206–210; Marsh, *Georgia's Frontier Women*, 97–107. Marsh persuasively demonstrates that the royal authorities in Georgia followed a policy that favored distributing land grants to men with families and widowed women as part of a strategy to stabilize the conditions within the colony. By contrast, the authorities rejected petitions from single, poor men and men with bad reputations. The decision to block single, poor men also reflected the authorities' desire to avoid conflict with the neighboring Indians. Individuals who fell into this category were believed to be responsible for much of the commotion and violence that took place between settlers in the interior and the Indians.

17. Flanders, *Plantation Slavery in Georgia*, 23.

18. Ralph Martin Bolzius, "Reliable Answers to Some Submitted Questions Concerning the Land Carolina, In Which Answer, However, Regard Is Also Paid at the Same Time to the Condition of the Colony of Georgia," *William and Mary Quarterly*, 3rd ser., 14, no. 2 (April 1957): 226–227.

19. Wood, *Slavery in Colonial Georgia*, 89. For an in-depth examination of the colony's early demography, see Marsh, *Georgia's Frontier Women*, chapter 4.

20. David R. Chestnutt, "South Carolina's Expansion into Colonial Georgia,

1720–1765" (Ph.D. diss., University of Georgia, 1973), 202–206; Wood, *Slavery in Colonial Georgia*, 91–93; Marsh, *Georgia's Frontier Women*, 99–102.

21. John Gerar William DeBrahm, *Report of the General Survey in the Southern District of North America*, ed. Louis De Vorsey, 141–142 (Columbia, S.C., 1971).

22. Minutes of Gov. and Council, in *The Colonial Records of the State of Georgia*, ed. Allen D. Candler and Lucian L. Knight, (Atlanta, Ga., 1904–1916), vol. 9, pp. 135–136, 284, 366, 382, 482, 506–507, 577, 642; vol. 6, p. 442 (hereafter cited as *Colonial Records*).

23. Oglethorpe insisted on the removal of the slaves after it became clear to him that their presence was detrimental to the colony's mission. By the 1740s, however, slaves could be found in small numbers in the colony once again. The largest concentration was located in the backcountry near Augusta, an area largely beyond the authority of the governing officials in Savannah. See Wood, *Slavery in Colonial Georgia*, 16–17, 76.

24. Ibid., 89.

25. Elizabeth Donnan, *Documents Illustrative of the History of the Slave Trade to America*, vol. 4, *The Border Colonies and the Southern Colonies* (New York, 1965), 608–634. According to Ben Marsh's calculations, based upon the Trans-Atlantic Slave Trade database, at least thirty-three slave ships from Africa arrived in Georgia between 1766 and 1774, carrying 5,617 Africans. The average size of each cargo was 196 people (Marsh, *Georgia's Frontier Women*, 120).

26. Bolzius, "Reliable Answers to Some Submitted Questions Concerning the Land Carolina," 233; Harold E. Davis, *The Fledgling Province: Social and Cultural Life in Colonial Georgia, 1773–1776* (Chapel Hill, 1976), 135.

27. Flanders, *Plantation Slavery in Georgia*, 37.

28. Donnan, *Documents*, 624–625. James Habersham Sr., who held several positions in Georgia's colonial government, including a brief stint as governor, played an instrumental role in establishing the firm Clay & Habersham; he provided capital for his son and his nephew, Clay, to begin their operation. Clay and the younger Habersham remained in business for approximately five years before ending their partnership. Clay remained a major figure in the slave importation business in the years that followed, forming partnerships with a number of prominent men in Georgia, including Joseph Habersham (the second son of James Habersham Sr.), Seth John Cuthbert, and Edward Telfair.

29. Wood, *Black Majority*; Wood, *Slavery in Colonial Georgia*, 103; Michael A. Gomez, *Exchanging Our Country Marks: The Transformation of African Identities in the Colonial and Antebellum South* (Chapel Hill, 1998), 40, 41, 69, 70; Marsh, *Georgia's Frontier Women*, 120. According to Marsh's calculations 41 percent of the Africans who arrived in Georgia between 1766 and 1774 were from Senegambia, while another 22 percent were from Sierra Leone and the Windward Coast. These estimates are roughly in line with Betty Wood's conclusions, based upon her survey of twenty-five hundred African slaves imported to Georgia between 1766 and 1771.

30. For more on the role of West African slaves in the development of low-country rice cultivation, see Judith Carney, *Black Rice: The African Origins of Rice Cultivation in the Americas* (Cambridge, Mass., 2001); Edda L. Fields-Black, *Deep Roots: Farmers in West Africa and the African Diaspora* (Bloomington, Ind., 2008); Wood, *Black Majority*, 56–62; Daniel Littlefield, *Rice and Slaves: Ethnicity and the Slave Trade in Colonial South Carolina* (Baton Rouge, 1981), 74–114. For an alternative interpretation on the influence of slaves in the development of lowcountry rice cultivation, see Morgan, *Slave Counterpoint*, 182–183. See also David Eltis, Philip Morgan, and David Richardson, "Agency and Diaspora in Atlantic History: Reassessing the African Contribution to Rice Cultivation in the Americas," *American Historical Review* 112, no. 5 (December 2007), 1329–1358.

31. DeBrahm, *Report of the General Survey in the Southern District of North America*, 162. Writing more than a decade earlier, Johann Martin Bolzius asserted that it cost at least £456 to establish a plantation with a minimum of ten slaves. This amount did not include the owner's home or the land. See Bolzius, "Reliable Answers to Some Submitted Questions Concerning the Land Carolina," 260–261.

32. Chaplin, *An Anxious Pursuit*, 208.

33. James Habersham to Earl of Hillsborough, 24 April 1772, *The Letters of James Habersham* (Savannah, Ga., 1904), 171.

34. Gallay, *The Formation of a Planter Elite*, 101.

35. Davis, *The Fledgling Province*, 141.

36. Milton S. Heath, *Constructive Liberalism: The Role of the State in Georgia to 1860* (Cambridge, Mass., 1945), 63–65; Smith, *Slavery and Rice Culture in Low Country Georgia*, 24–26; Walter J. Fraser Jr., *Savannah in the Old South* (Athens, Ga., 2003), 61–62; Abbot, *The Royal Governors of Georgia*, 20–31.

37. Abbot, *The Royal Governors of Georgia*, 23.

38. DeBrahm, *Report of the General Survey in the Southern District of North America*, 163–164.

39. James Habersham to William Knox, 17 July 1765, *The Letters of James Habersham*, 38. For more on the danger posed by hurricanes to lowcountry planters, see Walter J. Fraser Jr., *Lowcountry Hurricanes: Three Centuries of Storms at Sea and Ashore* (Athens, Ga., 2006).

40. Abbot, *The Royal Governors of Georgia*, 9–12.

41. Ibid., 30–31.

42. Davis, *The Fledgling Province*, 126–130; Wood, *Slavery in Colonial Georgia*, chapter 7.

43. Ibid.

44. Petition of James Habersham, N. Jones, Lewis Johnson, N. W. Jones, John Milledge, Archibald Bulloch, and William Ewen, 19 May 1768, *The Letters of James Habersham*, 71; Committee of Correspondence to Benjamin Franklin, 23 May 1770, *The Letters of James Habersham*, 79.

45. Committee of Correspondence to Benjamin Franklin, 23 May 1770, *The Letters of James Habersham*, 79.

46. "AN ACT For Ordering and Governing Slaves Within this Province, and for Establishing a Jurisdiction for the Trial of Offences Committed by Such Slaves, and other Persons therein mentioned, and to Prevent the Inveigling, and Carrying Away Slaves from their Masters, Owners, or Employers, May 1770," in Candler and Knight, eds., *Colonial Records*, vol. 19, pt. 1, pp. 209–249.

47. Bolzius, "Reliable Answers to Some Submitted Questions Concerning the Land Carolina," 242.

48. Davis, *The Fledgling Province*, 97; Wood, *Slavery in Colonial Georgia*, 83.

49. Davis, *The Fledgling Province*, 97–98.

50. Petition of Edmond Tannatt, John Graham, Alexander Wylly, Lewis Johnson, William Handley, and others, in Candler and Knight, eds., *Colonial Records*, vol. 16, pp. 269–270.

51. Davis, *The Fledgling Province*, 58.

52. Flanders, *Plantation Slavery in Georgia*, 51; Davis, *The Fledgling Province*, 105, 107, 110, 113.

53. For more on the labor involved in rice cultivation, see Carney, *Black Rice*, chapters 3 and 4; Daniel C. Littlefield, *Rice and Slaves: Ethnicity and the Slave Trade in Colonial South Carolina* (Baton Rouge, 1981), 74–114; Wood, *Black Majority*, 56–62; Morgan, *Slave Counterpoint*, 156–159. For more on the impact of the environment on lowcountry residents' health, see Wood, *Black Majority*, chapter 3.

54. Bolzius, "Reliable Answers to Some Submitted Questions Concerning the Land Carolina," 258; Carney, *Black Rice*, 117–132.

55. Bolzius, "Reliable Answers to Some Submitted Questions Concerning the Land Carolina," 245. For more on the task system, see Philip D. Morgan, "Work and Culture: The Task System and the World of Lowcountry Blacks, 1700–1880," *William and Mary Quarterly* 39, no. 4 (1982): 563–599; Philip D. Morgan, "Task and Gang Systems: Organization of Labor on New World Plantations," in *Work and Labor in Early America*, ed. Stephen Innes, 189–219 (Chapel Hill, 1988). For more on slave women in markets, see Robert Olwell, "'Loose, Idle, and Disorderly': Slave Women in the Eighteenth-Century Marketplace," in *More Than Chattel: Black Women and Slavery in the Americas*, ed. David Barry Gaspar and Darlene Clark Hine, 97–110 (Bloomington, Ind., 1996).

56. Carney, *Black Rice*, 98–101. For an alternative viewpoint on the emergence of the task system in the lowcountry, see Morgan, *Slave Counterpoint*, 182–183.

57. Quote from Bolzius, "Reliable Answers to Some Submitted Questions Concerning the Land Carolina," 244; Davis, *The Fledgling Province*, 105–107.

58. Flanders, *Plantation Slavery in Georgia*, 43.

59. Davis, *The Fledgling Province*, 99.

60. James Habersham to Thomas Broughton, 1 December 1770, *The Letters of James Habersham*, 99. For another example, see Johann Martin Bolzius, "Johann Martin Bolzius Answers a Questionnaire on Carolina and Georgia, Part II," ed. Klaus G. Loewald, Beverly Starika, and Paul S. Taylor, *William and Mary Quarterly* 15, no. 2 (April 1958): 240.

61. For example, James Habersham to Henry Laurens, 3 June 1771, *The Letters of James Habersham*, 132.

62. Bolzius, "Reliable Answers to Some Submitted Questions Concerning the Land Carolina," 233–234. For more on the use of slave drivers in the lowcountry and relations between drivers and planters, see Morgan, *Slave Counterpoint*, 218–225, 342–346.

63. Davis, *The Fledgling Province*, 153.

64. Bolzius, "Reliable Answers to Some Submitted Questions Concerning the Land Carolina," 233–234. For more on the demography of South Carolina, see Wood, *Black Majority*, 131–166.

65. James Habersham to William Knox, 18 July 1772, *The Letters of James Habersham*, 193.

66. As Joyce Chaplin notes, "The new emphasis on the principle of humanity stressed the importance of sympathy, the emotion that bonded humans together, the innate positive regard people had for each other. . . . The principle of humanity thus enlarged the sphere of an individual's moral responsibility to include all people, rather than any smaller social grouping. It did not, however, necessitate political equality; it emphasized general human needs, not specific political rights." (Joyce Chaplin, "Slavery and the Principle of Humanity: A Modern Idea in the Early Lower South," *Journal of Social History* 24, no. 2 [winter 1990]: 301.)

67. Flanders, *Plantation Slavery in Georgia*, 23; Coleman, *Colonial Georgia*, 229; Davis, *The Fledgling Province*, 127. Historians have documented the influence of South Carolina on the development of slavery in Georgia. The cash crop, the system of labor, and even the individuals who formed a significant portion of the planter elite all had their origins in Georgia's northern neighbor. For that reason, it was only natural that, when drafting their earliest slave codes, Georgia's authorities initially turned to South Carolina as a model slave society. Of the historians who study early Georgia, Betty Wood has done the most to highlight the links between the two colonies as reflected in their respective slave laws. In her important work *Slavery in Colonial Georgia*, Wood notes similarities in the language used in the slave codes of Georgia and South Carolina. Pointing to changes in the form of punishments and restrictions on slaves, she demonstrates the degree to which Georgia's authorities relied on their more experienced counterparts in South Carolina.

68. See Governor James Wright to the Board of Trade, 8 June 1768, in Candler and Knight, eds., *Colonial Records*, vol. 28, pt. 2, p. 55.

69. James Habersham to N. Jones, Lewis Johnson, N. W. Jones, John Milledge, Archibald Bulloch, and William Ewen, 19 May 1768, *The Letters of James Habersham*, 71.

70. Duc de la Rochefoucauld-Liancourt, "La Rochefoucauld-Liancourt, 1796," in *The Rambler in Georgia: Desultory Observations on the Situation, Extent, Climate, Population, Manners, Customs, Commerce, Constitution, Government, etc., of the State from the Revolution to the Civil War Recorded by Thirteen Travellers*, ed. Mills Lane, 14 (Savannah, Ga., 1973).

71. James Habersham to William Knox, 11 February 1772, *The Letters of James Habersham*, 163.

72. James Habersham to William Knox, 17 July 1765, *The Letters of James Habersham*, 38.

73. Quotes drawn from Chaplin, "Slavery and the Principle of Humanity," 306, 307, 309, 310.

74. James Habersham to Countess of Huntingdon, 19 April 1775, *The Letters of James Habersham*, 242.

75. As quoted in Davis, *The Fledgling Province*, 138.

76. James Habersham to Countess of Huntingdon, 19 April 1775, *The Letters of James Habersham*, 242; Chaplin, "Slavery and the Principle of Humanity," 304–306, 308.

77. Davis, *The Fledgling Province*, 132; Wood, *Slavery in Colonial Georgia*, 163.

78. James Habersham to Thomas Broughton, 1 December 1770, *The Letters of James Habersham*, 99; James Habersham to William Knox, 26 November 1770, *The Letters of James Habersham*, 95; James Habersham to Cornelius Winter, 6 June 1771, *The Letters of James Habersham*, 135; Davis, *The Fledgling Province*, 142–144.

79. James Habersham to Thomas Broughton, 1 December 1770, *The Letters of James Habersham*, 99.

80. Herbert Aptheker, "Maroons within the Present Limits of the United States," *Journal of Negro History* 24, no. 2 (April 1939): 167–170; Wood, *Slavery in Colonial Georgia*, chapter 10; Berlin, *Many Thousands Gone*, 169–170; Morgan, *Slave Counterpoint*, 449–451; Davis, *The Fledgling Province*, 139. For more on runaway slaves in general, see John Hope Franklin and Loren Schweninger, *Runaway Slaves: Rebels on the Plantation* (New York, 1999). Although its temporal scope is the nineteenth century, the book nevertheless provides a useful vantage point for understanding the motivations and actions of slaves who resisted their status in the late eighteenth century as well.

81. Flanders, *Plantation Slavery in Georgia*, 31; Davis, *The Fledgling Province*, 130; Wood, *Black Majority*, 292.

2. The Contagion of Liberty

1. Harvey H. Jackson, "The Rise of the Western Members: Revolutionary Politics and the Georgia Backcountry," in *An Uncivil War: The Southern Backcountry during the American Revolution*, ed. Ronald Hoffman, Thad W. Tate, and Peter J. Albert, 276–320 (Charlottesville, 1985); Edward J. Cashin, "'But Brothers, It Is Our Land We Are Talking About': Winners and Losers in the Georgia Backcountry," in Hoffman, Tate, and Albert, eds., *An Uncivil War*, 240–275.

2. J. E. Hays, ed., "Proceedings of the Georgia Council of Safety, 1775 to 1777," in *Collections of the Georgia Historical Society* (Savannah, 1901), vol. 5, pt. 1, p. 70.

3. Joseph Clay to Henry Laurens, 21 October 1777, in Joseph Clay, *Letters of Joseph Clay, Merchant of Savannah, 1776–1793, and a List of Ships and Vessels Entered at the Port of Savannah, for May 1765, 1766 and 1767* [Savannah, ca. 1913], 52–57.

4. For more on revolutionary Georgia, see Kenneth Coleman, *The American Revolution in Georgia, 1763–1789* (Athens, 1958); Edward J. Cashin, *The King's Ranger: Thomas Brown and the American Revolution on the Southern Frontier* (Athens, 1989); Edward J. Cashin, *William Bartram and the American Revolution on the Southern Frontier* (Columbia, S.C., 2000); Gallay, *The Formation of a Planter Elite*; Sylvia R. Frey, *Water from the Rock: Black Resistance in a Revolutionary Age* (Princeton, 1991); Leslie Hall, *Land and Allegiance in Revolutionary Georgia* (Athens, 2001).

5. Joseph Clay to Henry Laurens, 21 October 1777, in *Letters of Joseph Clay,* 52–57.

6. W. W. Abbot, "Structure of Politics in Georgia, 1782–1789," *William and Mary Quarterly* 14, no. 1 (January 1957): 47–65.

7. Gary Nash, *Forgotten Fifth: African Americans in the Age of Revolution* (Cambridge, Mass., 2006).

8. Frey, *Water from the Rock*, 86. See also Benjamin Quarles, *The Negro in the American Revolution* (Chapel Hill, 1961), 60–67; Pete Maslowski, "National Policy toward the Use of Black Troops in the Revolution," *South Carolina Historical Magazine* 73, no. 1 (January 1972), 6–17; Chaplin, *An Anxious Pursuit*, 56–58, 364–365. For the most thorough account of John Laurens's efforts to raise black troops, see Gregory D. Massey, "The Limits of Anti-Slavery Thought in the Revolutionary Lower South: John Laurens and Henry Laurens," *Journal of Southern History* 63, no. 3 (August 1997): 495–530.

9. General Nathanael Greene to Governor John Rutledge, 9 December 1781, Nathanael Greene Letters, ms 329, Georgia Historical Society. General Wayne proposed "embodying a corps of negroes" the following year as well, but his suggestion met a similar response. General Wayne to Governor Martin, 19 February 1782, Force Transcripts, Georgia Records, Council of Correspondence, 1782–1789, and Governors Correspondence, Letters of Governors, 4–5, GDAH.

10. For more on the long history of using slave soldiers, see Christopher Leslie Brown and Philip D. Morgan, eds., *Arming Slaves: From Classical Times to the Modern Age* (New Haven, 2006).

11. Wood, *Black Majority,* 124–130.

12. Landers, *Black Society in Spanish Florida,* particularly chapter 2.

13. Wood, *Slavery in Colonial Georgia,* 118–119.

14. Hall, *Land and Allegiance in Revolutionary Georgia.* For more on British policies toward slaves and slavery in general during and after the Revolutionary War, see Simon Schama, *Rough Crossings: Britain, the Slaves, and the American Revolution* (New York, 2006); Cassandra Pybus, *Epic Journeys of Freedom: Runaway Slaves of the American Revolution and the Global Quest for Liberty* (Boston, 2007).

15. For more on the role of black soldiers in the British Army during the

American Revolution, see Quarles, *The Negro in the American Revolution*; Frey, *Water from the Rock*; Nash, *The Forgotten Fifth*.

16. Joseph Clay to Henry Laurens, 9 September 1778, in *Letters of Joseph Clay*, 105; Joseph Clay to George Abott Hall, 10 March 1779, in *Letters of Joseph Clay*, 111; Joseph Clay to Bright and Pechin, 23 March 1779, in *Letters of Joseph Clay*, 129; Lachlan McIntosh Jr. to Lachlan McIntosh, 22 July 1776, in Lilla M. Hawes, *The Papers of Lachlan McIntosh, 1774–1779* (Savannah, 1957), 52; Lachlan McIntosh Jr. to Lachlan McIntosh, 14 August 1776, in *Papers of Lachlan McIntosh, 1774–1779*, 54; Chaplin, *An Anxious Pursuit*, 217, 235.

17. Chaplin, *An Anxious Pursuit*, 208–220.

18. Lachlan McIntosh to [?], 8 March 1776, in *Papers of Lachlan McIntosh*, 1; Joseph Clay to [?], 1 September 1778, in *Letters of Joseph Clay*, 99; Joseph Clay to Abraham Markoe, 15 December 1777, in *Letters of Joseph Clay*, 63.

19. "Proceedings of the Georgia Council of Safety," in Hays, ed., *Collections of the Georgia Historical Society*, vol. 5, pt. 1, pp. 30, 96, 122; Frey, *Water from the Rock*, 91.

20. "Account of the Siege of Savannah, 1779, From a British Source," in Hays, ed., *Collections of the Georgia Historical Society*, vol. 5, pt. 1, pp. 130, 138; Charles Stedman, *The History of the Origin, Progress, and Termination of the American War* (London, 1794), 2:128–132; Frey, *Water from the Rock*, 95–99.

21. Frey, *Water from the Rock*, 102. For more on the role of black French troops in the Siege of Savannah, see George P. Clark, "The Role of the Haitian Volunteers at Savannah in 1779: An Attempt at an Objective View," *Phylon* 41, no. 4 (1980): 356–366.

22. Hall, *Land and Allegiance in Revolutionary Georgia*, 119.

23. Ibid., 161–163.

24. Ibid., 162.

25. See Schama, *Rough Crossings*; Pybus, *Epic Journeys of Freedom*.

26. General Jackson to Governor of Georgia, 1787, document 85, folder 10, box 1, Joseph Vallence Bevan Papers, ms 71, Georgia Historical Society (hereafter cited as GHS).

27. General James Jackson to the Governor of South Carolina, 26 December 1786, folder 1, box 82, Telamon Cuyler Collection, Ms 1170, Hargrett Rare Book and Manuscript Library, University of Georgia (hereafter cited as Hargrett).

28. General Jackson to Governor of Georgia, 1787, document 85, folder 10, box 1, Joseph Vallence Bevan Papers, ms 71, GHS; General James Jackson to the Governor of South Carolina, 26 December 1786, folder 1, box 82, Telamon Cuyler Collection, Ms 1170, Hargrett.

29. General James Jackson to the Governor of South Carolina, 26 December 1786, folder 1, box 82, Telamon Cuyler Collection, Ms 1170, Hargrett.

30. For more on maroons in the Savannah River area, see Timothy Lockley, ed., *Maroon Communities in South Carolina: A Documentary Record* (Columbia, S.C., 2009), especially chapter 3.

31. Governor of South Carolina to Governor of Georgia, 2 April 1787, document 83, folder 10, box 1, Joseph Vallence Bevan Papers, ms 71, GHS.

32. James Gunn to General James Jackson, 5 May 1787, document 84, folder 10, box 1, Joseph Vallence Bevan Papers, ms 71, GHS.

33. General Jackson to Governor of Georgia, 1787, document 85, folder 10, box 1, Joseph Vallence Bevan Papers, ms 71, GHS.

34. Chaplin, *An Anxious Pursuit*, 235.

35. George Baillie to John Mackintosh Jr., 7 September 1783, John McIntosh, Jr., Papers, ms 525, GHS.

36. Joseph Clay to Nathaniel Hall, 16 April 1783, in *Letters of Joseph Clay*, 184.

37. Joseph Clay to Joachim Noel Famming, 23 April 1783, in *Letters of Joseph Clay*, 190.

38. U.S. Census, 1790.

39. C. L. R. James, *The Black Jacobins: Toussaint L'Ouverture and the San Domingo Revolution*, 2nd ed. (New York, 1963), 68–75. For more on Vincent Ogé and *gens du couleur*, see Stewart R. King, *Blue Coat or Powdered Wig: Free People of Color in Pre-Revolutionary Saint Domingue* (Athens, 2001). See also Robin Blackburn, *The Overthrow of Colonial Slavery, 1776–1848* (New York, 1988), chapter 6.

40. For the most comprehensive account of the Haitian Revolution, see Laurent Dubois, *Avengers of the New World: The Story of the Haitian Revolution* (Cambridge, Mass., 2004).

41. During the early 1790s, white Georgians only gradually became concerned with threats emerging in the aftermath of the rebellion in St. Domingue. Newspaper accounts in Georgia initially downplayed the threat posed by the rebels in St. Domingue. It took almost three months for a report of the revolt led by Ogé to appear in either of the newspapers in Georgia, and when it did in early 1791 the account included no names and only a brief description of the incident. (*Augusta Chronicle and Gazette of the State*, 5 February 1791; *Georgia Gazette*, 3 February 1791.) News of the outbreak of an "alarming" slave revolt in St. Domingue in the summer of 1791 brought greater attention to the escalating violence in the French colony. Still, John E. Smith, the editor of the *Augusta Chronicle and Gazette of the State*, managed to put a brave face on the transpiring events. Although he acknowledged that "only God" knew the final outcome of the "dreadful disturbances," he remained confident in the eventual defeat of the black rebels. He assured readers that the slaves would soon return to their plantations because they were running out of provisions and were on the verge of starvation. (*Augusta Chronicle and Gazette of the State*, 12 November 1791.)

42. For more on the spread of the Haitian Revolution throughout the slave societies of the Atlantic World, see Julius Sherrard Scott III, "The Common Wind: Currents of Afro-American Communication in the Era of the Haitian Revolution" (Ph.D. diss., Duke University, 1986). See also David Barry Gaspar and David Patrick Geggus, eds., *A Turbulent Time: The French Revolution and the Greater Caribbean* (Bloomington, 1997).

43. *Augusta Chronicle and Gazette of the State*, 12 October 1793, 26 October 1793.

44. *State Gazette of South Carolina*, 3 October 1793, 5 October 1793, 10 October 1793, 17 October 1793. For more on the fear of slave insurrection in Charleston in connection with the refugees from St. Domingue, see Robert Alderson, "Charleston's Rumored Slave Revolt of 1793," in *The Impact of the Haitian Revolution in the Atlantic World*, ed. David P. Geggus, 93–111 (Columbia, S.C., 2002). For more on émigrés of African descent who arrived in the United States, see Alfred N. Hunt, *Haiti's Influence on Antebellum America: Slumbering Volcano in the Caribbean* (Baton Rouge, 1988).

45. *Augusta Chronicle and Gazette of the State*, 2 November 1793.

46. *Acts of the General Assembly of the State of Georgia, 1793* (Augusta, 1794), 24; *Augusta Chronicle and Gazette of the State*, 21 December 1793. Legislators debated whether to place restrictions on the importation of Africans, but the amendment was defeated 21 to 8 (*Augusta Chronicle and Gazette of the State*, 21 December 1793).

47. "A Proclamation," Executive Minutes, 11 June 1798, 300, GDAH.

48. The legislature in South Carolina banned the importation of slaves for two years in 1792 (*Augusta Chronicle and Gazette of the State*, 9 March 1793). The authorities reopened the trade in 1803, however. In the five-year interval that followed, thirty-five thousand Africans were imported into South Carolina. See Berlin, *Many Thousands Gone*, 308–309.

49. *Augusta Chronicle and Gazette of the State*, 16 November 1793, 7 December 1793.

50. This was drawn from a survey of marine lists in the *Georgia Gazette* in 1795. Villano, Commander, 15 July 1791; Andrés del Villán, Commander, 18 July 1791; Jeremy Garraud to Mr. Tiote, 23 June 1792; François Garraud to Mr. Tiot, 24 June 1792; pass from Baudouin Des Marrettes, 30 December 1794; receipt from Leonard Simonet, 28 January 1795; T. M. [Call?] to Charles Tiot, 31 December 1795; James Reston to James Tiot, [December 1795?], all in Thiot Family Papers, manuscript no. 297, box 1, folder 1, Special Collections, Emory University.

51. Savannah City Council Minutes, 1 October 1793, 16 October 1793, 23 May 1794, 23 October 1794, GDAH.

52. Ph. Wright and G. Debien, *Les colons de Saint Domingue passés à la Jamaïque (1792–1835)*, Bulletin de la Société d'Histoire de la Guadaloupe, no. 26 (Basse-Terre, 1975).

53. *Journals of the Assembly of Jamaica, Vol. IX from 25th October, 1791, to 4th August, 1797* (Jamaica, 1805), 350, 352, 356.

54. Savannah City Council Minutes, 1 July 1795, GDAH.

55. Ibid., 2 July 1795, GDAH. The Committee of Inspectors included Dr. Jon Buckell, Owen Owens, Mathew Johnston, Justus H. Schenber, Joseph Roberts, Robert Bolton, James Robertson, William [illegible], George Jones, Nichol Turnbull, William Moore, John Armour, William H. S[illegible], Peter S. Lafitte, James

Clark, Thomas Hogg, Robert Watts, William Belcher, William Coats, Frederick Shrek. The committee's duty was to oversee the city's various wards and implement City Council resolutions.

56. Savannah City Council Minutes, 1 July 1795, 2 July 1795, 13 July 1795, 21 July 1795, GDAH; James Jackson to John Glenn, 20 June 1798, Executive Minutes, GDAH.

57. Savannah City Council Minutes, 30 September 1795, GDAH.

58. Ibid., 29 November 1795, GDAH.

59. An Act to organize the Militia in the several new counties of this state, passed on 22 February 1796 and published in *Augusta Chronicle and Gazette of the State*, 19 March 1796.

60. Elizabeth Donnan lists a handful of slave ships that arrived in 1796–1797 as a sample, but her count is far from exhaustive. By contrast, Alan Kulikoff estimates that forty-eight thousand African slaves were imported in the 1790s and early 1800s. This number seems far too high, especially considering that Georgia banned the importation of all slaves, both by land and sea, in 1798. (Allan Kulikoff, "Uprooted Peoples: Black Migrants in the Age of the American Revolution, 1790–1820," in *Slavery and Freedom in the Age of the American Revolution*, ed. Ira Berlin and Ronald Hoffman, 147–152 [Charlottesville, 1983].) In the last ten months before the ban was implemented in October 1798, tax records from Savannah indicate that 724 African slaves were imported into the city. (Chatham County Tax Digests, 1798–99, GDAH.) This tally fits with the estimate offered by the French traveler the Duc de la Rochefoucauld, who estimated in 1796 that six hundred to seven hundred African slaves were introduced to Georgia per year.

61. La Rochefoucauld, "La Rochefoucauld-Liancourt, 1796," in Lane, ed., *The Rambler in Georgia*, 9

62. *Columbia Museum and Savannah Advertiser*, 24 February 1797; *Augusta Chronicle and Gazette of the State*, 4 March 1797. For more on African slaves running away in groups in the late eighteenth and early nineteenth centuries, see Morgan, *Slave Counterpoint*, 446–450. For more on tensions between African-born and American-born slaves, see Charles Ball, *Fifty Years in Chains; or, The Life of an American Slave* (Detroit, 1971). In his memoir, Ball asserted, "The native Africans are revengeful, and unforgiving in their tempers, easily provoked, and cruel in their designs" (219). See also Michael A. Gomez, *Exchanging Our Country Marks: The Transformation of African Identities in the Colonial and Antebellum South* (Chapel Hill, 1998), 194–195; Morgan, *Slave Counterpoint*, 459–463.

63. *Augusta Chronicle and Gazette of the State*, 23 December 1797.

64. Ibid., 2 December 1797, 9 December 1797.

65. Ibid., 17 February 1798; *Acts of the General Assembly of the State of Georgia, Passed at Louisville, in January and February, 1798* (Augusta, 1798), 7–8. The ban on slaves imported from Africa and elsewhere was to take effect six months from the passing of the act; the ban on the importation of "domestic" slaves took effect

three months from the passing of the act. Delegates to the 1798 Constitutional Convention modified the law to allow slave owners who settled in Georgia to bring their slaves. See "The Constitution of the State of Georgia," *Augusta Chronicle and Gazette of the State*, 30 June 1798. The provision is in Article IV, Section II, of the document.

66. *Augusta Chronicle and Gazette of the State*, 4 March 1797. For more on the importance of ethnicity among African slaves imported into the United States, see Gomez, *Exchanging Our Country Marks*.

67. *Columbia Museum and Savannah Advertiser*, 24 February 1797.

68. *Augusta Chronicle and Gazette of the State*, September 16, 1797.

69. Ibid., 7 October 1797.

70. For more on amelioration, see Edward Brathwaite, *The Development of Creole Society in Jamaica, 1770–1820* (Oxford, 1971), 243–265, 292–293.

71. David Geggus, "The Enigma of Jamaica in the 1790s: New Light on the Causes of Slave Rebellions," *William and Mary Quarterly*, 3rd ser., 44, no. 2. (April 1987): 274–299.

72. *Augusta Chronicle and Gazette of the State*, 7 October 1797. For another example of promoting benevolent patriarchy, see *Columbia Museum and Savannah Advertiser*, 14 March 1797.

73. 1798 Georgia Constitution, Article IV, Section 12.

74. *Journal of the 1798 Constitutional Convention of the State of Georgia*. The law returned to the standard established by the trustees in the 1750 slave code, but the legislators were likely unaware of this fact.

75. Joseph Clay to James Seagrove, 5 February 1783, in *Letters of Joseph Clay*, 174; Joseph Clay to Joachim Noel Flamming, 23 April 1783, in *Letters of Joseph Clay*, 190; Samuel Edward Butler Diary, Ms 432, Hargrett; Melvin Herndon, ed., "The Diary of Samuel Edward Butler, 1784–1786, and the Inventory and Appraisement of His Estate," *Georgia Historical Quarterly* 52 (1968): 203–220.

76. *Augusta Chronicle and Gazette of the State*, 8 June 1799.

77. Ibid., 13 June 1801. The quote was taken from *The State v. William Aftline*, before Judge Walton in Richmond County, 9 June 1801.

78. *Augusta Chronicle and Gazette of the State*, 25 September 1801.

79. Various presentments by frontier county grand juries: "Presentments and Recommendations of the Grand Jury of Columbia County," *Augusta Chronicle and Gazette of the State*, 26 September 1801; "Georgia, Warren County," *Augusta Chronicle and Gazette of the State*, 12 July 1800; "Presentments of the Grand Jury of Columbia County," *Augusta Chronicle and Gazette of the State*, 21 September 1799. A letter from "A Friend to the States and the Laws," in *Augusta Chronicle and Gazette of the State*, 31 August 1799, called on public officials to abide by the laws regarding the ban on the introduction of slaves into Georgia.

80. Douglas R. Egerton, *Gabriel's Rebellion: The Virginia Slave Conspiracies of 1800 and 1802* (Chapel Hill, 1993). For more on Gabriel's Rebellion, see James Sidbury,

Ploughshares into Swords: Race, Rebellion, and Identity in Gabriel's Virginia, 1730–1810 (New York, 1997).

81. *Augusta Chronicle and Gazette of the State,* 27 September 1800.

82. Ibid., 27 September 1800.

83. Ibid., 12 June 1802, 26 June 1802.

84. *Journal of the House of Representatives of the State of Georgia, for the Year 1801* (Louisville, 1801), 9, 11, 14, 15, 21, 27, 35–38, 42; *Journal of the House of Representatives of the State of Georgia, 1802* (Savannah, 1803), 11, 13, 16, 19, 23–25, 29; *Journal of the Senate of the State of Georgia, 1801* (Louisville, 1801), 34; *Journal of the Senate of the State of Georgia, 1802* (Savannah, 1803), 29–33.

85. *Journal of the House of Representatives of the State of Georgia, 1802,* 4–5.

86. Wood, *Slavery in Colonial Georgia,* 128. For examples of scholarship on free people of African descent in antebellum Georgia, see Edward F. Sweat, "The Free Negro in Antebellum Georgia" (Ph.D. diss., Indiana University, 1957); Edward F. Sweat, "Social Status of the Free Negro in Antebellum Georgia," *Negro History Bulletin* 21, no. 6 (September 1958): 129–131; Edward F. Sweat, *Economic Status of Free Blacks in Antebellum Georgia* (Atlanta, 1974); Edward F. Sweat, *Free Blacks and the Law in Antebellum Georgia* (Atlanta, 1976); Ralph B. Flanders, "The Free Negro in Antebellum Georgia," *North Carolina Historical Review* 9, no. 3 (July 1932): 250–272.

87. "George Galphin's Will," in "Creek Indian Letters, Talks, and Treaties" (hereafter cited as CILTT), 1:8–15, GDAH; *Bowers v. Newman,* 2 McMull. 472 (S.C., 1842); Thomas McArdory Qwen, *History of Alabama and Dictionary of Alabama Biography* (Chicago, 1921), 3:832.

88. For more on George Galphin, see J. Leitch Wright Jr., *Creeks and Seminoles: The Destruction and Regeneration of the Muscogulge People* (Lincoln, 1989), 81, 290, 303; Andrew K. Frank, *Creeks and Southerners: Biculturalism on the Early American Frontier* (Lincoln, 2005), 70–71, 115.

89. "George Galphin's Will," CILTT, 1:8–15, GDAH.

90. For more on white traders and Indian women, see Theda Perdue, *"Mixed Blood" Indians: Racial Construction in the Early South* (Athens, 2003), 13–26; Frank, *Creeks and Southerners,* 26–40.

91. In the past half-century, the 1765 naturalization law has attracted the attention of a number of historians. Yet in that time no consensus on either the law's origins or its significance has emerged. For example, in a 1962 essay on racial attitudes among the English colonists in the Americas, Winthrop Jordan argued that mainland colonists held starkly different views on race than did their counterparts in the British West Indies. The former were more rigid while the latter were more flexible. Yet, he admitted, "A single exception to these generalizations stands out sharply from the mass of colonial legislation." Referring to the 1765 law, Jordan described it as "a begrudging kind of citizenship [that] was extended to free mulattoes," a decision he attributed to the "colony's weak and exposed condition," which "made Georgians eager for men who might be

counted as white and thus strengthen the colony." Winthrop Jordan, "American Chiaroscuro: The Status and Definition of Mulattoes in the British Colonies," in *The Slavery Reader*, vol. 1, ed. Gad Heuman and James Walvin (New York, 2003), 642–643. A decade after the publication of Jordan's essay, Carl Degler considered the law in his seminal work *Neither Black nor White: Slavery and Race Relations in Brazil and the United States*. Imputing slightly less cynical motives than Jordan, Degler contended that the 1765 law demonstrated that "the idea of defining a Negro by ancestry was not a foregone conclusion among Englishmen." Despite the fact that it failed to become law, its relevance, Degler insisted, lay in its passage alone. It was the sole instance in which a mainland English colony "came close to legalizing the mulatto escape hatch just as was done in Jamaica." Degler's comparison was interesting. He, like Jordan, compared the rigidity of racial attitudes on the mainland with the fluidity that characterized racial attitudes on the islands. But, he suggested, the Georgia law represented a road not taken, a possibility of what could have emerged rather than the racial system that did take hold.

In the four decades since the publication of *Neither Black nor White*, our understanding of colonial slavery has become more nuanced, yet the 1765 law has remained an enigma. Among the historians who've taken on the law is Betty Wood, who labeled it "puzzling." She argued that economic motives most likely spurred the legislature to include the provision. She speculated that the authorities in Georgia hoped the law would attract skilled black workers to the colony to drive down the price of labor. More recently, Ben Marsh offered an analysis of the naturalization law that has seemingly brought the argument full circle. Marsh labeled the provision "an exceptional piece of legislation" reflecting the "interracial idiosyncrasy" that marked the racial order in Georgia prior to the 1750s and 1760s. Echoing Winthrop Jordan, he identified the law as an anomaly, "begrudgingly" undertaken by the authorities (*Georgia's Frontier Women*, 145).

92. "AN ACT For the better Ordering and Governing Negroes and other Slaves in this Province and to prevent the inveigling or carrying away Slaves from their Masters or Employers, 1765," in Candler and Knight, eds., *Colonial Records*, vol. 18, pp. 649–688.

93. See Governor James Wright to the Board of Trade, 8 June 1768, in Candler and Knight, eds., *Colonial Records*, vol. 28, pt. 2, p. 55.

94. For contemporary white accounts of distinctions among free people of color in Jamaica, see Bryan Edwards, *The History, Civil and Commercial, of the British West Indies* (London, 1819), 2:18–38; Edward Long, *The History of Jamaica: Reflections on its Situation, Settlements, Inhabitants, Climate, Products, Commerce, Laws, and Government* (London, 1774), 2:320–337. See also Edward Brathwaite, *The Development of Creole Society in Jamaica, 1770–1820* (Oxford, 1971), 166–175, 188–192; Mavis Christine Campbell, *The Dynamics of Change in a Slave Society: A Sociopolitical History of the Free Coloreds of Jamaica, 1800–1865* (Rutherford, N.J., 1976), 39–117; Gad Heuman, "The Free

Coloreds in Jamaican Slave Society," in Heuman and Walvin, eds., *The Slavery Reader*, 1:654–667.

95. For a comparison of the language used by Jamaica's legislature when elevating the legal status of free people of color, see *Acts of Assembly, passed in the island of Jamaica, from the year 1681 to the year 1769 inclusive. In two volumes....* (Kingston, Jamaica, 1787), 1:17–18, 20, 22–25, 30; 2:3, 8–11, 15. In 1733, the assembly granted John Golding and his family "the Rights and Privileges of Englishmen, born of white Ancestors" (1:14). In subsequent decades, the legislature continued the practice of extending special status to certain free people of color, though the language in the acts changed slightly. Like the provision in the 1765 Georgia slave code, the Jamaican authorities granted certain free people of color the "same rights and privileges with English subjects, born of white parents." Later in the eighteenth century, most of the acts began to include the phrase "under certain restrictions." Almost all of the individuals who received this status were the wives or children of white men.

96. Joseph Clay to John Wright, 17 February 1784, in *Letters of Joseph Clay*, 201.

97. U.S. Census, 1790; U.S. Census, 1800.

98. For more on Vincent Ogé and *gens du couleur*, see Stewart R. King, *Blue Coat or Powdered Wig: Free People of Color in Pre-Revolutionary Saint Domingue* (Athens, 2001). See also Robin Blackburn, *The Overthrow of Colonial Slavery, 1776–1848* (New York, 1988), chapter 6.

99. *Augusta Chronicle and Gazette of the State*, 3 August 1793.

100. Ibid., 2 November 1793.

101. *Acts of the General Assembly of the State of Georgia Passed at their session, begun and holden at Augusta, the fourth November, one thousand seven hundred ninety three, and continued, by the adjournments, to the nineteenth December following* (Augusta, 1794), 24.

102. *Augusta Chronicle and Gazette of the State*, 2 November 1793.

103. The provision required all "free negroes, mulattoes, or mustizoes" who came to the state after the passage of the act to enroll in the clerk's office of the county where they resided within thirty days of their arrival. Within six months they had to "procure a certificate of two or more magistrates of the county" attesting to their "honesty and industry, to entitle them to privilege of residence" in the state. Those who failed to abide by the law were subject to a three-month jail sentence.

104. Register of Free Persons of Color, 81/4, 1780–1865, 1837–1849, 1861–1864, GDAH. The documents clearly include various registers of free persons of color; however, the dates are less certain. I have used them to point out links in general rather than to suggest any temporal connection.

105. For examples of Richard Stites's connections to free blacks, see Richard Stites to Mr. Drayton, 7 October 1811, Wayne-Stites-Anderson Papers, ms 846, box 11, GHS; Richard Stites to Mr. Drayton, 3 December 1811, Wayne-Stites-Anderson Papers, ms 846, box 11, GHS. The correspondence includes a letter of

introduction from Stites for Simon Jackson, a free person of color and tailor by trade. Stites served as Jackson's guardian and helped finance his business transactions. Jackson was one of Savannah's most respected tailors. Stites referred to Jackson as "very generally respected for his industry and correct deportment in life," qualities he had displayed in the fifteen years since he had moved to Savannah in 1796. In the letter, Stites requested that Drayton facilitate Jackson's purchase of property in Charleston that once belonged to Norman Young. For more on Stites's financial relationship with Jackson, see the document "Dr. Simon Jackson in Acct Current with Richard M. Stites," contained in the same collection. The document covers 1811. In one instance, Simon Jackson actually sold a slave to Stites (Simon Jackson to Richard M. Stites, 5 August 1807). For more on Simon Jackson, see Whittington Bernard Johnson, *Black Savannah, 1788–1864* (Fayetteville, 1996), 63, 70. For examples of Stites's transactions involving rented slaves, see box 2, folder 23, Wayne-Stites-Anderson Papers, ms 846, GHS.

106. For a different interpretation of the relationship between free people of African descent and whites in the lowcountry, see Lockley, *Lines in the Sand*. In his monograph, Lockley focuses on relations between African Americans and nonelite whites in lowcountry Georgia between 1750 and 1860. However, not all relations between whites and free people of African descent followed this pattern in Savannah. Savannah was home to a relatively significant number of wealthy free people of color. While not as large as their counterparts in Charleston or New Orleans, elite free people of color in Savannah and the surrounding area had long connections to the local planter elite. The guardian system provided a different means of bringing together the races; it gave official recognition to relations between elite whites and elite free people of color. While Lockley does an excellent job exploring the links between nonelite whites and slaves and poor free blacks, he does not address the relationships between the white elite and free people of color in the same depth. Yet, these relationships included large numbers of individuals from both communities. They were not inconsequential. They demonstrate that members of the white elite preferred to deal with nonwhites when conducting certain parts of their affairs. They reveal that the white elite sometimes perceived class rather than race as the key factor in determining an individual's fate in society.

107. For example, several of Chatham County's wealthiest free people of color had the same last names as Georgia white elite families.

108. Savannah City Council Minutes, 24 December 1794, GDAH.

109. Ibid., 15 October 1792.

110. Frey, *Water from the Rock*, 288–290.

111. Ira Berlin, *Slaves without Masters: The Free Negro in the Antebellum South* (New York, 1974)

112. For more on divisions between elite free people of color and slaves in the Lower South, particularly in the early national period, see Berlin, *Slaves without*

Masters, 271–283; Michael P. Johnson and James L. Roark, *Black Masters: A Free Family of Color in the Old South* (New York, 1984); Kimberly S. Hanger, *Bounded Lives, Bounded Places: Free Black Society in Colonial New Orleans, 1769–1803* (Durham, 1997), 55–108.

113. Timothy Lockely's *Lines in the Sand* highlights the many complex ways in which blacks and whites interacted during this long period of time. He points out that there were multiple moments in time and particular geographies where members of the two groups came together to struggle against the white elite. Living and working near each other, he notes, brought the two groups together physically and, at times, ideologically. "The attitudes this proximity engendered in the minds of nonslaveholding whites and African Americas," he states, "establish that, within certain limitations, race could defer to self-interest, friendship, cooperation, and brotherly or sisterly solidarity in the minds of the poorer black and white members of lowcountry Georgia society" (xviii). As Lockley makes clear, the races crossed lines often in their illicit activities and socializing and conspiring in grog shops and in the city's poor neighborhoods. He does acknowledge that divisions strained relations and produced conflict, at times violent, yet his account seems to underplay its frequency and depth.

114. For example, Peter Daugherty and Peter Coalman were both summoned to appear before the Savannah City Council and fined $10 for entertaining Negroes (Savannah City Council Minutes, 29 September 1795, 19 January 1796, GDAH).

115. Savannah City Council Minutes, 1794–1796, GDAH. In 1808, the General Assembly enacted an even more stringent measure to control illicit trade. The legislation forced tavern- and shopkeepers who sold liquor to get a license and take an oath that they would not buy from or sell anything to unauthorized slaves. The law imposed a $30 penalty for each infraction and required the perpetrator to post a $200 bond guaranteeing their good behavior for a year. Two years later the law was amended and the oath repealed, but the new statute called for much larger fines ($200 to $300) for each violation.

116. Scott, "The Common Wind"; Laurent Dubois, *A Colony of Citizens: Revolution and Slave Emancipation in the French Caribbean, 1787–1804* (Chapel Hill, 2004).

117. Savannah City Council Minutes, 29 June 1795, GDAH.

118. *Georgia Gazette*, 2 July 1795.

119. Savannah City Council Minutes, 7 July 1795, GDAH.

120. The quotations are from testimony given at the Savannah City Council (Savannah City Council Minutes, 7 July 1795, GDAH).

121. *Columbia Museum and Savannah Advertiser*, 15 September 1797, 29 September 1797; *Georgia Gazette*, 14 February 1798, 2 March 1798, 6 April 1798; Executive Minutes, 22 January 1798, 9 February 1798, 20 February 1798, 26 February 1798, 9 March 1798, 20 March 1798, GDAH.

122. *Georgia Gazette*, 21 March 1798. For more on the controversy over the

Exuma, see *Columbia Museum and Savannah Advertiser*, 15 September 1797, 29 September 1797, 16 February 1798, 2 March 1798, 6 April 1798; Executive Minutes, 22 January 1798, GDAH.

123. Horatio Marbury and William Crawford, eds., *Digest of the laws of the state of Georgia, from its settlement as a British province, in 1775, to the session of the General assembly in 1800, inclusive* (Savannah, 1803), 203–207.

124. *Acts of the General Assembly of the State of Georgia: Passed at Louisville, in January and February, 1799* (Louisville, Ga., 1799), 148–149.

125. *Louisville Gazette*, 18 June 1799; *Acts of the General Assembly of the State of Georgia: Passed at Louisville, in January and February, 1799* (Louisville, Ga., 1799), 148–149; Marbury and Crawford, eds., *Digest of the laws of the state of Georgia*, 203–207.

126. For examples of free people of color obtaining special rights and privileges in Jamaica in the late eighteenth century, see *Journals of the Assembly of Jamaica, From 25th October, 1791, to 4th August, 1797 (32d to 37th Geo. III.)* (Jamaica, 1805), 162, 169, 190, 316. For more examples, see *Acts of Assembly Passed in the Island of Jamaica, From the Year 1784 to the Year 1788 inclusive* (Kingston, Jamaica, 1789), vi–ix, xi, xv–xvi; *Acts of Assembly passed in the island of Jamaica, in the years 1789 and 1790* (Kingston, Jamaica, 1790?), iii. See also, Edward Brathwaite, *The Development of Creole Society in Jamaica, 1770-1820*. According to Brathwaite, at least 67 petitions involving 512 free coloreds (and only one free black) passed the Jamaican Assembly between 1772 and 1796. Of those, 176 were mulattoes, 245 quadroons, and 90 mustees (291–292).

127. *Acts of the General Assembly of the State of Georgia: Passed at Louisville, in January and February, 1799* (Louisville, 1799); *Acts of the General Assembly of the State of Georgia: Passed at Louisville, in November and December, 1799* (Augusta, 1800), 5–6.

128. "Virginia Council and General Court Records, 1640–1641," *Virginia Magazine of History and Biography* 11, no. 3 (January 1904), 281; Paul Heinegg, *Free African Americans of North Carolina, Virginia, and South Carolina, from the Colonial Period to about 1820*, vol. 1 (Baltimore, 2001), 410–428. Because Moses Going disappeared from the records in Virginia by 1787, Heinegg speculates that he had died (423). More likely, however, Moses Going is the man listed in other records under the same name in Georgia beginning in 1786. See for example, Grace Gillam Davidson, ed., *The Early Records of Georgia*, vol. 1, *Wilkes County* (Macon, 1933), 256, 262; Grace Gillam Davidson, ed., *The Early Records of Georgia*, vol. 2, *Wilkes County* (Macon, 1933), 111.

129. Heinegg, *Free African Americans of North Carolina, Virginia, and South Carolina, from the Colonial Period to about 1820*, vol. 1, 416. The two joined the 14th Virginia Regiment under Colonel Charles Lewis, and Sherwood (also listed as Sherrod) reenlisted in 1780 for an additional eighteen months, according his pension application.

130. Marbury and Crawford, eds., *Digest of the laws of the state of Georgia*, 205

131. *Acts of the General Assembly of the State of Georgia: Passed at Louisville, in January and February, 1799*. The exact language in the act specified that Thomas Going was to

be "vested with and entitled to all the rights privileges and immunities belonging to a free citizen of this state." These rights did not, however, extend to serving as a juror, testifying against whites in most cases, voting, or holding office. Paul DeForest Hicks, *Joseph Henry Lumpkin: Georgia's First Chief Justice* (Athens, 2002), 11–12. Hicks notes that a free black man named "Gowen" was a successful doctor in Lexington in the early 1800s until he was forced to leave when his affair with the wife of white merchant became public.

132. Davidson, ed., *The Early Records of Georgia*, vol. 1, 318, 326. According to lottery records, Drury Goin, William Goin Jr., and John Going received plots from the 1803 land lottery; Drury Goin and John Goyne (Goin) received draws in 1806.

133. For more on French policies in the 1790s regarding former slaves, see Dubois, *A Colony of Citizens*.

134. *Journal of the Senate of the State of Georgia, 1801* (Louisville, 1801); *Journal of the House of Representatives of the State of Georgia, 1801* (Louisville, 1801). After 1801, several free people of color petitioned the legislature to be made "citizens of the state," but none were successful. See *Journal of the House of Representatives of the State of Georgia* (Louisville, 1803), 23, 42; *Journal of the Senate of the State of Georgia, for the year 1804* (Washington, Ga., 1805), 26, 28; *Journal of the House of Representatives of the State of Georgia, at the Annual Session of the General Assembly, begun at Milledgeville, on the first Monday in November, 1808* (Washington, Ga., 1808), 47,52.

135. *Journal of the Senate of the State of Georgia, 1801* (Louisville, 1801), 25–26; *Journal of the House of Representatives of the State of Georgia, 1801* (Louisville, 1801), 13–15, 17–18, 21, 25, 31.

136. *Columbia Museum and Savannah Advertiser,* 11 February 1800; *Augusta Chronicle and Gazette of the State,* 15 February 1800.

3. The Trans-Oconee Republic

1. The Trans-Oconee Republic has received relatively little attention from scholars, in contrast to similar instances of rebellion in the 1780s and 1790s. George Gilmer published one of the first accounts in his book *Sketches of Some of the First Settlers of Upper Georgia, of the Cherokees, and the Author* (1855). In the first half of the twentieth century, the Trans-Oconee attracted the attention of a trio of scholars: Merton Coulter, "Elijah Clark's Foreign Intrigues and the Trans-Oconee Republic," *Mississippi Valley Historical Association Proceedings* 10 (1918–1921): 260–279; Louise Frederick Hays, *Hero of Hornet's Nest: A Biography of Elijah Clark, 1733 to 1799* (New York, 1946); Richard K. Murdoch, *The Georgia-Florida Frontier, 1793–1796: Spanish Reaction to French Intrigue and American Designs* (Berkeley, 1951).

2. For more on the "Whiskey" rebellions, see Thomas P. Slaughter, *The Whiskey Rebellion: Frontier Epilogue to the American Revolution* (New York, 1986); Mary K. Bonsteel Tachau, "The Whiskey Rebellion in Kentucky: A Forgotten Episode of Civil

Disobedience," *Journal of the Early Republic* 2, no. 3 (1982): 239–259. For another example of rebellion in the post-revolutionary era, see Kevin T. Barksdale, *The Lost State of Franklin: America's First Secession* (Lexington, Ky., 2008).

3. Edward Cashin, "But Brothers, It Is Our Land," 241; Kenneth Coleman, *Colonial Georgia*, 226–227; Candler and Knight, eds., *Colonial Records*, vol. 38, pt. 1A, p. 120; Wright to the Earl of Halifax, 23 December 1763, in Candler and Knight, eds., *Colonial Records*, vol. 37, pt. 1, pp. 69–71; Wright to Hillsborough, 12 December 1771, in Candler and Knight, eds., *Colonial Records*, vol. 28, pt. 2, p. 356; Governor Wright to the Earl of Dartmouth, 10 August 1773, in Candler and Knight, eds., *Colonial Records*, vol. 38, pt. 1A, p. 80.

4. For more on rise of the backcountry after the Revolutionary War, see Abbot, "Structure of Politics in Georgia"; Cashin, "But Brothers, It Is Our Land"; Jackson, "The Rise of the Western Members"; Harvey H. Jackson, "Consensus and Conflict: Factional Politics in Revolutionary Georgia, 1774–77," *Georgia Historical Quarterly* 59 (1979): 388–401.

5. For more on the military campaign in Georgia during the War of Independence, see Coleman, *The American Revolution in Georgia, 1763–1789*; Hoffman, Tate, and Albert, eds., *An Uncivil War*; Cashin, *William Bartram and the American Revolution on the Southern Frontier*; Cashin, *The King's Ranger*; and David K. Wilson, *The Southern Strategy: Britain's Conquest of South Carolina and Georgia, 1775–1780* (Columbia, S.C., 2005).

6. Abbot, "Structure of Politics in Georgia"; Cashin, "But Brothers, It Is Our Land"; Jackson, "The Rise of the Western Members."

7. For more on the role of the state in American territorial expansion into the Southwest, see Adam Rothman, *Slave Country: American Expansion and the Origins of the Deep South* (Cambridge, Mass., 2005).

8. Alex M. Hitz, "Georgia Bounty Land Grants," *Georgia Historical Quarterly* 38 (1954): 347–348.

9. Richard Henderson to John Martin, 23 September 1782, CILTT, 1:33, GDAH; Richard Henderson to John Martin, 23 December 1782, CILTT, 1:42–44, GDAH; Patrick Carr to Governor Houstoun, 22 August 1784, CILTT, 1:63–64, GDAH; James Durouzeaux to William Clark, 25 May 1785, CILTT, 1:76, GDAH; James Durouzeaux to Governor Elbert, 10 August 1785, CILTT, 1:79–81, GDAH; Ulrich B. Phillips, *Georgia and State Rights: A Study of the Political History of Georgia from the Revolution to the Civil War with Particular Regard to Federal Relations* (Washington, D.C., 1902), 41. For more on diplomacy between the United States and the Creeks in the 1780s, see Randolph C. Downes, "Creek-American Relations, 1782–1790," *Georgia Historical Quarterly* 21 (1937): 142–184; Lucia Burk Kinnaird, "The Rock Landing Conference of 1789," *North Carolina Historical Review* 9 (1932): 349–365; J. Leitch Wright Jr., "Creek-American Treaty of 1790: Alexander McGillivray and the Diplomacy of the Old Southwest," *Georgia Historical Quarterly* 51 (1967): 379–400; and Corkran, *The Creek Frontier, 1540–1783*.

10. John Berrien to James Jackson, 30 September 1788, CILTT, 1:185–186,

GDAH; James Jackson to Governor Elbert, 3 October 1788, CILTT, 1:187–188, GDAH; Roger Parker Saunders to Governor Walton, 29 March 1789, CILTT, 1:194, GDAH.

11. The totals were as follows: militia of Franklin County, £756; militia of Greene County, £2,008; militia of Washington County, £2,861. Compare those amounts with the £121 spent for the militia of Camden County. (CILTT, 1:219, GDAH.)

12. "A Talk Delivered by the Fat King and other Indians of the Creek Nation," 5 April 1784, John Houstoun Letters, ms 397, 4–7, GHS.

13. Alexander McGillivray to [?], 2 September 1785, CILTT, 1:85, GDAH; Alexander McGillivray to James Durouzeaux, 15 August 1785, CILTT, 1:87–88, GDAH; Alexander McGillivray to William Clark, 24 April 1785 [1786?], CILTT, 1:89–90, GDAH.

14. Alexander McGillivray is the focus of several studies. For example: John W. Caughey, McGillivray of the Creeks (Norman, 1938); Michael D. Green, "Alexander McGillivray," in American Indian Leaders: Studies in Diversity, ed. R. David Edmunds, 41–63 (Lincoln, 1980); Lawrence Kinnaird, "International Rivalry in the Creek Country, Part I, The Ascendancy of Alexander McGillivray," Florida Historical Quarterly 10 (1931): 59–85; J. M. O'Donnell, "Alexander McGillivray: Training for Leadership, 1777–1783," Georgia Historical Quarterly 49 (1965): 172–183; Thomas D. Watson, "Strivings for Sovereignty: Alexander McGillivray, Creek Warfare, and Diplomacy, 1783–1790," Florida Historical Quarterly 58 (1980): 400–414; Arthur P. Whitaker, "Alexander McGillivray, 1783–1789," North Carolina Historical Review 5 (1928): 181–203; Arthur P. Whitaker, "Alexander McGillivray, 1789–1793," North Carolina Historical Review 5 (1928): 289–309; Saunt, A New Order of Things. For more on the place of "mixed-blood" individuals in Indian society, see Theda Perdue, "Mixed Blood" Indians: Racial Construction in the Early South (Athens, 2003).

15. Alexander McGillivray to [?], 2 September 1785, CILTT, 1:85, GDAH; Alexander McGillivray to James Durouzeaux, 15 August 1786, CILTT, 1:87–88, GDAH; Alexander McGillivray to William Clark, 24 April 1785, CILTT, 1:89–90, GDAH; Alexander McGillivray to James Durouzeaux, 12 September 1785, CILTT, 1:93–99, GDAH; J. Clemente to Edward Telfair, 6 May 1786, CILTT, 1:103, GDAH.

16. Extract of a letter from Alexander McGillivray that appeared in Augusta Chronicle and Gazette of the State, 9 April 1791.

17. Augusta Chronicle and Gazette of the State, 29 May 1790.

18. Address to the President of the United States from the Joint Committee of the General Assembly, 22 December 1789, Joseph V. Bevan Collection (Washington, D.C., 1984).

19. Augusta Chronicle and Gazette of the State, 15 May 1790.

20. Ibid., 15 May 1790, 4 September 1790.

21. Supplement to the Augusta Chronicle and Gazette of the State, No. 204, "Definitive Treaty," in ibid., 4 September 1790.

22. Wright, *Creeks and Seminoles*, 138–140.

23. "A Talk Delivered by the Fat King and other Indians of the Creek Nation," 5 April 1784, John Houstoun Letters, ms 397, 4–7, GHS.

24. See Article 12 of the treaty in *American State Papers: Indian Affairs* (Washington, D.C., 1831–1861) (hereafter cited as *ASPIA*), 1:81–82. The provision calls for the Creek Nation to be "led to a greater degree of civilization, and become herdsmen and cultivators." For more on the civilizing plan, see Bernard W. Sheehan, *Seeds of Extinction: Jefferson Philanthropy and the American Indian* (Chapel Hill, 1973), 119–181.

25. *Augusta Chronicle and Gazette of the State*, 26 November 1791.

26. Ibid., 4 June 1791.

27. Ibid., 12 June 1790.

28. Ibid., 4 June 1791.

29. For more examples of white traders among the southeastern Indians, see Perdue, *"Mixed Blood" Indians*, chapter 1.

30. Phillips, *Georgia and State Rights*, 43–44; George R. Lamplugh, *Politics on the Periphery: Factions and Parties in Georgia, 1783–1806* (Newark, Del., 1986), 64–65.

31. *Augusta Chronicle and Gazette of the State*, 1 May 1790.

32. For example, see the *Augusta Chronicle and Gazette of the State* from September 1790 until well into 1791.

33. *Augusta Chronicle and Gazette of the State*, 30 October 1790.

34. Ibid., 12 October 1791.

35. Elijah Clark to General Elholm, 19 February 1793, CILTT, 1:268, GDAH. For reactions of the federal officers to examples of settler violence, see Henry Gaither to Governor Edward Telfair, 15 February 1793, CILTT, 1:267, GDAH; Lieutenant Van Allen to Henry Gaither, 18 October 1793, CILTT, 1:343, GDAH.

36. "The Charge of the Honorable William Stith," *Augusta Chronicle and Gazette of the State*, 23 February 1793.

37. Elijah Clark to Governor Edward Telfair, 13 June 1792, CILTT, 1:248–253, GDAH; Elijah Clark to Governor Edward Telfair, 15 October 1792, CILTT, 1:261, GDAH.

38. Affidavits of John Felder, Joshua Browning, James Fielder, Duncan Camron, William Rogers, Nathan Barnett, Michael Cupp, Thomas Findly, 22 April 1793, CILTT, 1:285–287, GDAH; affidavit of Elihu Lyman, 22 April 1793, and affidavit of Michael Cupps, 22 April 1793, both in Joseph V. Bevan Collection; *Augusta Chronicle and Gazette of the State*, 27 April 1793, 4 May 1793.

39. *Augusta Chronicle and Gazette of the State*, 9 June 1792, 27 October 1792, 8 June 1793, 15 June 1793.

40. Ibid., 27 January 1793.

41. Ibid., 15 June 1793.

42. Ulrich B. Phillips accepted this account, which downplayed divisions among white Georgians (*Georgia and State Rights*, 43, 44).

43. *Augusta Chronicle and Gazette of the State*, 22 June 1793; "A Volunteer," 13 July

1793 [mislabeled on the front page of the newspaper as 11 July 1793], 10 August 1793, 20 July 1793.

44. For example, see Nathaniel Pendleton to William Stephens, 4 June 1790, in William Stephens Collection, GHS. For more on the sectional conflict in Georgia during the 1780s, see Lamplugh, *Politics on the Periphery*, chapters 2 and 3.

45. *Augusta Chronicle and Gazette of the State*, 6 July 1793.

46. Ibid., 22 June 1793.

47. Ibid.

48. James Seagrove to Governor Telfair, 3 October 1793, in *Augusta Chronicle and Gazette of the State*, 26 October 1793; James Seagrove to Governor Telfair, 14 October 1793, in *Augusta Chronicle and Gazette of the State*, 2 November 1793; Lieutenant Van Allen to Henry Gaither, 18 October 1793, CILTT, 1:343, GDAH.

49. James Seagrove to Secretary of War, 9 October 1793, *ASPIA*, 1:411.

50. Lieutenant Van Allen to Henry Gaither, 18 October 1793, CILTT, 1:343, GDAH.

51. *Augusta Chronicle and Gazette of the State*, 9 November 1793.

52. "A Querist," *Georgia Gazette*, 31 October 1793.

53. Governor George Mathews to James Seagrove, 3 February 1794, CILTT, GDAH.

54. *Augusta Chronicle and Gazette of the State*, 29 July 1793, 3 August 1793, 24 August 1793, 16 November 1793, 23 November 1793, 14 December 1793, 8 November 1794; *Georgia Gazette*, 25 July 1793.

55. *Augusta Chronicle and Gazette of the State*, 8 November 1793.

56. Ibid., 3 August 1793.

57. For more on the Nelson episode and white Georgians' attitudes toward the French Revolution, see Michele Gillespie, *Free Labor in an Unfree World*, 45, 50–51. As Gillespie notes, white Georgians were divided over the events in France, particularly after the execution of Louis XVI, yet certain geographical patterns did emerge.

58. Elijah Clark to Governor George Mathews, 18 February 1794, Elijah Clark Collection (File 11), GDAH; Harry Ammon, *The Genet Mission* (New York, 1973), 166.

59. "French Invasion of Florida," East Florida, West Florida Papers (hereafter cited as EFWF), GDAH. The quote is from the seventh article. For more on the Genêt affair, see Ammon, *The Genet Mission*; Murdoch, *The Georgia-Florida Frontier, 1793–1796*.

60. Thomas Houghton, Robert McAlpin, G. W. Foster, and John Armor to Governor George Mathews, 16 March 1794, CILTT, 2:366–369, GDAH; Lilla Mills Hawes, ed., "The Frontiers of Georgia in the Late Eighteenth Century: Jonas Fauche to Joseph Vallance Bevan," *Georgia Historical Quarterly* 47 (1963): 90–91; James Seagrove to Governor George Mathews, 26 May 1794, CILTT, 2:384–385, GDAH.

61. *Augusta Chronicle and Gazette of the State*, 8 March 1793; "A Copy of a Letter from the Governor to the Secretary of War," 19 August 1794, *ASPIA*, 1:495.

62. Murdoch, *The Georgia-Florida Frontier, 1793–1796*.

63. Thomas Houghton to Governor George Mathews, 20 May 1794, in Elijah Clark Collection (File 11), GDAH.

64. Ibid.

65. For more on family relations in the backcountry, see Gilmer, *Sketches of Some of the First Settlers of Upper Georgia, of the Cherokees, and the Author*.

66. Jonas Fauche to Governor George Mathews, 18 October 1794, CILTT, 2:418–419, GDAH.

67. Alex M. Hitz, "The Earliest Settlements in Wilkes County," *Georgia Historical Quarterly* 40, no. 3 (September 1956): 260–280. According to Hitz, the "Governors and the Council of the Province encouraged and sanctioned two settlements in the Indian lands some sixteen years" before the land cession of 1773. Among the men who received warrants for land were Gideon Chevers and Matthew Chevers, both of whom were free blacks. They each received one hundred acres in 1759 (260, 262).

68. U.S. Census, 1790.

69. Ibid., 1790, 1800.

70. Hays, *Hero of Hornet's Nest*, 57–58.

71. "An Act to Emancipate and set free Austin a mulatto, also Harry, a Negro fellow," 14 August 1786, vol. D, Enrolled Acts and Resolutions, House and Senate, Legislature, RG 37-1-15, GDAH; Marbury and Crawford, eds., *Digest of the laws of the state of Georgia*, 203–204; "Austin Dabney Petition for Land Grant for 250 acres of Washington County, Georgia" (1786), in Negroes, Box 1, GDAH; "In council 4th Feb. 1788, From Executive Council Journal, Jan. 7–Feb, 15, 1788," 56–59, in Austin Dabney File, GDAH; "Pension Statement of Austin Dabney, Free Person of Color from the National Archives and Records Service, Washington, D.C.," in Austin Dabney File, GDAH.

72. For admiring depictions of Austin Dabney by antebellum white Georgians, see Gilmer, *Sketches of Some of the First Settlers of Upper Georgia, of the Cherokees, and the Author*, 164–167; George White, *Historical Collections of Georgia*, 584–585. For an interpretation that stresses the role of whites in fomenting racial divisions between blacks and Indians in the colonial Southeast, see William S. Willis, "Divide and Rule: Red, White, and Black in the Southeast," *Journal of Negro History* 48, no. 3 (July 1963): 157–176. For an interesting examination of the origins of Indian racial attitudes toward blacks, see James M. Merrell, "The Racial Education of the Catawba Indians," *Journal of Southern History* 50, no. 3 (August 1984): 363–384.

73. Thomas Houghton to Governor George Mathews, 20 May 1794, in Elijah Clark Collection (File 11), GDAH.

74. *Georgia Gazette*, 4 September 1794.

75. *Augusta Chronicle and Gazette of the State*, 23 August 1794.

76. Ibid., 13 September 1794.

77. Ibid.

78. Ibid., 11 October 1794.

79. Ibid., 6 September 1794.

80. Ibid., 20 December 1794.

81. Ibid., 13 September 1794.

82. Ibid., 11 October 1794.

83. "Discharge of General Clarke by the Justices of Wilkes County," *ASPIA*, 1:496; Gilmer, *Sketches of Some of the First Settlers of Upper Georgia, of the Cherokees, and the Author*, 149; Elijah Clark to Committee of Safety, 5 September 1794, Elijah Clark Collection, GDAH; "Copy of a Letter from Elijah Clark to the Committee of Safety," *ASPIA*, 1:501.

84. Gilmer, *Sketches of Some of the First Settlers of Upper Georgia, of the Cherokees, and the Author*; Constant Freeman to the Secretary of War, 29 September 1794, *ASPIA*, 1:500.

85. Jonas Fauche to Governor George Mathews, 19 October 1794, CILTT, 2:418–419, GDAH.

86. Thomas Houghton to Governor George Mathews, 20 May 1794, in Elijah Clark Collection (File 11), GDAH.

87. Freeman Constant to Governor George Mathews, 1 January 1794, CILTT, 2:352–353, GDAH; Bird Tail King to Governor George Mathews, no date, CILTT, 2:354, GDAH.

88. Freeman Constant to Governor George Mathews, 10 May 1794, CILTT, 2:378, GDAH; Jared Irwin to Colonels Melton and Watts, Major Irwin, 4 July 1794, CILTT, 2:387, GDAH.

89. Elijah Clark to Major David Adams, 17 May 1794, CILTT, 2:380, GDAH.

90. Declaration of Charles Abercrombie et al., 11 June 1796 [listed as 1794 in other documents], CILTT, 2:478–479, GDAH.

91. Charles Abercrombie to President George Washington, no date, CILTT, 2:486–487, GDAH.

92. Louise Frederick Hays, "Chronology of Georgia, 1773–1800, particularly as related to Elijah Clark," GDAH; James Seagrove to Governor George Mathews, 26 May 1794, CILTT, 2:384–385, GDAH.

93. Elijah Clark to Jared Irwin, 24 September 1794, CILTT, 2:407, GDAH; Elijah Clark to Jared Irwin, 26 September 1794, CILTT, 2:408, GDAH; John Twiggs, 2 October 1794, CILTT, 2:411, GDAH.

94. Jared Irwin to Timothy Barnard, 3 October 1794, CILTT, 2:412, GDAH; Jonas Fauche to Governor George Mathews, 19 October 1794, CILTT, 2:418–419, GDAH.

95. Thomas Houghton to Governor George Mathews, 20 May 1794, in Elijah Clark Collection (File 11), GDAH.

96. Lieutenant Van Allen to Henry Gaither, 18 October 1793, CILTT, 1:343, GDAH.

97. Jared Irwin to Timothy Barnard, 3 October 1794, CILTT, 2:412, GDAH.

98. Jonas Fauche to Governor George Mathews, 19 October 1794, CILTT, 2:418–419, GDAH.

99. *Augusta Chronicle and Gazette of the State*, 13 February 1796. For lengthier treatments of the Yazoo controversy in Georgia, see Lamplugh, *Politics on the Periphery*; Samuel Guyton McLendon, *History of the Public Domain of Georgia* (Atlanta, 1924); Peter Magrath, *Yazoo: Law and Politics in the New Republic, the Case of Fletcher v. Peck* (Providence, 1966).

100. *Augusta Chronicle and Gazette of the State*, 26 September 1795.

101. Coleman, ed., *A History of Georgia*, 96.

102. For a comparison of remonstrances against the Yazoo sale, see "Presentments of the Grand Jury of Chatham County," *Augusta Chronicle and Gazette of the State*, 14 March 1795; "Presentments of the Grand Jury of Hancock County," *Augusta Chronicle and Gazette of the State*, 4 July 1795.

103. *Augusta Chronicle and Gazette of the State*, 13 February 1796; Gilmer, *Sketches of Some of the First Settlers of Upper Georgia, of the Cherokees, and the Author*, 154.

104. "Treaty Between the United States and his Catholic Majesty," *Augusta Chronicle and Gazette of the State*, 7 May 1796.

105. For more on the Treaty of Colerain, see Saunt, *A New Order of Things*, 192–195.

106. Jonas Fauche to Governor George Mathews, 19 October 1794, CILTT, 2:418–419, GDAH; Hawes, ed., "The Frontiers of Georgia in the Late Eighteenth Century," 90–94.

107. Juan Nepomuceno de Quesada to George Matthews, 8 October 1795, EFWF, GDAH; Juan Nepomuceno de Quesada to George Matthews, 12 October 1795, EFWF, GDAH; Murdoch, *The Georgia-Florida Frontier, 1793–1796*, 91–92.

108. Elijah Clark to Dr. McDonald, 9 December 1794, in Hays, "Chronology of Georgia, 1773–1800, particularly as related to Elijah Clark," chapter 22, GDAH.

109. *Augusta Chronicle and Gazette of the State*, 23 December 1797.

110. Ibid., 5 January 1799.

111. Jacob Kingsberry to Governor Milledge, 6 May 1803, CILTT, 3:672–673, GDAH.

112. Jared Irwin to Governor George Mathews, 2 October 1795, CILTT, 2:445, GDAH; H. Hampton to Governor George Mathews, 5 October 1795, CILTT, 2:446, GDAH; James Seagrove to Governor George Mathews, 2 October 1795, CILTT, 2:455, GDAH; Timothy Pickering to Governor Mathews, 12 November 1795, CILTT, 2:456–457, GDAH.

113. William Scarbrough Deposition, 9 January 1796, CILTT, 2:462–463, GDAH.

114. H. Hampton to Governor George Mathews, 5 October 1795, CILTT, 2:446, GDAH.

115. *Augusta Chronicle and Gazette of the State*, 5 March 1796.

116. James Seagrove to Governor Jared Irwin, 9 April 1796, CILTT, 2: 470–476.

117. *Augusta Chronicle and Gazette of the State*, 1 October 1796.

118. Ibid., 13 May 1797.

119. Coleman, ed., *A History of Georgia*, 97. For more on James Jackson's impact on politics in Georgia, see Lamplugh, *Politics on the Periphery*.

120. *Augusta Chronicle and Gazette of the State*, 21 December 1799.

121. Ibid., 20 January 1798.

122. Ibid., 6 January 1798, 20 January 1798, 31 March 1798, "Message of the Governor," 19 January 1799, "Presentments of the Grand Jury of Hancock County," 31 March 1799.

123. The new state constitution included the following provisions in Article I: Each county retained one senator and, depending on the population, one to four representatives to the House of Representatives. Each county with three thousand residents received two members, each county with seven thousand got three members, each county with twelve thousand residents received four members, but every county received at least one member. According to the new framework, Bullock and Byran counties each received one representative, Camden, Effingham, Franklin, Glynn, Jackson, Lincoln, McIntosh, Montgomery, and Scriven each received two, Burke, Columbia, Elbert, Greene, Jefferson, Liberty, Oglethorpe, Richmond, Warren, and Washington got three, and Chatham, Hancock, and Wilkes counties received four representatives apiece.

124. For more on the sale of the western land to the federal government, see McLendon, *History of the Public Domain of Georgia*; Lamplugh, *Politics on the Periphery*, especially chapter 9; Heath, *Constructive Liberalism*, 139–143.

125. Coulter, "Elijah Clark's Foreign Intrigues and the Trans-Oconee Republic"; Hays, *Hero of Hornet's Nest*; Murdoch, *The Georgia-Florida Frontier, 1793–1796*.

4. The State of Muskogee

1. William Bartram, *The Travels of William Bartram*, ed. Mark Van Doren (n.p., 1928), 182–184.

2. For more on the emergence of the Seminoles, see William C. Sturtevant, "Creek into Seminole," in *North American Indians in Historical Perspective*, ed. Eleanor Burke Leacock and Nancy Oestreich Lurie, 92–128 (New York, 1971); Saunt, *A New Order of Things*, 34–36; James A. Covington, *The Seminoles of Florida* (Gainesville, 1993), 12–17; Robbie Ethridge, *Creek Country: The Creek Indians and Their World* (Chapel Hill, 2003), 30; Christina Snyder, *Slavery in Indian Country: The Changing Face of Captivity in Early America* (Cambridge, Mass., 2010), 213–217; Kathryn E. Holland Braund, *Deerskins and Duffles: The Creek Indian Trade with Anglo-America, 1685–1815*, 2nd ed. (Lincoln, 2008), 7.

3. For more on the Creeks, see Ethridge, *Creek Country*; Saunt, *New Order of Things*; Braund, *Deerskins and Duffles*; Steve C. Hahn, *The Invention of the Creek Nation* (Lincoln, 2004); Michael D. Green, *The Politics of Indian Removal: Creek Government and Society in Crisis* (Lincoln, 1982); John R. Swanton, *Early History of the Creek Indians and*

Their Neighbors (Washington, D.C., 1922). For more on mestizo Creeks, see Frank, *Creeks and Southerners;* Theda Perdue, *"Mixed-Blood" Indians.*

4. Covington, *The Seminoles of Florida,* 12–25.

5. Saunt, *A New Order of Things,* 35–37.

6. For more on the emerging conflict among the Creeks see Saunt, *A New Order of Things,* 116. Saunt persuasively argues that the introduction of new notions of property ownership fundamentally altered Creek society. For studies that downplay the impact of consumerism among the Creeks see Ethridge, *Creek Country,* chapter 8, and Kathryn E. Holland Braund, *Deerskins and Duffels: The Creek Indian Trade with Anglo-America, 1685–1815* (Lincoln, 1993), 127–132.

7. For more on the agricultural economy of the Seminoles, see Brent Weisman, "The Plantation System of the Florida Seminole Indians and Black Seminoles during the Colonial Era," in *Colonial Plantations and Economy in Florida,* ed. Jane G. Landers (Gainesville, 2000). For a broader discussion of Creek agriculture and husbandry in the late eighteenth and early nineteenth centuries, see Ethridge, *Creek Country,* chapters 7 and 8.

8. For more on attitudes toward modernity in the Lower South, see Chaplin, *An Anxious Pursuit.*

9. Stephen Minor to Governor Gayoso, 5 August 1799, Lockey Papers, box 9, file 1799, August–October, P. K. Yonge Library, University of Florida (hereafter cited as PKY).

10. For more on the agricultural economy of the Seminoles, see Weisman, "The Plantation System of the Florida Seminole Indians and Black Seminoles during the Colonial Era."

11. Kenneth Wiggins Porter, "Negroes on the Southern Frontier, 1670–1763," *Journal of Negro History* 33, no. 1 (January 1948): 53–78; Peter H. Wood, *Black Majority: Negroes in Colonial South Carolina, from 1670 through the Stono Rebellion* (New York, 1974), 239–270.

12. Jane Landers, *Black Society in Spanish Florida* (Chicago, 1999), 79–81.

13. For more on runaways in the colonial era, see Wood, *Slavery in Colonial Georgia, 1730–1775,* chapter 10; Davis, *Fledgling Province,* 137.

14. William Bartram, *Travels of William Bartram,* 164–165, 182–184. For contemporary accounts of the relationships between native and black Seminoles and Creeks in the 1810s and 1820s, see Thomas S. Woodward, *Woodward's Reminiscences of the Creeks, or Muscogee Indians Contained in Letters to Friends in Georgia and Alabama* (Montgomery, 1859), 21, 33, 36, 41, 44, 77, 92–100, 106–112; William Hayne Simmons, *Notices of East Florida, with an Account of the Seminole Nation of Indians* (Charleston, 1822), 32–96. For historical treatments of these relationships, see Saunt, *A New Order of Things,* chapter 5; Wright, *Creeks and Seminoles,* chapter 3.

15. John Kinneard to [?], 25 May 1793, East Florida Papers, reel 43, PKY.

16. John Hambly to Lieutenant Colonel Howard, 8 May 1793, East Florida Papers, reel 43, PKY.

17. Wright, *Creeks and Seminoles*, 75–76; Saunt, *A New Order of Things*, 130–133.

18. Elijah Clark to Governor George Mathews, 13 April 1787, CILTT, 1:147–148; Jared Irwin to Governor George Mathews, 11 June 1787, CILTT, 1:156; James Robertson to John Sevier, 1 August 1787, CILTT, 1:157; Arthur Fort to George Mathews, 28 September 1787, CILTT, 1:160; Elijah Clark to Governor George Handley, 2 February 1788, CILTT, 1:164; Elijah Clark to Governor George Handley, 8 February 1788, CILTT, 1:166; Elijah Clark to Governor George Handley, 26 March 1788, CILTT, 1:166; Benjamin Lanier to Governor James Jackson [?], 14 February 1788, CILTT, 1:167; Israel Bird to Brigadier General James Jackson, 14 February 1788, CILTT, 1:168; John Crawford to Governor Jared Irwin, 3 March 1788, CILTT, 1:170; John Twiggs to Governor Jared Irwin, 4 March 1788, CILTT, 1:171; Jared Irwin to Governor George Handley, 6 March 1788, CILTT, 1:172; J. Meriwether to [?], 13 March 1788, CILTT, 1:173; Jared Irwin to Governor George Handley, 13 March 1788, CILTT, 1:174; John Berrien to Brigadier General James Jackson, 30 September 1788, CILTT, 1:185–186; Brigadier James Jackson to Governor George Handley, 3 October 1788, CILTT, 1:187–188. For more on the economic impact of the raids on the state's southern border, see file "Indian War, Glynn County, 1788" at GDAH and file "Liberty Co., Indian Depredations, 1788" at GDAH.

19. Alexander McGillivray to Richard Winn, 26 January 1789, CILTT, 1:193.

20. Snyder, *Slavery in Indian Country*, 214; Brent Richard Weisman, *Unconquered People: Florida's Seminoles and Miccosukee Indians* (Gainesville, 1999), 14–25.

21. J. Leitch Wright, *Creeks and Seminoles: The Destruction and Regeneration of the Muscogulge People* (Lincoln, 1986), 138–140.

22. Affidavit of David Shaw, 2 June 1792, CILTT, 1:247.

23. For more on the transformation of gender roles among the Creeks in the late eighteenth century, see Saunt, *A New Order of Things*, chapter 6.

24. General James Jackson to Governor Edward Telfair, 16 March 1793, CILTT, 1:271, GDAH; James Seagrove to Governor Edward Telfair, 17 March 1793, CILTT, 1:272–274, GDAH; J. Houston to Governor Edward Telfair, 18 March 1793, CILTT, 1:275, GDAH; William McIntosh to General James Jackson, 18 March 1793, CILTT, 1:276, GDAH; James Seagrove to Chief Payne, 14 April 1793, CILTT, 1:283, GDAH; General James Jackson to Governor Edward Telfair, 9 May 1793, CILTT, 1:309–310, GDAH; General James Jackson to Governor Edward Telfair, 27 May 1793, CILTT, 1:314–316, GDAH; John Kinneard to Cuseta King, Hollowing Tung [?], 25 May 1793, East Florida Papers, reel 43, PKY.

25. Timothy Barnard to [?], 2 July 1793, Joseph V. Bevan Collection. For other examples of Americans attesting to the "peaceful" intentions of the Cussetas, see Richard Call to Governor Edward Telfair, 29 April 1792, CILTT, 1:246, GDAH. The Cusseta chiefs made clear their desire for peace in letters to James Seagrove and the Mikasuki: "Cussatah King, Cussatah Warrior King, Opoy Mico, and Hollowing King" to James Seagrove, 5 October 1792, CILTT, 1:255–256, GDAH;

Cuseta King to "Burgess and the Headmen of the Simmeloneys," 9 June 1793, East Florida Papers, reel 43, PKY.

26. White Lieutenant to James Seagrove, 15 August 1792, CILTT, 1:254, GDAH; White Lieutenant to James Seagrove, 23 June 1793, Joseph V. Bevan Collection; James Seagrove to Secretary Henry Knox, 1 November 1794, Joseph V. Bevan Collection; "Cussatah King, Cussatah Warrior King, Opoy Mico, and Hollowing King" to James Seagrove, 5 October 1792, CILTT, 1:255–256, GDAH; John Kinnard to James Seagrove, 5 October 1792, CILTT, 1:257, GDAH; James Seagrove to Governor Edward Telfair, 5 October 1792, CILTT, 1:259, GDAH; Alex Cornels to James Seagrove, 14 June 1793, CILTT, 1:323–324, GDAH; "A Talk from the Mad Dog and Big Warrior of the Tuckabatches, in behalf of the Creek nation, to James Seagrove, Esq. Agent for Indian Affairs," 22 April 1795, and "An Extract of a Talk from the White Lieutenant, great Chief of the Oakfuskees, in behalf of the whole Creek Nation, to James Seagrove, Agent of Indian Affairs for the United States," 1 May 1795, in *Augusta Chronicle and Gazette of the State*, 30 May 1795. The differences between the approaches of Seagrove and Hawkins toward the Creeks created tensions soon after Hawkins assumed the post of Indian agent (Abner Hammond to Governor James Jackson, 8 November 1798, CILTT, 2:533–536, GDAH). In time, Hawkins managed to forge solid relationships with a number of chiefs. For examples of Creek headmen pledging to work with Benjamin Hawkins, see "Creek Chiefs" to Benjamin Hawkins, 25 November 1799, Joseph V. Bevan Collection. As mentioned, the headmen who made deals with the Americans faced opposition from their fellow Creeks as well as from white Georgians who attempted to incite conflict between the two nations. For some the results proved fatal. At the height of the violence in 1793, for example, soldiers and white settlers killed David Cornels, a trusted Creek translator, and three other Indian men as they traveled to meet James Seagrove to negotiate an end to the conflict. Cornels's killers targeted him specifically because of his efforts. The soldier assigned to accompany the Creek men to the meeting with Seagrove reportedly played a central role in the murders, informing troops stationed at Colerain of their route so that they could waylay the party. The incident proved sufficiently embarrassing to the authorities in Georgia to spur the prosecution of the soldiers. In the end, however, the local militia officers who oversaw the proceedings declared the men not guilty. William Johnston to Governor Edward Telfair, 30 June 1793, CILTT, 1:326, GDAH; Timothy Barnard to James Seagrove, 3 July 1793, CILTT, 1:326, GDAH; Jacob Townsend to General James Jackson, 1 July 1793, CILTT, 1:327, GDAH; General James Jackson to Governor Edward Telfair, 8 July 1793, CILTT, 1:329–330, GDAH; affidavit of James Kirby, 22 July 1793, CILTT, 1:338–339, GDAH; Untitled (Opinion of Court of Inquiry), 23 October 1793, CILTT, 1:345–348, GDAH.

27. "A Talk from James Seagrove," *Augusta Chronicle and Gazette of the State*, 21 May 1796.

28. *ASPIA*, 1:603–610.

29. The "failure" of the treaty prompted accusations and recriminations from white Georgians and the commissioners appointed to negotiate with the Creeks. For examples, see *Augusta Chronicle and Gazette of the State*, 23 July 1796, 16 July 1796, 27 August 1796, 3 September 1796, 24 September 1796, 10 December 1796.

30. William Johnston to Governor Edward Telfair, 30 June 1793, CILTT, 1:326, GDAH; Timothy Barnard to James Seagrove, 3 July 1793, CILTT, 1:326, GDAH; Jacob Townsend to General James Jackson, 1 July 1793, CILTT, 1:327, GDAH; General James Jackson to Governor Edward Telfair, 8 July 1793, CILTT, 1:329–330, GDAH; Affidavit of James Kirby, 22 July 1793, CILTT, 1:338–339, GDAH; Untitled (Opinion of Court of Inquiry), 23 October 1793, CILTT, 1:345–348, GDAH.

31. Here I am not suggesting that the organization of the national council represented a completely new political concept to the Creek Indians. As other scholars have pointed out, chiefs from the Creek Confederacy had met on occasion before Hawkins's appointment as Indian agent, a process that Alexander McGillivray tried to harness in his attempts to centralize authority (or claims to authority). I do, however, agree with Claudio Saunt, who argues that the national council's actions, particularly its claims to speak for all Creeks and its use of coercive tactics, signified a departure from the political and legal systems that preceded it (*A New Order of Things*, 179–183). For interpretations of the national council that stress continuity with earlier forms of political organization, see Ethridge, *Creek Country*, 105–107; Green, *The Politics of Indian Removal*, 33–38; Hahn, *The Invention of the Creek Nation*, 275–276.

32. Saunt, *A New Order of Things*, 216–219.

33. Benjamin Hawkins, "Sketch of the Creek Country," in *The Collected Works of Benjamin Hawkins, 1796–1810*, ed. H. Thomas Foster II, 67s-68s (Tuscaloosa, 2003); Benjamin Hawkins to Secretary of War, 6 January 1797, "Letters of Benjamin Hawkins" in Foster, ed., *The Collected Works of Benjamin Hawkins, 1796–1810*, 57–58. For more on Benjamin Hawkins, see Henri Florette, *The Southern Indians and Benjamin Hawkins, 1796–1816* (Norman, 1986).

34. For more on the civilizing plan, see Bernard W. Sheehan, *Seeds of Extinction: Jefferson Philanthropy and the American Indian* (Chapel Hill, 1973), 119–181; Anthony F. C. Wallace, *Jefferson and the Indians: The Tragic Fate of the First Americans* (Cambridge, Mass., 1999), 160–240; William G. McLoughlin, *Cherokee Renaissance in the New Republic* (Princeton, 1986), 34–40; Ethridge, *Creek Country*, 13–16, 18, 148–149; Florette, *The Southern Indians and Benjamin Hawkins, 1796–1816*, chapter 4.

35. "Letters of Benjamin Hawkins," in Foster, ed., *The Collected Works of Benjamin Hawkins, 1796–1810*, 314–315.

36. Ibid., 321.

37. "Efau Haujo, of Tuckabatchee, to his friends, the Sinanolees," 2 August 1798, "Letters of Benjamin Hawkins," in Foster, ed., *The Collected Works of Benjamin Hawkins, 1796–1810*, 492–494.

38. *New York Spectator,* 10 July 1799, in Florida Newspaper Collection, University of Florida Digital Library Center, http://fulltextt6.fcla.edu/cgi/t/text/text-idx?c=flnp;idno=UF00002333;sid=0a29cebc0174dc27a245d7570c8968ec;cc=flnp;view=header;subtype=citation (accessed 1 May 2007).

39. Stephen Minor to Governor Gayoso, 5 August 1799, Lockey Papers, box 9, file 1799, August–October, PKY; Report of Stephen Minor and Andrew Ellicott on Northern Boundary Line, 8 April 1800, Lockey Papers, box 9, file 1800, January–April, PKY.

40. Dan McGillivray to William Panton, 9 October 1799, Cruzat Papers, box 1, folder 1799, PKY.

41. Report of Tustunnue Haujo and Robert Walton to Benjamin Hawkins, 4 November 1799, Joseph V. Bevan Collection; Benjamin Hawkins to William Panton, 9 October 1799 [date appears mislabeled], Cruzat Papers, box 1, folder 1799, PKY; Hawkins, "Sketch of the Creek Country," in Foster, ed., *The Collected Works of Benjamin Hawkins, 1796–1810,* 67s-68s. For other accounts of this incident, see Wright, *Creeks and Seminoles,* 150–151; James A. Covington, *The Seminoles of Florida* (Gainesville, 1993), 22–23; Saunt, *A New Order of Things,* 181–183.

42. William Augustus Bowles, *Authentic Memoirs of William Augustus Bowles, Esquire, Ambassador from the United Nations of Creeks and Cherokees to the Court of London* (London, 1791); *Life of General W. A. Bowles: A Native of America—Born of English Parents, in Frederic County, Maryland, in the Year 1764* (London, 1803); Alexander Stephens, *Public Characters of 1801–1802* (London, 1804), 4:117–154; Laurence Kinnaird, "The Significance of William Bowles' Seizure of Panton's Apalachee Store in 1792," *Florida Historical Quarterly* 9 (January 1931): 156–192; Duvon C. Corbitt and John Tate Lanning, "A Letter of Marque Issued by William Augustus Bowles as Director General of the State of Muskogee," *Journal of Southern History* 11 (May 1945): 246–261; Elisha Douglass, "The Adventurer Bowles," *William and Mary Quarterly,* 3rd series, 6, no. 1 (January 1949): 3–23; Lyle N. McAlister, "William Augustus Bowles and the State of Muskogee," *Florida Historical Quarterly* 40 (April 1962): 317–328; J. Leitch Wright Jr., *William Augustus Bowles, Director General of the Creek Nation* (Athens, 1967). Wright's biography remains the best and most comprehensive account of Bowles's life.

43. "Declaration of T. H. Fergusson," 16 June 1800, Greenslade Papers, box 1, folder 1800–01, PKY.

44. Stephens, *Public Characters of 1801–1802,* 4:117–154.

45. Thomas Forbes to William Panton, 25 August 1799, Cruzat Papers, box 1, folder 1799, PKY.

46. T. Forbes to Panton, 25 August 1799, Cruzat Papers, box 1, folder 1799, PKY.

47. For example, see Kinnaird, "The Significance of William Bowles' Seizure of Panton's Apalachee Store in 1792," 156–192; Corbitt and Lanning, "A Letter of Marque Issued by William Augustus Bowles as Director General of the State

of Muskogee," 246–261; Douglass, "The Adventurer Bowles," 2–23; McAlister, "William Augustus Bowles and the State of Muskogee," 317–328.

48. For example, Michael D. Green describes Bowles as "an adventurer" whose chief interest among the Creeks was personal enrichment (*The Politics of Indian Removal*, 35). Claudio Saunt, too, labels Bowles an "adventurer," though he does acknowledge that Bowles "did a better job than Alex McGillivray," a mestizo Creek chief and rival of Bowles, "in shedding his European American heritage and adopting the dress and lifeways of the Creeks" (*A New Order of Things*, 86). In *McIntosh and Weatherford, Creek Indian Leaders* (Tuscaloosa, 1988), Benjamin W. Griffith Jr. describes Bowles as "bizarre" (48). More recently, in *Slavery in Indian Country: The Changing Face of Captivity in Early America* (Cambridge, 2010), Christina Snyder charges that Bowles was a "pompous and often delusional fellow" (220).

49. *ASPIA*, 1:677.

50. Payne Mico to Governor White, 5 June 1802, East Florida Papers, reel 43, PKY.

51. Richard Lang to Governor James Jackson, 26 June 1800, EFWF, 119, GDAH; John King to Governor James Jackson, 12 July 1800, EFWF, 127–128, GDAH; Thomas King to Governor James Jackson, 29 October 1800, EFWF, 135–137, GDAH; Wright, *Creeks and Seminoles*, 73–100; Saunt, *A New Order of Things*, 111–135.

52. Governor James Jackson to the Chehaw Chief, 5 March 1799, CILTT, vol. 3, GDAH.

53. Andrew Walthour to Governor Irwin, 30 December 1806, CILTT, vol. 3, GDAH. For more examples of runaways fleeing from Georgia to Florida, see Jared Irwin to Governor of East Florida, 21 January 1797, East Florida Papers, reel 42, PKY; [untitled document listing forty-three Georgia slaves who fled to East Florida since 1790], 9 May 1797, East Florida Papers, reel 42, PKY; James Seagrove to Henry White, 13 May 1797, East Florida Papers, reel 42, PKY; letter from "A. Planter," dated 24 June 1800, in *Augusta Chronicle and Gazette of the State*, 12 July 1800. The flow of runaways across the Georgia-Florida border was not unidirectional, however. Some slaves held in bondage in Florida sought freedom or hoped to improve their conditions by escaping to Georgia. For examples of slaves fleeing from Spanish Florida to Georgia, see Pallinear [?] to Henry White, 13 May 1797, East Florida Papers, reel 42, PKY; Thomas King to Henry White, 19 October 1797, East Florida Papers, reel 42, PKY; Thomas King to Henry White, 26 October 1797, East Florida Papers, reel 43, PKY.

54. Saunt, *A New Order of Things*, 207–212.

55. For example, see Wright, *William Augustus Bowles*, chapters 8 and 9.

56. "Declaration of T. H. Fergusson," 16 June 1800, Greenslade Papers, box 1, folder 1800–01, PKY; Joseph Hunter to William Augustus Bowles, 5 March 1800, Greenslade Papers, box 1, folder 1800–01, PKY. Edward Forrester claimed that Bowles returned to the Southeast in 1799 with a "good deal of powder &

ball" as well as "75 to 100 white troops of different nations" (Edward Forrester to William Panton, 6 October 1799, Cruzat Papers, box 1, folder 1799, PKY). Thomas King to Governor James Jackson, 29 October 1800, EFWF, 135–137, GDAH.

57. A Talk from the Chiefs of the Creek Nation to the Governor General at New Orleans, 5 October 1802, Lockey Papers, box 9, file 1802, September–December, PKY. Bowles's recruiting efforts apparently bore fruit, prompting Thomas King to complain that "sevl. of the young men" from Camden County "have been led astray by their talks" (Thomas King to Governor James Jackson, 29 October 1800, EFWF, 135–137, GDAH).

58. Governor James Jackson, "A Proclamation," *Augusta Chronicle and Gazette of the State*, 19 July 1800.

59. John King to Governor James Jackson, 12 July 1800, EFWF, 127–128, GDAH; Thomas King to Governor James Jackson, 15 October 1800, EFWF, 130–131, GDAH; William Jones to William A. Bowles, 17 August 1800, EFWF, 132–133, GDAH; Thomas King to Governor James Jackson, 29 October 1800, EFWF, 135–137, GDAH.

60. Murdoch, *The Georgia-Florida Frontier, 1793–1796*; Hoffman, *Florida's Frontiers*, 230–252. Many of these same men were involved in a plot in 1795 to depose the Spanish authorities in Florida. Lieutenant Henry Gaither to Governor George Mathews, 20 August 1795, EFWF, 88, GDAH; Lieutenant Henry Gaither to Governor George Mathews, 29 September 1795, EFWF, 89, GDAH; Manuel Rengitte to Juan Nepomuceno de Quesada, John King, and John Burrowes, 3 October 1795, EFWF, 90, GDAH; Juan Nepomuceno de Quesada to Governor George Mathews, 8 October 1795, EFWF, 91–92, GDAH; Juan Nepomuceno de Quesada to Governor George Mathews, 12 October 1795, EFWF, 97, GDAH; Jonas Fauche to Governor George Mathews, 14 October 1795, EFWF, 99, GDAH.

61. "Proclamation Addressed to Richard Lang from William A. Bowles," 5 June 1800, Joseph V. Bevan Collection. The Georgia-Florida border became a hotbed of intrigue in 1800 as the Spanish and American authorities competed with the leaders of the State of Muskogee for the loyalty of the residents of the region. Richard Lang played a central role in the machinations. Richard Lang to William A. Bowles, 17 August 1800, Joseph V. Bevan Collection; Governor James Jackson to Acting Secretary of State Charles Lee, 12 July 1800, EFWF, 116, GDAH; Richard Lang to Governor James Jackson, 26 June 1800, EFWF, 119, GDAH; affidavit of Richard Lang, 26 June 1800, EFWF, 121, GDAH; Thomas King to Governor James Jackson, 15 October 1800, EFWF, 130–131, GDAH; William Jones to William A. Bowles, 17 August 1800, EFWF, 132–133, GDAH; Thomas King to Governor James Jackson, 29 October 1800, EFWF, 135–137, GDAH.

62. We might assume that Bowles was the mastermind behind the citizenship policies of the State of Muskogee, as he assumed such a prominent position.

But Bowles acted as an intermediary and so was necessarily prominent. He was in all likelihood acting with the approval, even perhaps upon the instructions, of Kenighe and other Mikasuki chiefs. For a nuanced portrait of Indian-white power relations in the colonial era, see Kathleen DuVal, *The Native Ground: Indians and Colonists in the Heart of the Continent* (Philadelphia, 2006).

63. Letter from "A. Planter," dated 24 June 1800, *Augusta Chronicle and Gazette of the State,* 12 July 1800; *Augusta Chronicle and Gazette of the State,* 8 November 1800; Thomas King to Governor James Jackson, 29 October 1800, EFWF, 135–137, GDAH.

64. Green, *The Politics of Indian Removal,* 34–35.

65. William Augustus Bowles to Governor José De Ezpeleta, 21 August 1789, Lockey Papers, box 7, file 1789, April, PKY; William Augustus Bowles to Governor Vicente Manuel De Zéspedes, Lockey Papers, 21 August 1789, box 7, file 1789, April, PKY; Daniel McGillivray to William Panton, 9 October 1799, Cruzat Papers, box 1, folder 1799, PKY; Florette, *The Southern Indians and Benjamin Hawkins, 1796–1816,* 132–134.

66. For Alexander McGillivray the connection between access to trade and power was clear. He asserted that Georgians wanted land cessions from the Creek Indians both to extend their control over the region and to "force our trade from its present channel the Floridas into their own hands which will at once make them our dictators in all matters." Of course, as a partner in the trading firm Panton, Leslie, and Company, McGillivray had an obvious conflict of interest. Alexander McGillivray to Estevan Miró, 24 June 1789, Lockey Papers, box 7, file 1789, May–July, PKY.

67. For example, the Spanish authorities temporarily halted the flow of goods to the Creeks and Seminoles in 1788 in an effort to thwart the Indians' offensive against Georgia's southern frontier. Although nominally their allies, the Spanish feared the growing power of the Indian confederacy. In addition, the Spanish hoped to improve relations with the Americans. When Bowles returned to the Southeast in 1799, the Spanish once again cut off the supply of trade goods to the Seminoles in an effort to compel them to turn him over. Even those who did not support Bowles appear to have been affected. James Burgess to William Augustus Bowles, 14 February 1800, Lockey Papers, box 9, file 1800, January–April, PKY; White to Prince Payne, Cholackochully, Opia, and other Chiefs of the Seminole Indians, 18 July 1800, East Florida Papers, reel 43, PKY; Vincente Folch to Andrew Ellicott, no date, 1800, Lockey Papers, box 9, file 1800, July–December, PKY

68. Florette, *The Southern Indians and Benjamin Hawkins, 1796–1816,* chapter 4.

69. The Spanish authorities demonstrated their resolve to prevent nonsanctioned trade with the Florida Indians in 1800 when they burned a trading post erected by the Muskogees and blockaded the river leading to the Mikasuki towns. Vincente Folch to Andrew Ellicott, no date, 1800, Lockey Papers, box 9,

file 1800, July–December, PKY; "Bowles's Proclamation of War," 5 April 1800, Lockey Papers, box 9, file 1800, January–April, PKY.

70. Saunt, *A New Order of Things*, 141.

71. Bartram, *Travels of William Bartram*, 182–184, 96. For more on the economic activities of the Seminoles, see Weisman, "The Plantation System of the Florida Seminole Indians and Black Seminoles during the Colonial Era"; Braund, *Deerskins and Duffels*; Wright, *Creeks and Seminoles*, chapter 2.

72. John Forrester to Governor White, 19 April 1801, East Florida Papers, reel 43, PKY.

73. Alex Walker to William Augustus Bowles, 8 July 1801, Lockey Papers, box 9, file 1800, May–December, PKY.

74. Peter Linebaugh and Marcus Rediker, *The Many-Headed Hydra: Sailors, Slaves, Commoners, and the Hidden History of the Revolutionary Atlantic* (Boston, 2000).

75. James Burgess to William Augustus Bowles, 14 February 1800, Lockey Papers, box 9, file 1800, January–April, PKY; John Forrester to Governor of Florida, 21 June 1800, East Florida Papers, reel 43, PKY; White to Prince Payne, Cholackochully, Opia, and other Chiefs of the Seminole Indians, 18 July 1800, East Florida Papers, reel 43, PKY; Edward Forrester to William Panton, 3 August 1800, Cruzat Papers, box 1, folder 1800, PKY.

76. Vincente Folch to Benjamin Hawkins, 8 December 1799, Lockey Papers, box 9, file 1799, November–December, PKY.

77. "Bowles's Proclamation of War," 5 April 1800, Lockey Papers, box 9, file 1800, January–April, PKY; William Augustus Bowles to Commandant of St. Marks, 17 April 1800, Lockey Papers, box 9, file 1800, January–April, PKY; *Augusta Chronicle and Gazette of the State*, 5 April 1800.

78. "Bowles's Proclamation of War," 5 April 1800, Lockey Papers, box 9, file 1800, January–April, PKY; William Bowles to Governor James Jackson, 6 June 1800, Joseph V. Bevan Collection.

79. William Bowles to Tostonee Opoie, 22 May 1800, CILTT, 3:587, GDAH; William Bowles to Governor James Jackson, 6 June 1800, CILTT, 3:590, GDAH; William Bowles to Richard Lang, 5 June 1800, Joseph V. Bevan Collection; Benjamin Hawkins to Governor James Jackson, 14 May 1800, Joseph V. Bevan Collection; Benjamin Hawkins to Governor James Jackson, 12 June 1800, Joseph V. Bevan Collection; Saunt, *A New Order of Things*, 208.

80. John Forrester to William Panton, 3 August 1800, Cruzat Papers, box 1, folder 1800, PKY; Benjamin Hawkins to Governor James Jackson, 18 July 1800, Joseph V. Bevan Collection; John Forrester to [Governor of East Florida], 16 July 1800, East Florida Papers, reel 43, PKY.

81. William Bowles to Richard Lang, 5 June 1800, Joseph V. Bevan Collection; Joseph Hunter to William Bowles, 5 March 1800, Greenslade Papers, box 1, folder 1800–1801, PKY; William Augustus Bowles to Vizente Folch, 2 July 1800, Lockey Papers, box 9, file 1800, July–December, PKY.

82. Daniel McGillivray to William Panton, 22 May 1800, Greenslade Papers, box 1, folder 1800–1801, PKY; John Forrester to [Governor of East Florida], 17 June 1800, East Florida Papers, reel 43, PKY; John Forrester to [Governor of East Florida], 21 June 1800, East Florida Papers, reel 43, PKY.

83. Benjamin Hawkins to William Panton, 11 June 1800, Cruzat Papers, box 1, folder 1800, PKY.

84. Letter from "A. Planter," dated 24 June 1800, in *Augusta Chronicle and Gazette of the State*, 12 July 1800. For other examples of slaves fleeing with the raiders, see John Forrester to [Governor of East Florida], 16 July 1800, East Florida Papers, reel 43, PKY; White to Prince Payne, Cholackochully, Opia, and other Chiefs of the Seminole Indians, 18 July 1800, East Florida Papers, reel 43, PKY; John King to Governor James Jackson, 12 July 1800, EFWF, 127–128, GDAH.

85. *Augusta Chronicle and Gazette of the State*, 20 February 1802.

86. Wright, *William Augustus Bowles*, 145–146.

87. Proceedings in the Court of Admiralty of the Bahama Islands, 31 March–29 May 1802, Cruzat Papers, box 1, folder 1802, PKY.

88. John Forbes to Governor Halkett, 6 March 1802, Cruzat Papers, box 1, folder 1802, PKY.

89. One of the captains in the State of Muskogee Navy was a man named John Gibson (referred to as "Gipson" by Wright). According to J. Hacket, Gibson was "one of the chief and most atrocious" pirates in the Muskogee Navy. His exploits, which included the seizure of several ships as well as "a most savage murder," made him a wanted man. The authorities in the Bahamas, where several other Muskogee sailors were convicted of piracy and executed, appealed to the governor of Georgia in November 1802 to locate the man since he was rumored to be staying in Savannah. The physical description of Gibson provided by Hackett suggests that he was possibly a person of African descent, though it is far from certain. According to Hackett, Gibson was a "stout looking man between thirty and forty years of age description—of a Brown complexion." He was believed to be in the company of a "yellow Colored Negro" who was likewise "a notorious Rogue." J. Hackett to Governor of Georgia, 20 November 1802, Lockey Papers, box 9, file 1802, September–December, PKY; "Marine Articles of War," ca. 1 April 1801, Lockey Papers, box 9, file 1801, January–April, PKY; John B. Delacy to William Augustus Bowles, 1 February 1802, Lockey Papers, box 9, file 1802, January–March, PKY; commission drafted by William Augustus Bowles, 1 February 1802, Lockey Papers, box 9, file 1802, January–March, PKY; John D. Delacy to William Augustus Bowles, 10 March 1802, Lockey Papers, box 9, file 1802, January–March, PKY; petition of John Booth and Freeman Johnson, 11 March 1802, Lockey Papers, box 9, file 1802, January–March, PKY.

90. John Forrester to Governor White, 19 April 1801, East Florida Papers, reel 43, PKY.

91. Payne Mico to Governor White, 5 June 1802, East Florida Papers, reel 43,

PKY; Governor White to John Kinnard and All Other Chiefs of the Creek Nation, 14 July 1802, East Florida Papers, reel 43, PKY; Dubreuil, "Report of Creek-Spanish Treaty (August 20)," 7 September 1802, Cruzat Papers, box 1, folder 1802, PKY. According to the report, Kenighe accompanied the other Seminole and Lower Creek chiefs to meet with the Spanish authorities in August 1802. While there, he and the other chiefs negotiated a peace. As part of the agreement, Kenighe was required to turn over slaves seized in raids and to disavow William Bowles. Dubreuil reported that Kenighe agreed to the terms "fully." Yet, in the wake of the meeting, Kenighe continued to meet with Bowles, which suggests that the Mikasuki chief may not have agreed with the principles adopted during the meeting.

92. Benjamin Hawkins to Secretary of War, 8 May 1802, "Letters of Benjamin Hawkins," in Foster, ed., The Collected Works of Benjamin Hawkins, 1796–1810, 418; "Talk of William Augustus Bowles to the Seminoles," ca. 1 January 1802, Lockey Papers, box 9, file 1802, January–March, PKY.

93. "Governor James Jackson's Proclamation," Augusta Chronicle and Gazette of the State, 19 July 1800.

94. Benjamin Hawkins to Secretary of War, 8 May 1802, "Letters of Benjamin Hawkins," in Foster, ed., The Collected Works of Benjamin Hawkins, 1796–1810, 418.

95. Florette, The Southern Indians and Benjamin Hawkins, 1796–1816, chapter 9.

96. "Extract of a Letter from a Gentleman, Fort Wilkinson," Connecticut Gazette and the Commercial Intelligencer, 9 September 1801, University of Florida Digital Library Center.

97. Commissioners Wilkinson and Hawkins noted that there were divisions among the chiefs attending the negotiations over whether they had a right to cede the Tallassee land because "the affected tribes, who reside low down on the Flint and Chattahoochee, and had declined attending the conference . . . might be incensed, and, out of revenge, would attack the frontier, and spill blood, in order to involve the nation in misfortunes." Consequently, they "entreated of us not to press them on this point." (James Wilkinson and Benjamin Hawkins to Secretary Henry Dearborn, 15 July 1802, ASPIA, 1:670.)

98. ASPIA, 1:678–679.

99. Ibid., 1:669. See Article 1 for an explanation of land cession.

100. "Efau Haujo to the Seminoles," ASPIA, 1:680.

101. According the commissioners, it was not only the Seminoles whom the chiefs feared. The chiefs were apprehensive about ceding the land on the Oconee as well because they worried that "their young warriors" would join "the partisans of Bowles, divide the nation, wrest the government from those who at present administer it, and, by some hasty and impudent act, involve their country in ruin." (James Wilkinson, Benjamin Hawkins, and Andrew Pickens to Secretary Henry Dearborn, 17 June 1802, ASPIA, 1:680.)

102. Talk of the Chiefs of the Creek Nation, 25 November 1799, Joseph V. Be-

van Collection. Also listed as "Indian Talk to Governor of Pensacola and Panton," in Greenslade Papers, box 1, folder 1799, PKY, under the same date.

103. James Burgess to William Augustus Bowles, 3 July 1801, Lockey Papers, box 9, file 1801, May–December, PKY; James Burgess to William Augustus Bowles, 17 July 1801, Lockey Papers, box 9, file 1801, May–December, PKY.

104. "Proclamation," 31 October 1799, Joseph V. Bevan Collection.

105. William A. Bowles to Cowoppe, 30 November 1799, Joseph V. Bevan Collection.

106. *Augusta Chronicle and Gazette of the State*, 25 June 1803.

107. William Augustus Bowles to the Commandant at St. Marks, 15 January 1802, Lockey Papers, box 9, file 1802, January–March, PKY; William Augustus Bowles to Commandant at St. Marks, 14 January 1802, Lockey Papers, box 9, file 1802, January–March, PKY; William A. Bowles to Jacob Dubreuil, 23 January 1802, Lockey Papers, box 9, file 1802, January–March, PKY; James Durouzeaux to Vincente Folch, 2 May 1802, Lockey Papers, box 9, file 1802, April–June, PKY; Wright, *William Augustus Bowles*, 152–153.

108. John D. Delacy to William Augustus Bowles, 12 March 1802, Lockey Papers, box 9, file 1802, January–March, PKY.

109. For example, see the transcript of the *Nassau Gazette*, 4 March 1802 (listed as 1802), "Article on conditions in 'State of Muscogee' presented for publication in the *Nassau Gazette*," in Cruzat Papers, box 1, folder 1802, PKY; John D. Delacy to William Augustus Bowles, 12 March 1802, Lockey Papers, box 9, file 1802, January–March, PKY.

110. Proceedings in the Court of Admiralty of the Bahama Islands, 31 March–29 May 1802, Cruzat Papers, box 1, folder 1802, PKY; John D. Delacy to William Augustus Bowles, 1 February 1802, Lockey Papers, box 9, file 1802, January–March, PKY; John D. Delacy to William Augustus Bowles, 10 March 1802, Lockey Papers, box 9, file 1802, January–March, PKY; petition of John Booth and Freeman Johnson, 11 March 1802, Lockey Papers, box 9, file 1802, January–March, PKY; John Booth and Freeman to William Augustus Bowles, 1 May 1802, Lockey Papers, box 9, file 1802, April–June, PKY.

111. Proceedings in the Court of Admiralty of the Bahama Islands, 31 March–29 May 1802, Cruzat Papers, box 1, folder 1802, PKY.

5. Borders of Freedom

1. *Savannah Republican*, 27 February 1812, 28 March 1812, 9 April 1812, 23 May 1812, 2 June 1812.

2. In recent years, the Georgia-Florida border has been the focus of several excellent studies. These include Claudio Saunt's *A New Order of Things* and Jane Landers's *Black Society in Spanish Florida*. Along with Kenneth W. Porter's work, Saunt's and Lander's scholarship has greatly increased our understanding of life

in the Southeast and interactions among the various people who inhabited the region. Saunt examines these disputes from Indians' perspectives. Landers explores the conflicts from the Spanish perspective. Few scholars explore the perspective of Georgians, both black and white. For an exception, see Rothman, *Slave Country*.

3. Eugene D. Genovese, *Roll, Jordan, Roll: The World the Slaves Made* (New York, 1974), 587–598. Genovese elaborated on his arguments in *From Rebellion to Revolution: Afro-American Slave Revolts in the Making of the Modern World* (Baton Rouge, 1979), which analyzed the history of slave insurrections throughout the Americas. For another study of slave insurrections in the United States, see the pioneering work of Aptheker, *American Negro Slave Revolts*.

4. "Trade in Negroes," *Niles' Register*, 12:323. The *Niles' Register* was also called the *Niles' Weekly Register* and the *Weekly Register*, but all versions of this newspaper are commonly referred to as the *Niles' Register*, so I have used that title throughout.

5. Chapter 3 discusses in greater detail George Mathews's terms as executive of the state and his tense relationship with Elijah Clark.

6. I use the term "Anglo-Floridian" to refer to white loyalists who fled from Georgia to Florida during the American Revolution and opted to remain there after the war. The group was joined by other Georgian émigrés (and their slaves) after the Spanish authorities relaxed restrictions on land ownership in 1790. For more on the change in land policy, see Landers, *Black Society in Spanish Florida*, 74–75. For more on the exodus of Georgia loyalists to Florida, see Hall, *Land and Allegiance in Revolutionary Georgia*, chapter 7.

7. Rembert W. Patrick, *Florida Fiasco: Rampant Rebels on the Georgia-Florida Border, 1810–1815* (Athens, 1954), 40–54.

8. *Savannah Republican*, 26 March 1812, 2 April 1812, 9 April 1812.

9. For more on the effects of the raids conducted by British forces under Oglethorpe and their Indian allies on Fort Mose, see Landers, *Black Society in Spanish Florida*, 37–53.

10. *Savannah Republican*, 23 April 1812, 28 April 1812, 30 April 1812.

11. For more on the status of blacks in Florida, see Landers, *Black Society in Spanish Florida*.

12. *Niles' Register*, 3:21–22.

13. Patrick, *Florida Fiasco*, 162–163.

14. *Savannah Republican*, 23 April 1812, 21 May 1812.

15. "Constitution of East Florida," in EFWF, 204–212, GDAH.

16. Saunt, *A New Order of Things*, 240.

17. Quoted in Patrick, *Florida Fiasco*, 155 (dated 30 July 1812), and in Kenneth Wiggins Porter, "Negroes and the East Florida Annexation Plot," *Journal of Negro History* 30, no. 1 (January 1945): 24 (dated 24 January 1813).

18. Governor David B. Mitchell to Secretary of War Monroe, 12 July 1812, as quoted in Landers, *Black Society in Spanish Florida*, 222.

19. *Savannah Republican*, August 6, 1812; Benjamin Hawkins to Deputation from

Kenhegee and Paine, 5 December 1812, in Benjamin Hawkins, *Letters, Journals, and Writings of Benjamin Hawkins*, vol. 2, 1802–1816 (Savannah, 1980), 623 (hereafter cited as *LJWBH*).

20. *Niles' Register*, 3:311.

21. Saunt, *A New Order of Things*, 238.

22. General John Floyd to William H. Crawford, 26 March 1812, quoted in Patrick, *Florida Fiasco*, 109–110.

23. Patrick, *Florida Fiasco*, 185–194.

24. In addition to attacking the American troops, warriors raided plantations for potential recruits. See Abraham Bessert to Governor David Mitchell, 15 August, 1812, CILTT, 3:757–758, GDAH; William Kinnear to Mother and Brother, [n.d.], reel 42, East Florida Papers, PKY; T. Frederick Davis, ed., "United States Troops in Spanish East Florida, 1812–1813, Part 2," *Florida Historical Society Quarterly* 9, no. 2 (October 1930): 110–111.

25. *Savannah Republican*, 24 September 1812, 10 October 1812; Porter, "Negroes and the East Florida Annexation Plot," 20–21. For more on the combat between the Seminoles and American troops, see Thomas Smith's correspondence in T. Frederick Davis, ed., "United States Troops in Spanish East Florida, 1812–1813, Part 3," *Florida Historical Society Quarterly* 9, no. 3 (January 1931): 135–155; Davis, ed., "United States Troops in Spanish East Florida, 1812–1813, Part 2," 96–116.

26. *Niles' Register*, 3:171; "Newnan's Expedition," *Niles' Register*, 3:235–237; *Savannah Republican*, 8 October 1812; Porter, "Negroes and the East Florida Annexation Plot," 21–24.

27. "Newnan's Expedition," *Niles' Register*, 3:235–237; *Niles' Register*, 3:171; *Savannah Republican*, 8 October 1812, 20 October 1812; Governor Mitchell to James Monroe, 19 September 1812, as quoted in Saunt, *A New Order of Things*, 245.

28. D. B. Mitchell to James Monroe, 13 October 1812, quoted in Saunt, *A New Order of Things*, 245.

29. "Message of the Gov. of Georgia," *Niles' Register*, 3:193–195; *Niles' Register*, 3:259–260.

30. *Savannah Republican*, 2 March 1813, 4 March 1813.

31. *Niles' Register*, 4:48, 67; *Savannah Republican*, 2 March 1813, 4 March 1813.

32. *Niles' Register*, 4:127.

33. William Ashley to Governor David Mitchell, 11 June 1813, contained in EFWF, 218, GDAH. See also affidavits by Abner Broadway, James Black, and James Hall, EFWF, 220–223, GDAH.

34. Ibid.

35. Major Francis Hopkins to Peter Early, 14 December 1813, contained in EFWF, 236, GDAH. The document includes affidavits by James Nephew and William A. Dunham.

36. *Columbia Museum and Savannah Advertiser*, 3 March 1814.

37. For more on the split among the Creeks during the civil war, see Claudio

Saunt, *A New Order of Things*, chapter 11; Ross Hassig, "International Conflict in the Creek War of 1813–1814," *Ethnohistory* 21 (1974): 251–271; Theron A. Nuñez Jr., "Creek Nativism and the Creek War of 1813–14," *Ethnohistory* 5 (1958): 1–47.

38. *Niles' Register*, 3:223, 4:180, 400–401; Benjamin Hawkins to David B. Mitchell, 26 April 1813, LJWBH.

39. The arrival of Benjamin Hawkins produced a rift among the Lower Creeks. When Hawkins moved to the nation, he established a model farm in Coweta. He planned to base his transformation of the Creeks from there. Under Hawkins's influence, some Creeks centered in Coweta adopted the tenets of the civilizing plan, including the use of slaves. For more on the rise of Coweta, see Green, *The Politics of Indian Removal*, 37–40; Saunt, *A New Order of Things*, 129, 155–158.

40. Benjamin Hawkins to John B. Floyd, 26 September 1813, LJWBH; Saunt, *A New Order of Things*, 263–266.

41. Saunt, *A New Order of Things*, 270–272.

42. Benjamin Hawkins to John Armstrong, 7 June 1814, LJWBH; Benjamin Hawkins to Peter Early, 15 June 1814, LJWBH. The Creek victors in the Redstick War were forced to give up close to 23 million acres in the Treaty of Fort Jackson. Parts of this land would later become the cotton belt in Georgia, Alabama, and Mississippi.

43. *Columbia Museum and Savannah Advertiser*, 29 August 1814, 1 September 1814, 15 September 1814, 26 September 1814, 2 October 1814, 10 October 1814, 13 October 1814, 14 November 1814.

44. *Niles' Register*, 6:194.

45. *Columbia Museum and Savannah Advertiser*, 10 October 1814.

46. *Savannah Republican*, 19 January 1815, 21 January 1815, 28 January 1815. See also Mary Bullard, *Black Liberation on Cumberland Island* (DeLeon, Fla., 1983).

47. *Niles' Register*, 9:82.

48. Bullard, *Black Liberation on Cumberland Island*, 101–104. Bullard contends that of the total number of slaves who left with the British, 833 were from Georgia.

49. Malcolm Bell Jr., *Major Butler's Legacy: Five Generations of a Slaveholding Family* (Athens, 1987), 126–153.

50. Philip D. Curtin, ed., *Africa Remembered: Narratives by West Africans From the Era of the Slave Trade* (Prospect Heights, Ill., 1967), 145–151; Allan D. Austin, *African Muslims in Antebellum America: A Sourcebook* (New York, 1984), 309–408; Gomez, *Exchanging Our Country Marks*, 70–87; T. Reed Ferguson, *The John Couper Family at Cannon's Point* (Macon, Ga., 1994), 93–114; John Solomon Otto, *Cannon's Point Plantation, 1794–1860: Living Conditions and Status Patterns in the Old South* (New York, 1984).

51. Austin, *African Muslims in Antebellum America*, 265–308; Gomez, *Exchanging Our Marks*, 70–87; E. Merton Coulter, *Thomas Spalding of Sapelo* (University, La., 1940), 81–86; Charles Spaulding Wylly, *The Seed That Was Sown in the Colony of Georgia: The Harvest and the Aftermath, 1740–1870* (New York, 1910). During his lifetime, Thomas

Spalding was renowned for his agricultural innovations. His writings appeared in several prominent journals, and he was credited with pioneering several techniques to improve cotton and sugar cultivation as well. Both of those crops were grown in the Bahamas, where Spalding purchased Bu Allah. Since Spalding was aware of his slave's agriculture knowledge before he bought him, and because Spalding relied on Allah to run his plantation, it is likely that the men discussed farming at length. Consequently, one wonders to what extent should Spalding's acclaim have been shared. For more on agricultural innovation in the lowcountry and Spalding, see Chaplin, *An Anxious Pursuit*, 112, 155; Coulter, *Thomas Spalding of Sapelo*, chapters 4, 5, and 6.

52. For more on the Negro Fort, see Landers, *Black Society in Spanish Florida*, 231–235; Saunt, *A New Order of Things*, chapter 12; Wright, *Creeks and Seminoles*, 180–184, 189–192, 197–200; James W. Covington, "The Negro Fort," *Gulf Coast Historical Review* 5, no. 2 (January 1990): 78–91; Herbert Aptheker, "Maroons within the Present Limits of the United States," *Journal of Negro History* 24, no. 2 (April 1939): 172–173.

53. Benjamin Hawkins to Andrew Jackson, 21 April 1816, LJWBH.

54. The contentious relationship between Hawkins and William Bowles is the focus of an earlier chapter. Benjamin Hawkins to Peter Early, February 20, 1815, LJWBH.

55. Benjamin Hawkins to Peter Early, 21 April 1815, LJWBH.

56. Benjamin Hawkins to William Crawford, 16 February 1816, LJWBH.

57. Ibid.

58. John Floyd to Peter Early, April 16, 1816, GDAH on-line.

59. Benjamin Hawkins to Peter Early, 21 April 1815, LJWBH.

60. Ibid.

61. Ibid.

62. Benjamin Hawkins to William Crawford, 3 February 1816, LJWBH.

63. John Floyd to David B. Mitchell, 12 April 1816, box 71, folder 11, Telamon Cuyler Collection, ms 1170, Hargrett.

64. Benjamin Hawkins to Tustannuggee Hopoie, 30 April 1816, LJWBH, 784–785.

65. Benjamin Hawkins to William Crawford, 2 April 1816, LJWBH, 779–781.

66. Benjamin Hawkins to General Gaines, 3 May 1816, LJWBH, 785.

67. As quoted in Landers, *Black Society in Spanish Florida*, 234.

68. "Negro Fort on Appalachicola," *Niles' Register*, 17:186–188.

69. Ibid.

70. Saunt, *A New Order of Things*, 288–289.

71. "Negro Fort on Appalachicola," *Niles' Register*, 17:186–188.

72. For more on the First Seminole War, see Kenneth Wiggins Porter, "Negroes and the Seminole War, 1817–1818," *Journal of Negro History* 36, no. 3 (June 1951): 249–280; John K. Mahon, "The First Seminole War, November 21,

1817–May 24, 1818," *Florida Historical Quarterly* 77, no. 1 (1998): 62–67; Landers, *Black Society in Spanish Florida*.

73. *American State Papers, Military Affairs* (Washington, D.C., 1832), 1:683; *Niles' Register*, 12:112.

74. *Niles' Register*, 13:216–217.

75. *American State Papers, Military Affairs* (Washington, D.C., 1832), 1:685; *Milledgeville Reflector*, 19 November 1817.

76. *American State Papers, Foreign Relations* (Washington, D.C., 1834), 4:586.

77. Ibid., 4:596.

78. John Floyd to David B. Mitchell, 12 April 1816, box 71, folder 11, Telamon Cuyler Collection, ms 1170, Hargrett.

79. *Milledgeville Reflector*, 2 December 1817. Kenneth Wiggins Porter, "Negroes and the Seminole War, 1817–1818," *Journal of Negro History* 36, no. 3 (June 1951): 249–280; Mahon, "The First Seminole War, November 21, 1817–May 24, 1818," 62–67; Landers, *Black Society in Spanish Florida*, 235–237.

80. *Milledgeville Reflector*, 14 April 1817, 16 December 1817.

81. Ibid., 16 December 1817, 23 December 1817, 6 January 1818, 20 January 1818, 27 January 1818, 24 February 1818; *Niles' Register*, 13:208, 216–219.

82. *Milledgeville Reflector*, 27 January 1818.

83. Ibid., 10 March 1818, 24 March 1818, 31 March 1818, 14 April 1818; A. B. Powell to Governor William Rabun, 14 March 1818, in Telamon Cuyler Collection, ms 1170, Hargrett.

84. *Niles' Register*, 13:396. For more on Andrew Jackson's tenuous relations with Indians, see Robert Vincent Remini, *Andrew Jackson and His Indian Wars* (New York, 2001); Anthony F. C. Wallace, *The Long, Bitter Trail: Andrew Jackson and the Indians* (New York, 1993); Sean Michael O'Brian, *In Bitterness and in Tears: Andrew Jackson's Destruction of the Creeks and Seminoles* (Westport, Conn., 2003).

85. *Niles' Register*, 14:218, 393–394, 15:269–270, 16:32–39; *Milledgeville Reflector*, 14 April 1818, 21 April 1818, 28 April 1818; 5 May 1818.

86. *Narrative of a Voyage to the Spanish Main in the Ship "Two Friends;" The Occupation of Amelia Island by M'Gregor, &c.—Sketches of the Province of East Florida; and Anecdotes Illustrative of the Habits and Manners of the Seminole Indians: With an Appendix, Containing a Detail of the Seminole War, and the Execution of Arbuthnot and Ambrister* (London, 1819), 217.

87. *Niles' Register*, 14:218, 16:33–39; *Milledgeville Reflector*, 28 March 1818, 5 May 1818.

88. *Niles' Register*, 14:218–219.

89. *Milledgeville Reflector*, 5 May 1818, 26 May 1818.

90. Ibid., 2 June 1818, 21 July 1818, 4 August 1818.

91. Ibid., 5 May 1818, 26 May 1818.

92. Ibid., 28 July 1818.

6. Making Georgia Black and White

1. In *Georgia and State Rights* (Washington, D.C., 1902), Phillips argued that white Georgians uniformly embraced Indian removal as the only solution to the seemingly intractable dilemma over the state's western lands. Moreover, he noted, the "Indian question" never produced any substantive political divisions because all white men could agree on the necessity of expelling the Indians to the lands west of the Mississippi. "Upon Indian affairs," he asserted, "the leaders of each party had ideas, sometime of decided character, but in each case these ideas happened to be practically the same" (111). In the century since the publication of Phillips's monograph, historians have largely hewed to this argument. For example, in his 1999 study, *Domesticating Slavery*, Jeffrey Young asserts that there was "nearly unanimous white support for Indian removal" among white Georgians (211). Scholars of Georgia's political history have embraced a similar position. Among those who have acknowledged the existence of political divisions over the question of Cherokee removal, they have assumed that these differences were inconsequential or failed to reflect genuine discrepancies in opinion concerning racial attitudes. For example, Donald A. DeBats acknowledges the use of the Cherokee controversy for partisan purposes, but he dates it to the gubernatorial campaign of 1837, not to when it first appeared in the 1831 contest between Wilson Lumpkin and George Gilmer. He notes that the Union Party castigated Gilmer for failing to look out for the interests of the settlers and claimed that he was a proponent of Indian rights, particularly the right to testify, which had been such an inflammatory issue six years earlier. DeBats asserts that there was no real basis for the attack on Gilmer and that it was a nonissue because all whites agreed. "The resulting clash did not stem from a fundamental difference in attitude of the party leaders to Indian removal; indeed if ever there existed a consensus in Georgia politics it was that all Indians should be removed as rapidly as possible" (Donald A. DeBats, *Elites and Masses: Political Structure, Communication, and Behavior in Ante-Bellum Georgia* [New York, 1990], 264). Mary Young mentions the differences of opinion over the "Cherokee question" in several articles, but she does not delve into the deeper significance of the division. For example, in "The Exercise of Sovereignty in Cherokee Georgia," *Journal of the Early Republic* 10 (1990): 43–63, Young contends that while all white Georgians "favored Indian removal," "not all Georgians agreed as to the tactics appropriate to achieve that desirable object" (44). Young, however, does not fully develop this thesis beyond noting that some lawyers and judges opposed the most draconian measures adopted by the General Assembly to remove the Cherokees.

2. For a lengthier examination of the removal of the Creeks, see Green, *The Politics of Indian Removal*.

3. *Savannah Republican*, 10 September 1816.

4. Ibid., 9 November 1819. For a dramatic account of Clark's selection and

the subsequent political fallout, see Gilmer, *Sketches of Some of the First Settlers of Upper Georgia, of the Cherokees, and the Author,* 211–216.

5. For more on George Troup and his early political activity, see Phillips, *Georgia and State Rights,* 94–97; Lamplugh, *Politics on the Periphery,* 150–151, 176–178; Edward J. Harden, *The Life of George M. Troup* (Savannah, 1859).

6. For more on John Clark, see Gilmer, *Sketches of Some of the First Settlers of Upper Georgia, of the Cherokees, and the Author,* 156–161; Phillips, *Georgia and State Rights,* 97–101.

7. *Journal of the House of Representatives of the State of Georgia at an Annual Session of the General Assembly, begun and held at Milledgeville, the Seat of Government, November and December,* 1821 (Milledgeville, 1821), 7.

8. *Journal of the House of Representatives of the State of Georgia at an Annual Session of the General Assembly, begun and held at Milledgeville, the Seat of Government, November and December,* 1819 (Milledgeville, 1819), 153–157.

9. Green, *The Politics of Indian Removal,* 56–59.

10. *Niles' Register,* 20:181–182.

11. *Acts of the General Assembly of the State of Georgia, Passed at Milledgeville, at an Extra Session, April and May 1821* (Milledgeville, 1821), 1:4–12.

12. Phillips, *Georgia and State Rights,* 53.

13. Coastal elites discerned a necessity to check the growing political power of the upcountry. Georgians had by 1821 succeeded in placing half of the land claimed by the state under its authority and already they had upset the sectional balance of power. Coastal elites feared that upcountry residents would soon secure the other half of the land claimed by the state and would then solidify their control over state politics. To prevent such an occurrence, they unsuccessfully proposed several bills that would have the effect of limiting the upcountry's representation in the General Assembly. (*Savannah Republican,* November 23, 1819.) In 1821, the General Assembly discussed another bill to reduce representation, but it too failed to pass.

14. *Journal of the House of Representatives of the State of Georgia at an Annual Session of the General Assembly, begun and held at Milledgeville, the Seat of Government, November and December,* 1823 (Milledgeville, 1823), 16–17.

15. Phillips recognized a shift in the state government's position relative to the federal authorities and the contested land, but he failed to discuss why Troup introduced this "new régime in Indian policy" (Phillips, *Georgia and State Rights,* 53–54).

16. *ASPIA,* 2:26–28.

17. "Indian Reservations in Georgia," *Niles' Register,* 26:100–101.

18. *Acts of the General Assembly of the State of Georgia, Passed at Milledgeville, at an Annual Session, in November and December 1823* (Milledgeville, 1823), 217–221.

19. Ibid.

20. *Journal of the House of Representatives of the State of Georgia at an Annual Session of the*

General Assembly, begun and held at Milledgeville, the Seat of Government, November and December, 1824 (Milledgeville, 1824), 20–29.

21. *Niles' Register*, 28:18. For more on the negotiations and the Treaty of Indian Springs, see Green, *The Politics of Indian Removal*, chapter 4.

22. Phillips, *Georgia and State Rights*, 56–57; Green, *The Politics of Indian Removal*, 93–97.

23. *Milledgeville Recorder*, 10 May 1825; *Georgia Messenger*, 18 May 1825; *Montgomery (Ala.) Republican*, 6 May 1825; *Niles' Register*, 28:49, 196, 197.

24. *Milledgeville Recorder*, 24 May 1825.

25. Green, *The Politics of Indian Removal*, chapter 5.

26. *Milledgeville Recorder*, 9 August 1825.

27. *Niles' Register*, 29:2; Green, *The Politics of Indian Removal*, 127.

28. *Georgia Journal and Messenger*, 28 September 1825.

29. *Milledgeville Recorder*, 27 September 1825.

30. For more on the sectional breakdown of the 1825 gubernatorial vote, see Phillips, *Georgia and State Rights*, 103–104.

31. Phillips, *Georgia and State Rights*, 59–64.

32. For more on the Cherokees' embrace of the civilization plan, see McLoughlin, *Cherokee Renascence in the New Republic*; and William G. McLoughlin, *Cherokees and Missionaries, 1789–1839* (New Haven, 1984).

33. For more on slaveholding among the Cherokees, see Theda Perdue, *Slavery and the Evolution of Cherokee Society, 1540–1866* (Knoxville, 1979); R. Halliburton Jr., *Red Over Black: Black Slavery among the Cherokee Indians* (Westport, Conn., 1977); William G. McLoughlin, *The Cherokee Ghost Dance: Essays on the Southeastern Indians, 1789–1861* (Mercer, Ga., 1984); Tiya Miles, *Ties That Bind: The Story of an Afro-Cherokee Family in Slavery and Freedom* (Berkeley, 2005); Tiya Miles, *The House on Diamond Hill: A Cherokee Plantation Story* (Chapel Hill, 2010).

34. For examples of white Georgians and elite Cherokees socializing, see testimonials in support of Judge Hooper, found in *The Charges Against the Hon. Judge W. Hooper, Judge of the Superior Courts of the Cherokee Circuit; Referred to the Committee of the House of Representatives for Investigation* (Milledgeville, Ga., 1835).

35. *Savannah Mercury*, 11 September 1829; DeBats, *Elites and Masses*, 28–29. According to Gilmer, he "was pressed to be a candidate for chief magistrate for the State, and consented. Major Joe Crawford was my opponent. The Clark party had no candidate. The majority of its members voted for me. I was consequently elected by a very large majority." Gilmer, *Sketches of Some of the First Settlers of Upper Georgia, of the Cherokees, and the Author*, 245.

36. George R. Gilmer to Tomlinson Fort, 27 August 1829, Fort Papers, Political Leaders Collection, Emory University; Gilmer, *Sketches of Some of the First Settlers of Upper Georgia, of the Cherokees, and the Author*; Phillips, *Georgia and State Rights*, 110; Paul Murray, *The Whig Party in Georgia, 1825–1853*, The James Sprung Studies in History and Political Science (Chapel Hill, 1948), 14–15. Gilmer won the 1829 election

by more than seventeen thousand votes out of over forty thousand cast. *Athens Athenian*, 20 October 1829, 27 October 1829.

37. *Acts of the General Assembly of the State of Georgia Passed in Milledgeville at an Annual Session in November and December, 1828* (Milledgeville, 1829), 88–89.

38. Judge Junius Hillyer Journal, chapter 17, "The Cherokee Indians," Hillyer Collection, Ms 76, Hargrett.

39. Governor George Gilmer to William Wirt, 19 June 1830, *Augusta Chronicle and Advertiser*, 1 September 1830.

40. "Indians Memorial," *Cherokee Phoenix and Indians' Advocate*, 29 April 1829; "From the Savannah Georgian," *Cherokee Phoenix*, 3 September 1828.

41. Junius Hillyer Diary, 221–223, Hillyer Collection, Ms 76, Hargrett.

42. The General Assembly debated bills in 1822 and 1826. The body passed the first, but for an unknown reason the governor did not sign it. The second attempt became law, but it restricted only those Indians who could not speak English from testifying. See *Georgia Journal*, 15 June 1829 and 19 September 1829, for more on the debate over these legislative actions. Quote from *Journal of the House of Representatives of the State of Georgia at an Annual Session of the General Assembly, begun and held at the State House in the Town of Milledgeville, on Monday the Second of November, 1829* (Milledgeville, 1830), 272–274.

43. "One of the Majority," *Georgia Journal*, 2 January 1830.

44. *Journal of the House of Representatives of the State of Georgia at an Annual Session of the General Assembly, begun and held at the State House in the Town of Milledgeville, on Monday the Second of November, 1829* (Milledgeville, 1830), 270–271.

45. *Acts of the General Assembly of the State of Georgia Passed in Milledgeville at an Annual Session in November and December, 1829* (Milledgeville, 1830), 98–101.

46. *Georgia Journal*, 19 December 1829.

47. "Message of the Governor of the State of Georgia," *Cherokee Phoenix*, 6 November 1830.

48. *Augusta Chronicle and Advertiser*, 15 December 1830. By advocating a plan to parcel out land in fee simple plots to elite Cherokees who wished to remain in Georgia, Gilmer articulated a vision of Georgia that included at least some Cherokees. This position stood in marked contrast to that of Gilmer's opponents, who lumped all Cherokees together and pushed for the complete expulsion of all Indians, regardless of their ancestry ("mixed-blood" or "full-blood") or the degree to which they had acculturated. For a more critical assessment of the federal government's program of granting fee simple allotments to Indians, see Mary E. Young, "Indian Removal and Land Allotment: The Civilized Tribes and Jacksonian Justice," *American Historical Review* 64 (1958): 31–45.

49. For example, the editor of the *Augusta Chronicle and Advertiser* stated, "Why cannot the Indians, since they are so averse to remove, be incorporated with our population, as citizens, subject to our laws; and regulations be made to divide their land among them individually, according their respective claims? We do

not believe this would be so consistent with their interest, as for them to remove West, for the reasons we have heretofore given; but since they must of necessity submit to the one or the other, and do determine positively against the latter, why should their will be forcibly opposed, when to do is against the interest of the State?" (*Augusta Chronicle and Advertiser*, 24 November 1830.)

50. *Augusta Chronicle and Advertiser*, 15 December 1830.

51. George Gilmer to William Wirt, 19 June 1830, *Augusta Chronicle and Advertiser*, 1 September 1830.

52. "Report of the Committee on the State of the Republic," *Augusta Chronicle and Advertiser*, 17 November 1830.

53. *Augusta Chronicle and Advertiser*, 1 December 1830.

54. Ibid.

55. *Milledgeville Journal*, 1 December 1830.

56. *Augusta Chronicle and Advertiser*, 1 December 1830.

57. The article appears in the *Cherokee Phoenix*, 6 November 1830. While moderate whites believed that the General Assembly would eventually adopt the correct course, the Cherokees possessed little faith. The *Cherokee Phoenix* entertained not the "least doubt that the legislature will do more than what is recommended" by Gilmer and would indeed survey the land and immediately distribute it to white Georgians. (*Cherokee Phoenix*, 6 November 1830.)

58. Gilmer, *Sketches of Some of the First Settlers of Upper Georgia, of the Cherokees, and the Author*, 246.

59. Wilson Lumpkin, *The Removal of the Cherokee Indians from Georgia* (New York, 1907) (hereafter *Cherokee Removal*), 2:303.

60. Ibid., 2:253.

61. Ibid.

62. *Milledgeville Federal Union*, 22 September 1831.

63. Ibid., 8 September 1831.

64. *Federal Union*, 10 November 1831. For the most part, historians of Georgia have failed to recognize how the Cherokee controversy factored into Gilmer's 1831 defeat. For example, see Phillips, *Georgia and State Rights*, 125–127; Anthony Gene Carey, *Parties, Slavery, and the Union in Antebellum Georgia* (Athens, 1997), 25–26; Murray, *The Whig Party in Georgia*, 22–25. One exception can be found in Mary Young's "The Exercise of Sovereignty in Cherokee Georgia." On page 62, Young states that Gilmer "probably lost his bid for reelection in 1831 because he publicly championed giving Indians full rights to testify in court." Young, however, does not elaborate on this statement, nor does she discuss the legislative conflict surrounding the debate over granting Indians the right to testify against whites.

65. Gilmer, *Sketches of Some of the First Settlers of Upper Georgia, of the Cherokees, and the Author*, 358. According to the 1831 election results, Gilmer lost badly in the counties on the Cherokee frontier, the same counties where he had performed so well two years before. In Hall County, Lumpkin received 953 votes to Gilmer's

657. In Habersham County, Lumpkin received 1,324 votes to Gilmer's 337. In Gwinnett County, Lumpkin received 1,001 to Gilmer's 833. (*Milledgeville Federal Union*, 30 October 1833.)

66. "Governor's Message," *Milledgeville Federal Union*, 10 November 1831.

67. Lumpkin's Address to the House of Representatives, 1 December 1831, *Milledgeville Federal Union*, 8 December 1831.

68. *Acts of the General Assembly of the State of Georgia, passed in Milledgeville at an Annual Session in November and December 1831* (Milledgeville, 1832), 141–149.

69. William W. Williamson to Governor Wilson Lumpkin, 28 April 1832, folder 3, box 49A, Telamon Cuyler Collection, ms 1170, Hargrett; John Coffee to Wilson Lumpkin, 17 June 1832, folder 46, box 1, Telamon Cuyler Collection, ms 1170, Hargrett.

70. *Milledgeville Federal Union*, 29 August 1833.

71. Based on election returns in the *Milledgeville Federal Union*, 30 October 1833.

72. "Message," published in *Milledgeville Southern Recorder*, 6 November 1833.

73. "Report," published in *Georgia Journal*, 28 November 1834.

74. *Acts of the General Assembly of the State of Georgia Passed in Milledgeville, at an Annual Session in November and December, 1833* (Milledgeville, 1834), 114–115; Wilson Lumpkin to John Forsyth, 30 May 1834, in Lumpkin, *Cherokee Removal*, 1:262.

75. *Acts of the General Assembly of the State of Georgia Passed in Milledgeville, at an Annual Session in November and December, 1833* (Milledgeville, 1834), 114–118.

76. Eli McConnell to Governor Wilson Lumpkin, 13 May 1834, in Lumpkin, *Cherokee Removal*, 1:274; D. R. Mitchell, John Brewster, and R. M. Holt to Governor Wilson Lumpkin, 13 May 1834, in Lumpkin, *Cherokee Removal*, 1:277; Howell Cobb and D. R. Mitchell to Governor Wilson Lumpkin, 13 May 1834, in Lumpkin, *Cherokee Removal*, 1:275–276.

77. *Milledgeville Journal*, 11 June 1834, 2 July 1834.

78. Ibid., 2 July 1834, 9 July 1834.

79. Governor Wilson Lumpkin to William Springer, 6 January 1834, *Documents Relative to the Judicial Administration of the Hon. John W. Hooper* (Milledgeville, Ga., 1835), 5; C. D. Terhune to Governor Wilson Lumpkin, 16 January 1834, *Documents Relative to the Judicial Administration of the Hon. John W. Hooper*, 9; Governor Wilson Lumpkin to John A. Cuthbert, 25 March 1834, *Documents Relative to the Judicial Administration of the Hon. John W. Hooper*, 17; William Springer to Governor Wilson Lumpkin, 25 October 1834, *Documents Relative to the Judicial Administration of the Hon. John W. Hooper*, 34; Judge Warner's Opinion in the case of *Adair v. Hugh Hamel*, *Documents Relative to the Judicial Administration of the Hon. John W. Hooper*, 25; Governor Wilson Lumpkin to William Springer, 1 February 1834, in Lumpkin, *Cherokee Removal*, 1:240; Governor Wilson Lumpkin to William Springer, 25 March 1834, in Lumpkin, *Cherokee Removal*, 1:252; Governor Wilson Lumpkin to William Springer, 28 March 1834, in Lumpkin, *Cherokee Removal*, 1:257.

80. "Judge Clayton's Charge to the Grand Jury of Clark County," *Cherokee Phoenix*, 10 October 1830.

81. Clayton often has been portrayed as a villain because he issued the ruling in the case of George Tassels, an Indian who was convicted of murder and sentenced to death. The *Tassels* case was argued up to the U.S. Supreme Court, which issued a writ to halt the execution, but Clayton ignored the higher court's injunction and carried out the sentence. For this, he is viewed as just another white Georgian bent on expelling the Indians. Yet a closer look at his record reveals a more complex portrait.

82. From *Southern Whig*, appearing in *Georgia Journal*, 5 December 1834.

83. *Georgia Journal*, 14 May 1834.

84. "Vindication of the Judiciary of Georgia," in *Georgia Journal*, 11 November 1834.

85. "Judge Hooper and His Supporters," *Milledgeville Federal Union*, 26 November 1834.

86. Testimony of William N. Bishop, *The Charges Against the Hon. John W. Hooper.*

87. William Springer to Governor Wilson Lumpkin, 25 November 1834, in *Documents Relative to the Judicial Administration of the Hon. John W. Hooper*, 34.

88. Governor Wilson Lumpkin to James M. Wayne, 2 January 1834, in Lumpkin, *Cherokee Removal*, 1:238–239; Governor Wilson Lumpkin to John A. Cuthbert, 25 March 1834, in *Documents Relative to the Judicial Administration of the Hon. John W. Hooper*, 17; John A. Cuthbert to Governor Wilson Lumpkin, 4 April 1834, in *Documents Relative to the Judicial Administration of the Hon. John W. Hooper*, 21; John A. Cuthbert to Governor Wilson Lumpkin, 8 August 1834, in *Documents Relative to the Judicial Administration of the Hon. John W. Hooper*, 23.

89. "Report of the Select Committee, on the Memorial of a Portion of the Citizens of the Cherokee Circuit," *Milledgeville Journal*, 28 November 1834; "Message," *Federal Union*, 5 November 1834; *Journal of the House of Representatives of the State of Georgia, at an Annual Session of the General Assembly, begun and held and Milledgeville, the Seat of Government, in November and December, 1834* (Milledgeville, 1835), 98, 232–233, 235–236, 247, 257, 271–273, 372, 412, 422; *Journal of the Senate of the State of Georgia, at an Annual Session of the General Assembly, begun and held and Milledgeville, the Seat of Government, in November and December, 1834* (Milledgeville, 1835), 88–94, 179–183. In both chambers of the General Assembly, there was protracted and contentious debate over how to proceed with the Hooper matter. Although a majority of the legislators called for sanctions, there was no consensus. Moreover, a significant portion of the legislators opposed taking any action against Judge Hooper.

90. The evidence related to the investigation is contained in two sets of documents: *The Charges Against the Hon. John W. Hooper* and *Documents Relative to the Judicial Administration of the Hon. John W. Hooper.*

91. For example, see the testimonies of Edward Hardin, Underwood, William Y. Hansell, Andrew J. Hansell, Samuel Rockwell, Thomas G. Barron, David Irwin, John Jolly, Robert Mitchell, Henry B. Shaw, William W. Holt, Lott Warren, and William E. Walker in *The Charges Against the Hon. John W. Hooper.*

92. For example, see the testimonies of William Springer, Francis Cone, William Bishop, William Brewster, Andrew McDonald, and Z. B. Hargrove in *The Charges Against the Hon. John W. Hooper.*

93. *Acts of the General Assembly of the State of Georgia Passed in Milledgeville at an Annual Session in November and December, 1834* (Milledgeville, 1835), 152–156.

94. "The Judiciary," from the *Augusta Chronicle and Advertiser,* in *Milledgeville Journal,* 24 November 1834. Union Party members also attempted to enact legislation that would place the selection of superior court judges in the hands of the voters, though the bill proved too controversial and was ultimately tabled for the remainder of the 1834 legislative session. (*Milledgeville Journal,* 28 November 1834, 2 December 1834.)

95. *Acts of the General Assembly of the State of Georgia Passed in Milledgeville at an Annual Session in November and December, 1834* (Milledgeville, 1835), 66.

96. Ibid., 152–156.

97. For more on the final stages of the removal of the Cherokees from Georgia, see Theda Perdue and Michael D. Green, *The Cherokee Nation and the Trail of Tears* (New York, 2007); Wallace, *The Long, Bitter Trail.*

7. The Democratization of Slavery

1. For an excellent overview of Olmsted's time in the South, see Lawrence N. Powell, introduction to Frederick Law Olmsted, *The Cotton Kingdom,* ed. Arthur M. Schlesinger Sr. (New York: Random House, 1984), ix–xxv. Olmsted published his observations under several different titles, but his work is commonly called *The Cotton Kingdom.*

2. U.S. Census, 1860. Dusinberre counts plantations rather than planters and tallies twenty-seven plantations with one hundred or more slaves in the Georgia lowcountry (Dusinberre, *Them Dark Days,* 461).

3. Olmsted offered a lengthy description of rice cultivation in *A Journey in the Seaboard Slave States, with Remarks on Their Economy* (New York, 1856), 466–477, and *The Cotton Kingdom,* 182–183. In his monograph *Them Dark Days,* Dusinberre notes, slaves considered it a "brutally harsh system" (428). He presents slavery as an overwhelming institution that destroyed slaves' lives and left them bereft of hope or agency. Dusinberre, however, conflates health statistics with the system of slavery. His proof is based on children's mortality rates. This tells us the work was hard and the physical environment harsh. But it does not speak to other aspects of slavery, namely the organization of labor. The task system and its advantages (compared to the gang system) must be considered when analyzing the development of slavery in Georgia. For another study of lowcountry slavery on the plantations of the elite, see Clarke, *Dwelling Place.*

4. Olmsted, *The Cotton Kingdom,* 189–192. For more on the task system in the lowcountry, see Morgan, "Work and Culture," 563–599.

5. Lafayette Delegal Allowed Claim, Liberty County, Georgia, Southern Claims Commission, RG 217, National Archives, College Park, Maryland.

6. Olmsted, *The Cotton Kingdom*, 185. For more on property ownership by slaves in the lowcountry, see Philip D. Morgan, "The Ownership of Property by Slaves in the Mid-Nineteenth-Century Low Country," *Journal of Southern History* 49 no. 3 (1983): 399–420; Dylan C. Penningroth, *The Claims of Kinsfolk: African American Property and Community in the Nineteenth-Century South* (Chapel Hill, 2003).

7. Olmsted, *A Journey in the Seaboard Slave States*, 478.

8. Basil Hall, "Basil Hall, 1828," in Lane, ed., *The Rambler in Georgia*, 66. Ebenezer Kellogg offered a similar assessment: "The culture of rice is more laborious than that of cotton, and is reckoned more unhealthy—and it makes more work for the negroes in winter, than a corn or cotton plantation. But the negroes prefer it commonly to cotton" (Ebenezer Kellogg, "A New Englander's Impressions of Georgia in 1817–1818: Extracts from the Diary of Ebenezer Kellogg," ed. Sidney Walter Martin, *Journal of Southern History* 12, no. 2 [1946]: 262).

9. Olmsted, *The Cotton Kingdom*, 193.

10. Ibid., 193–194.

11. Ibid., 188. For more examples of black drivers with exceptional skills and intelligence who enjoyed special privileges, see Clarke, *Dwelling Place*; Frances Anne Kemble, *Journal of a Residence on a Georgian Plantation in 1838–1839* (Athens, 1984); Dusinberre, *Them Dark Days*; Robert S. Starobin, *Industrial Slavery in the Old South* (New York, 1970), 152.

12. Olmsted, *The Cotton Kingdom*, 186.

13. Starobin, *Industrial Slavery in the Old South*, 25; John A. Eisterhold, "Savannah: Lumber Center of the South Atlantic," *Georgia Historical Quarterly* 57 (winter 1973): 527, 529, 533.

14. William A. Byrne, "The Burden and the Heat of the Day: Slavery and Servitude in Savannah, 1733–1865" (Ph.D. diss., Florida State University, 1979), 198–199; Starobin, *Industrial Slavery in the Old South*, 21; Richard Herbert Haunton, "Savannah in the 1850's" (Ph.D. diss., Emory University, 1968), 67.

15. Kemble, *Journal of a Residence on a Georgian Plantation in 1838–1839*, 54–55, 116–117, 168, 187; Clarke, *Dwelling Place*.

16. Charles C. Jones, *The Religious Instruction of Negroes in the United States* (Savannah, 1842). For more on Jones and his family, see Robert Manson Myers, *The Children of Pride: A True Story of Georgia and the Civil War* (New Haven, 1972); and Clarke, *Dwelling Place*.

17. Olmsted, *A Journey in the Seaboard Slave States*, 485.

18. Quote from Olmsted, *A Journey in the Seaboard Slave States*, 485; Kemble, *Journal of a Residence on a Georgian Plantation in 1838–1839*, 54–55. For more on punishment, see Dusinberre, *Them Dark Days*.

19. Census figures taken from tables in Richard C. Wade, *Slavery in the Cities: The South, 1820–1860* (New York, 1964), 327; Joseph Bancroft, *Census of the City of Savan-*

nah: *Together with Statistics, Relating to the Trade, Commerce, Mechanical Arts & Health of the Same; to Which is Added Historical Notices, and a List of the Incorporated Companies, and of the Charitable Societies* (Savannah, 1848).

20. Byrne, "The Burden and the Heat of the Day," 192.

21. Bancroft, *Census of the City of Savannah*, 16; Haunton, "Savannah in the 1850's," 71; Gillespie, *Free Labor in an Unfree World*, 128–129.

22. Wood, *Women's Work, Men's Work*, see chapter 5.

23. Bancroft, *Census of the City of Savannah*, 3.

24. Charles Ball, *Fifty Years in Chains; Or, The Life of an American Slave* (Detroit, 1971), 287, 417. For another example of a slave achieving a modicum of financial success through self-hire, see Dimmock Charlton, *Narrative of Dimmock Charlton, a British Subject, Taken from the Brig "Peacock" by the U.S. Sloop "Hornet," Enslaved while a Prisoner of War, and Retained Forty-five Years in Bondage* (Philadelphia, 1858). Several white foreign travelers developed an avid interest in the self-hire system while in Savannah. As with the task system, self-hire seemed to confound visitors' preconceived notions of how slavery operated. For example, Adam Hodgson believed that, rather than illustrating the flexibility of slavery as an institution, self-hire represented the first step toward freedom. The "system of allowing the Slaves to select their own work, and to look out for employment for themselves . . . is a great step toward emancipation, and an admirable preparative for it . . . through which the African will ultimately emerge from his degraded condition, and arrive at full enjoyment of his violated rights" (quote taken from Adam Hodgson, "Adam Hodgson, 1820," in Lane, ed., *The Rambler in Georgia*, 56).

25. William Grimes, *Life of William Grimes, The Runaway Slave, Brought Down to the Present Time* (New Haven, 1855), 60–61.

26. Byrne, "The Burden and the Heat of the Day," 185–186.

27. Richard H. Shryock, ed., *Letters of Richard D. Arnold, M.D., 1808–1876, Mayor of Savannah, Georgia, First Secretary of the American Medical Association* (Durham, 1929), 77. As historian Timothy Lockley notes, "the problem of self-hire of slaves was probably too big to be controlled by the legal system. Neither masters nor bondspeople had an incentive to curtail it. Self-hire gave masters a steady income without any of the responsibilities of caring for the slave, and it provided bondspeople with opportunities for self-aggrandizement and greater control over their own lives than they could have secured on the plantations or as domestics" (Lockley, *Lines in the Sand*, 65).

28. Wade, *Slavery in the Cities*, 41; Byrne, "The Burden and the Heat of the Day," 188–190; Wood, *Women's Work, Men's Work*, 82–83, 87, 108–110; Lockley, *Lines in the Sand*, 64–65, 70.

29. Savannah City Council Minutes, 25 October 1792, GDAH. For more on the origins and early years of the Savannah Mechanics' Association, see Gillespie, *Free Labor in an Unfree World*, 50–57.

30. Quote taken from Fraser, *Savannah in the Old South*, 215.

31. *Savannah Republican*, 28 October 1845, as quoted in Wade, *Slavery in the Cities*, 50.

32. *Savannah Republican,* 17 January 1818.

33. "Presentments of the Grand Jury of Chatham County, January Term 1818," *Savannah Republican,* 16 January 1818.

34. For another interpretation that focuses on differences between upcountry and lowcountry slavery, see Reidy, *From Slavery to Agrarian Capitalism in the Cotton Plantation South;* Anthony E. Kaye, *Joining Places: Slave Neighborhoods in the Old South* (Chapel Hill, 2007).

35. U.S. Census, 1830.

36. Figures drawn from O. C. Stine and O. E. Baker, *Atlas of American Agriculture,* Pt. V, Section A, Cotton (Washington, D.C., 1918), as quoted in Flanders, *Plantation Slavery in Georgia,* 66.

37. James Oakes, *The Ruling Race: A History of American Slaveholders* (New York, 1982). Oakes provides an intriguing portrait of middling and small slaveholders, their struggle for wealth and power, and their brutal treatment of blacks. For an opposing assessment that casts slaveholders in a more positive and paternalistic light, see Eugene Genovese's *Roll, Jordan, Roll* (1974).

38. For more on the development of cotton slavery in the upcountry, see Harris, *Plain Folk and Gentry in a Slave Society.*

39. John Brown, *Slave Life in Georgia: A Narrative of the Life, Sufferings, and Escape of John Brown, A Fugitive Slave* (Savannah, 1991), 22–23. In *Free Labor in an Unfree World,* Michele Gillespie argues that upward social and economic mobility remained within the grasp of artisans in Georgia in the early nineteenth century but became increasingly difficult to achieve by the 1830s, as the price of land and slaves rose and economic opportunities declined (135–137).

40. A. T. Havens Journal, ms 1337, Hargrett.

41. C. D. Arfwedson, "C. D. Arfwedson, 1833," in Lane, ed., *The Rambler in Georgia,* 105.

42. For more on overseers in the blackbelt, see William Kauffman Scarborough, *The Overseer: Plantation Management in the Old South* (Baton Rouge, 1966).

43. Gillespie, *Free Labor in an Unfree World,* 96–97, 121, 124.

44. U.S. Census, 1810, 1820, 1830, 1840, 1850, 1860; Flanders, *Plantation Slavery in Georgia,* 63. Flanders places the data into two fields: East and West. He doesn't explain what this means, however. He cites *A Century in Population Growth,* 133–134. For some reason, he concludes that the "growth of the slave regime was, therefore, gradual in the upland cotton belt" and cites Phillips's contention that Georgia "grew more rapidly in comparison with other states because of the small number at the beginning."

45. Brown, *Slave Life in Georgia,* 10–17. For scholarship on the internal slave trade, see Michael Tadman, *Speculators and Slaves: Masters, Traders, and Slaves in the Old South* (Madison, 1989); Walter Johnson, *Soul by Soul: Life Inside the Antebellum Slave Market* (Cambridge, Mass., 1999); Steven Deyle, *Carry Me Back: The Domestic Slave Trade in American Life* (New York, 2005).

46. Flanders, *Plantation Slavery in Georgia,* 185–187. Rias Body, born a slave in

1849 in Harris County, Georgia, traveled frequently with his owner to Columbus before the Civil War. There, he noted, slaves were sold from the auction block, which was located on one of the city's main streets (Broadway), after being driven "in droves—like cattle—by northern speculators." Prospective buyers flocked to the city from eastern Alabama and southwest Georgia "to visit the 'block' accompanied by doctors, who would feel of, thump, and examine" the slaves before purchasing them (WPA, vol. 12, pt. 1, p. 88). (The WPA slave narratives for Georgia are published in four volumes: George P. Rawick, ed., *The American Slave: Georgia Narratives, Parts 1 and 2* [Westport, Conn.: Greenwood, 1972], vol. 12; George P. Rawick, ed., *The American Slave: Georgia Narratives, Parts 3 and 4* [Westport, Conn.: Greenwood, 1972], vol. 13; George P. Rawick, ed., *The American Slave, Supplement, Series 1: Georgia Narratives, Part 1* [Westport, Conn.: Greenwood, 1977], vol. 3).

47. Deyle, *Carry Me Back*, 56. The 1860 figure was the average price for a prime male hand in New Orleans. Flanders, *Plantation Slavery in Georgia*, 188–194.

48. Former slaves noted that prices for black females with proven fertility were quite high in the antebellum era. Charles Ball recalled that while en route to Georgia the speculator was approached by a man in South Carolina who wanted to buy two pregnant female slaves whom he was transporting. "Our master replied, that these were two of the best breeding-wenches in all Maryland—that one was twenty-two, and the other only nineteen—that the first was already the mother of seven children, and the other of four." After considerable wrangling the trader accepted $1,000 for the pair (Ball, *Fifty Years in Chains*, 36–38). The WPA narratives also contain multiple references to slave women whose fecundity brought significant profits to their owners. By the mid-nineteenth century, the prices had increased tremendously. Isaiah Green reported that an owner could sell a good "breeding woman" for twice the usual amount (WPA, vol. 12, pt. 2, p. 50). Ferebe Rogers was placed on the auction block twice. Her owner, John Baggett, bought her because she was a "good breedin' woman" (WPA, vol. 13, pt. 3, p. 209). Lina Hunter noted that a "good breedin'" woman brought a hefty price (WPA, vol. 12, pt. 2, p. 260). Rias Body asserted that a "good 'breedin' woman'" could go for as high as $1,200; he also claimed that his owner allowed male slaves, including several of his brothers, to travel throughout the county serving as studs, impregnating women (WPA, vol. 12, pt. 1, p. 88).

49. The issue of female sexuality and slave "breeding" has generated considerable controversy among historians for decades. Richard Sutch offers one of the most compelling arguments that slave owners used their bondwomen to produce profits through the sale of children in "The Breeding of Slaves for Sale and the Westward Expansion of Slavery, 1850–1860," in *Race and Slavery in the Western Hemisphere: Quantitative Studies*, ed. Stanley L. Engerman and Eugene D. Genovese, 173–210 (Princeton, 1975). See also Jacqueline Jones, *Labor of Love, Labor of Sorrow: Black Women, Work, and the Family, from Slavery to the Present* (New York, 1985), 34–36; Daina Ramey Berry, *"Swing the Sickle for the Harvest Is Ripe": Gender and Slavery in Antebel-*

lum *Georgia* (Urbana, 2007), 77–84. For an opposing view, see Robert Fogel and Stanley L. Engerman, *Time on the Cross: The Economics of American Negro Slavery* (Boston, 1974), 78–86.

50. Johnson, *Soul by Soul*, 22–24; Deyle, *Carry Me Back*, 231–236.

51. Grimes, *Life of William Grimes*, 26.

52. Berlin, *Many Thousands Gone*, 269–272.

53. Reidy, *From Slavery to Agrarian Capitalism in the Cotton Plantation South*, 59.

54. Ball, *Fifty Years in Chains*, 49.

55. For examples of accounts of field hands' workdays, see WPA, vol. 12, pt. 1, pp. 22, 161, 185, 305; vol. 12, pt. 2, pp. 39, 345; vol. 13, pt. 4, p. 194. See also Flanders, *Plantation Slavery in Georgia*, 145–146; Genovese, *Roll, Jordan, Roll*, 309–324.

56. Joseph P. Reidy, "Obligation and Right: Patterns of Labor, Subsistence, and Exchange in the Cotton Belt of Georgia," in Berlin and Morgan, eds., *Cultivation and Culture*, 141, 145–147. For another example that illustrates the struggle between slaves and owners in the early development of the cotton upcountry, see Steven Miller, "Plantation Labor Organization and Slave Life on the Cotton Frontier: The Alabama-Mississippi Black Belt, 1815–1840," in Berlin and Morgan, eds., *Cultivation and Culture*, 155–169.

57. Ulrich B. Phillips, ed., *Plantation and Frontier Documents, 1649–1863, Illustrative of Industrial History in the Colonial and Antebellum South* (Cleveland, 1909), 1:126–129. In his memoir, *Slave Life in Georgia*, John Brown asserted that the task system was used in the cotton belt, but only on smaller plantations, "where the master does his own overseeing and flogs" his own slaves. In contrast to other contemporaneous accounts of the task system, Brown argued that slaves had little or no time after their daily quota was complete. Contrary to "some people" who claim "this system of task-work is the best for the slave," he noted, "I have not hesitation in saying that the system is very bad indeed for the negroes" (161–162).

58. Joseph Reidy, *From Slavery to Agrarian Capitalism in the Cotton Plantation South*, 35–37, 40–42.

59. For examples, see WPA, vol. 12, pt. 1, p. 161; vol. 12, pt. 2, p. 173; vol. 13, pt. 3, p. 149; vol. 13, pt. 4, p. 194; vol. 12, pt. 1, p. 300; vol. 12, pt. 1, p. 22.

60. WPA, vol. 13, pt. 3, p. 133; vol, 13, pt. 3, p. 61; vol. 12, pt. 2, p. 108; vol. 12, pt. 2, p. 73. In another example, an enslaved man named Primus endured a horrible beating from his owner, Thomas Stevens. The master enlisted the assistance of two neighboring planters to subdue Primus. The men snuck up on him; they then tied him to a carpenter's bench with his hands tied underneath as tight as possible. Stevens then beat him with a cobbing paddle, a broad, flat piece of wood measuring eighteen to twenty-four inches long with holes drilled into it. Before using the paddle, the men dipped it in water and rubbed in it sand. Two of the men took turns beating the slave until they were exhausted. The first beating produced blisters; the owner followed the initial procedure with a second round of flogging, which burst the blisters. When that was done, they rubbed his

cuts with red pepper and salt and water. All of Stevens's other slaves were brought in to watch. (Ball, *Fifty Years in Chains*, 57–59.)

61. Of course, not all slaves were field hands on cotton plantations. There were some skilled slaves, but they were relatively few in number. The biggest plantations had some carpenters, occasionally shoemakers, and, less often, blacksmiths. See WPA, vol. 12, pt. 1, pp. 91, 265; vol. 12, pt. 2, p. 48; vol. 12, pt. 2, pp. 127–130; vol. 13, pt. 3, p. 296; vol. 13, pt. 4, pp. 49, 73; vol. 3, pt. 1, pp. 111–117. Horace King was perhaps the most famous skilled slave in antebellum Georgia. He was a master craftsman who helped design and erect many of the bridges in southwest Georgia. See WPA, vol. 4, pt. 2, p. 368. In some places slaves also worked in various kinds of industries, performing both the unskilled and skilled labor. See, for example, WPA, vol. 12, pt. 2, p. 209. According to Laura Hood, her owner, Henry Banks, owned approximately fifty slaves and put most of them to work in his tannery in Griffin County.

62. For more on the agricultural transformation of the Upper South and its impact on the lives of slaves, see Berlin, *Many Thousands Gone*, 265–268; Alan Kulikoff, *Tobacco and Slaves: The Development of Southern Cultures in the Chesapeake, 1680–1800* (Chapel Hill, 1986), 157–161, 396–408; Lorena S. Walsh, "Slave Life, Slave Society, and Tobacco Production in the Tidewater Chesapeake, 1620–1820," in Berlin and Morgan, eds., *Cultivation and Culture*, 186–188, 190–197; Morgan, *Slave Counterpoint*, 170–175, 196–197, 204–205, 209–212, 214–216, 229–232, 239, 242, 246–248, 252.

63. Ball, *Fifty Years in Chains*, 205.

64. Ibid., 146–149.

65. During his travels throughout the cotton South, Frederick Law Olmsted encountered women performing "men's" work, such as plowing, without any trouble. "The plowing, both with single and double mule teams," he noted, "was generally performed by women, and very well performed too" (Frederick Law Olmsted, *A Journey in the Backcountry* [New York, 1860], 81). See also Jones, *Labor of Love, Labor of Sorrow*, 16–18; Kaye, *Joining Places*, 95–96.

66. WPA, vol. 12, pt. 1, p. 113.

67. WPA, vol. 12, pt. 1, p. 141.

68. WPA, vol. 13, pt. 3, pp. 210–211.

69. WPA, vol. 13, pt. 3, pp. 229–230.

70. For an opposing argument, that cotton cultivation had no impact on gender relations, see Genovese, *Roll, Jordan, Roll*, 495. Genovese acknowledges that a significant minority of those who plowed were women and that they often outperformed their male counterparts in picking cotton, but he downplays the relevance of these achievements, arguing instead that other, gendered activities, like corn shucking, provided owner-sanctioned activities and spaces for male slaves to assert their masculinity (318–319, 489–490). While the owners may have tried to inculcate a sense of patriarchy through this action, Genovese's claim

that women internalized these sentiments seems dubious based upon the recollections of former female slaves, and their children, who spoke proudly of their ability to outpace men.

71. For example, white Georgians in Monroe County in 1835 feared a slave rebellion.

72. While it is impossible to ascertain the exact number of the runaways who successfully escaped to the North, there were a number of high-profile cases in which ex-slaves wrote narratives detailing their experiences while in bondage in Georgia. For example, see William Craft and Ellen Craft, *Running a Thousand Miles for Freedom; or, the Escape of William and Ellen Craft from Slavery* (London, 1860); Brown, *Slave Life in Georgia*; Ball, *Fifty Years in Chains*. For an account of a runaway who fled from slavery in the Georgia lowcountry, see Grimes, *Life of William Grimes*. These slave narratives provided an invaluable firsthand account of the brutality of the southern slave system, which abolitionists employed to marshal support for the antislavery movement. For an in-depth examination of runaways in the antebellum South, the best account remains Franklin and Schweninger, *Runaway Slaves*. See also John Blassingame, *The Slave Community: Plantation Life in the Antebellum South* (New York, 1979), especially chapter 5.

73. Craft and Craft, *Running a Thousand Miles for Freedom*, 29–32, 40–80.

74. For a contemporary account of runaway slaves living in the woods, see Ball, *Fifty Years in Chains*, 247–261, 354–356. For more on slaves who fled from their plantations for extended periods of time, or engaged in "lying out" as the practice was known, see Franklin and Schweninger, *Runaway Slaves*, 98–109; Genovese, *Roll, Jordan, Roll*, 649–657; Kaye, *Joining Places*, 129–136. Runaways faced a host of difficulties beyond those inherent in living in the outdoors. As Kaye demonstrates, runaways could not always rely on fellow slaves to help or protect them. Runaways who hid in areas where they were unknown by the nearby slave population sometimes found themselves in conflict with local bondmen, who "were suspicious of slave strangers" just as they were of unfamiliar whites (132).

75. For more on the state government's policies toward infrastructure in Georgia, see Peter Wallenstein, *From Slave South to New South: Public Policy in Nineteenth-Century Georgia* (Chapel Hill, 1987), part I; Fletcher M. Green, "Georgia's Board of Public Works," *Georgia Historical Quarterly* 22 (June 1938): 117–137; Gates, "Building the 'Empire State of the South': The Political Economy, 1800–1860" (Ph.D. diss., University of Georgia, 2001), 70–90. For more on the use of slaves on internal improvement projects in the South, see Starobin, *Industrial Slavery in the Old South*, 28–34. As Starobin notes, the "wide use of industrial slaves by state and federal agencies suggests not only the centrality of industrial slavery to the southern economy but also the extent of southern control of the national political structure" (33).

76. Hamilton Fulton, "Report to the Joint Committee of Agriculture and Internal Improvement," published in *Georgia Journal*, 3 December 1827; Starobin, *Industrial Slavery in the Old South*, 199.

77. *Acts of the General Assembly of the State of Georgia, Passed in Milledgeville at an Annual Session in November and December, 1829* (Milledgeville, 1830), 139–145. In addition to authorizing how and where the slaves should work, the General Assembly determined their food and clothing rations. Slaves received three-quarters of a pound of bacon, or one pound of pork, and two pounds of "good corn meal" per day and one pint of molasses, half a pound of salt, and one-fourth of a pound of tobacco per week. Slaves were furnished with two "good suits of strong cotton cloth" for the summer and two "good suits of wool or cotton cloth for winter wear," one good blanket, a wool hat, and two pairs of "coarse shoes" per year (*Acts of the General Assembly of the State of Georgia, Passed in Milledgeville at an Annual Session in November and December, 1830* [Milledgeville, 1831], 189–190).

78. *Acts of the General Assembly of the State of Georgia, Passed in Milledgeville at an Annual Session in November and December, 1833* (Milledgeville, 1834), 305–308; *Acts of the General Assembly of the State of Georgia, Passed in Milledgeville at an Annual Session in November and December, 1834* (Milledgeville, 1835), 328–329. The $117,464 garnered from the auctions included proceeds from the sale of tools, wagons, mules, and horses used by public hands at the various worksites. Prior to the sale of the public hands, several escaped and remained at large at the time of the auction.

79. "Report of the Joint Committee on Agriculture and Internal Improvements," *Journal of the Senate of the State of Georgia, at an Annual Session of the General Assembly, begun and held at Milledgeville, the Seat of Government, in November and December, 1827* (Milledgeville, 1828), 253–259. The report can also be found in *Acts of the General Assembly of the State of Georgia, Passed in Milledgeville at an Annual Session in November and December, 1827*, 253–263; Starobin, *Industrial Slavery in the Old South*, 199.

80. "Report of the Joint Committee on Agriculture and Internal Improvements," *Journal of the Senate of the State of Georgia, at an Annual Session of the General Assembly, begun and held at Milledgeville, the Seat of Government, in November and December, 1827* (Milledgeville, 1828), 253–259. The report can also be found in *Acts of the General Assembly of the State of Georgia, Passed in Milledgeville at an Annual Session in November and December, 1827* (Milledgeville, 1827), 253–263.

81. Ulrich B. Phillips, *A History of Transportation in the Eastern Cotton Belt to 1860* (Norwood, Mass., 1908), 119–120; Fraser, *Savannah in the Old South*, 212.

82. Loammi Baldwin, *Report on the Brunswick Canal and Railroad, Glynn County, Georgia: with an Appendix Containing the Charter and Commissioners' Report* (Boston, 1837); Kemble, *Journal of a Residence on a Georgian Plantation in 1838–1839*, 122, 279; Phillips, *A History of Transportation in the Eastern Cotton Belt to 1860*, 356–357. For more on canals, see Gates, "Building the 'Empire State of South,'" 50–69.

83. Lockley, *Lines in the Sand*, 36–37.

84. Fraser, *Savannah in the Old South*, 232.

85. Kemble, *Journal of a Residence on a Georgian Plantation in 1838–1839*, 104–105. She noted that lowcountry planters in Georgia claimed "the Irish hate the Ne-

groes more even than the Americans do," and therefore it was necessary to keep them apart (124). For more on the Irish and slavery in the antebellum South, see David T. Gleeson, *The Irish in the South, 1815–1877* (Chapel Hill, 2001), especially chapter 8.

86. For more on Georgia's antebellum railroads, see Phillips, *A History of Transportation in the Eastern Cotton Belt to 1860*, chapters 5, 6, and 7; Coleman, ed., *A History of Georgia*, 156–162; Wallenstein, *From Slave South to New South*, part I; Gates, "Building the 'Empire State of South,'" particularly chapter 4.

87. Starobin estimates that southern railroads employed more than twenty thousand slaves (*Industrial Slavery in the Old South*, 28).

88. *Savannah Daily Georgian*, 5 January 1848, as quoted in Byrne, "The Burden and the Heat of the Day," 182. For more examples of newspaper advertisements from railroad companies and contractors seeking slaves to rent, see Flanders, *Plantation Slavery in Georgia*, 198; Smith, *Slavery and Rice Culture in Low Country Georgia*, 60.

89. Flanders, *Plantation Slavery in Georgia*, 197–198.

90. *Georgia Journal and Messenger*, 28 January 1852, as quoted in Flanders, *Plantation Slavery in Georgia*, 198.

91. As quoted in Starobin, *Industrial Slavery in the Old South*, 203. "Third Semi-Annual Report of the Engineer of the Central Railroad and Banking Company of Georgia, to the President, Directors and Stockholders," in *American Railroad Journal* 9 (1839): 83. For more on the Central Georgia Railroad, see Phillips, *A History of Transportation in the Eastern Cotton Belt to 1860*, 252–302. Phillips's study focuses chiefly on the economic history of the company and largely ignores issues related to slavery and the laborers. See also Wallenstein, *From Slave South to New South*, 38. The president of the Charleston & Savannah Railroad Company also recommended buying slaves as the most cost-efficient means of labor.

92. Starobin, *Industrial Slavery in the Old South*, 123–124. Starobin acknowledged that some railroad companies abandoned their use of slaves because of "uneven profits" in the 1840s and 1850s, but he rejected the notion that this represented a "general trend." Rather, he noted, "in the last antebellum decades many railroads were replacing free labor with slave labor, and many others either purchased or hired slaves as they had always done."

93. "Governor's Message," *Milledgeville Daily Federal Union*, 4 November 1858.

94. Wallenstein, *From Slave South to New South*, 67–68.

95. For more on the rise of manufacturing and industry in the Georgia up-country, see Gillespie, *Free Labor in an Unfree World*, chapter 3; Gates, "Building the 'Empire State of the South,'" chapters 5 and 6; John Richard Detreville, "The Little New South: Origins of Industry in Georgia's Fall-Line Cities, 1840–1865" (Ph.D. diss., University of North Carolina, 1985). For a broader discussion on the diversification of the southern economy in the antebellum era, see Starobin, *Industrial Slavery in the Old South*; Fred Bateman and Thomas Joseph Weiss, *A Deplorable Scarcity: The Failure of Industrialization in the Slave Economy* (Chapel Hill, 1981); Fogel and

Engerman, *Time on the Cross;* Carole E. Scott, "Why the Cotton Textile Industry Did Not Develop in the South Sooner," *Agricultural History* 68, no. 2, Eli Whitney's Cotton Gin, 1793–1993: A Symposium (spring 1994): 105–121; Herbert Collins, "The Southern Industrial Gospel before 1860," *Journal of Southern History* 12, no. 3 (August 1946): 386–402.

96. *Southern Whig,* 6 June 1846, as quoted in Gillespie, *Free Labor in an Unfree World,* 145. For a lengthier disquisition on the benefits of industry for southern progress and advancement, see Hon. J. H. Lumpkin, "The Industrial Regeneration of the South," *DeBow's Review* 12, no. 1 (January 1852): 41–50.

97. For more on the history of the antebellum textile industry in Georgia, see Gates, "Building the 'Empire State of the South,'" 124–149; Charles C. Jones Jr., "Pioneer Manufacturing in Richmond County Georgia," *Textile History Review* (July 1964): 69–83; Richard W. Griffin, "Antebellum Industrial Foundations of the (Alleged) New South," *Textile History Review* (April 1964): 33–43; Richard W. Griffin, "The Textile Industry in Greene County, Georgia, Before 1860," *Georgia Historical Quarterly* 48 (March 1964): 80–84; Richard W. Griffin, "The Origins of the Industrial Revolution in Georgia: Cotton Textiles, 1810–1865," *Georgia Historical Quarterly* 42 (December 1958): 355–375; Richard W. Griffin, "The Augusta (Georgia) Manufacturing Company in Peace, War, and Reconstruction, 1847–1877," *Business History Review* 32 (spring 1958): 60–73; J. G. Johnson, "Notes on Manufacturing in Ante-Bellum Georgia," *Georgia Historical Quarterly* 16 (September 1932): 214–231; R. H. Shryock, "The Early Industrial Revolution in the Empire State," *Georgia Historical Quarterly* 11 (June 1927): 109–128.

98. *Georgia Courier,* 24 April 1828, as quoted in Phillips, ed., *Plantation and Frontier Documents,* 358.

99. *Milledgeville Federal Union,* 28 November 1848. See also Gillespie, *Free Labor in an Unfree World,* 73–76.

100. *Macon Telegraph,* 6 November 1827.

101. James Silk Buckingham, *The Slave States of America* (London, 1842), 2:111–113.

102. Starobin, *Industrial Slavery in the Old South,* 119–122. Starobin recognized that white workers made "inroads into occupations traditionally dominated by industrial slaves in the 1850s" but asserted that historians have tended to overstate the extent of the conversion to white labor. Even in the textile industry, he claimed, slaves remained a critical part of the labor force in some areas of the South up until the war. While this seems to have been the case in South Carolina, a clear shift in favor of white laborers occurred in Georgia.

103. For an account of the rise and fall of Georgia's antebellum gold industry, see David Williams, *The Georgia Gold Rush: Twenty-Niners, Cherokees, and Gold Fever* (Columbia, S.C., 1993).

104. Major Philip Wager to General Alexander Macomb, 30 September 1830, in James W. Covington, ed., "Letters from the Georgia Gold Region," *Georgia Historical Quarterly* 39 (1955): 407–408; Williams, *The Georgia Gold Rush,* 26.

105. For more on Georgia's gold mining areas during the antebellum era, see Fletcher M. Green, "Georgia's Forgotten Industry: Gold Mining," *Georgia Historical Quarterly* 19 (1935): 1–19; Otis E. Young Jr., "The Southern Gold Rush, 1828–1836," *Journal of Southern History* 48 (August 1982): 373–392; Williams, *The Georgia Gold Rush*; David Williams, "Georgia's Forgotten Miners: African Americans and the Georgia Gold Rush of 1829," in *Appalachians and Race: The Mountain South from Slavery to Segregation*, ed. John C. Inscoe, 40–49 (Lexington, Ky., 2001).

106. Roy E. Bottoms, "History of the Franklin Gold Mine," *Northwest Georgia Historical and Genealogical Society Quarterly* 5 (October 1973): 3–7; Williams, "Georgia's Forgotten Miners," 42–44; Lloyd Marlin, *History of Cherokee County* (Atlanta, 1932), 147.

107. Robert L. Meriwether, ed., *The Papers of John C. Calhoun* (Columbia, S.C., 1959–2003), 12:555; Starobin, *Industrial Slavery in the Old South*, 24.

108. Henry B. C. Nitze and Henry A. J. Wilkens, *Gold Mining in North Carolina and Adjacent South Appalachian Regions* (Raleigh, N.C., 1897), 28.

109. Green, "Georgia's Forgotten Industry," 218.

110. Williams, *The Georgia Gold Rush*, 117–118, 120. Starobin notes that many of the forty-niners were southern slave owners who carried their bondmen out west (Starobin, *Industrial Slavery in the Old South*, 24).

111. Though most historians focus on commonalities among whites in the antebellum South, some historians do highlight class divisions. Most of the historians who examine class, however, focus on yeomen or "common" whites in rural areas. For one representative example on Georgia, see Hahn, *The Roots of Southern Populism*. For the scholarship on mechanics in the South, see Carl Bridenbaugh, *Colonial Craftsman* (New York, 1950); Richard Walsh, *Charleston's Sons of Liberty: A Study of the Artisans, 1763–1789* (Columbia, S.C., 1959); Ira Berlin and Herbert G. Gutman, "Natives and Immigrants, Free Men and Slaves: Urban Workingmen in the Antebellum American South," *American Historical Review* 88, no. 5 (December 1983): 1175–1200; Jean B. Russo, *Free Workers in a Plantation Economy: Talbot County, Maryland, 1690–1759* (New York, 1989); Christine Daniels, "'Wanted: A Blacksmith Who Understands Plantation Work': Artisans in Maryland, 1700–1800," *William and Mary Quarterly*, 3rd Series, 50, no. 4 (October 1993): 743–767; Johanna Miller Lewis, *Artisans in the North Carolina Backcountry* (Lexington, Ky., 1995). For work specifically on mechanics in Georgia, see Dudley Johnson, "William Harris Garland: Mechanic of the Old South," *Georgia Historical Quarterly* 53, no. 1 (1969): 41–56; Fred Siegel, "Artisans and Immigrants in the Politics of Late Antebellum Georgia," *Civil War History* 27, no. 3 (1981): 221–230; Gillespie, *Free Labor in an Unfree World*.

Over the past four decades, historians of Georgia have disagreed over how effective the state's white mechanics were at organizing to promote their interests. This debate has largely paralleled the broader debate in southern history over the relative power of planters in the antebellum era. In 1969, Dudley Johnson offered a portrait of the life of a southern urban mechanic as one of constant movement. Most white mechanics in antebellum Georgia, he argued, shifted jobs frequently, moving from city to city looking for opportunities. Johnson asserted that the white mechanics were decidedly apolitical, though. Fred Siegel offered a very different depiction of white mechanics in Georgia, in "Artisans and Immigrants in the Politics of Late Antebellum Georgia." Siegel's mechanics were well organized and politically astute. He noted the intense rivalry between "white and often immigrant city labor and slaveowning businessmen," which came to the fore in times of crisis, such as 1850 and 1860–1861. "When they were unable to compete with the planters' slaves in the marketplace, they turned to the ballot box to restrict the workings of the labor market" (223). The situation got worse during the 1840s, when the economy soured and slaves were sent to the cities in search of work. In contrast to Siegel, Michele Gillespie argues that mechanics in Georgia failed to coalesce into an effective political force to promote their interests because their interests were too broad. By the 1840s, social and economic changes linked to the spread of slavery reduced the opportunities for young white mechanics. Many failed to become master craftsmen and remained wage laborers their whole lives. Others, however, achieved substantial success and became planters in their own right. This fundamental divide, Gillespie asserts, meant that group cohesion of any type would have been difficult to achieve. While I agree with Gillespie that mechanics failed to sustain their reform efforts throughout the nineteenth century, that does not mean that they did not produce results. A close examination of the laws passed in the 1840s and 1850s, both at the state and local level, reflects the efforts of white mechanics to protect their industries from competition with slaves and free blacks.

For another study of southern mechanics that comes to similar conclusions, see Charles G. Steffen, *The Mechanics of Baltimore: Workers and Politics in the Age of Revolution, 1763–1812* (Urbana, 1984). Steffen argues that mechanics in Baltimore became a political force by the War of 1812. Their rise, more or less, coincided with the revolutionary era. Democracy in the new nation gave them broader access to power.

112. One of the key questions related to the historiography of the U.S. South concerns power relations in antebellum society. One group of historians argues that planters completely dominated all aspects of life in the South. For examples, see William E. Dodd, *The Cotton Kingdom: A Chronicle of the Old South* (New Haven, 1919); Ulrich B. Phillips, *Life and Labor in the Old South* (Boston, 1929); Lewis C. Gray, *History of Agriculture in the Southern United States to 1860* (Washington, D.C., 1933); Dickson D. Bruce, *And They all Sang Hallelujah: Plain-Folk Camp-Meeting Religion, 1800–1845* (Knoxville, 1974); Michael P. Johnson, *Toward a Patriarchal Republic: The Secession of Georgia* (Baton Rouge, 1977); Randolph B. Campbell and Richard G. Lowe, *Wealth and Power in Antebellum Texas* (College Station, Tex., 1977); Randolph B. Campbell, *An Empire for Slavery: The Peculiar Institution in Texas, 1821–1865* (Baton

Rouge, 1989); Christopher C. Morris, *Becoming Southern: The Evolution of a Way of Life, Warren County and Vicksburg, Mississippi, 1770–1860* (New York, 1995). In his various writings, Eugene D. Genovese has offered the most detailed and cogent analysis of this position. For examples, see *The Political Economy of Slavery: Studies in the Economy and Society of the Slave South* (New York, 1965) and *Fruits of Merchant Capital: Slavery and Bourgeois Property in the Rise and Expansion of Capitalism* (New York, 1983).

My work builds upon the scholarship of another group of historians, who contend that nonelite whites contested power. Though these historians disagree over the extent to which nonelite whites successfully resisted planters' efforts to dominate society, they reject the notion that planters enjoyed hegemonic control over the South. For examples, see Avery Craven, *The Coming of the Civil War* (New York, 1942); Fletcher M. Green, "Democracy in the Old South," *Journal of Southern History* 12, no. 1 (February 1946): 3–23; Frank L. Owsley, *Plain Folk of the Old South* (Baton Rouge, 1949); Fredrickson, *The Black Image in the White Mind*; Hahn, *The Roots of Southern Populism*; Lacy K. Ford Jr., *Origins of Southern Radicalism: The South Carolina Upcountry, 1800–1860* (New York, 1988); Bill Cecil-Fronsman, *Common Whites: Class and Culture in Antebellum North Carolina* (Lexington, Ky., 1992); Daniel Dupre, "Barbecues and Pledges: Electioneering and the Rise of Democratic Politics in Antebellum Alabama," *Journal of Southern History* 60, no. 3 (1994): 479–512; Charles C. Bolton, *Poor Whites of the Antebellum South: Tenants and Laborers in Central North Carolina and Northeast Mississippi* (Durham, 1994); Stephanie McCurry, *Masters of Small Worlds: Yeoman Households, Gender Relations, and the Political Culture of the Antebellum South Carolina Low Country* (New York, 1995); Lacy K. Ford, "Popular Ideology of the Old South's Plain Folk: The Limits of Egalitarianism in a Slaveholding Society," in *Plain Folk of the South Revisited*, ed. Samuel C. Hyde, 205–227 (Baton Rouge, 1997); Lockley, *Lines in the Sand*.

113. *Acts of the General Assembly of the State of Georgia*, 1827, 1829, 1830, 1831, 1832, 1833, 1834. The counties affected by the legislation were Burke, Jefferson, Scriven, Richmond, and Hancock. Interestingly, Liberty and McIntosh both followed this path in 1839, but they repealed the laws the next year. This went against custom in the region, a custom that proved agreeable to slaves and owners alike. For more on urban slavery in Georgia, see Donnie D. Bellamy, "Macon, Georgia, 1823–1860: A Study in Urban Slavery," *Phylon* 45, no. 4 (1984): 298–310; Wood, *Women's Work, Men's Work*; Johnson, *Black Savannah*; Reidy, *From Slavery to Agrarian Capitalism in the Cotton Plantation South*; Lockley, *Lines in the Sand*. For more on urban slavery in the broader South, see Richard C. Wade, *Slavery in the Cities: The South, 1820–1860* (New York, 1964); Claudia Dale Goldin, *Urban Slavery in the American South, 1820–1860: A Quantitative History* (Chicago, 1976); Berlin and Gutman, "Natives and Immigrants, Free Men and Slaves," 1175–1200; Stephen Whitman, "Diverse Good Causes: Manumission and the Transformation of Urban Slavery," *Social Science History* 19, no. 3 (1995): 333–370.

114. John Campbell Butler, *The Historical Record of Macon and Central Georgia, Contain-*

ing Many Interesting and Valuable Reminiscences Connected with the Whole State, Including Numerous Incidents and Facts Never Before Published and Of Great Historic Value (Macon, Ga., 1879), 167.

115. A. L. Hull, Sketches of Athens, Georgia, from 1830 to 1865 (Athens, 1893), 9.

116. Charles Lyell, A Second Visit to the United States of North America (New York, 1849), 2:78–82.

117. Athens Southern Banner, 13 January 1838. John J. Flournoy was a colorful character and prolific writer. He penned several volumes—books and pamphlets—related to race and class in the South. Using vitriolic prose, he assailed the negative impact of slavery on nonelite whites while demanding that white elites show greater deference to white supremacy. He called for the expulsion of "Africans" as a means to bring about greater white parity. For more examples of Flournoy's work, see Expulsion the Best Earthly Conservative of Peace (Athens, 1837), The Doctrine of Expulsion (n.p., 1836), and Essay on the Origin, Habits, &c. of the African Race (New York, 1835). For a sympathetic biographical treatment of Flournoy, see E. Merten Coulter, John Jacobus Flournoy: Champion of the Common Man in the Antebellum South (Savannah, 1942).

118. For example, see "Newton Superior Court," Milledgeville Federal Union, 15 April 1845; for Jasper County, see "Presentments," Milledgeville Southern Recorder, 19 December 1845; "Mayor's Office," Georgia Telegraph, 16 July 1844; and "Council Chamber," Georgia Telegraph, 28 October 1845. On 18 January 1845, the Columbus City Council outlawed slave self-hiring and prohibited free blacks from living by themselves. See Columbus Enquirer, 29 January 1845.

119. Acts of the State of Georgia, 1845 (Columbus, Ga., 1846), 49.

120. Lyell, A Second Visit to the United States of North America, 2:78–82.

121. Starobin regarded the 1845 law as a significant achievement for Georgia's white mechanics. In the years that followed, however, they "failed to strengthen the law of 1845" and the push to reform slavery flagged. As a result, he argued, the law represented their last major achievement. See Starobin, Industrial Slavery in the Old South, 212.

122. Most political histories of antebellum Georgia focus on the state level, examining elite whites, the development of the party system, and the competition for control of the legislature. For example, see Murray, The Whig Party in Georgia; DeBats, Elites and Masses; and Carey, Parties, Slavery, and the Union in Antebellum Georgia. By concentrating on politics at the state level, however, historians have largely neglected the rise in power among nonelite whites who exercised considerable control over elections and politics in urban areas in the 1840s and 1850s. The political struggles that took place at the local level had a tremendous impact on slavery and race relations. Indeed, these areas served as the battleground over the issue of slavery between elite and nonelite whites.

123. In 1825 Macon shipped out twelve thousand bales of cotton, and boosters expected the amount to nearly double the following season (Niles' Register, 30:4).

124. Reidy, *From Slavery to Agrarian Capitalism in the Cotton Plantation South*, 21. For more on the early history of Macon, see chapters 1, 2, and 3 in Reidy's study.

125. *Georgia Telegraph*, 15 May 1849.

126. For more on the early economic development of Macon, see Butler, *The Historical Record of Macon and Central Georgia*.

127. "Council Chamber," *Georgia Telegraph*, 28 October 1845; "Mayor's Office," *Georgia Telegraph*, 16 July 1844.

128. *Georgia Telegraph*, 13 June 1848.

129. Extensive extracts of the lecture appeared in the *Georgia Telegraph*, 20 November 1849.

130. *Georgia Telegraph*, 6 November 1849

131. Quoted in *Albany Patriot*, 17 August 1849, and in Flanders, *Plantation Slavery in Georgia*, 205.

132. *Georgia Telegraph*, 23 October 1849.

133. Ibid., 30 October 1849.

134. Ibid., 16 October 1849.

135. From *Rome Southerner*, as quoted in *Georgia Telegraph*, 18 September 1849.

136. Most historians focus on white southerners' agreement on the institution of slavery. Some historians identify white urban workers in the South as antislavery. I depart from both interpretations not in seeing agreement over slavery or uncovering significant antislavery or abolitionist sentiment but in discerning class-based disagreements over how slavery should best be organized. Here I agree with Starobin, who asserted: "White artisans did not object to the use of slaves in *all* industrial occupations, only to their use in certain skilled crafts. White artisans did seek not seek to abolish slavery altogether, only to exclude Negroes from certain trades and to curtail such pernicious practices as board money payments and self-hire privileges. . . . The net effect of most protests by white artisans was thus not to weaken slavery but to entrench it more firmly in southern society" (*Industrial Slavery in the Old South*, 212–213). For similar views by an historian of Georgia, see Gates, "Building the 'Empire State of South,'" chapters 6 and 7.

137. For more on abolitionism in Georgia, see Ruth Scarborough, *The Opposition to Slavery in Georgia Prior to 1860* (Nashville, 1933). In his memoir, John Brown recounted the tragic consequences that befell one of his owner's neighbors because of his abolitionist views. The man, a Scottish immigrant, chose to rely on free laborers, black and white, to cultivate his land rather than slaves and was outspoken in his belief that his laborers performed better than the slaves on the surrounding plantations. Slave owners living nearby conspired to cheat the man out of his land and succeeded in their endeavor. As many visitors to the state came to recognize, white Georgians brooked no dissent, from whites or blacks, when it came to slavery. See Brown, *Slave Life in Georgia*, 47–53.

138. *Georgia Telegraph*, 18 September 1849.

139. *Georgia Citizen,* 19 April 1851.

140. Ibid., 1 March 1851.

141. For example, mechanics formed societies in Atlanta, Americus, and Thomaston, as well as in Cobb, Drayton, and Dooly counties. See *Georgia Citizen,* 3 May 1851, 21 June 1851, 28 June 1851, 4 July 1851.

142. Ibid., 11 July 1851.

143. Ibid.

144. Ibid.

145. Lyell, *A Second Visit to the United States of North America,* 2:78–82.

146. For more on the sectional crisis of the 1850s and its impact on the political system in Georgia, see Coleman, ed., *A History of Georgia,* 140–152; Reidy, *From Slavery to Agrarian Capitalism in the Cotton Plantation South,* 82–107; DeBats, *Elites and Masses,* 95–119; Carey, *Parties, Slavery, and the Union in Antebellum Georgia,* 156–212; Phillips, *Georgia and State Rights,* 163–181. On the political divisions among white mechanics in Georgia, see Gillespie, *Free Labor in an Unfree World,* 140–148.

147. For a discussion of the impact of the Panic of 1857, see Edward L. Ayers, *Vengeance and Justice: Crime and Punishment in the 19th Century American South* (New York, 1984), 94–98.

148. *Columbus Enquirer,* 11 May 1858.

149. *Milledgeville Federal Union,* 6 July 1858 (taken from the *Brunswick Herald*).

150. Gillespie, *Free Labor in an Unfree World,* 85–86, 92.

151. Hahn, *The Roots of Southern Populism,* 26–27, 32–34, 40–49.

152. For example, in 1860 the counties surrounding Atlanta had relatively small black populations compared to the counties in the blackbelt or lowcountry: Cobb (w) 10,410, (b) 3,819; DeKalb (w) 5,798, (b) 2,000; Fulton (w) 11,441, (b) 2,955; Gwinnett (w) 10,358, (b) 2,551. North of these counties, the number of blacks dropped even lower. See U.S. Census, 1860.

153. Hahn, *The Roots of Southern Populism,* 91–116.

154. G. H. Stueckrath, "The Cities of Georgia—Atlanta," *DeBow's Review* 27, no. 4 (1859): 465–466; Thomas H. Martin, *Atlanta and Its Builders: A Comprehensive History of the Gate City of the South* (Atlanta, 1902), 1:153.

155. The population statistics are drawn from Martin, *Atlanta and Its Builders,* 1:73, 88, 128, 141, 149. The quote is taken from Stueckrath, "The Cities of Georgia—Atlanta," 464.

156. Martin, *Atlanta and Its Builders,* 1:88–89

157. Gillespie, *Free Labor in an Unfree World,* 161.

158. James Michael Russell, *Atlanta, 1847–1890: City Building in the Old South and the New* (Baton Rouge, 1988), 76.

159. Stueckrath, "The Cities of Georgia—Atlanta," 468.

160. Martin, *Atlanta and Its Builders,* 1:147.

161. *Atlanta Daily Intelligencer,* 8 October 1858.

162. *Atlanta Daily Intelligencer,* 20 January 1855. The candidates who lost in the

election claimed that they had been the victims of fraud. They alleged that "the majority was defeated by the votes of *non residents, aliens,* and others," and petitioned the mayor-elect to hold a new election. The appeal was rejected. For more on the election, see Martin, *Atlanta and Its Builders,* 1:122–124; Franklin M. Garrett, *Atlanta and Its Environs: A Chronicle of Its People and Events,* vol. 1 (Athens, 1954), 387–388.

163. The Democrats won the municipal election in 1855, 1858, 1859, and 1860. James M. Russell, "Elites and Municipal Politics in Atlanta, 1847–1890," in *Toward a New South? Studies in Post-Civil War Southern Communities,* ed. Orville Vernon Burton and Robert C. McMath Jr. (Westport, Conn., 1982), 55.

164. *Atlanta Weekly Intelligencer,* 2 December 1858.

165. According to James Michael Russell, in the antebellum era 16 percent of the city's mayors and council members were manual workers; this tally could be low since it does include the results of thirteen members whose occupations Russell could not positively identify. By contrast, planters and farmers held less than 2 percent of the offices. James M. Russell, "Elites and Municipal Politics in Atlanta, 1847–1890," in Burton and McMath, eds., *Toward a New South?* 44–45.

166. *Atlanta Daily Intelligencer,* 1 October 1857

167. Ibid. For more on the use of the term "boss" in antebellum America and the rise of class divisions, see Roediger, *Wages of Whiteness,* 54. For a broader discussion of the links between language, class, and race, see chapter 3.

168. *Atlanta Daily Intelligencer,* 3 October 1857.

169. Atlanta City Council Minutes, vol. 2, 25 September 1857, Atlanta History Center.

170. See examples in *Atlanta Daily Intelligencer,* 2 October 1857, 3 October 1857, 5 October 1857; 16 January 1858; 17 January 1858.

171. *Atlanta Weekly Intelligencer,* 22 January 1858.

172. Atlanta City Ordinance Book, 28 May 1852, 27 July 1855, Atlanta History Center.

173. Atlanta City Council Minutes, vol. 2, 5 March 1858.

174. Atlanta City Council Minutes, vol. 3, 4 January 1861.

175. The figures are drawn from Wade, *Slavery in the Cities,* 327.

176. Haunton, "Savannah in the 1850's," 12–17, 50–51; Byrne, "The Burden and the Heat of the Day," 203–204; Fraser, *Savannah in the Old South,* 254–255; Herbert Weaver, "Foreigners in Ante-Bellum Savannah," *Georgia Historical Quarterly* 37 (1953): 1–4; Herbert Weaver, "Foreigners in Ante-Bellum Towns of the Lower South," *Journal of Southern History* 13, no. 1 (February 1947): 66–67.

177. Ayers, *Vengeance and Justice,* 79; Haunton, "Savannah in the 1850's," 56–59; Byrne, "The Burden and the Heat of the Day," 203–204; Lockley, *Lines in the Sand,* 34–38.

178. Ayers, *Vengeance and Justice,* 80–81; Haunton, "Savannah in the 1850's," 57–58; Byrne, "The Burden and the Heat of the Day," 120–121; Lockley, *Lines in the Sand,* 46–48; Weaver, "Foreigners in Ante-Bellum Savannah," 1–2.

179. In *Lines in the Sand*, Timothy Lockley offers a different perspective. Though he acknowledges that conflicts arose between blacks and nonelite whites in Savannah, he emphasizes the moments when the two groups came together to resist the white elite. In the process, however, he underestimates the degree to which the animosities created deep divisions between the two groups.

180. Richard D. Arnold to Louisa McAllister, 6 December 1850, in Shryock, ed., *Letters of Richard D. Arnold*, 39; Richard D. Arnold to John W. Forney, 18 December 1850, in Shryock, ed., *Letters of Richard D. Arnold*, 47; Richard D. Arnold to John W. Forney, 9 September 1851, in Shryock, ed., *Letters of Richard D. Arnold*, 55; Haunton, "Savannah in the 1850's," 209–210; Fraser, *Savannah in the Old South*, 232, 291.

181. Lockley, *Lines in the Sand*, 73.

182. Ibid.; Wood, *Women's Work, Men's Work*, 143.

183. Goldin, *Urban Slavery in the American South*, 29.

184. Message of Joseph Brown, 7 November 1860, in Allen D. Candler, ed., *The Confederate Record of the State of Georgia* (Atlanta, 1909), 1:55–56.

8. Rewriting Georgia's Racial Past

1. White, *Historical Collections of Georgia*; George White, *Statistics of the State of Georgia: Including an Account of its Natural, Civil, and Ecclesiastical History; Together with a Particular Description of Each County, Notices of the Manners and Customs of its Aboriginal Tribes, and a Correct Map of the State* (Savannah, 1849).

2. White, *Historical Collections of Georgia*, v–vi.

3. Ibid., 162.

4. Ibid., 154–174.

5. Ibid., 173.

6. Ibid.

7. For the section on the Creeks, see White, *Historical Collections of Georgia*, 128–135. For the section on the Cherokees, see 136–153.

8. White, *Historical Collections of Georgia*, 236.

9. Ibid.

10. Gilmer, *Sketches of Some of the First Settlers of Upper Georgia, of the Cherokees, and the Author*.

11. Ibid., 334.

12. Ibid., 432.

13. Ibid., 287.

14. Ibid., 293.

15. Ibid., 137.

16. Ibid., 138–141.

17. Ibid., 142–156.

18. Ibid., 17, 34, 48, 50, 113, 402.

19. Lumpkin, *Cherokee Removal*, 2:253. For more on Lumpkin's actions while in office, see Carl J. Vipperman, "The 'Particular Mission' of Wilson Lumpkin," *Georgia Historical Quarterly* 66, no. 3 (fall 1982): 295–316.

20. Lumpkin, *Cherokee Removal*, 2:254.

21. Ibid., 2:255–257. Lumpkin explained his position in two letters to White: Wilson Lumpkin to Rev. George White, 25 July 1833, and Wilson Lumpkin to Rev. George White, 25 August 1833. Both letters are included in Lumpkin's memoir. See 2:257–266.

22. Lumpkin, *Cherokee Removal*, 2:318.

23. Ibid., 2:266.

24. Ibid.

25. Ibid., 2:300–317, quote on 306.

26. Ibid., 2:315.

27. Ibid., 2:305.

28. *Acts of the General Assembly of the State of Georgia, Passed in Milledgeville at an Annual Session in November and December, 1838* (Milledgeville, 1839), 68–69.

29. *Acts of the General Assembly of the State of Georgia, Passed in Milledgeville at an Annual Session in November and December, 1839* (Milledgeville, 1840), 32–33.

30. *Acts of the General Assembly of the State of Georgia, Passed in Milledgeville at an Annual Session in November and December, 1840* (Milledgeville, 1841), 31–32.

31. *Acts of the General Assembly of the State of Georgia, Passed in Milledgeville at an Annual Session in November and December, 1842* (Milledgeville, 1843), 49–50.

32. *Acts of the State of Georgia, 1845* (Columbus, Ga., 1846), 67.

33. Ibid., 65.

34. For more studies on Joseph Lumpkin and his role in slave law in Georgia, see Mason W. Stephenson and D. Grier Stephenson Jr., "'To Protect and Defend': Joseph Henry Lumpkin, the Supreme Court of Georgia, and Slavery," *Emory Law Journal* 25 (summer 1976): 579–608; John Philip Reid, "Lessons of Lumpkin: Review of Recent Literature on Law, Comity, and the Impending Crisis," *William and Mary Law Review* 23 (summer 1982): 571–624; Timothy S. Huebner, *The Southern Judicial Tradition: State Judges and Sectional Distinctiveness, 1790–1890* (Athens, 1999); Hicks, *Joseph Henry Lumpkin*.

35. Huebner, *The South Judicial Tradition*, 71–77.

36. Hicks, *Joseph Henry Lumpkin*, 56.

37. *American Colonization Society v. Gartrell*, 23 Ga. 464 (1857).

38. Helen Tunnicliff Catterall, *Judicial Cases Concerning American Slavery and the Negro* (New York, 1968), 1–94; Stephenson and Stephenson, "To Protect and Defend," 581–582; Hicks, *Joseph Henry Lumpkin*, 125.

39. *Niles' Register*, 28:238–240, 277, 325–316. Troup continued to reiterate his views in subsequent messages. In one instance, Troup warned of the dangers posed by the growing antislavery sentiments in the country and its potential impact on Georgia should residents fail to act to protect their property and way of life.

40. The literature on proslavery thought is vast and continues to grow. For a recent interpretation, see Ford, *Deliver Us from Evil*. For an informative and illuminating overview, see Drew Gilpin Faust, *The Ideology of Slavery: Proslavery Thought in the Antebellum South, 1830–1860* (Baton Rouge, 1981), 1–20.

41. *Milledgeville Federal Union*, April 21, 1836. See also Young, *Domesticating Slavery*, 164–167, 218–220.

42. "Governor's Message," published in *Milledgeville Southern Recorder*, 10 November 1835.

43. "Judge Lumpkin's Report on Law Reform," published in *Milledgeville Southern Recorder*, 4 December 1849.

44. Joseph Henry Lumpkin to daughter Callie, 13 October 1853, as quoted in Hicks, *Joseph Henry Lumpkin*, 131–132. See also Huebner, *The Southern Judicial Tradition*, 87.

45. *America Colonization Society v. Gartrell*, 23 Ga. 464 (1857). On the biblical curse, see Stephen R. Haynes, *Noah's Curse: The Biblical Justification of American Slavery* (New York, 2002).

46. Thomas Read Rootes Cobb, *An Inquiry into the Law of Negro Slavery in the United States of America: To Which is Prefixed, An Historical Sketch of Slavery*, ed. Paul Finkelman, clix–clx (Savannah, Ga., 1858; reprint, Athens, Ga., 1999).

47. Ibid., ccxi.

48. Ibid., ccxxxiii.

49. *America Colonization Society v. Gartrell*, 23 Ga. 464 (1857).

50. *Acts of the State of Georgia, 1845* (Columbus, Ga., 1846), 18.

51. For more on the creation of the state supreme court in Georgia, see Hicks, *Joseph Henry Lumpkin*, 86–97.

52. *Georgia Journal*, 7 April 1835.

53. "Message of the Governor," in *Journal of the House of Representatives of the State of Georgia, at an Annual Session of the General Assembly, begun and held at Milledgeville, the Seat of Government, in November and December, 1841* (Milledgeville, 1842), 18–19. Governor McDonald's predecessors made similar appeals in the second half of the 1830s. For other examples, see the messages to the General Assembly from Governor William Schley and Governor George Gilmer in the *Journal of the House of Representatives of the State of Georgia, at an Annual Session of the General Assembly, begun and held at Milledgeville, the Seat of Government, in November and December, 1836* (Milledgeville, 1837), 24–25, and the *Journal of the House of Representatives of the State of Georgia, at an Annual Session of the General Assembly, begun and held at Milledgeville, the Seat of Government, in November and December, 1838* (Milledgeville, 1839), 14–15, respectively.

54. *Acts of the State of Georgia, 1845* (Columbus, Ga., 1846), 18–24.

55. For more on the controversy surrounding Judge Hooper and the Cherokees, see chapter 5. The outcry over Hooper's rulings prompted the Union Party majority in the legislature to initiate the process of amending the state constitution to permit the creation of a state supreme court. The process required two

successive sessions of the General Assembly to approve the changes to the constitution. In 1835, the measure passed, though it would take another ten years for the General Assembly to finally pass legislation to establish the court. See *Acts of the General Assembly of the State of Georgia, 1834; Acts of the General Assembly of the State of Georgia, 1835.*

56. Hicks, *Joseph Henry Lumpkin,* 89–90.

57. "Judge Lumpkin's Report on Law Reform," *Milledgeville Recorder,* 4 December 1849.

58. Joseph Lumpkin, "Industrial Regeneration of the South," *DeBow's Review* 12 (1852): 41–50.

59. Catterall, *Judicial Cases Concerning American Slavery and the Negro,* 1–94; Stephenson and Stephenson, "To Protect and Defend," 581–582; Hicks, *Joseph Henry Lumpkin,* 125.

60. *Seaborn C. Bryan v. Hugh Walton,* 14 Ga. 185 (1853), 205–206.

61. *Acts of the General Assembly of the State of Georgia, passed at Milledgeville, at an Annual Session, in November and December, 1812* (Milledgeville, 1812), 105–109.

62. *Acts of the General Assembly of the State of Georgia, passed at Milledgeville, at an Annual Session, in November and December, 1816* (Milledgeville, 1816), 1816, 15–18.

63. *Acts of the General Assembly of the State of Georgia, passed at Milledgeville, at an Annual Session, in November and December, 1818* (Milledgeville, 1818).

64. *Acts of the General Assembly of the State of Georgia, 1829.*

65. *The State v. Philpot* (1831) in G. M. Dudley, ed., *Reports of the Decisions Made by the Judges of the Superior Courts of Law and Chancery of the State of Georgia* (Charlottesville, 1903): 375–385, quote on 377.

66. Ibid., 378.

67. *Acts of the General Assembly, of the State of Georgia, Passed in Milledgeville, at an Annual Session in November and December, 1833* (Milledgeville, 1834), 143–217; *Acts of the General Assembly, of the State of Georgia, Passed in Milledgeville, at an Annual Session in November and December, 1835* (Milledgeville, 1836), 264–269. See also Edward F. Sweat, "The Free Negro in Ante-Bellum Georgia" (Ph.D. diss., Indiana University, 1957), and Flanders, "The Free Negro in Antebellum Georgia," 250–272. For more on the comparison with white men who were compelled to leave their Indian families or become "Indian" themselves, see chapter 5.

68. *Acts of the General Assembly of the State of Georgia, Passed in Milledgeville at an Annual Session in November and December, 1842* (Milledgeville, 1843), 181–182.

69. *Acts of the General Assembly of the State of Georgia, Passed in Milledgeville at a Biennial Session in November, December, January, and February, 1853–4* (Savannah, 1854), 101–103, 105–107; *Acts of the General Assembly of the State of Georgia, Passed in Milledgeville at an Annual Session in November and December, 1859* (Milledgeville, 1860), 69–70.

70. The state supreme court issued rulings on the case in 1853, 1856, and 1864. Several recent studies have examined this fascinating case. For alternative interpretations of the *Bryan* case, see Martha Hodes, *White Women, Black Men: Illicit*

Sex in the 19th-Century South (New Haven, 1997) and Ariela Gross, *What Blood Won't Tell: A History of Race on Trial in America* (Cambridge, Mass., 2008).

71. *Seaborn C. Bryan v. Hugh [sic] Walton*, 14 Ga. 185 (1853), 197.

72. Ibid., 198.

73. Ibid., 202.

74. Ibid., 202.

75. Ibid., 198.

76. Many of the restrictions against free people of color that Lumpkin identified were enacted in 1829, after David Walker's *Appeal to the Coloured Citizens of the World* surfaced in Georgia, and in 1833 and 1835, when the legislature revised the state penal code. *Acts of the General Assembly of the State of Georgia, 1829*; *Acts of the General Assembly of the State of Georgia, 1833*; *Acts of the General Assembly of the State of Georgia, 1835*.

77. *Bryan v. Walton*, 20 Ga. 480 (1856), 492, 491, 495, 496, 501, 494. During the testimony in the trial, one of the witnesses, Joseph Bush, described James Nunez as "an American" whose "father was a Portuguese." He "passed as a white man." The witnesses in the trial gave strikingly different interpretations of James. Some suggested he was white or part Indian, while others depicted him as clearly a person of African descent. Of course, the testimony was based on recollections that were close to forty years old. James Nunez had died between 1809 and 1813.

78. U.S. Census, 1790, 1800, 1810, 1820, 1830, 1840, 1850, 1860. For early treatments of free people of color in Georgia, see Flanders, "The Free Negro in Antebellum Georgia," 250–272; W. McDowell Rogers, "Free Negro Legislation in Georgia Before 1865," *Georgia Historical Quarterly* 16 (March 1932): 27–37; Edward F. Sweat, "Social Status of the Free Negro in Antebellum Georgia," *Negro History Bulletin* 21 (March 1958): 129–131; Edward F. Sweat, "The Free Negro in Ante-Bellum Georgia" (Ph.D. diss., Indiana University, 1957); Edward Sweat, *Free Blacks and the Law in Antebellum Georgia* (Atlanta, 1976).

79. U.S. Census, 1790, 1800, 1810, 1820, 1830, 1840, 1850, 1860.

80. For more on free blacks in Atlanta see, Edward F. Sweat, "Free Blacks in Antebellum Atlanta," *Atlanta Historical Bulletin* 21, no. 1 (spring 1977): 64–71.

81. Atlanta City Ordinance Book, 20 May 1853, Atlanta History Center. Those free people of color who were arrested under the ordinance were to be "hired out at public outcry" to a person who would pay their fine.

82. *Atlanta Weekly Intelligencer*, 26 April 1855.

83. Atlanta City Ordinance Book, 20 May 1859, Atlanta History Center. See also Atlanta City Council Minutes, vol. 3, 6 May 1859, 13 May 1859, 20 May 1859, Atlanta History Center.

84. For examples of petitions, see Atlanta City Council Minutes, vol. 2, 26 January 1855, 6 March 1855, Atlanta History Center.

85. Atlanta City Ordinance Book, 29 April 1853, Atlanta History Center.

86. *Atlanta Daily Intelligencer,* 9 January 1860.

87. Atlanta City Council Minutes, vol. 2, 6 June 1856, Atlanta History Center.

88. Atlanta City Ordinance Book, 13 April 1860, Atlanta History Center. See also Atlanta City Council, vol. 3, 2 March 1860, 16 March 1860, 23 March 1860, Atlanta History Center.

89. Atlanta City Council Minutes, vol. 3, 15 July 1859, 19 July 1859, 8 February 1861, Atlanta History Center; Wallace P. Reed, *History of Atlanta:With Illustrations and Biographical Sketches of Some of Its Prominent Men and Pioneers* (Syracuse, 1889), 81; T. H. Martin, *Atlanta and Its Builders,* 1:145; Garrett, *Atlanta and Its Environs,* 453–454; Phillips, *Plantations and Frontier Documents,* 368. For more on Badger, see Allison Dorsey, *To Build Our Lives Together: Community Formation in Black Atlanta, 1875–1906* (Athens, Ga., 2004), 22–26; Ralph Benjamin Singer Jr., "Confederate Atlanta" (Ph.D. diss., University of Georgia, 1973), 83. I'd like to thank Bill Link for bringing these two sources to my attention.

90. Garrett, *Atlanta and Its Environs,* 453–454.

91. Ira Berlin, *Slaves Without Masters:The Free Negro in the Antebellum South* (New York, 1974).

92. For more on free people of color in Savannah, see Byrne, "The Burden and the Heat of the Day"; Smith, *Slavery and Rice Culture in Low Country Georgia;* Wood, *Women's Work, Men's Work;* Johnson, *Black Savannah;* Fraser, *Savannah in the Old South;* Lockley, *Lines in the Sand.*

93. Richard D. Arnold to A. P. Merrill, 23 May 1854, in Shryock, ed., *Letters of Richard D. Arnold,* 66; Richard D. Arnold to Sol Cohen, 29 September 1854, in Shryock, ed., *Letters of Richard D. Arnold,* 71.

94. Richard D. Arnold to Joe H. Gressoin, 15 November 1847, in Shryock, ed., *Letters of Richard D. Arnold,* 32.

95. J. P. Tustin, "Andrew C. Marshall, 1786–1856," in *Annals of the American Pulpit,* ed. William B. Sprague (Charleston, 1859), 258. See also Lyell, *A Second Visit to the United States of North America,* 2:2–3. For more on Marshall, see Whittington B. Johnson, "Andrew C. Marshall: A Black Religious Leader of Antebellum Savannah," *Georgia Historical Quarterly* 69 (summer 1985): 173–192.

96. Johnson, *Black Savannah,* 147–149.

97. Solomon Zeigler deposition, August and September 1871, David Waters Allowed Claim, Chatham County, Georgia, RG 217, National Archives, College Park, Maryland.

98. Sarah Ann Black deposition, April 14, 1874, Sarah Ann Black Allowed Claim, Chatham County, Georgia, RG 217, National Archives, College Park, Maryland.

99. For example, the number of free men of color in Savannah identified as craftsmen grew steadily over the antebellum era, increasing from forty-two in 1848 to 179 in 1860. According to the English traveler James Silk Buckingham, "coloured persons" dominated "the laborious trades," while slaves performed

"nearly all the severe and menial labor" (Buckingham, *The Slave States of America*, 1:122). Bancroft, *Census of the City of Savannah, 1848*, 16; Gillespie, *Free Labor in an Unfree World*, 165; U.S. Census, 1860.

100. Tustin, "Andrew C. Marshall, 1786–1856," 257; Byrne, "The Burden and the Heat of the Day," 193.

101. Whittington B. Johnson, "Free African American Women in Savannah, 1800–1860: Affluence and Autonomy amid Adversity," *Georgia Historical Quarterly* 76 (summer 1992): 273–275. See also Loren Schweninger, "Property-Owning Free African-American Women in the South, 1800–1870," *Journal of Women's History* 1 (winter 1990): 13–44.

102. Loren Schweninger, *Black Property Owners in the South, 1790–1915* (Urbana, 1990), 70; Johnson, *Black Savannah*, 62; Smith, *Slavery and Rice Culture in Low Country Georgia*, 196.

103. For example, see Adele Logan Alexander, *Ambiguous Lives: Free Women of Color in Rural Georgia, 1789–1879* (Fayetteville, 1991); Kent Anderson Leslie, *Woman of Color, Daughter of Privilege: Amanda America Dickson, 1849–1893* (Athens, 1995).

104. *Acts of the General Assembly of the State of Georgia, 1834.*

105. *Report of James P. Screven, Mayor of the City of Savannah, for the Year Ending September 30th, 1857, to Which is Added the Treasurer's Annual Report* (Savannah, 1857), 29–31; *Report of Thomas M. Turner, Mayor of the City of Savannah, for the Year Ending September 30, 1858, to Which is Added the Treasurer's Annual Report* (Savannah, 1858), 29–30. See also Byrne, "The Burden and the Heat of the Day," 194–196; Johnson, *Black Savannah*, 137–138; Lockley, *Lines in the Sand*, 39–40; Fraser, *Savannah in the Old South*, 293.

106. *Report of James P. Screven, Mayor of the City of Savannah . . . 1857*, 30.

107. "Annual Parade of the Fire Department," *Savannah Daily Morning News*, 26 May 1860.

108. *Savannah Daily Morning News*, 31 May 1851.

109. Ibid., 28 May 1853. For another example of a positive depiction of the parade in the newspaper, see the 27 May 1854 issue.

110. "Statement of Mr. James Oliver, Foreman of the Oglethorpe Fire Company," in *Savannah Daily Morning News*, 12 November 1853. See also Thomas Gamble Jr., *A History of the City Government of the City of Savannah, Ga., from 1790 to 1901* (s.n., 1900), 237; Haunton, "Savannah in the 1850's," 274–277.

111. "Proceedings of Council," *Savannah Daily Morning News*, 11 July 1856.

112. Ibid.

113. "Statement of Mr. James Oliver, Foreman of the Oglethorpe Fire Company," in *Savannah Daily Morning News*, 12 November 1853; "Proceedings of Council," *Savannah Daily Morning News*, 25 July 1856; "The Savannah Fire Department, and the Young America Fire Company," *Savannah Daily Morning News*, 9 July 1856.

114. "Statement of Mr. James Oliver, Foreman of the Oglethorpe Fire Company," in *Savannah Daily Morning News*, 12 November 1853.

115. "Savannah Fire Company," *Savannah Daily Morning News*, 7 November 1853;

Gamble, *A History of the City Government of the City of Savannah, Ga., from 1790 to 1901*, 196–197.

116. "Young America Fire Company," *Savannah Daily Morning News*, 13 August 1856.

117. "Savannah Fire Company," *Savannah Daily Morning News*, 7 November 1853.

118. "Proceedings of Council," *Savannah Daily Morning News*, 25 July 1856.

119. *Milledgeville Daily Federal Union*, 10 November 1858; Ernest C. Hynds, *Antebellum Athens and Clarke County, Georgia* (Athens, Ga., 2009), 162.

120. For more on the legislative debate, see *Milledgeville Daily Federal Union*, 17 November 1858, 18 November 1858; *Milledgeville Federal Union*, 23 November 1858; *Milledgeville Southern Recorder*, 23 November 1858, 30 November 1858.

121. *Milledgeville Southern Recorder*, 30 November 1858.

122. *Milledgeville Daily Federal Union*, 24 November 1858.

123. *Milledgeville Southern Recorder*, 18 December 1860.

124. Hicks, *Joseph Henry Lumpkin*, 89–90.

125. Cobb, *An Inquiry into the Law of Negro Slavery in the United States of America*; R. H. Clark, T. R. R. Cobb, and D. Irwin, codifiers, *The Code of the State of Georgia* (Atlanta, 1861). For biographical information on Cobb, see William B. McCash, *Thomas R. R. Cobb: The Making of a Southern Nationalist* (Macon, Ga., 1983), and Paul Finkelman's introduction in the 1999 reissue of *An Inquiry into the Law of Negro Slavery in the United States of America*, 1–23.

126. Flanders, "The Free Negro in Antebellum Georgia," 250–272.

SELECTED BIBLIOGRAPHY

PRIMARY SOURCES

Newspapers

Athens Southern Banner, 1832–1860
Atlanta Intelligencer, Daily Intelligencer, and Weekly Intelligencer, 1851–1861
Augusta Chronicle and Advertiser, 1822–1831
Augusta Chronicle and Gazette of the State, 1790–1808
Augusta Herald, 1798–1802
Cherokee Phoenix, 1828–1833
Columbian Museum and Savannah Advertiser, 1796–1814
Columbus Enquirer, 1828, 1832–1860
Georgia Citizen, 1850–1860
Georgia Gazette, 1790–1796
Georgia Journal, 1827–1845
Georgia Journal and Messenger, 1823–1825
Georgia Messenger, 1823–1847
Georgia Telegraph, 1826–1860
Louisville Gazette, 1799–1801
Macon Telegraph, 1826–1860
Milledgeville Federal Union and Daily Federal Union, 1830–1860
Milledgeville Reflector, 1817–1819
Milledgeville Southern Recorder, 1821–1830, 1849
Niles' Register, 1811–1836
Savannah Daily Morning News, 1850–1860
Savannah Mercury, 1828–1829
Savannah Republican, 1812–1820
Southern Sentinel, 1795
State Gazette of South Carolina, 1793
Statesman and Patriot, 1827–1830
Washington Monitor, 1802–1809

Government Records

Acts of the General Assembly, 1793–1860
Journal of General Convention of the State of Georgia, 1833
Journal of the Convention of the State of Georgia, 1798
Journal of the House of Representatives of Georgia, 1798–1842
Journal of the Senate of Georgia, 1798–1837
Journals of the Assembly of Jamaica, Vol. IX from 25th October, 1791, to 4th August, 1797. Jamaica: Alexander Aikman and Son, 1805.

Manuscript Collections

Emory University, Atlanta

Boles Collection
Virginia Myers McBlair Collection
Charles Thiot Papers
Fort Tomlinson Collection
Benjamin Watkins Collection

Georgia Department of Archives and History, Atlanta

Austin Dabney File
Chronology of Georgia, 1773–1800, Particularly Related to Elijah Clark
East Florida, West Florida Papers
Elijah Clark, File 11
Executive Minutes, 1798
Force Manuscripts
Negroes, 1773–1800
Savannah City Council Minutes, 1790–1804

Georgia Historical Society, Savannah

Richard Dennis Arnold Papers
Bailey Family Collection
George Baillie Jr. Collection
Samuel Barnett Collection
John Macpherson Berrien Papers
Joseph Vallence Bevan Papers
Jacob R. Brooks Collection
Dennis Cooley Collection
Basil Cowper Decision and Bonds
John M. Cox Collection
J. B. Cumming Collection
J. Evarts Collection
Jonas Fauche Collection
John Forsyth Collection

France Dept. of Foreign Affairs Collection
Ft. Hawkins Collection
Garvin and Meers Collection
Georgia Infirmary Board Collection
Nathanael Greene Letters
John Habersham Collection
Walter Hartridge Collection
John Houstoun Letters
John Inglis Collection
Jared Irwin Collection
Andrew Jackson Collection
William Jones Collection
Richard Leake Collection
Loyalists Collection
Macartan-Campbell Collection
George Mathews Collection
John McIntosh Jr. Papers
J. McIntosh-Kell Collection
James O'Fallon Collection
Ossabaw Island Collection
E. S. Rees Collection
Varner Rountree Collection
Savannah Merchants and Planters Collection
James Shorter Collection
James Smith Collection
James Spaulding Collection
St. Simons Lighthouse Collection
William Stephens Collection
John Adam Treutlen Collection
George M. Troup Collection
Nichol Turnbull Collection
John Twiggs Collection
Washington Guards Collection
Wayne-Stites-Anderson Papers
Joshua E. White Collection
Wilkes County Collection
Alexander Wright Collection

University of Georgia, Athens

Godfrey Barnsley Family Papers
David Crenshaw Barrow Sr. Family Papers
Telamon Cuyler Collection
James Eppinger Family Papers

Edward Harden Family Papers
Hillyer Family Papers
Reverend John Jones Family Papers
Ebenezer Kellogg Diary
Zachariah Lamar Papers
John Ray Papers

Books and Articles

Ball, Charles. *Fifty Years in Chains; or, The Life of an American Slave.* Detroit: Negro History Press, 1971.

Bartram, William. *The Travels of William Bartram.* Edited by Mark Van Doren. New York: Dover Publications, 1928.

Bolzius, Johann Martin. "Johann Martin Bolzius Answers a Questionnaire on Carolina and Georgia, Part II," ed. Klaus G. Loewald, Beverly Starika, and Paul S. Taylor. *William and Mary Quarterly* 15, no. 2 (April 1958): 228–252.

Bowles, William Augustus. *Authentic Memoirs of William Augustus Bowles.* London: R. Faulder, 1791.

Brown, John. *Slave Life in Georgia: A Narrative of the Life, Sufferings, and Escape of John Brown, A Fugitive Slave.* Savannah, Ga.: Beehive Press, 1991.

Butler, Pierce. *The Letters of Pierce Butler, 1790–1794: Nation Building and Enterprise in the New American Republic.* Edited by Terry W. Lipscomb. Columbia: Univ. of South Carolina Press, 2007.

Candler, Allen D., and Lucian L. Knight, eds. *The Colonial Records of the State of Georgia.* Atlanta, Ga.: The Franklin Printing and Publishing Co., 1904–1906.

Catterall, Helen T. *Judicial Cases Concerning American Slavery and the Negro.* Washington, D.C.: Carnegie Institution of Washington, 1926–1937.

Clay, Joseph. *Letters of Joseph Clay, Merchant of Savannah, 1776–1793, and a List of Ships and Vessels Entered at the Port of Savannah, for May 1765, 1766 and 1767.* [Savannah, Ga.: Morning News Printers, ca. 1913].

Cobb, Thomas Read Rootes. *An Inquiry into the Law of Negro Slavery in the United States of America: To Which is Prefixed, An Historical Sketch of Slavery.* Edited by Paul Finkelman. Savannah, Ga.: 1858. Reprint, Athens: Univ. of Georgia Press, 1999.

Coleman, Kenneth, and Milton Ready, eds. *Original Papers of Governor Wright, President Habersham, and Others, 1764–1789.* Athens: Univ. of Georgia Press, 1979.

Davis, T. Frederick, ed. "United States Troops in Spanish East Florida, 1812–1813, Part 2." *Florida Historical Society Quarterly* 9, no. 2 (October 1930): 96–116.

———, ed. "United States Troops in Spanish East Florida, 1812–1813, Part 3." *Florida Historical Society Quarterly* 9, no. 3 (January 1931): 135–155.

DeBrahm, John Gerar William. *Report of the General Survey in the Southern District of North America.* Edited by Louis De Vorsey. Columbia: Univ. of South Carolina Press, 1971.

Faust, Drew Gilpin, ed. *The Ideology of Slavery: Proslavery Thought in the Antebellum South, 1830–1860.* Baton Rouge: Louisiana State Univ. Press, 1981.

Gilmer, George R. *Sketches of Some of the First Settlers of Upper Georgia, of the Cherokees, and the Author,* rev. ed. Americus, Ga.: Americus Book Company, 1926.

Habersham, James. *The Letters of James Habersham, 1756–1775.* Savannah, Ga.: Savannah Morning News Print, 1904.

Harden, Edward J. *The Life of George M. Troup.* Savannah, Ga.: E. J. Purse, 1859.

Hawkins, Benjamin. *The Collected Works of Benjamin Hawkins, 1796–1810.* Edited by H. Thomas Foster III. Tuscaloosa: Univ. of Alabama Press, 2003.

———. *Letters, Journals, and Writings of Benjamin Hawkins.* Vol. 2. Savannah, Ga.: Beehive Press, 1980.

Hays, J. E., ed. *Collections of the Georgia Historical Society.* Savannah: Braid and Hutton, 1901.

Jackson, James. *The Papers of James Jackson, 1781–1798.* Savannah: Georgia Historical Society, 1955.

Kemble, Frances Anne. *Journal of a Residence on a Georgian Plantation in 1838–1839.* Athens: Univ. of Georgia Press, 1984.

Lane, Mills. *Neither More nor Less than Men: Slavery in Georgia: A Documentary History.* Savannah, Ga.: Beehive Press, 1993.

———, ed. *The Rambler in Georgia: Desultory Observations on the Situation, Extent, Climate, Population, Manners, Customs, Commerce, Constitution, Government, etc., of the State from the Revolution to the Civil War Recorded by Thirteen Travellers.* Savannah, Ga.: Beehive Press, 1973.

Lockley, Timothy James. *Maroon Communities in South Carolina: A Documentary Record.* Columbia: Univ. of South Carolina Press, 2009.

Lumpkin, Wilson. *The Removal of the Cherokee Indians from Georgia.* New York: Dodd, Mead and Company, 1907.

Lyell, Charles. *A Second Visit to the United States of North America.* New York: Harper and Brothers, 1849.

Marbury, Horatio, and William H. Crawford, eds., *Digest of the laws of the state of Georgia from its settlement as a British province, in 1755, to the session of the General assembly in 1800, inclusive. Comprehending all the laws passed within the above periods, and now in force, alphabetically arranged under their respective titles: also the state constitutions of 1777 and 1789, with the additions and amendments in 1795, and the constitution of 1798. To which is added, an appendix: comprising the Declaration of American independence; the Articles of confederation and perpetual union; the federal Constitution, with the amendments thereto: all the treaties between the United States and foreign nations; the treaties between the United States and the different tribes of Indians; and those between the state of Georgia and the southern and western Indians. With a copious index to the whole. Comp., arranged and digested from the original records, and under the special authority of the state.* Savannah, Ga.: Seymour, Woolhopter and Stebbins, 1803.

Olmsted, Frederick Law. *A Journey in the Backcountry.* New York: Mason Brothers, 1860.

———. *A Journey in the Seaboard Slave States, with Remarks on their Economy.* New York: Dix and Edwards, 1856.

————. *The Cotton Kingdom*. Edited by Arthur M. Schlesinger Sr. New York: Random House, 1984.

Phillips, Ulrich B., ed. *Plantation and Frontier Documents, 1649–1863, Illustrative of Industrial History in the Colonial and Antebellum South*. Cleveland: A. H. Clark Company, 1909.

Rawick, George P., ed. *The American Slave, Supplement, Series 1: Georgia Narratives, Part 1*. Vol. 3. Westport, Conn.: Greenwood, 1977.

————. *The American Slave: Georgia Narratives, Parts 1 and 2*. Vol. 12. Westport, Conn.: Greenwood, 1972.

————. *The American Slave: Georgia Narratives, Parts 3 and 4*. Vol. 13. Westport, Conn.: Greenwood, 1972.

Simmons, William Hayne. *Notices of East Florida, with an Account of the Seminole Nation of Indians*. Charleston, 1822. Reprint, Gainesville: Univ. of Florida Press, 1973.

White, George. *Historical Collections of Georgia: Containing the Most Interesting Facts, Traditions, Biographical Sketches, Anecdotes, Etc. Relating to its History and Antiquities, From its First Settlement to the Present Time*. New York: Pudney and Russell Publishers, 1854.

————. *Statistics of the State of Georgia, Including an Account of its Natural, Civil, and Ecclesiastical History, Together with a Particular Description of Each County, Notices of the Manners and Customs of its Aboriginal Tribes and a Correct Map of the State*. Savannah, Ga.: W. Thorne Williams, 1849.

Woodward, Thomas S. *Woodward's Reminiscences of the Creek, or Muscogee Indians, Contained in Letters to Friends in Georgia and Alabama*. Montgomery, Ala.: Barrett and Wimbish, 1859.

SECONDARY SOURCES

Books and Articles

Abbot, W. W. *The Royal Governors of Georgia, 1754–1775*. Chapel Hill: Univ. of North Carolina Press, 1959.

Albert, Peter J., Ronald Hoffman, and Thad W. Tate, eds. *An Uncivil War: The Southern Backcountry during the American Revolution*. Charlottesville: Univ. Press of Virginia, 1985.

Alexander, Adele Logan. *Ambiguous Lives: Free Women of Color in Rural Georgia, 1789–1879*. Fayetteville: Univ. of Arkansas Press, 1991.

Ammon, Harry. *The Genet Mission*. New York: Norton, 1973.

Aptheker, Herbert. "Maroons within the Present Limits of the United States." *Journal of Negro History* 24, no. 2 (April 1939): 167–184.

Austin, Allan D. *African Muslims in Antebellum America: A Sourcebook*. New York: Garland, 1984.

Baine, Rodney M. "Myths of Mary Musgrove." *Georgia Historical Quarterly* 76 (summer 1992): 428–435.

Baptist, Edward E. *Creating an Old South: Middle Florida's Plantation Frontier before the Civil War*. Chapel Hill: Univ. of North Carolina Press, 2002.

Bateman, Fred, and Thomas Joseph Weiss. *A Deplorable Scarcity: The Failure of Industrialization in the Slave Economy.* Chapel Hill: Univ. of North Carolina Press, 1981.

Bell, Malcolm, Jr. *Major Butler's Legacy: Five Generations of a Slaveholding Family.* Athens: Univ. of Georgia Press, 1987.

Berlin, Ira. *Slaves without Masters: The Free Negro in the Antebellum South.* New York: Pantheon, 1974.

Berlin, Ira, and Philip D. Morgan, eds. *Cultivation and Culture: Labor and the Shaping of Slave Life in the Americas.* Charlottesville: Univ. Press of Virginia, 1993.

Berry, Daina Ramey. *"Swing the Sickle for the Harvest Is Ripe": Gender and Slavery in Antebellum Georgia.* Urbana: Univ. of Illinois Press, 2007.

Bolton, Charles C. *Poor Whites of the Antebellum South: Tenants and Laborers in Central North Carolina and Northeast Mississippi.* Durham, N.C.: Duke Univ. Press, 1994.

Bonner, James Calvin. *Georgia's Last Frontier: The Development of Carroll County.* Athens: Univ. of Georgia Press, 1971.

———. *A History of Georgia Agriculture, 1732–1860.* Athens: Univ. of Georgia Press, 1964.

Brathwaite, Edward. *The Development of Creole Society in Jamaica, 1770–1820.* Oxford: Clarendon Press, 1971.

Bullard, Mary R. *Robert Stafford of Cumberland Island: Growth of a Planter.* Athens: Univ. of Georgia Press, 1995.

Campbell, Mavis Christine. *The Dynamics of Change in a Slave Society: A Sociopolitical History of the Free Coloreds of Jamaica, 1800–1865.* Rutherford, N.J.: Fairleigh Dickinson Univ. Press, 1976.

Carey, Anthony Gene. *Parties, Slavery, and the Union in Antebellum Georgia.* Athens: Univ. of Georgia Press, 1997.

Carney, Judith A. *The African Origins of Rice Cultivation in the Americas.* Cambridge, Mass.: Harvard Univ. Press, 2001.

Cashin, Edward J. *Governor Henry Ellis and the Transformation of British North America.* Athens: Univ. of Georgia Press, 1994.

———. *The King's Ranger: Thomas Brown and the American Revolution on the Southern Frontier.* Athens: Univ. of Georgia Press, 1989.

———. *Lachlan McGillivray, Indian Trader: The Shaping of the Southern Colonial Frontier.* Athens: Univ. of Georgia Press, 1992.

———. *William Bartram and the American Revolution on the Southern Frontier.* Columbia: Univ. of South Carolina Press, 2000.

Cecil-Fronsman, Bill. *Common Whites: Class and Culture in Antebellum North Carolina.* Lexington: Univ. Press of Kentucky, 1992.

Chaplin, Joyce E. *An Anxious Pursuit: Agricultural Innovation and Modernity in the Lower South, 1730–1815.* Chapel Hill: Univ. of North Carolina Press, 1993.

Clark, George P. "The Role of the Haitian Volunteers at Savannah in 1779: An Attempt at an Objective View." *Phylon* 41, no. 4 (1980): 356–366.

Clarke, Erskine. *Dwelling Place: A Plantation Epic.* New Haven, Conn.: Yale Univ. Press, 2005.

Coleman, Kenneth. *The American Revolution in Georgia, 1763–1789*. Athens: Univ. of Georgia Press, 1958.

———. *Colonial Georgia: A History*. New York: Scribner, 1976.

———, ed. *A History of Georgia*. Athens: Univ. of Georgia Press, 1977.

Cook, James F. *The Governors of Georgia, 1754–1995*. Macon, Ga.: Mercer Univ. Press, 1995.

Corkran, David H. *The Creek Frontier, 1540–1783*. Norman: Univ. of Oklahoma Press, 1967.

Coulter, E. Merton. *Georgia's Disputed Ruins: Certain Tabby Ruins on the Georgia Coast*. Chapel Hill: Univ. of North Carolina Press, 1937.

———. "Mary Musgrove, 'Queen of the Creeks': A Chapter of Early Georgia Troubles," *Georgia Historical Quarterly* 11 (1927): 1–30.

———. *A Short History of Georgia*. Chapel Hill: Univ. of North Carolina Press, 1960.

———. *Thomas Spalding of Sapelo*. University: Louisiana State Univ. Press, 1940.

Davis, Harold E. *The Fledgling Province: Social and Cultural Life in Colonial Georgia, 1773–1776*. Chapel Hill: Univ. of North Carolina Press, 1976.

Davis, Robert Scott. *Cotton, Fire, and Dreams: The Robert Findlay Iron Works and Heavy Industry in Macon, Georgia, 1839–1912*. Macon, Ga.: Mercer Univ. Press, 1998.

DeBats, Donald A. *Elites and Masses: Political Structure, Communication, and Behavior in Ante-Bellum Georgia*. New York: Garland, 1990.

Deyle, Steven. *Carry Me Back: The Domestic Slave Trade in American Life*. New York: Oxford Univ. Press, 2005.

Drago, Edmund L. *Black Politicians and Reconstruction in Georgia: A Splendid Failure*. Baton Rouge: Louisiana State Univ. Press, 1982.

Dubois, Laurent. *A Colony of Citizens: Revolution and Slave Emancipation in the French Caribbean, 1787–1804*. Chapel Hill: Univ. of North Carolina Press, 2004.

Dusinberre, William. *Them Dark Days: Slavery in the American Rice Swamps*. New York: Oxford Univ. Press, 1996.

DuVal, Kathleen. *The Native Ground: Indians and Colonists in the Heart of the Continent*. Philadelphia: Univ. of Pennsylvania Press, 2006.

Ferguson, T. Reed. *The John Couper Family at Cannon's Point*. Macon, Ga.: Mercer Univ. Press, 1994.

Fick, Carolyn. *The Making of Haiti: The St. Domingue Revolution from Below*. Knoxville: Univ. of Tennessee Press, 1990.

Finkelman, Paul, ed. *Free Blacks in a Slave Society*. New York: Garland, 1989.

———. *Proslavery Thought, Ideology, and Politics*. New York: Garland, 1989.

Flanders, Ralph B. "The Free Negro in Antebellum Georgia." *North Carolina Historical Review* 9, no. 3 (1932): 250–272.

———. *Plantation Slavery in Georgia*. Cos Cob, Conn.: J. E. Edwards, 1967 (ca. 1933).

Forbes, Jack D. *Africans and Native Americans: The Language of Race and the Evolution of Red-Black Peoples*. Urbana: Univ. of Illinois Press, 1993.

Ford, Lacy K. *Deliver Us from Evil: The Slavery Question in the Old South*. New York: Oxford Univ. Press, 2009.

Ford, Lacy K., Jr. *Origins of Southern Radicalism: The South Carolina Upcountry, 1800–1860.* New York: Oxford Univ. Press, 1988.

Fraser, Walter J., Jr. *Savannah in the Old South.* Athens: Univ. of Georgia Press, 2003.

Fredrickson, George M. *The Black Image in the White Mind: The Debate on Afro-American Character and Destiny, 1817–1914.* New York: Harper and Row, 1971.

Frey, Sylvia R. *Water from the Rock: Black Resistance in a Revolutionary Age.* Princeton, N.J.: Princeton Univ. Press, 1991.

Gallay, Alan. *The Formation of a Planter Elite: Jonathan Bryan and the Southern Colonial Frontier.* Athens: Univ. of Georgia Press, 1989.

———. *The Indian Slave Trade: The Rise of the English Empire in the American South, 1670–1717.* New Haven, Conn.: Yale Univ. Press, 2002.

Geggus, David Patrick. *Slavery, War, and Revolution: The British Occupation of Saint Domingue, 1793–1798.* New York: Oxford Univ. Press, 1982.

Genovese, Eugene D. *Roll, Jordan, Roll: The World the Slaves Made.* New York: Random House, 1974.

Gibson, James R. *European Settlement and Development in North America: Essays on Geographical Change in Honour and Memory of Andrew Hill Clark.* Toronto: Univ. of Toronto Press, 1978.

Gillespie, Michele. *Free Labor in an Unfree World: White Artisans in Slaveholding Georgia, 1789–1860.* Athens: Univ. of Georgia Press, 2000.

———. "Sexual Politics of Race and Gender: Mary Musgrove and the Georgia Trustees." In *The Devil's Lane: Sex and Race in the Early South,* edited by Catherine Clinton and Michele Gillespie, 187–201. New York: Oxford Univ. Press, 1997.

Goldin, Claudia Dale. *Urban Slavery in the American South, 1820–1860: A Quantitative History.* Chicago: Univ. of Chicago Press, 1976.

Gomez, Michael A. *Exchanging Our Country Marks: The Transformation of African Identities in the Colonial and Antebellum South.* Chapel Hill: Univ. of North Carolina Press, 1998.

Goveia, E. V. *The West Indian Slave Laws of the 18th Century.* Barbados: Caribbean Universities Press, 1970.

Gray, Lewis C. *History of Agriculture in the Southern United States to 1860.* Washington, D.C.: Carnegie Institution of Washington, 1933.

Green, Michael D. *The Politics of Indian Removal: Creek Government and Society in Crisis.* Lincoln: Univ. of Nebraska Press, 1982.

Hadden, Sally E. *Slave Patrols: Law and Violence in Virginia and the Carolinas.* Cambridge, Mass.: Harvard Univ. Press, 2001.

Hahn, Steven. *The Political Worlds of Slavery and Freedom.* Cambridge, Mass.: Harvard Univ. Press, 2009.

Hall, Leslie. *Land and Allegiance in Revolutionary Georgia.* Athens: Univ. of Georgia Press, 2001.

Harris, J. William. *The Hanging of Thomas Jeremiah: A Free Black Man's Encounter with Liberty.* New Haven, Conn.: Yale Univ. Press, 2009.

———. *Plain Folk and Gentry in a Slave Society: White Liberty and Black Slavery in Augusta's Hinterlands.* Middletown, Conn.: Wesleyan University Press, 1985.

Haunton, Richard Herbert. "Savannah in the 1850's." Ph.D. diss., Emory University, 1968.

Hays, Louise Frederick. *Hero of Hornet's Nest: A Biography of Elijah Clark, 1733 to 1799.* New York: Hobson Book Press, 1946.

Heuman, Gad J. *Between Black and White: Race, Politics, and the Free Coloreds in Jamaica, 1792–1865.* Westport, Conn.: Greenwood Press, 1981.

Heyrman, Christine Leigh. *Southern Cross: The Beginnings of the Bible Belt.* Chapel Hill: Univ. of North Carolina Press, 1997.

Hicks, Paul DeForest. *Joseph Henry Lumpkin: Georgia's First Chief Justice.* Athens: Univ. of Georgia Press, 2002.

Hodes, Martha Elizabeth. *White Women, Black Men: Illicit Sex in the Nineteenth-Century South.* New Haven, Conn.: Yale Univ. Press, 1997.

Hoffman, Paul E. *Florida's Frontiers.* Bloomington: Indiana Univ. Press, 2002.

Hoxie, Frederick E., Ronald Hoffman, and Peter J. Albert, eds. *Native Americans and the Early Republic.* Charlottesville: Univ. Press of Virginia, 1999.

Huebner, Timothy S. *The Southern Judicial Tradition: State Judges and Sectional Distinctiveness, 1790–1890.* Athens: Univ. of Georgia Press, 1999.

Hunt, Alfred N. *Haiti's Influence on Antebellum America: Slumbering Volcano in the Caribbean.* Baton Rouge: Louisiana State Univ. Press, 1988.

Ingersoll, Thomas N. *Mammon and Manon in Early New Orleans: The First Slave Society in the Deep South, 1718–1819.* Knoxville: Univ. of Tennessee Press, 1999.

Inscoe, John C., ed. *Georgia in Black and White: Explorations in the Race Relations of a Southern State, 1865–1950.* Athens: Univ. of Georgia Press, 1994.

Isham, Edward. *The Confessions of Edward Isham: A Poor White Life of the Old South.* Edited by Charles C. Bolton. Athens: Univ. of Georgia Press, 1998.

Jackson, Harvey H. *Lachlan McIntosh and the Politics of Revolutionary Georgia.* Athens: Univ. of Georgia Press, 1979.

Jackson, Harvey H., and Phinizy Spalding, eds. *Forty Years of Diversity: Essays on Colonial Georgia.* Athens: Univ. of Georgia Press, 1984.

Johnson, Michael P. *Toward a Patriarchal Republic: The Secession of Georgia.* Baton Rouge: Louisiana State Univ. Press, 1977.

Johnson, Michael P., and James L. Roark. *Black Masters: A Free Family of Color in the Old South.* New York: Norton, 1984.

Johnson, Whittington Bernard. *Black Savannah, 1788–1864.* Fayetteville: Univ. of Arkansas Press, 1996.

———. "Free Blacks in Antebellum Savannah: An Economic Profile." *Georgia Historical Quarterly* 64 (1980): 418–431.

Jordan, Winthrop D. *White over Black: American Attitudes toward the Negro, 1550–1812.* Chapel Hill: Univ. of North Carolina Press, 1968.

Kaye, Anthony E. *Joining Places: Slave Neighborhoods in the Old South.* Chapel Hill: Univ. of North Carolina Press, 2007.

King, Stewart R. *Blue Coat or Powdered Wig: Free People of Color in Pre-Revolutionary Saint Domingue.* Athens: Univ. of Georgia Press, 2001.

Klein, Rachel N. *Unification of a Slave State: The Rise of the Planter Class in the South Carolina Backcountry, 1760–1808*. Chapel Hill: Univ. of North Carolina Press, 1990.

Knight, Franklin W. *Atlantic Port Cities: Economy, Culture, and Society in the Atlantic World, 1650–1850*. Knoxville: Univ. of Tennessee Press, 1991.

Lambert, Frank. *James Habersham: Loyalty, Politics, and Commerce in Colonial Georgia*. Athens: Univ. of Georgia Press, 2005.

Lamplugh, George R. *Politics on the Periphery: Factions and Parties in Georgia, 1783–1806*. Newark: Univ. of Delaware Press, 1986.

Landers, Jane G. *Black Society in Spanish Florida*. Urbana: Univ. of Illinois Press, 1999.

———, ed. *Colonial Plantations and Economy in Florida*. Gainesville: Univ. Press of Florida, 2000.

Leslie, Kent Anderson. *Woman of Color, Daughter of Privilege: Amanda America Dickson, 1849–1893*. Athens: Univ. of Georgia Press, 1995.

Linebaugh, Peter, and Marcus Rediker. *The Many-Headed Hydra: Sailors, Slaves, Commoners, and the Hidden History of the Revolutionary Atlantic*. Boston: Beacon Press, 2000.

Lockley, Timothy James. *Lines in the Sand: Race and Class in Lowcountry Georgia, 1750–1860*. Athens: Univ. of Georgia Press, 2001.

Lovell, Caroline Couper. *The Golden Isles of Georgia*. Boston: Little, Brown, 1932.

Marsh, Ben. *Georgia's Frontier Women: Female Fortunes in a Southern Colony*. Athens: Univ. of Georgia Press, 2007.

Martin, Jonathan D. *Divided Mastery: Slave Hiring in the American South*. Cambridge, Mass.: Harvard Univ. Press, 2004.

McCash, William B. *Thomas R. R. Cobb: The Making of a Southern Nationalist*. Macon, Ga.: Mercer Univ. Press, 1983.

McFeely, William S. *Sapelo's People: A Long Walk into Freedom*. New York: Norton, 1994.

McLoughlin, William G. *Cherokee Renascence in the New Republic*. Princeton, N.J.: Princeton Univ. Press, 1986.

Miles, Tiya. *The House on Diamond Hill: A Cherokee Plantation Story*. Chapel Hill: University of North Carolina Press, 2010.

———. *Ties That Bind: The Story of an Afro-Cherokee Family in Slavery and Freedom*. Berkeley: University of California Press, 2005.

Morgan, Edmund S. *American Slavery, American Freedom: The Ordeal of Colonial Virginia*. New York: Norton, 1975.

Murdoch, Richard K. *The Georgia-Florida Frontier, 1793–1796: Spanish Reaction to French Intrigue and American Designs*. Berkeley: Univ. of California Press, 1951.

Narrative of a Voyage to the Spanish Main in the Ship "Two Friends;" The Occupation of Amelia Island by M'Gregor, &c.—Sketches of the Province of East Florida; and Anecdotes Illustrative of the Habits and Manners of the Seminole Indians: With an Appendix, Containing a Detail of the Seminole War, and the Execution of Arbuthnot and Ambrister. London: Printed for John Miller, Burlington Arcade, Piccadilly, 1819.

Oakes, James. *The Ruling Race: A History of American Slaveholders*. New York: Knopf, 1982.

O'Donovan, Susan E. *Becoming Free in the Cotton South*. Cambridge, Mass.: Harvard Univ. Press, 2007.

Otto, John Solomon. *Cannon's Point Plantation, 1794–1860: Living Conditions and Status Patterns in the Old South.* New York: Academic Press, 1984.

Patrick, Rembert W. *Florida Fiasco: Rampant Rebels on the Georgia-Florida Border, 1810–1815.* Athens: Univ. of Georgia Press, 1954.

Pearson, Edward A. "'A Countryside Full of Flames': A Reconsideration of the Stono Rebellion and Slave Rebelliousness in the Early Eighteenth-Century South Carolina Lowcountry." *Slavery and Abolition* 17, no. 2 (1996): 22–50.

Perdue, Theda. *"Mixed Blood" Indians: Racial Construction in the Early South.* Athens: Univ. of Georgia Press, 2003.

Perdue, Theda, and Michael D. Green. *The Cherokee Nation and the Trail of Tears.* New York: Viking, 2007.

Phillips, Ulrich B. *American Negro Slavery.* Baton Rouge: Louisiana State Univ. Press, 1966.

———. *Georgia and State Rights: A Study of the Political History of Georgia from the Revolution to the Civil War with Particular Regard to Federal Relations.* Washington, D.C.: Government Printing Office, 1902.

Porter, Kenneth Wiggins. *The Negro on the American Frontier.* New York: Arno Press, 1971.

Pybus, Cassandra. *Epic Journeys of Freedom: Runaway Slaves of the American Revolution and the Global Quest for Liberty.* Boston: Beacon, 2007.

Quarles, Benjamin. *The Negro in the American Revolution.* Chapel Hill: Univ. of North Carolina Press, 1961.

Reidy, Joseph P. *From Slavery to Agrarian Capitalism in the Cotton Plantation South: Central Georgia, 1800–1880.* Chapel Hill: Univ. of North Carolina Press, 1992.

Remini, Robert V. *Andrew Jackson and His Indian Wars.* New York: Penguin Books, 2001.

Richter, Daniel K. *Facing East from Indian Country: A Native History of Early America.* Cambridge, Mass.: Harvard Univ. Press, 2001.

Risjord, Norman. *The Old Republicans: Southern Conservatism in the Age of Jefferson.* New York: Columbia Univ. Press, 1965.

Roediger, David R. *The Wages of Whiteness: Race and the Making of the American Working Class.* London: Verso, 1991.

Rothman, Adam. *Slave Country: American Expansion and the Origins of the Deep South.* Cambridge, Mass.: Harvard Univ. Press, 2005.

Russell, James M. *Atlanta, 1847–1890: City Building in the Old South and the New.* Baton Rouge: Louisiana State Univ. Press, 1988.

Saunt, Claudio. *A New Order of Things: Property, Power, and the Transformation of the Creek Indians, 1733–1816.* Cambridge: Cambridge Univ. Press, 1999.

Schama, Simon. *Rough Crossings: Britain, the Slaves, and the American Revolution.* New York: HarperCollins, 2006.

Schweninger, Loren. *Black Property Owners in the South, 1790–1915.* Urbana: Univ. of Illinois Press, 1990.

Searcy, Martha Condray. *The Georgia-Florida Contest in the American Revolution, 1776–1778.* University: Univ. of Alabama Press, 1985.

Sheehan, Bernard W. *Seeds of Extinction: Jeffersonian Philanthropy and the American Indian.* Chapel Hill: Univ. of North Carolina Press, 1973.

Sidbury, James. *Ploughshares into Swords: Race, Rebellion, and Identity in Gabriel's Virginia, 1730–1810.* New York: Cambridge Univ. Press, 1997.

Smith, Julia Floyd. *Slavery and Rice Culture in Low Country Georgia, 1750–1860.* Knoxville: Univ. of Tennessee Press, 1985.

Smith, Mark M. "Remembering Mary, Shaping Revolt: Reconsidering the Stono Rebellion." *Journal of Southern History* 67, no. 3 (August 2001): 513–534.

Starobin, Robert S. *Industrial Slavery in the Old South.* New York: Oxford Univ. Press, 1970.

Steffen, Charles G. *The Mechanics of Baltimore: Workers and Politics in the Age of Revolution, 1763–1812.* Urbana: Univ. of Illinois Press, 1984.

Stiggins, George, Virginia Pounds Brown, and William Stokes Wyman. *Creek Indian History: A Historical Narrative of the Genealogy, Traditions and Downfall of the Ispocoga or Creek Indian Tribe of Indians.* Birmingham, Ala.: Birmingham Public Library Press, 1989.

Stowell, Daniel. *Balancing Evils Judiciously: The Proslavery Writings of Zephaniah Kingsley.* Gainesville: Univ. Press of Florida, 2000.

Sweat, Edward F. "The Free Negro in Antebellum Georgia." Ph.D. diss., Indiana University, 1957.

Sweet, Julie Anne. *Negotiating for Georgia: British-Creek Relations in the Trustee Era, 1733–1752.* Athens: Univ. of Georgia Press, 2005.

Thornton, John K. "African Dimensions of the Stono Rebellion." *American Historical Review* 96, no. 4 (October 1991): 1101–1113.

Tise, Larry E. *Proslavery: A History of the Defense of Slavery in America, 1701–1840.* Athens: Univ. of Georgia Press, 1987.

Ver Steeg, Clarence L. *Origins of a Southern Mosaic.* Athens: Univ. of Georgia Press, 1975.

Vipperman, Carl J. "The 'Particular Mission' of Wilson Lumpkin." *Georgia Historical Quarterly* 66, no. 3 (fall 1982): 295–316.

Wade, Richard C. *Slavery in the Cities: The South, 1820–1860.* New York: Oxford Univ. Press, 1964.

Wallace, Anthony F. C. *Jefferson and the Indians: The Tragic Fate of the First Americans.* Cambridge, Mass.: Harvard Univ. Press, 1999.

———. *The Long, Bitter Trail: Andrew Jackson and the Indians.* New York: Hill and Wang, 1993.

Wallenstein, Peter. *From Slave South to New South: Public Policy in Nineteenth-Century Georgia.* Chapel Hill: Univ. of North Carolina Press, 1987.

Ward, J. R. *British West Indian Slavery, 1750–1834: The Process of Amelioration.* New York: Oxford Univ. Press, 1988.

West, Charles N. *The Life and Times of William Harris Crawford of Georgia.* Providence, R.I.: Snow and Farnham, 1892.

Wharton, Vernon Lane. *The Negro in Mississippi, 1865–1890*. New York: Harper and Row, 1965.

Williams, David. *The Georgia Gold Rush: Twenty-Niners, Cherokees, and Gold Fever*. Columbia: Univ. of South Carolina Press, 1993.

Wilson, David K. *The Southern Strategy: Britain's Conquest of South Carolina and Georgia, 1775–1780*. Columbia: Univ. of South Carolina Press, 2005.

Wood, Betty. *Slavery in Colonial Georgia, 1730–1775*. Athens: Univ. of Georgia Press, 1984.

———. *Women's Work, Men's Work: The Informal Slave Economies of Lowcountry Georgia*. Athens: Univ. of Georgia Press, 1995.

Wood, Peter H. *Black Majority: Negroes in Colonial South Carolina from 1670 through the Stono Rebellion*. New York: Knopf, 1974.

Wright, J. Leitch, Jr. *Creeks and Seminoles: The Destruction and Regeneration of the Muscogulge People*. Lincoln: Univ. of Nebraska Press, 1986.

———. *William Augustus Bowles: Director General of the Creek Nation*. Athens: Univ. of Georgia Press, 1967.

Wright, Ph., and G. Debien. *Les colons de Saint Domingue passés à la Jamaïque (1792–1835)*. Bulletin de la Société d'Histoire de la Guadaloupe, no. 26. Basse-Terre, Guadeloupe: Archives departementales, 1975.

Wylly, Charles Spalding. *The Seed That Was Sown in the Colony of Georgia: The Harvest and the Aftermath, 1740–1870*. New York: Neale, 1910.

Young, Jeffrey Robert. *Domesticating Slavery: The Master Class in Georgia and South Carolina, 1670–1837*. Chapel Hill: Univ. of North Carolina Press, 1999.

INDEX

CPSIA information can be obtained at www.ICGtesting.com
Printed in the USA
BVOW071908110112

280252BV00002B/5/P